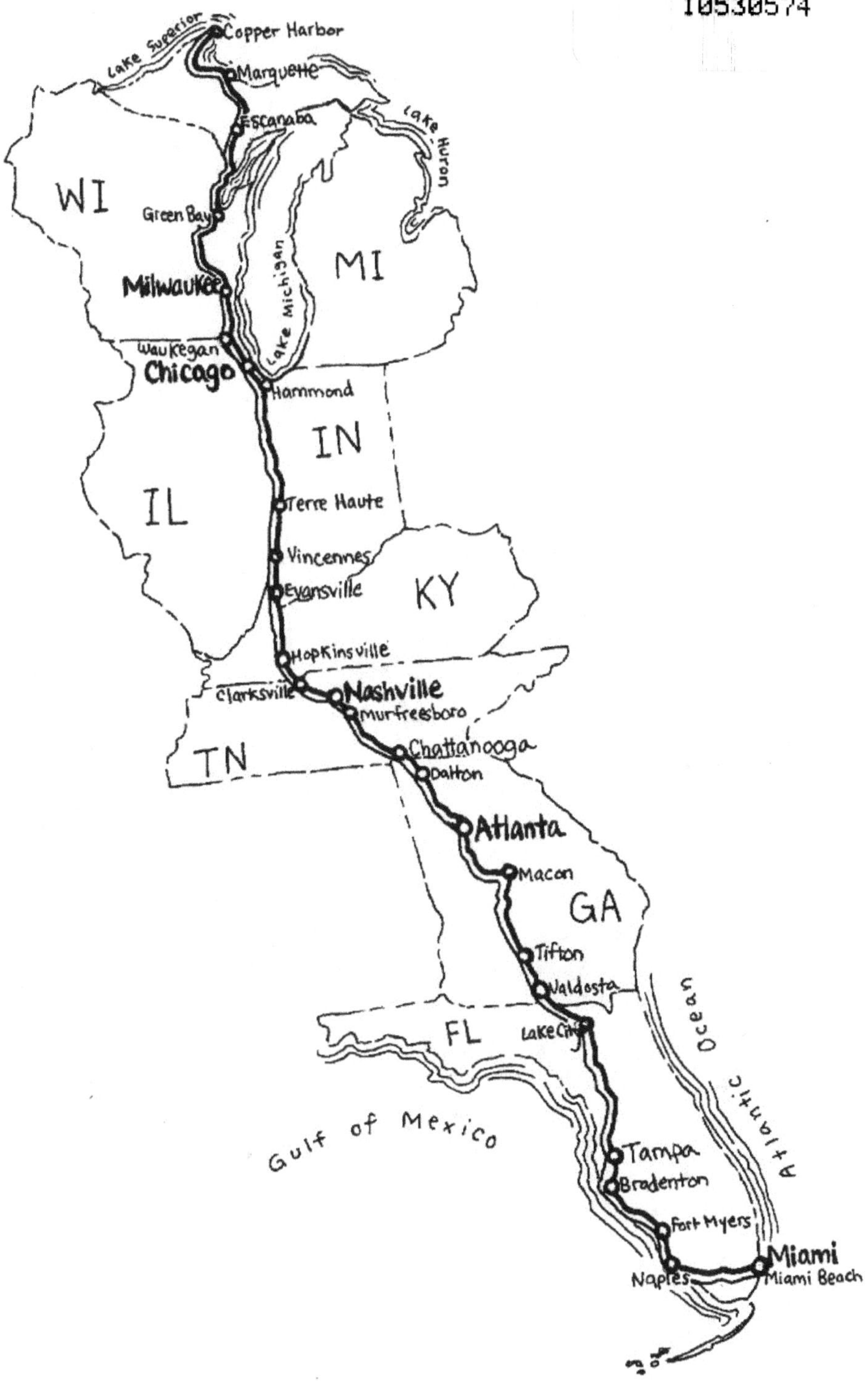

Copper Harbor

Lake Superior

Marquette

Escanaba

Lake Huron

WI

Green Bay

MI

Milwaukee

Lake Michigan

Waukegan

Chicago

Hammond

IN

IL

Terre Haute

Vincennes

Evansville

KY

Hopkinsville

Clarksville

Nashville

Murfreesboro

Chattanooga

Dalton

TN

Atlanta

Macon

GA

Tifton

Valdosta

Lake City

FL

Ocean

Atlantic

Gulf of Mexico

Tampa

Bradenton

Fort Myers

Miami

Naples

Miami Beach

UNEARTHING HIGHWAY 41

AN AMERICAN JOURNEY

CHRISTOPHER CLOTT

ILLUSTRATIONS BY
MOLLY MIKLOSZ

To Emily

TABLE OF CONTENTS

Part Three: South

Part Four: American Journey

PREFACE

When I was a kid, there was a locally produced television show called *Passage to Adventure*. It was mainly home movies taken by individuals on their travels throughout the country and world with some thoughts on what they had seen. This show sparked an idea in me: traveling to faraway places was something I badly wanted to do. As I came of age, I was part of a Boy Scout group that went to the storied Philmont Scout Ranch in New Mexico, and a year later I took a month-long Greyhound bus trip throughout the U.S. East Coast and Canada. Over the years, I would crisscross the country by train and car, see all 50 states, and be able to travel to many countries abroad. I worked in the global shipping industry and visited lots of cool (and uncool) places where companies were based. Later, as a college professor, I was able to create opportunities for students to study abroad in far-flung places.

I still love to travel. It broadens and informs in ways that sitting at home can never do. But it has become far more complicated in the current era: the allure of travel on the open road competes with in-home entertainment, theme parks, traffic congestion, and chain store homogenization. Tooling down the road to discover and explore what is out there is not what our Type A driven society would suggest is appropriate, yet I argue, this is needed now more than ever.

When I first thought of writing a book about Highway 41, I envisioned a "travel book"—something in-between a detailed observation suitable for a textbook study and an old-fashioned road trip book like so many authors had written before. After years of thinking and planning, the major upheavals of the COVID-19 pandemic over a three-year period starting in 2020 changed all manner of how I needed to consider writing about the road.

John Lennon famously observed that life happens while making other plans. So, the hoped-for several month road trip on Highway 41 from end to end over a summer would have to be a bit more chopped up than I would have liked. The silver lining is that it allowed me to distill parts of the road over a period of time—to think less of the miles of road traveled and more about all the places along the way. "Seeing is believing," is what a man told me long ago during a visit to Japan, and it's true here as well.

A journey on Highway 41 encompasses many different places and topics that range from the distant past to the immediate present. Think of this book as a guide to a swath of country threaded by the road itself over time. Some places engendered more detail than others and I wanted to avoid standard measures used by the media to describe places. I wanted to learn things and be surprised, and hopefully you will too.

So, without further ado, let's go on a journey through America via Highway 41.

INTRODUCTION
CROSSROADS OF AMERICA

"*Traveling on Highway No. 41 from any point does not present the usual tiresome prospect of just going from one place to another. On 41, you are going places and seeing things—observing new and wonderful beauties, finding new and interesting places, discovering scenic wonders that you had never believed existed so close around you—and this for every mile of its course.*"

— *Excerpt from the Evansville-Henderson Bridge
Dedication Celebration, July 4, 1932*

"*...And I was born on the back seat of a Greyhound bus/Rollin' down Highway 41.*"

— *"Ramblin' Man" (1973), The Allman Brothers Band*

An old bank building at 7th Street and Wabash Avenue in the small city of Terre Haute, Indiana has two plaques on its corner. The first mentions the "Old National Road," first proposed by George Washington as a path for development of the Northwest Territory that later became U.S. 40, *The Main Street of America*," and the first coast to coast highway.

The other plaque reads, *"The nation's major north-south highway; designated U.S. Highway 41 in 1926 reached from northernmost Michigan to Miami Florida. It was the commercial and cultural link between the Great Lakes & Chicago to all points south. It passed through Terre Haute's business district as Seventh Street and intersected U.S. 40, America's principal east-west federal highway at this site."*

Of the two roads, U.S. 40 is the better known, as it crosses the continent east to west in a movement that is still the way many think of the sweep of the country. "East and West" conveys excitement, occasional romance, and the mystery of the country between the coasts. "North and South" provides an altogether different experience, fraught with controversial historical and current issues that are part of the American journey.

This book is a long-overdue exploration of a great American road: U.S. Highway 41. Once the nation's principal north-south stem highway, it remains significant and vitally important for people and commerce as it passes through a varied eight-state section of the United States. Portions of 41 run through densely populated major cities and suburbs as well as small towns and rural portions that are some of the richest farmlands in the country. Some parts of the road today have been subsumed or eclipsed by the interstate highway system that parallels it in parts as the major means of conveyance by cars and trucks.

"Old 41" often exists in its original two-lane form nearby the current four- to six-lane highway that encompasses much of its distance. To explore what is currently on and near Highway 41 is to see the mundane—strip malls, lots of "dollar stores," car lots, billboards, highway congestion—and the sublime —Chicago's fabled lakefront, the Michigan forest, the Tennessee State Capitol in Nashville, and the Everglades in Florida, to name a few. Highway 41 has changed course throughout the states since its establishment a century ago and will most likely continue to be remapped and reengineered as states determine how best to make use of it. America may be seen in its best form among its less celebrated vistas—the geographies we often don't stop to notice simply because they continue to serve as important to day-to-day living. Travel today on Highway 41 will not be as exciting as the hyperbole from the 1932 Evansville-Henderson bridge dedication might have suggested, but very few roads are both historic and incredibly important to where we are as a country today.

While no book can convey all the places and events that exist along the 2000-mile distance of Highway 41, this travel guide/personal journey is an effort on my part to provide some observations on what I found interesting to note in my travels on the highway. You may only be aware of portions of the road as it goes by many different names: DuSable Lake Shore Drive in Chicago, the Tamiami Trail in Florida, Northside Drive in Atlanta, Ringgold Road in Chattanooga, etc. Few individuals realize the highway runs almost the entire length of the country. The journey on 41 presented here will cover travel on Highway 41, "Old 41", Interstate 41 (Wisconsin), Alternate 41 (Kentucky) and former iterations of 41 that now have different state numbers. An old-fashioned paper map or atlas can be a good companion to this book.

Highway 41 is not the celebrated "Mother Road" of historical Route 66, nor is it much of a tourist road today, although that was once a major reason for its existence. It is not posted with markers designating historical links like Route 30—the Lincoln Highway. It is not evocative on the level of the Nevada portion of Route 50, dubbed "The Loneliest Road in America." Nor does it offer spectacular views of the Pacific Ocean like the fabled Route 1. Rather, it is like much of America—plain, unassuming, practical, and still vital. A journey on the highway is one of discovery, seeing the evolution of a country built on an idea of individual rights and self-governance that is still trying to figure out what it wants to be close to 250 years after its creation.

For such an important and vital roadway, precious little has been written about it. The most important resource for me was the *American Guide Series*, authored by workers of the Federal Writers' Program of the Works Progress Administration (WPA). Written in the 1930s and 40s, the guides feature detailed descriptions of towns and historical happenings all along the highway. By providing jobs, the Writers Program saved the lives of a number of individuals who lived through the challenging times of the Great Depression. The guides date between 1937 and 1942—very useful for historical context but with limited relevance to the present. Through further research I came across old maps, engineering information, and studies of various points along the road, particularly regarding DuSable Lake Shore Drive in Chicago and the Tamiami Trail in Florida. Historical museums along the way also provided interesting descriptions of the road and the cities it has traversed since 1926. Suffice to say, this book is less about the highway itself than it is about all the places along the highway!

A drive on Highway 41 can be slow; interstates will get you where you want to be much faster. While portions of the current iteration of Highway 41 are four-lane highways, as a driver, you can also go through residential areas in towns with stoplights and turns that can lead you quickly astray. Many parts of the older road are two lanes, so one needs to pay attention to driving. Turn off your satellite navigation system—it will want to steer you to the fastest route possible, and that is generally not going to be Highway 41.

Plan on driving through and stopping to experience numerous small towns, parks, and recreation areas. Get out of the car and look around. Stop by a downtown store in a county square, museum, or public library (the road has quite a number of vintage Carnegie libraries along its traverse). Have lunch or dinner at a non-chain restaurant. Stay for the night at a nearby motel or bed and breakfast and, if you happen to get there for a holiday, festival, concert, parade, sports event, or anything else that brings people out, stick around. Understanding America and what makes places tick means seeing people enjoy themselves.

Road trips are a little different now from the idyllic time when Mom and Dad piled the kids, the family dog, and assorted suitcases into the station wagon for a long drive to a lakeside park, a campground, a cottage, etc. A highway like 41 is usually jumped on and off as a means to access other points as needed. Stoplights, railroad tracks, and open roads are all part of the highway.

Reading this book, you may not be looking to travel the 2000-mile entirety of Highway 41—in fact, I suggest you make multiple side trips to places along the way in your passage through the states. You will pass by multiple little roadside plaques memorializing long ago events along the road, and I urge you to stop at some and give a read to them. I have a suggested album playlist of music for each state you pass through, and it's best to have a travel companion who will be happy to move at a slow pace. Sometimes the best travel companions are the four-legged types.

Road trips these days also can be made on two wheels: a motorcycle or a bicycle covers the highway in a different way. Particularly with a bike, you actually can see at a stately pace nearby neighborhoods, town centers, and places that the car can't go with ease. I never owned a motorcycle, so I cannot tell you all the pleasures of motoring down the road at high speed with the wind in your face. The biker culture is an interesting one, and I have no doubt that companies like Harley-Davidson (not far from 41 in Milwaukee) want many more people to experience the open road on a motorcycle—a means of transportation that has been slowly growing over the past couple of decades. Maybe we will also see more electric motorcycles in the years to come. We are certainly seeing many more electric scooters and bicycles.

This book is also an effort to get you, dear reader, out to explore Highway 41 or any other forgotten roads and less celebrated vistas you are longing to see. In a digital age when we can see everything and be everywhere without ever leaving our home, you might wonder why a journey on a road is important. I think travel enables us to see and feel the past, the present, and perhaps glimpse into the future as well. Can a journey along Highway 41 explain the complicated American story? Perhaps a little. And you will discover America in ways you may not have thought about before.

We continue to be wedded to fossil fuels and thus to the price of a tank of gas; however, electric vehicles are becoming more common, and perhaps you will make the journey on 41 in one. More and more people are doing so, though these trips require an added layer of planning.

While there were numerous ways I could have constructed the story of Highway 41, I chose to simply write about the road in a linear way as it goes through each of the states. The geography of the states, dating from their formation in the early years of the country, is most certainly one that is less distinctive in an era of big urban mega-regions that can sprawl over several states but all too real for most of us in our daily lives. I write about places that were part of the "old 41" as well as new portions that often are parts of interstate highways. Some towns and cities along the road, particularly south of the Mason-Dixon line, have grown in population while others have declined. This reconfiguration of the population will have important ramifications on resources and connections to the rest of the country and the world.

The story of this historic and essential American highway begins with two introductory chapters that cover its beginnings. Long before it was conceived as a north-south highway that would speed travelers from small southern towns to northern cities and provide northerners with a "tropical tour" on the way to Florida, the road was a path for bison, Indigenous Americans, soldiers, settlers, fugitives from slavery, and immigrants. The

American Revolution, the establishment of the Republic, the Civil War, and industrialization are part of Chapter one. You will see population and university enrollment figures within the book. The figures are from 2024 unless otherwise denoted.

Chapter two takes a brief look at the sweeping cultural changes that have occurred to the country with the growth of automobile travel over the last 125 years and the origins of Highway 41, from the Dixie-Bee Highway to the advent of the Interstate to where we are today. Roads are catalysts for economic development and growth of the cities and towns they run through, and Highway 41 is no exception.

Chapters three to eleven detail my travel through the specific states that 41 runs through. This journey begins in the north, for no other reason than it was the easiest for me. You'll notice that I do not include things you would find in a more comprehensive guide such as addresses, accommodations, and other practical information that you can easily obtain from the internet. You will see some illustrated maps and other artwork and as well as photographs I took on the journey.

Chapter twelve is a final word from me on what I carried away from my travels and what I hope you can carry away as well. I have no doubt many readers will come back to me with things I missed, or misjudged, from life on the road.

And finally...this book is in no way intended as a survey. It is scholarly from the standpoint of researching to get facts right but written for general audience interest. While I have a great many thoughts to share, I will not attempt to spell out conclusions, good or bad, about any of the particular places I have visited along Highway 41. The book is the adventure of one man "badgered by the imp of curiosity" in the words of Studs Terkel, traveling through a space and time to see places from the past, the present, and very possibly, the future. This is my story.

PART ONE
THE PATH

CHAPTER ONE
BEFORE THE ROAD

"We must concern ourselves with the land that lies beside it and the clouds that float above it, and the streams that flow beneath the bridges. We must remember the people who pass along it and those others who passed that way in former years."

— *George R. Stewart, Author,*
U.S. 40: Cross Section of the United States of America

"The past is never dead. It's not even past."

— *William Faulkner, American Novelist*

Highway 41 traverses an area of the country rich in historical interest. A drive down all or parts of the road and its vicinity covers places and events that were immensely important to the formation of the country as we know it and that, in many cases, remain significant to where we are today. For many of us, there is only a hazy idea of how the country was formed taken from long ago history courses, old books, and movies, and perhaps a visit to an "old time" tourist site we might have taken as children.

This chapter covers aspects of American history from long before the highway existed. Many markers and museums exist along the road you might want to investigate further in your own journey along 41.

EARLY MIGRATIONS

Before there was a road, there was a path. The origins of Highway 41 date to the Pliocene Epoch in North America approximately 400,000 years ago when migratory herds of large animals crossed over a land bridge from Asia. Migration paths for food and water were developed by the great herds of bison that as late as 200 years ago numbered thirty to sixty million in North America, mostly in the Great Plains, but they migrated all through the area that Highway 41 now spans.

American bison or "buffalo" (the terms are often used interchangeably), have short horns, thick shaggy coats for a cold climate, and a massive hump that counterweights their low-mounted heads. Bison weigh up to 2,400 pounds, stand approximately six feet tall at the shoulder, and can move at speeds up to thirty-five miles per hour. With herds numbering in the millions, they easily broke 12-to-20-foot-wide paths through dense undergrowth while eroding solid rock to depths of twelve feet.

Buffalo traces—deep, hard-packed trails through dense forests to open grasslands, fresh water, and salt licks—are the original paths the buffalo followed and Indigenous peoples first traveled on. While often hard to find within forests, the traces still exist in areas around the highway. One of the best-known examples is the **Natchez Trace**, a 440-mile trail that extends from Nashville, Tennessee, to Natchez, Mississippi, linking the Cumberland, Tennessee, and Mississippi rivers. The **Vincennes Trace** extends between Louisville, Kentucky, and Vincennes, Indiana.

For thousands of years, Indigenous peoples followed the footpaths of the great bison herds and depended heavily upon these animals as a source of food, hides for clothing and shelter, tools, and jewelry. Bison were the inspiration for ceremonies. Indigenous peoples hunted the buffalo for thousands of years, perfecting the bow and arrow into a powerful weapon for hunting game. Such weapons were made from locally sourced or traded natural materials. For arrowheads, chert, flint, and obsidian were most often utilized. Because these rocks could not be found everywhere in North America, they were traded across vast distances over Indigenous trade routes.

Archaeological evidence indicates Indigenous populations quarried specific rock sites for over 10,000 years. As a result, complex systems of inter-tribal exchange flourished over a millennium. The slaughter of the bison in the United States by Europeans began in the 1700s with French hunters and traders and increased in earnest in the late 1830s courtesy of American hunters and settlers. As the railroads pushed farther west in the 1860s and 1870s, the buffalo were hunted to near extinction. Only through conservation efforts that began in the early 1900s have the bison slowly come back to a present-day population of around 500,000. A small herd of bison has been introduced to a wildlife area in northern Indiana where Highway 41 traverses, and several thousand bison live on farms and in nature areas within other states along the highway. Additional attempts are being made to restore bison herds on tribal lands, tapping Indigenous knowledge in the Western United States.

INDIGENOUS AMERICANS

Indigenous Americans came over a land bridge from Asia into the Americas sometime between 18,000 and 15,000 years ago. As the climate changed and the glaciers receded, Indigenous peoples slowly made their way from the west to the east as foragers and later as farmers. Fully developed societies developed around maize (corn) agriculture and evolved centuries before Europeans arrived. Millions of acres of primeval forests, stretching from Michigan to Florida, were home to people for at least ten thousand years and perhaps much longer before any Europeans arrived.

Much of the length of present-day Highway 41 was settled by various groups of Indigenous peoples. The sheer number of tribal civilizations and their importance to modern-day development suggest the need to provide a thorough documentation associated with the areas of the country the road travels through. That is an ongoing process with archeologists, professional and amateur historians, and individuals with tribal ancestry now keen to identify sites and artifacts associated with various Indigenous communities after long decades of shameful neglect. These include ancient villages and former sites of occupation, religious sites, burial sites, battle sites, monuments, memorials, and current settlements. I would encourage you to see some of the many small museums dedicated to Indigenous peoples interspersed along Highway 41 to see the artifacts that have been collected and to learn more about volunteer activities and efforts to uncover vanished civilizations.

Civilizations from the precontract Hopewell Culture (200 BCE to 500 CE) to the Mississippian Culture (800 CE) until the arrival of the European explorers, planted the "three sisters" (corn, squash, and beans) and developed genetic modifications that were adapted to shorter growing seasons in the far north. The three plants nurtured and supported one another, resulting in better crop yields and soil management. Sophisticated, populous cities such as **Cahokia** in Illinois near present-day St. Louis, Missouri, were founded in the Mississippi Valley region with huge earthen flat-topped mounds built for ceremonies and rituals much like those in Central America. Cahokia was the largest prehistoric indigenous community north of Mexico, and today it is a United Nations Educational, Scientific and Cultural Organization (UNESCO) World Heritage Site. The **Cahokia Mounds State Historic Site** is definitely worth a visit if you are in the area.

Mound sites near Highway 41, such as **Angel Mounds** near present-day Evansville in southern Indiana, were abandoned by their inhabitants by the 1400s for reasons that are still unknown. In northern Georgia, **Etowah Mounds**, dating from 1000 CE to approximately 1550, are the focus of the most intact Mississippian culture site in the southeast. Archeologists continue to excavate items that speak to paths between these ancient locations. At the beginning of the sixteenth century, approximately forty million Indigenous groups, speaking 500 distinct languages, lived in North America.

Etowah Indian Mounds State Historic Site, Cartersville, GA

EUROPEAN EXPLORATION AND COLONIZATION

The arrival of Europeans in North America in the early to mid-1500s brought unprecedented change to the continent. After plundering Mexico and Peru, Spain sent conquistadores on expeditions to "La Florida"—land of the flowers—searching for gold and other wealth of any kind. Ponce de Leon's 1521 expedition to Florida landed on the southwest coast of the peninsula, near what is now Charlotte Harbor, to start a colony. It lasted five months before de Leon was wounded in a native attack and died in Cuba.

The 1539–43 expedition of Hernando de Soto (1500–1542) landed near present-day Tampa Bay, Florida, and traversed much of the present-day American southeast. De Soto died of a fever in an Indigenous village on the banks of the Mississippi River in what is now Louisiana. The Spanish brought with them diseases: viral hepatitis, smallpox, chicken pox, and influenza that killed scores of Indigenous peoples who had no natural immunities.

The French entered North America in 1534 through present-day Canada and the Great Lakes states via the St. Lawrence River. Jacques Cartier claimed northern North America for France. The French brought manufactured metal goods and decorative items to trade for furs. Unlike the Spanish, the French showed a warm regard for Indigenous peoples and often married Indigenous women. French traders and settlers learned to speak native languages, used canoes, and adapted to the surroundings. Trapping furs to provide to the French traders changed Indigenous societies, creating dependencies that transformed farming, hunting, and gathering they had practiced over centuries. Later, there would be French missionaries such as Father Rene Menard (1605–1661), who arrived in Keweenaw Bay in 1660. By the early 1600's in present-day Michigan, Wisconsin, Illinois, and Indiana, Indigenous portage paths were utilized to bring French traders, missionaries, and explorers to North America including Jean Nicolet (1598–1642), Louis Jolliet (1645–1700), Jacques Marquette S.J. (1637–1675), and a host of other explorers who associated with the multiple Indigenous tribes who populated the area and gave their names to towns along the route.

With the defeat of the Spanish Armada in 1588, England began its own colonial exploration in North America. With Spain in the south and the French in the north, the English established their first colonies along the mid-Atlantic coast. Roanoke, off the North Carolina coast, was established in 1587 but disappeared under unknown circumstances. Jamestown, Virginia, was the first permanent colony in 1607. While the first colonies did not initially fare well, growing numbers of colonists pushed farther west. They too, brought diseases, particularly smallpox, that wiped out numerous Indigenous villages. The Dutch established a colonial presence in New York in the 1600s.

Slavery was introduced in the early 1600s on the Atlantic coast and took hold particularly in the coastal southern states, with the importation of African peoples. An estimated 12.5 million enslaved Africans were transported to the Americas on at least 36,000 voyages between 1619 and 1860, although the transatlantic slave trade was officially outlawed in 1808. Interestingly, slavery was initially banned in Georgia by the founders of the colony until pressure was put on them by planters arriving from South Carolina.

THE FRENCH AND INDIAN WAR AND AMERICAN REVOLUTION

As wealth and status changed in Indigenous societies in the 1700s due to contact with Europeans, so too did conflict among tribes with respect to their alliances with each other and with primarily French and English troops and settlers. Alliances of French and Indigenous tribes fought against alliances of English and Indigenous tribes. The **"Three Fires Confederacy"** was composed of Ojibwe, Odawa, and Potawatomi tribes that were largely in control of the western Great Lakes. They made alliances with the Europeans, as necessary, to keep the newcomers dependent upon native nations. Disease, however, as well as the introduction of alcohol, continued to lay waste to many tribes.

The competition among France, England, and Spain for the "New World" changed after 1763 when England defeated France in the **French and Indian War**. Colonists followed the British troops that claimed tribal lands and established forts around the Great Lakes and inland rivers within the interior of the country. The elimination of tribal nations became the goal of settlers. Smallpox and other illnesses continued to decimate Indigenous peoples. So did battles with British and later American troops.

The **American Revolution** began in 1775 and further isolated Indigenous nations. The Cherokee nation—spread over the Carolinas, Tennessee, Alabama, and Georgia—joined the British to drive out the colonials who were invading their land. Far-sighted Indigenous leaders such as Tecumseh (1768–1813) and Alexander McGillivray (1750–1793) attempted to unify disparate tribes and secure British backing to keep Indigenous lands out of the hands of settlers. For a time, they were successful, as the Spanish, French, and English were mainly on the east coast leaving the interior of the continent largely in Indigenous hands.

The American victory over Great Britain in the American Revolution and the subsequent withdrawal of British troops was pivotal for the demise of the Indigenous peoples in the areas traversed by Highway 41.

George Rogers Clark (1752–1818) and his small American army outmaneuvered the British garrisons through present-day Indiana and Illinois and pushed the British, who had hoped to ally with Indigenous nations, into what is now Canada. An impressive monument to Clark's achievements stands in the small city of Vincennes, Indiana. In the southeast, an extended series of small skirmishes known as the **Cherokee-American Wars** lasted from 1776 to 1794. With the formation of the new American republic, treaties and resettlement continued to shrink Indigenous territories. It is no wonder that indigenous nations could not successfully resist the European/American settler invasion. Reduced in number by disease and warfare, and scattered over huge areas, these nations had no effective way to stem the tide of white settlement.

George Rogers Clark plaque, Fort Massac State Park, IL

POST REVOLUTION

In the aftermath of the American Revolution, George Washington had wanted to "Americanize" the Indigenous peoples of the southeast. He appointed Benjamin Hawkins (1754–1816) a U.S. senator from North Carolina, to work with the so-called **"Five Civilized Tribes"**: Cherokee, Chickasaw, Choctaw, Creek, and Seminole, who had developed extensive economic ties with white settlers and adopted some settler culture attributes. Some members of these southeastern tribes adopted European clothing, spoke English, practiced Christianity, and even enslaved Africans.

While the United States government entered into more than 500 treaties with Indigenous nations between 1778 and 1871, virtually all of them were violated in some way or broken outright by the early republic. In 1871, Congress unilaterally abrogated treaty rights and excluded Indigenous peoples from citizenship. Indigenous nations are still fighting for their treaty rights in federal courts. Federal trial and appellate courts have issued more than 650 written opinions in cases dealing with Native American law each year with countless other cases still in litigation.

Upon his assumption of the presidency in 1801, Thomas Jefferson enacted policies more focused on westward expansion. This included expanding the United States by taking lands that belonged to Indigenous peoples and encouraging additional settlement by selling land the government did not own to white Americans. Jefferson purchased the Louisiana Territory (one-fourth of the present-day United States) in 1803 from Napoleon for around 3 cents an acre. William Henry Harrison's 1811 victory in the **Battle of Tippecanoe** near present-day Lafayette, Indiana, eventually led to his presidency and the loss of Indigenous homelands in Indiana. This was a precursor to tensions over differences regarding territorial expansion and British support for Indigenous nations that opposed U.S. settlement, which led, in part, to the War of 1812. That conflict resolved in a stalemate (both sides claimed and still claim victory) that ended the war via treaty in 1815. In turn, the war ended both British threats to American sovereignty and American military incursions into Canada.

THE NORTHWEST ORDINANCE AND THREE-FIFTHS COMPROMISE

The **Northwest Ordinance** of 1787, adopted at the Constitutional Convention, eventually led to the creation of the American states of Ohio, Michigan, Wisconsin, Indiana, and Illinois. Within the ordinance was prohibition of slavery in the states to be formed out of the territories. To gain ratification of the Constitution, the **Three-Fifths Compromise** was also installed as an agreement over the counting of slaves. Every enslaved person in the country would be counted as three-fifths of a person for taxation and representation purposes. At the time of the compromise, a few northern states had abolished slavery, but slavery was legal and still practiced in other northern states. The southern states where slavery had taken the strongest hold would end up having greater representation in Congress thanks to the compromise, and the "peculiar institution" continued until the end of the American Civil War in 1865, a war that claimed some 600,000 lives.

MANIFEST DESTINY, LAND TREATIES, GENOCIDE & INDIGENOUS SURVIVAL

By the end of the War of 1812, the concept of **Manifest Destiny,** a quasi-religious belief that the United States was divinely chosen by God to settle the continent, tame the wilderness, and "civilize" the west to the Pacific Ocean, had taken root in the American psyche. Indigenous peoples were forcibly removed from their native lands under the guise of Manifest Destiny. The idea that Indigenous Americans were not considered citizens in the same way as white Americans powered thinking into the twentieth century. In 1924, the **Indian Citizenship Act** finally conferred American citizenship on all Indigenous Americans. In 2022, the Vatican responded to Indigenous demands and formally repudiated the **"Doctrine of Discovery,"** theories within the Catholic faith derived from the fifteenth century that legitimized the colonial-era seizure of native lands.

Major General Andrew Jackson, the hero of the 1815 Battle of New Orleans against the British, and the 1814 Battle of Horseshoe Bend against the Creek, led American military forces in a series of engagements with Indigenous peoples, with the objective of forcing tribes to cede lands to the federal government. Jackson, a slaveholder, actively sought to dispossess and relocate the Indigenous so white settlers could control the land. Upon his election as president of the United States in 1829, he showed no concern for protecting the rights of the Cherokee or any other Indigenous nation.

Gold was discovered in North Georgia in Cherokee Territory in 1828. In 1830, Congress passed the **Indian Removal Act**, authorizing the government to create tracts of land west of the Mississippi on which to relocate specific southeastern nations after a planned forced migration. Leaders of the Cherokee nation wrote letters to Congress asking it to honor treaties previously made with them. They also appealed to the Federal Court, protesting removal. In 1832, the U.S. Supreme Court upheld the Cherokee claims on their lands in Georgia. President Jackson reportedly said, "John Marshall [Supreme Court Chief Justice] has made his decision; now let him enforce it." All Cherokee lands were seized, surveyed, and distributed by lottery to white residents. Cherokee rights were ignored by the state of Georgia and President Jackson.

In December 1835, the **Treaty of New Echota** was signed by a small group of unauthorized Cherokee agreeing to be removed to the west, to what is today eastern Oklahoma. The treaty was never approved by leaders of the Cherokee nation and was opposed by representatives from New England, other Indigenous nations, religious groups, and missionaries. The treaty passed in the Senate by a single vote. The National Cherokee Council claimed the treaty was invalid because the principal chief did not sign it, and the Cherokee who did were not authorized. The Council wrote that they had "full confidence that under such circumstances the voice of weakness itself will be heard in its cry for Justice." A petition in 1836 signed by 3,352 Cherokee urged the Senate not to ratify the treaty. Congress responded by tabling (laying aside) the petition. All but about 2,000 Cherokees ignored the treaty and refused to move to the west. This reaction was encouraged by Cherokee Chief John Ross and continued for nearly two years.

In 1838, the forced marches of the Cherokee, Choctaw, Chickasaw, and Creek, now known as the **Trail of Tears**, began. These Indigenous nations were forcibly removed from their lands and forced to march on a route from Georgia through present-day Tennessee, Kentucky, Illinois, and Missouri to what would later become Kansas and northeastern Oklahoma. Half of the 16,000 Indigenous men, women, and children who were rounded up and force-marched in the winter died on the journey. It's a story of suffering, genocide, intolerance, and, ultimately, survival. Along Highway 41 through Kentucky, Tennessee, and Georgia, you will see a variety of roadway signs signifying the 2,200-mile-long Trail of Tears historic route.

Meanwhile in Florida, the Seminole were also slated for removal, but they fought back effectively from 1835 to 1858. While several thousand Seminole were forcibly marched west, others refused to leave, hiding out in the Everglades. Generations later, their descendants still live on land along the **Tamiami Trail**, which is now part of Highway 41 to Miami, Florida. The Seminole were never fully conquered. African American fugitives from slavery lived among the Seminole, and the wars that ensued were as much slave wars as Indigenous wars. The status of the Seminole as legitimate residents of the United States was contested by the federal government until the middle of the twentieth century. In 1821, the United States assumed control over Florida from the Spanish by treaty, even though the Seminole were sovereign rulers of much of the state and had never been consulted on the matter.

Trail of Tears Auto Tour route sign, Trenton, KY

While the treatment of Indigenous peoples is a story of subjugation within the history of the United States, their cultures have remained uniquely durable to the present. From forest management to gaming enterprises, native peoples continue to play an important role within the country and to press cases of redress against the federal government in court. Today, all Americans are benefiting from increased scholarship that allows us to understand the role of Indigenous peoples in the creation of the country.

Below are several Indigenous nations of significance who have resided along what is now Highway 41 and the role they continue to play in the national story:

- The **Shawnee** were among the largest and most powerful nations in the southern Great Lakes. They consistently opposed white settlement beyond the Appalachians. The Shawnee fought under Tecumseh and his

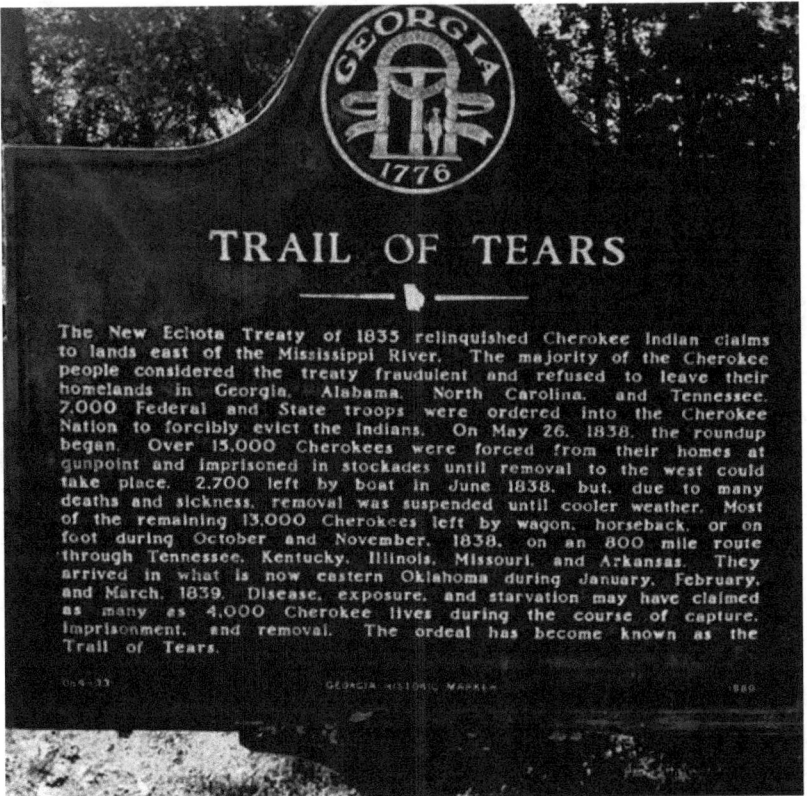

New Echota State Historic Site, Calhoun, GA

brother Tenskwatawa (The Prophet). In 1811, future U.S. President General William Henry Harrison defeated the Shawnee confederacy at the Battle of Tippecanoe in Indiana, and the nation never fully recovered. Today the **Shawnee Tribe** is a federally recognized sovereign nation with about 9,855 tribal citizens as of 2023, who live mainly in Oklahoma.

- **Potawatomi** territory extended south from Green Bay to present-day Milwaukee and Chicago. They had established numerous villages around Lake Michigan, including on the land where Chicago now lies, by the time the French arrived in the seventeenth century. The Potawatomi were first aligned with the French as Europeans began to arrive in North America. In present times, they have prospered with gaming and casinos. They are closely related to Ojibwe and Ottawa (pop. 14,000) nations. Today, the **Citizen Potawatomi Nation** has approximately 38,000 tribal members.

- The **Ojibwe (Chippewa)** (pop. 170,000) were once one of largest Indigenous nations in North America. Their territory spread into the Upper Peninsula, and they were involved in the fur trade with the French. They allied with the Ottawa and the Potawatomi to form the strong Three Fires Confederacy. Their land was rich in timber, iron, and arable soil, and the U.S. government pressed them to sell. The 1887 Dawes Act, sometimes called the General Allotment Act, allowed the federal government to break up tribal lands, depriving the Ojibwe of much of their territory. The Ojibwe exercised sanctuary rights written into treaties in Michigan and Wisconsin. Extensive cases in state and federal courts over land use clauses formed the basis for legal claims in the 1980s and 1990s. Today the Ojibwe live mainly on reservations in the upper Midwest where they operate casinos. An Ojibwe community resides on the Keweenaw Peninsula in Michigan.

The L'Anse Indian Reservation, the Village of Baraga, Baraga County, Michigan

- The **Kickapoo** were active in southern Wisconsin, Illinois, and Indiana, particularly along the Vermilion River near its confluence with the Wabash. As with many other Indigenous nations, the Kickapoo were forced to migrate west to reservations in Kansas and Oklahoma. Today, the **Kickapoo Tribe of Oklahoma** has a population of approximately 3,000 members. Its culture remains strong, and its language is still spoken.

- The **Sac and Fox** were hostile to the French who, in 1746, drove them from their homes along the rivers in Wisconsin. These nations eventually migrated southward to what is now southern Wisconsin and Iowa. They currently own more than 8,100 acres in Tama, Marshall, and Palo Alto counties in Iowa. **The Sac and Fox Tribe of the Mississippi** in Iowa (pop. 4,000) is the only federally recognized Indigenous nation in Iowa.

- The **Menominee** culture dates back 10,000 years. They allied with the French until the American Revolution. In 1854, the Menominee were restricted to a reservation located in northeastern Wisconsin. It is the largest existing Indigenous reservation east of the Mississippi River. The Menominee developed a successful forestry program that lasted until the 1954 Termination Act rescinded their land use rights. Then the U.S. government terminated the Menominee's reservation in 1961, declaring it Menominee County. Menominee activists petitioned the courts, and the nation was reinstated in 1973. The **Menominee Tribe** currently has about 8,700 members.

- The **Ho-Chunk Nation (Winnebago)** ranged throughout Wisconsin. The Winnebago factored in the **Black Hawk War** of 1832 in what is now Illinois and Iowa. Black Hawk, a hereditary Sac and Fox chief, was taken prisoner, but he petitioned the federal government for the Indigenous rights within U.S. law. He won his case but was remanded to the custody of a rival chief under whom he lived until his death at age seventy-one. At present, the Ho-Chunk Nation (pop. 10,000) operates several gaming establishments, including a large casino and resort near the Wisconsin Dells.

- The **Miami** were one of the larger tribes in the southern Great Lakes region. They worked cooperatively with the French and the British but had a contentious relationship with the Americans. A series of treaties and land transactions disempowered and impoverished most of the

Miami population before they, too, were forced to relocate west. At present, the **Miami Tribe** is based in Oklahoma and has about 5,600 members. The **Miami Nation of Indians of the State of Indiana** has about 2,500 members, but it does not have federal recognition.

- **The Seminole Tribe of Florida** (pop. 3,300) is one of three associated Seminole nations that are recognized by the federal government. The other two are the **Seminole Nation of Oklahoma** (pop. 17,000) and the **Miccosukee Tribe** in Florida (pop. 600). The Seminole Tribe of Florida is the only Indigenous nation never defeated by the U.S. government.

- The **Calusa** were based in southern Florida near Tampa with territory extending down the Gulf Coast. Once the most powerful Indigenous nation in south Florida, they were a nomadic people with a complex culture based on estuarine fisheries rather than agriculture. Smallpox and measles brought into their territory by European explorers contributed to the demise of the Calusa in the 1700s. A site complex northwest of Fort Myers has a research center dedicated to artifacts and sites related to the Calusa.

AMERICAN AND LATER EUROPEAN SETTLERS

Most of the lake and river ports now located along Highway 41 were settled by early waves of American migrants from the east beginning in the late eighteenth century and continuing throughout the nineteenth century. The majority of the towns and cities along the route were founded during this period. Finnish and Cornish emigrants settled in upper Michigan to work the copper mines, while French, English, and large numbers of Germans emigrated to Wisconsin. Illinois and Indiana had concentrations of German, Irish, and Italian immigrants who were later followed by Poles, Czechs, and Serbians into the twentieth century. Each of these ethnic groups left their mark in communities by building churches and cultural/social networks, many of which persist to this day.

Through sections of Kentucky and Tennessee, Highway 41 traverses parts of territory purchased from the Cherokee Nation by Richard Henderson and the Transylvania Company in 1775. (Yes, real estate speculation has been part of the American experience since the founding). Daniel Boone, James Robertson, and George Rogers Clark were among the notable early pioneers of Scots Irish descent to settle in this part of the country. English settlers arrived in Georgia in the 1730s, followed by Scots Irish and a pronounced concentration of enslaved African Americans to work in fields given to cotton cultivation. Georgia ultimately had almost as many enslaved residents as free citizens in the state. Florida remained under either Spanish or British control until the nineteenth century, with white settlers from Georgia and South Carolina taking up residence there as well as fugitives from slavery who sought safety with the Seminole.

The first white settlers in the southern states through which Highway 41 now runs were primarily farmers and individuals in some way connected to agriculture, and so were the generations that followed, but those demographics have changed markedly since the end of World War II. The invention of the air conditioner, the rise of tourism and retirement communities, and the increase in business and commerce established in the South have propelled diverse population growth in the region, with Latino, Asian, and Caribbean groups settling in significant numbers.

SLAVERY AND THE UNDERGROUND RAILROAD

No discussion of U.S. history is more uncomfortable than the race-based enslavement of Africans who were captured, transported, sold into slavery and forced to work here primarily in agriculture. My forebears left Eastern Europe to escape oppression to have a better life in America. But they did not arrive in chains as did an estimated 12.5 million African captives who spent the rest of their lives in bondage, followed by generations of their progeny, enslaved from birth with little to no hope of freedom, ever. Census tabulations taken from the founding of the American Republic until 1870 do not list the enslaved by name, as they were strictly viewed as commodities to be bought, owned, and sold.

Slavery existed in North America virtually from the very beginning of European colonization. Captured Indigenous peoples and Africans brought over by ship were enslaved by Spanish, British, and Dutch settlers. Indigenous peoples were not used to such treatment, and many of them ran away or simply died of despair. The Indigenous who were enslaved were more susceptible to disease, and it was cheaper to acquire Africans through capture and enslavement. The practice of slavery was initially widespread throughout the country but flourished in the South, particularly in labor-intensive tobacco growing and rice farming. After the invention of the cotton gin in 1794, cotton growing became profitable and encouraged the growth of plantations to be worked by enslaved people. By 1860, four million people of African descent were enslaved in the United States.

The states of Kentucky, Tennessee, Georgia, and Florida—through which Highway 41 runs—were all slave states prior to the Civil War. Signage notes the former existence of slave markets within cities and other aspects of the slave economy along the road that existed up to the Civil War.

Downtown Nashville, TN

The **Underground Railroad** was a network of clandestine routes and safe houses established in the United States during the early to mid-nineteenth century. African American fugitives from slavery used it primarily to escape into free states and Canada. Sections of the Underground Railroad are still located near Highway 41 in southern Indiana and in the cities of Chicago, Illinois, and Kenosha and Racine, Wisconsin. The city of Terre Haute, Indiana, was an important "station" with a network of safe houses and tunnels. A number of safe houses in the southern states are now open to the public for "heritage tours." Thanks to recent historical scholarship, there are now commemorative plaques and monuments along the route, as well as formerly forgotten cemeteries that have been uncovered to more fully tell the tale of slavery and efforts of individuals to fight it. Many travelers will find it worthwhile to learn more about African American settlements and the individual contributions of African Americans to commerce and development along the highway as they take their journeys.

THE CIVIL WAR AND ITS AFTERMATH

There are numerous active and historic military sites along or near Highway 41. These include established forts and armories, battle sites stretching from the French and Indian War through the American Civil War, and military installations that continue to be utilized, such as the Great Lakes Naval Training Center near Chicago and Fort Campbell, the large Army base on the Kentucky-Tennessee border. Throughout the route, particularly in Tennessee and Georgia, are sites of significant engagements during the **American Civil War** (1861–1865).

Important battles occurred at Nashville, Stones River, Murfreesboro, Missionary Ridge, Lookout Mountain, Chickamauga, Kennesaw Mountain, and Atlanta. General Sherman laid siege and burned Atlanta to the ground as he began his march to the sea in 1864. The fields where a host of smaller engagements were fought can be toured near the road as well. Civil War monuments abound in towns and cities throughout Highway 41, with multiple statues in all of the states honoring the fallen. In many cases, these statues are now part of larger groups of monuments to the fallen American soldiers in wars up to the present.

Montgomery County's Tribute to Her Heroic Dead
Crawfordsville, IN

Close to 160 years later, the American Civil War and its aftermath remain divisive topics. In recent years there has been much controversy over the disposition of Confederate monuments and their possible removal from public locations to be relocated in museums and other sites. Many of the statues were put up in the period from 1890 to 1930, but the largest—the **Stone Mountain** bas-relief carving just outside of Atlanta—was only completed in 1972. We will revisit this issue in our travels on Highway 41.

FARMS

A journey on Highway 41 goes through much agricultural country. Farming was one of the most important aspects of the American economy in the nineteenth century. In the 1800s, ninety percent of the American population lived on farms, and as late as 1920, there were thirty-two million people (nearly a third of the total U.S. population) living on farms. Today, less than one percent of Americans live on farms. There are many reasons for this change of course: the mechanization of farming, which requires fewer workers; better-paying opportunities in urban areas; the migration of farm workers seeking an escape from sharecropping oppression; and the consolidation of small farms into larger agribusiness entities. You will still see a great deal of farm country along Highway 41, but many of the houses and barns along the way are empty.

Near Hillsboro, TN

Along with the establishment of farms were county seats for the administration of government activities within the states. Historically, county seats were located near the geographic center of their respective counties to accommodate access to courts and business with government officials. County seats also became important centers of commerce where farmers brought crops to sell. Walmart Inc. developed its retail stores through the South during its early growth on the basis of locating stores just outside county seats. Highway 41 traverses through numerous county seats over the course of its distance.

Historic Citrus County Courthouse, Inverness, FL

THE RAILROADS

The coming of the railways in the mid-1800s killed off the stage coach trade, with almost all rural roads reverted to low-level local use mainly by horse-drawn carriage. The age of the rail, roughly from 1850 to 1950, created large cities in the interior of the country as "inland harbors" where commerce could be directed to and from. The cities of Chicago, Nashville, and Atlanta became important rail hubs as the country grew in population. Railroads also allowed people to travel from homes far from the city in newly created suburbs and nearby small towns lucky enough to have a railroad stop.

Railways built in the early part of the twentieth century still parallel Highway 41 along much of its route, and they continue to be vital to the nation's commerce. Many of the earliest rail track beds have been repurposed into bikeways and parkland. By 1910, horse-drawn carriages were about to give way to motorized vehicles, the subject of our next chapter. At present, Chicago remains the preeminent railroad center in the United States.

Newberry, FL

Electric interurban lines, powered by overhead electrical wires, were connecting many small towns with large cities at the beginning of the twentieth century. But these trains had lost out to the automobile for the most part after 1920. The interurban lines slowly disappeared, although one of the last interurban train lines, the **South Shore Line**, still operates between Chicago and South Bend, Indiana.

In addition to major rail lines, electric streetcars (trolleys) on "light rail" proliferated in areas within and near cities. Streetcars were gradually replaced by bus transportation and automobiles by the middle of the twentieth century. At present, some urban centers have brought light rail transportation back as an alternate means of transportation, such as the **TECO Streetcar** system that runs through downtown Tampa, Florida. Everything old becomes new again.

BICYCLES

Bicycles had been around for much of the nineteenth century when the design of the chain safety bicycle in 1885 and the inflatable pneumatic tire in 1888 caused a big jump in their efficiency. These inventions transformed the bike into a must-have product that could be ridden easily by women as well as by men. By the 1890s, hundreds of manufacturers had entered the bicycle business, and numerous repair shops were created to service them. The Wright Brothers were bicycle mechanics, as was teen-aged Carl Fisher, who owned a bike shop in Indianapolis and later figured heavily in the development of Highway 41.

Cyclists were the first group to use paved roads and to push for high-quality surfaces—"Good Roads" that would be built by cities, states, and ultimately the federal government. The first production motorcycles were developed toward the end of the decade, and the transfer of technology from cycling to automobile-making would take place over the 1890s as well. As automobile travel took hold, bicycles became an activity for children. In the 2000s, bicycle travel in the United States has enjoyed a resurgence of interest, particularly in cities that have created street lanes and paths for bike riders.

INDUSTRIALIZATION AND URBAN MIGRATION

Heavy industry developed in major cities along the highway as the nation grew. Manufacturing, refining, and food processing became prominent industries in Milwaukee, Chicago, northern Indiana, Evansville, Nashville, Chattanooga, and Atlanta. These cities grew as people left impoverished farms and large numbers of immigrants from Eastern and Southern Europe arrived in the early part of the twentieth century to work and live in the large inland urban centers.

The massive wealth created landed in a few hands, but most industrial workers faced low wages and unsafe working conditions. Violent strikes, such as the Pullman Strike of 1894, eventually led to more progressive policies to curb corruption and monopolistic big business practices that had been exposed by investigative journalism. The dawn of the twentieth century saw new technologies that changed the way people lived: the increased availability and use of electricity, telephones, phonographs, and "moving pictures." The first sustained human-controlled motorized flight took place in 1903. But the biggest impact on the country would be from the "horseless carriage," the subject of our next chapter.

CHAPTER TWO
WHEELS AND ROADS

Highway 41/DuSable Lake Shore Drive, Chicago, IL

"Automobiles are a useless nuisance. They'll never amount to anything but a nuisance. They had no business to be invented."

"I'm not so sure he's wrong about automobiles," Eugene Morgan responded. "With all their speed forward, they may be a step backward in civilization. It may be that they will not add to the beauty of the world, nor to the life of men's souls. I am not sure. But automobiles have come, and they bring a greater change in our life than most of us suspect. They are here, and almost all outward things are going to be different because of what they may bring. They are going to alter war, and they are going to alter peace. I think men's minds are going to be changed in subtle ways because of automobiles just how, though, I could hardly guess. But you can't have the immense outward changes that they will cause without some inward ones, and it may be that George is right, and that the spiritual alteration will be bad for us. Perhaps, ten or twenty years from now, if we can see the inward change in men by that time, I shouldn't be able to defend the gasoline engine but would have to agree with him that automobiles 'had no business to be invented.'"

—Passage from, The Magnificent Ambersons, by Booth Tarkington (1918)

The development of the automobile and the growth of roads in the United States are intertwined over the last 125 years. For better or worse, the profound changes that took place during this process have made the country we know today. To understand how the decades have unfolded since the introduction of the automobile and the development of Highway 41 is what this chapter is all about.

THE HORSELESS CARRIAGE

The invention of the automobile in Germany and France in the late 1800s changed the face of transportation in the world. While perfected in Europe, the United States was where the "horseless carriage" invention, first introduced in 1894 with eight registered vehicles, quickly took hold. At first, people did not think of automobiles as something useful; they were more like toys. Early cars were also expensive and unreliable. They always seemed to be breaking down, and tires went flat as often as once or twice a day on an all-day trip. "Git a hoss!" was the delightful expression often directed at a motorist stuck repairing a malfunctioning vehicle. However, the technology progressed, and the world would change in the new century. Automakers began building in larger quantities to lower the operating expenses and, hence, the purchase price.

The 1900s: The number of cars registered in the U.S. was 8,000 in 1900.

HENRY FORD AND THE BEGINNING OF THE AUTOMOTIVE AGE

In the early 1900s, a nation of farmers still needed a way to bring goods from farm to market. With its vast land area and scattered communities, the United States had a greater need for automotive transportation than Europe. In 1903, Henry Ford and eleven investors incorporated the Ford Motor Company in a converted Detroit wagon factory. Ford was a machinist by trade, and he was working on engines at the birth of the automobile age. Ford's creation of the affordable **Model T** car in 1908 was the catalyst for the end of rural isolation and the beginning of the automotive age. While the arrival of affordable automobiles brought urban amenities to rural towns, ushering in better medical care and schools, it also hastened the end of the traditional family farm.

Ford did not invent the automobile, but he was the first to understand the mass appeal it would have for people who were not wealthy but wanted affordable individual transportation. He was obsessed with building the best product and embraced mass production ideas that disregarded corporate conventions of the time where each item was hand-built separately. Long before modern management principles were codified, Ford constantly refined ways to build the auto by producing uniform products using repetitive and standardized processes. Durable, cheap, and easy to repair, the Model T was an "everyman's car" that was able to travel on dirt and log roads within the primitive road system then in place. Over fifteen million Model T's were made and sold between 1908 and 1927, transforming the car experience from a novelty to a necessity.

Although three-quarters of all the cars in use at the time were Fords, the automaker was not inclined to provide funds for private highway projects for the general public. He believed that the highways of America should be built at taxpayer expense.

Had Ford retired early, he would have been ranked high in the management pantheon, but it did not work out that way. He resisted change and did not understand the growing middle class was imbued with an interest in style and travel for other than work. The founders of what became General Motors instituted different car types to appeal to different market segments—a distinction Ford failed to realize. The Ford company lost its lead in car sales to GM in 1924 and would only regain it sixty-three years later. Ford's anti-union stance, ardent anti-Semitism, and health issues all affected the company's financial strength and popularity. It wasn't until after World War II that the Ford Motor Company began to regain significant market share.

The 1910s: The number of cars registered in the U.S. was 500,000 in 1910.

TRANSCONTINENTAL ROADS

Over time, many original animal trails, later followed by Indigenous peoples, had evolved to become bridle paths, wagon roads, paved roads, and highways. Some of which survive today, at least in part, along their original courses. From dirt and stone paths grew a series of differently named paved long-distance roads in the early days of the automobile with names such as the **Lincoln Highway**, the **Yellowstone Trail**, the **Dixie Highway**, and the **National Old Trails Highway**, creating much confusion among early automobile drivers.

Private road associations were formed to promote their own routes, particularly in smaller cities intent on providing thoroughfares for commerce and recreation when motoring was still considered a leisure activity. Boosters would select a route over existing—sometimes barely existing—roads, giving them colorful names, forming automobile associations to promote the trails, and collecting dues from businesses and towns along the way. The associations published maps and brochures, held annual conventions, and advocated for improvements in the highways. In downtown Chicago, a wonderful mural painted by John Warner Norton in 1928 is now on display in the former headquarters of the **Chicago Motor Club** (now the **Hampton Inn & Suites-Chicago**). It displays nineteen routes by the old trail names rather than the number designations that were just beginning to take hold in the country.

The Highway Mural in the former Chicago Motor Club,
now a Hampton Inn in Downtown Chicago, IL

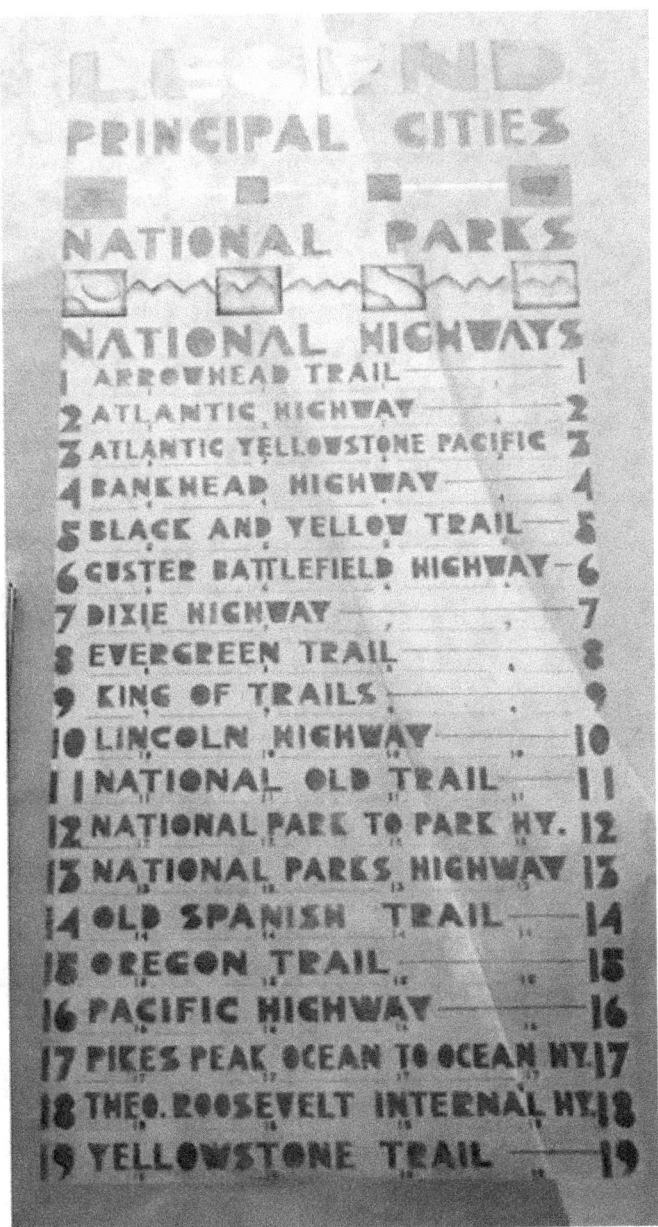

National Highways circa 1925

Historic National Automobile Route, Theresa, WI

VIGNETTE   MISS ALMA RITTENBERRY

Among the more interesting characters in the founding of U.S. 41 is Miss Alma Rittenberry (1858–1930), a resident of Birmingham, Alabama, and a member of the Birmingham Equal Suffrage Association, the Poetry Society of Alabama, and the United Daughters of the Confederacy. She would also become one of the first unlikely boosters of a major north-south highway.

An early proponent of transcontinental travel as well as the one of the few females in a leadership capacity, "Miss Alma," as she was known, conceived a route called the

"Jackson Highway" to honor President Andrew Jackson by linking Chicago and New Orleans as a "financial and cultural gain for the North and South." At that time, the few cars available were very expensive, and longer travel meant taking a train since most roads were nothing but wagon ruts in the mud. The Jackson Highway Association was organized at the National Good Roads Convention in 1911 in Birmingham.

After giving speeches around the country in tireless pursuit of public support for the road she lost control in January 1917 to a group of men who supported a different routing for the road. She resigned from the Association saying, "If Andrew Jackson knew the unchivalrous act of you men, he would turn in his grave; he was at least courteous to women." She developed a rival association to support a new route, initially called the "North-South National Bee-Line Highway" or "Dixie Bee" for short. It was like the Jackson Highway but routed farther east to pass through Nashville. Miss Alma, unfortunately, was never able to secure enough interest or financial backing for her alternate road. She died in 1930, but her ideas would live on and eventually become Highway 41 and Highway 31.

GOOD ROADS AND FEDERAL LEGISLATION

As more automobiles entered what had been local roads in the 1910s and 1920s, the pressure for bigger and better thoroughfares extending throughout the country became stronger. A loose coalition of rural farmers and bicyclist organizations, such as the League of American Wheelmen, had formed the **Good Roads Movement** in the latter part of the nineteenth century to advocate for improved roads to benefit commerce, agriculture, and tourism. Over time, the movement's focus turned toward cars. Being positioned close to a major highway route would also, over time, bring improvements to existing roads nearby. Dirt roads would be graveled to allow for faster speeds. Gravel roads would eventually be paved with macadam, asphalt, or concrete to smooth out travel, enabling farmers to bring their crops and livestock to market and generally advance a community's prospects.

Passage of the landmark **1916 Federal Aid Road Act** and the **1921 Federal Highway Act** provided much needed federal money for the development and construction of hard surfaced "post roads" (routes maintained for the transport of mail) and "interstate" highways.

CARL GRAHAM FISHER AND THE DIXIE HIGHWAY

Innovations in road building technology and design prompted more promotion of long-distance automobile highways and state and federal control over roads by advocates such as Carl Fisher (1874–1939), an entrepreneur who made a fortune manufacturing headlights for automobiles. Fisher became a real estate developer in Indianapolis and founded the Indianapolis Motor Speedway in 1911. He later figured heavily in the development of Florida, and Miami Beach in particular. (*Author's Note: A longer description of Carl Fisher is in Chapter eleven*). Long before it was accepted that road building was the task of government, Fisher was one of the earliest proponents of privately funding the coast-to-coast road for automobiles that would become the **Lincoln Highway (U.S. 30).**

Fisher's other idea was the multi-pronged **"Dixie Highway,"** stretching over 5,706 miles and connecting north and south through two mainlines that encompassed multiple roadways in Florida, Georgia, Tennessee, Kentucky, Indiana, Illinois, Ohio, and Michigan and extended north to Canada. An organizational meeting for the **Dixie Highway Association** occurred in 1915 in Chattanooga, Tennessee, where the association was headquartered. The roads comprising the east and west mainlines were completed by 1927, and the Dixie Highway Association disbanded. The route traversed now by Highway 41 was known prior to 1926 as the **"Dixie Bee Line."** Though technically never disbanded, the private Dixie Highway was subsumed by the federal highway system, becoming U.S. Routes 31, 41, 25, and 27 as well as other state route numbers over its length.

Today, a good case could be made for **Interstate 75** as the modern Dixie Highway running from Sault Ste. Marie in Michigan to Fort Lauderdale, Florida. The old Dixie Highway exists today through street names and Dixie Highway markers along its original route. Thanks to diligent roadway archeologists and great software, the highway has been mapped out for diligent travelers. See Two Lane Traveler Dixie Highway Map:

https://2lanetraveler.com/home/dhmaps/

The 1920s: The number of cars registered in the U.S. was 7.5 million in 1920.

The Dixie Highway, from the University of Tennessee at Chattanooga Archives

GROWTH OF AUTOMOBILE OWNERSHIP AND TRAVEL

By 1927, General Motors offered seventy-two different car models with extensive choices of colors and accessories—autos had become a way to express one's vanity and economic status. Sunday church services were replaced with Sunday drives for all members of the family. Cars designed expressly for female drivers who embraced the freedom of the automobile rolled off the assembly lines. Decentralization of housing began in the 1920s with once isolated villages becoming city suburbs. This trend accelerated after World War II with the development of suburban residential subdivisions designed with automobile ownership and use in mind.

Motorized trucks and buses became more practical and available in the years leading up to World War I, and railroads began losing business to trucking companies. Trucking helped spread factories deep into the countryside—the impetus for municipal zoning laws. Communities adopted low density layouts separating housing from jobs, creating more dependence upon the auto. Intercity bus transportation replaced interurban rail lines, whose tracks were subsequently torn up or paved over.

ROAD TRIPS

In the 1920s, the American love affair with the road trip was just beginning. Grace L. Shelley published the **Automobile Road Guide De Luxe** in 1922. It has maps of the national parks and highways. Rand McNally's first road atlas followed in 1924. Traveling for pleasure and adventure was something new on the American scene and was celebrated in film and song. The increasing popularity of the road trip gave birth to the need for hotels and inns in smalltown America. The first "tourist homes" included camps and cabin courts, which in turn, gave way to motor inns or "motels" to house travelers on their way to their destinations.

Roadside eating places introduced travelers to regional cuisines, while the concept of fast-food franchising began in 1925 with the first A&W Root Beer stands. Automobile service stations and dealerships sprung up along or near major roads, sporting big advertising signs to lure customers. Along Highway 41 are old drag racing and stock car racing tracks dating back to the early days of the auto. As cars became more efficient, they were able to pull small trailers.

In 1919, a group known as the Tin Can Tourists of the World (TCT) was set up by trailer enthusiasts. The TCT first met in Tampa, Florida, to create safe and clean campgrounds for people to visit. It's thought the name originated from the Ford Model T, or "Tin Lizzie," which was the preferred set of wheels for many TCT members at the time.

Automobile Road Guide 1922, Indiana State Archives

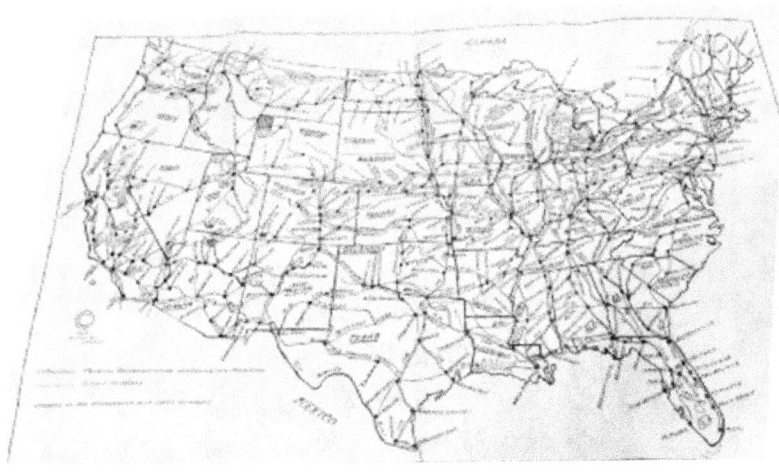

1922 road map, Indiana State Archives

THE ROOTS OF HIGHWAY 41
VIGNETTE ALVAN VERNON (A.V.) BURCH (1886-1973)

A.V. Burch of Evansville, Indiana, born in a log cabin and the owner of a farm implement company, was appointed by the governor of Indiana in 1921 to be the vice chairman, and later the chairman, of the new Indiana State Highway Commission. Burch is considered the "father of the Indiana highway system" and was one of the major boosters and designers of the Dixie-Bee Highway, as Highway 41 was then known.

He envisioned "the greatest highway in the Midwest" with Evansville as the midpoint. Not only did he sell the idea to Indiana, but he also sold it to other states along the proposed highway. Late in life, he fought to have 41 become part of the Interstate Highway System. Highway 41 remains one of the most heavily traveled thoroughfares in the country (other than interstate highways) through most of its passage.

Burch was a colorful character in Indiana who ran unsuccessfully for Congress, governor, and mayor of Evansville. He divorced his first wife after almost fifty years of marriage to marry a young hairdresser and then divorced again to marry the proprietor of a hat shop in the McCurdy Hotel in Evansville, headquarters of the U.S. 41 Association.

"U.S. Highway 41. "The Boulevard of America." The Bee-Line North and South. The shortest, fastest, best; most historical and most scenic route between the Great Lakes and the Florida Keys."

"From Northern blasts
To Southern sun
The shortest route
Is 41.

———————

From Southern heat
To Northern rest
Route 41
Is much the best."

"There is romance beyond every mirage along this wide, smooth ribbon of concrete that lies where Indian trails once wended their ways through primeval forests."

—*Early 1920s Promotional Pieces from the*
U.S. 41 Association—Indiana Historical Society

Americans' acquisition of mass-produced automobiles in the 1920s created a huge demand for reliable paved, well-marked roads. Cheap oil and the invention of stressed concrete along with asphalt for use as a roadbed allowed motorists unprecedented mobility. The ability to travel on a paved road to the north woods of Michigan and Wisconsin or to the palms and ocean beaches of Florida or almost everywhere in between was extraordinary for small-town and rural Americans.

Until the complete development of the Midwest interstate corridors (I-75 and I-65) in the late 1970s, Highway 41, completed in 1926, was the main stem road from Chicago to Miami. Depending on your age, you may remember when the interstate was not completely connected and there were epic traffic jams on 41 as it went through small cities with multiple stoplights before returning back to a highway.

In 1917, Wisconsin became the first state to legislate numbering rather than naming its roads. Other states soon followed suit. Work on the designation of a nationwide system of highways began in 1925 with the **Federal Aid Highway Act.** The federal action took previously disjointed roads and combined them into a significant whole, with uniform numbers and standardized shields rather than names and colored bands on telephone poles.

The new highway system was finalized and opened in 1926 with marked and numbered highways—ten main east-west transcontinental routes designated in multiples of ten and a series of important north and south routes numbered 1, 11, 21, 31, 41, etc. It was thought that the route numbering system would be beneficial to tourists in following through routes with even-numbered east and west routes and odd-numbered north and south routes. The advent of the Interstate Highway System in the mid-1950s would, for the most part, keep this designation as well.

The federal government designated the **American Association of State Highway Transportation Officials (AASHTO)**, a nonprofit, nonpartisan association representing highway and transportation departments throughout the country to foster the development, operation, and maintenance of the transportation system. This organization remains an important standard-setting body and liaison between state highway departments and the federal government.

1930–1950: The number of registered cars was 23 million in 1930, 26 million in 1940, and, due to manufacturing for the war effort, decreased to 25 million in 1950.

The rural composition of the country up to the 1930s encouraged the use of the automobile. Main streets designed for horse teams and wagons were changed to accommodate automobiles. The car vastly increased people's range of social contacts and recreational opportunities, opening previously isolated locations not served by passenger trains. By providing personal mobility on a scale never before known, the automobile changed the landscape and culture of the United States.

Cars meant freedom, choice, privacy, individualism, and self-reliance. Road trips and recreational opportunities became synonymous with America. The automobile, in the words of a historian, "freed common people from the limitations of their geography" and offered opportunities for people of modest means to journey to places far beyond the confines of their hometowns. Road trips became a rite of passage for men and women of all ages to explore the country by car for recreation, for romance, for excitement.

The Great Depression of the 1930s and advent of U.S. involvement in World War II in the early 1940s intervened and depressed auto ownership, and it would not fully recover until the 1950s. For those who could still afford to buy cars and travel, built-in trunks to store luggage in the back of cars became common. The year 1936 saw the invention of the iconic Airstream Clipper, an all-aluminum, riveted travel trailer that could be customized— another mode of transport that shaped the image of the American road trip in the decades to come.

THE GREAT MIGRATION AND AFRICAN AMERICAN TRAVEL

Similar to the need to fill in gaps in our understanding of the settlements and forced removal of Indigenous peoples from lands along Highway 41 is the need to document the African American travelers' experiences north and south. As one of the two main north-south routes within the center of the country, the Dixie-Bee Highway name served as a constant reminder to African American travelers of the oppression of slavery while conveying to white travelers the view of the old Confederacy as an idyllic era. Highway 41 was considered a "tourist road" in many early guidebooks, but it was also a conduit for the "Great Migration" of southern African Americans to the north—principally Chicago.

The Great Migration (1910–1970) of approximately five million people, remains the greatest mass movement of people in the history of the United States. During the Jim Crow era of racial segregation, which lasted from the end of Reconstruction through the mid-1960s, the **American Automobile Association (AAA)**, established in Chicago in 1902, actively discriminated against African Americans. They were not allowed to join the association.

The Negro Motorist Green Book (or simply the **"Green Book"** for short) was created in the 1930s as a guide to navigate services and tourist attractions that were relatively friendly to African Americans along the nation's highways. The book listed hotels, restaurants, and other Black-owned businesses until the mid-1960s, when the passage of the Civil Rights Act effectively ended Jim Crow laws in the South. In recent times there has been a reverse migration of sorts as African Americans return from northern cities back to the South to cities such as Atlanta.

THE 1950s POSTWAR AMERICA AND INTERSTATE HIGHWAYS

In the postwar years, cars became increasingly affordable, and many families were able to own them for the first time. This opened the world of road tripping up to a wider audience. A growing middle class with disposable income ventured on vacations with a new set of diners, motels, and tourist sites designed to serve them.

Traffic surged on Highway 41. This highway and other "vacation" routes created in the 1920s and 1930s were soon deemed insufficient to handle the increase. As traffic accidents multiplied, Highway 41 was dubbed "Killer 41" by locals. State highway departments began to build bypasses around towns and cities. In 1949, the terminus of Highway 41 in Naples, Florida was extended across the Everglades on what was known as the Tamiami Trail to Miami on the Atlantic coast.

After World War II, President Eisenhower and a new highway lobby in Congress pushed for more roads. The **Federal Aid Highway Act of 1956** provided a program for funding through the Highway Trust Fund to build an interstate highway system throughout the United States. Famously, as a young Army officer, Eisenhower was part of a 1919 convoy that took sixty-two days to go from Washington D.C. to San Francisco. The trip made a deep impression upon him, and it only intensified once he traveled on the German Autobahn at the end of World War II. Prior to the war, Congress had already passed the **Federal Highway Act of 1940**, which instituted the underpinning for the interstate system with some sections already under construction.

Unlike the earlier federally funded routes that passed directly through towns, the interstate superhighways featured a select number of exits utilizing on and off ramps rather than directly intersecting with other roads. The roads were designed during the Cold War to also carry troops and missiles. This allowed interstates to have higher speed limits, more lanes, and greater and safer traffic flow without stoplights. While the old highway routes often were more scenic as they wound through population centers and over physical obstacles such as rivers, the interstates were designed less for scenery than for speed and efficiency in travel. Tragically, many interstates in major cities were blasted through once vibrant neighborhoods, primarily in poor and minority sections. This intentional process led to urban blight, as well-documented in books such as *The Power Broker* (1974) by Robert Caro.

The majority of the interstate system was built between 1956 and the early 1970s. Federal funding for interstate projects ended in the late 1990s, and states now own and operate the roads. It is important to note that while there is uniform signage throughout the country, the maintenance, upkeep, and further development of both the interstate and highway systems are within the province of each state. State highway departments of transportation make decisions and institute rehabilitation projects as they see fit, along with the involvement of **Metropolitan Planning Organizations** in larger cities. Each state has its own rules for the regulation of traffic and works with neighboring states on interoperability issues. This might get complicated when driverless cars are introduced in the near future.

The 1960s: The number of cars registered in the U.S. was 61.6 million in 1960.

CAR CULTURE

The high point of the American automobile era was in the 1950s and 1960s with cheap fuel and station wagons for road trips to see relatives, to visit a vacation destination, and/or to travel to a shopping center in the expanding suburbs. The future was envisioned by Walt Disney's "Magic Highways" (1958) as a series of high-speed motoring destinations traveled by cars that function as rolling homes. The tourist boom in the 50s and 60s also accelerated a trend toward preserving more wildlife and recreation areas near highways. On TV, the adventures of Buz and Tod as they drove around the country in a Corvette were the subject of *Route 66* (1960–1964), while the movie *Easy Rider* (1969), starring Dennis Hopper and Peter Fonda, brought life on the road to multitudes of restless souls. Though it only lasted one season, *Then Came Bronson* (1969), an interesting TV show, featured Michael Parks tooling around the country on his motorcycle.

The 1970s: The number of cars registered in the U.S. was 118 million in 1970 —more than quadruple twenty years before.

With most money going to completion of the interstate system, the need for maintenance for the aging highway infrastructure and increasing congestion in certain sections of Highway 41 created problems often neglected until public pressure forced changes, such as expanding large portions of the former two-lane road into four-lane highways. From the standpoint of speed, this was a good thing. It allowed faster travel between destinations. But many of the interesting, adventurous aspects of places and attractions along the road could now only be found on what was titled "Old 41." Highway 41 was no longer the main north-south highway; it had been largely supplanted by I-75 from Tennessee to Florida, and Wisconsin had officially designated 41 as an interstate highway between Green Bay and the Illinois state line.

Ease of travel became more complicated in the early 1970s, when instability in the Middle East and OPEC oil embargoes in 1973 and 1979 limited the availability of gasoline and dramatically increased prices. Safety, environmental concerns, and efficient gas mileage became more important to the everyday motorist. New mandates required seat belts, and collapsible bumpers became standard on cars. Smaller cars, particularly imported cars that provided good gas mileage, became increasingly popular and sold in increasing numbers.

The 70s also brought demographic changes along the highway, as smaller towns and rural areas lost population to the larger cities. Starting in the 1970s and continuing to the present, a large influx of individuals from northern cities moved south to Florida, transforming the Gulf Coast communities along the road. Huge retirement and recreational complexes were developed, and Florida became the third most populous state in the country by 2014.

The 1980s: The number of cars registered in the U.S. was 121.6 million in 1980.

After a lag in the 1970s due to the oil crisis, travel resumed its upward trajectory in the 1980s with growth of the Recreational Vehicle (RV) industry. Popular movies whose storylines featured motorhomes cemented the RV's place in popular culture. The minivan was introduced in the mid-1980s and became the family vehicle of choice, supplanting station wagons. Few individuals had car phones until late in the decade, and folks on road trips could enjoy music recorded on cassette tapes. Without smartphones or GPS, travelers still relied on guidebooks, folding maps, and road atlases. The "Mother Road," iconic Route 66, was decommissioned in 1985 after newer, faster interstate routes had made it obsolete.

The 1990s: The number of cars registered in the U.S. was 193 million in 1990.

The 1990s saw the waning of the family sedan and the rise of SUVs (sport utility vehicles) and pickup trucks as popular vehicles of choice. SUVs offered more amenities, space, and cargo capacity. They became a dominant segment in the automotive market, offering a wide range of options to cater to different consumer preferences and needs. Improved fuel efficiency, climate control, and upscale interiors sealed in passengers, effectively disconnecting them from the passing road.

Pickup trucks became larger and were no longer used simply for utility. Now they are marketed to convey rugged and active lifestyle. The 1990s also saw a surge in car culture. Vehicles became more than mere modes of transportation—they became symbols of freedom, individuality, and expression.

Post 2000: The number of cars registered in the U.S. was 225.8 million in 2000, 250 million in 2010, 276 million in 2020, and 283 million in 2024.

Annual travel on the nation's highways reached an estimated 2.7 trillion vehicle miles in 2000, four times the level in 1960. In the first decade of the twenty-first century, a number of external economic shocks—chiefly the Great Recession of 2008–2009—disproportionately impacted small cities and towns in the mid-section of the United States. Populations declined dramatically in smaller towns as young people left for better opportunities in larger cities, and the "graying" population still in place was less willing or able to invest in stores and businesses that once personified small town living.

A shift in manufacturing capacity to Asia and the rise of corporate farming adversely impacted smaller cities dependent upon a less diverse business base. Tourism and factory location by some global companies enabled some places to maintain a healthy economy, but numerous communities lost their reason for being and became shells of what they once were. Tech skills, increasingly needed for most work, required higher levels of education and broadband accessibility that small towns often lacked. Some "winner" cities along the road prospered due to their location and allure: Nashville, Atlanta, Tampa, and Miami fit in that characterization, and their metropolitan areas have greatly expanded.

Many businesses remaining in small towns relocated closer to the highway to serve motorists less interested in stopping for prolonged visits. "Dollar Stores" proliferated on the outskirts of towns with smaller economic bases. In the 2000s, drivers no longer needed to worry about packing snacks for their road trips thanks to the proliferation of drive-thru fast-food outlets. Drive-thru pharmacies, grocery stores, liquor stores, coffee shops, and banks are now ubiquitous along the country's highways and byways by this point.

By the decade of the 2010s, technology had transformed the way drivers operated in motor vehicles. GPS technology started to appear on smartphones and later on dashboard screens for drivers. Paper maps and guidebooks were no longer essential to travel. Electric vehicles became more accepted, efficient, and profitable. Driver-assistance features utilized software with in-car operating systems connected to phones. Vehicles became "smart" with sensing features commonly including Artificial Intelligence (AI), Internet of Things (IoT), and advanced connectivity features. The aftermath of the Great Recession lasted well into the decade, engendering a new phenomenon of transient lifestyles as people traveled around the United States in search of seasonal work. More solo travel and the search for affordable living accommodations took place. Independent travel and remote work redefined professional and personal experiences for people.

American roads were moving ever-increasing numbers of people and goods, but studies suggested that over forty percent of the nationwide highway system was in poor or mediocre condition. As the backlog of rehabilitation needs grew, motorists were forced to pay over $1,000 every year in wasted time and fuel. The **Bipartisan Infrastructure Law** was passed in 2021 to provide urgently needed funding for a variety of projects, including road and bridge repairs.

Traffic fatalities, once on the decline, started to rise once again as speed limits were increased. The start of the 2020s threw a curveball at the travel industry: the COVID-19 pandemic. As of mid-2024, over 1.2 million people in the United States have died from the COVID-19 virus since March 2020. Popular destinations, such as Las Vegas, had their incomes from tourism almost completely slashed overnight as lockdowns took hold and flights were cancelled. However, when Americans were allowed to travel within the USA again, road trips experienced a renaissance. A whole new class of retired baby boomers were tooling around in RVs, flooding many national parks. The country's population grew .01 percent in 2021, the slowest rate since the nation was founded, but it has since moved upward by .04 percent, mainly due to international migration.

Another unexpected twist from the pandemic was the rise in remote working, which made long-term home workstations a genuinely feasible option for many. Digital workers no longer needed to be tied to traditional office commutes, planting a question mark on the future of downtowns in some large cities. Many people moved to select small towns, sunbelt locations, and a few big cities like Austin, Texas; Raleigh-Durham, North Carolina; and Orlando, Florida. Some individuals have migrated from the coasts to interior areas of the country due to the effects of climate change and rising housing costs, but this trend has been dwarfed by individuals moving to cheaper sunbelt cities for housing and economic opportunities.

Cities, towns, and countryside along Highway 41 continue to evolve in large and small ways. High fuel prices have impacted the way the road trip is viewed, but post-pandemic there has been a surge in road travel. Passenger train travel within the interior of the country unfortunately remains underdeveloped, but it has also increased along with air travel.

CONCLUDING THOUGHTS

Geography is destiny. We all carry maps of our country, however big or small, in our minds. If you live like much of the population, within or near one of the major metropolitan regions of the country, you are connected to employment, healthcare, recreation, culture, and educational opportunities.

But traditional small towns and cities with main streets, courthouses in county seats, neighborhood churches, and quiet residential avenues are still what many associate with the American experience. You can still find the old diners and motels from a bygone time along Highway 41.

Many smaller communities are thriving and have evolved to meet new needs and remain relevant. But there are also areas that have slowly disintegrated without a committed citizenry to provide vision and talent. Living costs, quality of life issues, and income play a large role in a traveler's vision along the road. A depressing sameness can afflict many places along America's main highways.

Today, for the American experience, it is important to try to venture beyond the franchises and chain stores to see where people live and what they do. I will have more to say later in our story about how changing patterns of American life are impacting communities along the road.

Car culture is still woven deeply into the American social fabric. This is emblematic on a trip down Highway 41. But rising fuel prices, inflation, sprawl and congestion, climate change, obesity, drug use, and senseless gun violence are also associated with automobile travel in the nation today.

As a road traveler, you may no longer achieve the romantic vision of automobile travel as promoted in the early days of the highway, but you will see a mature country grappling for what it wants to be in a new era—at once both hopeful and dystopian. Yes, there are many contradictions on the open road. Highway 41 is where you will see all of this in front of you.

So, we begin the journey through states along iconic Highway 41, starting in the woods of Michigan's Upper Peninsula.

ENDNOTES

For additional information on the early years of the road system in this chapter please see, *From Names to Numbers: The Origins of the U.S. Numbered Highway System,* by Richard Weingroff. Retrieved from https://www.fhwa.dot.gov/infrastructure/numbers.cfm.

Information on Tin Can Tourists is from *The History of our Tin Can Tourists* by Leroy Mills, 1946. Retrieved from https://tincantourists.com/2818-2/.

Highways are split into at least four different types of systems in the United States: Interstate Highways, U.S. Highways, State Highways, and County Highways. They are generally arranged by a route number or letter. These designations are generally displayed along the route by means of a highway shield. Each system has its own unique design to enable easy identification of the highway type. See signs on the next page.

PART TWO
NORTH

CHAPTER THREE
UPPER PENINSULA, MICHIGAN (THE U.P.)

"Gad that is great country."

— *Ernest Hemingway*

Highway 41 through Michigan is 279 miles and one of the main roads in the Upper Peninsula.

Key Towns/Cities: *Copper Harbor, Houghton, L'Anse, Negaunee, Ishpeming, Marquette, Escanaba, Menominee*

Michigan Counties along 41: *Keweenaw, Houghton, Baraga, Marquette, Delta, Menominee*

The Upper Peninsula (U.P.) is a separate and isolated region far different from the rest of the state of Michigan. It is connected to the Lower Peninsula of Michigan, which resembles a mitten, only by the Mackinac Bridge. However, the U.P. shares a 200-mile border with the state of Wisconsin.

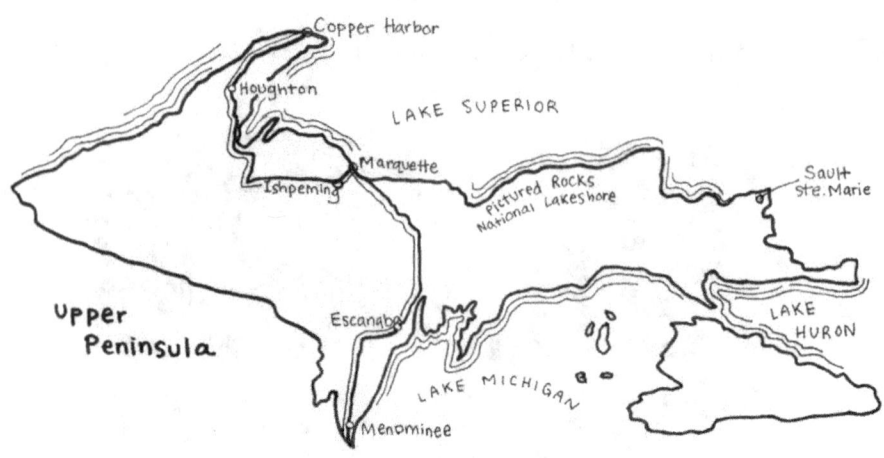

A U.P. ALBUM PLAYLIST

- Gordon Lightfoot: *Summertime Dream* 1976
- Lee Murdock: *Standing at the Wheel* 2002
- Duke Ellington: *Anatomy of a Murder* (soundtrack) 1959
- Sufjan Stevens: *Michigan* 2003
- Lord Huron: *Lonesome Dreams* 2012
- Bob Seger: *Stranger in Town* 1978
- T-Bizzy & The Management: *Welcome Home* 2018
- Alyssa Palmer: *Yooper Girl* 2022
- Phil Lynch: *Comin' Home* 2022
- Liquid Mike: *Paul Bunyan's Slingshot* 2024

ORIGINS

Indigenous cultures occupied the area of the U.P. for centuries before the arrival of Europeans. The Ottawa, Ojibwe (Chippewa), and Potawatomi nations populated the region and formed a loose alliance known as the "Three Fires." Small-scale mining, agriculture, fishing, hunting, and gathering activities formed the basis of life. The arrival of the French explorers in the late seventeenth century changed the dynamic of life for Indigenous peoples. French fur traders explored the area in search of beaver and other fur-bearing animals. They traded pelts with Indigenous nations for arms, ammunition, utensils, blankets, and cloth. Eventually, thousands of Indigenous peoples were employed within the fur trade which lasted until the beaver population became depleted in the early 1800s. French and, later, British traders in frontier outposts often took Indigenous wives, and the offspring of these mixed unions were called the *Métis*.

The end of the American Revolution led to the U.S.–Canadian boundary, dividing Lakes Superior, Huron, Erie, and Ontario as established by treaty in 1782, but the sheer remoteness of the U.P. promoted a weak sense of nationalism. You may be asking yourself, "Why isn't the U.P. part of Wisconsin?" That's an interesting historical sidelight that has to do with the founding of the United States and its acquisition of land from France after the American Revolution.

The Northwest Ordinance was adopted by the Confederation Congress in 1787 as it established a government for the Northwest Territory, outlining a process for admitting states into the Union, guaranteeing that the newly created states would be equal to the original thirteen states, protecting civil liberties, and prohibiting slavery in the new territories. This ordinance eventually led to the creation of the states of Ohio, Michigan, Wisconsin, Indiana, and Illinois.

Separate maps drawn by Ohio (the 17th state, admitted in 1803) and what was then the Michigan territory led to a confrontation over a piece of land along Lake Erie, known as the Toledo Strip, where the present-day city of Toledo is located. Ohio blocked Michigan's admittance into the union in Congress in 1833, commencing "The Toledo War." While this altercation involved angry speeches and much saber-rattling, fortunately the conflict resulted in no deaths. The "war" was ultimately resolved by President

Andrew Jackson in 1837: Ohio kept the Toledo Strip while Michigan was officially admitted as the 26th state and allotted a "consolation gift" of 9,000 square miles of the mineral- and timber-rich Upper Peninsula. Today, Michigan is the only state in the nation comprised of two peninsulas. In case you are wondering, Wisconsin was still a territory when all of this took place. It didn't become a state until 1848.

PERSPECTIVES

The land area of the U.P. is vast—equal to the combined areas of the states of Connecticut, Delaware, Massachusetts, and Rhode Island. Because of its physical separation and history, the U.P. has evolved a distinct culture. As author Rebecca Powers wrote in *The Washington Post* in 2021, "It puts the insular in peninsular." Within these buffered confines, the foods, traditions, and languages of Cornish and Finnish copper miners, French Canadians, and Indigenous peoples have merged as these groups burrowed in together within the deep snow and deeper forests. Indeed, residents of the U.P. are so fraternized that they affectionately refer to themselves as "Yoopers." (Incidentally, Michigan residents living south of the Mackinac Bridge are sometimes referred to as "trolls" since they are "under the bridge").

The Upper Peninsula is the least populated portion of the overall state of Michigan, whose 2020 population was just under ten million. The U.P. population in 2020 was 302,000 and has been declining since 2000 when the census recorded 317,000 individuals. This population decline is the result of an aging population combined with the struggle to attract the durable employment opportunities necessary to maintain younger adult populations in a beautiful, but isolated, region.

WEATHER

The U.P.'s climate is governed by its unique location nestled between Lake Superior to the north, Lake Michigan to the south, and, to a lesser extent, Lake Huron to the east. These three enormous Great Lakes produce their own microclimates, resulting in cooler temperatures and increased storm potential. Numerous rivers, small lakes, and forests also abound inland along the road. One significant U.P. weather event was immortalized in a popular song.

VIGNETTE   THE WRECK OF EDMUND FITZGERALD

Gordon Lightfoot (1938–2023) was a Canadian singer/songwriter who wrote a number of memorable songs over his long career. His biggest hit was a historical ballad called "The Wreck of the Edmund Fitzgerald" (1976) about the 1975 sinking of a Great Lakes ore-carrying freighter during a massive storm on the vast inland sea that is Lake Superior.

Few songs have better conveyed the power of the Great Lakes or the connections to the mining and shipping industries that have shaped Michigan's Upper Peninsula through the decades. The song is six minutes long—by pop standards an eternity—but Lightfoot's evocative description of life and death on the water in the midst of a storm still resonates.

There is a maritime museum in Marquette, Michigan, that contains some of the effects from the Edmund Fitzgerald. It is sobering to see and contemplate these artifacts.

MINING

The U.P. is part of the **Canadian Shield** (sometimes called the Laurentian Shield), a region underpinned by Precambrian rock formations that are more than 600 million years old. The area's mineral wealth includes iron ore that was extracted from the Marquette, Gogebic, and Menominee mountain ranges and copper that came from the Keweenaw Range. The copper mines in the Keweenaw Peninsula yielded the biggest and richest strike in American history during the 1840s. More miners rushed to Michigan in 1845 to strike it rich than ever made the trip to California for the 1849 gold rush. The copper mines were largely played out by the middle of the twentieth century, and there are interesting ruins to explore throughout the peninsula. Iron ore from the Marquette Range in the U.P. was mined continuously until 2016 when all but two mines ceased operation.

Recently, Michigan has seen an increase in mining interest for nonferrous (non-iron) minerals. This shift is due to new technology and higher metal prices. As of 2025, there are mineral exploration efforts underway in the Upper Peninsula. These efforts are focused on the discovery of major copper, nickel, gold, zinc, platinum, palladium, uranium, and cobalt ore bodies.

Within the U.P., and particularly on the Keweenaw Peninsula, are mining "ghost towns" and sites where you can see evidence of the industry boom and bust cycles of rapid population increases and declines as the mines played out. Among the interesting places to see nearby Highway 41 are the remnants of once-thriving towns such as **Freda, Wyoming, Osceola, Phoenix, Bete Grise, Gay, Central Mine,** and many more. If you have the time and a pair of good hiking shoes, it is well worth your time to explore these places but use caution around abandoned mining sites.

One thing you will see signs for throughout the route of Highway 41 in the U.P. are restaurants selling "pasties," portable, hearty hand pies stuffed with meat and with root vegetables. Cornish miners could easily carry pasties into the mines to help sustain them during their typical 12-hour workdays. A visit to the U.P. should include at least one lunch of pasties.

TIMBER AND THE BOREAL FOREST

The southward journey on Highway 41 begins in an enormous forest. It is part of the boreal forest that covers thousands of square miles of Michigan, Wisconsin, Minnesota, and central Canada. Boreal forests contain ash, aspen, balsam fir, white spruce, white pine, birch, maple, and northern white cedars. These trees are well adapted to the Great Lakes climate, which is characterized by high levels of humidity, heavy snowfall, lower summer temperatures, and summer fog and mist. The trees form a dense canopy over the ground. You can sometimes experience the sensation you are in a tunnel as you drive through the forest.

Today, there are 8.8 million acres of pine and hardwood forests in the U.P. but when the British and French arrived, there were many more. These first European arrivals initially used the hardwoods to build forts, ships, and other structures. Large-scale lumber operations began in the mid-1800s with wood from white pine and sugar maple trees being the most prized. Decades later, lumber trucks are still common on U.P. highways, transporting freshly cut logs to produce building lumber and paper in local mills.

Highway 41 going south from Copper Harbor, MI

AGRICULTURE

Perhaps surprisingly in this climate, the U.P. does entertain a short growing season. Farmland yields a harvest of corn, grain, and forage soybeans. You see much of this along 41, particularly on the lower part of the Peninsula. According to a 2023 newsletter by the Michigan State University (MSU) Extension, the region's number of traditional farms is decreasing, but the overall number of U.P. farms is increasing due to an influx of small, diversified farms supplying modest volumes of produce, poultry, and meat products. The specialized farms are selling through farmers' markets, community supported agriculture shares, on-farm stands, and, occasionally, to restaurants and institutions.

An online Upper Peninsula food resource portal called the U.P. Food Exchange supports local food projects of all kinds and is under development to stimulate growth in this sector. Land prices at approximately $6,400 per acre (2024) are relatively cheap for purchase or rent in comparison to other areas of the country. This might change appreciably in the near future, especially with climate change pushing populations northward—something to consider!

The MSU Extension suggests that aspiring farmers new to the area spend some time exploring as well as living through one of the long winters that can produce enormous amounts of snow before they commit to establishing an Upper Peninsula farm.

KEWEENAW PENINSULA–COPPER COUNTRY

The Keweenaw Peninsula is the northernmost section of Michigan's U.P. and arguably one of the most beautiful pieces of land in the Midwestern United States. It projects into Lake Superior and was the site of the U.S. copper boom, leading to its moniker "Copper Country." At the eastern tip of Copper Harbor lies a most unusual rock formation, "La Roche Verte," or the Green Rock. While its uniqueness established it as a navigational landmark, its primary importance lay in the utility of its composition. It is part of a vein of pure copper silicate mined for a millennium by Indigenous peoples before the Europeans showed up. Copper has been mined here for thousands of years and is some of the purest on Earth. It shows up in the artifacts of Indigenous peoples that date from the Bronze Age, 3300 BCE to 1200 BCE. There are some scholars who suggest based on ancient artifacts and DNA evidence that the ancient Minoans of the Island Crete in present-day Greece came here to excavate copper.

The copper strikes of 1843 and the resulting mines yielded the biggest and richest "strike" in American history. These strikes occurred when the Ojibwe still held title to the land. The U.S. Congress concluded a treaty with the Ojibwe as miners rushed in from Cornwall in England, Finland, and other parts of the United States in hope of striking it rich. Cornish and Finnish emigrants, in particular, brought their ethnic traditions and deep-mining techniques to the mines on the Keweenaw Peninsula.

The mines were largely played out by the middle of the twentieth century, and there are now interesting ruins to explore throughout the peninsula. You can find evidence of these old mines all around, including the **Cliff Mine**. Starting in 1845 and continuing for sixty years, it was the oldest and the richest of the mines associated with this mining boom. The copper mined in Michigan was crucial to the U.S. industrial revolution.

While most of the copper deposits were considered to have been exhausted decades ago, there have been recent feasibility studies conducted with advanced equipment that suggest there is still more copper in the ground here. New mines at the base of the Keweenaw may be opening soon as U.S. manufacturers scramble to secure domestic sources of high-tech metals.

THE TOP HALF OF THE U.P.–GITCHE GUMEE AND THE FOREST: COPPER HARBOR TO MARQUETTE

Highway 41 actually begins a couple of miles east of Copper Harbor. A nice sign designed by Byron Muljo, a highway worker, reads **"The Beginning of US 41"** at the cul-de-sac at the north end of the paved road.

Highway 41 sign, Copper Harbor, MI

FORT WILKINS HISTORIC STATE PARK

Fort Wilkins is located on the northern tip of the Keweenaw Peninsula and operated by the Michigan Department of Natural Resources. The park features a restored 1844 army military outpost with a history program provided by the Michigan History Center, as well as a quarter mile of rocky Lake Superior shoreline and **Lake Fanny Hooe**. Just to the south is pristine, tiny **Lake Manganese** that features a sandy beach which is good for swimming in the summer. The lake feeds **Manganese Falls**, a tourist attraction you can see from a brief hike.

Fort Wilkins was put up hastily by the federal government in 1844 to keep the peace with Indigenous nations before the copper rush began in earnest. It was also tasked with preserving mining interests from being attacked when thousands of settlers came to mine the copper deposits nearby. The fort never fired a shot. A peace treaty with the Ojibwe who owned and occupied the land, was proclaimed in 1843. The 105 men garrisoned at the fort fought boredom and snow until 1870 when the Army ended its occupation. The site became a state park in 1923.

The **Copper Harbor Lighthouse** stands nearby. Although it's a national landmark, the lighthouse is not accessible by land. The lighthouse is located on state park land, but the area between it and Fort Wilkins Historic State Park is situated on private property. Passage between the two is NOT allowed. To visit the lighthouse, take a boat tour from Copper Harbor Marina, located one-quarter mile west of Copper Harbor and just north of Highway 26.

Copper Harbor Lighthouse, Copper Harbor, MI

KEWEENAW ROCKET RANGE

A little farther beyond the official start of Highway 41 is a trail that requires a four-wheel drive vehicle or a mountain bike to traverse. It brings you to a marker for the site of the **Keweenaw Rocket Range**—an isolated launch pad once used for a joint research project between the University of Michigan and NASA that ran from 1964 to 1971. Small and medium "sounding" rockets were launched from this site to collect meteorological data. This may be one of the most remote points in Michigan, or the entire country for that matter. Those who make the trek are rewarded with a stunning view of Lake Superior and the knowledge that they are standing where scientists launched rockets during the early part of the Space Age.

COPPER HARBOR

From Fort Wilkins, the road winds into the tiny **Copper Harbor** at the tip of the Keweenaw Peninsula on the finger of land and farthest northern point of the Upper Peninsula. Copper Harbor is a touristy town with a few small motels, a campground, a souvenir store, an art gallery, a rock shop, and some places to eat. A local sign points south, indicating that Miami, Florida, is 1,990 miles away.

Road marker, Copper Harbor, MI

ISLE ROYALE NATIONAL PARK

The word *keweenaw* means "the crossing place" in the Ojibwe language. It refers to the fact that visitors must cross Portage Lake to reach the Keweenaw Peninsula. You can take a ferry in the summer months from Copper Harbor to **Isle Royale National Park**, the least-visited and most remote of the National Park Service wilderness parks within the lower forty-eight states. Isle Royale, part of the state of Michigan although much closer in distance to Minnesota and Ontario, was acquired in peace talks following the Revolutionary War. Rumors that the island might contain massive copper deposits proved unfounded; mineral resources there turned out to be minimal. The main resources of the island are its beauty and solitude. The island remains one of the few pristine wilderness areas left in the United States. It is wild, rugged, roadless, and isolated. You will see more wildlife than people there. As of 2024, the National Park Service was trying to increase the wolf population to maintain a natural limit on the island's abundant moose herd.

KEWEENAW SNOW GAUGE

There used to be a sign in Copper Harbor that said, "You are now breathing the purest, most vitalizing air on earth." (For some reason, you can now see the sign in Houghton, forty-seven miles to the south). And certainly, facing Lake Superior you are far from anywhere else.

For lovers of snow and winter activities, the Upper Peninsula is the place to visit, as it receives, on average, 270 inches of snow each winter thanks to the proximity of the lake. The **Keweenaw Snow Gauge**, a roadside attraction in the village of **Mohawk**, says everything you need to know about U.P. winters. The deepest snowfall, recorded as of 2025, was 390.4 inches in 1978–1979. The snow can stick around well into April and even May on occasion.

COPPER HARBOR TRAILS FEST–MOUNTAIN BIKING

Attention mountain biking enthusiasts: among the recreational attractions of the area are multiple trails for mountain biking. The Copper Harbor area is known as one of the top-rated trail systems in the world by the International Mountain Bicycling Association (IMBA). A variety of gateway, cross-country, flow, and gravity trails exist with services for bike riders. In

Keweenaw Snow Gauge, Mohawk, MI

September, the **Copper Harbor Trails Fest** features mountain-bike races at all levels.

BROCKWAY MOUNTAIN DRIVE

Nearby 41 is **Brockway Mountain Drive**, a 9.5-mile scenic drive with breathtaking views of Lake Superior and the thousands of acres of forest on the Keweenaw Peninsula. It is the highest above-sea-level drive between the Rockies and the Alleghenies. It is designated as an official **Michigan Wildlife Viewing Area**. Its biggest wildlife attraction is the annual migration of hawks and other birds of prey, which lasts from mid-April to mid-June. Near the west end of the mountain drive is the cascading **Silver River Falls** that features a bridge dating from 1930 and is listed on the National Register of Historic Places.

EAGLE RIVER

East of Copper Harbor is Eagle Harbor and the town of **Eagle River**, the county seat of Keweenaw County. With a population of 2,189, it is Michigan's least-populated county. The **Eagle River Timber Bridge** enables picturesque views of **Eagle River Falls**.

Eagle River Falls and Dam, Eagle River, MI

Nearby the Eagle River is a monument to Douglass Houghton, the first geologist for the state of Michigan. He surveyed the peninsula, identified the large copper deposits in 1840, and pioneered economic development of the U.P. Houghton foresaw that the copper ores were of superior quality, and that many speculators would "end in disappointment and ruin."

Houghton drowned during a storm on Lake Superior near Eagle Harbor in 1845 while making a survey of mineral lands in the U.P. He was thirty-six years old. In addition to being a geologist, he was a physician, a professor at the University of Michigan, and was elected to a term as mayor of Detroit. Houghton gave his name to the town of Houghton as well as to Houghton County, Houghton Lake, and Houghton Falls, among other places.

LIGHTHOUSE AT EAGLE HARBOR

Copper Harbor was the main port of shipment from the mines, and Eagle Harbor, just down the road, was a copper port developed in 1845. The red brick **Eagle Harbor Lighthouse** dates from 1871 (an earlier wooden lighthouse existed from 1851 to 1871) and features a light that is still in operation by the U.S. Coast Guard, guiding ships away from Superior's rugged shore. The lighthouse itself is now part of a regional museum devoted to the history of the area, its maritime past, and commercial fishing. The lighthouse and museum complex are open from mid-June to early October.

MOUNT BOHEMIA

Off Highway 41 near the unincorporated community of Delaware on Gay Lac La Belle Road is **Mount Bohemia Extreme Ski Resort**, which offers steep vertical drops and views of Lake Superior for expert skiers and snowboarders. Mount Bohemia does not have groomed runs and is not appropriate for beginners.

BEACH ZONES

There are several waterfront turnoffs along Highway 41 through the Keweenaw Peninsula that allow you to get out and walk the beaches next to the shores of Lake Superior—the largest freshwater lake in the world. You can find agates on many of the beaches. Agates are banded gemstones of finely grained micro-crystalline quartz. Each agate is unique in its color banding patterns making the translucent gemstone sought after. Agates are often used in the making of jewelry.

The Ojibwe called Superior "Gitche Gumee"—the Great Water. Henry Wadsworth Longfellow starts his poem *The Song of Hiawatha* with the line, "By the shores of Gitche Gumee." Lake Superior is the coldest and deepest of the Great Lakes. If you seek solitude, you can find it here within the deep forests, open lands, rocky shores, and rushing streams that surround it.

Unfortunately, from mid-May to mid-July, you might also find yourself in the company of biting black flies along Lake Superior. The flies are most active several hours after sunrise and an hour or two before sunset due to the humidity of the air and position of the sun. When the air is dry, flies may seek moisture in leaf litter on the ground, making ankles a source of concern to protect against the biting flies. Wearing protective clothing, socks and shoes, and a hat will limit your chances of being bitten.

CALUMET

From Copper Harbor to the town of Calumet, the highway is a forested stretch that is a canopy of green in the summer and of red, orange, and gold in the fall. **Kuusi Modern Mercantile**, "The Last Place on Earth" housewares and provisions store in Phillipsville just past the village of Allouez, contains an eclectic mix of vintage finds, collectibles, art, woodwork, and candlelight copper. Near the town of Calumet is a stone boat from the early 1930s made entirely of locally mined copper.

A plaque near the stone boat mentions in the depths of the Great Depression the price of copper, the area's only commodity, dropped to a point where most of the mines shut down and workers were destitute. Through the Works Progress Administration (WPA) of the 1930s, a number of local projects involving construction, road building, and canning provided employment. The WPA was created to alleviate the mass unemployment of the Great Depression, and by the time the program ended in 1943, it had put over eight and a half million Americans back to work. It is interesting to see the number of WPA buildings along the highway that are still in use.

Calumet is an interesting town worth a stop, and it seems to be on the upswing. When I visited about twenty years ago, it had an abandoned ghost town feel and holds the title of the snowiest small town in America. The town owes its existence to the nearby but now abandoned **Calumet and Hecla (C&H) Mine**. A statue of Alexander Agassiz (1835–1910), the president of the C&H Mining Company, stands outside of its former main office, which now houses the Keweenaw History Center. Calumet was a classic boom town boasting over 60,000 residents in the area by 1900. The **Calumet Historic District** comprises most of the village and is now a national heritage historic landmark district. Its downtown streets were the first in Michigan to be paved. There is a restored town hall and a showplace opera house theatre, first opened in 1900, designed in an Italian Renaissance style of architecture. It has a red sandstone exterior with copper accents and arches.

Downtown businesses include a coffeehouse, a brewpub, and several retail stores. Stop in to see the décor at the **Michigan House Café** and **Shute's 1890 Saloon**. Despite its tiny population of 680 in 2024, Calumet has a vibrant downtown that residents are restoring to avoid becoming a ghost town again.

Copper Country History Museum (former fire station), Calumet, MI

Calumet Theatre, Calumet, MI

THE ITALIAN HALL DISASTER ON CHRISTMAS EVE, 1913

Once located just north of Elm and Seventh streets in downtown Calumet, the **Italian Hall** was a two-story structure for civic gatherings. In 1913, returns from the C&H Mine had started to dwindle. A violent miner's strike caused Calumet's population to start declining. On December 24, 1913, as striking miners and their families gathered to celebrate Christmas Eve in the Italian Hall, a cry of "Fire!" triggered a stampede. The victims who lost their lives in the Italian Hall disaster included seventy-three people who were crushed and suffocated; many of them were children. The perpetrator who yelled "Fire!" was never apprehended, but eight witnesses swore the man wore an anti-union button on his coat. Woody Guthrie's song "1913 Massacre" accuses men from the C&H Company of holding the doors shut so the crowd could not exit. The Italian Hall was razed in 1984 and a memorial to the victims was erected in a local park, which is part of the **Keweenaw National Historical Park**. The C&H Mine finally closed in 1968.

Alexander Agassiz, President of C&H Mining, Calumet, MI

LAURIUM

South of Calumet is the town of Laurium, where many of the managers of the C&H Mine had their homes. The **Laurium Manor Inn** has been restored into a historic mansion hotel where you can stay overnight. Built for Thomas H. Hoatson, owner of Calumet & Arizona Mining Co. and his wife Cornelia, no expense was spared building this forty-five-room mansion. At a time when miners were making twenty-five cents per hour, this house was built at a cost of $50,000 with $35,000 of furnishings added.

Laurium is also the hometown of George Gipp, noted on a sign at the edge of town. Gipp was a Notre Dame football star who died of pneumonia. According to most accounts, during the 1928 Army game, Knute Rockne, the famed Notre Dame coach, gave the famous "Win one for the Gipper" half-time speech. Ronald Reagan played "the Gipper" in the 1940 movie *Knute Rockne, All American*, a fact constantly referred to when he became president in 1980.

QUINCY MINE

Farther down the road, by Keweenaw National Historical Park, are the ruins of the **Quincy Mine**, an extensive warren of mine shafts, hoist houses, and a copper smelting complex on the shore of Portage Lake. The mine was owned by the Quincy Mining Company and operated between 1846 and 1945, although some activities continued through the 1970s. The mine was designated a National Historic Landmark District in 1989. Visitors can ride down the mine shaft in the **Nordberg Steam Hoist**, built in 1918 and the largest steam hoisting engine in the world. It sits on the largest reinforced concrete engine foundation ever poured. The **Hoist House** has been listed on the National Register of Historic Places since 1970.

HANCOCK

Highway 41 pulls into the city of **Hancock** just north of its sister city of Houghton, which lies across the Portage River. Hancock has a strong Finnish heritage with many older residents of Finnish background. They are the descendants of Finnish immigrants—miners who worked in Copper Country. Hancock was once the home of **Finlandia University**, a private

Lutheran-affiliated university founded in 1896. It closed in 2023 due to declining enrollment and a high debt load. The Finnish American community in the United States wants to preserve the Finnish heritage center that was part of the university.

The streets in the Hancock's historic downtown are one-way before U.S. 41 crosses the **Houghton Hancock Portage Lake Lift Bridge**, an engineering landmark and the only bridge of its type in Michigan. When it was completed in 1959, it was the heaviest aerial lift bridge ever constructed. A double-deck bridge, the lower deck is designed for railroad traffic with the upper deck for highway traffic.

Houghton Hancock Bridge, (Portage Lake Lift Bridge), Houghton County, MI

HOUGHTON–MICHIGAN TECH

Houghton is home of **Michigan Technological University–Michigan Tech** (enrollment 7000). The school was established in 1885 for training miners and has become a respected engineering school. The university's **Great Lakes Research Center** was established to study the natural resources of the area. In addition, the school has an innovation/entrepreneurship maker space called "Husky Innovate," which is developing startup ideas for commercialization and development. Michigan Tech today is a recognized research university and technology hub that has been cited nationally for excellence in cyber defense contributions. There has been a steady increase in the number of female students; women now comprise nearly thirty percent of the student body. Houghton is the largest city on the Keweenaw Peninsula and celebrates winter activities with a Winter Carnival held each year. The NCAA Division 1 Michigan Tech men's hockey team is usually one of the most competitive in the country.

VIGNETTE VERNA MIZE

Verna Grahek Mize (1913–2013) of Houghton and Calumet campaigned to end the practice of dumping mining waste into Lake Superior, which led to government-set pollution standards. Mize lived in Maryland but returned to her childhood home in Houghton every summer. In 1967, on a trip home, Verna noticed that the clarity of Lake Superior was not the same as she had remembered from her childhood. Through extensive research, she learned that the Reserve Mining Company was dumping 67,000 tons of waste tailings annually into Lake Superior in Two Harbors, Minnesota. Verna embarked on a thirteen-year battle to save Lake Superior.

Returning to her Maryland home, she began writing letters to senators, congressmen, and President Nixon. By 1971, Verna had typed over 5,000 letters and visited the offices of senators and congressmen. In the span of only ten days, she collected 5,182 signatures on a petition that accompanied a letter to President Nixon asking for an investigation.

Verna was once quoted in a 1971 news article as saying, "Sometimes I wonder how in the world I had the courage to do what I have done. I really think that if someone said, Verna, you'll have to sacrifice your life for the lake I'd do it. What's my life compared with the lake?"

The EPA brought the mining company to trial in 1973. It was one of the longest, most costly, and most bitterly fought environmental cases at the time, which, thanks to Verna's tireless efforts, led to the end of the company's waste dumping into Lake Superior on March 16, 1980. A park in Houghton is named for Verna Mize.

From Houghton, the highway proceeds east across the peninsula, skirting **Portage Lake**, a haven for bass fishing, before going south along Keweenaw Bay. Some of the oldest copper mines in the area are found along this route. For those interested in what a working mine was like in the 1880s, the **Adventure Copper Mine** near the town of Greenland offers tours of a long-ago copper mine.

Along the way south on the peninsula, looking across the bay, is the town of **Pequaming**, built by Henry Ford in 1923 as a processing point for mining and timber is now mainly a ghost town, largely abandoned in the 1940s. The town is about eight miles north of L'Anse on the shore of Lake Superior. On my visit, Pequaming had a few residents and lots of "Private Keep Out" signs. Just off the highway, **Carla's Restaurant, Motel, and Cozy Inn** offers a nice place to have a fish dinner and a beautiful view of **Keweenaw Bay**.

Sunrise from Carla's Inn Motel, Keweenaw Bay, Baraga, MI

BARAGA–L'ANSE

A good place to get a cup of coffee along the road is **Nana's Den**, a tiny place just outside of the town of **Baraga** that sits within the Keweenaw Bay Ojibwe Reservation. Between Baraga and L'Anse is the Shrine of Bishop Baraga, with a large copper statue of **Bishop Baraga** (1797–1858), "The Snowshoe Priest," who ministered to the Indigenous peoples. Father Baraga became the first bishop of the Upper Peninsula and was also called the "Apostle of the Great Lakes." A small gift shop and picnic area are near the statue.

L'Anse, a village founded by Jesuit missionaries in the late 1600s, is the Baraga County seat, and was once a campground for French explorers, trappers, and missionaries. A historic sign provides information about the L'Anse-Lac Vieux Desert Trail that runs from L'Anse to the Lac Vieux Desert in Wisconsin. This trail has been used by humans since prehistoric times, including Indigenous peoples, fur traders, surveyors, and settlers.

Bishop Baraga Shrine, L'Anse, MI

HURON MOUNTAINS

East of L'Anse are the **Huron Mountains**, the location of **Mount Arvon**, at 1,979 feet. The summit provides great views, but it's not easy to get used to driving on old logging roads. Blue diamond-shaped signs (approximately every mile) mark the route to Mt. Arvon.

ALBERTA

Just before the village of **Alberta**, you'll see the word F-O-R-D spelled out in the grass just a little off the highway. This marks the spot of the old Ford Sawmill, now a museum and the site of a company town established by the Ford Motor Company to harvest and cut timber used for auto bodies. Henry Ford bought up several hundred thousand acres of forest in the U.P. in the early twentieth century. A Ford auto plant, one of the nation's first charcoal factories, commercial forests, and sawmills were scattered throughout the U.P. There were even rumors of an experimental Ford chicken farm. After World War II, when less wood was being used in the auto industry, Ford donated the sawmill and 3,700 acres to Michigan Tech University, which now uses it as a field camp for majors in the College of Forest Resources and Environmental Science. A bust of Henry Ford presides over the guest book in the **Ford Visitor Center**.

Ford Center and forest, L'Anse, MI

The drive from L' Anse south and east toward Ishpeming is especially beautiful. There are stops at **Canyon Falls Roadside Park** and **Tioga Creek Roadside Park** where you can take short hikes into the woods. Continue on the highway to the area around **Three Lakes**, a picturesque series of small lakes along the road. You can stop to admire the lakes as well as canoe or kayak on them. The road continues past **Michigamme**, now a resort community, founded in the early 1870s by lumbering and mining concerns. Much of the town's early growth was dependent upon the iron ore mine.

Michigamme was also the dividing line between geologic mineral resources of copper and nickel within Michigan's copper range and iron ore deposits. Iron ore was first discovered here, in what is today known as the Marquette Range, in 1844 by William Burt, a government surveyor. The Michigamme Mine was established in 1873 and closed in 1905 after yielding nearly one million tons of ore.

Tioga Creek Roadside Park, Baraga County, MI

ISHPEMING AND NEGAUNEE

Highway 41 continues into the small city of **Ishpeming**. The town's name means "high place" in Ojibwe and is so named because it is situated on the divide between Lakes Superior and Michigan. Ishpeming is a historic old mining town with nearby deep shaft and open pit iron mines that kept its economy going for many years. Now it is a satellite community of Marquette, fifteen miles to the east.

After years of decline and blight, the town has rebounded and repurposed many of the old storefronts, bringing new business and energy into the area. The **Velodrome Coffee Company** has lots of ski and mountain bike related gear. Stop along the way at **Da Yoopers Tourist Trap**, an old-fashioned gift and rock shop.

"Old Ish" Downtown Ishpeming, MI

Lake George, Lincoln Township, Clare County, MI

Da Yoopers Tourist Trap, Ishpeming, MI

Next to Ishpeming is the city of **Negaunee**, also with old storefronts and buildings that date from the days when the mines just outside the town were booming. The buildings are being restored with one of them housing the **Upper Peninsula Brewing Company**. This brewpub, named for the first brewery in the region, is located in a former slaughterhouse located along the **Iron Ore Heritage Trail**.

The local **Michigan Iron Industry Museum** recounts the history of mining in the area. The community has lots of areas to walk and hike around and civic leaders of these cities believe that outdoor recreation and tourism are where they can achieve economic growth. Some evidence also points to "climate migrants" moving into the area due to it being less susceptible to major weather events. Outdoor enthusiasts who can work remotely from anywhere also seem to be attracted to the area.

TILDEN MINE

Mining for nickel and copper is still occurring in a couple locations not far from Negaunee. The **Tilden Mine** is the last remaining large, active iron mine in the U.P. It is in an area known as the Marquette Iron Range and produces eight million tons of iron ore pellets annually. The mine and ore reserves are owned by Cleveland-Cliffs Inc., which also operates iron ore mines in the Mesabi Range of Minnesota. The ore from the Tilden Mine goes by rail from the mine to the nearby Port of Marquette, where it is loaded onto Great Lakes freighters destined for the steel mills of Indiana on the shores of Lake Michigan.

You'll also find the **National Ski and Snowboard Hall of Fame and Museum** between Ishpeming and Negaunee. Ishpeming was the birthplace of organized skiing in the United States when Scandinavian immigrants brought the sport to the area in the late 1880s. On display are vintage sets of skis, some old snow equipment, some Olympic patches, and many plaques recounting honored members in the Hall of Fame.

The U.S. Ski Association was founded here by Carl Tellefsen, a Norwegian immigrant, in 1905. He organized the first ski-jumping competition at nearby Suicide Hill, where there is still a ninety-meter ski jumping site and an annual ski jumping tournament. While the locus of skiing long ago shifted out to the west (the Ski Association is now headquartered in Park City, Utah), the Hall of Fame celebrates its roots in Ishpeming by providing lasting recognition for American skiers and snowboarders who excelled nationally and internationally. The museum is open daily from 8 am to 2 pm. There is a beautiful glass mosaic at the entrance to the museum.

There is some U.S. road history on this stretch of Highway 41. The first center line on a state highway was hand-painted in 1917 in white on the portion of the Marquette–Negaunee Road known as **"Dead Man's Curve"** to separate traffic moving in opposite directions. It was the work of Kenneth Ingalls Sawyer, who was a superintendent of the county board of road commissions. Michigan and California were the first states to pass legislation standardizing center lines on all main roads in 1917, and these lines became a national requirement in 1935.

U.S. Ski & Snowboard Hall of Fame, Ishpeming, MI

BIG BAY AND ANATOMY OF A MURDER

Twenty-three miles northwest of the city of Marquette is tiny unincorporated Big Bay, situated alongside the **Big Bay** of Lake Superior. In 1944 it was the site of a Ford Motor Company auto plant and a retreat for Henry Ford and top company executives. You can stay at the **Thunder Bay Inn**, built in 1911 and converted to an inn by Henry Ford. At the tip of Big Bay is the **Big Bay Point Lighthouse B&B**. Set atop a cliff overlooking Lake Superior, this historic bed and breakfast lies four miles from the village of Big Bay and is housed in one of the nation's few remaining resident lighthouses.

Big Bay's **Lumberjack Tavern** is a slice of local history and popular culture. The tavern was first opened in 1938 as Rose's Tavern and renamed Lumberjack Tavern as a nod to the area's logging history and the famous lumberjacks. The book *Anatomy of a Murder* by Robert Traver (1958) is based on a real life 1952 murder that occurred at the Lumberjack. A movie version of this courtroom drama was released in 1959 with James Stewart and Lee Remick in the leading roles. The movie soundtrack has a great jazz musical score by Duke Ellington. In addition to Big Bay, scenes were filmed in Marquette, Ishpeming, and Michigamme.

MARQUETTE

Marquette, with a population of 22,000, is situated along Lake Superior, and the largest city in the Upper Peninsula. It is also the home of **Northern Michigan University**. NMU's enrollment is approximately 7,000 students, but there is some concern about the decline in high school students within the U.P. interested in attending college. Thus, the school makes a concerted effort to recruit students from lower Michigan and elsewhere.

The campus's big wooden sports dome, the Superior Dome (a.k.a. the **"Yooperdome"**), is home to the football team, the women's lacrosse team, women's track and field team, and the marching band, as well as a host of other campus and community events. It also houses the National Training Site for Olympic training programs in Greco-Roman wrestling and weightlifting. The school touts, according to its website, that NMU is one of the most affordable and safest public universities in Michigan.

Marquette has long been a major shipping hub for iron ore and now exists as a regional administrative hub in the U.P. for the state of Michigan. The city is a service center and tourist jumping-off point for recreational attractions that include hunting, fishing, mountain biking, skiing, and boating. Marquette had been settled for centuries by the Ojibwe before French fur traders made it a destination point.

The Port of Marquette was founded in 1849 near what is now Presque Isle State Park to serve the nearby iron range. While there is far less mining than in the past, freight trains still transport taconite pellets (low-grade iron ore used to make steel) from local mines to the ore dock for loading onto lake freighters bound for Great Lakes ports such as Detroit, Gary, and Cleveland. The hulking **Lower Harbor Ore Dock** near downtown Marquette is a historical landmark, a relic of bygone days when iron ore was loaded directly from railcars onto lake freighters. Much of the city center's waterfront now features pricey condominiums for vacationers and second homeowners. There is a new hotel and a walking path along this waterfront.

We have visited my wife's sister and brother-in-law and their family who have lived there over twenty-five years and have watched it evolve from a declining industrial city to much more of a recreational and tourist destination. Marquette's location right on Lake Superior means the city receives lots of winter snow that can stick around often right till the end of May. It's far north enough that residents and visitors can also view the spectacular Northern Lights from the shore. If you can, plan a trip in early October when the fall colors are at peak and the city is a little quieter.

Downtown Marquette has a number of old stone buildings that speak to Marquette's importance in years past. Many are being repurposed from their initial use. An old movie theater has been refurbished into a bistro on one side of West Washington Street, and on the other side is a theater refurbished as a whiskey distillery. You'll also find **Donkers**, the little ice cream and candy shop President Barack Obama visited in 2011 while in Marquette. Other famous visitors include the Rolling Stones, who in 2002 attended the funeral of Royden "Chuch" Magee, a resident of Marquette and the band's road manager for many years.

Marquette is benefiting from an influx of people drawn by the multiple recreational opportunities—boating, skiing, biking, hiking, fishing, hunting, etc.—nearby. The **Iron Ore Heritage Trail**, completed in 2013, is a forty-seven-mile bike path that passes through Marquette and surrounding areas. It has iron rail markers and art along the route. The **Greywalls Golf Course**, part of the Marquette Golf Course, was constructed in 2005 and is considered one of the premier golf courses in Michigan.

Marquette has a beach, a historic lighthouse, and a maritime museum close to its downtown, as well as the lovely **Presque Isle State Park**, one of the most visited sites in Marquette County, a mile away. The city has become more of a destination point with a children's museum, two artisanal bread bakeries, and a choice of several brewpubs as well. There is a hipster vibe now present in the city, with clothing stores and interesting specialty shops that are transforming some of the old downtown.

Even though Marquette is becoming more attractive for new potential residents, a lack of affordable housing for the millennial generation remains a current problem. The average cost of a single-family home within the city of Marquette is currently $400,000. Similar to many small cities along Highway 41, there is a strip of national retail chain outlets just outside of the old downtown. Still, Marquette is a very attractive small city to reside despite being very remote from larger population centers, provided one can handle long winters.

Delft Theatre, Marquette, MI

Marquette Harbor Lighthouse, Marquette, MI

Highway 41 runs east along Lake Superior as it passes out of Marquette. You can connect to State Route 28 for a side trip to Munising to see waterfalls and, just beyond, to visit **Pictured Rocks National Lakeshore Park**. The park is known for its dramatic, colorful cliffs and sandstone rock formations such as Miner's Castle. A boat cruise is the best way to see the rocks, and two- to three-hour cruises depart Munising all summer long. The park has seen a surge in visitors in recent years.

Tahquamenon Falls State Park is another place of interest in the area. It encompasses nearly 50,000 acres and is home to the 200-foot-wide **Upper Falls**, one of the largest waterfalls east of the Mississippi River. Continuing east on M-28 will take you to the city of **Sault Ste. Marie**, the Soo Locks, and the international bridge into Canada.

HIGHWAY 41 SOUTH TO LAKE MICHIGAN

As the highway heads south through a sparsely populated, heavily wooded area, you'll see many logging trucks and, every now and then, an entrance to a campground. The small city of **Gladstone**, fifty-eight miles to the south of Marquette, sits near the top of the **Little Bay de Noc**. Named for the Indigenous Noquet "Noc" who once lived along these shores, this smaller bay opens onto Green Bay on Lake Michigan. Founded as a rail-lake terminal, the town of Gladstone was originally named "Minnewasca" by the Soo Line Railroad. This Ojibwe name means "white water." When the name was filed with the county and Michigan Secretary of State, William Washburn, a U.S. Senator from Minnesota with an interest in the railroad, pushed to change the name to Gladstone in honor of the British Liberal statesman and prime minister William Gladstone because the railroad was partially funded by British capital.

GREEN BAY—MICHIGAN

Green Bay is an inlet of Lake Michigan that extends along the southeastern shore of the U.P. into Wisconsin to the mouth of the Fox River. **Hiawatha National Forest** and **Menominee State Forest** each lie along the bay's northern shore. The bay was an important portage route for the fur trade and later a shipment point for iron ore.

Deep within the Hiawatha Forest is the **Milkweed Inn** that offers a fine dining experience created by Illiana Regan, the chef of Michelin-starred Elizabeth Restaurant in Chicago, and her wife Anna Hamlin. Guests can stay on the grounds in some makeshift cabins. (Note: The inn is a full-service bed and breakfast. Currently, they do not offer an option to dine without booking the full accommodation). The inn is rumored to be fully booked for the next couple years.

ESCANABA

The city of **Escanaba** along the shore of Green Bay's Little Bay de Noc is the next stop along Highway 41. With a population of slightly over 13,000, it is the third-largest city in the Upper Peninsula after Marquette and Sault Ste. Marie. Historically, Escanaba was built as a manufacturing city to serve nearby timber-based industries. It also served as a distribution point for coal and other raw materials. The city is close to Wisconsin-based population centers and benefits from this proximity. The typical set of chain retail stores and restaurants greet you as the road runs into the city.

The name *Escanaba* derives from the Ojibwe word for the flat rock that the bottom of the Escanaba River, which borders the city to the east, is made of. The river runs some fifty miles inland. It is known for excellent trout fishing and figures into Longfellow's epic poem *The Song of Hiawatha*.

Escanaba, or "Esky" to residents, is the Delta County seat and a center for cultural activities presented by the **William Bonifas Fine Arts Center**, the **Waterfront Art Festival**, the **Players de Noc**, the **Bay de Noc Choral Society**, the **Escanaba City Band**, and many smaller arts organizations, art galleries, and musical groups. The Bay de Noc area, as part of Lake Michigan, is popular for fishing, cross-country skiing, and snowmobiling. The **Upper Peninsula State Fair** is held in Esky every August with up to 100,000 visitors. Escanaba is also the headquarters of the vast Hiawatha National Forest just to the east of the city. The forest extends from Lake Michigan in the south to Lake Superior in the north.

In downtown Escanaba, Ludington Street has a welcoming sign as well as several shops and restaurants, the historic House of Ludington Hotel built in 1864, a new library, and a new courthouse. There are old, shuttered movie theaters on the street, and I worry that they will disappear before I visit again.

Sayklly's, a famous old candy company and the creator of the famous Yooper Bar, Snappies, and Yooper Trail Mix, has been making and selling homemade chocolates and candies from their factory and store in Escanaba since 1906. The company ships candy all over the world.

Sand Point Lighthouse, at the end of Ludington Street, was established in 1867 to guide ships through squalls and shoals into the harbor. Fire destroyed the original structure in 1886, but the lighthouse was rebuilt and served the public until 1939. Now an electronic light guides boats into the harbor, and the historic old lighthouse has been restored as a maritime museum. Escanaba remains a port city and is still called on by lake freighters. Cruise ships, which once thrived on the Great Lakes before all but disappearing in the 1970s, are making a comeback on the inland seas and have begun to call at the port in recent years. Marketed as "expedition cruising," the ships deliver tourists and their spending money to ports that for decades were used primarily to ship iron ore and other raw materials.

Sand Point Lighthouse, Escanaba, MI

There are two ways to journey south from Esky toward Menominee and the Wisconsin border. The M-35 route hugs the Lake Michigan shore and features many views of the lake and lakefront cottages along the way. Highway 41 takes a route through the forest that is part of the Hannahville Potawatomi tribal community. The **Island Resort and Casino** is an eleven-story casino/hotel complex in Harris, about ten miles outside of Escanaba that is owned by the Hannahville Potawatomi. The resort has a big water park, a professional golf course, and all the bells and whistles for gaming.

Michigan Theater, Escanaba, MI

Delft Theatre, Escanaba, MI

VIGNETTE NATIVE AMERICAN GAMING IN THE UPPER PENINSULA

Along Highway 41 in the U.P. (and along the road through virtually the entire length of the highway), travelers will come across a number of casinos and gaming establishments. A significant number of them are operated by Indigenous nations. The history of gaming in the U.P. begins in the early 1980s when Indigenous reservations began to seek tribal revenue and jobs for members by opening bingo operations and blackjack tables in violation of state laws that prohibited most gambling.

Outside of the state of Nevada, casino gambling was illegal in virtually every state at that time. In 1987, two separate U.S. Supreme Court cases—one in Florida and the other in California—made it clear that Indigenous nations had broad rights to engage in gaming activities on reservation land. Due to these rulings, in 1988, Congress created a framework for a relationship between state gaming regulations and Indigenous gaming activities called the Indian Gaming Regulatory Act (IGRA). The bill was passed and signed into law by President Reagan. After negotiations concerning video gambling devices and percentage of revenue provided to the state of Michigan, the signatory tribal governments were given exclusive rights to operate casinos in the state in 1993.

Legal gaming has had a significant and positive economic impact on tribal budgets since its introduction in the mid-1990s. There are presently ten casinos in the U.P., and three of them (in Baraga, Marquette, and Harris) are right along Highway 41. The casinos are now among the largest employers in the U.P.

Highway 41 turns south toward Menominee at the town of Powers. For more forest adventures, you can follow U.S. Highway 2 at Powers. This route proceeds through state and national forests before reaching **Porcupine Mountains Wilderness State Park.** The Porcupine Mountains are fondly known as "the Porkies" and feature 60,000 acres of old-growth forest, roaring waterfalls, Lake Superior shoreline, rivers, trails, and ridges. Michigan's largest state park is a popular destination for camping, hiking, snowmobiling, fishing, and more.

Traveling on Highway 41 through this lower part of the peninsula is not for the faint-hearted. The main industry in this area appears to be the lumber industry. The highway passes several large sawmills on the road to Menominee, and motorists will pass lots of logging trucks on this stretch of road as well.

Lumber harvesting was one of the key drivers of the U.P. economy in the last century, and it continues to be one of the key aspects of the economy. The immense old-growth forests of Michigan were decimated by clear cutting up to the early part of the twentieth century. A concerted effort during the Great Depression resulted in the planting of some 485 million trees from 1933 to 1942. The regenerated forest is susceptible to a variety of diseases, pests, and fungi that threaten the watershed, the flora, and all of the fauna that call the forest home. Areas such as the Hiawatha National Forest have strict curbs on logging, but local areas that are not set aside for tourism are open to over-logging.

MENOMINEE

The city of **Menominee**, named after the Ojibwe word for "wild rice," is at the southern end of the U.P. on the Lake Michigan/Green Bay shore. A bridge over the Menominee River leads to its sister city of Marinette, Wisconsin. The city bills itself as "Where the Best of Michigan Begins." Menominee is the Menominee County seat and was once a prominent lumbering and shipping point with a population of over 30,000 at the turn of the twentieth century. Once the pine forests were cut down, the city began a slow decline. As of 2023, the population was approximately 8,200.

The downtown historic district contains some grand old buildings that are now on the National Historic Register. The **Spies Library** was built in 1903 as a gift from Augustus Spies, a prominent Menominee businessman, and remains a beautiful building and important anchor to the community although for a while local rumor predicted it would close.

The **Menominee Opera House** was built in 1902 by lumber barons to bring culture to the community. It has been vacant for decades, but a determined group is working on securing funding from the state to restore it.

The old downtown contains some beautifully restored, well-kept, old, but quite empty office buildings. **Henes Park** is an old but very lovely lakefront park within the city limits that features a Shakespeare nature trail.

Right on the highway just before downtown, the **Lloyd Flanders Furniture Company** produces its wares in a very cool old building dating from 1906. That was the year Marshall Lloyd opened the company and developed a unique process for creating fine woven wicker heirloom furniture. The company features a video about the making of furniture in the factory on the company website: https://www.lloydflanders.com/about.

Menominee Opera House, Menominee, MI

Spies Public Library, Menominee, MI

TO WEED OR NOT TO WEED

One of Menominee's current issues is whether or not to open businesses that sell marijuana. Cannabis dispensaries have been touted as a godsend to struggling small cities such as Menominee, but some view them as a blight on communities. The public is fairly split on the issue. Given the murkiness of state and federal laws on the sale of marijuana, it might be some time in the future before this issue is settled.

The Interstate Bridge between Menominee and Marinette, Wisconsin, carries Highway 41 over the Menominee River. The current bridge, dedicated in late 2005, replaced a span that was built in 1929 just as the Great Depression took hold. Midway in the river is **Stephenson Island Park**, which actually lies in Wisconsin. The park features the **Marinette County Historical Museum**, which includes many examples of logging equipment from the region. Crossing into Wisconsin from Michigan provides an opportunity to reflect on a journey through the U.P.

CONCLUDING THOUGHTS

Travel on Highway 41 through the U.P. is rural, wild, and very beautiful—something that you can easily behold. You can truly "get away from it all" when you journey along this part of the road. The scenery is incredible, and you don't need to pursue all of the different recreational opportunities the area affords to enjoy it. The remoteness of the U.P. is part of its allure and also one of its challenges.

It seems like every little town in Michigan names its high school teams and lists their championships on a welcome sign as you enter. Some farming is ongoing in the area. But neither farming nor the other industries that used to fuel the U.P.'s economy are thriving enough to keep or attract a larger population. This is darkly illustrated by a closed and abandoned elementary school located by the highway near the small town of Daggett in Menominee County.

The U.P. is undergoing demographic change. Recent population studies suggest that the "Yoopers," descendants of previous generations who came to work the mines, harvest timber, and farm, are aging quickly. Death rates increased during the period of the COVID-19 pandemic, and birth rates have not sufficiently sustained the population. An aging population requires healthcare infrastructure to become a priority for the region.

Many younger people raised in the U.P. are relocating elsewhere for better higher education options and job opportunities in larger cities, and they are not returning to the region. The decline in the number of individuals of prime working age (25–34) impacts what industries remain. Mining and logging were the base of the area economy for over a century, and neither now requires a lot of workers. Two songs by the musician Lee Murdock lamenting the changing economy you can watch on YouTube are "Marquette Range" and "The Soo Line." The state of Michigan is well aware of these trends and has set up the "Growing Michigan Together Council" to focus on population growth through attracting talent and providing expanding opportunities for young professionals. Attracting and keeping residents is one of the primary challenges facing the U.P.

A study of the area's needs by researchers from Michigan Tech University suggests that the U.P. can attract "amenity migrants" who can bring economic activity, talented labor, and capital for investment. But the study also points out that these individuals are often remote workers who are fickle and tend to leave if they cannot find affordable housing or do not feel welcomed within communities. Current residents can see these population changes in a negative light and leave as well.

The U.P. does not have a diverse population at present. It is overwhelmingly white, and this, too, may be viewed as a negative. Thus, city planners must try to balance the complex possibilities such as how to welcome individuals migrating due to climate change, while not undermining the communities already in place. The cities of Houghton and Marquette are both home to mid-sized universities that drive local economies and provide some cultural diversity in these towns. Marquette is the major regional hub and will attract much of the investment and population growth with spillover to nearby towns. Menominee can become an attractive place for new residents as well, provided there is affordable housing.

The U.P. is in transition. A new generation of residents are transforming this unique part of the state of Michigan. Managing tourism, recreation, entrepreneurship, and stewardship of the land will be important for an area that may see many more climate change migrants in the decades to come.

Closed Elementary School near Daggett, MI

ENDNOTES

The full text on the WPA plaque outside of the town of Calumet reads as follows:

Copper County WPA

The WPA Stone Boat built here is the product of a WPA work group, constructed in 1933–1934. It is one of many WPA projects constructed throughout the copper country.

In the early 1930's, the Michigan Copper Country was firmly in the grip of the Great Depression. Mines closed as the price of copper slid from 18 to 5.25 cents per pound. Since copper mining was the areas only industry, this drop in copper prices destroyed the local economy.

The Depression prompted President Franklin D. Roosevelt's administration to develop a number of relief measures to aid the nation. His belief was that people would rather work than accept charity. Harry Hopkins, President Roosevelt's welfare administrator, estimated in 1934 that the Copper Country had more people on relief than any other comparable area across the nation.

Federal money was allocated to the state and local agencies to hire people for const-

ructive work projects, beginning in the Fall of 1933 as the Civil Works Administration (CWA), the program renamed the Works Progress Administration (WPA), a year later and continued through 1943. Only one job slot was allowed per family. In 1939, the WPA paid thirty-four cents per hour for unskilled and forty-nine cents per hour for skilled laborers.

Among the Copper Country WPA projects we still benefit from today are the Keweenaw Mountain Lodge and Golf Course, Brockway Mountain Drive, M-26, McClaine and Fort Wilkins State Parks, Rice Lake Boy Scout camp, Calumet Post Office, George Gipp Memorial and numerous other buildings, utilities, parks and playgrounds. Road work was given a high priority with 5000 men assigned to Houghton County Road projects widening building and digging ditches. These men are responsible for a majority of the roads we depend on today. Horse and buggy trails were upgraded to roads that could accommodate two-way auto traffic.

Women, who made up eight to ten percent of the WPA workforce, contributed clerical support and worked on sewing and canning projects. The local WPA also featured a writer's project and historical records survey. The Houghton County WPA band entertained thousands with public concerts.

As you drive our roads, enjoy our parks, admire the colorful WPA mural in the Calumet Post Office or wonder about WPA folk art like the stone boat built here, also pause to remember the hard times of the WPA laborers and their families surviving a difficult time in this nation's history, the Great Depression of the 1930's.

CHAPTER FOUR
WISCONSIN

"You can leave Wisconsin, but it never leaves you."

—Anonymous

"Wisconsin isn't a state; it's a state of mind; and gentle good humor is the coin of the realm."

—Scott Jacobs, Artist

Highway 41/Interstate 41 through Wisconsin is 225 miles.

Key Towns/Cities: *Marinette, Green Bay, Appleton, Oshkosh, Fond du Lac, Menomonee Falls, Wauwatosa, Milwaukee, Racine, Kenosha*

Wisconsin Counties along 41: *Marinette, Oconto, Brown, Outagamie, Winnebago, Fond du Lac, Dodge, Washington, Waukesha, Milwaukee, Racine, Kenosha*

Crossing the Menominee River, Highway 41 leaves Michigan's Upper Peninsula and enters the eastern section of the state of Wisconsin. Travel on Highway 41 through Wisconsin is primarily on the Interstate system; it was officially added in 2015. U.S. 41 is no longer acknowledged from intersecting routes or along highway guide signs in the state. There is, however, some interesting signage along the way that indicates the highway has now become an interstate. Some signs have the old 41 route shield as well as the 41 interstate highway shield to explain that they are now one and the same.

Like all interstates, this route has limited access, which allows for much faster travel provided you are not in a section under construction. There is little to see along most interstate highways except other cars and a great deal of truck traffic, and the highway through much of Wisconsin is no exception. Parts of the original four-lane interstate near Green Bay are slated to be widened to six lanes soon for expected increases in traffic.

Travel on what used to be Highway 41 is still possible along **State Road 175**, which is more interesting from the standpoint of seeing small towns and farm country. It's also a jumping-off point for exploring the city of Milwaukee.

The highway follows the shore of Lake Michigan through the city of Green Bay before going west through the Fox Valley, circling by Lake Winnebago, then returning east to go through Milwaukee, Wisconsin's largest city. South of Milwaukee, the road skirts by the older manufacturing cities of Racine and Kenosha to the Illinois border.

WISCONSIN

Marinette

Oconto

GREEN
BAY

Appleton

Osh Kosh

Fond
du Lac

Menomonee Falls

Milwaukee

Racine

Kenosha

A WISCONSIN ALBUM PLAYLIST

- Les Paul: *The Best of Les Paul* 2001
- Al Jarreau: *Glow* 1976
- Violent Femmes: *Violent Femmes* 1983
- Garbage: *Garbage* 1995
- Steve Miller: *Fly Like an Eagle* 1976
- BoDeans: *Love & Hope & Sex & Dreams* 1986
- Carlie Hanson: *Wisconsin* 2023
- House of Pain: *House of Pain* 1992
- Jerry Lee Lewis: *Another Place, Another Time* 1968
- Hanson: *Middle of Nowhere* 1997
- John Prine: *Sweet Revenge* 1973

CULTURAL, INDUSTRIAL, AGRICULTURAL ROOTS

Multiple Indigenous nations have made their home in the state and continue to have a presence. Some of the oldest European settlements in the country were established by French fur trappers and explorers in Wisconsin dating to the early 1600s. In the early 1800s, Yankee (New York/New England) settlers moved west to Wisconsin for farming opportunities. A terrific description of the early settler days in Wisconsin is contained in the book *Wau-bun: The Early Day in the Northwest*, authored in 1855 by Juliette Augusta Magill Kinzie (1806–1870).

The territory was known as the "Badger State," not because it was a habitat of these animals but because miners burrowed homes in the hills during the 1820s lead rush were described as "living like badgers." Large migrations of settlers came from Germany and Austria in the late 1840s, and later waves of immigrants from Scandinavian countries, Poland, Bohemia, Slovakia, and Slovenia followed suit. Still later, in the middle of the twentieth century, African Americans came from the South to work in manufacturing facilities in Milwaukee and nearby. In the last fifteen years, there has been an increase in the Hispanic population. The state has a large agriculture footprint that includes dairy farms (Wisconsin is known as America's Dairyland), agricultural crops, and significant service industries in addition to manufacturing. The state has also emerged as a political battleground in recent times with intense partisan politics.

BY THE NUMBERS

Wisconsin had an estimated population of 5.93 million as of 2024, up slightly from 5.9 million in 2020 and 5.4 million in 2000. By contrast, in 1980 the population was 4.8 million. Recent projections predict a slow growth to over 6 million by the mid-2020s, with the largest population increase located on the eastern side of the state. The four-county Milwaukee metropolitan area is the most densely populated part of the state with approximately 1.46 million people as of 2024. Growth in the population will need to occur from outside migration since there are now more deaths than births within the state. Wisconsin's aging baby-boom generation in expanding the population of retirees, while the number of youths under the age of eighteen has declined in recent years.

WEATHER

Wisconsin has long and cold winters with lots of snow, contrasting with often hot and humid summers. A portion of the highway skirts Lake Michigan, a huge inland sea that produces its own microclimate. This results in cooler temperatures near the shore and storms that can engulf close-by locations in floods. Spring can come slowly to the state, but its truly spectacular fall foliage in September and October attracts many tourists.

IDENTITY

As with all of the geographic areas traversed by Highway 41, the route through the state of Wisconsin is distinct. There are many stereotypes of Wisconsin, and, as with all stereotypes, this leads to an oversimplification of what is actually true. Similar to Michigan's Upper Peninsula, the relative isolation of Wisconsin has meant the development of a separate identity built around its history, natural resources, migrants, and means of making a living. The state has a long history of active civic- and community-focused involvement due to the need for people to rely upon each other during the harsh winters.

There are many notable American figures (past and present) with Wisconsin ties. Among them are architect Frank Lloyd Wright (born in Richland Center), movie director and auteur Orson Welles (born in Kenosha), Israeli Premier Golda Meir (childhood, high school, and early work in Milwaukee), astronaut James Lovell, talk show host Oprah Winfrey (childhood and some high school in Milwaukee), and many more.

Wisconsin is also the fictitious birthplace of the Barbie doll (Willows). Wisconsin's significant tourism/recreational industry is due to many inland lakes and parks that provide opportunities for camping, hiking, fishing, hunting, snowmobiling, golfing, etc. Going "up north" is understood by Wisconsinites to mean spending time at cottages on inland lakes, camping in the woods, fishing on a river, and hiking or biking along numerous trails.

Wisconsin is a highly social state with many supper clubs and lots of drinking establishments (called a "local"). A recent study on binge drinking in the United States lists ten Wisconsin cities in the top twenty! The dairy and cheese-making industries are historically significant, and beer, sausages and a host of ethnic foods are part of the story. This is also a manufacturing state, churning out everything from toilet seats to motorcycles to washing machines.

While National Football League fans from opposing teams might be tempted to characterize all Wisconsin residents as "cheeseheads" who wear funny hats, that would be seriously off the mark. Demographics are changing, and the state has had to come to grips with how to attract a younger, more ethnically diverse population to relocate into the state. Many Wisconsin locales show up on "Best Places to Live" sites based on affordable housing, good schools, and recreation opportunities. The state's reputation as a scenic, tolerant location to plant roots has long been one of its strengths. But difficult issues encompassing the decline of family farms and Wisconsin's manufacturing workforce, an aging infrastructure, and social problems that include alcoholism, drug use, family dissolution, crime, discrimination, and the effects of climate change are very real within the state.

MARINETTE

Crossing the Menominee River, Highway 41 leaves the city of Menominee, Michigan, and enters its twin city of **Marinette**, Wisconsin. Named in honor of the Indigenous trading post owner known as Queen Marinette, the city, with a population of 11,000 is slightly larger than Menominee. It is the seat of Marinette County. The county is the self-proclaimed "waterfall capital of Wisconsin," with over fourteen waterfalls within a one-day drive. From the Menominee River near Niagara to the village of Crivitz, you can observe picturesque waterfalls located primarily in Marinette County's Parks System.

Similar to its Michigan neighbor, Menominee, Marinette was a lumbering center with some handsome old turn of the twentieth century downtown buildings, notably the Queen Anne style **1902 Dunlap Square Building**; unfortunately, many are vacant. A historical logging museum and the handsome 1903 Stephenson Library—funded with a gift from Isaac Stephenson—a wealthy lumber baron and philanthropist and U.S. senator from Marinette, are on the riverfront. A bronze statue of Stephenson also overlooks the Menominee River. Down the street from the library, historic Riverside Avenue features a number of large turn of the century mansions built by prominent individuals of days gone by.

Dunlap Square Building
Marinette, WI

Isaac Stephenson statue,
Marinette, WI

EMPLOYMENT LEADERS IN MARINETTE

The large **Kimberly-Clark** manufacturing facility in Marinette produces paper towels for household and consumer use, and there are several other small foundries and factories on the river close to Lake Michigan.

The city's largest employer is **Fincantieri Marinette Marine**, a large U.S. maritime contractor that builds ships for the U.S. Navy and other government operations. A prominent sign on the factory wall states, "Our Work Keeps America Safe." The U.S. Navy awarded Fincantieri a $5.5 billion dollar contract to build a new generation of ships, which guarantees much economic development in and around the shipyard to accommodate the project. This is great for the area's economy if they can find the workers. News reports suggest that there was political pressure to build ships in Marinette, and the Littoral Combat Ships coming out of the Fincantieri factory are highly suspect of not working correctly.

Small cities such as Marinette are at a disadvantage in not having enough workers who are of prime working age living nearby. An additional problem is the lack of affordable housing for employees, necessitating employees to make long commutes outside of the area to work. Existing housing stock nearby is often in need of repairs and owned by an aging group of homeowners no longer in the workforce. Building new housing is costly and has not met the demand. This is a particularly acute problem in largely rural-based locations.

RESTAURANTS AND RETAIL IN MARINETTE

Highway 41 through Marinette has a number of chain retail stores and restaurants before it exits to a four-lane highway. **The Brothers Three** is an old-time pizza place along the road, and across the street is one of the multiple **Culver's** fast-food franchises—started in Wisconsin and now nationwide—that abound in the state. A mall just outside the city struggles to compete in the shadow of a Walmart Supercenter.

A few miles south of town is **Seguin's House of Cheese**, the first of many cheese shops along Highway 41's route through Wisconsin. Cheese, meats, spreads, souvenirs—these shops offer everything for the tourist on the road. I love the family-owned, independent "tourist traps" that are holdovers from driving trips of yore. Seguin's aging owners sold the business to a local guy who has vowed to keep the same type of merchandise enjoyed by customers over the decades.

PESHTIGO

The small city of **Peshtigo**, "The City Rebuilt from the Ashes," is the next stop along the highway. Peshtigo's main claim to fame is that it was the site of the **Great Peshtigo Fire** on October 8, 1871,—the most destructive forest fire in American history. The fire consumed well over a million acres of land and caused over 1,200 casualties.

In a terrible coincidence, the fire began on the same day as the Great Chicago Fire of 1871 that destroyed much of that city and received the most attention from the outside world. (Interesting fact: Across Lake Michigan on the same day, the city of Holland, Michigan, also caught fire in a devastating event that destroyed two-thirds of the community and left hundreds homeless).

The fire in Peshtigo was the result of a prolonged drought, logging and clearing of land for agriculture and industry, and a lack of local understanding of the threat of fire. The city has a museum devoted to the

Peshtigo fire that is open during the summer tourist season. It is located in a former church where many of the perished and those who survived now rest. Today Peshtigo advertises itself as a good place to reside and locate a business. Per the local website, residents would really like a hardware store to operate in Peshtigo.

Peshtigo Fire Memorial, Peshtigo, WI

POPULAR CULTURE IRONIES

The **Northpoint Exotic Dance Club**—"an adult entertainment club open at 4 p.m. every day"—lies a little outside of Peshtigo's city limits. It seems to be in the middle of nowhere, but I'm sure there is substantial traffic for the club. Just down the highway from the dance club is an old marker from 1938 that announces you are at 45 degrees North latitude, the theoretical halfway point between the North Pole and the Equator (about 3,000 miles in each direction). It's interesting, and a little weird to contemplate just past the strip club.

OCONTO

The small historic city of **Oconto** is the seat of the county of the same name and sits on the Oconto River near Lake Michigan. It is home to **Copper Culture State Park**, site of an ancient burial ground with remains dated to around 5000–6000 BCE.

The Menominee have lived in the area for thousands of years. The French arrived in the area in the 1600s, and a marker in the downtown area honors Nicholas Perrot, a diplomat, explorer, and fur trader who understood Indigenous languages and apparently settled a dispute between the Potawatomi and Menominee in 1668.

The **First Christian Science Church**, erected in 1886, is on the list of historic places as the first purpose-built Christian Science church in the world. While the city was once a major port for commercial fishing and lumber transportation, Oconto today is a small exurb north of Green Bay with an attractive marina, a restaurant, and a park with panoramic views of Lake Michigan, Sturgeon Bay, and Egg Harbor in Door County across the bay.

GREEN BAY

The city of Green Bay sits at the mouth of the Fox River, an arm of Lake Michigan. It is a small city with a population of 107,000 that, combined with the surrounding suburbs, has a metropolitan population of 326,000. That makes it the third-largest metro area in Wisconsin and the largest city in the northern portion of the area traversed by Highway 41. Built as a trading post in 1634 on the site of an ancient Indigenous village, it is the seat of Brown County and one of the oldest permanent European settlements in the United States.

VIGNETTE   JEAN NICOLET AND VINCE LOMBARDI

Two very different individuals put the small city of Green Bay on the map along the northwestern waters of Lake Michigan.

Jean Nicolet (1598–1642) founded the city of Green Bay, Wisconsin, in 1634 while he was reputedly in search of passage to the Orient. Nicolet, born in Cherbourg, France, signed on with the Compagnie des Marchands to go to what was then known as New France to serve as interpreter and ambassador of sorts with the various Indigenous peoples in the area. He worked with the Menominee and Ho-Chunk to smooth out relations with the French fur traders, and helped develop trade and commerce at this strategic location before returning to Quebec. He succeeded in his short life by recognizing and establishing a commercial outpost at Green Bay.

Vince Lombardi (1913–1970) was the legendary football coach of the Green Bay Packers who accepted a position as head coach in 1959 at what was then considered the traveling *Siberia of the National Football League. Lombardi was a New York City native who went on to great fame as the Packers coach who won five NFL football championships and the first two Super Bowls. Many consider him to be the greatest coach in football history. The Lombardi Trophy is awarded each year to the winning team of the National Football League.*

There are several historical sites to see in the city. The **Brown County Historical Society** is housed in **Hazelwood,** the Greek revival home of the influential Martin family from 1838 to 1931. A few structures from the early settler era were moved to **Heritage Hill State Historical Park**, opened in 1977, primarily for visitation in the summer months.

The **National Railroad Museum**, the only congressionally designated railroad museum in the United States, is located in Green Bay and continually increases its collection of old freight equipment and unique locomotives from U.S. railroad history. Among its attractions are the Union Pacific #4107 "Big Boy," the Pershing and Dwight D. Eisenhower locomotives, and numerous other pieces. More than 100,000 visitors visit annually from across the country and around the world. The museum holds seasonal train rides and special events.

Green Bay's strategic location made it a key point for the lumber industry. In 1901, Northern Paper Mills introduced the first "sanitary tissue," called Northern Tissue. But this toilet paper was quite uncomfortable because it contained wood splinters. The first "splinter-free toilet paper" was introduced by Northern Tissue in 1935, and the city was accorded the title of the "Toilet Paper Capital of the World." A number of paper product producers are still in operation in the city and nearby areas.

Green Bay is also home to several meatpacking firms. The Indian Packing Company gave its name to the Green Bay Packers. Curly Lambeau, a shipping clerk for the company, got the owner to provide money for jerseys and the use of the company's athletic field in 1919.

Green Bay has also become a major medical hub for northeastern Wisconsin. Green Bay hosts a branch of the **Medical College of Wisconsin**, several hospitals (including a children's hospital), and medical equipment providers. A large sports medicine facility is located near Lambeau Field.

The city of Green Bay was picked by *US News and World Report* as the "Best Place to Live in 2023-24." Housing affordability, quality of life, safety, and both employment and educational opportunities are factored into this ranking. Perhaps due to this publicity, the price of housing is climbing quickly within the city.

The **University of Wisconsin Green Bay**, with an enrollment of 9,800, is one of the fastest-growing campuses in the UW system. The downtown area of Green Bay is a bit less well-defined than that of other nearby cities with a few hotels and offices. For a true old-time Green Bay experience, venture to **Kroll's East** for a hamburger (they also have a restaurant close to Lambeau Field).

GREEN BAY PACKERS

Then, there is the football team. Green Bay is the smallest U.S. city by far with a professional sports team. The Packers were founded in 1919, making it the third oldest franchise in the National Football League. Professional football in America brings in enormous investment, and the team is currently valued at $5.6 billion dollars according to *Forbes Magazine*. It is the only community-owned franchise in American professional sports. There are approximately 539,000 "shareholders" who own a piece of the team—they hold stock certificates that pay no dividends and cannot be traded.

The Packers are also the only publicly owned team that releases annual financial figures showing the soaring value of pro football teams (twenty years ago the team value was $609 million). Since the Packers have no real owner, the yearly profits are all reinvested into the team, its employees, and facilities. Tens of millions of dollars have been invested in **Lambeau Field Stadium** where the team plays. The Packers' storied history is on display in the **Packers Hall of Fame**, and during tours of the stadium—all available for a fee.

A modern "gastropub" called **1919 Kitchen and Tap** is located within the stadium. I last visited Lambeau Field about twenty years ago, and the stadium from that era is unrecognizable. Today, it seems like a vast TV studio.

You get the sense in Green Bay that everything is secondary to the Packers. It helps that the team has been very competitive over the last few decades and has had marquee athletes playing for them. They have the most wins of any NFL franchise. The Packers are a storied professional football team, and it is not hard to see why. While the Packers are the home team for Wisconsin, they have a rabid fan base that extends throughout the country.

The land adjoining Lambeau Field is called **"Titletown"** and features townhouses and office space. There is a big exposition center across the street from the stadium that features hotels, restaurants, and a business incubator and startup venture capital firm called **Titletown Tech**.

Just down the road is **Schneider National**, a large transportation and logistics firm headquartered in Green Bay that has opened its own innovation center called **The Grove**. The growth of innovative startups combined with investments leveraging the NFL will certainly change the character of the area.

DE PERE AND THE ONEIDA NATION

Just past the city of Green Bay is the town of **De Pere** on the Fox River. It boasts an attractive downtown and large old homes. It features the campus of **St. Norbert College**, a small Catholic liberal arts institution. St. Norbert has a topflight Center for Global Engagement that presents speakers and offers multiple study abroad opportunities for its students. St. Norbert attracts many students from the Chicago area.

St. Norbert College, De Pere, WI

The historic **Union Hotel** in De Pere dates from 1883 and is one of the famous old "supper clubs" owned and operated by the Boyd family since 1918. Although it no longer operates as a hotel, it is where Gerald "Dad" Barisher, equipment manager for the Packers, lived for forty years. He is credited with designing the "G" for the Green Bay Packers logo in his spare time.

To the west of De Pere is the **Oneida Nation**, a sovereign government and federally recognized Indigenous nation in Wisconsin. The Oneida Nation operates the **Oneida Casino**, "the Official Casino of the Green Bay Packers," next to **Green Bay Austin Straubel Airport**. The Oneida Nation also operates a small museum that features exhibits and educational information about the Oneida and Iroquois culture and history. The Oneida Nation is one of the largest employers in Brown and Outagamie counties and provides a court system, healthcare, and social services for its members.

SEYMOUR

Just west of the Oneida Nation and Green Bay is the little town of **Seymour**, which proclaims itself the "home of the hamburger." In 1885, fifteen-year-old "Hamburger Charlie" Nagreen reputedly sold the first burger at the Outagamie County Fair by smashing meatballs into patties and serving them on bread to allow for convenience while eating. Charlie peddled burgers until his death in 1950. In 2007, the Wisconsin legislature issued a proclamation that Seymour is the original home of the hamburger. A fourteen-foot statue of Charlie with hamburger in hand, is prominently displayed in downtown Seymour, and the town holds a Burger Fest every August.

KEWAUNEE AND DOOR COUNTIES

To the east of Green Bay are Kewaunee County, with farms, agriculture, and fishing communities, and Door County, "the Cape Cod" of the Midwest. **Door County**, with 250 miles of coastline, is located on a peninsula that juts northeastward out into Lake Michigan and contains numerous resorts and vacation homes. Its rocky shores, sandy beaches, and eleven lighthouses are reminiscent of a New England seashore. It is a premier Midwestern tourist destination, attracting over 2.5 million visitors annually. Door County's long, scenic shoreline features many attractions and recreational opportunities, including swimming, boating, kayaking, fishing, biking, cross-country skiing in season, and a host of other activities. It is a huge draw for visitors.

When visiting Door County, be sure to stop in at **Al Johnson's Swedish Restaurant** in **Sister Bay**. At certain times of the year, you can see goats grazing atop the grass roof.

THE FOX RIVER VALLEY

South of Green Bay, Highway 41 becomes Interstate 41 to a bit south of Wisconsin's state border with Illinois. Through this area of the journey, the road skirts the western side of **Lake Winnebago**, the largest inland lake in the state, covering a distance of about 215 square miles. The **Fox Valley**, an area of small cities bordering the Fox River, which flows from Lake Winnebago into Green Bay, is known as the "Paper Valley," an area synonymous with paper mills and early growth of the paper industry. While there still are paper mills in the area, the costs of raw materials have contributed to some plant closures. Like many areas of the country, the Fox Valley is dealing with the scourge of illegal drugs, such as fentanyl, that has skyrocketed of late in seizures and overdoses.

APPLETON

Appleton, the seat of Outagamie County with a population of 75,000, has become a medical, financial, and insurance center and is often considered one of the best cities to live and work in the state. It's a historic city with some beautiful turn-of-the-century residences.

In 1882, a small hydroelectric plant was built along the Fox River, and Appleton became one of the first cities in the country to use electricity for streetcars and lights. **"Hearthstone,"** the historic mansion of industrialist Henry Rogers, became the first residence in the country to be electrified from a hydroelectric plant.

Lawrence University, a small liberal arts university founded in 1847, was one of the first co-educational universities in the country. The school has a well-known music conservatory and is just on the outskirts of the downtown. A former industrial area, "Eagle Flats" on the Fox riverfront, has been reconfigured for apartments and commercial development along a walking path.

Long ago, Appleton was a "sundown town" where African Americans were prohibited from settling or spending the night. Sundown towns became common in the Midwest, the South, and other parts of the United States during the Jim Crow era, roughly between the 1890s and the 1960s. In addition to African Americans, other groups—including Jewish Americans, Asian Americans, Native Americans, and Latinos—were often similarly targeted. Federal law was enacted in 1968 to prohibit racial discrimination in the sale of housing. Green Bay and Fond du Lac were also sundown towns along Highway 41. In present-day Appleton, efforts have been made to incorporate more diversity, equity, and inclusion into company hiring practices with the intention of becoming a welcoming community. However, Grand Chute, an Appleton suburb, also remains the headquarters of the ultra-right-wing John Birch Society.

VIGNETTE   EDNA FERBER AND HARRY HOUDINI

Many individuals who grew up and lived in Wisconsin have achieved fame and fortune elsewhere. Edna Ferber (1885–1968) and Harry Houdini (1874–1926) are two examples from the Fox Valley city of Appleton.

Ferber was one of the most widely read authors of the 1920s and 1930s. A 1924 Pulitzer Prize winner for the novel So Big and the author of Showboat, Cimarron, Giant, and several other novels and plays, Ferber was a Jewish American whose family lived in Appleton where she attended high school and Lawrence University. One of her classic novels, Come and Get It, is a family saga set in northeastern Wisconsin during the lumber boom. Ferber's books have strong female characters and distinctive American settings. She was a member of the famed literary Algonquin Round Table in New York City, where she lived most of her life. Her novels helped highlight the diversity of American culture for those who did not have the opportunity to experience it.

Houdini was a famous magician and escape artist who became a worldwide sensation for his numerous death-defying stunts. Houdini, born with the name Erich Weisz, was from an immigrant family whose Rabbi father briefly headed a Jewish reform synagogue in Appleton before moving to Milwaukee and, ultimately, to New York City. After some time on the American vaudeville circuit, Houdini was booked in Europe where he performed escape acts, card tricks, and other "magic" stunts. He became one of the world's highest paid entertainers. He served as the president of the Society of American Magicians, was an early aviator who flew in Europe and Austr-

alia, and made a practice of debunking spiritualists who claimed they could summon the dead. Houdini died at age fifty-two from acute appendicitis possibly caused by blows to his abdomen from a man claiming to test his stomach muscles. Even a century after his passing, he remains one of the world's most well-known magicians. A street in Appleton is known as Houdini Plaza, and a history museum in the town features a display in his honor.

A short drive from Appleton along the north shore of Lake Winnebago on the High Cliff escarpment will bring you to **High Cliff State Park**. An escarpment is a rock slope separating areas of land at different heights. The High Cliff area is part of the Niagara Escarpment, known as "the ledge," which stretches nearly a thousand miles from Wisconsin through Michigan and Ontario into New York, where it ends at Niagara Falls. Limestone, used for plaster and cement, was quarried from the area where you can still find abandoned pits. You can find the ruins of an old lime kiln that operated here from 1855 to 1956 above the northeast shoreline.

NEENAH

Traveling south from Appleton, it's a short journey on Highway 41 to **Neenah**, a smaller version of Appleton. The city's website describes the town as "a friendly, spirited 'hometown,' where life is safe, comfortable and secure." Like Appleton, Neenah has been a paper making location for well over 100 years. **Kimberly-Clark**, the producer of Kleenex, Scott Paper, Kotex, and other paper products was founded in Neenah in 1872, but its corporate headquarters are now outside of Dallas.

The **Neenah Foundry** has been in business since 1872 and is known for the production of the cast iron manhole covers that can be found throughout the country providing access to sewer systems below city streets. Neenah has an attractive historical downtown, lots of landmark homes, and an active chamber of commerce.

OSHKOSH

A little farther south of Neenah on Lake Winnebago is **Oshkosh**, the seat of Winnebago County with a population of 66,000. There are several historic buildings in the downtown area that date from the locality's lumber and wood manufacturing era. It has a classic library built in 1900 with a domed rotunda and two bronze lions that guard the front door. The city is also home to **The Grand Oshkosh**, a performing arts venue built in 1883. The **University of Wisconsin, Oshkosh** campus, with an enrollment of 15,000, is one of the larger satellite institutions within the UW system.

Oshkosh has been home to a few companies, best known being OshKosh B'gosh, the children's apparel company. It was founded in Oshkosh but is now a subsidiary of Carter's Inc. and headquartered in Atlanta. The company first specialized in work clothes and overalls. Like most apparel companies in the United States, it long ago closed its domestic operations to outsource internationally.

The Grand Oshkosh, Oshkosh Opera House, Oshkosh, WI

Oshkosh is also home to **"EAA AirVenture Oshkosh,"** an event hosted each year by the Experimental Aircraft Association. It features an annual airshow in late July that shows off supersonic jets, vintage planes, aerobatics, and all types of light and experimental aircraft. Attendance is huge, with upwards of 650,000 people coming from ninety-two countries to see over 10,000 varieties of aircraft. Many participants spend the night at the adjacent **Camp Scholler** campground "where new friends meet, and old friends reunite." The show makes a special effort to interest children in flying. The **EAA Aviation Museum,** also located in Oshkosh, is a year-round destination for those interested in exploring world-class aviation, aircraft displays, and galleries.

FOND DU LAC

South of Oshkosh, at the mouth of Lake Winnebago, is **Fond du Lac,** seat for the county of the same name, which translated from the French that means "bottom of the lake." The city is the world headquarters for **Mercury Marine**, a venerable maker of outboard motors, propellers, and assorted watercraft-related products since 1939. The company features a Mercury Marine Museum to show off its old outboard motors. An old machine tool company called **Fives Giddings and Lewis, LLC** has been manufacturing in Fond du Lac since 1859.

Fond du Lac has a population of 44,000 and is a bit grittier and blue-collar than some of its neighbors, perhaps due to it being a manufacturing center and a railroad town. There still is an interesting old **Army-Navy** store with a sign advertising Ghillie suits—camouflage wear for hunting—and **Dutch's Trading Post**, your one-stop local shop for all your hunting and fishing needs.

A statue of a soldier stands near the waterfront as a "MEMORIAL TO THOSE WHO SERVED IN THE WAR WITH SPAIN 1898 to 1902." I don't think I have ever before seen a Spanish-American War memorial.

Before leaving Fond du Lac, I had to take a picture of **Leon's Corner Pub**, evocative of the of the many local neighborhood taverns you will find in Wisconsin. Leon's is a member of the Tavern League of Wisconsin, a non-profit lobbying group seeking to assist the many establishments that sell alcohol within the state as they strive to remain viable.

Spanish-American War Memorial, Fond du Lac, WI   *Leon's Corner Pub, Fond du Lac, WI*

FDL Army-Navy Store, Fond du Lac, WI

If you are interested in experiencing what it is like to drive the Old Highway 41, you can easily take State Highway 175 from Fond du Lac into Milwaukee. However, most of the locales covered in my journey are quite close to Interstate 41 and accessible by both highways.

SIDE TRIP TO RIPON

A half hour from Fond du Lac to the west is the small city of **Ripon**, the birthplace of the Republican Party in a little white schoolhouse that has recently been moved to the edge of town. The party was founded in 1854 by individuals convinced political compromise was impossible after the Kansas-Nebraska Act was passed in Congress.

Ripon College (enrollment 754) is a small, prestigious college on the outskirts of the downtown area that began in 1851 as a college preparatory school. It became a four-year college in 1863. Its first graduating class comprised four women in 1867, noteworthy at a time when few women went on to higher education. Ripon has always been considered a national leader in innovative liberal arts education. Additionally, it is a very pretty campus to walk around.

Downtown Ripon is a real gem of a small town with historic restored Italianate buildings that house a mix of different stores, pubs, restaurants, and coffee shops. The vintage **Campus Cinema**, a single-screen theater that first opened in 1935, is still showing first-run movies. The **Ripon Chamber of Commerce** occupies a former library; it is one of the Carnegie libraries that dates from 1902.

Ripon Chamber of Commerce, Ripon, WI

Birthplace of the Republican Party, Ripon, WI

HORICON NATIONAL WILDLIFE REFUGE

South and slightly west of Fond du Lac is the site of the 70,000-acre **Horicon National Wildlife Refuge**, established in 1941 to provide an undisturbed sanctuary for migratory birds and waterfowl. **Horicon Marsh** is the largest cattail marsh in the United States. To see it in person from an elevated vantage point is an amazing experience; the cacophony of bird calls makes visitors realize just how essential this wildlife refuge is to the environment. We need birds—healthy birds—to populate the ecosystem. They are essential to our well-being. Some 300 species of birds, including Canada geese, Sandhill cranes, trumpeter swans, cormorants, pelicans, herons, osprey, wood ducks, grebes, and many more have been sighted at Horicon Marsh.

The town of Horicon, situated next to the marsh, has a **John Deere** tractor factory. Deere is the major employer in town and one reason the area remains economically viable. A "Help Wanted" sign was displayed outside the factory—once again an indication of the problem that many rural towns have in attracting skilled, able-bodied workers.

AMERICA'S DAIRYLAND

From Horicon the drive south through the little towns of Byron, Lomira, and Theresa features often idyllic, pastoral scenes of red barns, grazing cows, and fields of crops. Sometimes you'll pass a small farmstand selling local produce. This is "America's Dairyland," as the Wisconsin state license plates proclaim. Unfortunately, the Dairyland is not in good shape. In 1968, there were 71,000 dairy farms in Wisconsin. Thirty years later, that number had dropped to 23,000. By the end of 2016, the number of licensed dairy farms had ebbed to 9,400, and, as of January 2024, the number was 5,661, a drop of nearly 65,000 individual dairy operations in just over half a century.

Dairy farm near Horicon, WI

A number of reasons can be cited for the decline of dairy farms:

1. Mechanized farming with costly, specialized tractors and other equipment requires a large operation to cover costs.
2. State and federal incentives for dairy farming in the 1980s and 1990s encouraged larger farms at the expense of smaller operations.
3. An aging farming population paired with the enterprise's declining profitability have discouraged younger people from farming as an occupation.
4. Rising land and feed costs have contributed to the consolidation of existing farms and agricultural specialization.
5. Smaller farms with fewer heads of cattle are no longer economically viable within a business model that emphasizes production quantity.

While the production per cow has increased, the cultural and societal cost of losing all of those farms is still being assessed. What you see from the road are a number of empty farmhouses and empty silos which point to the fact that rural areas are becoming more depopulated as prime farmland is left fallow. Small farm towns that had stores and services for the nearby population no longer have a customer base, which has resulted in vacant storefronts. Today, Wisconsin's dairy industry is comprised of a small number of large mega-dairy farms. This is where things seem to be headed at the moment.

THERESA

Old 175 (old 41) passes through the small town of **Theresa**, where it appears every home has a satellite dish for TV. Theresa exists on a historic auto route, the **Yellowstone Trail Route, 1912–1930,** which begins at the Atlantic Ocean in Plymouth, Massachusetts, runs through Montana to Yellowstone National Park in Wyoming, and from there, on to Seattle, Washington and the Pacific Ocean. The road's slogan was "A Good Road from Plymouth Rock to Puget Sound." There is some signage to note this fact. The best-known business in Theresa is **Widmer's Cheese Sellers** (https://www.widmerscheese.com), with lots of flags and, reputedly, an international client base. Widmer's is most famous for its Wisconsin brick cheese, which brings us to the importance of cheese to the state.

Farmland outside Theresa, WI

Wisconsin leads the nation in the production of cheese thanks to the state's dairy farms and production know-how. The state has more than 126 cheese plants producing over 350 varieties of cheese. Consolidation has occurred in cheese-making factories due to large contracts from a few big customers and high barriers to entry for smaller operators. Successful small operators, such as Widmer's, have a retail outlet in addition to bulk sales to large buyers. Cheese production is an outgrowth of the Wisconsin dairy industry, which sells some ninety percent of its milk to make cheese. Wisconsin ranks second in nationwide milk production to California. The frozen pizza industry in Wisconsin is also quite large, producing several national brands such as DiGiorno, Tombstone, and Jack's.

The cheese industry in Wisconsin has had brushes with organized crime. Wisconsin mozzarella, used in the making of pizza and favored by Italian pizza shops in New York City, was cornered by the Al Capone syndicate. One of Capone's many tactics was to pressure pizzerias into buying cheese from farms he owned in Wisconsin. It has been alleged that if a pizzeria denied his offer, he'd have it set ablaze. Later, the Joseph Bonanno mob family entered the cheese business. A March 1980 report from the Pennsylvania Crime Commission stated that Bonanno, "...initiated a conspiracy to control the specialty cheese business in the United States in the early 1940s, and that he and his associates control[led] the activities of the largest and most prosperous specialty cheese companies." Presumably, organized crime is no longer involved in cheese production.

HOUSES OF WORSHIP

If you stay on 175, you'll pass by **St. Lawrence Church**. Erected in 1882, it is one of the many old rural churches, primarily Catholic or Lutheran, that you'll pass by on the road. This area was settled by Germans who were very religious, very conservative, and very resistant to the tides of change that affected more urban denominations. While church attendance has declined nationwide, small-town churches sometimes defy national trends by serving as an anchor for communities.

To the west of 175 is the **Holy Hill Basilica and National Shrine of Mary Help of Christians**, a Roman Catholic church built on a bluff in 1926. The church's scenic tower rises 192 feet from its base to the tip of its spire. Those who complete the 178-stair climb will find a breathtaking panoramic view of the Kettle Moraine area. According to the church, over half a million people from all over the world visit each year.

KETTLE MORAINE STATE FOREST

To the east of 175 and Interstate 41 is the **Kettle Moraine State Forest**, a massive recreation area comprising over 30,000 acres of glacial wooded hills, kettle lakes, and prairies. Trails abound for hiking, mountain biking, horseback riding, and groomed cross-country ski trails in the winter. Numerous campsites and several locations for swimming are within the area as well. Approximately 600,000 people visit the forest annually, with July being the busiest month.

ADDISON TO SLINGER

Continuing south on 175 you pass through the small rural town of **Addison** that is made up of several unincorporated areas with the largest being **Allenton**, just off Interstate 41. You still have a distinct feel of old time Wisconsin here with old brick homes, a grain elevator, rail tracks, and a few small stores.

Nine miles to the south is the village of **Slinger**, about thirty-five miles outside of Milwaukee. Slinger shows up on real estate "Best Places to Live" lists. This area is seeing an increase in suburban housing developments, single-family homes, and the willingness of residents to make long car commutes. Suburban spread is common throughout our Highway 41 drive near large cities. It will definitely change the small rural locations near metropolitan areas.

MILWAUKEE METRO

Metropolitan **Milwaukee** begins a densely populated urban "Megaregion" stretching along Lake Michigan through Chicago into Northwest Indiana to the Michigan border. The Chicago-Milwaukee-Gary region and surrounding area is home to approximately thirteen million people who are increasingly linked by highways, commuter railroads, and largely similar quality of life issues surrounding how to manage flooding, water supplies, business expansion, and affordable housing. The linkages between the three states the region runs through are, unfortunately, not always easily addressed within the political process. Rivalries between the Chicagoland region and the State of Wisconsin that covers much of northeastern Illinois and southeastern Wisconsin have sometimes limited cooperation on projects, such as direct rail links between airports that would benefit residents of the entire area.

VIGNETTE JANE BRADLEY PETTIT

Jane Bradley Pettit (1918–2001) was an American philanthropist who left a giant imprint on her hometown of Milwaukee. The daughter and heiress to of one of the founders of Allen-Bradley (now Rockwell Automation), she donated more than $250 million to a variety of institutions including the Bradley Center, a multipurpose arena (since demolished); Bradley Tech, a public high school; the Pettit National Ice Center with two Olympic-sized hockey rinks; the Milwaukee Institute of Art & Design; the Milwaukee Art Museum; and the United Way. She owned a percentage of the Milwaukee Brewers baseball team. The Jane Bradley Pettit Foundation continues to fund programs and projects in the city that serve low-income and disadvantaged individuals, women, children, and the elderly.

WAUKESHA COUNTY

Interstate 41 and State Road 175 pass through the northern portion of Waukesha County enroute to Milwaukee. With a population of approximately 416,000 as of 2024, it is the third most populous county in Wisconsin.

MENOMONEE FALLS

The large village of Menomonee Falls is the northernmost of the many suburban towns that ring the central city. **Kohl's Corporation** is headquartered here. Like all big-box department store chains, Kohl's is trying to remain relevant in a post-pandemic era when online retail has become the dominant means of acquiring goods. One of its strategies is to introduce more contemporary brand names, such as Sephora cosmetics, to appeal to younger consumers. Just beyond Menomonee Falls, State Road 175 and Interstate 41 enter the city of Milwaukee.

WAUKESHA

South of Menomonee Falls and west of Milwaukee is the city of **Waukesha**, the county seat and a large, prosperous suburb. In 2013, Waukesha applied for permission to withdraw water from Lake Michigan, thirty-five miles away. The Great Lakes Compact made the city ineligible to withdraw water from the lake without approval from the governors of Illinois, Indiana, Michigan, Minnesota, New York, Ohio, Pennsylvania, and Wisconsin—all states that are situated along the lakes. Waukesha's application was accepted, and in 2023 the city switched from groundwater spring wells, for which it was once known, to Lake Michigan water. There will be many more locales outside of the Great Lakes area that will be pressing for water in the future.

Waukesha is home to **Carroll University** (enrollment 1,098), a private Presbyterian university and the oldest college in Wisconsin which opened in 1846.

Two strange and terrible events have afflicted Waukesha. The first was in 2014 when two twelve-year-old girls lured a friend into the woods and stabbed her repeatedly to appease a fictional online character known as "Slender Man." The victim survived the attack, and the two girls were sentenced to long periods in mental health institutions. Then in 2021, an individual with an extensive criminal record drove a vehicle through the city's Christmas Parade, killing six and injuring sixty others, including the Milwaukee Dancing Grannies, who lost three members that day. The offender was captured, convicted, and sentenced to life in prison. Public violence such as this has, unfortunately, become more common in the country. The city has continued the parade with a hardened security barrier to prevent a recurrence.

MILWAUKEE COUNTY

Interstate 41 and State Highway 175 continue into Milwaukee County, the most populous county in the state with approximately 940,000. To the north of the central city are the suburbs of Brown Deer and Glendale and along the lakefront are the communities of Fox Point, Whitefish Bay and Shorewood.

WHITEFISH BAY

In the affluent lakefront village of **Whitefish Bay** sits **Jack Pandl's Whitefish Bay Inn**, a traditional "supper club" restaurant established in 1915. Supper clubs are unique cornerstones of old-time Wisconsin. They are independently owned and rely heavily on traditional American fare such as Friday fish fry, Saturday prime rib, and Sunday broasted chicken and ribs. There is usually a relish tray with crackers and cheese at the bar. Most supper clubs have collections of memorabilia on display and a bartender who can make an excellent brandy Old-Fashioned cocktail; Wisconsinites consume more brandy than any other state. The waiters and waitresses at Jack Pandl's have been serving customers for decades, and they greeted me as an old friend when I patronized the establishment on the recommendation of my wife. Hopefully, the old-style supper clubs will continue to be viable as consumer preferences evolve.

HMONG TOWN

Back on old 41 (SR175, also called Appleton Avenue) in the northern reaches of Milwaukee, I stopped at **Hmong Town**, a grocery store and other shops catering to the expatriate Hmong population that lives in the area. In their native Laos, the Hmong were United States allies during the long Vietnam conflict and paid a heavy price in lives for doing so. Approximately 100,000 Hmong fled to the United States as political refugees from the mid-1970s to the 1990s. Religious organizations assisted in resettling many of the Hmong in Wisconsin and Minnesota where they have established a foothold, particularly in the Milwaukee metropolitan area.

The path of a refugee is never easy, and the Hmong have endured racial discrimination as they seek education, job opportunities, and advancement. They have established a distinctive Asian culture within Wisconsin and are a rapidly growing population. The Hmong are well known at art fairs and farmers' markets within the state for their garden produce and intricate embroidery.

If you continue south on SR 175, you will come to a concentration of recreational and tourist establishments, including the **Miller Brewery**. A slick guided tour in "Miller Valley" shows how beer making has changed over 165 years of brewing history and offers visitors a chance to sample some brews along the way and after the tour. Seventy-minute tours, offered on Thursdays and Fridays, cost $20, and require participants to negotiate a number of stairs through the brewery buildings. Located just to the west is the desirable close-in suburb of **Wauwatosa** (known informally to locals as "Tosa"), and the **Milwaukee County Zoo.**

When State Road 175 ends, you can proceed east on National Park Road (59) into the heart of Milwaukee. Along the way is the **Mitchell Park Horticultural Conservatory**, known by locals as the "Domes." The conservatory is housed in three eighty-five-feet high beehive-shaped buildings, each with a different climate: the Floral Dome for flowers, the Arid Dome for desert plants, and the Tropical Dome for rain forest plants, which features a waterfall and live tropical birds flying freely within.

MILWAUKEE

Milwaukee, with a population of 569,000, is the largest city in Wisconsin and the first big city encountered on our north to south journey on Highway 41. It is ninety miles north of Chicago on Lake Michigan, and in many ways the two cities share a very similar feel. The city is different from the rest of the state with respect to its population diversity. Milwaukee is vibrant, distinctive, diverse, and even quirky. The city that was once stereotypically known for "beer, brats, and bowling" has transformed over the last ten years. It is well worth a visit of several days to explore the neighborhoods and all the city has to offer.

THE NAME

There is a great line in the movie *Wayne's World* by Alice Cooper about the origins of the name Milwaukee as "The Good Land."

Historians suggest that the word comes from the Potawatomi or Ojibwe language and signifies a "Gathering Place" by the water.

NICKNAMES

Milwaukee is known as "Cream City," not because of the dairy industry, but due to the many public, corporate, and residential buildings that were constructed of distinctive yellow, cream-colored bricks throughout the nineteenth century. The bricks were made from a local clay that contained high levels of calcium and magnesium, producing a soft, golden-yellow color. The clay was found in the Menomonee River Valley and on the western banks of Lake Michigan. Many of these historic buildings are still in use today.

A more recent nickname is the "City of Festivals" due to the number of permanent festivals and street festivals, fairs, and parties year-round.

ORIGINS

Indigenous nations had lived in the area for thousands of years when Jesuit missionary Father Jacques Marquette became the first European to camp on the site of the city in 1674. Real estate speculators in the 1830s bartered with Indigenous peoples for the land. Milwaukee became a city and an important wheat market center in 1846. It was once an important shipping/railroad point for the lumber and mining districts to its north and west.

By the mid-1800s, the city was home to a concentration of tanneries, making it one of the largest producers of leather in the world. Local farms and meatpackers provided the hides while hemlock tanbark from northern Wisconsin provided the tannin necessary to turn hides into leather. The tanning industry would remain a major employer until the 1980s when automation and synthetic materials as well as more focus on environmental pollution closed most of the tanneries. A handful of local tanneries still exist, including the **Seidel Tanning Corporation**, which has produced specialty leather goods since 1945. Many of the old buildings that once housed the tanning firms have been repurposed into condominiums and restaurants.

Industries came to Milwaukee in the late 1800s making it a major tool and die center as well as a prominent location for heavy equipment manufacturing. Eastern European immigrants poured into the city for this work. African Americans followed in the period after World War I and faced economic discrimination. These struggles continued well into the 1980s, by which time all of Milwaukee's major industries were under economic duress as factories moved from northern cities to cheaper locations in the American South, Mexico, and China. The city is no longer as reliant on the manufacturing sector as it once was.

MOTORCYCLES

In 1903, William Harley and his childhood friend Arthur Davidson founded a partnership that eventually launched the **Harley-Davidson Motorcycle Company**, long headquartered in Milwaukee. Through many ups and downs over the decades in a competitive global market, this company has managed to survive and thrive, manufacturing its iconic brand of the American motorcycle for a loyal worldwide following. The **Harley-Davidson Museum** on the company premises is where you can see classic motorcycles made over the decades by the company and is well worth a visit. H-D celebrated its 120th anniversary in July 2023 with a four-day homecoming festival in Milwaukee.

BEER

In the 1840s, large numbers of Germans started arriving in the Midwest making Milwaukee one of their favorite destinations. The city's beer industry was created by individuals who learned the art of brewing in Germany. Four notable immigrant entrepreneurs were Frederick Miller, Joseph Schlitz, Frederick Pabst, and Valentin Blatz. They all gave their names to their beers, and the fortunes of all their beer companies underwent multiple twists and turns over the next two centuries.

Schlitz—"the beer that made Milwaukee famous"—introduced a disastrous change of recipe in the 1970s. Now it is produced by Pabst Brewing Company from the "classic 60's formula" that Schlitz created and made famous in the first place. Pabst Brewing is now headquartered in San Antonio, Texas and produces Pabst Blue Ribbon; a beer better known as "PBR" in every dive bar around the country. Blatz Beer is also still made through Pabst Brewing. The only beer of these original names that is made in Milwaukee is Miller—"the champagne of beers." But even though the Miller brewery is headquartered in Milwaukee, it is now a subsidiary of Molson Coors, which is headquartered in Chicago.

The **Pabst Mansion**, built in 1892 by Captain Frederick and Maria Pabst at a cost of just over $254,000 (over $8,000,000 in 2024 dollars), is filled with artwork and treasures collected by the family. It was spared demolition in the 1970s and is now a popular historic house museum tourist destination. The mansion is on the National Register of Historic Places and shows what the gilded age provided for a lucky few.

Today, Milwaukee's beer making expertise has been harnessed by a new generation of local brewers who are establishing popular craft beers and microbreweries. **Lakefront Brewery**, housed in a former utility building, is emblematic of the new age of Milwaukee beer making. The close-in suburb of Glendale is home to the **Sprecher Brewing Company**, which brews both alcoholic craft beers and a much-loved root beer.

OTHER NOTEWORTHY MILWAUKEE COMPANIES, PAST AND PRESENT

Briggs & Stratton: In business since 1908, Briggs & Stratton makes outdoor power equipment that continues to be sold worldwide. While the manufacturing has been outsourced, Briggs & Stratton remains headquartered in Milwaukee.

Allen-Bradley (Rockwell Automation): In business since 1903, Allen-Bradley developed many factory automation devices before it was eventually bought by **Rockwell Automation** in 1985, which owns it today. The founding Bradley family have been notable philanthropists for the city of Milwaukee. The **Allen-Bradley Clock Tower** is a Milwaukee landmark with the largest four-sided clock in the Western Hemisphere.

Northwestern Mutual: In business since 1857, Northwestern Mutual is a large financial services organization headquartered in downtown Milwaukee.

Harnischfeger Corporation/Komatsu: In business since 1884, Harnischfeger Corporation sells material handling and mining equipment. It was acquired by **Komatsu**, a Japanese multinational, in 2017.

Koss Corporation: In business since 1953, Koss Corporation introduced the first high fidelity stereo phones. Known for its witty billboards and print advertising, the company continues to make headphones in Mexico while maintaining its headquarters in Milwaukee.

INNOVATION

The beer barons and industrial families who once dominated Milwaukee businesses have moved on through the generations. Unfortunately, Milwaukee never developed the regional strength of Chicago and Minneapolis to retain local ownership of many of its large firms. The city is in the process of reinventing itself to become more of a technology center. The city is now home to more than 600 tech companies, employing more than 35,000 people. An affordable cost of living, open office space, and a strong talent pool from nearby universities provides an attractive location for new businesses.

Milwaukee is the location of the **Global Water Center**, home to more than 120 water-related companies, the BREW 2.0 post-accelerator program, and the Oasis Co-working Community—a soft landing spot for water entrepreneurs arriving in or visiting Wisconsin. The Water Council is an industry cluster organization and the official North American partner of the Alliance for Water Stewardship which is responsible for overseeing the alliance's comprehensive global standard across the continent.

PORT OF MILWAUKEE

One of the best-run shipping ports on the Great Lakes is the **Port of Milwaukee**. In addition to being a cargo port, it is becoming a port for cruise ships. This is where you can board the Lake Express Ferry to take you across Lake Michigan to Muskegon, Michigan.

POLITICS: MAYORS AND ACTIVISTS

MAYORS

Milwaukee has had some interesting mayors throughout its history. The German heritage of many residents led to the election of several Socialist mayors who ran on good government planks over the years. Frank Paul Zeidler (1912–2006) served three terms as mayor from 1948 to 1960 and is known as the last Socialist mayor of a major American city. He was considered one of the best mayors in the country. Zeidler expanded Milwaukee's geographic base from forty-six to ninety-six square miles, allowing the city to broaden its tax base. He pushed for the establishment of the University of Wisconsin–Milwaukee and the founding of Channel 10, Milwaukee's public television station.

After Zeidler, Milwaukee was led by Henry Maier (1918–1994) from 1960 to 1988. While adept at obtaining federal dollars and increasing the efficiency of city government, he was tone-deaf to the Civil Rights movement and opposed most open-housing legislation. He was the father of **Summerfest**, an annual lakefront celebration that began in 1968 and is now billed as the world's largest music festival. The fest is a huge event that celebrated its fifty-sixth year in 2024 with over 625,000 people in attendance. **Henry Maier Park**, where the fest is held, is named in his honor.

John Norquist (b. 1949) was the mayor from 1988 to 2004 and led a revival of Milwaukee neighborhoods and new downtown housing. More public amenities such as walkable streets were constructed during his term, as well as a reorientation away from freeway development. In 2022, Cavalier Johnson (b. 1986) became the first African American elected as mayor of Milwaukee.

VIGNETTE ACTIVISTS VEL PHILLIPS AND FATHER JAMES GROPPI

Vel Phillips (1924-2018) was one of the most prominent and accomplished figures of Milwaukee's African American community. She graduated from Milwaukee's North Division High School and Howard University in Washington D.C. She returned to Wisconsin to attend the University of Wisconsin–Madison Law School and received her law degree in 1951. In 1956, at the age of thirty-two, she became the first African American and first woman elected to the Milwaukee City Council.

In 1962, she introduced a bill that outlawed housing discrimination to her peers on the council. The bill, however, was defeated 18–1 with only her vote in favor. Between the years of 1963 and 1967, Phillips would reintroduce the housing bill three additional times, only to have it defeated each time. Finally, in 1968, the Fair Housing Law that Phillips had written was approved by the city council. In 1971, Governor Patrick Lucey appointed Phillips to the Milwaukee County Circuit Court, making her Wisconsin's first African American judge. In 1978, she once again made history when she became the first African American to be elected as secretary of state. A street and a school in Milwaukee are named after her, and in 2021, a statue of Phillips was erected on the grounds of the Wisconsin State Capital.

James Groppi (1930-1985) was a Roman Catholic priest who was a central figure in the Civil Rights movement in Milwaukee during the 1960s. He served at St. Boniface Church in the predominately African American Inner Core neighborhood from 1963 to 1970. The church served as a hub for 200 consecutive days of open housing marches from the fall of 1967 to the spring of 1968. When Vel Phillip's Fair Housing Law was finally passed, Father Groppi turned his attention to welfare rights, Indigenous rights, and opposition to the Vietnam War. Eventually, Father Groppi left the priesthood, married, and fathered three children. In 1977, Groppi became a bus driver for the Milwaukee County Transit system and would remain so until his death from complications of cancer. In 1988, the 16th Street Viaduct crossing the Menomonee River in Milwaukee was renamed the **James E. Groppi Unity Bridge***. The* **James E. Groppi High School***, an alternative high school for at-risk youth in Milwaukee, is also named in his honor.*

HOUSING

Milwaukee is a conglomeration of neighborhoods that you can see firsthand on your drive through the city if you proceed on the old route of 41 (Appleton Avenue). Rates of home ownership, poverty, and public health vary widely between White, African American, and Latino residents. The city and county were among the most racially segregated in the nation for many years, and it still struggles with that legacy. Community activists worry that ongoing gentrification of some close-to-downtown, formerly working-class neighborhoods such as **Walkers Point** and **Bay View** will push out longtime residents of color.

The city has seen some population loss since the COVID-19 pandemic of 2020–2021 similar to what Chicago is experiencing. Lower birth rates, smaller households, and more people moving out than are moving in is a dynamic not easily changed. City officials are adding bike lanes and pushing for more affordable housing.

In a 2023 statement, Milwaukee County Executive David Crowley said the county's strategic plan aims to retain residents, in part by focusing on people who have been historically underserved. "Milwaukee County remains at the top of some of the worst lists when it comes to race and health equity, and we've been at the top for the better part of the decade—this hurts everyone," Crowley said. "If we're concerned about the exodus from the County then we must make the investments to make our region a place people want to stay, settle down, and contribute to the community around them."

According to U.S. Census Bureau data, Milwaukee has the second-highest poverty rate among the top fifty most populated cities in the United

States, with 24.6% of the city living in poverty.

LANDMARKS

Downtown Milwaukee has several landmark buildings worth taking a stroll to see. I was particularly impressed with the **Mitchell Building**, an ornate structure built in 1876 and recently restored.

Mitchell Building , Milwaukee, WI

"The Bronze Fonz" is a statue of Arthur Fonzerelli, a fictional character made popular by the hit 1970s TV series *Happy Days*, which was set in Milwaukee. Played by actor Henry Winkler and nicknamed Fonzie, or "the Fonz," his big shtick was turning both thumbs upward and exclaiming, "Ayyyy!" The Fonz also contributed the idiomatic term "Jumping the Shark," a pejorative phrase used to suggest that a creative work appears to have reached a point where it has exhausted its story. You can see the Bronze Fonz in downtown Milwaukee.

"Bronze Fonz" by Gerald P. Sawyer, Milwaukee, WI

Another noteworthy downtown statue is **Gertie the Duck** on East Wisconsin Avenue. The statue memorializes Gertie (a duck) and her ducklings on a bridge crossing the Milwaukee River that captivated the war-weary city in 1945, the final year of World War II. A kind bridge tender looked after Gertie as she raised her ducklings.

Gertie the Duck, designed by sculptor, Gwendolyn Gillen, Milwaukee, WI

West of the city, near the city of Waukesha, is **Ten Chimneys**, the summer home of Broadway legends Alfred Lunt and Lynn Fontanne from the 1920s to the 1970s. The home is now a national landmark and offers tours of Lunt's collection of theater memorabilia and other items of interest and offers theater and arts training as well.

MILWAUKEE ART MUSEUM

Among the many things to see in Milwaukee, you should definitely make an effort to see the **Milwaukee Art Museum**. Its spectacular structure on Lake Michigan was designed in 2001 by Santiago Calatrava and unfurls into wings like a giant bird taking flight. Inside is an impressive collection of works by Georgia O'Keefe (a Wisconsin native) as well as collections of other pieces by noted artists. While I was there, I was able to check out a really great exhibit of Scandinavian design in the United States.

Milwaukee Art Museum, Milwaukee, WI

AMERICA'S BLACK HOLOCAUST MUSEUM

In the Bronzeville neighborhood north of the central city, **America's Black Holocaust Museum**, founded by Dr. James Cameron, a lynching survivor, was originally opened in 1988. Dr. Cameron passed away in 2006, and the museum was closed in 2008 during a severe economic downturn. Thanks to the efforts of community activists, the museum reopened in 2022. In addition to its physical location, ABHM has a virtual online presence with exhibits that seeks to educate individuals on the African American experience from pre-captivity in Africa to the present day. The museum's website also curates and aggregates stories from African American journalists around the country.

FOOD AND DRINK

BARS/BOWLING

Numerous historic taverns abound in every part of the city. One of the most notable, due to its ubiquitous bumper stickers, is **Wolski's Tavern**, which opened in 1908 on Milwaukee's lower east side. If you stay late, you might earn an "I Closed Wolski's" sticker to post wherever in the world you are.

There are some great old bowling alleys in the city as well. **Bay View Bowl** in the Bay View neighborhood on the south side of the city is located in a building constructed in 1925 and is well worth a trip. **East Brady Street** in the Lower East Side neighborhood has a number of unique restaurants and bars.

RESTAURANTS

Restaurants in Milwaukee appeal to every taste. The **Milwaukee Public Market** is in the trendy **Historic Third Ward** of the city that offers numerous restaurants with lots of different artisan and ethnic foods to take home. It offers cooking classes as well. If you like chili, I recommend **Real Chili** downtown that has been around since 1931.

Fiesta Garibaldi Restaurant, Lincoln Village neighborhood, Milwaukee, WI

If you want authentic, old-school German food, go to **Mader's Restaurant** downtown, which has been in business since 1902, or **Kegels Inn**, which has been serving since 1924 near American Family Field.

For authentic Serbian food, **Three Brothers Restaurant** has been in business since 1956. If it's Friday night in Wisconsin, you may want to find a place for a fish fry, a cherished, deeply ingrained part of the state's culture. Try the **Swingin' Door Exchange Saloon and Eatery** in Milwaukee for an authentic fried fish meal. Near the Brewers ballpark is **Daddy's Soul Food and Grille**, and there are several good Mexican restaurants in the Lincoln Village neighborhood. Check out **La Casa De Chivolin, Taqueria La Sierrita**, and **La Salsita**, to name three. The high-profile **3rd Street Market Hall** opened downtown in January 2023 and looks to be a major venue for food.

SCHOOLS

Milwaukee is home to several universities of note. The **University of Wisconsin–Milwaukee** (enrollment 27,000) is the largest university in the city and a member of the UW system. **Marquette University** (enrollment 11,000) is a well-known private Jesuit university. The **Milwaukee School of Engineering** (enrollment 2,700) is a private, non-profit university focusing on engineering, business, and nursing. **Alverno College** (enrollment 2,100) is a private Roman Catholic women's college. Finally, the **Medical College of Wisconsin** (enrollment 1,500) is a private medical school, pharmacy school, and graduate school based in Milwaukee.

SPORTS AND GAMING

BASKETBALL

The **Milwaukee Bucks** were champions of the National Basketball Association in 2021 and have a very appealing superstar player, Giannis Antetokounmpo, a.k.a. "The Greek Freak." The Bucks play in **Fiserv Forum**, a recently built multi-purpose arena close to the downtown area in the **Deer District**—a rethought urban area with apartment lofts, restaurants, and entertainment venues designed to appeal to individuals seeking to be downtown. This development points to an evolving city that is appealing to young professionals.

"Our Lady of Guadalupe" mural, by Chaco Lopez and Mauricio Ramirez,
Lincoln Village, WI

Mural by artist Mauricio Ramirez, Downtown Milwaukee, WI

BASEBALL

The Milwaukee Brewers are part of the city's rich legacy of baseball. Milwaukee is the birthplace of the American League of Major League Baseball founded in 1900 at the Republican House Hotel. The Braves moved from Boston to Milwaukee in 1953 and were one of the premier teams of the 1950s, winning it all in 1957 with Hall of Fame players Hank Aaron, Warren Spahn, Eddie Matthews, and Red Schoendienst. Alas, the Braves left for Atlanta in 1965; Milwaukee gained the Brewers in 1970.

The Brewers have a devoted fan base and play in **American Family Field** (formerly Miller Park), located in the western portion of the city right off old Highway 41. The facility boasts a retractable roof that can be opened and closed in ten minutes. You can watch mascot Bernie Brewer slide into a

144

giant mug of beer each time the home team hits a home run.

SPEED SKATING

The **Pettit National Ice Center** is an Olympic Training Site for the U.S. speed skating team in West Allis, just west of Milwaukee. Many Olympic champions have trained at this facility.

AUTO AND MOTORCYCLE RACING

The oval **Milwaukee Mile Speedway** has been operating since 1903 at the Wisconsin State Fair Grounds west of the central city.

CARD GAMES

The card game **Sheepshead** is most commonly played in Wisconsin. In 1983, it was declared the official card game of the city of Milwaukee. I once had a Milwaukee native try to teach me how to play on a long overseas plane flight, but I still cannot tell you how to do it!

Another Wisconsin passion is the card game **Euchre** to which Sheepshead is somewhat similar. My brother-in-law, who lived in Wisconsin for many years, is an ardent Euchre player.

OTHER IMPORTANT PLACES

WISCONSIN STATE FAIRGROUNDS

The **Wisconsin State Fair** has been held every August in West Allis since 1892. It annually hosts about one million fairgoers and is considered one of the best state fairs in the United States. A longtime favorite treat is the **Original Cream Puff**, a pastry that's been sold at the fair for a century! And there's the **Milk House**, where a dollar can buy a glass of this ice-cold drink in various flavors! The fair also features agriculture demonstrations, with a main show ring and barns holding sheep, cattle, rabbits, poultry, and goats. Another fair delight is **"Saz's Famous Racing Pigs,"** where you can cheer on your favorite swine.

WOOD NATIONAL CEMETERY

Nearby the fairgrounds is **Wood National Cemetery**, established as a gravesite for veterans of the U.S. Civil War in 1871. The cemetery contains more than 30,000 graves, including those of members of the first Union unit of African American soldiers and several Medal of Honor recipients. The cemetery, which is located next to Interstate 94, has added some acreage for the graves of veterans from World War II, the Korean War, and the Vietnam War. The cemetery's most prominent monument is the Soldiers and Sailors Monument. Located at the northeast corner of the cemetery, it is a granite monument that rises sixty-five feet.

USINGER'S AND WISCONSIN CHEESE MART

Near downtown Milwaukee is **Usinger's Famous Sausage Factory** and shop, which declares "The Usinger family has been making sausages in Milwaukee for over 140 years. Recipes have remained unchanged since 1880." They claim they have "never altered in order to meet a competitive price." Close by is the **Wisconsin Cheese Mart**, opened in 1938, serving hundreds of varieties of cheese.

LIBRARY

The downtown **Milwaukee Central Public Library** is a beautiful Renaissance style building dating from 1898. A national competition was held in 1893 to pick a design for the building, including a submission from Frank Lloyd Wright. The entrance to the library features mosaic floor tiles hand-laid by Italian craftsmen who had settled in Milwaukee. The building is now listed on the National Register of Historic Places.

CITY HALL

Milwaukee City Hall dates from 1895 and was the city's tallest building until 1973. The Flemish-Renaissance-inspired building has mosaic and marble flooring with a grand open atrium rising eight stories in the building's center, topped with a skylight. According to one of the guards I talked to at City Hall, another 70s sitcom, *Laverne and Shirley*, about two friends who work at a brewery, opened with a shot of the City Hall and "Welcome to Milwaukee" graphics.

Milwaukee City Hall, Milwaukee, WI

THE PFISTER HOTEL

Long regarded as a premier historic hotel in downtown Milwaukee, the **Pfister Hotel** was opened in 1893 and billed as the "Grand Hotel of the West." The hotel has been extensively renovated over the decades and has a Victorian Art collection, a beautiful lobby, and a terrific lounge. The Pfister is believed to be haunted by its namesake, businessman Charles Pfister who it's said keeps a watch over the hotel and its guests.

The hotel frequently hosts visiting baseball teams, and several of its high-profile guests have had some interesting things to say about their stays. Bryce Harper of the Washington Nationals claimed that his belongings and furniture moved while he was sleeping, while Brandon Phillips of the Boston Red Sox said his radio repeatedly turned on and off for no reason.

CITY TRENDS

Milwaukee is far more than a relic of another era as portrayed by old television shows. I was impressed by the energy and reinvention taking place to revitalize Milwaukee into a city for young, educated people—a city of technology and social life. In the downtown area and nearby, that attempt seems to have been successful. The city has multiple challenges to meet to ensure that it is a welcoming place for all of its citizens. Milwaukee is a major city that is continuing to evolve.

SOUTH OF MILWAUKEE TO THE ILLINOIS BORDER

As you leave Milwaukee on I-41, you will pass by **Milwaukee Mitchell International Airport**. In addition to greater Milwaukee residents, it attracts passengers from the far north suburbs of Chicago as an alternative to O'Hare International Airport.

Continue south toward Illinois as I-41 and I-94 merge into one eight-lane mega-expressway that is routinely filled with trucks, and turn off east at State Road 20 toward the city of Racine. Before Racine, you will go by the village of Mount Pleasant. Take a turn south on 150th Street, and you will come to land zoned for industrial use. A huge power station and a big sphere are visible behind fences and street barricades. This is the location of the Foxconn factory—or rather what was supposed to be the Foxconn factory.

VIGNETTE FOXCONN

Foxconn is the international name for Hon Hai Precision Industry, a Taiwanese multinational company established in 1974. The founder is Terry Gou, a Taiwanese billionaire who would like to become president of Taiwan. Foxconn is one of the primary assemblers of Apple iPhones.

With much fanfare, in October 2017, Foxconn announced they would be building a multi-billion-dollar LCD flat panel TV factory. The project was touted as an investment of up to $10 billion that would deliver 13,000 jobs to the region. Mount Pleasant offered $860 million in tax incentives to attract Foxconn, and it borrowed funds to do so. The state legislature passed a $2.85 billion tax incentive package, and the company also received a $150 million break in sales taxes for a total state package of $3 billion.

The deal required buying out landowners in Mount Pleasant and tearing down dozens of homes. A number of landowners sued to stop the village's use of eminent domain laws to benefit a private company. The Wisconsin Department of Natural Resources also approved a request to pull millions of gallons of water daily from Lake Michigan to serve a new Foxconn Technology Group manufacturing plant, thus helping the Taiwanese electronics giant clear a major regulatory hurdle.

Mount Pleasant and Foxconn benefited from a loophole in the Great Lakes Compact, an agreement between the Great Lakes states, Ontario, and Quebec that prohibits diverting water from the lakes' basin. Communities such as Mount Pleasant straddle the basin boundary, so they can withdraw Great Lakes water for public use. Municipalities such as Racine, which supply straddling communities with water, can make a withdrawal request on behalf of those communities.

Ground was broken with much fanfare in June 2018. President Donald Trump, former House Speaker Paul Ryan, in whose Congressional district the project was located, and former Governor Scott Walker all shoveled dirt with Terry Gou. Construction that was supposed to start in 2018 never began. The company has never explained why.

In April 2023, Microsoft agreed to buy a $50 million, 315-acre parcel of land in southeastern Wisconsin initially meant for Foxconn to build a data center. Typically, these data centers employ about 200–300 workers. In a recent election, the four village trustees who signed off on the Foxconn deal were narrowly reelected. Foxconn has not been forthcoming with further information. My drive around the factory campus in April 2023 was through much empty land.

Foxconn also has an office building in downtown Milwaukee that was planned to be a state-of-the-art headquarters displaying its "continuing innovation in leading-edge technologies." When I passed by, there was a Foxconn sign, but the building appeared to be vacant. Numerous lawsuits have been filed against the company, and many commentators have decried the "corporate welfare" that enabled this deal to move *forward. As a sidelight, bankrupt Lordstown Motors in Ohio has filed for Chapter 11 and is suing its investment partner Foxconn for breach of contract and fraud (June 2023).*

As of 2024, Microsoft was proceeding with $3.3 billion toward the construction of a new AI (Artificial Intelligence) data center on the former Foxconn site.

RACINE

You will pass a number of chain shopping and retail establishments on State Road 20 before entering the city of **Racine**. It is the fifth-largest city in Wisconsin and boasts one very important reason to stop in what is, mostly, a small old industrial "rustbelt" city. The **S.C. Johnson & Son Company Headquarters** in Racine occupies a building designed and furnished by America's most famous architect, **Frank Lloyd Wright**. Wright was a pioneer of modern architecture, and all of his homes and buildings around the country are venerated. The Johnson Wax Headquarters is the only surviving office building designed by Wright that was built between 1936 and 1939. Like so many of Wright's buildings, it is the interior that matters; in this case, it features a series of columns within the building that spread to the ceiling, emitting light to the open "Great Workroom." There are far too many details to describe here; you will simply have to see it for yourself, and, fortunately, building tours are provided. Needless to say, people from all over the world come to see the Johnson Wax Headquarters.

In downtown Racine, visitors can explore the **Racine Art Museum** which holds one of the largest craft collections in North America, and the **Racine Heritage Museum**, housed in what was once a Carnegie-donated library built in 1904. The city has a classic old downtown that, aside from a few empty storefronts, is in good shape. Racine was known historically for glass blowing, and you can visit **Hot Shop Glass** downtown for tours and lessons. Stop at the old-school **Kewpee Hamburgers** for lunch.

A large tractor manufacturer with a worldwide footprint, **CNH**, was founded as the J.I. Case Corporation in Racine in 1842, initially named Racine Threshing Works. After mergers with International Harvester and New Holland Machine Company, *CNH* is an acronym for Case–New Holland. CNH still maintains a small presence in Racine but is currently headquartered in England.

Photo mural, artist unknown, Racine, WI

Like many former industrial, waterfront cities, Racine has spruced up its lakeside area with a large marina, a hotel, a brewpub, and a wide expanse of shoreline called **Racine North Beach.** Next to the beach is the **Racine Zoo.** Farther north is **Wingspread**, a retreat and conference center designed by Frank Lloyd Wright. Also, just north of the city, is the **Wind Point Lighthouse**—a national historic landmark built in 1880 with lovely grounds made for a stroll.

Downtown Racine, WI

Racine is also the home of Danish Kringle, Wisconsin's official state pastry. A Kringle is made with layers of sweet, flaky pastry filled with fruit, nuts or a gourmet filling, and topped with sweet icing. With a high concentration of Danish settlers immigrating to southern Wisconsin in the early 1900s, Racine became known as the Kringle capital of the world. To sample the true authentic pastry, stop at **Bendtsen's Bakery**, in business since 1934, or **O&H Danish Bakery**, in business since 1949.

As famously portrayed in the film *A League of Their Own*, the Racine Belles of the All-American Girls League played in the city from 1943 to 1950.

Heading south on Sheridan Road along the lakefront, you can stop at **HobNob**, a classic Wisconsin supper club since 1954 that advertises it has "the best food in town." Even if you don't plan to eat there, at least stop to admire the classic martini glass mural in front.

Windpoint Lighthouse, Racine, WI

HobNob Supper Club, Kenosha, WI

KENOSHA

The final lakefront city on our southward trek through Wisconsin, **Kenosha** is the fourth-largest city in the state. It's a proud old "rustbelt" city that has gone through many iterations. Unfortunately, it has also been at the epicenter of some difficult events of late.

For decades, Kenosha, named after a Potawatomi village, was an industrial location. The Nash Automobile company, founded in 1917, morphed into American Motors Corporation, the automaker that manufactured the Gremlin, the Pacer, the Javelin, and the Jeep, among other models at its plant in the city. A partnership with the French automaker Renault led to its sale to Chrysler in 1987, and Chrysler promised to continue auto production at the factory. Alas, the factory was closed in 1988 and demolished in 1990.

There were other plant closings in Kenosha during this period, including a lakeshore steel mill. This spurred its transition to a service economy, and Kenosha slowly became a distant bedroom suburb of Chicago, a process that is still ongoing.

The local **Kenosha Station** is served by Metra Union Pacific North, a commuter rail line that runs south to downtown Chicago. **Snap-On-Tools**, a manufacturer of high-end tools and equipment for professional use, and **Jockey International**, a manufacturer and retailer of underwear, sleepwear, and sportswear, still maintain headquarters in Kenosha.

Where the factories once stood are many new lakefront condominiums. The city has repurposed some old electric streetcars to provide transportation between downtown Kenosha and the Lake Michigan shoreline. The University of Wisconsin has a **UW Parkside** campus in Kenosha with an enrollment of 4,800, and **Carthage College**, a private liberal arts college of 2,600 students, has a campus on Lake Michigan.

The **Civil War Museum** on the Kenosha lakefront eloquently highlights the conflict from the perspective of the people of the seven states of the upper Midwest, as well as addressing some of the enduring issues from the Civil War the nation still struggles with. In downtown Kenosha, an old post office building houses the **Dinosaur Discovery Museum**. It focuses on the link between meat-eating dinosaurs and birds.

Other old structures of interest in Kenosha include **Franks Diner**, the oldest continuously operating "lunch car" diner in the United States, and **Simmons Field**, home of the Kenosha Kingfish. Opened in 1920, this baseball stadium features minor league and semi-pro games. The **Kenosha Velodrome**, built in 1927, is the nation's oldest operating facility for track cycling. Kenosha also hosts a large annual vintage car show called the **Kenosha Classic Cruise-In**. If you're in town on Labor Day weekend, you can check it out.

VIGNETTE   KENOSHA'S RECENT HISTORY

In August 2020, a local white Kenosha police officer shot and seriously injured Jacob Blake, an African American man. Many people felt that the use of deadly force was unwarranted, and the event sparked protests and general civil unrest. There was rioting and arson in the downtown area on the night of August 25th, during which three individuals were shot. Two of the victims died and a third was wounded. The perpetrator was seventeen-year-old Kyle Rittenhouse, who claimed self-defense. Rittenhouse had come to the protests from Illinois, carrying an AR-15 assault rifle—a gift from his mother.

Shortly after the shooting, both Presidential candidates Donald Trump and Joe Biden visited Kenosha during the tense 2020 political campaign. Rittenhouse became a hero to conservative news personalities and gun-rights advocates.

In November 2021, the jury trial of Kyle Rittenhouse commenced. The city remained in the public eye throughout the trial. Rittenhouse claimed that he was protecting property and therefore acted in self-defense. The jury found him not guilty of any charges. Rittenhouse's defense was bankrolled by several individuals. Some protests occurred directly after the verdict, but Kenosha has remained peaceful since then.

In the years since his acquittal, Rittenhouse has remained in the spotlight, attending numerous events hosted by conservative organizations and celebrities, including Tucker Carlson, and Matt Gaetz. Rittenhouse is currently the outreach director for Texas Gun Rights, a state affiliate of the National Association for Gun Rights advocacy group.

This is not something that Kenosha tourist literature wants to talk about.

BEYOND KENOSHA

On the outskirts of Kenosha, just off I-41, is the **Mars Cheese Castle**. I don't think any visit to Wisconsin is complete without a stop at Mars. Go to see all of the cheeses and sausages and stay to enjoy a beer and a brat or a pretzel with cheese spread at the bar/restaurant in the store. Don't forget to pick up a Danish Kringle, cheese curds, and some beer.

New Glarus Spotted Cow, a beer that is "only sold in Wisconsin," is a necessary purchase. The store is in a much bigger building now than it used to be. I preferred the old, more ramshackle place, but it was torn down in 2011.

Near I-41 to the south and west of Kenosha is the village of **Pleasant Prairie**. It has no real downtown. Rather, it is occupied by multiple distribution centers, and more are being built on what was once farmland. The village has instituted tax incentives to provide infrastructure improvement. Amazon, Uline, FedEx, Meijer, and Kohl's all have large cross-dock facilities within the area.

A question that comes to mind: will distribution centers become the white elephants (dead malls) of tomorrow? Big-box distribution centers have popped up outside of most central cities to provide access to goods, mainly by truck. It appears that the Wisconsin–Illinois border will eventually be little more than a logistics warehouse complex.

A **Jelly Belly Candy Factory and Store** used to stand off I-41 in Pleasant Prairie for many years but the **Haribo** opened a manufacturing facility in

2023 to make its widely known "Gummy Bear" candy. Unfortunately, they do not allow tours at this time.

An outlet mall for fashion brands is also located just off the highway in Pleasant Prairie. Outlet malls were originally used to sell overstock items at discount prices, but as of late, designers and vendors are creating fashion brand items specifically for their outlets at lower cost and quality. Time will tell whether outlet malls will return to doing big business or if they will thin out as online retailing grows.

Chiwaukee Prairie stretches from the southeast corner of Pleasant Prairie along the Lake Michigan shoreline to the Illinois state line. It features 400 acres of preserved grasslands, wetlands, shoreline, tall oaks, and even sand dunes, and it is officially recognized as a National Landmark.

Finally, near the Wisconsin–Illinois state line, is the site of the **Bristol Renaissance Faire**, a Renaissance-themed park in the village of Bristol that is open from July to early September. It recreates a sixteenth century English town during the reign of Queen Elizabeth I, with jousting tournaments, stage shows, and all kinds of actors in costume. It's very kitschy, but fun. Closed during the pandemic, it is back to packing in the visitors.

CONCLUDING THOUGHTS

So, how to sum up the journey on Highway 41 through Wisconsin? The state faces issues of demographic change, affordable housing, shifting industry, and rural shrinkage. The recreational and tourist opportunities that draw visitors to the state remain in place, but for residents, there is a mixed bag. Wisconsin is a "purple state," with intense partisan politics that are often at odds with the fun-loving public hospitality face the tourist industry would like to portray. The state is political yet friendly for the most part. How that affects life in Wisconsin going forward is a question mark. "Getting things done" to help the state as a whole is often subject to lots of interference from outside political interests with little understanding of the state dynamics.

Traveling through the length of Wisconsin and stopping along the way enables travelers to gain an understanding of the intense loyalty of previous and current residents. Winters can be very long and cold, and mosquito season in the summer is only one of the challenges state residents deal with.

Despite, or perhaps because of enduring climate variations, the residents are friendly, happy, hardworking, and unpretentious. They place more stress on commonalities than divisions in day-to-day living.

Yet that does not necessarily mean they accept new people easily. New residents from Latin America, Africa, and Asia are welcomed to Wisconsin as necessary workers, but their economic and cultural contributions are not often part of the social fabric of the state with its Central European roots. African Americans in the state may be lionized for their athletic accomplishments, but they struggle with being accepted as full-fledged Wisconsinites in a state with few pockets of population diversity. Indigenous peoples who have lived in Wisconsin for centuries are also oftentimes excluded from this state persona, despite giving their names to many of the locations within it and providing critical employment opportunities to many communities.

Wisconsin will continue to transition from its manufacturing and agricultural origins to a greater technology orientation. It will need to continue being a good steward to all of the natural attractions the state has to offer, and it needs to be more inclusive of new residents. That is a tall order, but a positive attitude can enable the state to propel itself forward into a new period of growth. That can also include lots of beer, brats, cheese curds, and Kringle.

CHAPTER FIVE
ILLINOIS

"Illinois is the heart of the nation."

—*Abraham Lincoln*

"It is hopeless for the occasional visitor to try to keep up with Chicago—she outgrows his prophecies faster than he can make them. She is always a novelty; for she is never the Chicago you saw when you passed through the last time."

—*Mark Twain*

"There is an open and raw beauty about that city that seems either to kill or endow one with the spirit of life."

— Richard Wright

"Chicago is a town, a city that doesn't ever have to measure itself against any other city. Other places have to measure themselves against it. It's big, it's outgoing, it's tough, it's opinionated, and everybody's got a story."

— Anthony Bourdain

Highway 41 through Illinois is sixty-five miles. That's the shortest stretch of the eight states covered by the highway.

Key Towns/Cities: *Waukegan, Highland Park, Northbrook, Glenview, Wilmette, Skokie, Evanston, Chicago*

Illinois Counties along 41: *Lake, Cook*

Between the Wisconsin and Indiana state lines, Highway 41 crosses through the flatland of Illinois. The state is considered to be the "most normal" of the whole of the United States, with its spread of demographics across race, religion, education, and income, along with its mix of diverse urban, industrial, and agricultural settings. While the bulk of Illinois would easily qualify as a rural farming state akin to neighboring Iowa, the track of Highway 41 goes through an ancient crossroads of travel and trade that has played a key role in the making of modern, urban America. The greater **Chicago Metropolitan Area** with a population of nine million starts almost immediately as you cross from Wisconsin into the northeastern corner of Illinois and remains a national economic, social, and cultural crossroads that continues to exert influence, good and bad, upon the rest of the country.

The far northern route of 41 in Illinois passes by a mix of older cities and parkland before running into an area of affluent suburbs bordering the shores of Lake Michigan, collectively known as the **North Shore**. The highway then enters the **North Side** of the city of **Chicago** and traverses from north to south along the lakefront, where it is commonly known as **DuSable Lake Shore Drive**, one of the most iconic parts of the entire national highway. The highway continues through the **South Side** of Chicago before passing into Indiana.

AN ILLINOIS ALBUM PLAYLIST

- Sufjan Stevens: *Illinoise* 2005
- Aliotta Haynes Jeremiah: *Lake Shore Drive* 1971
- Muddy Waters: *The Chess Box* 1989
- Buddy Guy: *Damn Right, I've Got the Blues* 1991
- Sam Cooke: *Sam Cooke* 1958
- Chicago: *Chicago Transit Authority* 1969
- Styx: *The Grand Illusion* 1977
- The Smashing Pumpkins: *Siamese Dream* 1993
- Cheap Trick: *Heaven Tonight* 1978
- Mavis Staples: *You Are Not Alone* 2010
- Herbie Hancock: *Headhunters* 1973
- Steve Goodman: *Somebody Else's Troubles* 1972
- John Prine: *John Prine* 1971
- Koko Taylor: *Koko Taylor* 1969
- Common: *Be* 2005
- Chance the Rapper: *Acid Rap* 2013
- Wilco: *Yankee Hotel Foxtrot* 2002

ORIGINS

Indigenous peoples settled in the area about 2000 BCE. The Miami, Illinois, Sauk, Chippewa, Potawatomi, Sac, Fox, and Ottawa lived within the area where they hunted, fished, and grew small crops. In the late seventeenth century, the Great Lakes region experienced profound changes due to the arrival of European powers. Robert Cavalier de LaSalle (1643–1687), the great French explorer, predicted upon seeing the area in 1682 that a great city would arise on the banks of the lake, and it would command a New World empire.

Not far from **Chicago Midway International Airport** is the **Chicago Portage National Historic Site**. French explorers Jacques Marquette (1637–1675) and Louis Jolliet (1645–1700) arrived in the area in 1673 as they followed ancient Indigenous trade routes from the Mississippi River to the Illinois River. Indigenous peoples showed them a shortcut portage passage through the ten-mile-long marsh called Mud Lake, which divided what we know today as the Des Plaines and the Chicago rivers. This portage brought them to "Checagou" on Lake Michigan. Jolliet realized that a canal through the portage could easily cut the time of travel and simplify trade and exploration. It would be well over 175 years before his vision would be realized in the form of the **Illinois and Michigan Canal**, completed in 1848. The wider **Chicago Sanitary and Ship Canal** was built in 1900, and Chicago became the country's busiest inland port.

The northern Illinois region remained contested and dangerous from the mid-1700s to the 1820s, with numerous clashes between Indigenous peoples, French and British soldiers, American soldiers, and the newly arriving settlers pouring into the Northwest Territory of the recently created United States thanks to improvements in the transportation network.

BY THE NUMBERS

Illinois had an estimated population of 12.86 million in 2024, an increase from 12.59 million in 2020. After a review of 2020 data, the U.S. Census Bureau announced that Illinois' population had been under-counted by nearly two percent. That means the state's population grew by nearly 250,000 from 2010 to 2020 and now has over 13 million people for the first time in its state history. The state had 12.4 million in 2000 and 11.4 million

Chicago Portage National Historic Site, Forest View, IL

in 1980. Two thirds of Illinois's population reside in the Chicago Metropolitan Area.

Highway 41 travels through two densely populated counties before reaching Indiana. The northernmost, Lake County, has an approximate population of 708,000. Cook County, with an estimated population of 5.1 million, as of 2024, is the second most populous county in the United States, second only to Los Angeles County.

HIGHWAY 41 NORTH OF CHICAGO

The current iteration of Highway 41 in Wisconsin blasts along the multi-lane interstate as I-94/41 before crossing the state line into Illinois. A Highway 41 turnoff appears very shortly after you enter Illinois, turning onto what was once known as **Skokie Highway**. This route continues as a four-lane, limited-access highway from the Wisconsin border to the city of Highland Park, where it flows back into **I-94**, also known as the **Edens Expressway**, but before it does so, it runs through the marshes and savannas of several forest preserves prior to giving way to a miles-long strip of corporate offices, warehouses, high-end car dealers, and other retail establishments.

In the 1939 Federal Writers' Project *WPA Guide to Illinois* (1930), the author(s) suggest, "U.S. 41 is an uninteresting express highway. Such charm as it may possess lies more in its clean-cut lines and freedom from dangerous intersections than in beauty of scene or history of settlement." Some eighty-five years later that is still the case for at least the first thirty-eight miles of the highway's Illinois traverse.

With the surge in automobile use in the 1920s, the north-south thoroughfare of **Sheridan Road** (once known as Illinois Route 42 and now State Road 137) along Lake Michigan grew congested. Cities along the road were anxious to deviate the increasing truck traffic away from their local streets. A new highway farther to the west through less-populated marshland was proposed in 1931, but construction was slowed by the Great Depression.

Upon its completion in 1937, U.S. 41, the "Chicago–Milwaukee Superhighway," was touted as the nation's longest highway of four lanes or more in width. Today, the bulk of heavy north-south traffic travels on the I-94 tollway a few miles to the west, but Highway 41 still serves as major alternate route (with no tolls) that is closer to the lakefront communities.

Author's Note: Most of the descriptive comments on places in the northern portion of the highway route will be about cities and locales several miles away from Highway 41, particularly areas near the lakefront along Sheridan Road.

VIGNETTE THE EDENS EXPRESSWAY AND THE UNBUILT CROSSTOWN EXPRESSWAY

THE EDENS EXPRESSWAY

In 1951, Illinois dedicated its first expressway to William Grant Edens (1863–1957), "the man who pulled Illinois out of the mud." It seemed only fitting. Edens had a sixth-grade education and worked as a mail carrier and a railroad conductor before becoming a banker. He is best remembered, though, as an advocate for good roads to accommodate the growing number of automobiles in the early part of the twentieth century. Through his efforts, a bond issue was passed in Illinois that enabled the building and maintenance of a new road system within the state. The "Edens Superhighway," touted as the "most beautiful highway in the country when finish-

ed," was officially opened on a snowy day in December 1951. Unlike most highways in Illinois, which are named after political figures, the Edens was named for someone directly connected to the road system.

THE CROSSTOWN EXPRESSWAY

The Crosstown Expressway (I-494) was a proposed urban freeway loop that would offer an alternate route around downtown Chicago. Championed by then-Chicago Mayor Richard J. Daley, the proposed road paralleling IL-50 (Cicero Avenue) on the West Side of the city would have required the demolition of thousands of homes as it connected with the Edens Expressway. Intensive community opposition, environmental issues, and a national concern in the 1970s about constructing more freeways in urban areas led to delays in the start of construction. Mayor Daley's death in 1976 killed further interest in the plan, and funds for the proposed interstate were officially repurposed to pay for the mass transit project that established rail connections from the Loop to O'Hare and Midway airports.

At the village of Wilmette, Highway 41 breaks off the Edens Expressway onto **Skokie Boulevard** and continues through the village of Skokie. Just to the north of the village of Lincolnwood, the road connects to **Lincoln Avenue** as it continues into the city of Chicago.

PART ONE: NORTHERN LAKE COUNTY

Lake County is situated in the northeastern corner of Illinois and borders Wisconsin to the north along the Lake Michigan shore. The county is primarily suburban, with some urban and rural areas. Due to its location immediately north of Cook County, Lake County is one of the five so-called "collar counties" of the Chicago metropolitan area. The Hispanic population has seen significant increases since 2010 in nearly all areas of the county and comprised twenty-four percent of the county's population in 2024.

RUSSELL

Situated just across the state line is the **Russell Military Museum**. Open only on weekends, it has a collection of artifacts from the various foreign wars in which the United States has been involved in over the last eighty years. It looks kind of like a military junkyard, but if you are interested in what old military helicopters, planes, patrol boats, jeeps, and tanks looked like in reality, this is the place to visit. Take the Russell Road exit off I-94.

WINTRHOP HARBOR & ILLINOIS BEACH STATE PARK

Traveling east on Russell Road, you will pass through a forest preserve area before arriving at the lakefront at **Winthrop Harbor**. This village is known primarily for **North Point Marina**, the largest marina on the Great Lakes, with mooring facilities for over 1,500 boats. North Point Marina is adjacent to **Illinois Beach State Park**, which stretches 6.5 miles along the Lake Michigan shoreline. The park preserves the last remaining natural shore in the state and features natural coastal dunes and wetlands. One of the interesting things I learned on my visit there was the difficulty of keeping the beaches sandy due to erosion and the blocking of natural coastal sand movement by communities farther north in Wisconsin. Many beaches in this section of Illinois along Lake Michigan are replenished by sand that is brought in from elsewhere.

Illinois Beach State Park, Zion, IL

ZION

Some small motels line Sheridan Road before you enter the city of **Zion**. Today, Zion is a distant suburb of Chicago with a pleasant downtown and nearby **Shiloh Park**, which features **Christ Community Church**, a large evangelical, non-denominational church founded in 1896 by Dr. John Alexander Dowie. Zion's founding and history are unique. Dr. Dowie established the city in 1901 as a religious utopia and a planned industrial community. **Shiloh House**, a twenty-five-room mansion built in the same year, was Dowie's residence and now houses the Zion Historical Society.

VIGNETTE JOHN ALEXANDER DOWIE, EVANGELIST, FAITH HEALER, AND FOUNDER OF ZION, ILLINOIS

John Alexander Dowie (1847–1907) was a Scottish Australian minister who emigrated to the United States in 1888. He began his mission in San Francisco with a faith healing practice before moving to Chicago and opening a church near the site of the 1893 World's Fair. Word spread of Dowie's seemingly miraculous healing powers at the fair. Medical doctors and Protestant ministers denounced Dowie as a charlatan, but that did not stop the growth of his faith-healing business or deter the thousands of followers he acquired.

He bought a large parcel of land in 1899 north of Chicago, which he named Zion, proclaiming it was governed by "the will of God." Dowie owned everything in Zion— the businesses, the general store, the bank, and the homes of the followers who settled there with him. He forbade saloons, pork, and medical practices, and "swearing and bad language of any sort [were] not allowed." Dowie proclaimed himself to be Elijah the Restorer, sent by God to prepare the world for the second coming of Christ. "The time has come," he announced. "I tell the church universal everywhere, you have to do what I tell you . . . because I am the Messenger of God's covenant."

By 1902, Zion's population had grown to 10,000, and Dowie had amassed a fortune in excess of $10 million. He lived in a huge mansion in luxury. But then a faith-healing venture in New York City carried out by Dowie and his "Zionites" ended in disaster, and he was soon under investigation by members of his church for using Zion's bank as "his personal piggy bank."

In 1905, he was deposed as head of the church and fled the country to Mexico to escape his creditors. The laws Dowie had created were repealed or ignored, and today Zion is much like other Chicago suburbs.

WAUKEGAN

Continuing south on Sheridan Road, you will enter **Waukegan**, an old industrial town on the lakefront. It is the county seat and largest city in Lake County. *Waukegan*, the Potawatomi word for "trading post," was first visited by Jacques Marquette in 1673 and is one of the oldest communities in Illinois.

The city was for many years a company town for the large wire mill established there in 1891. This mill manufactured barbed wire among other products. That plant closed years ago, in 1979, but there are other aging aspects of local industry that have closed or are barely hanging on. A downtown mural depicts famous folks who have called Waukegan home, including noted author Ray Bradbury (1920–2012), actor Jerry Orbach (1935–2004), football great Otto Graham (1921–2003), and comedian Jack Benny (1894–1974), who is also honored by a downtown statue. If you're hungry on your visit, I recommend a stop at **La Casa de Samuel**, a Mexican restaurant in the downtown area for freshly made tortillas.

"The Waukegan Story" mural, painted by a team of artists led by Patrick Tufo, Waukegan, IL

Jack Benny statue, by artist Mark Fredenberg, Waukegan, IL

GURNEE

If you have kids or the urge to shop, you will want to stay on U.S. 41 crossing the Wisconsin border until arriving at State Road 132, which will take you to the village of **Gurnee**. Gurnee is known for two things: **Six Flags Great America**, with its state-of-the-art roller coasters, and **Gurnee Mills**, a massive outlet shopping complex.

My kids made many journeys to Great America as they were growing up, and they will, no doubt, bring their kids at some point. Me? I get dizzy on the merry-go-round and am absolutely terrified on the mildest roller coaster. Expect very large crowds during the summer season.

SIDE TRIP TO VOLO

For a fun side trip, travel west of Highway 41 on IL-120, approximately fifteen miles to the little town of **Volo** where the **Volo Car Museum** is located. Lots of vintage cars, particularly "muscle cars" from the late 1960s and early 1970s, are actually for sale at the location. The museum has all kinds of weird attractions outside of cars including a dinosaur exhibit, old campers and TV show kitsch.

Near the car museum is the **Volo Antique Malls** complex, where you can spend lots of time picking through a potpourri of collectibles, oddities, and all kinds of antique stuff. Allegedly, one of the four antique malls on the grounds is haunted by a Civil War soldier!

NORTH CHICAGO

The city of Waukegan merges into **North Chicago**, which boasts the huge AbbVie pharmaceutical contract manufacturing plant and the equally huge **Naval Station Great Lakes (NSGL)**. Opened in 1911, NSGL is the Navy's largest training installation and the home of the Navy's only boot camp. Located on over 1,600 acres overlooking Lake Michigan, the installation includes 1,153 buildings. Thirty-nine of those are on the National Register of Historic Places.

The official **National Museum of the American Sailor** is on the site and open to the public. On any given weekend in downtown Chicago, you will see clumps of young sailors on liberty, having fun in the big city. Well over 20,000 sailors, Marines, soldiers, and civilians employed by the Department of Defense live and work at Naval Station Great Lakes.

PARKS AND GOLF COURSES NORTH OF CHICAGO

Throughout the northern section of Highway 41 are parks, forest preserves, and LOTS of golf courses. Some well-maintained bike paths pass through the area as well. The **Green Bay Bike Trail, Robert McClory Bike Trail, North Branch Bike Trail**, and **North Shore Bike Trail** are good ones, and I highly recommend you try to bike in some of the areas if possible.

FOREST PRESERVES–TRAVELING NORTH TO SOUTH

- Pine Dunes, Antioch
- Van Patten Woods, Wadsworth
- Wadsworth Savanna Forest Preserve, Wadsworth
- Sedge Meadow Forest Preserve, Wadsworth
- North Dunes Nature Preserve, Zion
- Oak Hickory Forest, Zion
- Greenbelt Forest Preserve, North Chicago
- Skokie River Nature Preserve, Lake Forest
- Northcroft Park, Lake Forest
- Heller Park, Highland Park
- Skokie River Woods, Highland Park
- Chicago Botanic Gardens, Glencoe
- Skokie Lagoons, Glencoe
- Erickson Woods, Winnetka
- Watersmeet Woods, Northfield
- Blue Star Memorial Woods, Glenview
- Emily Oaks Nature Center, Skokie
- Henry Proesel Park, Lincolnwood

GOLF COURSES–TRAVELING NORTH TO SOUTH

- Shepherds Crook Golf Course, Zion - Public
- Thunderhawk Golf Club, Zion - Public
- Bonnie Brook Golf Course, Waukegan - Public
- Foss Park Golf Course, North Chicago - Public
- Lake Bluff Golf Club, Lake Bluff - Public
- Knollwood Club, Lake Forest - Private
- Deerpath Golf Course, Lake Forest - Public
- Conway Farms Golf Club, Lake Forest - Private
- Onwentsia Club Golf Course, Lake Forest - Private
- Old Elm Club, Highland Park - Private
- Exmoor Country Club, Highland Park - Private
- Sunset Valley Golf Club, Highland Park - Public
- Northmoor Country Club, Highland Park - Private
- Glencoe Golf Club, Glencoe - Public

- Skokie Country Club, Glencoe - Private
- North Shore Country Club, Glenview - Private
- Winnetka Golf Club, Winnetka - Public
- Indian Hill Club, Winnetka - Private
- Sunset Ridge Golf Club, Northfield - Private
- Westmorland Country Club, Wilmette - Private
- Chick Evans Golf Course, Morton Grove - Public
- Evanston Golf Club, Skokie - Private
- Bryn Mawr Country Club, Lincolnwood – Private

PART TWO: NORTH SHORE

LAKE BLUFF AND LAKE FOREST

As you follow Sheridan Road south into the village of **Lake Bluff**, a stretch of affluent Chicago suburbs known collectively as **North Shore** begins. These are some of the wealthiest communities in the United States. Lots of trees and a suburban lakefront setting describe most of these towns, with many large homes along the way. North Shore communities all have picturesque downtowns near the Metra commuter rail line stations that link them with Chicago.

In Lake Bluff you'll pass by **Crab Tree Farm**, the only working farm located on Lake Michigan in the state of Illinois. Originally a large commercial dairy operation, many of the farm buildings have been renovated over the last thirty years into a private museum of arts and crafts, containing furniture and decorative arts. The site is still a working farm, however. It is just not as expansive an enterprise as it once was.

Lake Bluff merges into **Lake Forest**, a bastion of old wealth virtually since its founding in 1861. **Lake Forest College** spreads along Sheridan Road as one comes into downtown Lake Forest. One of the top resort hotels in the Midwest, the **Deerpath Inn**, is located downtown. This super fancy hotel has been a stop for people of means since 1929.

The community is noteworthy in the history of the game of polo, established here in 1896. Lake Forest also gets mentioned in the first chapter of F. Scott Fitzgerald's iconic novel *The Great Gatsby* for being the place of polo ponies and the hometown of Daisy Buchanan, Gatsby's obsession. The city has been the site of several movies including *Ordinary People*, the 1980 Oscar winner for Best Picture.

Lake Forest Rail Station, Lake Forest, IL

Lake Bluff and Lake Forest have strong links to African American history. Aided by residents who were associated with the Abolitionist movement, one section of the merged communities was settled by fugitives from southern slavery who traveled north on the Underground Railroad and settled in the area. Both Lake Bluff and Lake Forest once had Black-owned businesses as well as strong African American community organizations, churches, and cultural centers. Over time though, the African American community gradually moved out of the towns, and these early community sites were razed for new development.

Several well-known people have ties to Lake Forest. Vince Vaughn has property in the city and Robin Williams lived a portion of his childhood in Lake Forest. Character actor Lawrence Tero, (born Laurence Tureaud), aka "Mr. T." infamously bought property in Lake Forest and cut down many of the old-growth trees on it. Lake Forest has many wealthy residents with a recent survey placing it second nationwide of the wealthiest retirement communities.

FORT SHERIDAN & HIGHWOOD

Fort Sheridan is a residential neighborhood within the cities of Lake Forest, Highwood, and Highland Park. It was originally established in 1887 as an Army post named after Civil War cavalry general Philip Sheridan. The majority of the fort was decommissioned in 1993 and is now a National Historic Landmark District. Some lovely old Army officers' quarters have been converted into private homes. For the visitor, Fort Sheridan features a forest preserve and free public access to Lake Michigan. The area is also known for excellent birdwatching.

The working-class town of **Highwood** used to be known for its preponderance of Italian Americans. Now it is a heavily Latino enclave that is also a nightlife destination for the North Shore neighborhoods. It boasts several restaurants, coffee shops, and bars within its city limits.

HIGHLAND PARK

The North Shore suburb of **Highland Park** has a larger downtown than some of the nearby communities and is notable as the location of a number of late twentieth century movies. The films *Risky Business* (1983), *Ferris Bueller's Day Off* (1983), *Sixteen Candles*, (1984), *Weird Science* (1985), *The Color of Money* (1986), *Uncle Buck* (1989), *Home Alone* (1990), and *Prelude To A Kiss* (1992) all featured a Highland Park backdrop. Legendary Director John Hughes (1950–2009) was enamored with Highland Park as a setting for many of his iconic 1980s films.

Several members of the championship Chicago Bulls basketball team, including Michael Jordan and Scottie Pippen, lived in Highland Park during the 1990s. Highland Park is also home to **Ravinia Park**, the summer home of the Chicago Symphony Orchestra and hosts numerous concerts during the summer months. First opened in 1904, Ravinia has hosted nearly every major music entertainer in every musical genre imaginable from classical to rock. A seated pavilion and a large lawn expanse for picnicking make this a great place to hear music. Full meals can be brought in and consumed at concerts, including alcoholic beverages. Food, drink, and souvenir concessions are also on the premises.

Metra Union Pacific North line trains run from downtown Chicago to still stop at Ravinia's historic entrance, making it the only private train stop left in Illinois. If you can squeeze in a concert at Ravinia, it is well worth your time. The Ravinia Festival attracts about 600,000 attendees over its three-month summer season.

GUN VIOLENCE

Highland Park and the nation were rocked by gun violence on July 4, 2022, when an individual who fired from a rooftop shot and killed seven people and left scores injured as they were attending a downtown July 4th parade.

This mass shooting has put this town in the same unfortunate place as Newtown, Connecticut, and so many other localities across the country where unspeakable (and preventable) gun violence has occurred. Maybe the tragedy will help spur more common-sense gun controls. A memorial has been erected in the downtown to the fallen, and many windows display a decal saying, "Highland Park Strong."

BANNOCKBURN & DEERFIELD

To the west of Highland Park are the wealthy North Shore suburbs of **Bannockburn** and **Deerfield**. Bannockburn was founded in the early 1920s by William Aitken, a native of the town in Scotland with the same name. The village was created as a development with "country estates," the largest of which were suitable for stabling horses. Adjacent to Bannockburn, Deerfield, founded in 1903, is another wealthy North Shore community that is home to several large corporate headquarters including **Walgreens Boots Alliance** and **Baxter Healthcare**.

COOK COUNTY

When Highway 41 crosses Lake Cook Road, it enters **Cook County**. Forty percent of all residents of Illinois live in Cook County. The county's historic growth since its founding in 1831 has been due to its transportation access and network. Within the county borders, you'll find the Port of Chicago and a river system leading to the Mississippi River, an extensive railroad network encompassing virtually all major cross-country rail links, an interstate expressway system, and one of the busiest airports in the world. Despite the heavily urban nature of the area, the **Forest Preserve District of Cook County** covers nearly 70,000 acres and is one of the oldest and largest forest preserve districts in the United States.

GLENCOE, WINNETKA, KENILWORTH

As you proceed south from Highland Park, you will pass through the villages of **Glencoe, Winnetka,** and **Kenilworth**; all are on the list of the top ten wealthiest communities in the United States. The village of Glencoe is bordered on the west by the **Chicago Botanic Garden**, owned by the Cook County Forest Preserve and managed by the Chicago Horticulture Society. The Botanic Garden is quite large, with twenty-seven separate display gardens and multiple exhibits that draw large crowds in the spring and summer. Next to the garden is the **Skokie Lagoon**, which provides a wonderful nature preserve for fishing, kayaking, and hiking.

In Winnetka, you can drive by the "Home Alone" house, a private residence that was a star in the 1990 film. Also in Winnetka are two local churches, the **Winnetka Congregational Church** and **Christ Church Winnetka**, which are renowned for their biannual rummage sales that bring in shoppers from many far-flung locations—some of whom arrive by the busload.

Kenilworth was developed by Joseph Sears as a planned community in 1889 on the Lake Michigan shore with large lots and park lands. The village has an active historical society with a mission "...to preserve, interpret, and celebrate the unique history, architecture, and traditions of the village...." The village is an exclusive area with multi-million-dollar homes.

VIGNETTE   LAURIE DANN AND WINNETKA

Before the numbing frequency of school shootings began with Columbine High School in 1999 and continuing unabated with so many more, including Sandy Hook Elementary School (2012), Parkland High School (2018), Robb Elementary School (2022), Apalachee High School (2024), there was Hubbard Woods Elementary School.

On May 20, 1988, Laurie Dann, a deeply disturbed and lethally armed woman, entered the Winnetka school, where she opened fire in a second-grade classroom, killing one student and wounding five others. From there, she entered a home and shot a young man in the chest before killing herself when she realized she was surrounded by police. That young man, Philip Andrew, survived and grew up to become an FBI agent. At the time, the shooting shocked the nation. The fact that such a person was able to easily obtain a weapon and enter a school was considered an aberration. Decades later, such a scenario is, unfortunately, all too common.

NORTHBROOK, GLENVIEW, NORTHFIELD, MORTON GROVE

To the west of Highway 41 within Cook County are the established railroad suburbs of **Northbrook, Glenview, Northfield,** and **Morton Grove**. These suburbs boast a large number of homes, businesses, restaurants, and retail shopping areas. Northbrook was nicknamed the "Speedskating Capital of the World" thanks to the many athletes who have trained for some seventy years at the Northbrook Speed Skating Club of Illinois.

Morton Grove was in the national news in the early 1980s for voting to ban handguns within the village. Subsequent U.S. Supreme Court decisions overturned most gun laws, and Morton Grove removed the ban in 2008.

WILMETTE

The North Shore mansions end on southbound Sheridan at the village of **Wilmette**, where a number of high-rise condominiums greet you as you enter. Wilmette has a large harbor and a pumping station on the lakefront. It is the mouth of the North Branch of the Chicago River, which flows into Lake Michigan. Nestled by the high-rises is the Plaza del Lago, built in 1928 and considered the second oldest shopping center in the United States designed for automobile use. The oldest, Country Club Plaza in Kansas City, Missouri, was built in 1923. Once upon a time, this plaza was part of an undeveloped area called **No Mans' Land**. Neither part of Wilmette nor Kenilworth, it briefly became a haven for shady activities and wild times until it was annexed by Wilmette in the 1960s and redeveloped.

Downtown Wilmette is similar to other North Shore communities with a commuter rail stop, but it is also the northern terminus for the **Chicago Transit Authority (CTA) "L"** trains.

Wilmette was the home of the Murray family whose five siblings, Brian, Nancy, Bill, Joel and John, became successful actors. Bill Murray and his brothers caddied at the Indian Hill Club Golf Club in Winnetka, an experience that served as the inspiration for the 1980 movie *Caddyshack*.

BAHÁ'Í

Once you pass by the high-rises and gracious homes along Sheridan Road, you will come upon the **Bahá'í House of Worship**, a spectacular domed temple dedicated in 1953 as a devotional space for the Bahá'í faith. Open to the public, the interior is a place of quiet contemplation, while the intricate details carved into its creamy white concrete exterior invite the awe of visitors. Lovely gardens surround the temple. Please stop and take in this beautiful site.

EVANSTON

Sheridan Road soon brings you into the city of **Evanston**, where it passes by the historic **Grosse Point Lighthouse** (built in 1873) and through the **Northwestern University** campus, which has a total enrollment of approximately 21,000. Northwestern also has a downtown Chicago campus and facilities worldwide, but this is the main university campus. Northwestern is a private "Big 10" school and one of the top universities in the country. It is particularly known for journalism, music, and theater, as well as having one of best-known graduate business programs in the world. This beautiful campus is located on Lake Michigan. Take a look if you can.

Evanston has a diverse population, five National Register Historic Districts, and a large downtown filled with stores and dining establishments. Historic home tours are available and information on tour options is provided by the **Evanston History Center**, located in the **Dawes House,** former home of Charles Dawes (1865–1951). U.S. vice president under Calvin Coolidge (1925–1929), Dawes also served as ambassador to Great Britain and was awarded the 1925 Nobel Peace Prize. I suggest booking a walking or biking tour to see some of the homes on and near the lakefront, such as the recently restored **Oscar Mayer** mansion on Forest Avenue. This was the home of the son of the founder of the **Oscar Mayer** company, known for meat and cold cuts.

One little-known organization headquartered in Evanston is the **Women's Christian Temperance Union (WCTU).** The mission of the WCTU is "to educate all people, with the help of God, to total abstinence from alcohol, illegal drugs, and tobacco as a way of life." Once extraordinarily powerful, the WCTU was instrumental in getting the 18th Amendment prohibiting alcohol passed in 1919 and making Prohibition the law of the land until the 21st Amendment repealed the ban in 1933.

You can visit the **Frances Willard House Museum**, "also known as Rest

Cottage," which is listed as a National Register of Historic Landmarks. Frances Willard (1839–1898) was the founder of the WCTU and influenced reforms in the United States that helped transform the role of women in nineteenth century America. Thanks to the WCTU's involvement in Evanston, the city was "dry" until 1973 when the ban was lifted and restaurants were allowed to serve alcohol, but only if they also served food. Finally in 1984, the City Council voted to allow liquor sales within the city. Evanston continues to uphold more restrictive liquor license regulations than neighboring communities.

Evanston's **Gichigamiin Indigenous Nations Museum** features lots of permanent and updated exhibits about Indigenous peoples. One of the permanent exhibitions is "A Regional Tour of American Indian Cultures" that covers the 1,200 federally recognized Indigenous tribes and nations living within the United States and Canada. The museum has a library and offers docent-led tours of its exhibits.

Evanston has five public beaches on its Lake Michigan waterfront. These are free to residents of the city, but you will need to pay an entrance fee and obtain a pass if you hail from elsewhere.

Recently, a controversy erupted in Evanston over the demolition of **Ryan Field**—originally built in 1926 and refurbished in the 1990s. A new Ryan Field is under construction and slated to be completed in 2026. Major community opposition to the field centered on the potential for concerts and other types of activities in a larger stadium within a residential area. After many lawsuits, both Evanston and Wilmette gave the green light to build the new stadium. Time will tell if it serves to better the community.

SKOKIE

West of Evanston is the village of **Skokie**, promoted for many years as the "The World's Largest Village." In addition to many single- and three-flat apartment buildings, Skokie has the **North Shore Center for the Performing Arts,** the upscale Old Orchard shopping center, and a number of restaurants with a diverse offering of cuisines.

Once a heavily Jewish enclave with many Holocaust survivors, the village has become more diverse in recent years. Now, about thirty percent of the population is of the Jewish faith, and a dozen synagogues are located within village environs.

Decades before the 2017 Neo-Nazi march in Charlottesville, Virginia, Skokie was the center of an important First Amendment Supreme Court case involving the right of the American Nazi party to march in the streets of the village. The Skokie march, originally scheduled for April 1977, was never held due to public pressure (although the Nazis did march in April 1978 in downtown Chicago instead), but the village became inextricably linked with the court battle. It galvanized the Jewish community to form the **Illinois Holocaust Museum and Education Center**, which opened in Skokie in 2009.

LINCOLNWOOD

Bordering Skokie and Chicago, Highway 41 becomes **Lincoln Avenue** as it proceeds through the village of **Lincolnwood,** a close-in suburb. Lincolnwood was once home to the "Purple Hotel," which opened in 1960 and was demolished in 2013. The hotel had a purple brick exterior and was also known as the Hyatt House Hotel. It offered entertainment, wild parties, and celebrity stays, and was even the infamous site of a mob hit. The hotel closed due to health violations in 2007 and was briefly put on the National Register of Historic Places before demolition. Now this location is just a nondescript mixed-use condominium complex that features a huge mural by artist Emmy Star Brown to provide some visual interest.

If you are pining for a Wisconsin-type supper club experience, the **L. Woods Tap & Pine Lodge,** which has been in business for more than twenty-five years, is located a short way southeast along the highway.

PART THREE: CHICAGO

Continuing southeast on Lincoln Avenue will bring you into the city of **Chicago,** the Cook County seat, the largest city in Illinois, and the third-largest city in the United States. Lincoln Avenue passes through the **Lincoln Square** neighborhood, where it connects to **West Foster Avenue** and bears east toward Lake Michigan.

On the Chicago lakefront, Highway 41 meets up with and follows **Jean Baptiste Pointe DuSable Lake Shore Drive (DuSable Lake Shore Drive)** south almost all the way to Indiana. The road parallels Lake Michigan until 67th Street, when it becomes **South Shore Drive** in the South Shore neighborhood before being routed east to become **South DuSable Lake Shore Drive** as it travels through land that was formerly occupied by U.S. Steel South Works. It then crosses the Calumet River on the historic **Ewing Avenue Bridge** to become **South Ewing Avenue** then continues south as part of **U.S. 12/20** through the East Side neighborhood. There, it crosses under I-90, also known as the Chicago Skyway, and becomes **South Indianapolis Avenue** before it crosses the state line into Indiana.

Chicago has been called many things, not all of them kind. It's a world city with architecture, art, food, music, professional sports teams, company headquarters, and universities that have a global presence and put the city on almost anyone's list of vital locations. Recent U.S. president, Barack Obama, once called Chicago home. It's the most important and essential city in the center of the United States. It is a transportation hub with one of the busiest airports in the world, the most important rail freight point in the country, and highways that disperse people and products to all points. It is cosmopolitan, diverse, and slightly less expensive than its competitor cities of New York and Los Angeles on the east and west coasts.

Unfortunately, it also has some of the most violent street gangs in the country. Chicago is a city that is both reviled and envied, sometimes in the same breath. I suggest you try to spend at least a week here to get a glimpse of what the place is all about. Chicago has been voted the "Best Big City" in the U.S. for eight consecutive years by *Conde Nast Traveler's* Readers' Choice Awards.

IDENTITY

What makes a Chicagoan? Some of that depends upon where in the vast Chicago area one lives. City residents have a number of different identities, depending on neighborhood, financial circumstances, and ethnic ties. "South Siders" and "North Siders" often see themselves as having different identities. And not just because of which baseball team they root for! If a person is from one of the multiple Chicago suburbs, there is an additional layer of identity. If you are a visitor, you have undoubtedly been fed the multiple and dated stereotypes of what constitutes a Chicagoan. Just like New York City or Los Angeles—cities that Chicago is often compared to— most Chicagoans share a particular mindset despite their many differences. You will see glimpses of this if you spend enough time in this place. I will take a stab at what you should know about the area.

CHICAGOESE

Within the city and close-in suburbs, some people speak "Chicagoese," a colorful language all of its own, with terms and usages that vary by age and ethnicity of the speakers. Suffice to say, it is slowly dying out as the city becomes less insular and young people throughout the city speak more like newscasters. If you want to hear true Chicago-speak, it's a good idea to try to get to a neighborhood bar—the older the tavern the better.

THE LAKE

Without Lake Michigan, it would be difficult to conceive of Chicago. The city owes its spectacular skyline to the lakefront. Lake Michigan is a huge inland sea that is both inviting and intimidating. It is the largest freshwater lake located in one single country. If you have not been to the lake for some form of recreation—parks, beaches, museums, boating, etc.—you have been missing a vital part of the reason for coming to Chicago. The lake is also a giant body of water that rises and falls with the powerful storms that it can engender.

The lake is the area's water source. To protect the lake from pollution, the flow of the Chicago River was reversed in the nineteenth century. An engineering feat still funnels water from the lake to the Chicago Sanitary and Ship Canal. To further protect the lake, the **Tunnel and Reservoir Plan,** known as TARP or "The Deep Tunnel," was established in the 1970s. TARP is a system of deep tunnels and vast reservoirs throughout the metropolitan area intended to reduce flooding and improve water quality.

THE WEATHER

The weather in the Chicago metro area is a source of constant conversation thanks to its unpredictability. Fronts can come off the lake, or they can arrive from the Great Plains, the Gulf of Mexico, or Canada. Famously, a sharp wind can come off the lake. Known locally as "the Hawk," this wind can cut through layers of clothing. Winters are commonly long and cold, but this may change in the future as Earth's climate changes. Spring is often too short. Summer is over too quickly. Fall can be spectacular, if all the ingredients are in place.

TRAFFIC

According to the 2024 Inrix Global Traffic Scorecard, Chicago currently ranks behind only Istanbul and New York City for the title of the city with the world's worst traffic. Highways are super-congested, and rush hour extends to cover quite a bit of the day and night. Unlike many big cities, Chicago's Metro area has a robust and long-standing commuter rail system that helps to ease commutes somewhat. Within the city and close-in suburbs, the **Chicago Transit Authority (CTA)** operates a rapid transit system (famously called the **"L,"** as much of it is elevated above ground) that also helps alleviate traffic congestion. Public transit ridership is still recovering from the COVID-19 pandemic in the early part of the 2020s.

The Chicago area is also an important logistical center within the United States. That means lots of distribution centers, heavy freight rail traffic, and an immense amount of truck traffic. A huge concentration of warehouses and distribution centers have been built forty miles west of the central city. Needless to say, the region often has air pollution issues that are quite concerning. Some freight rail pollution issues have been addressed, but much more needs to be done, particularly regarding trucking.

FOOD

Chicago is a celebrated foodie paradise. Restaurants serving every imaginable cuisine are available. The biggest challenge is to try to keep up with the never-ending variety thanks to all of the different cultures that call the area home. Yes, it has great deep-dish pizza, hot dogs, ribs, and Italian beef, but Chicago also features some of the best chefs and most experimental restaurants in the country.

A short list of noted chefs and restaurants in the city is at the end of this chapter. Plan on several nights of great dining but be sure to make reservations in advance.

ARCHITECTURE

The birthplace of the skyscraper and the place that spawned Frank Lloyd Wright, Louis Sullivan, Mies van der Rohe, and so many more great architects, has a stunning skyline. Chicago is a mecca for people around the world who come to see its buildings. The outlying areas of the city have celebrated homes, places of worship, and monuments galore.

POLITICS

From Abraham Lincoln to Mayors Daley (I & II) to Harold Washington to Barack Obama to the many politicos who have landed in jail, Illinois has had its share of outsized characters in the political world. Chicago's size and national prominence, primarily regarding its Democratic politicians, has always been a factor for those who reside here.

THE FLAG

The flag of Chicago is a striking design with stripes of sky blue and white. The two blue stripes represent Lake Michigan and the Chicago River, and the white stripes represent all of the neighborhoods where Chicagoans reside. (Actually, the white stripes represent the North, South, and West sides of the city). The four red stars in the middle white stripe represent significant events in the city's history. The first star is for Fort Dearborn, the second for the Great Chicago Fire, the third for the 1893 World's Fair, and the fourth for the 1937 World's Fair. The flag is not only a symbol of the city's past but also a representation of its resilience and unity. The flag logo is displayed throughout the city.

SPORTS

Every professional sports league, from baseball to women's soccer, has a team based in Chicago. The fans are passionate, and loyalty is intense. The presence of "Da Bears," the Bulls, the Cubs, the White Sox, the Blackhawks, the Wolves, the Fire, the Sky, and the Red Stars means there is always a game to attend.

PROFESSIONAL SPORTS TEAM LOCATIONS

- Bulls (basketball) and Blackhawks (hockey): United Center on the West Side
- Cubs (baseball): Wrigley Field in Wrigleyville on the North Side
- White Sox (baseball): Guaranteed Rate Field (The Rate) in Bridgeport on the South Side
- Bears (football) and Fire (soccer): Soldier Field at the lakefront
- Red Stars (soccer): Seat Geek Stadium in suburban Bridgeview
- Sky (basketball): Wintrust Arena in the South Loop

MUSIC

Plan on seeing some great live music on a trip to the city and suburbs. The blues, gospel, jazz, country, folk, rock, house, and hip-hop all have deep roots in Chicago. The **Chicago Symphony Orchestra** is one of the world's best. **The Green Mill, Jazz Showcase, The Hideout, Park West, Metro Chicago, Schubas Tavern, Thalia Hall, Aragon Ballroom, The Riviera Theatre, Auditorium Theater, Chicago Theatre, Millennium Park, Ravinia, Chicago Symphony Center, Lyric Opera of Chicago,** and more are all fantastic places to experience wonderful music.

And finally,

NIGHTLIFE

Nightlife in Chicago is legendary. Comedy clubs, bars, live theater, magic shows, dance clubs, karaoke bars—every form of entertainment you can imagine—are likely available in Chicago. Plan on lots of choices for evening entertainment.

A BRIEF CHICAGO HISTORY

VIGNETTE   JEAN BAPTISTE POINTE DuSABLE

In the late 1780s, Jean Baptiste Pointe DuSable, a fur trader of mixed West African and French ancestry, began developing a farm near the mouth of the Chicago River or "Eschecagou" (later shortened to "Checagou") as it was known to Indigenous inhabitants; the name means "the land of wild onions." Pointe DuSable married a

Potawatomi woman named Kitihawa, who took the name Catherine.

He is acknowledged as the first permanent non-Indigenous resident of what became the city of Chicago. Born in the port town of St. Marc in western Haiti in 1745, DuSable was said to have spoken French, English, Spanish and several Indigenous languages. He was a successful trader who had extensive contacts from what is now Missouri up to the city of Peoria along the Illinois River and was living near present-day Michigan City, Indiana, when the British arrested him in 1779 on suspicion of harboring rebel sympathies. Upon his release, DuSable built a farm in Chicago and erected a five-room mansion with a long-covered porch where he entertained Indigenous locals, explorers, French fur traders, and military troops of several nationalities who passed over the portage from Lake Michigan and the Chicago River to the Des Plaines River, the Illinois River, and ultimately the Mississippi River—the major highways of the time.

DuSable prospered with a trading post for livestock and agricultural commodities. But unbalanced treaties between the new American government and the Indigenous as well as the racial attitudes of new white American settlers caused him to sell his property in 1800 and move farther south where the more tolerant French still held influence. Upon the death of his wife, DuSable gave most of his money to his children. He was briefly arrested and imprisoned on charges of nonpayment of debt in 1814 and lived out the remainder of his life in poverty. He died in 1818 in St. Charles, Missouri, and was buried in an unmarked grave in the St. Charles Borromeo Church Cemetery there until a granite marker was erected by the state of Illinois in 1968.

A statue of DuSable also stands in Chicago's Pioneer Court, erected in 2009 on the site of DuSable homestead on Michigan Avenue next to what was then known as the Michigan Avenue Bridge. The bridge was renamed "DuSable Bridge" in 2010. DuSable Harbor is located nearby Highway 41 where Randolph Street meets Lake Michigan. Yet to be developed three-acre DuSable Park is planned for the land at the mouth of the Chicago River.

DuSable's contributions to Chicago's growth were expunged for well over a century until African American residents of Chicago worked to reestablish his legacy. DuSable High School opened in the 1930s in the Bronzeville neighborhood on Chicago's South Side, and the DuSable Black History Museum and Education Center opened in 1961. In 1968, DuSable was finally recognized as Chicago's founder, and after a long controversial battle in the City Council, Lake Shore Drive was officially renamed "Jean-Baptiste Pointe DuSable Lake Shore Drive" in 2021. DuSable's long-ago vision of a trading center has evolved into the third-largest city in the United States.

DuSable statue overlooking the Chicago River, Chicago, IL

The Chicago area remained a frontier backwater through the 1820s when the construction of the Illinois & Michigan Canal linked the Chicago and Illinois rivers. On March 4, 1837, Chicago was incorporated as a city and grew quickly as a central marketplace for agricultural products from farmlands to the south and west.

The advent of railroads in the 1840s created a national network of trade, manufacturing, and distribution with Chicago at its center, making the city a national hub of transportation and distribution. As America's rail capital, the city and nearby region experienced tremendous growth over the next hundred years. It became a food processing and manufacturing center, bringing thousands of jobs to northeastern Illinois.

The devastating great Chicago Fire of 1871 that destroyed much of the downtown area led to explosive growth in the final decades of the nineteenth century. In 1893, the World's Columbian Exposition along the city's lakefront hosted some twenty-five million visitors and left several buildings that are still in use today. Irish, Italian, and Eastern European immigrants, and beginning in the twentieth century, African American migrants poured into the city and surrounding suburbs to work at the factories. Chicago's population peaked at 3.6 million in 1945.

The growth of industry and population in the early twentieth century created great wealth and enormous social convulsions within the city. The Great Migration of African Americans from the South occurred from 1910 to 1970. It led not only to much racial strife but also to the development of real political power by local African Americans. The onset of Prohibition (1920–1933) after World War I led to the growth of organized crime and the notoriety of Al Capone (1899–1947), who, unfortunately, is still one of Chicago's best-known historical figures. The end of Prohibition overlapped the early years of the Great Depression and spawned the Chicago Democratic "Machine" that dominated city politics for decades.

In the early part of the 1900s, streetcars and commuter railroad lines kept most people within the city limits or in small clusters of development around outlying railroad stations. Starting in the early 1950s, construction of the Chicago area expressway system, which radiated from the central city, allowed the population to decentralize.

The Highway Act of 1956 created the federally funded interstate system and propelled explosive growth outside of the Chicago city limits. Auto ownership increased, and federal policies allowing for the deduction of mortgage interest and property taxes provided incentives to vacate the inner city for the suburbs. Cheap land in "collar counties" and metropolitan fringe areas allowed for the area around Chicago to grow beyond the now mature "railroad suburbs." The introduction of the jet aircraft in the late 1950s led O'Hare Airport to become one of the busiest airports in the United States as well as a magnet for nearby suburban growth. Shopping malls with large parking lots were built to serve residents of primarily single-family homes.

World War II and its aftermath led to rapid transit growth, urban renewal, a downtown building boom, and continued migration, starting with the Mexican and Puerto-Rican Latino communities followed by Middle Eastern, East and South Asian immigrants. Currently, Central and South American immigrants have continued to change the demographics of the city. Culturally, the city has spawned Second City, *Playboy* magazine, Gay Pride, the birth control pill, the blues, house music, Oprah Winfrey, and Michael Jordan.

The city's meatpacking plants, stockyards, and steel mills slowly moved out. Most of these were gone by the early 1980s. Segregation, blockbusting, redlining, and racial disturbances led to "white flight," which caused many Chicago neighborhoods to go from majority white to majority African American and Latino in the 1960s and 1970s. Chicago's downtown and Loop continued to be occupied by office buildings until the mid-1980s, when gentrification began to affect the downtown core. Downtown Chicago became more desirable for young professionals seeking to be closer to workplaces and entertainment venues. Numerous high-rises were constructed in areas of the city once largely blighted and abandoned.

Since the Great Recession of the late 2000s, the Streeterville, West Loop, and South Loop neighborhoods—all adjacent to the Loop Central Business District—have become hot markets for new residential developments.

The 2020s have posed new challenges to the region, starting with the COVID-19 pandemic in the early part of the decade, which emptied downtown (and suburban) office buildings of their historic use. Proposals to turn much of the central business district into a mixed-use residential neighborhood still needs further development.

The aftermath of George Floyd's murder at the hands of a Minneapolis police officer brought mayhem to Chicago's downtown in 2020 not experienced since the mayhem of the 1968 Democratic convention. High-profile, violent crime has increased in certain neighborhoods. Lack of affordable housing and subsequent homelessness are pressing issues. Chicago is a big city with all the issues emblematic of big U.S. cities. And that will always be the case.

VIGNETTE DANIEL BURNHAM, EDWARD BENNETT, AND IRA BACH

Chicago owes its architectural legacy and multiple parklands to the vision of three men: Daniel Burnham (1846–1912), Edward Bennett (1874–1954) and Ira Bach (1907–1985). Burnham and Bennett were architects and co-authors of the 1909 Plan of Chicago (also known as the Burnham Plan), which continues to influence city developers to this day. This plan called for an integration of parks, buildings, and streets that borrowed heavily from the nineteenth century redevelopment of Paris, France. Its flexibility has particularly impacted the design of Chicago's lakefront parks, which boast cultural enhancements such as the **Field Museum of Natural History***.*

Daniel Burnham is known for his exhortation, "Make no little plans. They have no magic to stir men's blood and probably will not themselves be realized. Make big plans, aim high in hope and work, remembering that a noble, logical diagram once recorded will never die, but long after we are gone will be a living thing, asserting itself with ever growing insistency."

Edward Bennett was born in England and attended technical school before immigrating to San Francisco to work in an architectural office. He would study in Paris and work in New York before coming to Chicago and teaming up with Burnham to co-author the Plan for San Francisco in 1905. Bennett served on the Chicago Plan Commission and became one of the most important city planners in the country. He would later develop plans for Minneapolis; Detroit; Portland, Oregon; and San Juan, Puerto Rico. Regional planning in the United States owes a great debt to Bennett.

Ira Bach was an MIT-trained architect, who became Chicago's City Commission of Planning Director in the late 1950s, a position he held into the early 1980s. He published many reference books about Chicago during his life and influenced many urban planning decisions, including the development of mass public transit from O'Hare Airport to downtown Chicago. His name ranks with Burnham and Bennett in the history of Chicago planning. His bust holds a place of honor in the Chicago Cultural Center.

SOME BRIEF OBSERVATIONS OF CHICAGO

Author's Note: The bookshelves are groaning with excellent books about Chicago. Read the At a Glance section at the end of this chapter for some titles and other quick reference information. For this section, I will provide a thumbnail sketch of the many things you can learn about the city in more depth.

THE NAME

Like almost all things about Chicago, you will get an argument about the derivation of the name. The "most accepted" meaning comes from the Algonquin or Miami tribal name "shikaakwa" meaning "striped skunk" or "onion." The current popular theory that it refers to a species of wild onion that once carpeted the region has more support, but even that idea has been contested. The first known reference to Chicago as we know it, comes from the explorer Robert de LaSalle. In his memoir of late September 1687, he writes, "We arrived at the said place called "Chicagou" which, according to what we were able to learn of it, has taken this name because of the quantity of garlic which grows in the forests in this region."

NICKNAMES

New and old nicknames for Chicago include the "Windy City," the "Second City," "Chicagoland," "Chi Town," the "City of Big Shoulders," the "City in a Garden," the "White City," the "City that Works," the "City by the Lake," "Chiberia," a "City on the Make," "Chiraq," and the "312."

TELEVISION

For better or worse, Chicago is known to much of the world for its characterization in movies and television. An expanded list of movies about or set in Chicago appears at the end of this chapter in the *At a Glance* section.

Some of the more recent television shows have been *Shameless* (2011–2021), *The Bear* (2022–), *South Side* (2019–2022), *Chicago P.D.* (2014–), *Chicago Fire* (2012–), *Chicago Med* (2015–), *The Good Wife* (2009–2016), *The Good Fight* (2017–2022), and *The Chi* (2018–). Older shows constantly referenced are *ER* (1994–2009) and *Married with Children* (1987–1997).

I worked at a travel bookstore in the summer of 1999 and was amazed at the number of people who wanted directions to the "Married with Children Fountain." That is Buckingham Fountain, a Chicago landmark and one of the largest fountains in the world. It is discussed in more detail later in the chapter.

HOUSING

Historically, Chicago has been a very segregated city. If you were to take the Red Line Elevated train from the northern city limits to its far south terminus, you would see Chicago's largely white and Asian north give way to a largely African American and Latino south and west. Gentrification and an enduring legacy of racist real-estate practices and policies have contributed to demographic gaps in home ownership. Communities of color remain highly concentrated in neighborhoods on the south and west sides of Chicago. Chicago's African American population has declined citywide in the last decade, while Latino and Asian populations have grown.

The costs of home ownership and rents have substantially increased throughout the city, particularly in neighborhoods favored by young professionals. The city is grappling with a large homeless population that lacks basic services and a migrant population of individuals escaping failed nations such as Venezuela, which has taxed the city's ability to remain a "sanctuary city" for all. Despite all of these challenges, the city remains a magnet for young people, many of them from small cities and towns in the Midwest that lack the opportunities and amenities that are only found in a big city.

THE "PROJECTS"–PAST AND PRESENT

Public housing projects exist in many American cities to house the many Americans who cannot afford to live in a home or apartment without some form of assistance. Many high-rise "projects" were built in the early 1960s with minimal amenities. They became warehouses for the poor, comprised primarily of African Americans. Some of the most notorious projects in the United States have been in Chicago, less than a mile away from Highway 41. On the North Side of the city the Cabrini-Green Project, housing 15,000 residents was completed in 1962 and slowly torn down starting from 1995 through 2011. The location of the former Cabrini project has had much redevelopment.

On the South Side were the Robert Taylor Homes—once the largest and most infamous public housing project in the country. Twenty-seven thousand people lived in twenty-eight high-rises that fronted the Dan Ryan Expressway (Interstate 94). Built in 1962 and finally demolished in 2007, the overcrowded and underfunded project was a haven for every urban ill that could be put on its despairing residents.

With the demise of the large projects, several smaller scale public housing projects remain in the city. Efforts have been made by the Chicago Housing Authority to create a greater supply of subsidized "Section 8" housing, designed to enable low-income families to obtain residences. This has produced mixed results. In April 2025, the **National Public Housing Museum** was opened on the Near West Side to provide visitors with an understanding of public housing and its impact on communities.

CHURCHES

Chicago has a plethora of interesting churches to see. Much of this is due to the multiple groups of immigrants and migrants from other parts of the United States who have called the city home since its founding. A fair number of churches are endangered or have closed as their congregations shrink. The following are among the more interesting places of worship to visit in Chicago and their neighborhood location:

- Holy Trinity Orthodox Cathedral, Ukrainian Village (survivor of the Great Chicago Fire)
- St. John Cantius Church, Goose Island
- Old St. Patrick's Church, West Loop (survivor of the Great Chicago Fire)
- St. Michael Catholic Church, Old Town (survivor of the Great Chicago Fire)
- St. James Cathedral, Near North
- St. Peter's Church, Downtown
- Holy Name Cathedral, Downtown
- First United Methodist Church Chicago Temple, Downtown
- St. Mary of the Angels, Bucktown
- St. Stanislaus Kostka Church, Pulaski Park (the Kennedy Expressway; I-90/94 was moved to preserve this church)
- Unity Temple, Oak Park (designed by Frank Lloyd Wright and listed as a UNESCO World Heritage Site)
- Fourth Presbyterian Church, Magnificent Mile
- Holy Family Catholic Church, Near West Side
- St. Adalbert Church, Lower West Side
- Pilgrim Baptist Church of South Chicago (birthplace of Gospel music)

NEARBY COLLEGES AND UNIVERSITIES

- University of Illinois, Chicago West Loop (enrollment 33,500)
- University of Chicago, Downtown & Hyde Park (18,500)
- DePaul University, Downtown & Lincoln Park (21,348)
- Loyola University Chicago, Downtown & Rogers Park (16,900)
- Northwestern University, Downtown & Evanston (22,700)
- Roosevelt University, Downtown (4,000)
- Columbia College, South Loop (6,400)

BUSINESS

Chicago has numerous corporations that are headquartered in the city or have substantial business within it. The diversity of businesses has somewhat shielded the city from the economic declines that have impacted other cities dependent upon one industry. The city remains a hub for tech firms, printing/publishing, insurance, transportation, financial trading, services, and food processing.

Among the major companies doing business within the city are:

- Accenture
- Allstate
- Aon
- Archer Daniels Midland (ADM)
- Blue Cross Blue Shield Association
- CME (Chicago Mercantile Exchange)
- CNA Financial Corporation
- Echo Global Logistics
- Exelon
- Hyatt Hotels Corp.
- ITW
- Jones Lang LaSalle
- Kraft Heinz
- McDonald's
- Molson Coors Beverage Company
- Mondelez
- Morningstar
- OCC (Options Clearing Corporation)
- Sidley Austin LLP

- United Airlines
- Walgreens Boots Alliance

NEIGHBORHOODS

Chicago has seventy-seven designated "community areas" but well over one hundred more or less distinct "neighborhoods" that can overlap into different community areas. If this sounds confusing for visitors, it is! Suffice to say that neighborhood borders tend to be what local residents consider their location to be part of. Travel on Highway 41 enables one to see many interesting areas of the city. Here are some locations along the road or nearby to explore.

DEVON AVENUE

Highway 41 crosses from Lincolnwood into Chicago at **Devon Avenue**. I highly recommend a trip east on Devon Avenue to **Little India** in the West Ridge neighborhood. Although Little India is the title of this stretch of West Devon between North Seeley and North California avenues, it could also be Little Pakistan and Little South Asia, with Little Israel thrown in the mix. This area of West Ridge is one of the most diverse in the city. Many restaurants serve Indian food, and it is a great location to find authentic South Asian grocery items and window-shop for a sari, a kurta, a salwar kameez, jewelry, and everything in between.

If your tastes run more toward the classic Chicago-style hot dog (mustard, onions, pickle relish, dill pickle, tomato, pickled peppers, and celery salt on a poppyseed bun), fries, and milkshakes, turn west on Devon Avenue and proceed to **Superdawg Drive-In**, located in Norwood Park. Known for Maurie and Flaurie, the hot dog figurines on the rooftop, and in business since 1948, Superdawg has been written in national publications as one of the places to go for a true drive-in experience, including carhops, of course. Your "Superdawg" will be delivered to your car window, resting in a little box atop a layer of "Superfries."

KOREATOWN

South of Devon Avenue in the **Peterson Park** neighborhood, Highway 41 enters an area of dining establishments and shops collectively known as **Koreatown**, which serves the area's greater Korean community. It's well worth a stop at one of its great Korean restaurants if you have not had your food fill already. If you still need another traditional Chicago hot dog, **Wolfy's** in West Ridge is nearby on Peterson Avenue (Route 14).

Superdawg, Chicago, IL

MOTEL ROW

Along the stretch of Highway 41/Lincoln Avenue that runs from Devon to Foster Avenue, are a few survivors of what was once known as **Motel Row**. Many of these motels were built after World War II but prior to the interstate—a time when Highway 41 was still the main road bringing travelers into Chicago. These motels were moderately priced and served road travelers well over the years before they became more commonly associated with activities such as prostitution and drug dealing. The city made efforts to close many of these motels in the early 2000s, but a few still remain. Gentrification and new businesses will probably hasten an end to the strip soon, so see them while they are still in business. A cool church to see along the strip is **Holy Nativity Romanian Orthodox Church** in West Ridge.

Holy Nativity Romanian Orthodox Church, Peterson Park, Chicago, IL

LINCOLN SQUARE & RAVENSWOOD

Continue on Lincoln Avenue, and you will arrive at the **Lincoln Square/Ravenswood** community. Here, where Lincoln intersects with Foster Avenue, is where to turn left (east) to follow U.S. 41, but I suggest you take some time to explore Lincoln Square. If you stick to Lincoln Avenue south of Foster, you will reach the **Old Town School of Folk Music–Lincoln Square** just south of Wilson Avenue. This venerable music school and performance venue has been offering vocal and instrumental lessons and presenting top-of-the-line musical acts for decades.

If you're in the mood for a movie, check out the **Davis Theater**, just north of the Lincoln/Wilson intersection. This movie theater has been a fixture of the neighborhood for more than a century. Opened in 1918 as a vaudeville house called the Pershing Theater, it's been the Davis ever since films began playing there. Although it was a revival house for a stretch in the late twentieth century, it now presents first-run films.

Lincoln Square/Ravenswood is a hip area with lots of interesting restaurants and shops. And if you want to see more of the nearby North Side neighborhoods of Chicago west of the lakefront, continue south on Lincoln Avenue. When you are ready to return to the route, backtrack on Lincoln to Foster, hang a right, and head for the lake.

The three-flat apartment buildings along Foster Avenue and surrounding streets have soared in value as more young professionals move here. Highway 41 within this neighborhood has a more local vibe. Gentrification is occurring rapidly in the area, and teardowns for new construction are bringing in more modern structures.

Foster Avenue passes by **Amundsen High School**, where more than fifteen languages are officially spoken, and students of multiple ethnic backgrounds represent the crazy-quilt diversity of Chicago's North Side. Foster Avenue continues into **Andersonville**, a neighborhood that was once heavily Swedish. Some beautiful old nineteenth century row houses are located here.

The **Swedish American Museum**, which celebrates Nordic culture and history, is located on Foster, as well as a Middle Eastern bakery and grocery. A Belgian Gastropub called **Hopleaf**, just off Foster on Clark Street, features a great beer selection. You will also pass by the **Chicago Waldorf School** at Foster and Ashland Avenue, a Pre-K to Grade 12 school based on the educational philosophy of Rudolf Steiner, who favored a holistic approach to learning.

To the west of 41 on Foster Ave is the **Bohemian National Cemetery**, an old burial ground known for its limestone gatehouse, statues, and decorated columbaria niches for the funeral urns that honor the many Czech Americans interred there.

OTHER NORTH SIDE NEIGHBORHOODS NEAR HIGHWAY 41

ROGERS PARK

North of Highway 41/Foster Avenue between Devon Avenue and the Chicago/Evanston border is the neighborhood of **Rogers Park**. An extremely diverse population, good free beaches (**Loyola Beach** is a personal favorite), interesting architecture, good bars and restaurants, and a generally calm, laid-back vibe are earmarks of this far-north neighborhood. Take an opportunity to stop and look around if you can.

As parking can be challenging, I recommend taking a bicycle or public transportation if possible. The lakefront of the city in this area has been hit in recent times by high lake levels that have unfortunately created some problems for residents with homes and apartment buildings along the shore.

Within Rogers Park is **Loyola University**, a highly ranked Catholic Jesuit university with an enrollment of approximately 16,000. Similar to Northwestern University, Loyola also has a downtown Chicago campus. Its Rogers Park campus is smaller and more compact than Northwestern's, and is also a lovely place to see on the lakefront. There is a CTA elevated line (L) stop right next to the school.

UPTOWN

The **Uptown** neighborhood is just south of Foster Avenue. Once known mainly as a place that attracted many recent migrants, both from abroad and from Appalachia, Uptown remains one of the most ethnically diverse neighborhoods in the city.

The **North Broadway Avenue** commercial district features some iconic entertainment venues including **The Green Mill**, established at its present location in 1935, which hosts primarily jazz acts; the **Riviera Theatre (The Riv)**, and the **Aragon Ballroom**—two vintage concert venues that host many well-known bands.

Just south of Uptown lies the 120-acre, heavily forested **Graceland Cemetery,** the burial site for many famous Chicagoans. It is the final resting place of athletes, politicians, industrialists, and many of the finest architects of the last century, such as Louis Sullivan and Mies van der Rohe. While walking around Graceland Cemetery be sure to visit **"Eternal Silence,"** a bronze statue marking the grave of Dexter Graves, one of Chicago's early settlers. The 1909 sculpture by Lorado Taft represents a cloaked figure draped with a hood. Legend once had it that the statue was haunted and if you looked into the eyes, you would see your own death. Yikes!

Another interesting cemetery to see in the area just to the north of 41 is the **Rosehill Cemetery** between Peterson and Bryn Mawr avenues. Rosehill is the final resting place for other famous Chicagoans including Oscar Mayer, Richard Sears, and Aaron Montgomery Ward. The most photographed monument in Rosehill is the sculpture over the grave of Frances Pearce Stone and her infant daughter that is encased in glass enclosure to shield it from the weather.

EDGEWATER

North of Uptown and south of Rogers Park lies the **Edgewater** neighborhood. If you follow 41 toward the end of Foster Avenue, the road will take you by the ultra-exclusive **Saddle & Cycle Club**, a pricey and secretive club that I can't talk about without authorization. The club serves as a venue for wedding receptions and other events, so you might experience the club's interior if you are lucky enough to be invited.

If you stay on Foster, it will take you directly to the lakefront at **Foster Avenue Beach**. This is the northern end of Lincoln Park with its bike paths, playing fields, and parklands. If you need a respite before resuming your 41 drive, stop here and park but be prepared to pay.

VIGNETTE   THE PARKING METER FIASCO

Just about everywhere you can find a possible parking place along Chicago's lakefront and in much of the rest of the central city, you will also encounter the ubiquitous parking meters. The meters accept credit cards and are serious moneymakers—just not for Chicago. In one of most shortsighted civic moves ever, the city sold the parking meters to an investment group—the creatively named Chicago Parking Meters LLC, backed by money from the Kingdom of Qatar.

Chicago Parking Meters paid $1 billion to the city for a seventy-five-year lease. This allowed the city to plug a hole in its 2008 budget, but the terms of the lease assure that the investors have already made back their initial investment and will reap several billions more out of the deal by the end of the term of contract. Several attempts have been made to undo this deal, but none have made it to a hearing. In late 2023, the latest effort to void the contract for public parking in the city was turned away by the U.S. Supreme Court when it declined to hear the case.

WRIGLEYVILLE

To the south of Graceland Cemetery is the baseball shrine **Wrigley Field**, home of the Major League Baseball Chicago Cubs. The historic park is the centerpiece of a neighborhood that long ago was working class but is now a gentrified tourist location. Lots of bars and restaurants surround the ballpark, originally built in 1914 and heavily renovated over the last decade.

The old three-story apartment buildings where spectators could watch the ballgame from rooftop bleachers are slated to be demolished in favor of more modern structures. Wrigley was declared a National Historic Landmark in 2020 and, along with Fenway Park in Boston, is one of only two Major League ballparks that date from the early part of the twentieth century. The Cubs were world champions in 2016 after a hiatus of over 100 years. Many young professionals live in the area. Up the street from Wrigley Field is **Metro**, a great concert venue.

VIGNETTE THE CURSE

The Cubs are one of the oldest teams in the major leagues, having started play in 1876. They won back-to-back World Series in 1907 and 1908, and then the winning streak stopped. From their final National League pennant win in 1945 until the 2016 championship, the Cubs were bedeviled by the famed "Billy Goat curse."

A local Chicago saloon owner named William "Billy Goat" Sianis tried to enter Wrigley Field in game four of the 1945 series with the Detroit Tigers with his pet goat Murphy. He was told that he could attend but not his goat. Reputedly, Billy Goat asked, "Why not the goat?" and the Cubs owner, P.K. Wrigley, answered, "Because the goat stinks." With that, Billy Goat threw up his arms and exclaimed, "The Cubs ain't gonna win no more. The Cubs will never win a World Series so long as the goat is not allowed in Wrigley Field." With the curse on, the Cubs lost the Series and subsequently became one of the worst teams in baseball for years after. In 1984, the goat and Sianis were allowed back into Wrigley Field, but it would take until 2016 for the curse to finally be lifted when the Cubs ended their 108-year World Series drought.

THE DRIVE

Starting at Hollywood Avenue at its northern end and continuing to 71st Street at its southern end is the **Jean Baptiste Point DuSable Lake Shore**

Drive, the official name given to this stretch of Highway 41. (Note that Highway 41 technically does not begin until the entrance from Foster Avenue). The land areas bounding this stretch of road are as dear to me as any I can think of. "The Drive," as I will call it, is one of the most iconic urban parkways in America. It stretches approximately sixteen miles through the city of Chicago along Lake Michigan.

On the lake side (always east) running the length of the Drive are separate bike and walking paths bordering beaches, parks, a golf course, piers, museums, marinas, and a convention center. On the land side (west) is also parkland bordering the "Gold Coast," downtown Chicago, and luxury high-rises. The Drive is the front door and the front yard to the city of Chicago. It is symbolic of the city and always a point of pride—as well as a source of much controversy. What was once a promenade for wealthy property owners is now a divided multi-lane highway with multiple stoplights. Normal rush hours can be congested and crawling. This spectacular road can, unfortunately, often seem to resemble a high-speed expressway separating Chicago residents from the lakefront. Some serious future thought must be given to making the road a scaled-back boulevard as it once was.

The views of Lake Michigan and downtown buildings from the Drive are spectacular and ever changing. Every year around Memorial Day the Drive is closed to motor vehicle traffic for one morning for "Bike the Drive," when bicycles can travel the length of it. It is wonderful to be on the road at a slower speed and take in the beauty of the city. Suffice to say without an open lakefront, "The Drive" would not be much to talk about.

A LITTLE BIT OF HISTORY

The Drive was originally a path for horse-drawn carriages carrying affluent Chicagoans. Almost alone among major cities in the United States, the 1836 founding map of the city of Chicago proclaimed the Lake Michigan waterfront to be "Public Ground—A Common to Remain Forever Open, Clear and Free of any Buildings, or Other Obstruction whatever." That edict has been subject to much interpretation over the intervening years.

In 1882, Potter Palmer, the business entrepreneur responsible for much of the development of downtown Chicago, persuaded the city to connect his mansion at 1350 N. Lake Shore Drive to the downtown area. Daniel Burnh-

Bike the Drive event, held on Memorial Day weekend, Chicago, IL

am, an architect and city planner, wanted to make the lakeshore a chain of lagoons and grassy islands from the city's northern boundary to its southern, all free and open. While the "Burnham Plan" of 1909 never reached full fruition, portions of it have continued to guide city planners over the years. With the invention of the automobile and continual lengthening of the road over the decades, the Drive has been extended to its northern terminus at Hollywood Avenue (5700 North) and Marquette Road (6600 South) at its southern end. Much of the highway was built during the Great Depression of the 1930s, and parts still retain sculptures from that time. Many of the tunnels built then for pedestrian access to the lakefront are deteriorating. So are many of the oldest bridges along the highway.

A seawall was built for part of the Drive, and there have been continual efforts to reinforce the Lake Michigan shoreline to avoid flooding and road closures due to inclement weather. Because of canals dug over a century ago to keep waste from flowing from the Chicago River to the Lake, which also supplies the city's drinking water, the surface of Lake Michigan is usually only a few feet lower than the roadbed of the Drive. Due to increasingly extreme swings in the water levels of Lake Michigan, caused by the local cycles of precipitation, evaporation, river flow and believed to be exacerbated by climate change, Chicago and the metropolitan area are very vulnerable to heavy rains that increase lake levels and lead to flooding. Billions of dollars have been spent on tunnels dug deep below the surface of the metropolitan area to redirect rainwater, but the bottom line is that building a massive city on what were once broad lakeshore wetlands has resulted in a constant threat of flooding and undermined land.

Landfill from construction projects—some of it dating back to the Great Chicago Fire of 1871—has been used to extend the Lake Michigan shoreline next to the Drive.

In 1979, Friends of the Parks—an advocacy group—pushed for an eighteen-mile **Chicago Lakefront Trail** from Hollywood Avenue to 71st Street. The trail is still in place and has been widened in most sections to have a walking/running trail separate from a bicycle trail. A bike/pedestrian rail bridge across the **Chicago River** was finally completed in 2021 to allow bikers and pedestrians to avoid heavy automobile traffic. In the mid-1980s, the notorious, traffic-stopping "S-curve" with its two 90-degree turns where the Drive crosses over the Chicago River, was smoothed out, and the road became even more like a major highway. There is still another S-curve where the Drive skirts by Michigan Avenue and the beginning of downtown Chicago.

In the 1990s, medians with trees and shrubs were installed on North Lake Shore Drive, and two pedestrian bridges were built over South Lake Shore Drive. In April 2021, after protracted and highly charged hearings and debates in the city council, the name "Lake Shore Drive" was officially changed to "Jean Baptiste Pointe DuSable Lake Shore Drive" to honor the city's first non-Indigenous settler and the recognized founder of Chicago. DuSable, who was of African descent, was only marginally recognized until advocates in recent decades pushed to name the Drive for this Chicago pioneer. Most maps and signage now refer to the road as **DuSable Lake Shore Drive**.

Plans for redesigning the heavily used northern part of the Drive have been floated for many years. Tunneling the Drive to add more park and lakefront space and converting lanes to bus lanes and bike lanes have been in consideration. An initiative called **Redefine the Drive** was launched in 2013 to promote adding more lakefront green space, build more bike and pedestrian access, and smooth out the remaining S-curve near Oak Street. A final plan was supposed to be unveiled in 2025, but several groups want the state to halt the redesign project to figure out a new design that dissuades car use. To date, the road has had resurfacing projects but no final decision on how to rework the current configuration.

So, where to start? Long ago, the 1970s rock group Aliotta Haynes Jeremiah penned "Lake Shore Drive" in honor of the road, and the song does a great job of conveying the magic you can experience tooling down the road in search of adventure and excitement. Because the Drive travels north to south along the length of the city, drivers can take in the postcard beauty of the lakefront. Each season transforms the Drive, of course, and it can be treacherous in a storm when high lakefront waves endanger the road. It's also much better to be a passenger who can look around rather than a driver who must negotiate the busy city highway.

I strongly suggest a visitor to the city should ditch the auto, if possible, and walk or bike the **Lakefront Trail** east of the road and the paths in the parks that line the west side of the road. Try to go on a weekday if possible because on a weekend summer day, the Lakefront Trail can be as congested with bikers, skaters, joggers, walkers, strollers, and people crossing to beaches and parks and just being part of the scene as the Drive is crowded with cars. The parks are all heavily used, and it's best to leave plenty of time to explore everything along the road.

THE BEACHES

NORTH SIDE BEACHES

You will find some of the best beaches in the Midwest along the Drive. In fact, it is fair to say that Chicago is part of a very short list of major cities, mainly on the east and west coasts, that have beaches in short proximity to their downtown. The beaches are officially opened and staffed with lifeguards from Memorial Day to Labor Day, but individuals come all year to swim, kayak, and stroll along the lakefront. Ask a resident to name their favorite beach, and you will get a wide assortment of answers.

To the north is **Loyola Beach** in Rogers Park, **Kathy Osterman Beach** (best to walk or bike here due to the lack of parking), **Foster Beach** (soft sand, small crowds of peaceful swimmers, volleyball players, an unusual trapeze set up), and **Montrose Beach**. Montrose is the largest of these with lots of parking, a dog beach, and a bird sanctuary.

Across the Drive from Lincoln Park is **North Avenue Beach**, one of the most popular of the beaches. It lures a cross-section of the city and is the site of the annual **Air and Water Show**. Volleyball palyers congregate on the sand courts, and if you want one of the best views of the city, go to the **Castaways Beach Club** on the second floor of the iconic boat house on the beach.

Steps away from the Magnificent Mile downtown shopping area is **Oak Street Beach**, a small beach that can get very crowded because of its location. A little farther south is **Ohio Street Beach**, one of my favorites. Not as crowded as Oak Street Beach and North Avenue Beach, Ohio Street Beach offers great views of the Chicago skyline that surrounds it.

Entry to Oak Street Beach, Chicago, IL

SOUTH SIDE BEACHES

South of the downtown area are a number of beaches. This array of beaches starts at the **Museum Campus** area with **12th Street Beach**. It is located on Northerly Island, right next to the Planetarium. Heavily used **31st Street Beach/Margaret T. Burroughs Beach** (adjacent to the 31st Street Boat

Harbor), is farther south, followed by **Oakwood Beach** at 41st Street. Here, a pedestrian bridge crosses the Drive and provides great lake views.

By the University of Chicago and across the Drive from the **Griffin Museum of Science and Industry** you'll find **57th Street Beach**; **63rd Street Beach** is a few blocks farther south. It features a great old, restored bathhouse. **South Shore Beach** is located at 71st Street just behind the South Shore Cultural Center.

Finally, **Rainbow Beach** is at 75th Street on the far South Side. Of these, 31st Street Beach is the most popular for families, but all the beaches are quite well attended in the summer. If you are young, or young at heart, in the summer there is no better place to soak up what is Chicago than the beach.

LINCOLN PARK

Situated on both sides of the Drive from virtually the north end of the Drive south to North Avenue is **Lincoln Park**, one of the most heavily used parks in the city. On the west side of the Drive, the park encompasses 1,200 acres home to the highly regarded, attended, and free **Lincoln Park Zoo**; ball fields, bird sanctuaries, the **Peggy Notebaert Nature Museum**; **North Pond Nature Sanctuary**; a boat harbor, golf driving range, **Lincoln Park Conservatory**; the **Alfred Caldwell Lily Pool** (a hidden gem); and **North Pond Café**; one of the many premier restaurants in Chicago that sits in a beautiful location. Much of the park was once a vast cemetery with thousands of unmarked graves. Yes, much of this popular park lies over skeletons!

The **Chicago History Museum** is located at the southern end of the park and is worth visiting to learn about the city. Two major post-Civil War statues stand in the park. One honors President Ulysses S. Grant. The other is "Abraham Lincoln: The Man," a famous statue cast by the noted artist Augustus Saint-Gaudens. Bordering Uptown in the far reaches of Lincoln Park, is a statue of Dr. José Rizal (1861—1896), a Philippine revolutionary martyr and national hero from the Spanish Colonial period. The statue was dedicated in 1999, funded by various Filipino American organizations.

On the lakefront, the parkland fronts Montrose Beach. **Montrose Harbor, Belmont Harbor, Sydney Marovitz Golf Course**, tennis courts, soccer fields, and nature preserves are all accessible along the Lakefront Trail. Lots of local anglers are out early in the morning casting their lines. Past Belmont Harbor is **Belmont Rocks**, once a haven for gay bathers. It now attracts a diverse audience of people taking in the views. The **AIDS Garden** is a park commemorating the HIV/AIDS crisis. It features a huge Keith Haring statue, flowers, and a scattered array of benches.

THE LINCOLN PARK NEIGHBORHOOD

West of the park is a residential area also called **Lincoln Park**, which is known for its beautiful brownstone rowhouses with arched windows and often beautiful doors. These homes are among the most expensive properties in the city. The neighborhood also boasts notable entertainment and restaurant venues such as **Kingston Mines**—a famous blues club and a definite stop—as well as **Glascott's Saloon**, an Irish Pub first opened in 1937. Down the street from Glascott's is the **Victory Gardens Theater**, once known as the Biograph. Depression-era bank robber John Dillinger met his demise just outside the infamous movie house. **Pequod's Pizza**, named the number one pizza in the country by Yelp, is located in Lincoln Park. DePaul University's main campus (enrollment 21,000) is a private Catholic institution also located in Lincoln Park.

OLD TOWN

To the south of Lincoln Park, the very hip **Old Town** neighborhood has always been tourist friendly. In the 1960s, it was one of the few places in Chicago that was tolerant of "the hippies." Many Victorian-era buildings, eclectic shops, and a variety of restaurants comprise the neighborhood.

The Second City is one of Old Town's most popular destinations. This storied "improv" comedy theater offers nightly shows. Second City is also a school of sorts for sketch comedy and attracts many aspiring comedians. The list of noted performers who have been affiliated with Second City over the years is a long one.

A similarly noteworthy list of performers has acted in live theater at Old Town's **Steppenwolf Theatre Company**. Many plays that debuted at Steppenwolf have gone on to Broadway and beyond.

Zanies, a decades-old comedy club, is also located in Old Town. Other attractions include the **Midwest Buddhist Temple**, **Twin Anchors Restaurant & Tavern**, and **Old Town Ale House**, a great dive bar.

THE GOLD COAST

The Gold Coast neighborhood is quite prestigious. It is a mixture of mansions, historic row houses, and high-rise apartments. It's also a great area to walk around and admire. The **Archdiocese of Chicago Cardinal Mansion**, the **Original Playboy Mansion**, the **Charnley-Persky House** (designed by Louis Sullivan and Frank Lloyd Wright), the **McCormick Mansion** (designed by Stanford White), and the historic **Ambassador Hotel** are all located in the Gold Coast. A hidden gem of a museum, the **International Museum of Surgical Science** with its collection of weird surgical instruments from the old days, is just a block east of the Cardinal Mansion.

RUSH STREET

To the west of the Gold Coast is **Oak Street**, a well-known restaurant and nightlife entertainment area replete with designer stores, is situated around the intersection of Oak and **Rush Streets**. Rush Street is the place for folks to see and be seen. Back in the day, this area boasted famous nightclubs such as Mister Kelly's, where audiences could see big-name entertainers in a small venue. Long before African American performers and customers could be assured of a warm welcome in many places, they could visit Mister Kelly's and other Rush Street establishments. Most of these nightclubs closed in the 1970s and 1980s as performers migrated to larger stages.

Restaurants such as **Gibson's Bar & Steakhouse** and **Hugo's Frog Bar & Fish House** opened in their place. For a period in the early 2000s, this area was known as the "Viagra Triangle," where rich old dudes came to look for love with beautiful young women. The area now has a number of restaurants that spill out to the sidewalk in the summer. Nearby is the **Newberry Library**, free and open to the public since 1887, and the **Loyola University Water Tower Campus**.

STREETERVILLE

The neighborhood known as **Streeterville** borders the Drive from Oak Street to the Chicago River and west to Rush Street. Named for a ne'er dowell scammer who once laid claim to the area in the early twentieth century, Streeterville was once full of warehouses. Now it is known for its lakefront high-rises, huge hospital complex, the **Museum of Contemporary Art**, and **Northwestern Pritzker School of Law**.

Downtown Chicago starts as Highway 41 makes a bend around Oak Street beach. If you want, you can exit the Drive at **North Michigan Avenue** and travel what is known as the **Magnificent Mile**, the city's premier commercial district. Landmarks include the historic **Chicago Water Tower**, **Water Tower Place** shopping center, upscale stores, restaurants, hotels, and two of Chicago's most famous buildings: the **Tribune Tower** and the terracotta **Wrigley Building**. The "Mag Mile" is still recovering from the COVID-19 pandemic, and several storefronts are still vacant, but the area is bouncing back for tourists.

Wrigley Building, Chicago, IL

As you take the remaining S-curve on 41, you will pass by the historic **Drake Hotel**, which is listed on the National Register of Historic Places. Behind it is the **Palmolive Building**—formerly the Playboy building. Beyond that is the 100-story mixed-use building presently known as **875 North Michigan Avenue** but known locally as the John Hancock Center. Great views can be seen from the observatory at the top, but the 96th-floor Signature Room, where you could drink and dine as you admired the view, closed in 2023.

Oak Street Beach, Chicago, IL

Some classic apartment buildings overlook the lakefront along this stretch of the Drive. One good example is **860/880 Lake Shore Drive**. These two renowned twenty-six-story glass curtain apartment buildings, designed by Mies van der Rohe, were built in 1949. They have clear views of **Ohio Street Beach** and **Olive Park**, which fronts the **Jardine Water Purification Plant** and **Navy Pier**.

Now a tourist attraction, Navy Pier was built in 1916. It has been a port, a warehouse, a World War II training facility, and a campus for the University of Illinois. It was the home of the "Chicagofest" music festival from 1978 to 1982. After languishing for years, the pier was redeveloped in 1994 and reopened in 1995 with a children's museum, restaurants, theaters (including Chicago Shakespeare Theater), tour boats, carnival attractions, and a huge Ferris wheel (replaced with the current Centennial Wheel in 2016). Given landmark status, Navy Pier is one of Chicago's most-visited destinations, attracting over eight million visitors annually.

DuSable Lake Shore Drive, Lake Point Tower, Navy Pier, and DuSable Harbor
Chicago, IL

VIGNETTE THE NAMESAKE OF OLIVE PARK

Private First-Class Milton L. Olive III (1946–1965) was a posthumous Medal of Honor recipient. A true hero, in 1966 Olive became the first African American soldier to be awarded the Medal of Honor in the Vietnam Conflict. He grew up on Chicago's South Side and moved to Mississippi where he stayed with his grandparents and worked during the Freedom Summer of 1964, registering African American voters. He joined the military on his eighteenth birthday and became a paratrooper in the U.S. Army's 173rd Airborne Brigade. Olive was known as "Preacher" for his quiet demeanor and his tendency to avoid cursing. A plaque in the Chicago Park that bears his name reads as follows:

"Citation: For conspicuous gallantry and intrepidity at the risk of his life above and beyond the call of duty. Pfc. Olive was a member of the 3d Platoon of Company B, as it moved through the jungle to find the Viet Cong operating in the area. Although the platoon was subjected to a heavy volume of enemy gunfire and pinned down temporarily, it retaliated by assaulting the Viet Cong positions, causing the enemy to flee. As the platoon pursued the insurgents, Pfc. Olive and four other soldiers were moving through the jungle together when a grenade was thrown into their midst. Pfc. Olive saw the grenade and then saved the lives of his fellow soldiers at the sacrifice of *his by grabbing the grenade in his hand and falling on it to absorb the blast with his body. Through his bravery, unhesitating actions, and complete disregard for his safety, he prevented additional loss of life or injury to the members of his platoon. Pfc. Olive's extraordinary heroism, at the risk of his life above and beyond the call of duty, are in the highest traditions of the U.S. Army and reflect great credit upon himself and the Armed Forces of his country."*

THE PLAYPEN

Along the Drive is a lakefront area of water just north of Navy Pier where yachts and powerboats congregate known locally as **"The Playpen."** This is where a see-and-be-seen crowd drinks, dances, and socializes along the skyline. Lots of buff bodies are on display. A couple of recent accidents with injuries may cause the Playpen to become a bit tamer going forward than it has been in years gone by.

LAKE POINT TOWER

Next to Navy Pier is a seventy-story, curved glass condominium building known as **Lake Point Tower**. Constructed in 1968 by two students of Mies van der Rohe, for a time it was the tallest apartment building in the world. A loophole in local zoning policy led to the development of this building, as well as two others at the mouth of the Chicago River, despite the "Forever Open, Clear, and Free" edict that protects Chicago's waterfront from such development. The loophole was fixed in the early 1970s, and when the S-curve of the Drive was straightened out, Lake Point Tower was the only residential building east of Lake Shore Drive. A 2.5-acre park, complete with playground, waterfalls, and views of the city and lake is located on the third-floor terrace of the building.

VIGNETTE THE SPIRE

*The **Chicago Spire** was a skyscraper project that was started between 2007 and 2008. It was located on a spit of land beside the Chicago River and next to the Franklin Delano Roosevelt Bridge, but it was never completed. It was cancelled during the Great Recession of 2008. One of the most famous Chicago buildings that never was, the Spire was designed by architect Santiago Calatrava to be 150 floors, which would have made it the tallest building in the Western Hemisphere.*

For years after the plan fell through, all passers-by saw was a huge seventy-six-foot hole in the ground where the building was to stand. The property was redeveloped in 2024, and two seventy-story residential towers are now under construction at the site. The first tower is projected to be completed in 2027.

THE CHICAGO RIVER

Once an incredibly polluted river, the **Chicago River** has undergone a renaissance of sorts over the last two decades. Pedestrians can now walk from the **Chicago River Lock**, which prevents the river from flowing into Lake Michigan under the Drive, along a scenic river walk that has become a major people magnet over the last decade. Several restaurants line the walkway, along with terraced sitting areas, fishing piers, boating docks, and a **Vietnam Veterans Memorial**. The walkway extends to the bend where the north and south branches of the Chicago River meet.

On St. Patrick's Day, the river is famously dyed Kelly green, and kayakers, pleasure boaters, and spectators on multiple tour boats gather to admire both the sight and the splendid downtown architecture, which is constantly changing. In the summer, river travelers can see a cool light show projected on the wall of the historic **Merchandise Mart**. The **Chicago Architecture Center River Cruise** (and competitors) operate boat tours from spring through fall on the river. My wife has served as docent for the Architecture Center for several years on these tours. It is considered one of the "must dos" for visitors to the city.

NEW EASTSIDE

Where the Drive crosses over the Chicago River on the **Franklin Delano Roosevelt Bridge**, a view comprises the lake on one side and multiple high-rises on the other of a neighborhood called the **New Eastside**. A small park called **Lakeshore East Park**, and several large hotels are tucked among the high-rises as well. If you are fortunate to know someone who lives in the New Eastside, some of the best views of the city and lake can be seen.

DuSable Harbor and the Columbia Yacht Club, both located on the lakeshore, can be accessed by a pedestrian walkway. This area is a good place to watch fireworks shows featured weekly over the lake at Navy Pier throughout the summer.

Chicago River, Chicago, IL

THE LOOP

The central business district and public transportation hub for the city of Chicago is known as **"The Loop,"** named after the historic elevated commuter rail track that circles the area. The Loop is composed of numerous distinctive high-rise buildings and public art. I highly recommend a walking tour of the area led by an experienced docent from the **Chicago Architecture Center**. Hotels, shops, theaters, and restaurants abound within the area, which appears to be witnessing a transformation due to the aftereffects of the COVID-19 pandemic rendered the area a ghost town for most of 2020 and 2021. Several plans have been floated to convert now empty or sparsely leased downtown office buildings into residential units. A short list of buildings and structures worth visiting follows:

- **Willis Tower** (still known by locals as Sears Tower): Once the tallest building in the world at 110 stories, it has an observation deck that enables visitors to see four states on a clear day. Visibility from the Skydeck is approximately forty to fifty miles.
- **Chicago Board of Trade:** This iconic Art Deco tower is crowned with a statue of Ceres, the goddess of agriculture.

- **Chicago Cultural Center:** Opened in 1897 as the Chicago Public Library, this Chicago landmark building is famous for its Tiffany Dome and Grand Army of the Republic (GAR) Hall and Rotunda.
- **The Rookery Building:** One of the most historically significant buildings in Chicago, the Rookery Building was designed by Daniel Burnham and features a lobby designed by Frank Lloyd Wright.
- **Daley Plaza:** This space is where you'll find Chicago's statues by Picasso and Joan Miro. The city's Marc Chagall mosaic, called "The Four Seasons," is two blocks south.
- **Auditorium Theater:** An architectural gem designed by Adler & Sullivan; this venue was completed in 1889.
- **Fine Arts Building:** This 1885 building is famous for its Art Nouveau murals inside.
- **Carson Pirie Scott Building:** Once a famous downtown department store designed by Louis Sullivan, this building still boasts a flamboyant wrought-iron entryway even though it's now a **Target** store.
- **Chicago Theatre:** This landmark theater with its iconic Chicago marquee was built in 1921.
- **Harold Washington Library Center, Chicago Public Library:** Named in honor of former Mayor Harold Washington, construction on the building began in 1988 and was completed in 1991. The design of Chicago's main public library incorporates many elements representing the city's history.
- **Palmer House Hilton Hotel:** This historic hotel was built in 1925 and remains a landmark destination for travelers to Chicago.

VIGNETTE NEWSPAPER COLUMNISTS

Ever since the days of Ben Hecht and Charles MacArthur (writers of the play The Front Page), Chicago has had its share of well-known journalists. Two of the best were Irv Kupcinet and Mike Royko.

Irv Kupcinet (Kup) (1912–2003) was a popular newspaper columnist for the Chicago Sun-Times for over six decades. His daily "Kup's Column" was a gossipy piece that chronicled the many celebrities who lived in or visited Chicago during that time period. Kup and his wife Esther (Essee) (1915–2001) were fixtures on the Chicago nightlife scene and seemingly knew everyone who mattered (at least, socially) in the city. Kup was a television talk show host and radio personality as well. The Kupcine-

ts' lives were upended by the death of their daughter Karyn (1941–1963), an actress who was murdered in Los Angeles in a still-unsolved case. A statue of Kup called "Mr. Chicago" stands in the Loop on Wacker Drive next to the Chicago River.

Mike Royko (1932-1997) was a daily newspaper columnist for the Chicago Daily News, the Chicago Sun-Times, and the Chicago Tribune over his thirty-year career. He won a Pulitzer Prize for commentary in 1972, and his book Boss: Richard J. Daley of Chicago (1971), is considered one of the best books ever written about city politics. He was the street smart "voice of the working guy," and his writing is still studied for his unique ability to connect with readers.

MILLENNIUM PARK

Continuing south on the Drive, you will reach more of the places that make the city the draw that it is. Please, park your car if you have not already done so and proceed to **Millennium Park**. First dedicated in 2004 after what seemed an eternity of construction issues, the park has proven to be a huge tourist draw. It is the top tourist destination in Chicago with upwards of twenty-five million annual visitors. The centerpiece of the park's 24.5 acres is **Jay Pritzker Pavilion**, a bandshell designed by architect Frank Gehry as an outdoor venue for all types of musical performances, movies, and picnics, and every visitor can enjoy this city experience for free.

Also within the park is the Anish Kapoor "Cloud Gate" sculpture that everyone knows as **"The Bean,"** the **Crown Fountain** with its changing video faces, and the **Lurie Garden**, which always has some variety of wildflowers in bloom. From Millennium Park, one can take the serpentine stainless steel paneled, 925-foot-long **BP Pedestrian Bridge**, designed by Frank Gehry. The bridge crosses over Columbus Avenue to **Maggie Daley Park**, named for the wife of former Mayor Richard M. Daley. It contains a skating rink, a climbing wall, tennis courts, and a fanciful, modern kids' playground.

VIGNETTE   THE DRIVING FORCE BEHIND MILLENNIUM PARK

John H. Bryan (1936–2018) was one of the unsung heroes who made Millennium Park a reality. Bryan was the CEO of the Chicago-based Sara Lee Corporation from 1975 to 2001. Originally from Mississippi, Bryan came to Chicago in 1968 to oversee a family business in specialty foods, which eventually became Sara Lee.

He sat on numerous corporate boards and was involved in a number of philanthr-

opic projects for the Lyric Opera of Chicago, the Chicago Symphony Orchestra, and the Art Institute of Chicago. Thanks to Bryan, over $200 million in private funding was raised for Millennium Park. Without the corporate funding that Bryan was able to shepherd, it is doubtful the park would be the civic attraction it is today.

ART INSTITUTE OF CHICAGO

South of Millennium Park is the **Art Institute of Chicago**, founded in 1879 and one of the oldest, largest, and most prestigious art museums in the world. A pair of 1893 bronze lion sculptures stand guard in front of the entrance. Even if you are from town, there is so much to see. As a suggestion, plan on spending several hours to visit the multiple galleries (there are over 200) of major works of art from around the world. Famous for its masterworks from the Impressionist School and the Post-Impressionist period, the Art Institute features some of the most well-known works of art including, *American Gothic*, *Nighthawks*, and *A Sunday Afternoon on the Island of La Grande Jatte*.

The **School of the Art Institute of Chicago (SAIC)** is housed here. It is one of a handful of independent schools of art and design in the world.

BUTLER FIELD

Butler Field lies across Columbus Drive from the Art Institute and next to the Drive. The **Petrillo Band Shell**, located here, was the scene of most outdoor concerts and other events until the arrival of the Pritzker Pavilion. The band shell has seen better days but still hosts a number of concerts and festivals. **Monroe Harbor**, across 41 on the lakefront, offers 390 mooring cans for the sailboats that help create the Chicago skyline's central panorama.

GRANT PARK

Stretching along the Drive from Monroe Street to Roosevelt Road is **Grant Park,** "Chicago's Front Yard." The park is a venue for softball, tennis, picnics, festivals, celebrations, demonstrations, running races—you name it, Grant Park has probably hosted it for the city over the last century.

A small plaque at the 11th Street pedestrian bridge honors Aaron Montgomery Ward (1843–1913), founder of Montgomery Ward, a pioneering

Chicago skyline, Chicago, IL

mail-order business and department store chain that operated between 1872 and 2001. (Montgomery Ward has operated online since 2004). Ward fought multiple business interests in court over a twenty-year period to ensure that Grant Park remained a park and not just a series of buildings. Ward is one of the many unsung heroes who helped keep the lakefront open.

Of special note in Grant Park's long history was the visit of Pope John Paul II in 1979 and Barack Obama's presidential election acceptance speech in 2008. The park is home to the nation's largest remaining stand of historic elm trees that have not been impacted by Dutch Elm disease. The park also has gardens, statues, and green spaces for leisure.

For the last couple decades, the entire park is taken over for about three weeks each August for the four-day **Lollapalooza** music festival, which brings some 400,000 people to the park. "Lolla" is operated by a private concern and is currently one of the premier music events in the country. Lolla provides revenue for the city, but the huge set-up and take-down for the event impacts the ability to walk around and enjoy the park. Another huge event, the annual **Chicago Marathon**, takes place in the park each fall.

In the last few years, a third major event has been added which may or may not become an annual fixture. The **NASCAR Chicago Street Race** has taken place in early July in both 2023 and 2024. The daunting amount of set-up and take-down necessary for the race area poses one of the many questions about whether or not the city gains anything from hosting this event. Be that as it may, the race adds something else to the crowded Grant

Park summer calendar. The race has impacted **Taste of Chicago**, an annual free admission food and music festival that was typically held in Grant Park over a week in early July and since moved to early September. "Taste" provides a venue for multiple small restaurants to serve up culinary specialties.

BUCKINGHAM FOUNTAIN

The centerpiece of Grant Park is **Buckingham Fountain**. While it does not look like much for half of the year when the fountain is not in operation, for the remainder of the year (May until October), it is a glorious sight and another iconic piece of Chicago. Millions of photos have been taken of people in front of the fountain, and more than a few marriage proposals, wedding parties, *quinceaneras*, and family gatherings have had the backdrop of Kate Buckingham's 1927 gift to the city in honor of her brother Clarence. (The fountain's official name is "The Clarence F. Buckingham Fountain"). At night, the fountain puts on a light show, and when the hour changes it shoots a plume of water 150 feet into the air. Directly across the Drive, on the lakeside, is **Queen's Landing**, where a young Queen Elizabeth came to visit the city on the Royal yacht in 1959.

MUSEUM CAMPUS

From Grant Park, a walkway on the lakeside of the Drive will take you south to what is known as the **Museum Campus**. The Drive was reconfigured in 1998 to create a sort of island home for three long-established Chicago treasures—the **Field Museum**, the **Adler Planetarium**, and the **Shedd Aquarium**. The aquarium, with its dolphin and whale shows, has become Chicago's most-visited cultural institution. The Field Museum's big draw is "Sue," a huge skeletal T. rex dinosaur. The museum features a host of changing exhibits of the natural world and human history. The Adler Planetarium has received a facelift as of late and, because of where it sits, offers perhaps the best free view of the Chicago skyline. Nearby stands the **Thaddeus Kosciuszko Monument**, which honors one of the Polish heroes of the American Revolution.

Just beside the Museum Campus is access to **Northerly Island**. This human-made island was once the site of the 1933 Century of Progress World's Fair. Later the location of Meigs Field, a small business airport, the site has now been converted into a nature preserve, a boat harbor, a concert venue, and **12th Street Beach**.

SOLDIER FIELD

The Drive goes by **Soldier Field**, a stadium owned by the Chicago Park District. It is the current home of the Chicago Bears football team and the Chicago Fire soccer team. The stadium was built in 1924 and has hosted many major events in its time, from athletic events to rock concerts. Once upon a time, it was a national landmark with distinctive Roman colonnades. That lasted until 2003, when the interior was rebuilt as part of a major renovation project to modernize the facility. Inside, it provides better sight lines for spectators, but from the outside it looks like a toilet bowl or flying saucer was placed on top of the old stadium. Soldier Field was de-listed as a national historic landmark in 2006. This modernization scheme was paid for in part by state of Illinois taxpayers, and it remains a costly issue. Needless to say, it has been a source of ongoing controversy.

Recently, the Chicago Bears' ownership has indicated that they want to leave the current stadium, which has one of the smallest seating capacities in the NFL, to build a multi-billion-dollar domed stadium on the lakefront nearby to be paid for with public funding. Previously, the team's ownership had indicated it wanted to build a new stadium in the northwest suburbs on the site of a previous horse racing track. Whether anything gets built at all, will be an interesting question.

Next to Soldier Field is the **Gold Star Family Memorial**, a grassy, five-acre park with sculptures and a memorial wall honoring fallen Chicago police officers.

Constant controversy and litigation have followed what can and/or should be allowed along the lakefront. George Lucas, director of the *Star Wars* and *Indiana Jones* movies, and his wife Mellody Hobson, a financier and Chicago native, wanted to build a private museum on a parking lot by the lakefront. After numerous protests and lawsuits, Lucas decided to build his museum in Los Angeles instead.

STATUES

At the southern end of Grant Park near the walkway to the lakefront and the Museum Campus, a statue of Christopher Columbus had been in place since its installation in 1933. (For locals, it always looked like Columbus was hailing a taxi). The historical myth of the heroic Columbus, discoverer of the New World and namesake to multiple public works, has been revised in recent years in light of his responsibility for the deaths of thousands of Indigenous peoples and his promotion of slavery.

In the wake of the George Floyd protests during the summer of 2020; a group of protestors made a concerted effort to pull the statue down. They were stopped by police, who were pelted by frozen water bottles, firecrackers, and other items in the fray. Several officers were severely wounded. Rather than placing a twenty-four-hour guard at the statue, the city pulled it up in the dead of night, and the mayor created a commission on public monuments to review the Columbus statue and other potentially problematic monuments around the city.

At this writing, the statue is still not back on its pedestal, and it may be some time before a decision is reached on what to do with it. On the lakefront near Soldier Field stands a Roman column that was a gift from the Fascist government of Italy in the 1930s. It still remains—but with a fence around it.

McCORMICK PLACE

McCormick Place is the largest convention center in North America, with over 2.6 million square feet of exhibit space. It is hard to miss from the Drive as you pass by. It consists of four interconnected buildings and one indoor arena sited on and near the shore of Lake Michigan, about two miles south of downtown Chicago. McCormick Place has hosted numerous large trade shows and meetings over the decades and normally serves about three million visitors per year. The Lakefront Trail runs between the lake and the back of the Lakeside Center, the oldest of McCormick Place's convention facilities, dating from 1971.

PART FOUR: THE SOUTH SIDE

The South Side of Chicago is immortalized in song and story as being the tough part of town and often thought by individuals who do not know the city to be a place where tourists should not travel. But to miss it would be to only know half of the story of Highway 41 in its traverse through Chicago. A newspaper for the area, *The Daily Southtown* (now published by the *Chicago Tribune*) has had a popular slogan "People Up North Just Don't Get It." On your travel itinerary make time to see the South Side. By special note, I am a former "South-Sider," having raised a family and worked in what is considered the South Side of the city.

Chicago addresses are divided into north, south and west sides, although there is a very small east side close to the lake. **Madison Street** in downtown Chicago is the dividing point between north and south addresses, but the South Side really begins at Roosevelt Road, the south border of Grant Park. From there, the South Side stretches to the Indiana border (where U.S. 41 leaves Chicago and Illinois) and beyond to 138th Street, Chicago's southern border. The South Side has historically been the more industrial region of the city. It was also where the largest concentration of African Americans first lived when they came north during the Great Migration.

South of McCormick Place, at 2600 S. Martin Luther King Jr. Drive, is the **Monument to the Great Northern Migration**, a bronze figure by sculptor Alison Saar that honors the thousands of African Americans who migrated to Chicago in the early twentieth century. Many fine books have been written about that era. If you want to learn more. I highly recommend *The Warmth of Other Suns: The Epic Story of America's Great Migration* (2010) by Isabel Wilkerson.

VIGNETTE   THE SOUTH SIDE HISTORIAN

Dempsey Travis (1920–2009) was a real estate entrepreneur and civil rights activist who became a prominent historian later in life. A World War II veteran, he founded the Travis Realty Corporation, a successful property development firm on Chicago's South Side. He participated in the Civil Rights movement and served as a coordinator of Dr. Martin Luther King Jr.'s 1960 March on Chicago, one of the first civil rights marches in the nation. Travis worked with presidents Johnson, Nixon, and Ford on urban housing issues. Travis was also a noted author who published over twenty books, including An Autobiography of Black Chicago (1981) and An Autobiography of Black Politics (1987), both considered to be among the best chronic-

les of the African American experience in Chicago.

THE SOUTH LOOP

The large area known as the **South Loop** begins at Ida B. Wells Drive and extends south to McCormick Place. It encompasses historic **Printer's Row**, a neighborhood that once was the location of numerous printing companies, and **Dearborn Station**, a former train station with an iconic clock tower.

In the early 1970s, South Loop was one of the first areas on the south side of the city to gentrify, and it contains a number of interesting, rehabbed buildings. Michigan Avenue and Roosevelt Road in the South Loop now have some of the tallest residential buildings in the city. Two terrific entertainment venues here are the **Jazz Showcase** (within Dearborn Station) and **Buddy Guy's Legends**, a blues club on Wabash Avenue.

Along Michigan Avenue within the South Loop are three classic old hotels. **The Congress Plaza Hotel & Convention Center**, across the street from the Auditorium Theater, was built in 1893 to house travelers visiting the World's Columbian Exposition. **The Blackstone**, built in 1910, was the site of the "smoke filled room" where Republican leaders and party brokers met secretly to nominate Warren G. Harding as their party's candidate for president. **The Hilton Chicago**, built in 1927, was once the largest hotel in the world that continues to host many events. The hotel was also the location of the infamous confrontation between police and anti-war protesters during the 1968 Democratic National Convention.

Across the street from the Hilton on Michigan Avenue is the prominent **General John Logan Monument**, which commemorates a Civil War commander from Illinois. The bronze statue sits atop a staircase. If you climb up to the statue, you will be rewarded with a nice view of the city and Grant Park.

South of Roosevelt Road in the South Loop is the **Prairie Avenue Historic District**. At the founding of the city, Prairie Avenue was where the wealthy lived. One of the most significant homes in the district is **Glessner House**, designed by architect H. H. Richardson. Glessner House was saved from the wrecking ball in 1996 by a dedicated group of people who formed what is now the **Chicago Architecture Center**.

General Logan and skyscrapers, Grant Park, Chicago, IL

BLUES TRAIL

The Great Migration brought numerous African American musicians to Chicago who changed the face of modern music. A plaque memorializing the **"Blues Trail: Mississippi to Chicago"** is located at the corner of Michigan Avenue and Roosevelt Road, just west of the Drive. The long-ago Central Station was located here. It was where musicians such as Muddy Waters, Howlin' Wolf, and Willie Dixon arrived from the south by train in the 1940s and 1950s, bringing a new sound that was immortalized as Chicago Blues. The blues, gospel, soul, jazz, and early rock and roll music have significant ties to Chicago's South Side.

Another plaque at 2120 S. Michigan Avenue honors the location of **Chess Records**, the label that pioneered recording and marketing African American artists. Today, you can tour historic **Chess Studio**, which is located inside the home of the Blues Heaven Foundation. More recently, Chicago House Music (electronic dance music), hip-hop, and heavy metal have all had South Side roots. *See the At a Glance section at the end of this chapter for some notable Chicago-area musicians and writers.*

COMMEMORATIVE PLAQUES

Along the Lakefront Trail south of McCormick Place before 31st Street Beach is a memorial to the 1919 race riots, which were triggered by the beating death of Eugene Williams. Williams was an African American kid swimming in Lake Michigan on a hot summer day when he passed through an imposed but not physical barrier at the time to an area frequented by white bathers. A riot ensued that spread much farther than the beach. Numerous individuals, mainly African Americans, died in one of the more painful pieces of city history. The repercussions of that incident are still reverberating in the city.

In the redeveloped South Loop neighborhood across the railroad tracks from Soldier Field at 18th and Calumet Avenue, a plaque honors another site of violence—the 1812 Fort Dearborn massacre, where settlers fleeing the fort were slain by the Potawatomi. Left untold until relatively recently are the numerous incidents triggered by the military officers and settlers against the Potawatomi that contributed to the massacre.

DOUGLAS TOMB AND BRONZEVILLE

Located past 31st Street Beach on the west side of the road at 35th Street (accessible from the Lakefront Trail by a pedestrian bridge) is the **Douglas Tomb State Historic Site**. Stephen Douglas was instrumental in the early development of the city of Chicago. Though he is known mainly for the Lincoln-Douglas debates where he took the side of states' rights to keep slavery, Douglas lost to Lincoln in the 1860 presidential election, which triggered the Civil War. Not boasting the greatest legacy, this historic site is rarely visited and is little noted by current residents of the area.

Highway 41 proceeds south along the lakefront. Just inland is the historic **Bronzeville** district. Bronzeville was the business and cultural hub of the South Side African American community for decades during the years when segregated housing policies prevented people of color from moving to many areas of the city and suburbs.

Urban renewal and lack of investment caused the area to decline for many years, but Bronzeville is now being redeveloped with new restaurants and rehabbed housing. Tour the area to see several architectural landmark buildings including **The Forum, The Wabash YMCA, The First Church of Deliverance,** and **S.R. Crown Hall (Illinois Institute of Technology College** of **Architecture**). The annual **Bud Billiken Parade**—the largest African American parade in the United States—is held each August in Bronzeville.

HYDE PARK, KENWOOD

Continuing south on the road will bring you to the neighborhoods of **Hyde Park** and **Kenwood**. Lovely old homes and apartment buildings grace this area where the University of Chicago (total enrollment 17,000) is located. One of the most highly selective and renowned academic institutions in the country, the university has had 100 Nobel Prize winners and is famous for economics, law, and science. The university is located along the **Midway Plaisance** (locally known as the Midway), which was also the location of the 1893 Columbian Exhibition. Nowadays, much of the Midway offers soccer and other game fields and an ice skating rink.

Some of the many interesting things to see on and near the Midway include:

THE CHENEY-GOODE MEMORIAL

An old limestone bench is tucked under the railroad embankment at the east end of the Midway Plaisance. It looks across at the Obama Center, currently under construction. The bench is covered in black paint and is flanked by a stand that once supported a sundial. The bench bears a very faded inscription: *"Leaders who devoted their lives to the civic betterment of their neighborhood, city, and state; Katherine Hancock Goode 1872–1928; Flora Sylvester Cheney 1872–1929."*

Goode and Cheney were nationally renowned women who worked for women's rights and civic improvements during the period when the 19th Amendment, which certified women's right to vote, was ratified and added to the U.S. Constitution. Goode and Cheney were also political crusaders in Illinois who fought corruption and pushed for honest elections. In their honor, the **Cheney-Goode Memorial** bench was dedicated in 1932 to become the focal point of a memorial garden dedicated to Goode's and Cheney's "righteous indignation against special privilege and the exploitation of the helpless." Unfortunately, the garden was never planted, and the bench has been covered in graffiti over the years. Hopefully, a restoration can be made one day.

THE MASARYK MEMORIAL

The **Masaryk Memorial**, sculpted by Albin Polásek, is a large statue of a knight on horseback honoring Czechoslovakian statesman and scholar Tomáš Garrigue Masaryk (1850–1937). He led his country to independence during World War I and went on to serve as the first president of Czechoslovakia from 1918 to 1935. Earlier in his life, Masaryk spent time in the United States as a visiting professor of Slavic Studies at the University of Chicago.

THE CARL VON LINNÉ (LINNAEUS) MONUMENT

Near the university, the **Carl von Linné Monument**, sculpted by Frithiof Kjellberg, features a bronze statue of the Swedish botanist atop a granite base. Linné (1707–1778) is known as the Father of Taxonomy. As portrayed in this statue, he holds the flower he identified, *Linnaea borealis*, which became Sweden's national flower. One of his books is tucked under his arm. The monument was erected in Lincoln Park in 1891 to honor the Swedish community and moved to the University of Chicago in 1976.

HARPER LIBRARY AND ROCKEFELLER MEMORIAL CHAPEL

Across the street from the Linné monument are two beautiful university buildings, the **William Rainey Harper Memorial Library** (1912) and **Rockefeller Memorial Chapel** (1928). The library honors the first president of the University and was built in the "College Gothic" style then prevalent on many campuses. (College Gothic was a style using Gothic Revival architecture for college and high school buildings in the United States in the late nineteenth and early twentieth centuries). The Rockefeller Chapel shares the same Gothic style. Within the chapel is the **Laura Spelman Rockefeller Memorial Carillon**. Fashioned with seventy-two bells and a hundred tons of bronze, it is the single largest musical instrument ever built.

INSTITUTE FOR THE STUDY OF ANCIENT CULTURES & ROBIE HOUSE

Steps away from the Memorial Chapel is the **Institute for the Study of Ancient Cultures (ISAC)** (formerly the Oriental Institute). It is not a huge museum, but it's a terrific place to see artifacts from ancient civilizations.

ISAC displays archeological artifacts from many excavations, including some outstanding pieces from ancient Egypt and North Africa.

Across the street from the ISAC is the **Frederick C. Robie House**, completed in 1910 and one of the masterpieces among Frank Lloyd Wright's Prairie style houses. You can tour the house, but it's best to book ahead of time to assure access.

THE FOUNTAIN OF TIME

At the end of the Midway is the **Fountain of Time** by sculptor Lorado Taft (1860–1936). While you may have to dodge some traffic, the fountain is well worth your time to see. Considered to be Taft's masterpiece, the sculpture is one of Chicago's most significant historic public works of art. It's a little worn from the elements, but is a detailed and interesting work. The monument is composed of a cloaked figure of Father Time looking over a reflecting basin towards a wavelike procession of 100 human figures. Babies and children are on the eastern end. Soldiers, workers and lovers are in the center, and elderly figures are at the western end defining the arc of life.

Taft spent more than a decade on the project, which he described as "his best thought." He was inspired by a poem by Henry Austin Dobson entitled "The Paradox of Time." The poem includes the following repeating couplet: "Time goes, you say? Ah, no: Alas! Time stays; we go!"

"Fountain of Time," sculpted by Lorado Taft, George Washington Park, Chicago, IL

WASHINGTON PARK

Located beyond the Midway and the Fountain of Time is **Washington Park**. It's a huge, beautiful park that encompasses lagoons, nature areas, athletic fields (including cricket pitches), a pool, an arboretum, and two excellent museums: the **DuSable Black History Museum and Education Center** and the **Smart Museum of Art**. Although, unfortunately, the park does not get the volume of visitors it deserves due to the negativity too often associated with the South Side, it is well worth visiting.

PROMONTORY POINT

On the lakefront side of the Drive, accessible through a pedestrian tunnel, is **Promontory Point**, a scenic peninsula and picnic area that juts into Lake Michigan. One of my all-time favorite places on Earth to walk around, its spectacular city views are much to be admired. Created by the Works Progress Administration in the 1930s, there is a beautiful Alfred Caldwell field house where numerous weddings are held. "The Point" was added to the National Register of Historic Places in 2018. A limestone revetment adds to the beauty of the place.

JACKSON PARK & GRIFFIN MUSEUM OF SCIENCE AND INDUSTRY

A stoplight on the Drive at 57th Street puts you in front of the magnificent **Griffin Museum of Science and Industry**, originally the Palace of Fine Arts in the 1893 World's Columbian Exposition and now one of the largest science centers in the country. It offers constantly changing exhibits and popular permanent ones, including a German submarine from World War II, an accurate facsimile of a working coal mine, and a huge model railroad. If you go to this museum, plan on spending most of the day—and you may want to go on a day when there are fewer school visits.

Close behind the museum are beautiful blossoming cherry trees with an authentic Japanese garden known as **Garden of the Phoenix**. This hidden gem in the city is very beautiful and well maintained. The garden was a gift to Chicago from Japan for the 1893 World's Columbian Exposition. The museum and gardens are part of **Jackson Park**, a large expanse with an eighteen-hole public golf course, ball fields, a marina, and lots of parkland, including **57ᵗʰ Street Beach** and **63ʳᵈ Street Beach**. Near the **Jackson Park Golf Course** and **Jackson Park Inner Harbor** is a gilded bronze sculpture by Daniel Chester French titled ***The Republic***. It was dedicated in 1918 to commemorate the 25ᵗʰ anniversary of the 1893 World's Fair. The sculpture was restored in 1992 to celebrate the fair's 100ᵗʰ anniversary.

Statue of the Republic, Jackson Park, Chicago, IL

THE OBAMA PRESIDENTIAL CENTER

Jackson Park is also the location of the upcoming **Obama Presidential Center**, a project developed to commemorate the presidency of Barack Obama. The center will house a museum, a library, and more. Barack and Michelle Obama still maintain a residence in the nearby Kenwood neighborhood, although they are seldom there. As with all things close to the lakefront, the building of the Obama Center was mired in controversy due to its location on public parkland. The center is expected to become a major tourist location when it opens its doors—an event anticipated for 2026.

SOUTH SHORE

DuSable Lake Shore Drive ends in Jackson Park, as Highway 41 turns into Marquette Drive and then into South Shore Drive. **The South Shore Cultural Center Park** is located on the lake side of this road. Formerly a restrictive, private club that did not allow African Americans, the 1916 Cultural Center building is now a public and National Landmark. A nine-hole golf course, the **South Shore Golf Course**, lies directly along the lakefront. The grounds also include **South Shore Beach**, picnic areas, and a stage that hosts many arts productions. Within the Cultural Center is the **Oak Room** where private catered events are held, and **NAFSI**, a fine dining restaurant that serves soul food. The Chicago Police Department maintains its horse stables here as well.

South Shore Cultural Center, Chicago, IL

From the Cultural Center, U.S. 41 enters a more residential area in the **South Shore** neighborhood. Close by the lakefront are some lovely homes and one of the city's oldest garden park areas. The **Rainbow Beach Victory Garden** was created during World War I as an urban vegetable and herb garden to contribute to the war effort. The garden continues the tradition of

233

urban farming on the Chicago lakeshore and was featured by former First Lady Michelle Obama in her 2012 book, *American Grown: The Story of the White House Garden and Gardens Across America.*

Rainbow Beach, a large expanse with beautiful views of the Chicago city skyline is located here. This beach was once a place of racial conflict as more African Americans moved into the area. A plaque commemorates the 1961 "freedom wade-in" that effectively brought integration to the beach. South Shore is now a largely African American community that has suffered from disinvestment, leaving it vulnerable to increased crime.

Jackson Park Highlands is a historic district tucked into the South Shore neighborhood just south of Jackson Park Golf Course. Featuring some large homes that date from the early twentieth century, this lovely area is virtually unknown except to its residents.

ADDITIONAL AREAS OF INTEREST NEAR U.S. 41

Avalon Regal Theater is a classic 1927 theater in the Avalon Park neighborhood with a beautiful interior designed with a Moorish theme. Unfortunately, it is still in a state of disrepair and needs much work before it can once again be used by the community. Check out the mural on the side of the building.

The Nation of Islam National Center and Mosque Maryam is the headquarters of the Nation of Islam (NOI), located on Stony Island Avenue in the South Shore neighborhood. The NOI is a controversial religious and political organization, founded in 1930 to advocate for Black nationalism and self-improvement.

Oakwood Cemetery lies just beyond South Shore in the **Grand Crossing** neighborhood. Covering 187 acres, Oakwood is the final resting place of several famous Chicagoans, including Harold Washington, Ida B. Wells, Jesse Owens, and Enrico Fermi. The cemetery features a mass grave and memorial for Confederate prisoners of war from Camp Douglas called the Confederate Mound.

Additional South Side neighborhoods to see include **Woodlawn, Chatham,** and **Englewood**; however, I would suggest you take a tour with an experienced guide. Several tour operators offer Chicago South Side Tours.

HIGHWAY 41 RELOCATION

In 2013, a new configuration of Highway 41 was built. The highway once again took the name South DuSable Lake Shore Drive as it was extended from 79th Street to South Harbor Drive just west of the Calumet River. This changed the route of Highway 41 from the residential streets it once traveled to a large space of open land that was once the U.S. Steel South Works. Opened in 1882, the foundry closed in 1992 and was demolished soon after, providing access to the lakefront that was previously off-limits.

Many different ideas have been put forward over the years about ways this area, which is as large as the Chicago Loop, could be better utilized, but it remains distressingly vacant. If you have a bike, it's a fascinating ride around this largely vacant tract of land. A massive ship dock, left over from the former steel mill, has been transformed into a climbing wall as part of **Steelworkers Park**, which now occupies part of the site. This park also includes walking paths that wind among interesting artifacts from its former industrial era.

"Tribute to the Past," sculpture by artist Roman Villarreal,
Steelworkers Park, Chicago, IL

In the summer of 2024, plans were made public for what will be called the **Illinois Quantum & Microelectronics Park** to be developed on the former U.S. Steel South Works site. The campus will be anchored by PsiQuantum, a Palo Alto, California, company, which plans to build the nation's first commercially useful quantum computer at the site. The 440-acre campus will be completed in phases over a four-to-six-year period. If all goes according to plan, the site is projected to have a $50 to $65 billion economic impact upon the region and create thousands of jobs. After many years of promises to develop the area, this one might actually occur.

SOUTH CHICAGO

The surrounding residential neighborhoods in this part of the city are known collectively as **South Chicago**. It's a working-class area that once housed the families of those who worked in the nearby steel mills. Physically cut off from the rest of the city by the Calumet River makes this area feel like an entirely different place. For that reason, I suggest you spend a little time exploring a place that very few tourists to the city ever see. The homes and streets of this blue-collar area have seen little change over the years.

In a neighborhood called **The Bush**, where Highway 41 formerly traversed and which fronts the former steel mill location, a chunk of land is still being remediated for the slag buried underground. Generations of African Americans and immigrants from Eastern Europe and Mexico who worked in the steel mills called this area home. On 91st Street is **Our Lady of Guadalupe Church**, the first Mexican parish established in the city. A memorial located beside the church honors the many individuals from the neighborhood sent to fight in the Vietnam conflict and other wars. **The National Shrine of St. Jude**, the saint of impossible causes, is also located next to the church. Past Steelworkers Park, just off U.S. 41, is the **Urban Growers Collective**, a Black and women-led non-profit farm.

Leaving South Chicago, Highway 41 crosses the **Ewing Avenue Draw Bridge**, built in 1913 over the Calumet River, where the road enters the **Illinois International Port District**, also known as **Iroquois Landing**. This is where the **Port of Chicago** is located. Ships entering the port area can berth at facilities along the Calumet River to Lake Calumet.

Years ago, I worked in the shipping industry with customers who utilized the port to move goods into the Great Lakes and through the St. Lawrence Seaway to the Atlantic Ocean and points beyond. While commerce still moves through the area, the port has declined from its heyday from the 1960s to the early 1980s.

A links-style golf course called **Harborside International** has been developed on some of the port land. The marshy area adjacent to the port is now a nature preserve around **Big Marsh Park**, which features an off-road bike park and areas for hiking and bird watching. Make a point of turning west on 95th Street (U.S. 20), just across the 95th Street bridge and stopping at the tiny **Calumet Fisheries** shack for smoked fish-another hidden gem in the big city.

SIDE TRIP TO PULLMAN NATIONAL HISTORICAL PARK

A great side trip is only a few miles away to the west of U.S. 41 on the South Side. Go west on 95th Street to South Stony Island Avenue and turn left (south). Turn right (west) at 111th Street and enter the **Pullman National Historical Park** and the **A. Philip Randolph Pullman Porter Museum**. Ensure to leave time to walk around the Pullman neighborhood. Pullman was a planned industrial community created in the 1880s to house workers at the nearby Pullman Railroad Car factory. The area figures heavily into labor history and became a National Historical Park as of December 2022. *Author's Note: My wife and I were married at the historic* **Greenstone Church** *in Pullman and had our wedding reception nearby at the* **Hotel Florence**.

CALUMET PARK

Back on the road, Highway 41/South Ewing Avenue passes the fieldhouse at **Calumet Park**, listed on the National Register of Historic Places. The park dates from 1905 and has lots of open land to stroll around. Its vintage fieldhouse was erected in 1924 and is known as **Calumet Park Cultural Center/Fieldhouse. Calumet Park Beach** is a small bathing area next to the **U.S. Coast Guard Station**, both within the park and just outside its southern border you'll pass the **Calumet Yacht Club**. The very next point of interest is the Illinois–Indiana border, which leads to the next chapter in our story.

Pullman National Historical Park, Chicago, IL

OTHER CHICAGO NEIGHBORHOODS, SUBURBS

There are so many interesting places to visit within the vast Greater Chicago region. Ideally two weeks, or if you can make multiple trips, will give you the opportunity to really see and experience the city.

Here are some recommendations:

CHICAGO NEIGHBORHOODS

- **Chinatown/Bridgeport:** Chinatown boasts great restaurants and shops for browsing. From its original boundaries, Chinatown spilled over into Bridgeport, formerly an Irish American enclave but far more diversified in recent years. The Chicago White Sox play at **Guaranteed Rate Field** in Bridgeport (locally known as Sox Park). The field has good food as ballparks go but it is surrounded by parking lots. The team is investigating moving to a different location.

- **Pilsen:** Chicago's large Latin American community is scattered throughout the city, but one of its beating hearts is the Pilsen neighborhood with its colorful murals and the **National Museum of Mexican Art**. The area has become more redeveloped due to its proximity to the Loop, so it is quite diverse. Check out the landmark music venue **Thalia Hall** for concerts.
- **West Loop:** Once a decaying industrial area, the West Loop is now one of the hottest neighborhoods for young professionals. Boasting many cutting-edge restaurants and new construction for residences and businesses makes this an attractive location to live and work.
- **Wicker Park/Bucktown/Logan Square:** These collective neighborhoods add up to a hipster's paradise. Plenty of restaurants, bars, and nightlife, these neighborhoods are trendy places to live in and visit.
- **Beverly/Morgan Park:** Located on the far southwest side of the city, these adjacent residential neighborhoods feature many historic homes. This is where to see the annual **South Side Irish St. Patrick's Day parade**, which is the largest community-based St. Patrick's Day parade outside of Ireland.

SUBURBS

- **Oak Park:** Frank Lloyd Wright's home and many homes he designed are here in this mecca for architecture buffs. The **Unity Temple** on Lake Street is one of his masterworks and is a UNESCO World Heritage Site.
- **Riverside:** This upscale community was the first planned suburb in the United States, designed in 1869 by Calvert Vaux and Frederick Law Olmsted who designed New York City's Central Park. It features a beautiful public library and a number of historic homes.

CONCLUDING THOUGHTS

"Yet once you've come to be part of this particular patch, you'll never love another. Like loving a woman with a broken nose, you may well find lovelier lovelies. But never a lovely so real."

—Nelson Algren, *Chicago: City on the Make* (1951)

Chicago has been called the last great American city. Unlike its counterparts on the east and west coasts of the United States, Chicago is a crossroads where experimentation is the norm. For more than a century, people have come to this city from all over the world and all walks of life to make a go of it. There is nothing more interesting to me than to see people walking the lakefront speaking dozens of different languages. The city has endured difficult times and sometimes curious leadership but remains a place where interesting things can occur. And that is why people continue to call the city home.

Author's Note: On May 8, 2025 the worldwide Roman Catholic Church elevated Cardinal Robert Prevost to become Pope, the first American to have that position. Pope Leo XIV, as he is now known, was born and raised on the South Side of Chicago and the adjoining suburb of Dolton. Pope Leo is now one of the most famous individuals with Chicago ties. And he is a White Sox fan!

AT A GLANCE: CHICAGO LISTS AND RESOURCES

FAMOUS CHICAGO CHEFS AND RESTAURANTS

- Grant Achatz, "Alinea"
- Curtis Duffy, "Ever"
- Rick Bayless, "Frontera Grill"
- Stephanie Izard, "Girl & the Goat"
- Sarah Grueneberg, "Monteverde"
- Paul Kahan, "The Publican"
- Joe Flamm, "Rose Mary"
- Erick Williams, "Virtue"

CHICAGO MUSICIANS

Classical: CSO Conductors–Riccardo Muti, Sir Georg Solti, Fritz Reiner, Pierre Boulez, Daniel Barenboim

The CSO orchestra is one of the great classical orchestras in the world.

Gospel: Thomas Dorsey, Mahalia Jackson, Sallie Martin, Albertina Walker

The Chicago Gospel Festival is an annual event that takes place in early June.

Blues: Ma Rainey, Big Bill Broonzy, Muddy Waters, Howlin' Wolf, Willie Dixon, Tampa Red, Buddy Guy (still alive and kicking with his own Blues joint), Bo Diddley, Elmore James, Big Walter Horton, Little Walter, Sonny Boy Williamson II, Charlie Musselwhite, Paul Butterfield, Junior Wells,

James Cotton, Koko Taylor, Siegel-Schwall Band, John Lee Hooker

Blues Record Producers: Chess Records, Alligator Records

The **Chicago Blues Festival** is an annual event that takes place in mid-June.

Jazz: King Oliver, Jelly Roll Morton, Louis Armstrong (who hit it big first in Chicago before moving to New York), Jimmy McPartland, Bix Beiderbecke, Benny Goodman, Gene Krupa, Earl Hines, Von Freeman, Ramsey Lewis

The **Chicago Jazz Festival** is an annual event that takes place in late August.

R&B/Soul: Sam Cooke, Curtis Mayfield, Lou Rawls, The Staple Singers, Mavis Staples, Earth Wind & Fire, Rufus (Funk Band), Chaka Khan, The Chi-lites, Jennifer Hudson, Chuck Berry

Pop: Quincy Jones, Nat King Cole

House Music: Frankie Knuckles, Ron Hardy, Hot Mix 5

Rock: Chuck Berry, The Buckinghams, Chicago, The Shadows of Knight, The Cryan' Shames, The Ides of March, New Colony Six, Styx, Survivor, REO Speedwagon, Cheap Trick, Veruca Salt, Liz Phair, Urge Overkill, The Smashing Pumpkins, Wilco, Neko Case, Umphrey's McGee, Steve Albini

Folk: John Prine, Steve Goodman, Jim Post, Bonnie Koloc, Bob Gibson, Fred Holstein, Win Stracke, Sons of the Never Wrong, Art Thieme

Hip-Hop: Kanye West, Common, Chance the Rapper, Vic Mensa

CHICAGO LITERARY AUTHORS OF NOTE

Studs Terkel, Gwendolyn Brooks, Lorraine Hansberry, Nelson Algren, Carl Sandburg, Saul Bellow, Richard Wright, Joe Meno, Sara Paretsky, Rebecca Makkai

CHICAGO MOVIES

- *The Beginning of the End*, 1957
- *Medium Cool*, 1969
- *Cooley High*, 1975
- *Looking for Mr. Goodbar*, 1977
- *The Blues Brothers*, 1980
- *Risky Business*, 1983
- *About Last Night*, 1986

- *Ferris Bueller's Day Off*, 1986
- *The Untouchables*, 1987
- *Backdraft*, 1991
- *The Fugitive*, 1993
- *Hoop Dreams*, 1994
- *While You Were Sleeping*, 1995
- *My Best Friend's Wedding*, 1997
- *High Fidelity*, 2000
- *Road to Perdition*, 2002
- *The Dark Knight*, 2008

BOOKS ABOUT THE CITY (A SHORT LIST)

- *A Raisin in the Sun*, Lorraine Hansberry
- *AIA Architecture Guide to Chicago*
- *Chicago*, Dominic Pacyga
- *Chicago's Lake Shore Drive*, Bernard Judge and Neal Samors
- *Chicago: City on the Make*, Nelson Algren
- *Chicago: A Novel*, Brian Doyle
- *Chicago*, David Mamet
- *Chicago Poems*, Carl Sandberg
- *City of the Century*, Donald Miller
- *Encyclopedia of Chicago*, Edited by James Grossman, Ann Durkin Keating, Janice Reiff
- *The Adventures of Augie March*, Saul Bellow
- *The Jungle*, Upton Sinclair
- *Sister Carrie*, Theodore Dreiser
- *The Devil in the White City*, Erik Larson
- *The Great Believers*, Rebecca Makkai
- *The House on Mango Street*, Sandra Cisneros
- *There Are No Children Here*, Alex Kotlowitz
- *The Third Coast: When Chicago Built the American Dream*, Thomas Dyja

CHAPTER SIX
INDIANA

"A lot of smart young people have come out of Indiana. The smarter they are, the faster they come out."

— *George Ade*

Highway 41 through Indiana is 282 miles.

Key Towns/Cities: *Hammond, Schererville, St. John, Kentland, Attica, Rockville, Terre Haute, Sullivan, Vincennes, Princeton, Evansville*

Indiana Counties along 41: *Lake, Newton, Benton, Warren, Fountain, Parke, Vigo, Sullivan, Knox, Gibson, Vanderburgh*

Indiana Counties nearby 41 that are worth visiting: *Vermillion, Tippecanoe, Montgomery, Posey*

Author's Note: Part of the journey on Highway 41 in Indiana is through an area where I grew up, northern Lake County. Although some nostalgia may enter into the descriptions of this part of the journey, my goal is to paint a realistic picture of the present.

Crossing the border with Illinois, Highway 41 in Indiana runs 282 miles due north and south skirting the western border with Illinois for its entire length. Prior to the complete installation of Interstate 65 in the 1970s, it was the main road of travel to and from the Chicago area for points south.

Beyond the far reaches of the Chicago Metro area as you drive south on the highway, you will see a number of large grain elevators. This area of the road is dominated by agriculture. If you are driving in the summer along this route at dusk, stop and admire the sunset over the fields of corn and soybeans. A brief note on agriculture: much of the central portion of Indiana is cropland. Thanks to millions of years of glaciers, swamps, and decay, some of the richest black topsoil on Earth, rich in nutrients and organic matter, is situated here, leading to high crop yields. Indiana ranks fourth in the country in the production of soybeans, and the state is the nation's fifth-largest corn producer. These two cash crops make up approximately sixty percent of the agricultural products sold by the state. There are just over 55,100 farmers in the state, with the average age of a farmer being fifty-seven years old. The average farm size in Indiana is about 269 acres.

Bodies of water are prevalent along the route in Indiana. Highway 41 crosses the 981-mile-long Ohio River into Kentucky just south of the city of Evansville. At the northern end is the forty-five-mile-long Indiana shoreline of Lake Michigan. Running parallel to Highway 41 for much of its length, the 503-mile-long Wabash River forms part of the state's boundary with Illinois. The Wabash enters the Ohio River, which has shifted boundaries over time, leaving a small portion of the state of Kentucky north of the river.

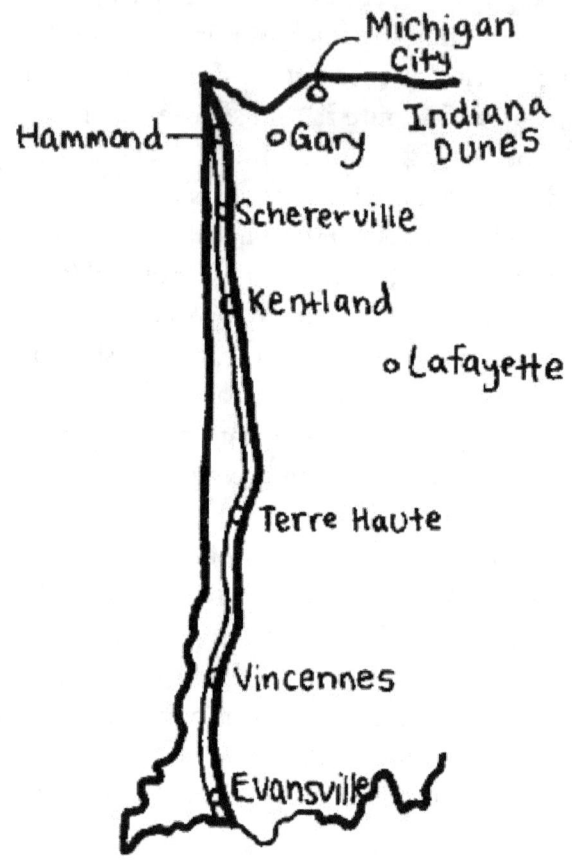

AN INDIANA ALBUM PLAYLIST

- John Mellencamp: *Mr. Happy Go Lucky* 1996
- John Mellencamp: *Scarecrow* 1985
- Michael Jackson: *Thriller* 1982
- Cole Porter: *It's De Lovely—The Authentic Cole Porter Collection by Cole Porter* 2004
- Guns N' Roses: *Appetite for Destruction* 1987
- Hoagy Carmichael: *Hoagy Sings Carmichael with the Pacific Jazzmen* 1956
- Janet Jackson: *Rhythm Nation 1814* 1989
- Wes Montgomery: *The Incredible Jazz Guitar of Wes Montgomery* 1960
- Kenneth "Babyface" Edmonds: *Face2Face* 2001
- Freddie Hubbard: *Red Clay* 1970
- The Jackson 5: *ABC* 1970

HISTORICAL PERSPECTIVES

Western Indiana has an abundance of early American history. Indigenous peoples had long settled the area prior to the arrival of the French in the 1600s. The Shawnee, the Miami, the Wea, the Potawatomi, the Illinois, and many others traversed and established outposts in the area. Several state parks near the highway provide information on and recognition of Indigenous settlements.

The Battle of Vincennes, also known as the Siege of Fort Sackville, was fought during the American Revolution in 1779. This American victory over a British garrison secured the western territories for the new republic. American commander George Rogers Clark is celebrated with statues and a large memorial building in the city of Vincennes.

In 1811, the Battle of Tippecanoe was fought near present-day Lafayette between American troops led by William Henry Harrison—who later became a U.S. president—against Indigenous nations associated with the Shawnee leader Tecumseh and his brother Tenskwatawa, better known as "The Prophet." The American victory resulted in the end of Indigenous control of the Indiana territory. Significant settler populations soon arrived from the south to populate the territory, which became a state in 1816.

During the American Civil War, several small skirmishes were fought near the Ohio River. The Newburgh Raid, perpetrated by Confederate partisans in 1862 near Evansville, led to a permanent force of Union soldiers being stationed in Indiana.

Several points near Highway 41 were part of the Underground Railroad, which enabled many fugitives from slavery to escape to the North. Safe houses were established in Evansville, Terre Haute, Merrillville, and other towns. Due to the extreme secrecy surrounding routes and stations (or houses associated with Underground Railroad), much research has been performed in recent years to uncover this history.

In the 1800s, American settlers established numerous farms to take advantage of the fertile land. Over 220,000 farms had been established in the state by 1900. Farming towns were established along the path of the highway to provide for the needs of a largely rural population that has declined over the decades.

Coal was discovered on the banks of the Wabash River in 1736. Coal is abundant in southern Indiana, thanks to a geological formation known as the Illinois Basin. Proximity to urban-industrial markets of the Middle West, electric power utilities, and the steel industry contributed to the growth of coal mining in the region until the 1950s, when power sources shifted from coal to oil and natural gas. Environmental regulations and a current shift toward cleaner energy alternatives have further reduced the need for coal in recent years. Coal is essential to the production of steel. The high-capacity factor and consistent heat rate in coal gives steel its strength, which is important for its use in infrastructure and automobiles. A number of towns along Highway 41 owe their existence to the presence of coal mines and served to house the miners.

In the early twentieth century, large steel mills were established along Lake Michigan. Iron ore was transported by rail from the Lake Superior region to lake ports. From there it was transported by ore boats to mills in Chicago, Gary, and other Great Lakes cities. Large numbers of immigrants from Germany, Poland, and other countries in Eastern Europe arrived to work in the mills. They were followed by individuals from Appalachia and African Americans who arrived from the south in large numbers from 1930 to 1950 during the Great Migration to work in the mills and other factories in the area. The mills thrived until the 1970s when production from overseas and a continued use of outdated steel-making processes led to a long decline.

Investments in new technologies stabilized production in the 1990s, but the new methods required fewer individuals to operate the mills. The steel industry remains important in Indiana in a reduced form.

Many manufacturing operations were created in Indiana over the decades, and a number of them are associated with the transportation industry. The state has one of the highest levels of employment in manufacturing in the country, but it is lagging in productivity according to recent reports. The state needs to attract, develop, and retain skilled talent with advanced training in areas such as automation and artificial intelligence to avoid losing new manufacturing opportunities. This requires increases in the wage rates paid to Indiana factory workers, as they are well behind the national average.

LIBRARIES

One of the good things about travel through western Indiana on Highway

41 is the number of historic local public libraries located in small towns. Many are "Carnegie" libraries, funded by the philanthropic gifts of Andrew Carnegie between 1900 and 1920. Carnegie funded the construction of more libraries in Indiana than in any other state in America. This may have had to do with state legislation act passed in 1895 that allowed local entities to levy a tax for libraries. Typically, the Carnegie libraries were built in the Neoclassical Greek or Roman styles or in Craftsman-Prairie Tradition styles. Many of Indiana's Carnegie libraries are listed on the National Register of Historic Places as well as on the Indiana State Register of Historic Sites and Structures.

IDENTITY

Indiana's official motto is "The Crossroads of America." Unofficially, some residents will add that you can't really travel anywhere more interesting in the country without having to pass through or fly over Indiana. Many well-known individuals have grown up in Indiana and then left for greener pastures. The state remains a draw for people from elsewhere due to affordable housing and a low cost of living relative to its neighbors.

"Hoosiers," the nickname for residents of the state, are generally friendly and aware that their state is often perceived as a "flyover state." Nevertheless, the "Hoosier State" lives in the imagination of many as full of apple-cheeked, quirky people in idyllic small towns, who are tolerant, sports-loving, and primarily white and middle class with a few minorities in the mix. Think of the TV shows *Parks and Recreation* (2009–2015) and *The Middle* (2009–2018). While some of that myth actually exists, the reality is far more complicated.

VIGNETTE HOOSIERS

People from Indiana have been called "Hoosiers" for well over a century and a half. While the origin of the term is not known with certainty, the most serious study of the matter was conducted by Jacob Piatt Dunn Jr., the long-time Secretary of the Indiana Historical Society.

Dunn noted that hoosier was frequently used in many parts of the South in the nineteenth century to identify woodsmen or rough hill people. Dunn traced the word back to hoozer in the Cumberland dialect of England. In this dialect, the word meant anything unusually large, such as a hill. Thus, hoozer was attached to a hill dweller or highlander. As Cumberland descendants immigrated to the hills of Southern Indiana, they brought with them the name Hoosier. Hoosiers bear their nickname proudly. Many generations of Hoosier achievements have endowed the term with connotations that are strong and friendly.

BY THE NUMBERS

Indiana is estimated to have a population of 6.84 million as of 2024 up from 6.75 in 2020 and 6.1 million in 2000. In 1980, the population was 5.5 million. The 2020 Census showed that the state population continues to diversify with twenty-five percent of Hoosiers now identified as part of a minority or ethnic group. Most of the urban population (approximately two million) is concentrated in the Indianapolis metropolitan area and northwest Indiana near Chicago (831,000). Evansville (115,000), in southwestern Indiana, is the largest population center Highway 41 passes through in the state.

LAKE COUNTY AND THE REGION

The journey through the Indiana portion of Highway 41 actually starts in Illinois, at the southeast border of Chicago. The old nineteenth century factory neighborhoods of the **East Side, The Bush, Hegewisch,** and **South Deering** are cut off from the rest of the city by the Calumet River. The area was home primarily to Hungarians, Czechs, Poles, and Ukrainians in the early part of the twentieth century and later Mexican immigrants became the primary residents. Now these neighborhoods are mostly populated by Central American Latinos on the first rung of the ladder of American immigrant experience.

The **Calumet Region,** or simply "the Region," has no fixed boundaries, but it roughly incorporates the area around the Grand Calumet and Little Calumet Rivers. (*Calumet* is said to come from French interpretations of the Potawatomi name for the rivers). On the Illinois side of the state line are some suburbs adjacent to Chicago: the tiny village of Burnham (a reputed Al Capone hangout) and the towns of Calumet City, Lansing, and South Holland. On the Indiana side are the cities and towns of Gary, East Chicago, Hammond, Highland, Griffith, Munster, Merrillville, Schererville, Hobart, Whiting, Crown Point, Dyer, Saint John, and Valparaiso. The area has been heavily industrialized since the 1890s, with steel mills, oil refineries, chemical plants, automobile factories, and an assortment of other manufacturing clustered along the south shore of Lake Michigan.

For centuries before European contact, this swampy area was the sparsely populated home to the Miami, Potawatomi, Kickapoo, and Shawnee. The politicians who created the state line between Illinois and Indiana from the Northwest Territories in the early 1800s had little regard for the geography or demographics of the area. They simply drew a line extending some 200 miles from near the tip of Lake Michigan south to the Wabash River, which separates the two states and acts as a border. U.S. 41 runs almost straight south on the Indiana side of the border, but it is so close to Illinois that the term *Illiana* can encompass the two states' close geographic proximity.

For many people in metropolitan Chicago and individuals driving through on I-80/90 to points east or west, the Region is a forty-five-mile endurance test through Indiana on heavily traveled highways dominated by trucks and seemingly always under construction. True Chicagoans' eyes will glaze over when conversation turns to Indiana—it might as well be a million miles away except for the casinos, gas stations, firework stands, tobacco stores, and lower taxes luring some businesses and individuals to the Indiana side of the border.

Lake County, **Indiana**, where most of the Region is located, has always been different from the rest of Indiana. Its proximity to Chicago—a city that many Hoosiers despise and envy at the same time— as well as its heavy industry, diverse population, blue-collar labor workforce, and historically Democratic political control has always pegged Lake County as an anomaly within Indiana. This is changing as an influx of new residents from Illinois settle in south suburban Lake County. The Region is in the Central time zone and is considered part of the Chicago Metro area, but remains a world apart from its gigantic neighbor and distinct from the rest of Indiana. Highway 41 is the only north-south highway from one end of Lake County to the other.

The Region also personifies "The Rust Belt." Once upon a time, its heavy industries provided lots of employment opportunities for immigrants and African Americans. Racial tensions, plant closings, and economic decline hollowed out the formerly thriving downtowns of Gary and Hammond in the 1960s and 1970s. Many individuals in the northern part of Lake County moved farther south to suburban areas and the formerly agricultural parts of Lake County during the "white flight" of the 1970s and 1980s. Commercial development followed, and formerly small farm towns have grown in population and density.

The Region now is a place of economic contrasts: Gary, Hammond, and East Chicago have endured years of decay and stagnation as heavy industries required ever fewer blue-collar workers. Meanwhile, southern Lake County has become more similar to other suburban bedroom communities of Chicago. Envisioning this, the Northwest Indiana Commuter Transportation District (NICTD) is constructing the West Lake Corridor Commuter Rail Project, an eight-mile southern branch extension of the South Shore Commuter Rail Line through Hammond, Munster, and Dyer. It will provide direct commuter rail service from Chicago to the high-growth areas of central and southern Lake County, Indiana with the intent of operating trains by mid-2025.

THE BOUNDARY MARKER

To see the location of the original **boundary marker** between Illinois and Indiana, take Highway 41 in Chicago to 100th Street and go under a railway underpass. From there, follow old brick streets to Chicago's **Calumet Park** along Lake Michigan. Keep walking or riding south past Calumet Yacht Club. That will bring you to a small stone column. This is the boundary marker, erected in about 1830 and believed to be one of the oldest standing objects in the two states. Time, wind, development, nearby railroad tracks, and isolation make the marker something that you must find your way to. The marker indicates it is 159.359 miles due north from the Wabash River.

The marker has been refurbished and moved a short distance to just outside a former power plant that opened in 1929, closed in 2012, and eventually demolished to make way for a state-of-the-art data center called **Digital Crossroad**, which provides fiber assets to create connections for the internet. All that is left of the former coal-fired power plant is the Art Deco entrance. Now you can freely walk all the way to the water's edge. Huge United States and Indiana state flags fly above the shore. The only way to the marker and this "park" of sorts in Indiana is via streets in Chicago.

Illinois-Indiana state line boundary marker, between Chicago, IL and Hammond, IN

VIGNETTE   VIEWING THE MARKER

In a 2022 summer visit to the marker, I observed a cement sidewalk that was being created around the obelisk for viewing purposes. A skinny, shirtless worker was setting up the location for concrete to be dropped. We had a brief conversation—he reminded me of my cousin—and we talked about how remote the marker is and, of course, why two states so much alike suddenly are very different. Says he, "I was talking to two Chicago cops, and I said, 'Hey, if I step over here can I carry my gun?'" (Indiana allows the open carry of guns if individuals meet certain criteria. Chicago *and Illinois have very strict gun laws). He did not say how the cops answered. We walked around in the brush trying to find the original placement point for the marker but came up empty. It is a pretty barren location.*

There is a bikeway next to the facility. The **Marquette Greenway** starts here. It is a sixty-mile bike path to Michigan that follows the shoreline of Lake Michigan, but this is not a beautiful part of the lake. While the industrial area around the Lake Michigan is slowly receding, it still has an "edge of the earth" feel. In the wintertime "the Hawk,"— the icy-cold damp wind that blows into the city off of Lake Michigan—whips in cold and gray.

Back on the highway, U.S. 41 becomes Indianapolis Avenue through the heavily Latino "East Side" neighborhood of Chicago. This area is brimming with war memorials for the sons and daughters who served and died in the armed forces. The population here is blue-collar and ethnic. Long ago, the multiple steel mills nearby supplied employment, but all of the mills on the Illinois side were closed and demolished decades ago. This is hallowed ground for organized labor, with an annual Memorial Day event held by the United Steelworkers to commemorate the ten protesters killed by Chicago police outside Republic Steel's plant as the company attempted to break a strike for better pay and working conditions. A plaque in the Chicago neighborhood of Hegewisch honors the victims.

Overhead looms the **Chicago Skyway**, an elevated toll road connecting I-94 (Dan Ryan Expressway) in Chicago to I-90 (Indiana Toll Road). The Skyway includes a 125-foot-high bridge crossing the Calumet River. Built in 1958, the Skyway was operated by the City of Chicago until 2004 when it was sold by the city in a ninety-nine-year lease arrangement. The buyer subsequently sold it in 2016 to a group of Canadian Pension Funds. In 2022, the Australian toll road operator **Atlas Arteria Ltd.** entered an agreement to acquire a majority stake in the Chicago Skyway for more than $2 billion. Tolls for the Skyway have risen repeatedly since the city leased it to private operators. Cars paid $2 in 2004. The toll as of 2025 is $7.80.

The Skyway merges into the Indiana Toll Road (I-90), which becomes I-80 farther east. The **Indiana Toll Road** is also privately owned by investors under the auspices of the **ITR Concession Company LLC**. These public-private partnerships were considered a major means of getting infrastructure developed, but they often have failed to live up to agreements regarding maintenance and repair.

HAMMOND & WHITING

U.S. 41 begins its Indiana journey across the state line through the city of **Hammond** neighborhood known as Robertsdale. Several gas stations, smoke shops, fireworks shops (legal in Indiana), and a Walmart greet you as you enter. Train tracks abound—this is a heavily traveled section of railway for freight and passengers. The highway skirts by the **Horseshoe Casino** in Hammond. There is a purpose-built road directly to the casino. The casino is "a boat" permanently moored in Lake Michigan and greatly expanded since arriving in 1996. Casinos are also based in neighboring East Chicago and Gary, and there is an effort to bring a casino to Calumet City, which adjoins Hammond. The Horseshoe brands itself as the closest to downtown Chicago, and at present, it is until one is built in the city. The casino is also the largest private employer in Hammond and one of the largest employers in the state. Two venerable Region restaurants closed as the casino became the sole destination point: **Phil Smidt's** (2007), famous for its frog legs, and **Vogels** (1997), known for its perch. Residents of the area still lament their demise.

There is a small marina and beach on this section of Lake Michigan; long ago it was completely inaccessible and polluted. Odors from the **Lever Brothers** soap factory and the **Cargill** plant (once called American Maize), where corn syrup is processed, can still be redolent. There is less visible pollution than there was decades ago, but heavy industry still retains a grip here.

Just a few blocks east of Hammond is the small city of **Whiting**. Not far away is the **BP Whiting** refinery, first established by Standard Oil of Indiana in 1889. It is the sixth-largest refinery in the United States. Whiting hosts a well-attended annual summer festival called **"Perogie Fest,"** a nod to the Polish dumpling and to the many Poles and other East European immigrants who settled here in the early 1900s to find work on the railroads and in steel mills.

NEARBY POINTS OF INTEREST

Farther east of U.S. 41 lies **East Chicago**, where there is another giant steel mill now called **Cliffs Indiana Harbor,** and **Gary**, "the Steel City"created by U.S. Steel Corporation in 1906 and the hometown of Michael Jackson, Janet

Jackson, and the "Jackson 5" family before they became famous and moved to California in 1969. Railroads, factories, and the interstate complete the picture for travelers new to the area. This part of the Region is a hardscrabble place, mostly populated by descendants of the Polish, Slavic, and Lithuanian cadres, followed by African Americans, Mexicans, and Central Americans.

I suggest taking an interesting side trip to **Marktown**, a historic English-style village designed by Howard Van Doren Shaw in 1917 as an urban-planned workers' community in East Chicago. It is surrounded by heavy industry. The Marktown Historic District was added to the National Register of Historic Places in 1975.

VIGNETTE   STEVE TESICH AND FOUR FRIENDS

Steve Tesich (1942–1996) was a Yugoslav-born playwright and an Academy-Award-winning screenwriter who settled in East Chicago with his family when he was fourteen. He is best known for two very fine films, Breaking Away (1979) and The World According to Garp (1982). But his homage to the Region is the film Four Friends (1981). Set during the turbulent 1960s, it traces four high school friends as they become adults. Directed by Arthur Penn, it is well worth watching.

Heading a bit farther east to the heavily used **Indiana Dunes National Park** is well worth your time. Three key individuals saved the Dunes from destruction: Senator Paul Douglas of Illinois; Henry Cowles, a University of Chicago botanist; and Dorothy Buell, a resident of the area and an English teacher. On February 15, 2019, Congress authorized the name change from Indiana Dunes National Lakeshore to Indiana Dunes National Park (Public Law No: 116-6; written into House Joint Resolution 31), making it the nation's 61st national park. The park has multiple trails, two excellent beaches, and several restored homes that were originally built for the 1933–1934 Chicago World's Fair Century of Progress, and moved to the Dunes area by barge. An annual tour of these homes occurs each September. Note: in between portions of the national park is **Indiana Dunes State Park**, with three miles of beach, nature trails, and the restored 1930s-vintage **Dunes Pavilion.**

HAMMOND

Highway 41 proceeds south through Hammond and becomes Calumet Avenue along **Wolf Lake**. This area is cut off geographically from the rest of the city. The Indiana Tollway is overhead with marshes, light industry, and franchise stores at street level. The challenging **Lost Marsh Golf Course** was carved out of the marsh in 2013. Since 2004, the city of Hammond has put on the **Festival of the Lakes** with musical entertainment, food, and carnival rides each July.

Hammond once had a thriving downtown with department stores, movie theaters, and businesses. Little but the buildings still remain in the downtown area; many saw the wrecking ball in the 2000s. A downtown revitalization plan to breathe life into the area has been introduced with a "prosperous sustainable community" as the end goal. Among the old buildings that have survived is the Art Deco **Hammond City Hall**, dedicated in 1935. The city population has been depleted from its high point in the early 1960s when it reached 111,000.

School closings and consolidations have occurred as the population continues to decrease. A new high school (Hammond Central) was recently built to replace the former Hammond High, whose building dated from the 1920s.

Like many old former industrial cities, Hammond is trying to find a new identity. There is less pollution now than there once was, but increasing poverty rates, high unemployment, and declining neighborhoods of modest homes built to house factory workers means a struggle as the city figures a way forward. How does a city that rose with a manufacturing economy, producing all kinds of products people needed, cope in a world where those operations have been made obsolete by new technologies? The larger homes in Hammond that housed factory managers and professionals were clustered at the far south end of the city near the Illinois border, and they remain desirable locations to live within the city. Edison School, my grammar school in Hammond many years ago, was demolished in 1992 and rebuilt. I once lived just down the street from the school.

Jean Shepherd (1921–1999), author, humorist, and narrator of the perennial Christmas movie, *A Christmas Story*, grew up in Hammond before making his way to fame and fortune in New York City. He was best known for penning several best-selling books about his childhood in the town of "Hohman," as he called it. Shepherd described his hometown as "a place people never really come to but mostly want to leave." Another great description of Shepherd's is (Hohman) "clings precariously to the underbody of Chicago like a barnacle clings to the rotting hulk of a tramp steamer."

A jog in Highway 41 shifts you to Interstate 94 for one exit before the off-ramp returns you to Indianapolis Boulevard. It's not much of a boulevard these days. There is a big **Cabela's Outdoor** store and a **Walmart** big-box store. Hammond Gavit High School, now closed, was once considered one of the best high schools in the country.

VIGNETTE INDIANA HIGH SCHOOL BASKETBALL AND TWO LIVES

Long before the 1986 movie Hoosiers, the state of Indiana was associated with boys' high school basketball. Until 1997, there was a single class elimination format, which meant that every school in the state, regardless of its size, had a shot at winning the state championship. The term "Hoosier Hysteria" had much to do with the boys' state tournament that took place in March. (Girls' basketball in the state was quite popular in the early decades of the twentieth century, but it fell on hard times during the Great Depression. It was revived when Title IX went into effect in 1972).

Two of the finest championship teams to ever come out of the Calumet Region were from the city of East Chicago in consecutive years: E.C. Roosevelt High School in 1970 and E.C. Washington High School in 1971. Roosevelt's star player was Jim Bradley, who went on to play at Northern Illinois University and then for Kentucky and Denver in the old American Basketball Association. Sadly, Bradley's life was cut short in 1982 when he was found dead in an alley in Portland, Oregon, shot in the back in a drug-related deal. Washington's star player was Ulysses "Junior" Bridgeman (1953–2025), who went on to play at the University of Louisville, followed by a twelve-year career in the National Basketball Association, mainly with the Milwaukee Bucks. After retiring from basketball, Bridgeman went on to an extremely successful business career. He was a billionaire and one of the wealthiest former athletes in the United States at the time of his passing.

SUBURBAN LAKE COUNTY

Highway 41 crosses from Hammond into the town of **Highland**. Long ago, a fish-and-tackle store and an old fishpond would greet you here, along with a parking lot for the bus to Chicago airports. **Wicker Park Golf Course** is along the way.

Wicker Park Pool, where I learned to swim, was demolished in 1993. For many years there was a prominent Christ figure at the entrance to Wicker Park Pool. Across the street were department stores, which now house an antique mall. What to do with empty department stores is a problem in much of the country.

Continuing east on Ridge Road (U.S. Highway 6) brings you into downtown Highland. Highland was once visited by President Calvin Coolidge and many years later by candidate Barack Obama, who won the usually Republican state of Indiana in the 2008 election and went on to the presidency. Highland was once home to the **Town Theatre**, a quirky movie house that showed foreign films and other independent offerings—pretty spicy stuff for a blue-collar town. At intermission, audience members would go in the lobby to have coffee and cake. The theater owner sat there with his dog to greet the moviegoers. Sadly, the theater was demolished in 2018.

Continuing west on Ridge Road takes you to **Munster**, the wealthiest community in Lake County and the town where I went to high school. Munster is home to lots of physicians, lawyers, and middle managers at the nearby factories. For many years it was all white—a small town initially composed of emigrant Dutch truck farms and, later, tract homes for returning veterans of World War II and the Korean War. Munster grew as white flight brought in new residents from Gary, Hammond, and farther afield, including the Chicago neighborhoods of Roseland, Pill Hill, and South Shore. The town now has a large hospital and all kinds of ancillary medical establishments serving the increasing numbers of elderly retirees who have opted to age in place. Back in the early 1960s, Munster had a Cold War era Nike missile base on the town's outskirts. I had no idea that missiles were in place at the base to deter a nuclear attack less than a mile from where we lived until many years later.

The **Highway of Flags Serviceman Memorial** sits at the Corner of Ridge Road and Highway 41. It opened in May 1975 and was the brainchild of Mary Lou Kieswetter, "the Flag Lady." There once were governor proclamations framed on the back of the memorial, including one by then Georgia Governor Jimmy Carter, proclaiming Highway 41 to be the "Highway of Flags." All the proclamations vanished long ago. Mary Lou established the National Council for the Encouragement of Patriotism, which disappeared at the time of her passing in 2012.

A few blocks farther down Indianapolis Boulevard is **Jansen's Blue Top**, an old-fashioned drive-in with car hops serving the customers. Blue Top was famed for its multitudes of high school cruisers and still retains a clientele of aging baby boomers with classic cars.

Just down the street from Blue Top is **Miner-Dunn**, a hamburger diner established in the Depression and little changed in decades. You can still sit at the counter and get the "Hungry Steelworkers" lunch order of burgers, fries, and a little sherbet dessert. A row of stores along this part of U.S. 41 have closed as the population has steadily moved south for housing and land.

New restaurants for new times have opened along the highway, offering Chinese, Hispanic, Korean, and East European foods. A shopping center has been established as the population continues to sprawl from the old cities to the north. Traffic becomes thicker along this stretch with several strip malls containing stores, restaurants, and hotels as Highway 41 intersects with U.S. 30, **"The Lincoln Highway,"** through the town of **Schererville**, which bills itself as the "Crossroads of the Nation." It's the first of many Indiana towns along the north-south route through the state that call themselves a crossroads. Population growth in the formerly small farm towns of Schererville, Dyer, and St. John has accelerated, and what was once available land is now built up with homes.

Through **Dyer**, just east of Highway 41 on U.S. 30, is a road that is called **Sauk Trail** in Illinois. Sauk Trail is an ancient Indigenous trail that ran from Rock Island, Illinois, on the Mississippi River to Detroit, Michigan, near the western shore of Lake Erie. **Tiebel's Family Restaurant**, in business since the 1920s, is located at the crossroads of U.S. 41 and U.S. 30. Tiebel's was the place to come for a special occasion: a birthday, an anniversary, Mother's Day, etc. It still serves great fried chicken and perch, but most recent patrons are grey-haired. **Tandoor Indian Cuisine**, a newer restaurant close by, serves East Indian food, illustrating the more diverse population of Lake County. **Sauzer's Kiddieland** amusement park used to lie across the highway from Tiebel's. When I was a child, I enjoyed the rides in this little park, and so did my children, decades later. Alas, it closed in 1993. Highway 41 has had more recent development south of U.S. 30 with many chain stores now lining the road.

The road continues into the town of St. John, where the **Shrine of Christ's**

Passion sits right along Highway 41. Heavily advertised on roadside billboards, the shrine is a stop for the faithful from around the country, and it is definitely worth stopping even if you are not religious. You know you are there when you see the thirty-three-foot-tall "Our Lady of the Millennium" statue near the entrance. You'll pass through a gift shop replete with every type of Christian religious item that you can think of for sale. There are a number of statues and sculptures on display outside. Somber music plays in the background, accompanied by narration by Bill Kurtis, a former Chicago television newscaster. A prayer loop can be followed around the shrine. Entry is free, and the shrine is open at all times.

St. John is now a Chicago "exurb" with numerous homes built on former cornfields. The local population rose from 4,000 in 1980 to 21,000 in 2022. There are many real estate signs with housing developments within sight. As St. John and Schererville grew, a 1989 newspaper article emphasized the need to redevelop Highway 41 or face a "potential traffic nightmare." This is similar to many roads designed decades ago, and little has changed. But everything around these roads has changed. Today, signs indicate construction to widen U.S. 41 to accommodate the influx of heavier traffic.

Proceeding farther down the road, you will pass by **Great Oaks Banquets**. It's now an events restaurant, but in the past, it was a nursing home, a supper club, a factory for leather harnesses, and, most famously, for a spell in the 1970s, a drive-in theater showing X-rated films. Nearby was a go-kart shop and **Cedar Lake**, a small lake packed with revelers, many quite drunk, on any weekend in the 1960s and 1970s. The surrounding town of **Cedar Lake** now has many new housing developments and more upscale homes surrounding the lake. Nearby **Lake Dalecarlia** is a human-made lake created in the 1930s and dotted with surrounding cottages.

Highway 41 next passes by the town of **Lowell**, which is named after Lowell, Massachusetts. The town features a number of antique stores and the Three Creeks Monument, an old statue honoring soldiers from long ago wars. Lowell has grown of late as a far exurb of metropolitan Chicago. It has a Labor Day parade and a Legend of Sleepy Hollow event each September. The strip malls finally end just outside of Lowell, and the farmland begins. If you take the trip in the winter or early spring, the horizontal nature of the vacant surroundings is surreal.

At the southern end of Lake County is the tiny town of **Schneider**, just north of the Kankakee River. Schneider is an old railroad town. You can be on the community's one main street and see no one at all. If you really want to get away from it all, Schneider could be the place.

NEWTON COUNTY

Moving out of Lake County, Highway 41 crosses the Kankakee River into **Newton County**, home to a large nature and wildlife preserve. While this area is still considered the far exurbs of the Chicago metropolitan area, the scenery becomes decidedly more rural. The county has a total area of approximately 400 square miles and a demographic breakdown that is over ninety-five percent white. Within its boundaries there are a number of interesting sights and the area of some strange events.

WILLOW SLOUGH AND WILDLIFE AREA

Willow Slough and Wildlife Area near the town of Morocco provides habitat for several plant and animal species, as well as offering outdoor recreational activities for visitors. At the center of the property is a reservoir called J.C. Murphey Lake, which was created in 1951 to provide a resource for migrating waterfowl. The fish and wildlife species and recreational opportunities are currently declining due to degrading habitat quality and, as such, a renovation began in March 2022 enabling conservation-minded patrons opportunities to volunteer in fish salvage, lakebed clean-up, and fish structure construction. The renovation project was completed in 2025 with fish restocked for recreational use.

KANKAKEE SANDS

The **Kankakee Sands** are 8,400 acres of prairies and wetlands, owned and managed by the Indiana chapter of the Nature Conservancy. The land was once part of the Grand Kankakee marsh system and has been referred to as "the Everglades of the North." There is a PBS documentary of the same name describing the rich history of the land that is well worth watching. https://www.pbs.org/video/the-story-of-the-grand-kankakee-marsh-evt7wb/

More than 600 species of native plants thrive in the prairies of the Kankakee Sands. As a result, abundant native wildlife, including more than

240 bird species, 70 species of butterflies, and 900 species of moths are found in the habitat. Dragonflies, bees, frogs, lizards, snakes, badgers, and bison all hover, slither, and roam at Kankakee Sands.

Here, you can also see bison, brought back to roam the prairie much as they did before white settlers came to the area. The Bison Viewing Area is open from 7:00 a.m. until dusk, and rangers are available by appointment to answer questions. If you have never seen buffalo up close, this is your opportunity.

Buffalo herd on the Kankakee Preserve, Newton County, IN

LaSALLE FISH AND WILDLIFE AREA

LaSalle Fish and Wildlife Area provides outdoor recreational opportunities while maintaining 4,511 acres of hardwood forests, marshes, and open water. The property is dominated by wetlands that lie along the Kankakee River that attract migratory birds. Popular activities include hunting, fishing, birding, hiking, and kayaking.

SUMAVA RESORTS

Along this stretch of Highway 41 is a community known as **Sumava Resorts**. It was established in 1926 and named for the "Bohemian Forest," which is called the "Sumava Forest" in the Czech Republic. Czech immigrants from Chicago once traveled to the resort by train for the weekend or for extended summer stays. It's a bit down at the heels now. The proximity of the resort to the **Kankakee River** resulted in major flooding in 1950, 1967, and 1976, while a 1993 levee break forced a more encompassing intervention. Ultimately, the U.S. Army Corps of Engineers constructed a $7 million dollar dike around the entire community, eliminating future flood risk.

ROSELAWN

Just east of Highway 41 is the town of **Roselawn**, known primarily for the two ongoing nudist resorts—the **Ponderosa Sun Club and Sun Aura**—operating within its boundaries. Decades ago, Sun Aura was known as "Naked City" in the 1970s and early 1980s. It was managed by Dick Drost (1920—1996) who fancied himself a competitor to Hugh Hefner and put on a Ms. Nude America pageant for several years. Naked City was closed in 1986 after Drost was convicted on several counts of exhibition of an obscene performance, offering to distribute obscene matters, displaying matters harmful to minors, and sponsoring an obscene performance depicting a person under the age of sixteen years, the last being a Class D felony.

Among the more curious roadside attractions along Highway 41 is the **Giant Lady's Leg Sundial** at Sun Aura. It is sixty-three feet long and positioned to tell time for nudists. If you want to take a picture of the leg, the front desk will let you come to the camp during business hours and you don't need to take off your clothes!

THE HIGHWAY KILLER

Farther down the road is the little town of **Lake Village**, which boasts a real-life crime drama. On Oct. 18, 1983, two people hunting for mushrooms near an empty barn just north of Lake Village came across the decomposed body of a young man. Investigators later found three more bodies of young men buried in shallow graves nearby. All four victims were connected to Larry Eyler, a serial killer thought to be responsible for the deaths of twenty-three young men in the Midwest. Dubbed "The Highway Killer," Eyler confessed to murdering the four in Newton County but did not know their names. Two victims were quickly identified, and a third was identified in 2021. Four decades later, in July 2023, the fourth victim was finally identified with the use of DNA. Eyler died in prison in 1994.

CONRAD SAVANNA NATURE PRESERVE

A little down the road from Lake Village is the **Conrad Station Savanna Nature Preserve**, a 360-acre sand savanna with black and white oaks growing on rolling sand hills. This preserve physically connects with the Kankakee Sands nature area. In the early 1900s, a small town called **Conrad** was near the present site; it just disappeared in the 1940s. The town was founded in 1908 by Jennie Conrad, a wealthy widow and heiress with a profitable agricultural business over several thousand acres of land. The town had a train depot, a hotel, a post office, a general store, a church, a cement block factory, and several shops. From all accounts, Jennie Conrad was eccentric, interesting, cultured, and traveled, but she was also quite argumentative with neighbors. She patrolled her land on horseback with a shotgun at her side to drive strangers away. When she died in 1939, the town of Conrad pretty much died with her and became a ghost town. Remnants of the town within the forest are all that is left of Conrad.

PEMBROKE TOWNSHIP, ILLINOIS

Across the western Indiana state line is **Pembroke Township**, a historically African American farming community. Founded in the 1860s by fugitives from slavery and one of the poorest communities in Illinois, the locality has many African American families that go back generations. Within the township is the **Pembroke Savanna**, a high quality, large-scale ecosystem of national significance.

ENOS

Back on the highway, which passes through more farmland near unincorporated **Enos**, is the site of one of the more infamous mob hits. In 1986, the bodies of Anthony "Tony the Ant" Spilotro, a high-ranking member of the Chicago Outfit organized crime syndicate in Las Vegas in the 1970s and 1980s, and his younger brother Michael, were found in a shallow grave in a cornfield. They had been beaten to death. The scene was recreated in Martin Scorsese's 1995 film *Casino*. Anthony was the model for the character "Nicky Santoro," and "Dominick Santoro" was based on Michael Spilotro. Some of the details of the murder were also part of the 1990 Scorsese film *Goodfellas*.

VIGNETTE   THE SPILOTRO BROTHERS

Anthony "Tony" Spilotro was a Chicago mobster who was "made man" (a fully initiated member of the Mafia). He relocated to Las Vegas in 1971 to manage the affairs of the "Chicago Outfit" in Las Vegas. While in Las Vegas he formed the "Hole in the Wall Gang" known for drilling through walls to burglarize businesses. Ultimately this would lead to his being blacklisted from casinos and angering the mob bosses in Chicago. Tony's brother Michael, had once aspired to be an actor. He was friends with some noted Hollywood actors of the time. After landing some bit parts, the younger Spilotro brother shifted into bookmaking, drug dealing, prostitution, robbery, and extortion.

The Spilotro brothers did not fare as well in Las Vegas as they did in Chicago. They disappeared on June 14, 1986, from Michael's Oak Park home. On June 22nd, their bodies were found, one on top of the other, stripped down to their underwear and buried near Enos, Indiana. The freshly turned earth had been noticed by a farmer who thought that a poacher had buried the remains of a deer killed out of season there. In 2007, it was determined that the Spilotro brothers were killed in a basement in Bensenville, Illinois, where Michael was going to be inducted into "The Outfit" as a "made man." It was reported in court testimony that Tony realized what was about to occur and requested time to "say a prayer."

This was not the first Hollywood moment for Enos. The unincorporated area is also the supposed location of "Prairie Stop 41," where the famous scene of Cary Grant being chased by the crop duster plane in the Alfred Hitchcock film *North by Northwest* was alleged to be shot. The actual scene was shot near Bakersfield, California, but the fictional location lives on. One clue that gives the actual location away is that the Highway 41 sign in the movie is square. State highways have square signs. Because 41 is a U.S. highway, it is always afforded a six-pointed shield sign.

SIDE TRIP TO FAIR OAKS FARM

To the east of Enos on State Road 14 near I-65 is **Fair Oaks Farm**, a forty-acre agritourism operation that is open every day except Thanksgiving and Christmas. The farm claims to have over 500,000 visitors a year. The founders of the farm, Mike and Sue McCloskey, launched it in 2004 to showcase the practices and innovations of contemporary dairy farming.

The farm is the largest dairy producer in Indiana and one of the largest in the country, producing 2.5 million pounds of milk a day. Cows are milked on small carousels three times a day. The farm also houses a birthing station where visitors can witness calves being born.

The farm also emphasizes environmentally conscious practices such as the conversion of cow manure into energy through the production of methane. According to McCloskey, use of the conversion process "will reduce the amount of diesel that the milk tanker/trailers use by two million gallons in one year."

In 2019, Fair Oaks Farm was in the spotlight after an undercover investigation of abuse and cruelty involving the farms' calves was shown on video. Three former employees were charged, and one was sentenced to a year of probation. Additionally, the McCloskey's took several additional steps to ensure animal welfare: initiating continuous employee training and education, installing cameras where there are human-animal interactions, monitoring camera footage constantly, and hiring animal welfare experts.

MOROCCO

Just down the road from Enos is the town of **Morocco**, with a billboard that says, "Home of Baseball Hall of Famer Edgar "Sam" Rice," a star on the Washington Senators in the 1920s. Check out the memorabilia room in the public library, which features lots of old pictures and trophies from long-ago basketball games. From the town's website: "If you are looking for a small-town living with world-class amenities nearby, you may have found it in the Town of Morocco, Indiana! Let us tell you about our town and all we offer for those who live, work, and learn here."

VIGNETTE   CAR RACING TRACKS

Just outside of Morocco is the **US 41 Motorplex**, *once called "US 41 Dragstrip" and* *recently reopened for business under the new name. The track is one of several car racing tracks that were built along Highway 41 in Indiana. Many were developed in 1940s and 1950s when more people started owning automobiles. Some tracks have disappeared over the years, but several tracks continue such as US 41 Motorplex and the **Tri-State Speedway**, farther south in Haubstadt.*

KENTLAND

The highway passes by the Newton County seat of **Kentland**. The Kentland town motto from their website is "Boldly Moving Forward," indicating that, "We're a fun, small town located halfway between Chicago and Indianapolis, and we are moving forward!" During my visit, it was pretty quiet.

KENTLAND CRATER

The **Kentland Crater**, just outside of Kentland, was first discovered in 1880 by two farmers quarrying crushed rock at the site. By the late 1960s, geologists concluded that the Kentland Crater was caused by impact from a falling object as opposed to the remnant of a theorized volcanic event. Researchers estimate that 980 feet eroded after the initial strike, followed by a shallow deposit of glacial sediment during the Wisconsin Glacial Period, which took place from 70,000 to 11,000 years ago. The impact deformation is so extensive that rock formations from vastly different geologic periods can commonly be seen in similar horizontal planes.

VIGNETTE GEORGE ADE

*Writer and humorist George Ade (1866–1944) was born in Kentland and made millions from his writing and real estate purchases. An 1887 graduate of Purdue University, he continued an association with the school throughout his life, serving on the Board of Trustees and becoming one of the largest donors in the University's history. He personally donated funds for the construction of the university's Memorial Gymnasium and Memorial Union Building. With David Ross, Ade contributed land and funding for the construction of Purdue's **Ross-Ade Stadium**, named in their honor in 1924.*

Upon graduating from Purdue, Ade made his way to Chicago, where he became a reporter for the Chicago Daily News. Ade's reporting style, utilizing everyday language and street slang, endeared him to the public, and he began to experiment with using slang to write stories in fable form. He became a nationally syndicated columnist, offering humorous observations of everyday life. He authored over twenty books and acquired notable fans, including authors Mark Twain and H.L. Mencken. Later, he wrote Broadway plays and helped establish the musical comedy genre.

Ade's writing brought him financial success. He retired to Newton County, where he invested his earnings in farmland. He built a country manor called "Hazelden" in 1904 just outside of the small town of Brook, Indiana, and it became a cultural mecca of the time. Ade initially planned to build a summer cottage on his land, but Billie Mann, a Chicago-based architect and fellow fraternity brother, designed a two story, fourteen-room Tudor Revival country manor for Ade that cost an estimated $25,000 ($858,683 in 2023 dollars). The frame dwelling featured leaded glass windows and beamed vaulted ceilings. Ade made additional improvements including landscaped grounds, a swimming pool, a greenhouse, a barn, a caretaker's cottage and an adjacent golf course and country club in 1910. Hazelden was used for political gatherings (William Howard Taft had a campaign rally here in 1908), parties, community gatherings and golf tournaments.

For forty years, Ade presided over elaborate festivities at Hazelden, including the annual Children's Picnic held each summer for all children under twelve years old from Newton and surrounding counties. This was one of the highlights of community gatherings. Ade died of a heart attack in 1944. He is considered to be one of the greatest writers of the early 1900s, with his fables in slang earning him the nickname of the "Aesop of Indiana." Unfortunately, his works have been largely forgotten in recent decades.

Hazelden is on the National Register of Historic Places, but unfortunately the home and grounds need substantial work, and the memorial association disbanded in 2018. A statue of George Ade sits outside of the home. Next to Hazelden is the George Ade Memorial Health Care Center.

BENTON COUNTY

Highway 41 progresses south into rural and scenic **Benton County**. Located on this stretch of the road is a vast amount of traditional farmland, as well as a number of more contemporary wind farms. The pastoral lands abutting the large turbine windmill farms provide a very interesting visual contrast.

Hazelden and George Ade statue, Brook, IN

Windmills, Benton County, IN

Earl Park (pop. 358) is home to Indiana's first large wind farm. The Benton County Wind Farm began operation in April 2008 and consists of eighty-seven GE Energy 1.5 MW wind turbines.

The Earl Park area is home to many species of wildlife including deer, mink, beaver, badger, heron, pheasant, quail, rabbit, coyote, fox, racoon, opossum, and numerous birds of prey. Its local annual Fall Festival attracts about 45,000 visitors.

VIGNETTE   MATILDE MOISANT AND BARNSTORMING

Earl Park was the birthplace of Matilde Moisant (1878–1964). A pioneer aviator, she was the second woman in the United States to obtain a pilot's license certified by the Aero Club of America. She pursued a career in exhibition flying or "barnstorming." Barnstormers were pilots who traveled the country performing stunt aviation in what were known as "flying circuses." The term **barnstorming** *came about because pilots had to use a local farm as a runway from which to stage an airshow. After securing a field, aviators would fly over the village and drop promotional flyers advertising their performances. In some small towns, the arrival of a barnstormer, or a flying circus, would shut down the town as everyone attended the show.*

Barnstorming drew not only former military men, but also female performers. Bessie Coleman, an African American woman, thrilled audiences with her performances in the air. She used her influence as a celebrity to combat segregation. Perhaps the most well-known barnstormer was Charles Lindbergh. A barnstorming tour in 1923 led him to pursue further formal instruction with the U.S. Army Air Service.

Moisant stopped flying when her plane crashed on April 14, 1912 (the same day the Titanic struck the iceberg), but she was able to recover from her injuries. During World War I, she volunteered at the front in France.

Continuing on Highway 41, you'll pass by the small farm town of **Boswell**. With a population of only 800, the town's nickname is unapologetically the "Hub of the Universe." Unfortunately, there is not much of a town left for the Hub.

The town of **Fowler** is home to the Fowler Ridge Wind Farm, the second utility-scale wind power plant in Indiana. The project was constructed in two phases starting in 2008, and it has a capacity of 600 megawatts.

If you are a vintage movie theater buff, be sure to check out Fowler's cool

Boswell, IN

old movie theater, the **Fowler Theatre**, which first opened on March 1, 1940. It is an Art Deco gem on the prairie. The theater originally seated an audience of 442, but an ongoing renovation has reduced that number to 196. A volunteer-based non-profit called the Prairie Preservation Guild restored every component of the theater, using old photos as a guide. The facade and marquee were restored in 2008, followed by the lobby in 2012. The lobby's original ceiling frieze was restored, and the concessions area is flanked by original glass tube columns backlit with blue and pink neon.

The theater might also be haunted! Very active ghosts are alleged to be roaming its halls. The restless spirits are thought to be those of the original owner of the theater, a manager who committed suicide in 1968, and a child. You can do some paranormal investigations for a fee with a volunteer guide provided by "My Haunted Fowler" after movie showings on Friday or

Saturday evenings. Note that the theater is open only on weekends. Arrangements must be made in advance.

Fowler Theatre, Fowler, IN

SIDE TRIP TO TIPPECANOE COUNTY

To the east of Fowler is State Road 52, which you can take approximately thirty miles to the city of **Lafayette** (pop. 70,000), the seat of Tippecanoe County, and West Lafayette (pop. 56,000), home of **Purdue University**, a Big Ten school with an enrollment at the main campus of over 50,000 students. That makes Purdue the 12th largest university in the United States. Purdue is a land-grant university that was founded in 1869 after Lafayette businessman, John Purdue donated land money to establish a college of science, technology, and agriculture in his name. It is most known for its school of engineering. Purdue has had many illustrious graduates, including twenty-six astronauts. Gus Grissom, one of the original Mercury Seven; Neil Armstrong, the first person to walk on the moon; and Eugene Cernan, the last person to this date to walk on the moon, were all Purdue alumni. Lately, the university has moved aggressively to offer online programs through Purdue University Global.

One block from the University is **Purdue State Bank**. The historic building was designed by Frank Lloyd Wright's mentor Louis Sullivan and completed in 1914. This is the smallest and least expensive of all the "Jewel Box" banks Sullivan designed near the end of his career. The building cost $14,600 ($446,309 in 2023) of which only ten percent was paid to Sullivan. Each of the building's two long sides feature a horizontal row of recessed windows, separated by brick piers and surrounded by a floral band of green ceramic tiles. Typical of Sullivan, the brick parapets each have a single yellow tile that shines with a jewel-like quality.

Louis Sullivan "Jewel Box" Bank, Lafayette, IN

Louis Sullivan designed eight small, rural banks between 1902 and 1920. There are three in Iowa, two in Ohio, and one each in Wisconsin, Minnesota, and Indiana. The "jewel box" nickname given to his first in Owatonna, Minnesota, referred to its modern, box-like shape and its richly ornamented interior.

TIPPECANOE BATTLEFIELD PARK

Nearby West Lafayette and close to Interstate 65 is the town of **Battle Ground**. Located within is **Tippecanoe Battlefield Park & Museum**, a ninety-six-acre picnic and hiking area, historical museum, and home to the **Wah-ba-shik a Nature Center**. While the park is open every day from dawn until dusk, the museum is closed on Wednesdays.

An eighty-five-foot-tall marble obelisk, erected in 1908, commemorates the site of the November 7, 1811, Battle of Tippecanoe between United States forces led by William Henry Harrison and warriors led by Tenskwatawa ("The Prophet"). The museum, which is curated by the Tippecanoe County Historical Association, details the events prior to the battle, the specifics of the actual engagement, and the events after the combat exchange, including the War of 1812 and the election of Harrison to the presidency of the United States.

The **Tippecanoe Battlefield History Store**, located within the museum, has a vast selection of books for readers of all ages on the following topics: 1800s Indiana, military history, and Native American history and culture.

Of the ninety-six acres currently housing the Tippecanoe Battlefield Park, sixteen acres were deeded to the State of Indiana by John Tipton, a veteran of the battle and the general in charge of the forced Potawatomi march from Indiana to Kansas, known as the Potawatomi Trail of Death. He made this donation on November 7, 1836, the 25th anniversary of the battle. The site was used for political rallies, most notably for the presidential candidacy of William Henry Harrison as he capitalized on his involvement in the battle at Tippecanoe. Thirty thousand people were said to have attended his rally there on May 29, 1840.

Despite interest in the location for sesquicentennial of the battle in 1961 (it had been designated a National Historic Landmark in 1960), the site was abandoned in 1971, and the location was neglected for quite some time. A citizen's group acquired the property in 1990 and created the museum, which was extensively renovated in 1995.

POTAWATOMI TRAIL OF DEATH ROUTE

Nearby the museum is a rock with a plaque placed in 1996 memorializing the **Potawatomi Trail of Death Route**. Enforcing the Indian Removal Act of 1830, the U.S. government marched a caravan of 859 Potawatomi at gunpoint 660 miles from Twin Lakes, Indiana, to Osawatomie, Kansas. The journey began on September 4, 1838, spanning over sixty-one days in arid conditions and claiming the lives of forty-two people, twenty-eight of whom were children.

The Trail of Death was declared a Regional Historic Trail in 1994 by Indiana, Illinois, and Kansas, and in 1996, by Missouri. As of 2013, eighty markers were located along the route in all four states, placed every fifteen to twenty miles marking where the group camped each day. Historic highway signs signal each turn along its way in Indiana through Marshall, Fulton, Cass, Carroll, Tippecanoe, and Warren counties.

PROPHETSTOWN STATE PARK

Next to Tippecanoe Battlefield site is **Prophetstown State Park**, established in 2004 and located where the Tippecanoe River meets the Wabash. The park encompasses the Indigenous village once known as Prophetstown. The park offers such activities as camping, swimming, hiking, biking, birding, and wildlife observation.

WARREN COUNTY

You can return to Highway 41 from Lafayette via State Road 26 or proceed on State Road 25 to connect to 28, which will bring you into the town of Attica. Most of the area between Boswell and Williamsport on U.S. 41 is farmland. About six miles north of Williamsport, you will encounter a turn off for State Road 63—a limited access highway leading south to the city of Terre Haute. State Road 63 is close to the Illinois border and the old manufacturing city of **Danville, Illinois**, birthplace of actors Dick Van Dyke and Gene Hackman and pianist Bobby Short. Past the turnoff for State Road 63, Highway 41 becomes a two-lane road.

WILLIAMSPORT

Williamsport, the Warren County seat, is indeed a crossroads, with U.S. 41; State Roads 28, 63, 55, and 26; as well as Interstate 74 all intersecting in the county. The town was named for General William Henry Harrison in 1828. A ferry operated crossing the Wabash River for several years. The town drew shipping traffic by constructing a spur of the Wabash and Erie Canal to the town in 1852, leading to its nickname, "Side-Cut City." The route followed by U.S. troops under General Harrison to the Battle of Tippecanoe runs through this area.

I suggest you make a stop in Williamsport to see **Williamsport Falls**. Located on the Fall Branch of the Wabash River and accessible by means of an easy hike, it's the highest free-falling waterfall in Indiana. The waterfall flows over a sandstone ledge between the older and new sections of the town. While the flow was forceful enough to support a mill in the nineteenth century, diversion of natural water for farm irrigation has minimized the current volume and energy potential of this natural resource.

Williamsport is also where Indiana native Paul Dresser (1857–1906) wrote the state song and his biggest hit "On the Banks of the Wabash." Dresser was a vaudeville entertainer in New York City before shifting to songwriting. Published in 1897, the song earned comparisons with Stephen Foster's "Old Folks at Home"— also known by the song's first line, "Way Down upon the Swanee River" (the state song of Florida, with revised lyrics in 2008). On this portion of Highway 41 as it spans the Wabash River is a sign identifying the road as the "Paul Dresser Memorial Highway."

VIGNETTE   THE WABASH RIVER

The Wabash is Indiana's most famous river. Located almost entirely within the state, it flows to its confluence with the Ohio River. In addition to being the official state river, the Wabash is also the longest free-flowing river east of the Mississippi. The river is usually muddy and slow moving as it drains much of the state's farmland.

KRAMER

North of Williamsport is the unincorporated village of **Kramer**, where the ruins of the **Hotel Mudlavia** are located. Mudlavia was a grand health hotel built on the site of a natural mineral spring in 1890. The resort was known for the spring water and its mud baths, as well as its spa atmosphere. It targeted middle-class mid-westerners, enticing them to take "the cure," which meant soaking in mud baths. The hotel boasted not only the therapeutic mineral waters and mud treatments, but steam heat, electric lights, call bells, long-distance telephone service, fine cuisine, golfing, and other recreational activities. Transportation was provided to the hotel for

Wabash River, IN

those patrons arriving by rail in the nearby town of Attica. This luxury was novel for health hotels in the day. Guests would often stay for weeks at a time, basking in mud baths as well as enjoying all of the other amenities.

Notable guests such as John Sullivan, Paul Dresser, John Dillinger, and Al Capone were said to have stayed at the hotel before it burned to the ground in 1920. The Great Depression, coupled with medical advances, made it fiscally unsound to rebuild what was once there. However, a newer, smaller structure was later built, succumbing to the same fate as its spacious predecessor. It burned and was abandoned in 1974. You can still see some of the ruins of the old hotel. Although the hotel is gone, water from the local mineral springs is still bottled and sold by Perrier Group of America.

FOUNTAIN COUNTY

Crossing the Wabash River, you'll arrive in the town of **Attica. Harrison Steel**, a steel castings company, greets you on the way with a sign that says "Welcome to Attica. The Place to Be." The historic downtown has many buildings that date from between 1840 and 1942. Unfortunately, there are a lot of vacant storefronts. A bright spot in the old downtown is **Robie's Restaurant & Bar**. This is a good, unpretentious place for lunch or dinner. The bulk of the ongoing retail commerce now lies on the outskirts of the city center where land is available for purpose-built operations.

Attica is the birthplace of George Dewey Hay, founder of the Grand Ole

Opry. "The Solemn Old Judge," as he became known, always made two suggestions for those who appeared on the Opry stage. They sprang from a philosophy inherent in his hometown: "Keep it down to earth," and "make it from the heart."

VIGNETTE DR. JOHN EVANS

Dr. John Evans (1814–1897) was one of Attica's most famous citizens. He lived with his family in Attica from 1838 to 1848 before moving to Chicago. Evans founded the Chicago Mercy Hospital and was one of the founders of Northwestern University. The college town of Evanston, Illinois, was named in his honor. Investments in railroads made him wealthy and politically influential—he was friends with Abraham Lincoln. He was appointed the territorial governor of Colorado in 1862 and used his railroad connections to secure the city of Denver as one of the main stops on the developing transcontinental railroad. Working with Colonel John Chivington, Evans co-founded what is now Denver University. Both Northwestern and Denver University have professorships in his honor.

Evans and Chivington were both implicated in the Sand Creek massacre, which took place in November 1864. Federal troops under Chivington's command attacked Cheyenne and Arapaho bands led by Black Kettle, who were camped peacefully beside the creek. They killed twenty-eight unarmed men and 105 women and children. In 1865, two congressional committees accused Evans of covering up the massacre, and he was forced to resign the Colorado governorship.

Evans spent the rest of his life working to cement the city of Denver as the future hub of the railroad industry. He was instrumental in Denver becoming the commercial capital of the Rocky Mountain region.

As you leave Attica, you will pass by the former Shawnee Bowling Alley. It's disheartening to see old-time bowling alleys close, but unfortunately many have done so over the last few years. The COVID-19 pandemic did not help this trend. Highway 41 from Attica is lightly traveled and passes through lots of farmland. In the summertime, you can see very high corn on one side of the road and soybeans on the other side.

To the east, next to the Wabash River, is the former community of **Fountain**, originally called Portland and established in 1828. The Wabash and Erie Canal formerly passed through the community and was a major conduit of trade for the area's residents. The town once had several stores and a considerable population until the canal was replaced by the railroad in the late 1800s. Next to Fountain is **Portland Arch Nature Preserve**, a state preserve with the largest natural sandstone arch in the state. It is an enjoyable place to hike in a unique environment.

Indiana farmland, Parke County, IN

Portland Arch Nature Preserve, Fountain County, IN

The highway continues through the town of **Veedersburg** at the cross-roads of U.S. 41 and I-74. The buildings are well kept but, again, the community has lots of empty storefronts. Stop by the **Old "41" Diner** in Veedersburg for good food, good service, and a hometown atmosphere.

Old "41" Diner, Veedersburg, IN

SIDE TRIP TO MONTGOMERY COUNTY

Twenty miles to the east of 41 on state road 32 is the city of **Crawfordsville**, the seat of Montgomery County and the site of **Wabash College** (enrollment 840), one of only three all-male liberal arts colleges remaining in the United States. The college played host to one of the earliest intercollegiate basketball games between Wabash and Purdue in 1894 at the city's YMCA.

Crawfordsville was incorporated in 1834 and deemed a desirable settlement partly due to its proximity to Sugar Creek, a southern tributary of the Wabash River. In 1836, the city was nicknamed the "Athens of Indiana" due to its wealth of prominent authors and cultural heritage. Most books written at the town's literary pinnacle are now found only in antiquarian book sellers, with the exception of Lew Wallace's *Ben-Hur: A Tale of Christ.*

VIGNETTE   GENERAL LEW WALLACE

Indiana native Lew Wallace (1827–1905) was a lawyer, a Union general in the Civil War, a politician, a diplomat, an artist, and an author. He wrote Ben-Hur: A Tale of the Christ in Crawfordsville, often working as he sat outdoors during the summer under a favorite beech tree near his home. The tree was later named the Ben-Hur Beech. It was cut down in 1908 after being damaged in a storm. There is a statue of Wallace where the tree once stood.

Published in 1880, the widely translated novel depicts the oppressive Roman occupation of ancient Palestine in parallel with the historical origins of Christianity. Its main character, a young Jewish nobleman, loses his freedom and that of his family because of an injustice by a Roman officer. Judah Ben-Hur eventually triumphs through his own abilities and the intervention of Christ.

The novel's themes of betrayal, conviction, and redemption loosely borrow from Wallace's personal experiences during his command at the Battle of Shiloh on April 6–7, 1862, after which he was relieved of his duty and returned home to Crawfordsville before being once again called to serve in the Union Army. Wallace later became governor of the New Mexico Territory and U.S. Minister to Turkey.

Crawfordsville has twelve properties listed on the National Register of Historic Places, of which three are museums: **General Lew Wallace Study, Henry S. Lane House,** and **Rotary Jail Museum**, which houses the only remaining mechanically operated rotary jail in the country. The Montgomery County Jail was built to house sixteen prisoners, with three cells for quarantine prisoners. The rotary mechanism was disabled in the late 1930s, but in 1975, the Montgomery County Cultural Foundation renovated the structure to create a museum.

The rotary jail was an interesting albeit, highly flawed, concept. The pie-slice-shaped cells rotated around a core with a hygienic plumbing system, considered an unusual luxury in 1881. The cell block could be rotated using a crank, which was connected to gears that rotated the entire cell block on a ball-bearing surface. The rotary jails encountered problems immediately, with inmates' limbs being crushed, sometimes as they sought to deliberately interfere with cell block rotation. Only a few rotary jails were built, but most of them had to be welded in a fixed position and retrofitted with individual cell accesses after only a few years.

The **Montgomery County Courthouse Clock Tower** is also of historic interest. The previous clock tower on the 1876 building had to be taken down in 1941 due to structural concerns.

Investment in Crawfordsville is not just historical. In 1989, **Nucor Steel** broke ground on its first sheet steel mill and galvanizing line at its billion-dollar facility in Crawfordsville. It is home to the world's first thin-slab casting mini mill. In June 2023, Nucor announced that it will build a second state-of-the-art production facility adjacent to its original steel mill. It is expected to create 200 full-time jobs in a highly automated, advanced galvanizing operation to support renewable energy projects such as a nationwide network of EV charging stations.

PARKE COUNTY

Continuing south into **Parke County** is an area known for its covered bridges and the **Parke County Covered Bridge Festival**, Indiana's largest festival. This event is held in mid-October and attracts many thousands of visitors. Parke County calls itself the "covered bridge capital of the world," with thirty-two covered bridges that are visible time capsules from another era. This is one of the prettiest parts of the drive on the Indiana portion of Highway 41.

Historic Mecca covered bridge, Mecca, IN

TURKEY RUN STATE PARK

A short distance from the town of **Kingman** is a turnoff for **Turkey Run State Park**. Indiana's second-recognized state park is a beautifully scenic recreational area. You can hike, canoe/kayak, tube, horseback ride, traverse a suspension bridge originally built in 1917 over **Rocky Hollow Falls Canyon**, view historic structures (including covered bridges), and even lodge overnight. Turkey Run lies in the traditional territory of the Kickapoo, the Peoria, the Potawatomi, and the Miami. First France and then Great Britain, through the Treaty of Paris of 1763, claimed control of the area from these Indigenous nations.

The region's first white settler was Salmon Lusk, who migrated from Vermont. Lusk, who served under William Henry Harrison at the Battle of Tippecanoe in 1811, received a tract of land at Turkey Run in 1825 as compensation for his military service. The **Lusk Home and Mill Site** is but one of the structures within the park that is listed on the National Register of Historic Places.

The **Richard Lieber Log Cabin** (also known as the Old Log Cabin) within Turkey Run was added to the National Register in 2001. Lieber was the conservationist who advocated for the creation of Indiana's state parks system as a permanent memorial to Indiana's centennial anniversary of statehood. After the Lusk family died out, Lieber became involved with preserving Turkey Run in 1916 when he was appointed chairman of the State Parks Memorial Committee of the Indiana Historical Commission. Thanks to Lieber's efforts, the natural environment was preserved.

THE MANSFIELD SANDSTONE

The major physical features of Turkey Run are its rock formations. Known as the Mansfield sandstone, named after Mansfield, Indiana, these rock beds form Turkey Run's cliffs. Over time, erosion has created a stunning display of canyons and gorges. Appreciation of this picturesque natural environment is reflected in the park's popularity: it attracts some 700,000 visitors annually. A walk into one of the ravines takes the visitor on a geological trip through time, with the sandstone walls and gorges displaying 300 to 600 million years of nature's handiwork. Many millions of years ago, flowing water deposited sand, which eventually was compressed into sedimentary rock. Wind and water initially cut into the sandstone, but glacial movement during the ice age shaped the sandstone into observable forms.

As the glacier, which covered the north portion of Turkey Run, melted and deposited debris from the moving ice, stones of many shapes and sizes were ground against the softer sandstone. This constant grinding carved out the Sugar Creek streambed, and remnants of these hard round stones, known as glacial till, can be found in stream beds today. The present formations are very likely what inhabitants viewed throughout the last hundreds of years.

The road winds through forest before coming into the town of **Rockville**, the county seat and very much a place that comes alive at festival time. The fall colors in Parke County are probably the best in the state. Note that visiting in the middle of the week in autumn might help you avoid traffic jams on the weekends from "leaf peepers" eager to see the fall foliage.

The topography of Parke County is also unlike most of this western portion of Indiana. Highway 41 is a winding two-lane road through the county's woodlands. Some pretty agricultural vista overlooks are situated along the road, as are a couple of junkyards. This was also shaft-mining coal country once upon a time, and there are lots of old-time towns along the road. You'll encounter a covered bridge along the way. The **Mecca Tavern** in the tiny town of **Mecca** has been serving tenderloin sandwiches since 1899. Come with an appetite as the tenderloin is quite big.

Jungle Park, Parke County, IN

10 O'CLOCK LINE

Outside of Mecca is a plaque for the **10 O'clock Line**—the boundary agreed upon in 1809 by William Harrison and a consortium of Indigenous nations for almost three million acres of land in what became known as 10 O'clock

Treaty when it was signed in 1810. The 10 O'clock Line is sixteen miles in length. Of the nations, the Miami were the only ones to initially oppose the treaty. Legend has it that, in dealing with Governor Harrison, Miami Chief Little Turtle did not trust the white man's surveying equipment. He would only accept a line created by the shadow of a spear thrown into the ground at ten o'clock in the morning.

The Ten O'Clock Line, Gosport, IN

Mecca Tavern, Mecca, IN

SIDE TRIP TO VERMILLION COUNTY

West of the highway along State Road 63 is the town of **Newport**. Newport's claim to notoriety was the existence of the Army's **Newport Chemical Depot**, where the Cold War VX nerve gas stockpile was located. Originally known as the Wabash River Ordnance Works, the site was built in 1942 by the E.I. Dupont de Nemours & Company. The area was selected due to its labor market, access to water, electricity, rail lines, and its location at least 200 miles away from international borders or coastal waters.

The facility's original purpose was the manufacturing of the military high explosive RDX during World War II. RDX was used in mixtures with TNT for a higher explosive impact. By 1943, the site also added a "heavy water" plant as an element of the Manhattan Project's construction of nuclear weapons. Heavy water was a component of early nuclear energy research.

In 1959, the Army added the Newport Chemical Plant to produce a VX nerve agent. VX is a human-made chemical warfare agent. It is tasteless and odorless. Exposure to VX can cause death. By 1964, the Wabash River Ordnance and the Newport Chemical Plant had merged into the Newport Army Ammunition Plant, where the entire U.S. stockpile of VX nerve agent was produced.

In 1997, when the Chemical Weapons Convention Treaty went into effect prohibiting the development, production, stockpiling, and use of such products, the Newport Chemical Agent disposal facility was created for the sole purpose of destroying the 1,000 tons of chemical agents at this location. The start of operations was delayed for several years until a solution could be found for the disposal of wastewater. Beginning in May 2005, the Army neutralized all of the VX nerve agent, accomplishing the task by August 2008.

Disposal of the gas and deactivation of the base began in 2008, followed by closure in 2010. The town has created an industrial park called the **Vermillion Rise Mega Park** on the old site as well as an endangered species habitat.

DANA

South of Newport, near the state border, is the small town of **Dana**, in Vermillion County. Here stands the house where Ernie Pyle was born.

Ernie Pyle monument marker replica, Dana, IN

VIGNETTE ERNIE PYLE

Ernie Pyle was born on August 3, 1900, in rural Vermillion County to tenant farmers who lacked schooling beyond the eighth grade. Pyle, their only child, aspired to leave the farm as soon as possible and become a globe-trotting journalist. As a roving reporter of human-interest stories for the Scripps-Howard newspaper syndicate, Pyle's column, the "Hoosier Vagabond" appeared six days a week and became so popular with readers that he was already receiving national recognition before WWII catapulted him to fame.

Pyle covered the European theater of WWII extensively, from the Battle of Britain in 1940 to the later military campaigns in North Africa, the Normandy, France, landings; and the invasion of Sicily, Italy. He lived and worked directly alongside the U.S. servicemen he was reporting about for the benefit of those not serving in battle.

On June 7, 1944, Pyle landed with the American troops at Omaha Beach aboard an LST (landing ship tank) and was again in France in August 1944 to witness the liberation of Paris firsthand.

Pyle reluctantly headed for the Pacific theater of WWII in January 1945 where he reported on naval action during the Battle of Okinawa, the largest amphibious assault in the war with Japan. By this time, Pyle had premonitions of his own death, with the long duration of the war taking its toll. On April 17, 1945, Pyle came ashore on IeJima, a small island northwest of Okinawa. The vehicle he was riding in came under fire from a Japanese machine gun. While taking cover in a ditch, a bullet entered Pyle's left temple just under his helmet.

Pyle was buried alongside other servicemen. A monument at the site of his death reads, "At this spot the 77th Infantry Division lost a buddy, Ernie Pyle, 18 April 1945." General Dwight Eisenhower wrote, "The G.I.s in Europe—and that means all of us—have lost one of our best and most understanding friends." President Harry Truman also offered, "No man in this war has so well told the story of the American fighting man, as American fighting men wanted it told. He deserves the gratitude of all of his countrymen."

A replica of the monument in IeJima stands in a small park just outside of the town of Dana on State Road 36. The Pyle homestead was slated for demolition until the "Friends of Ernie Pyle" raised enough funds to move the house from its original rural location into the town of Dana. The site was rededicated with a WWII museum in 1995 and operated by the State of Indiana until limited resources necessitated the ownership to be transferred to the "Friends of Ernie Pyle." On January 1, 2012, the site was renamed the **Ernie Pyle WWII Museum.**

Farther south between Highway 41 and State Highway 63 is the little town of **Clinton**, a former coal mining community. Its downtown is a National Historic District, but the commercial center is struggling and has many abandoned storefronts. Clinton was established in 1829, populated primarily by immigrants from northern Italian coal mining towns. This contrasts to the rest of the United States, where most Italian immigrants hailed primarily from southern Italy. When the coal mining industry in Clinton ceased, many Italian settlers remained.

Since 1966, Clinton has been hosting the Little Italy festival with crowds estimated near 100,000. After the first festival, the Jaycees of the town bought a genuine Venetian gondola from Italy for $1,627 ($15,351 in 2023). The townspeople used this authentic Italian-made gondola to transport festivalgoers along the Wabash River from 1967 to 1979. While the boat has since been retired, it still serves as a symbol of Clinton's annual Little Italy festival.

VIGO COUNTY

U.S. 41 becomes a more robust highway as it enters Vigo County, widening to four lanes as you near the city of **Terre Haute**. Named "high ground" by the French, Terre Haute is soaked in the history of the United States. It sits on the Wabash River in the fertile Wabash Valley, where a fort was constructed in 1811; the city was founded in 1818. It became a center for farming, milling, food processing, and the coal mining going on in the surrounding area.

Stag Magazine, a former men's periodical, labeled Terre Haute as "Sin City" in the 1950s and 1960s for the gambling spots and the busy "red light district" operating within its limits. Urban renewal in the 1970s eliminated the district, and the prominent gambling houses disappeared.

If you grew up in the 1960s through the pre-Internet early 1990s, you might remember that Terre Haute was the location of the fulfillment center for the **Columbia House Record Club**. Customers mailed their twelve-albums-for-a-penny forms to the Columbia House Record Club at 1 Music Lane. Unfortunately, Columbia House closed its Terre Haute operation in 2009 and ceased to exist a few years later.

Terre Haute has been called the "Crossroads of America" by virtue of its location at the historic intersection of Highways 40 and 41, as mentioned in the Introduction. Perhaps the city was historically also the Crossroads of America as a key stop on the Underground Railroad to Canada and freedom from slavery.

Near the Crossroads plaques is a statue and plaque honoring Max Ehrmann (1872–1945), a Terre Haute native best known as the author of the inspirational prose poem "Desiderata." The poem with the memorable opening, "Go placidly amid the noise and the haste, and remember what peace there may be in silence. As far as possible, without surrender, be on good terms with all persons," has been widely read since it was first copyrighted in 1927. Unfortunately, a number of different publications printed the poem without permission or attribution, and Ehrmann's work achieved fame only after his death. The poem is now recognized to be in the public domain.

In the 1940 census, Terre Haute had a population of 85,000. By 2023, the city's population had declined to 58,000. In addition, the "Queen City of the Wabash," as Terre Haute was also known, has grappled with the closure of several manufacturing facilities, an aging housing stock, and increasing numbers of residents living below the poverty line, making it one of the poorest metro areas in the country. The downtown is attempting to revitalize with the help of tax increment financing (TIF)—an economic development tool used to spur development or redevelopment of blighted or underperforming areas. It hopes to rehab old office buildings and better utilize nearby Indiana State University. Much of the retail business has relocated south of the central city near Interstate 70, which connects Terre Haute with the larger cities of Indianapolis to the east and St. Louis to the west.

The **Vigo County Museum** downtown extols past Terre Haute innovations, such as the iconic design of the Coca-Cola bottle by the Root Glass Company. Across the street from the museum is a downtown convention center built in 2022 with the hopes of attracting meetings and events. Housed within the convention center is the newly opened **Larry Bird Museum**. The museum is completely free to the public and showcases memorabilia from every stage of Larry Bird's career.

A new **Terre Haute Casino Resort** was opened in April 2024, and the city hopes it will provide some additional stimulus for visitors to frequent the downtown area. Attracting new residents and retaining the ones it has, particularly young people, is something that the city knows it must do. How to do that after a destructive three-year pandemic and the changing economics over the last few years is a major challenge, not only for Terre Haute but also for hundreds of towns and cities throughout the country.

VIGNETTE INDIANA STATE & LARRY BIRD

Terre Haute and Little Indiana State University were put on the national map in 1978–79. Larry Bird, "the Hick from French Lick" attended Indiana State from 1976 to 1979. In the '78/79 season, Bird led the ISU basketball team, the Sycamores, through an undefeated regular season and all the way to the NCAA championship game, where they squared off against Earvin "Magic" Johnson and the Michigan State Spartans. To date, it is the all-time most viewed college basketball game, with some thirty-five million viewers watching as Michigan State won the game. Bird and

Magic emerged from the game as superstars and faced off over the next decade on their respective NBA teams, the Boston Celtics (Bird) and the Los Angeles Lakers (Johnson). Both are members of the NBA Hall of Fame. After retiring as a player for the Celtics, Bird continued with the franchise in an executive capacity for several years. In 1997, Bird took on the role of coach for the Indiana Pacers NBA team and later served as president of the Pacers' basketball operations. He still works for the team in an advisory capacity, as a consultant. The state of Indiana is still identified with basketball and has produced countless great players over the years, but probably none are as recognizable as Larry Bird.

The neighborhood of **Twelve Points** just off Highway 41 in Terre Haute is a National Register Historic District. Efforts are now being made to revitalize the area after years of decline. The collection of buildings represents the earliest suburban development in the city of Terre Haute. A little west of the highway is **St. Mary of the Woods** (enrollment 793), a private Catholic liberal arts institution. On the campus grounds is the **Grotto of Our Lady of Lourdes**. The Grotto, located on the grounds of a religious community of Catholic nuns, can be seen from the road. It was built to resemble the famous grotto in Lourdes, France, where the Virgin Mary is said to have appeared to a young peasant girl named Bernadette Soubirous. A few stones from Lourdes are embedded within the Indiana grotto. *The Song of Bernadette* was a 1943 Academy-Award-winning movie depicting the story of Lourdes and Bernadette.

Close to downtown Terre Haute is **Indiana State University** (enrollment, 7,895). ISU's enrollment has declined quite a bit since 2017, when over 13,000 students were enrolled. An administrator mentioned to me that they have struggled to compete for students in the state with Indiana University and Purdue University. Unfortunately, the school is not much to look at from the highway, but it boasts **Normal Hall**, a 1910 building on the National Historic Register with a recently restored glass cupola. The **Vigo County Courthouse** lies just past the ISU campus. It is an imposing building dedicated in 1888. A Vietnam conflict memorial and some grain elevators are just off the road here as well.

Just east of the Indiana State campus grounds is the **Eugene V. Debs Museum.** If you are interested in the history of organized labor in the United States, this is an important stop to make. The home of Eugene Debs and his wife Katherine "Kate" Debs has a great deal of labor memorabilia on display and a fantastic painted mural on the third floor of the home. In the backyard are plaques honoring members of the labor movement. The home was designated as a National Historic Landmark of the United States in 1966. Debs's home is owned by the Debs Foundation and operated as a museum. Vermont Senator Bernie Sanders has been a lifelong admirer of Debs and has a plaque dedicated to him in his Congressional office. Sanders produced a 1979 documentary where he described Debs as "probably the most effective and popular leader that the American working class has ever had."

Eugene V. Debs museum, Terre Haute, IN

VIGNETTE   EUGENE DEBS

Eugene Victor "Gene" Debs (1855–1926) was an American socialist and labor organizer who was a five-time U.S. presidential candidate. A Terre Haute native and prominent figure in the community, he represented Terre Haute in the Indiana General Assembly early in his career. Debs worked on the railroad and organized one of the first industrialized unions for unskilled workers in the United States: The American Railway Union (ARU). He was a charismatic speaker, and this enabled him to organize as he evolved in his views.

After effectively negotiating the Great Northern Railway Strike of 1894, Debs and the ARU were reluctantly pulled into the Pullman Strike of 1894. He agreed to represent the workers of the Pullman Car community, and his leadership made the strike, known as "Debs Rebellion," nationally significant. Because the strike affected U.S. Mail delivery, the federal government obtained an injunction and sent the U.S. Army to enforce it. Thirty strikers were killed, and thousands were blacklisted from employment. Debs was found guilty of contempt of court and sent to federal prison for six months. Debs emerged from prison as a committed Socialist.

In 1905, with other labor activists, Debs founded the Industrial Workers of the World (IWW). Debs was a reluctant leader who found himself caught in a rift between the Socialist Party and the IWW. This weakened both organizations just when they had begun to make inroads into the American political system. Debs was firmly opposed to United States involvement in World War I and urged resistance to the military draft because he considered the war to be in the interest of capitalism. He was charged with sedition and sentenced to ten years in the Atlanta Federal Penitentiary. He made a memorable speech at the time of his sentencing in 1918. In 1920, while still in prison, Debs ran for president and won 3.41 percent of the vote, which remains the all-time high percentage of votes for a Socialist Party candidate in a U.S. presidential election.

In December 1921, President Warren Harding commuted Debs's sentence due to health reasons. Upon release, he was greeted in Terre Haute by a crowd of 50,000. Debs died in an Elmhurst, Illinois, sanitarium in 1926 at the age of seventy. His funeral was attended by 5,000 mourners. In 1976, Congress posthumously restored Debs's citizenship retroactive to 1919.

Following is an excerpt from Deb's classic speech at his sentencing hearing on September 14, 1918, said to be one of the most inspirational passages in the English language.

"When the mariner, sailing over tropic seas, looks for relief from his weary watch, he turns his eyes toward the Southern Cross, burning luridly above the tempest vexed ocean. As the midnight approaches the Southern Cross begins to bend, and the whirling worlds change their places, and with starry finger-points the Almighty marks the passage of time upon the dial of the universe; and though no bell may beat the glad tidings, the look-out knows that the midnight is passing—that relief and rest are close at hand. Let the people take heart and hope everywhere, for the cross is bending, midnight is passing, and joy cometh with the morning."

Eugene V. Debs museum, Terre Haute, IN

Eugene V. Debs museum, Terre Haute, IN

Farther east in Terre Haute is **Rose-Hulman Institute of Technology** (enrollment 2,150), a private, highly ranked engineering and technology college. Rose-Hulman's national reputation has achieved a significant milestone: for twenty-five consecutive years it has been a highly ranked undergraduate engineering college in *U.S. News & World Report's Best Colleges Guide*.

A different institution is located farther south on Highway 41. The **U.S.**

Penitentiary Terre Haute is a maximum-security federal prison for male inmates. It houses a Special Confinement Unit for inmates who have been sentenced to death, as well as a federal execution chamber. After a hiatus from 2009 to mid-2024 based upon the cost of appeals and the cost of execution drugs, the state of Indiana will resume executions of inmates.

Timothy McVeigh was executed in Terre Haute on June 11, 2001. McVeigh was a Gulf War veteran who hoped to inspire a revolution against the federal government by perpetrating the 1995 bombing of the Alfred Murrah Federal Building in Oklahoma City, killing 168 innocent people. Another well-known inmate of the penitentiary is Aldrich "Rick" Ames, currently serving a life sentence without the possibility of parole. Ames was convicted of espionage on behalf of the Soviet Union and Russia in 1994. In court, Ames admitted that he had compromised "virtually all Soviet agents of the CIA and other American and foreign services known to me" and had provided the U.S.S.R. and Russia with a "huge quantity of information on United States foreign, defense and security policies."

Leaving Terre Haute, Highway 41 is awash in strip mall businesses—mainly chain stores such as Walmart, Sam's Club, Lowes, Tractor Supply Co. etc. This mirrors many small cities with a declining downtown and strip malls outside of the central city where people now shop, eat, and have fun.

Traveling on, you can stop in **Pimento**, an unincorporated area that has an old 1925 high school on the National Historic Register. The small town of **Shelburn** is also along this section of the route. Shelburn was the home of an interurban depot. Interurbans were intercity electric railways that connected small towns with big cities. They were popular in the early 1900s. Indiana had one of the most extensive interurban systems in the country. Today, the only remaining interurban in the state and one of the few remaining in the country is the South Shore line that links South Bend with Chicago. Shelburn was a stop along the statewide interurban that connected to Terre Haute and Evansville, much farther south. The old Shelburn depot was restored in 2015 and is listed on the National Register of Historic Places. It is all set up to be a bar or restaurant if the right investor comes along.

SULLIVAN COUNTY

Arriving in the small city of **Sullivan**, the Sullivan County seat, you'll see a community that is a throwback to another era. It has an old courthouse square. Check out the well-preserved 1905 Carnegie public library just off the town square. The library has a domed tower, which is unusual for a Carnegie structure. The town also boasts the historical Downtown Sullivan High School Gym Building, which hosts boxing matches among other events.

Sullivan was the site of the most devastating mining accident to date in Indiana history. On February 20, 1925, an explosion rocked the City Coal Company mine, killing fifty-one out of the 121 men working at the time. Miners were badly burned, crushed, or suffocated. The victims left behind forty widows and eighty-seven fatherless children, imparting a tremendous social impact on the town. The loss of life in Hoosier mine country disasters was not uncommon at that time, as there were fifty to sixty mines operating in the state in the early 1900s. However, the accident in Sullivan began the push for stricter mining safety. Today, shifting consumer reliance on fossil fuels is impacting the mining industry. Currently, there are only four active underground coal mines in the state of Indiana, with fewer than 1,500 employees generating thirteen tons of clean coal annually.

On the night of March 31, 2023, Sullivan was struck by an EF3 tornado containing 165 mph winds, causing catastrophic damage in the city and surrounding area. At least three people perished, several were injured, and at least 200 structures sustained damage. As of 2024, the town is still rebuilding from the devastation. The Sullivan County Long Term Recovery Coalition was formed in the months following the tornado to keep helping those in need.

VIGNETTE WILL HAYS & THE HAYS CODE

Sullivan was the hometown of William Hays (1879–1954), the manager of Warren Harding's successful campaign for president in 1920 and subsequently appointed Postmaster General. He is best known, however, for his chairmanship of the Motion Picture Producers and Distributors of America from 1922 to 1945. As chairman, Hays oversaw the Motion Picture Code—the infamous "Hays Code"—which censored movie content from the 1930s until 1968. The code put puritanical rules for films in place that mandated separate beds for married couples, rules about length of kisses, banning any hint of homosexuality, etc.

Studios found ways to circumvent the code until 1934 when Catholic boycotts and financial backers changed the dynamic. With resources in question, studios ultimately granted Hays full authority to enforce a strict regime of self-censorship. Hays subsequently hired a Catholic, antisemite Joseph Breen, to censor films that spoke out against Nazism and Fascism. Hays also created a 117-name list of performers whose personal lives, he thought, made them unfit to appear in films. This certainly foreshadowed the Joseph McCarthy era of the 1950s.

Hays underestimated the creative talents of those he was censoring. In fact, Director Edward Dmytryk said, "If we wanted to get something across that was censorable, we had to do it deviously. We had to be clever. And it usually turned out to be much better than if we had done it straight."

Ultimately, shifting consumer preferences doomed the Hays Code. Hollywood needed to offer the public more than what they could get on the newly expanding entertainment medium known as television. Furthermore, the studios needed to keep pace with foreign films, which had no such censorship. The linchpin moment came with the 1952 Supreme Court decision that held that motion pictures were entitled to First Amendment protection and could not be banned.

Following the obsolete Hays Code came the 1968 Motion Picture Association of America (MPAA) rating system, based upon age appropriateness. There are many critics of the current system. The MPAA does not provide information on why certain decisions are made and will not reveal to the filmmaker the specific scenes that are prohibiting an alternative rating. If history repeats itself, the industry will find its current rating system obsolete as well.

Sullivan Carnegie Library, Sullivan, IN

MEROM

To the east of Sullivan, right along the Wabash River, is the little town of **Merom**. With a population of only 207, it is the smallest town in the country with a Carnegie library and considered "the most beautiful small town in Indiana," though it's hard to track down just what publications have anointed it with that title.

Merom played a small role in the War of 1812 and was a stop along the Underground Railroad, but it is mostly known for its annual **Merom Bluff Chautauqua**, which was held from 1905 to 1936. The Chautauqua was revived in the 1960s and has become an annual event. Since 1874, Chautauqua's have brought speakers and culture to rural communities throughout the United States. Every year in early June thousands of people gather at **Merom Bluff** "amid the perfect influences of nature and enjoy the best literature, oratory and music, and intellectual and religious culture." At an elevation of 200 feet, Merom Bluff is the highest point on the Wabash River. It provides a stunning view from its summit that includes a vista of neighboring Illinois.

CARLISLE

Back on Highway 41, the drive continues past the unincorporated area of Paxton. I counted nine cemeteries along the way. Throughout travel along the highway are roadside cemeteries of settlers long gone. The road goes by the little town of **Carlisle**, named after Carlisle, Pennsylvania. One of the oldest towns in Indiana, it was settled in 1803 and formally founded in 1815 with the motto "We have faith in our past and hope in our future." Unfortunately, Carlisle's present seems rather bleak—its downtown was almost entirely boarded up when I traveled through.

Just outside of Carlisle is a plaque memorializing the westernmost naval battle of the American Revolution, which occurred in 1779 on the nearby Wabash River. Shortly after George Rogers Clark captured Fort Sackville at Vincennes from the British, Captain Leonard Helm, who commanded three boats and fifty volunteers from Vincennes, captured a British reinforcement fleet of seven boats carrying forty soldiers and valuable supplies. This small naval battle completed the Continental forces' destruction of British military strength in the Wabash Valley. The plaque is located outside a Dollar General Store you drive by as you enter or exit Carlisle.

Downtown Carlisle, IN

KNOX COUNTY

Highway 41 proceeds into Knox County, the oldest county in Indiana and one of the two original counties created in the Northwest Territory in 1790. The other is St. Clair County in Illinois. The county seat of Vincennes is one of the most historic cities in the interior of the United States and comprises the bulk of what we cover on our journey through this county.

In the 1960s, automobile traffic on this portion of the old two-lane road increased, leading Highway 41 to receive the dubious title of "Killer 41" for the number of fatal traffic accidents that followed. This stretch of Highway 41 is now a four-lane highway, built in the early 1970s, that runs all the way to Evansville. This has been good for traffic, but it also provides an easy drive for people headed to shopping malls in Terre Haute and Evansville, which is not good for retail in small towns between the two. The old road still exists, though, and there is signage to allow you take the old "Killer 41" highway route if you like.

OAKTOWN/SHAKERTOWN

One mile north of the tiny town of **Oaktown** on Highway 41 is a marker acknowledging **"Shakertown."** Shakers were a "United Society of Believers in Christ's Second Appearing" and were firmly established in New England. Missionaries who wanted to spread the faith walked on foot to establish new communities in the expanding frontier. Much effort was put into establishing the West Union Community in Knox County.

A number of the approximately 400 Shakers who settled in the area were Revolutionary War veterans, but free African Americans also diversified the community. The Shakers espoused communal ownership of property, gender equality, celibacy, and economic cooperation. Shaker practice encouraged children raised in the community to become "covenanting" members at age eighteen. Not surprisingly, celibacy was a major deterrent to the growth of the population.

The West Union Shakertown community was vexed with additional adversity. Illness continuously plagued the settlement. A tornado struck in May 1819, severely damaging the orchard and buildings. In 1820, heavy spring flooding damaged the mills. By 1826, the community decided that the settlement should be closed, and the land was sold. Many of the inhabitants relocated to a new Shaker settlement near Cincinnati, Ohio, and the Indiana settlement was abandoned. Today the land once occupied by the Shakers is privately owned, active farmland.

Vincennes University Agricultural Center is located several miles north of the city of Vincennes. You can stop in and see the latest in farm equipment and learn a bit about agribusiness. The center is a state-of-the-art facility that will prepare the next generation of farmers and agriculture professionals. Students have access to cutting-edge laboratories, Purdue University's food safety hub, a greenhouse, bee colonies, and much more.

FORT KNOX II

Three miles north of Vincennes on a bluff called Petit Rocher that overlooks the Wabash River lies the former site of **Fort Knox II**. This military installation was used by the United States Army from 1803-1813. Captain Zachary Taylor, a future U.S. president, was put in charge of the fort. Fort Knox was the mustering location of the army Governor William

Henry Harrison brought together to fight the battle of Tippecanoe in November 1811. The Fort Knox II site is now preserved as a state and national historic site close to present-day **Ouabache Trails Park**. The park has a campground and some excellent hiking trails near the Wabash River.

VINCENNES

The city of **Vincennes** is the oldest city in Indiana, founded by the French in 1727. Vincennes is an interesting city, as a great deal of the formative history of the United States exists in this region of the state. To see for yourself, take Business Highway 41 into the city. Unfortunately, the road passes through an area of retail strip malls before reaching Vincennes' historic district.

VINCENNES UNIVERSITY

North of the city center is **Vincennes University** (enrollment 17,862), a public undergraduate liberal arts school founded in 1806. V.U. has the distinction of being the oldest public institution of higher learning in the state of Indiana. The school has a pleasant campus right along the Wabash River.

The **Red Skelton Performing Arts Center** was dedicated in February 2006 on the campus of Vincennes University, one block from the family home where he was born. The building includes an 850-seat theater, classrooms, rehearsal rooms, and dressing rooms. Its grand foyer is a gallery for Skelton's paintings, statutes, and film posters. The adjacent **Red Skelton Museum of American Comedy** houses his personal and professional materials, which he collected since the age of ten. The town of Vincennes has held the Red Skelton Festival since 2005. The associated "Parade of a Thousand Clowns" is billed as the largest clown parade in the Midwest.

VIGNETTE RED SKELTON

Near the V.U. campus is the childhood home of Red Skelton (1913–1997), a well-known entertainer from the days of radio to movies and television. Skelton was born in Vincennes two months after his father, Joseph, passed away. Joseph, a grocer, had once been a clown in a circus, and this may have been the driver for Skelton's seventy-year-long career in show business and art. Skelton wanted to be described as a clown rather than a comic: "A comedian goes out and hits people right on. A clown uses pathos. He can be funny, then turn right around and reach people and touch them with what life is like. I just want to be known as a clown because to me that's the height of my profession. It means you can do everything—sing, dance and above all, make people laugh." *In addition to performing, Skelton was a prolific writer, composer, photographer, and painter.*

Skelton began painting in 1943, but did not have his first public showing until 1964 at the Sands Hotel in Las Vegas, where he was performing at the time. Skelton found painting a better vehicle to visualize the imaginary props he used in his pantomime routines. At the time of his death in 1997, Skelton had created over 1,000 oil paintings of clowns, making more money from his paintings than from his television work. When asked why his artwork focused on clowns, he said at first, "I don't know why it's always clowns." *After a moment he corrected himself,* "No, that's not true—I do know why. I just don't feel like thinking about it."

GROUSELAND

Visitors will also find **Grouseland**, the home of President William Henry Harrison, on the Vincennes campus. It is now a National Historic Landmark. President John Adams appointed Harrison as the first governor of the Indiana territory, and Vincennes was the capital from 1800 to 1813. Lewis and Clark stopped by in 1806 on their return east after exploring the lands of the Louisiana Purchase.

Nearby Grouseland, overlooking the Wabash River, is a statue of Chief Tecumseh (1768–1813), the Shawnee Chief, orator, military leader, and advocate of an intertribal alliance formed to promote resistance to U.S. expansion onto Indigenous lands, who met with Harrison to defend the rights of his people. (See Chapter One: Before the Road for more information). Harrison called Tecumseh "one of those uncommon geniuses, which spring up occasionally to produce revolutions and overturn the established order of things." While Tecumseh continued to negotiate peace and unity among Indigenous nations, Harrison petitioned the U.S. government for more soldiers and made plans to intimidate and break up Tecumseh's confederacy.

Also, on the Grouseland grounds is a small plaque that honors Sarah Knox "Knoxie" Taylor (1814–1835). Sarah was born at Fort Knox II in Vincennes and was the daughter of Zachary Taylor, the 12th U.S. president and a descendant of the notable Lee family. She married military officer Jefferson Davis, future president of the Confederacy. Taylor died of malaria three months after their wedding.

Adjacent to Grouseland is the **Indiana Territorial Capitol Building**, dating from 1800. When Vincennes was the capital of the Indiana territory, it included Indiana, Illinois, Wisconsin, and the eastern half of Minnesota from 1800 to 1809. The territory also included the western half of Michigan from 1800 to 1805 and the eastern half of Michigan from 1803 to 1805. There are some old structures dating from the French establishment of the city nearby.

William Henry Harrison's Grouseland, Vincennes, IN

SUGAR LOAF MOUND

East of Vincennes University is **Sugar Loaf Mound**, part of a small public park in a residential neighborhood. It is a natural landform that was used by prehistoric Woodland Era Indigenous peoples for burials (circa 900 CE). Long ago, travelers heading to Vincennes along the **Buffalo Trace**, a trail from Louisville, used it as a landmark. The mound also served as a marker along the Underground Railroad for fugitives from slavery seeking freedom in the North.

KNOX COUNTY COURTHOUSE AND MARY CLARK

The **Knox County Courthouse** is located in downtown Vincennes. It is an imposing structure, built in 1876. Among the war memorials that surround the courthouse is a plaque honoring Mary Clark (1795–1840). Clark was born enslaved, purchased in Kentucky by B.J. Harrison, and brought to Vincennes in 1815 indentured as his servant. In 1816, G.W. Johnston purchased her indenture for twenty years. In 1821, Clark and her attorney petitioned the Knox County Court to terminate her indenture because she was held illegally as enslaved. The Court ruled against her, but on appeal, the Indiana Supreme Court ruled that Clark's service was involuntary, violating Indiana's 1816 Constitution. She won her freedom, and the precedent-setting ruling ended indentured servitude in Indiana.

Mary Clark plaque outside Vincennes Courthouse, Vincennes, IN

FORT SACKVILLE

Vincennes historic downtown was once the location of **Fort Sackville**, where a Continental victory during the Revolutionary War ended British hopes of controlling the West. This whole area is drenched in history. The

Old State Bank building was completed in 1838 in the Greek Revival style, made to look like the front of a Greek temple. The **Old Cathedral Catholic Church** (Basilica of St. Francis Xavier), first constructed by the French in 1732, was rebuilt in 1826 and still holds services. A "French and Indian" cemetery lies next to the church—many soldiers and patriots of the American Revolution are buried there. The historic city center of Vincennes has some appealing shops and restaurants, including **Old Chicago Pizza + Taproom** in a converted movie theater. I hope the city's downtown develops more businesses in these historic buildings in the future.

LINCOLN MEMORIAL BRIDGE

In the midst of downtown Vincennes is the **Lincoln Memorial Bridge**, a concrete arch structure constructed in 1931. The bridge carries U.S. Highway 50 across the Wabash into Illinois. On either side of the bridge in Indiana are two massive decorative pylons that depict Indigenous peoples. If you walk across the bridge to Illinois, you will see the **Lincoln Trail State Memorial**, a sculpture commemorating Lincoln's travel to Illinois as a young man in 1830. North of the Lincoln Memorial Bridge, there is a statue of François-Marie Bissot, Sieur de Vincennes (1700–1736), the founder of Vincennes. He built a fort on the site in 1732 and claimed the area for France. Vincennes met a gruesome end—he was burned at the stake by the Chickasaw, near present-day Fulton, Tennessee.

Lincoln Bridge Memorial, Westport, IL

GEORGE ROGERS CLARK MEMORIAL

Adjacent to and south of the bridge in Vincennes is the **George Rogers Clark Memorial**, a massive structure similar in size to the Jefferson Memorial in Washington, D.C. The building was completed in 1933 and features a series of seven murals painted by Ezra Winters, which surround a statue of Clark. It is the kind of memorial you rarely find anywhere other than Washington D.C., that conveys the importance given to the achievements of Clark and his associates. Franklin Delano Roosevelt dedicated the memorial in 1936, and it is administered by the National Park Service.

On my visit, I viewed a documentary about Clark and had an informative chat with a park department ranger inside the Memorial. I was the only visitor. Clark (1752–1818) was a hero of the American Revolution and a chief explorer of the Old Northwest, but he died in poverty and obscurity. His brother, William Clark, is celebrated for co-commanding the Lewis and Clark Expedition to explore the West.

George Rogers Clark Memorial, Vincennes, IN

In recent years, the importance of Clark's role in U.S. history has been the subject of much debate among historians. Clark earned the nickname "Conqueror of the Old Northwest" when the British ceded the entire Northwest Territory to the United States in the 1783 Treaty of Paris. However, the "conquest" was against weakly fortified enemies, and it was little more than a temporary occupation. Clark had a reputation as an "Indian hater" who once declared that he would like to see the whole race of

Indians extirpated [destroyed], that for his part he would never spare man, woman or child of them on whom he could lay his hands. It was rumored that Clark was often drunk on duty and submitted fraudulent claims to the state of Virginia for military campaigns he financed with borrowed funds.

A monument to Clark erected at the University of Virginia in 1921 was removed in 2021 as the nation grappled with increasing attention to the violence committed by early European explorers, settlers, and their descendants against African Americans, Indigenous peoples, and other people of color. Monuments to Clark around the country are being defaced and/or removed. It will be interesting to see how changing attitudes about Clark's exploits impact this memorial in future years.

I spent the night at a hotel on the outskirts of Vincennes where a great many migrant workers were staying. The bus they rode in on was out on the road at dawn. Each year, thousands of migrant workers follow the harvest from Florida, Georgia, and other parts of the south to northern states such as Indiana, Ohio, and Michigan. They pick and pack asparagus, melons, tomatoes, and other fruits and vegetables that grace American dinner tables. They settle, sometimes for months, into roadside motels, apartment buildings, and mobile home parks in farm towns across the country. Vincennes is right in the middle of farming country and thus a stop along their way.

VIGNETTE DESHEE FARMS

Leaving Vincennes and heading south puts you back in farmland. Although there is no sign, you will pass by **Deshee Farms***, a unit of the Wabash Farm collective, which was a part of a larger national collective farm project. Conceived in 1938, the farm operated as a "cooperative" implemented by the Resettlement Agency of the Farm Security Administration to house and employ low-income tenant farmers who had been hit the hardest by the Great Depression. Deshee Farms was one of seventeen cooperative farms constructed around the nation. Later, the farm was accused of being a "Russian Farm" promoting communist views as it attempted to educate family farmers on the best techniques to utilize their land. The farm was shuttered in 1946, but the ideas surrounding its development have been newly embraced, often by independent farmers and ranchers who operate small to midsize farms and utilize fair labor practices along with ecological farming and ranching practices.*

GIBSON COUNTY

Continuing south on the highway will bring you into Gibson County and the Greater Evansville metropolitan area. Traffic volume along the highway is much greater as you proceed south. The county seat for Gibson is the town of **Princeton**. A striking iconic 1884 Romanesque Revival County Courthouse dominates the downtown which is on the National Register of Historic Places.

Princeton is probably better off than many of the other towns along this stretch of 41 in Indiana by virtue of the massive Toyota auto plant, located right along the highway on the outskirts of the city. According to the facility's website: **"Toyota Motor Manufacturing, Indiana** (TMMI) uses high-tech manufacturing systems to assemble some of the most technologically advanced vehicles on the road today. TMMI has assembled more than six million vehicles—and counting. Since the plant's groundbreaking in 1996, Toyota has invested $6.6 billion to make high-quality vehicles through smarter, flexible manufacturing and innovation." About 5,600 people work at the plant, making it by far, the largest employer in Gibson County.

A side trip west of Princeton is the restored **Lyles Station Historic School and Museum**. Lyles Station was a settlement of African Americans who had been emancipated from enslavement in the 1840s. Their descendants still live and farm in the area.

Continue on Highway 41 past the town of Fort Branch and stop for a meal in **Haubstadt**, a bedroom community of Evansville where you can dine at **The Log Inn**. Built in 1825 as a noonday stagecoach stop and trading post, the inn is officially recognized as the oldest restaurant in Indiana. I recommend dining in the same room as Abraham Lincoln, who visited in 1844. Note that the restaurant is only open for dinner.

VANDERBURGH COUNTY

Highway 41 runs directly into the city of **Evansville**. It is the Vanderburgh County seat and Indiana's third most populous city after Indianapolis and Fort Wayne. As the one city of size between St. Louis, Nashville, and Louisville, Evansville is the hub of commercial and cultural activity for the tri-state area of Illinois, Indiana, and Kentucky. The city sits along the Ohio River with a charming downtown of many stately old homes and beautifully kept buildings. Several new condo buildings intended to attract young professionals are currently under construction, but I did not see many people at all during my weekday early afternoon visit on a beautiful day—quite strange. Nearby is the **Ford Center**, a big multipurpose arena built in 2011. A large casino, **Bally's Tropicana**, is situated on the riverfront, and permanently docked nearby is the World War II era **USS LST 325**, the last fully functional landing ship tank remaining in the country that is open for tours.

The land Evansville now occupies has been populated for a very long time. There is evidence in the area of Indigenous settlement from at least 8,000 BCE. There are several ancient sites in and near the city—**Angel Mounds State Historic Site** is the most complete. The site was built and occupied from 1000 to 1450 and features earthen mounds built by the Mississippian culture. Evansville was founded in 1812. It became a major stop for steamboats on the Ohio River. Today, the city is often referred to as the "Crescent Valley," the "River City," or the derisive "Stoplight City"—a name conferred by truck drivers frustrated by all the city's stoplights on U.S. 41 and, more recently, on the Lloyd Expressway.

Highway 41 carves a path right through the middle of the city, and it is still an important throughway. In the early days of the automobile, around 1915, this part of U.S. 41 was called the **Dixie Bee Line**. (See Chapter Two: Wheels and Roads for more information). The U.S. 41 Association was created in 1926 to promote the road. It operated out of the **Hotel McCurdy**, now a historic residential building in Evansville's Riverfront District.

Downtown Evansville, IN

VIGNETTE EVANSVILLE NATIVES, HALSTON & DON MATTINGLY

Roy Halston Frowick (1932–1990), better known simply as "Halston," moved to Evansville from Des Moines, Iowa, with his family at age fourteen and graduated from Benjamin Bosse High School in 1950. He briefly attended Indiana University before coming to Chicago in 1952 to attend the School of the Art Institute and become a designer of women's hats. Halston first achieved fame for designing the pillbox hat worn by Jacqueline Kennedy to her husband's presidential inauguration in 1961. After expanding into women's wear, Halston opened a boutique in New York City in 1968. As an American fashion designer, he became internationally famous in the 1970s for redefining women's clothing with a minimalist approach and clean lines. His frequent appearances at the infamous Studio 54 discotheque were often in the news as he partied with friends such as Andy Warhol, Bianca Jagger, and Liza Minnelli. Halston went on to design women's ready-to-wear clothing for the J.C. Penney retail chain—a controversial move at the time, as no high-end designer had ever licensed their designs to a mid-priced retail store. Halston lost control of his company in the 1980s and tested positive for HIV in 1988. He died of AIDS in 1990.

Don Mattingly (b. 1961) is a Major League Baseball coach currently with the Toronto Blue Jays and a former player. Nicknamed "the Hit Man" and "Donnie Baseball," he spent his entire fourteen-year playing career with the New York Yankees. He later managed the L.A. Dodgers and the Miami Marlins and is currently a bench coach for the Toronto Blue Jays (2025). An Evansville native, Mattingly played for the Reitz Memorial High School baseball team, which won a state-record fifty-nine straight games through the 1978-79 season. He signed with the Yankees in 1979 and made his MLB debut in 1982. Mattingly was named to the American League All-Star team six times and won nine Gold Glove Awards, the 1984 AL batting title, and the 1985 AL Most Valuable Player. He was the team captain of the Yankees from 1991 to 1995, when he retired as a player. The Yankees retired Mattingly's uniform number 23, making him the only Yankee to have his number retired without his ever having won a World Series with the team. During the late 1980s and early 1990s, Mattingly owned a restaurant in Evansville called "Mattingly's 23," after the uniform number he wore for most of his career.

Although an old Business Route 41 exists, I recommend taking in the sights of the city by getting off the highway. Near the intersection of Highway 41 and State Road 66 in the middle of the city is **Wesselman Woods Nature Preserve**, a 200-acre stand of virgin, old-growth forest; it is the largest such tract within any city limits in the United States and a National Natural Landmark.

If you visit Evansville in the summer, you should definitely plan on taking in a minor league baseball game with a visit to **Bosse Field**, home of the Evansville Otters of the Frontier Minor League. Built in 1915, Bosse Field is one of the oldest baseball stadiums still in use today, along with Fenway Park in Boston and Wrigley Field in Chicago. The 1992 movie *A League of Their Own* was filmed there.

The city has several old neighborhoods (Riverside, Bayard Park, Lincolnshire, Culver, Baptisttown) that are listed on the National Register of Historic Places. Neighborhood walking tours are available through the **Evansville Convention and Visitors Bureau**, and you can visit the **Reitz Home Museum**, the only Victorian home open to the public. The **Victory Theatre** is a restored vintage theater that houses the Evansville Philharmonic Orchestra.

The **University of Evansville** (enrollment 1,763) is a private university affiliated with the Methodist Church and located close to the highway. It is a small liberal arts school, but it competes in the Division 1 level of the NCAA. It is known for its arts program and operates a campus in England as well. Just outside of the central city is the **University of Southern Indiana** (enrollment 9,750), a public university with many areas of study. Other sights include the **Evansville African American Museum**, the **Children's Museum of Evansville**, the **Evansville Museum of Arts, History & Science, Mesker Park Zoo and Botanic Garden**, a plaque honoring one of the Underground Railroad sites in downtown, and the **Willard Library**, built in 1885. It is the oldest public library in Indiana and a very cool building to tour inside.

VIGNETTE   THE I-69 ROAD CONTROVERSY

The Interstate Highway System, conceived in the 1950s, ignored Evansville and left the city without a direct route to the state capital in Indianapolis. The closest interstate was I-64, opened in 1969, which is located some twenty-six miles north of the city, tying it to Louisville and St. Louis. The shortest route to Indianapolis was a two-lane state road, and many local businesses believed this was creating problems for the southwestern Indiana economy. The solution was to build a new interstate that would connect Evansville directly with Indianapolis and run through or by the small city of Washington where David Graham (1927–2020), an influential businessman and "the father of I-69," lived.

The proposed interstate would also run close to the town of Crane, where there is a big Naval Sea System Command base, and Bloomington, home of Indiana University. The Mid-Continent Highway Coalition group, formed by Graham and comprised primarily of large transportation companies, lobbied state and federal officials to designate Interstate 69 as part of the so-called "NAFTA Highway" that would eventually run from the Mexican border in Texas to the Canadian border at Port Huron, Michigan. (The North American Free Trade Agreement— "NAFTA"— was renegotiated in 2020, and the new name is the U.S. Mexico Canada Agreement (USMCA), which somehow does not trip off the tongue as easily as the old name). Since globalization is no longer as popular as it once was, the "Mid-Continent Highway" from Canada to Mexico is now the route's semi-official name.

The problem is that I-69 was not part of the original Interstate system, planned decades ago, so it required funding and road designation from multiple states for completion. The only state that has completed its portion of I-69 to date is Michigan, and the road is a very low priority for several southern states that it is slated to run through. I-69 from the Michigan border to Indianapolis was completed in the early 1970s and considered done at that time. Federal legislation created the mandate to extend I-69 from southwestern Indiana to Texas, but it did not provide any funding for its construction. After much delay, many lawsuits, and numerous protests from foes of the highway—such as property owners, the city of Vincennes (which also lacked a convenient interstate connection), and individuals concerned about losing the bucolic nature of southern Indiana—construction on this new section of the road began in 2012.

The highway was originally conceived as a toll road and, later, as public-private-partnership. Money from a gasoline tax and leases from the existing Indiana toll road was used to secure the final costs of building the new interstate highway. The corridor connecting Evansville to Indianapolis was completed in August 2024. The completion of the project means it's now theoretically possible to drive from Evansville all the way to the Canadian border at Port Huron, Michigan, without hitting a single stop light. Time will tell if the new highway pays off in greater development for southwestern Indiana.

SIDE TRIP TO NEW HARMONY

The unique and historic town of **New Harmony** is well worth a side trip,

Willard Public Library, Evansville, IN

even though it is located in Posey County, east of Highway 41's route through Vanderburgh County. New Harmony became a National Historic Landmark in 1965. From Evansville, you can take State Road 66 east for twenty-five miles to reach the town.

New Harmony has an interesting history right up to the present. It was founded as a utopian community in the early 1800s by German settlers and, later, Scotsman Robert Owen, as a place to seek enlightenment. That community fell apart, although there were later attempts over the decades to revive New Harmony as a special place. Owen's granddaughter, Jane Owen (1915–2010) was a patron of the arts, an author, and the heir to the Humble Oil (later ExxonMobil) fortune. She and her husband helped resettle New Harmony, and she commissioned construction of the **Roofless Church**, designed by architect Philip Johnson.

Another appealing building is the **Athenaeum**, designed by acclaimed architect Richard Meier, which also serves as the visitor center for **Historic New Harmony**. Conferences and meetings are held there. Also, make a point in seeing the **Harmonist Labyrinth**, a manicured privet hedge planted in concentric circles. The labyrinth evokes the serenity and peacefulness the utopians were seeking. Decades before Andrew Carnegie bequeathed libraries to many small towns, Scottish immigrant William Maclure established a library for laborers in 1838 called the **New Harmony Working Men's Institute**. It is the oldest continuously operating public library in Indiana.

I highly recommend spending the night in New Harmony walking or riding a bike around to see all of the interesting structures and artwork in this town. Stay at the **New Harmony Inn Resort & Conference Center** if possible. This unique resort is steps away from the center of town and features rooms with Harmonist decor. It is surrounded by beautifully groomed landscapes, lakes, and gardens.

A historic 1928 bridge, the **Harmony Way Bridge**, crosses the Wabash River to Illinois here. Visitors to and residents of the town once used the bridge heavily to cross from Posey County, Indiana to White County, Illinois, until it was deemed unsafe in 2012 and closed. Recent (2024) infrastructure grants have been awarded to continue the engineering design for the bridge's restoration. This structure is vital to the regions on both sides of the Wabash, as crossing at New Harmony used to take three minutes, but it currently takes thirty minutes.

New Harmony Bridge, New Harmony, IN

Athenaeum, New Harmony, IN

The Roofless Church, housing the statue, The Descent of the Holy Spirit
New Harmony, IN

CONCLUDING THOUGHTS

Travel on Highway 41 through western Indiana may seem boring at first glance, but it would be a mistake to avoid looking carefully at many of the interesting aspects of the journey discussed in this chapter. Most Americans and foreign visitors know very little about Indiana aside from the occasional sports reference. Details about the state that often come to

316

mind are agriculture, manufacturing, conservative politics, songs about small towns by Indiana native John Mellencamp, county fairs, tractors, the Indy 500, and basketball. But along Highway 41 travelers will also find an enormously broad slice of American history.

The Indiana Association of Realtors has as its new catch phrase, "Home Again, IN Indiana," on its website, along with interviews of individuals who left the state and returned. This is an effort to combat the designation that Indiana is a place where people grow up and then leave. The factors that entice people to live in the state now are a low cost of living relative to other Midwestern locations and a good educational system. The city of Indianapolis, in the center of the state, is a large urban location that is accessible to virtually every part of the state. Proximity to Indianapolis, or Evansville to the south, or Chicago to the north, is a big determinant of where the majority of the state's population near Highway 41 resides.

Indiana may never be in the vanguard of change in America, but that would seem to be just fine for many residents. Neal Peirce, an author studying the state in the early 1970s wrote, "the people are clannish, protective of property, suspicious of government, patriotic, and insecure." That said, a journey on Highway 41 through Indiana is a window on the country as a whole.

PART THREE
SOUTH

CHAPTER SEVEN
KENTUCKY

"Heaven must be a Kentucky kind of place."

— Daniel Boone

"I hope to have God on my side, but I must have Kentucky."

—Abraham Lincoln

"If the world ends, I'll just head on down to Kentucky because they're always 20 years behind."

—Mark Twain

Highway 41 through Kentucky is 106 miles.

Key Towns/Cities: *Henderson, Madisonville, Hopkinsville, Guthrie*

Kentucky Counties along 41: *Henderson, Webster, Hopkins, Christian, Todd*

Kentucky Counties nearby 41 that are worth visiting: *Daviess, McCracken*

A KENTUCKY ALBUM PLAYLIST

- Bill Monroe: *Knee Deep in Bluegrass* 1958
- Loretta Lynn: *Coal Miner's Daughter* 1971
- Chris Stapleton: *Traveller* 2015
- W.C. Handy: *Memphis Blues* 1912
- My Morning Jacket: *Z* 2005
- Cage the Elephant: *Melophobia* 2013
- Sturgill Simpson: *A Sailor's Guide to Earth* 2016
- The Judds: *Why Not Me* 1984
- Dwight Yoakam: *Guitars, Cadillacs, Etc., Etc.* 1986
- The Everly Brothers: *The Everly Brothers* 1958
- Alison Krauss: *A Hundred Miles or More: A Collection* 2007

IDENTITY

After crossing the Ohio River, Highway 41 proceeds south through the western section of the state of Kentucky. The road goes through a rolling terrain underpinned by the **Pennyroyal Plateau**. More commonly known as "the Pennyrile," it is an extensive area of grassland that became a major tobacco producing region, but it also yields corn, soybeans, rapeseed, and a variety of other crops. Abundant coal deposits exist in western Kentucky, and the region was extensively mined until recently, as industries have switched to less polluting forms of energy, such as natural gas. Many traditional coal-mining areas in western Kentucky have little to no coal production at present. Many former miners have gone into new areas of employment such as manufacturing within the booming Kentucky economy. Western Kentucky is prime cave country. To the east of 41 is **Mammoth Cave**, the longest known cave system in the world. It will be suggested as a side trip.

BOURBON

Bourbon is barrel-aged American whiskey made primarily from corn. It is closely associated with Kentucky, where it has been distilled since the eighteenth century. The popularity of bourbon has been a boon to the state's tourism industry. **The Bourbon Trail** comprises tasting and travel tours to Kentucky's myriad distilleries. The majority of these distilleries are farther east near Louisville and the state capital of Frankfort, but several are located along the Highway 41 corridor. Three of these individual distilleries worth visiting for the smaller crowds and more relaxed atmosphere are **Casey Jones Distillery** in Hopkinsville, **MB Roland Distillery** in Pembroke, and the **Bard Distillery** in the town of Graham, slightly east of Madisonville. I stopped to sample the Kentucky bourbon at the Bard Distillery and checked out the repurposed 1920s school site that houses the distillery.

Highway 41 is paralleled for much of its length by the **Pennyrile Parkway**, which is also Interstate-69/169, and the CSX railroad. The drive is largely along a two-lane road through picturesque rural country punctuated by small towns. Historically, between Henderson and Nashville, the route was a "post road" (a road over which mail was carried) called the "Buttermilk Road." Farmers along the route would set aside crocks of buttermilk and dippers for travelers, prior to its 1926 incorporation into the national highway system, U.S. The highway has taken at least four distinctly different routes through Kentucky over the past eighty-five years, including crossing the Ohio River by ferry at the foot of Second Street in downtown Henderson, now miles from its current route. There is also Highway 41A that starts in Henderson and runs slightly to the east of Highway 41 through some small towns before rejoining the main road at Madisonville.

About thirty miles east of Henderson is the city of **Owensboro**, home to the **Bluegrass Music Hall of Fame and Museum**, which honors the musical style that originated in Western Kentucky. Bluegrass music derives from settlers who lived in remote areas of Appalachia and wrote songs about life on the farm or in the hills. It was influenced by gospel, jazz, and blues music and received wide recognition when introduced by Bill Monroe, the acknowledged father of bluegrass, in 1945. Bluegrass is high energy, fast-tempo country music and is widely known from its use in movies and television by artists like Earl Scruggs, Lester Flatt, Doc Watson, Jimmy Martin, Maybelle Carter, and Roy Acuff. Owensboro is also famous for its barbecue—the city holds an International Bar-B-Q Festival each May.

To the west of Hopkinsville is the **Land Between the Lakes**, a 170,000-acre national recreation area that spans the Kentucky/Tennessee border between Lake Barkley and Kentucky Lake. The latter is the largest man-made lake in the eastern United States. Kentucky Lake was a TVA (Tennessee Valley Authority) project created from dams constructed on the Tennessee and Cumberland Rivers during the Great Depression. It was intended to extend electricity throughout this region. The area is known for its wildlife, hiking trails, fishing, boating and other forms of recreation. A two-lane road called **The Trace** bisects the Land Between the Lakes. Nearby is the historic Ohio River city of **Paducah**, founded by William Clark in 1827. Nicknamed "Quilt City USA" and home to the **National Quilt Museum**, this restored city is a thriving arts center.

Kentucky is a border state. It is not intensely southern or northern, but a blend of both. You will get little consensus from Kentucky natives on this dichotomy, but in general, the state is more Midwestern in its geographical location but more southern in its cultural sensibilities. During the Civil War, Kentucky separated the Confederate states of the South and the Union states of the North and was considered strategic by both sides. Several battles were fought within the state. The 1862 Battle of Perryville, near the capital city of Lexington, was one of the bloodiest battles of the Civil War. Slavery existed in Kentucky until the end of the war in 1865.

Paducah, KY

BY THE NUMBERS

Kentucky had an estimated population of 4.50 million in 2023. The state has grown modestly in the past few decades, with 4.47 million in 2020, 4.05 million in 2000 and 3.6 million in 1980. Most of Kentucky's urban population is concentrated in the eastern part of the state, including the Louisville and Lexington metropolitan areas and greater Cincinnati, Ohio. Along Highway 41, Henderson, to the north, is part of metropolitan Evansville, Indiana, and Fort Campbell Army base to the south is part of metropolitan Clarksville, Tennessee.

THE INDIANA BORDER TO HOPKINSVILLE

Due to the shifting Ohio River, the state of Kentucky actually begins just south of Evansville, Indiana on what is called Green River, before crossing the Ohio River. **Ellis Park Racing & Gaming** (formerly Dade Park) has been a fixture along the river since 1922. Horse racing is featured in season, with slot machines and an upstairs level with televisions all tuned to horse racing across the world. In its 100 years of existence, the park has experienced ownership changes, barn fires, floods, and tornadoes.

Highway 41 presently crosses the Ohio River on the **Bi-State Vietnam Gold Star Twin Bridges**. The bridge's southbound span was built in 1965, and the original span, built in 1932, travels northbound.

A new bridge over the Ohio River to be built on what will become I-69 is slated to start construction in 2025 with a projected completion by 2031. You can see the construction taking place just outside of Henderson. By completion, the oldest span of the original bridge will be taken out of service. A new interchange will connect Highway 41 with the existing I-69 corridor. Civic officials in Kentucky hope this will be an economic boost for western Kentucky. Local residents are hoping for a less congested road than Highway 41 will possibly be upon completion.

Looking south toward the Bi-State Vietnam Gold Star Twin Bridges
from the Ellis Park Racetrack, KY

JOHN JAMES AUDUBON STATE PARK

Just across the bridge is the **John James Audubon State Park**. This park offers some easy walking and hiking trails in hills along the Ohio River. The **Audubon Museum and Nature Center** is housed on-site in a beautiful WPA-era building constructed in 1938. The museum houses one of the largest collections of materials in the world related to Audubon (1785–1851).

Audubon was a noted ornithologist, naturalist, artist, and slaveholder, who resided and operated a dry goods store in Henderson from 1810 to 1820. Audubon's family gave his name to long-lasting conservation efforts in the form of the National Audubon Society, founded in 1905, cementing a portion of his legacy by protecting birds and their habitats. However, Audubon was a complex and difficult man; he enslaved African Americans, promulgated the superiority of the white race, plagiarized the work of others, killed many birds for purposes of art, and stole human remains. Similar to other naturalists of the era, Audubon, along with another ornithologist, John Kirk Townsend, raided Indigenous burial sites and the gravesites of enslaved African Americans and picked up human skulls he found in his explorations.

He sent them to Dr. Samuel Morton, a Philadelphia-based "craniologist" who was intent on promulgating theories of racial hierarchy suggesting that Caucasians had larger brain capacity. This fed the racist logic of the time that claimed such "studies" as evidence why people of African descent should continue to be enslaved.

Audubon remains the most famous American bird artist who achieved some measure of fame during his life. In Henderson, plaques, statutes, and artwork in the library commemorate this famous resident. Unfortunately, he is also a man of the times and leaves, as do so many other historical figures, an uncertain legacy. At this writing, numerous city chapters of the national Audubon society have decided to drop *Audubon* from their names due to his problematic actions.

Audubon Museum & Nature Center, Henderson, KY

Audubon State Park, Henderson, KY

HENDERSON

Henderson is a small, pleasant, and picturesque city. Founded in 1797 and one of the oldest cities along the Ohio River, it is now a suburb within the greater Evansville, Indiana, metropolitan area. This metro region is known locally as the Tri-State Area because it lies where the borders of Illinois, Indiana, and Kentucky meet along the Ohio River.

Although Henderson's historic and well-kept downtown has some empty storefronts in the business center, it also features a number of renovated buildings and several colorful murals depicting local flora, fauna, and charitable organizations. From downtown, you can see the **Henderson Bridge**, a striking, long railroad bridge built in the 1930s and still in use, as it crosses the Ohio River from Indiana. When I visited Henderson in 2023, the "American Queen" paddlewheel steamboat was docked at the Henderson River Front; however, the company operating the boat ceased to do business in 2024. River cruises have become quite popular in recent years visiting historic locations such as Henderson, and I would expect that an alternative company will be in business soon.

Audubon Mill Park fronts the Ohio River in the downtown area offering both open parkland and recreation areas. Located at the original site of John James Audubon's original grist mill, the park features century-old shade trees, riverfront views, and picnic tables. It is the site of many seasonal festivals.

Henderson was a center for the export of "dark tobacco" (a category of tobacco plant that produces exceptionally dark leaves with a strong taste or aroma) in the nineteenth century, and a number of the city's largest, most expensive homes in town were built from earnings in that industry. A walking tour of historic homes near downtown allows visitors to see how the wealthy lived 150 years ago. Be sure to check out **Central Park**, once called "Transylvania Park." Opened in 1797, it is believed to be the first municipal park west of the Allegheny Mountains. The park contains a gazebo, mature trees, and a twenty-six-foot fountain named "Rebecca," a replica of the original 1890 fountain installed in 2003.

You'll find the **Henderson Public Library** (established in 1904 and renovated in 2020) across the street from the park. Well worth a visit, this Carnegie library was awarded to the town by Andrew Carnegie himself after a golf game with one of the local business leaders. The rotunda ceiling has murals depicting the Greek muses of art, science, music, and literature, as well as the names of classical authors. A brass chandelier hangs from the stained-glass skylight. A portrait in the library honors Mary Towles Sasseen (1860–1906), schoolteacher and librarian who is recognized as the originator of "Mother's Day" in the United States. In August 2023, the library added a two-story painted mural titled *The Lady of the Park*, which features a silhouette of the Central Park "Rebecca" fountain surrounded by some 200 books detailing the history of Henderson and Kentucky.

Henderson Railroad Bridge over the Ohio River

"Rebecca" fountain in Central Park, Henderson, KY

*"The Lady in the Park, " Henderson Public Library, Henderson, KY,
(photo courtesy of Henderson Public Library)*

Henderson Public Library, Henderson, KY
(photo courtesy of Henderson City Public Library)

WILLIAM CHRISTOPHER (W.C.) HANDY

W.C. Handy (1873–1958) was another famous former resident of Henderson. A composer and musician, Handy referred to himself as the "Father of the Blues." He lived in Henderson from 1893 to 1903 and is credited with introducing a music style known regionally as Delta blues into the national consciousness. According to legend, the Alabama-born composer and his band were traveling home from the postponed Chicago World's Fair in 1892 when they ran out of money in St. Louis. Work was scarce there, so Handy left the rest of the band and headed to Evansville, Indiana. In need of funds, Handy worked with a street paving crew and joined a local band that performed throughout the region. When the group played at a Henderson barbecue, he met Elizabeth Price, who soon became his wife.

Henderson holds the **W.C. Handy Blues & Barbecue Festival** annually.

This event has become one of the largest free music festivals in the nation, drawing attendees from just about every state and many countries. The festival is a celebration of the life and legacy of W.C. Handy. The festival books some of the hottest national and local blues talent each year. The opening day of the festival is highlighted by the "Taste of Henderson Barbecue," where attendees can enjoy barbecue sold by local vendors and listen to great live music in Audubon Mill Park. Total attendance is estimated to exceed 50,000 each year.

VIGNETTE DANIEL BOONE, RICHARD HENDERSON, AND TRANSYLVANIA

Daniel Boone (1734–1820) was an early frontiersman, farmer, hunter, and pathfinder who grew up in the wilderness of Pennsylvania. Boone was employed by Richard Henderson (1735–1785), a jurist and land speculator, who formed the Transylvania Company in 1775 with other speculators to negotiate their own purchase of western lands from the Cherokee Nation. In exchange for several wagon loads of goods, the Cherokee signed over some eighteen million acres to the company, most of which is now present-day Kentucky. Virginia and North Carolina objected to the deal and voided the agreement in 1783. This led to years of armed conflict with the Cherokee. Richard Henderson gave his name to the city and county of Henderson, Kentucky, and he later sold the land that became the city of Nashville, Tennessee.

Boone was employed in 1775 by the Transylvania Company to blaze a trail through the Cumberland Gap—the pass through the Appalachian Mountains to central Kentucky and points west—for settlers to the Transylvania territory. Boone later led a militia to defend the territory during the American Revolution and worked as a surveyor along the Ohio River after the Revolution. Eventually, Daniel Boone drifted through several business ventures and followed one of his sons to Missouri, where he lived out his days near St. Louis.

Daniel Boone's early biographers began their mythmaking of the frontiersman as a folk hero soon after his death. The English romantic poet Lord Byron depicted Boone as such in one of his epic poems, Don Juan in 1822. Legends and books followed, later supplemented by movies. A TV show in the mid-1960s that featured actor Fess Parker in the role of Boone was a huge hit with children and caused a fad for raccoon-skin caps. Contrary to his television caricature, the real Daniel Boone wore a broad brimmed hat, not a coonskin cap. The more complex story of Daniel Boone at the birth of the American nation is one of negotiation, violence, and conflict with Indigenous peoples over coveted land and the early American justice system. Some forty-six million people in the U.S. today are descendants of the pioneers and settlers who passed through the Cumberland Gap. Many places in the United States are named for Boone, including the Daniel Boone National Forest in Kentucky.

SEBREE

Leaving Henderson and proceeding south, you'll pass through farmland into the small town of Sebree, an old railroad point. Along this portion of the road, I noted a food store catering to the Guatemalan and Mexican residents of the area, some of whom possibly worked at the local Tyson Foods Feed Mill and Americold Logistics distribution center nearby. About thirty-five percent of Sebree's current population is of Hispanic descent.

FRONTIER JUSTICE ON HIGHWAY 41A

A side trip west of Sebree of about fifteen minutes on Highway 41A will bring you to **Harpe's Head Road State Historic Site**. It received its name from the gruesome end met by Big Harpe, an outlaw in the early American republic who was slain in 1806 and had his head placed on a pole near an oak tree by the roadside. The Harpes were a gang of bandits who terrorized travelers in the area. Harpe's head was meant to serve as a deterrent to other potential highway robbers and murderers in the Kentucky territory. A historic marker titled "Frontier Justice" provides context at the site. Note that Highway 41A is a lightly traveled alternative to the main Highway 41, if you like pastoral surroundings. The little town of **Dixon** located along 41A is the seat of Webster County and the site of a WPA courthouse that dates from 1941.

THE I-69 CORRIDOR

Farther south on Highway 41 you'll pass farms and the busy CSX rail line going down to Nashville. The town of **Hanson** advertises itself as a strategic location for economic development just off the Pennyrile Parkway, which is soon to be part of the advertised **I-69 Corridor**. The corridor is part of an ambitious effort to create an interstate highway through the United States stretching from the Mexican border to the Canadian border. Each state along the route of this interstate is responsible for construction and timelines within state limits. Kentucky is farther advanced than most states in the development of its part of this corridor, which may be decades away from completion.

Frontier Justice plaque on 41A, Webster County, near Dixon, KY

Webster County Courthouse, Dixon, KY

MADISONVILLE

Highway 41 continues into Madisonville, the "Best Town on Earth" (or so says a sign on its Administrative Building). The town has a song, and a YouTube video titled "Best Town on Earth" to promote itself.

Madisonville is the seat of Hopkins County, with a courthouse square where a monument erected in 1908 to honor the Confederate dead stands. The town was a coal and tobacco center in the old days and has evolved into a manufacturing hub for western Kentucky. Several companies operate in the area. Major employers include distributors of apparel and restaurant supplies, aircraft engine and automotive components manufacturing, and manufacturers of firearms parts for assault weapons.

Madisonville's town square boasts some handsome old buildings and a cool ghost sign on what is now the Hopkins County Library. It advertises "Dulin's Ready-to-Wear Dry Goods." Madisonville is a quaint small town and a pleasant place to stop for lunch, as I did at **Country Cupboard**. If you have the time, visit the **Mahr Park Arboretum**, a 265-acre city park with trails, a disc golf course, and fishing ponds.

MORTONS GAP

Traveling south from Madisonville, you will pass through the little former coal mining towns of **Earlington** and **Mortons Gap**. Check out the City Hall building in Mortons Gap, now a barber shop, that dates from 1922. At Mortons Gap, you can view a historical marker noting the birthplace of Oliver Loving who became a cowboy in Texas, driving cattle with his partner Charles Goodnight on what came to be called the Goodnight-Loving trail. Larry McMurtry's 1985 Pulitzer Prize-winning novel *Lonesome Dove* and the television series it inspired, are based on their adventures.

From there, the road passes by more farms growing corn, soybeans, winter wheat, and tobacco, and through the small railroad towns of Nortonville—another "Crossroads of America" as stated on their website—and Crofton before arriving in Hopkinsville.

Madisonville, KY

Old City Hall, Mortons Gap, KY

HOPKINSVILLE

Hopkinsville, known by locals as "Hoptown," is the seat of Christian County and the most populous city along the Kentucky portion of Highway 41. Hoptown is an old city, incorporated in 1804, and a strategic location during the American Civil War. Both Confederate and Union forces controlled the city during the war. In December 1864, Confederate troops under General Hylan B. Lyon captured the town and burned down the Christian County courthouse. Remnants of the scorched decorative fence that once surrounded the old courthouse are on display at the local Pennyroyal Area Museum.

In addition to its long-standing role as the center for business and culture in this tobacco growing region, the southern portion of the city is expanding with hotels and restaurants along the 41-ALT four-lane road leading to Fort Campbell Military Base. A number of Japanese-owned auto suppliers have facilities nearby. Kentucky is a "right to work" state, which makes it illegal for a worker to be required to join or remain in the union of a unionized workplace. Most of the recent Japanese auto-related investment is going to states with low union membership.

Hopkinsville's city center has several restored buildings, including the **Pennyroyal Area Museum**—formerly the city's post office—which provides an exhibit about the role of tobacco-growing in the region. Since the early

Hopkinsville, KY

1800s, the city has been one of the leading "dark-fired" tobacco markets in the country. Grown in Kentucky and Tennessee, this type of tobacco is robust and smoky, with a strong flavor and aroma. The tobacco leaves are cured by exposing them to open fires or in heated barns, which gives them their distinctive dark color and intense flavor. Dark-fired tobacco is often used in pipe tobacco, chewing tobacco, and a variety of cigars. Kentucky ranks second in total tobacco production in the nation.

Downtown Hopkinsville, KY

The **Woody Winfree Fire-Transportation Museum** in the old Hopkinsville Fire Station is also located in Hopkinsville's downtown. The museum houses old buggies, wagons, gas pumps, antique fire trucks, and classic cars. No visit to Hoptown is complete without a stop at **Ferrell's Snappy Service**, a little eight-stool hamburger joint with an iconic sign outside. Ferrell's has been in business since 1935 and is an official Kentucky landmark.

Ferrell's Hamburgers, Hopkinsville, KY

HOPKINSVILLE AND THE TRAIL OF TEARS

Hopkinsville was a significant stop along the northern route of the "Trail of Tears," the forced displacement of approximately 60,000 Indigenous peoples by the United States government between 1830 to 1850. The **Trail of Tears Commemorative Park**, south of Hopkinsville's downtown, has a Heritage Center/Museum, a statue ground, and burial markers for Fly Smith and Chief Whitepath—two important Cherokee leaders who died during the removal. The site is part of the National Park Service and is on the National Register of Historic Places.

As you continue south from Hopkinsville through the little towns of Pembroke and Trenton, you will come across signs for the Northern portion of the **Trail of Tears Auto Route**, which extends through Western Kentucky and Tennessee. Highway 41 mirrors the Trail of Tears from Hopkinsville to the Tennessee border. To put the Trail in perspective, imagine following it on foot as most of the Indigenous people had to do.

While some Indigenous peoples traveled a water route via region's major

Trail of Tears Commemorative Park, Hopkinsville, KY

rivers—the Tennessee, the Ohio, the Mississippi, and the Arkansas—the majority were forced on a grueling overland journey on foot that lasted from November 1838 to March 1839. It is estimated that approximately 4,000 Indigenous peoples died of cold, hunger, and disease as they tried to complete the trip. The overland route ran from southeastern Tennessee into southwestern Kentucky. They then crossed the Ohio River into southern Illinois, walked across the Mississippi River and through southern Missouri, and finally stopped in what was then called "Indian Territory." This region was eventually reduced to the boundaries of the current state of Oklahoma after the Civil War. The **Trail of Tears National Historic Trail** was authorized in 1987 to help recognize this tragic part of U.S. history and to commemorate the struggles of the Indigenous peoples during this time.

VIGNETTE TWO NOTED HOPKINSVILLE RESIDENTS

Edgar Cayce (1877–1945) was a noted psychic, clairvoyant, faith-healer, and forerunning proponent of the holistic health movement, whose family lived in Hopkinsville. He founded the non-profit Association for Research and Enlightenment (A.R.E.), in 1931 with the mission of transforming lives through mind, body, and spirit wisdom. Cayce's work prefigured the New Age movement that currently promotes holistic, natural, and therapeutic treatments for some of the most common health concerns. He was a controversial figure within the health community, and his work remains controversial today.

bell hooks, the pen name of Gloria Jean Watkins (1952–2021), was a noted professor, scholar, author, and social activist best known for her writings on race, feminism, and class. bell hooks, an African American, grew up in Hopkinsville and attended segregated schools before attending Stanford University. She had a long career in academia at the University of Southern California before becoming the Distinguished Professor in Residence at Berea College in Kentucky. The bell hooks institute was founded in 2014 at Berea as an inclusive space for underrepresented students motivated by her insights that "patriarchy has no gender" and that "feminism is for everybody." A mural featuring her portrait is painted on the western wall of the Christian County Historical Society, one of the downtown buildings in Hopkinsville.

PINK ELEPHANTS

Along the highway south of Hoptown is the first of two GIANT pink elephants. The first one, near the town of Pembroke, advertises the **Pit Stop Drive In**, a drive-through liquor store. This elephant has a "Whiskey" sign next to it. The second, about fifteen miles south, stands outside of a gas station/convenience store in Guthrie. These are the kind of weird roadside attractions that make driving on the highway interesting!

Pink elephant outside Hopkinsville, KY

FAIRVIEW

Slightly to the east of Hopkinsville on U.S. Highway 68 not far from Highway 41 in the small farming town of Fairview (pop. 149), sits an unusual historical monument. Fairview was the birthplace of Jefferson Davis (1808–1889), a former U.S. Representative who became president of the Confederate States of America. To honor him, the Orphan Brigade, made up of Kentucky veterans who had fought on the side of the Confederates in the Civil War, put up an obelisk that looks like the Washington Monument in Washington, D.C. It is known as the **Jefferson Davis State Historic Site**. Started in 1907 and completed in 1924, it was meant to be one of a series of Confederate monuments for auto tourists to stop by and see. Today, you'll have to take a short but interesting side trip to see the edifice and the modest location it inhabits. You can take a vintage elevator ride to the top for a wide view of the surrounding area.

Jefferson Davis State Historic Site, Fairview, KY

KENTUCKY'S ROLE IN THE CIVIL WAR

In most of the county seats in Kentucky, there are monuments or historic markers commemorating soldiers of the Confederacy. Kentucky's government was on the side of the Union in the Civil War, but much of the population was sympathetic to the Confederacy. Ironically, to get to the Jefferson Davis historic site in Fairview, visitors must drive down Dr. Martin Luther King Jr. Way past Martin Luther King Jr. Elementary School in Hopkinsville.

Opinions about the Civil War will always be complicated due to the different lenses through which the conflict is seen. "The Lost Cause" is an interpretation of the American Civil War as the "War Between the States" that preserves the honor of the South as fighting a just and heroic war without any mention of the central role of slavery in the conflict. This deification of the war began shortly after its conclusion and increased into the 1960s as the Civil Rights movement gained support. Today, the monuments and markers are often paired with markers honoring soldiers from later conflicts up to the present. Though the Civil War took place over 160 years ago, we are still debating its legacy.

GUTHRIE

Highway 41 exits Kentucky at the small border town of Guthrie. Originally the site of the Pondy Woods stagecoach stop in the 1840s, Guthrie was later a railroad center incorporated by and named for James Guthrie, president of the Louisville & Nashville Railroad, in 1867. Once Guthrie was also an important tobacco center. A historical marker in town commemorates where a group of tobacco growers formed the Dark Tobacco District Planters' Protective Association of Kentucky and Tennessee (PPA) in 1904. This cooperative was established so these farmers could pool their crops in protest to the price fixing actions of James Duke and the American Tobacco Company, which were creating economic hardship to growers. A restoration of Guthrie's downtown was undertaken in the early 2000s, and if you are an aficionado of "ghost signs," there's a classic Coca-Cola ghost sign on the wall of one of the downtown buildings.

VIGNETTE NIGHT RIDERS AND TOBACCO WARS

Highway 41 in Kentucky traverses historic tobacco country. The Night Riders were

341

a militant faction of farmers opposed to the tobacco monopoly of the late 1800s and early 1900s promulgated by James B. Duke. Duke owned the American Tobacco Company (ATC), which had a tobacco monopoly; it controlled over ninety percent of the American cigarette market. Duke cut prices paid to tobacco farmers, which led to the Black Patch Tobacco Wars, that lasted from 1904 to 1909. The ATC priced tobacco so low that farmers were unable to make any profit. While groups of planters formed cooperatives to boycott the ATC, the Night Riders were far more militant. They targeted and destroyed ATC tobacco warehouses and actively terrorized farmers who sold to the ATC. In 1908, the Kentucky National Guard raided the group and arrested most of the leaders of the Night Riders, which diminished the organization. Several Night Riders were tried in court for violence and acquitted. In 1910, the US Supreme Court ruled that the ATC was a monopoly and ordered it to be disbanded, resulting in farmers once again receiving competitive prices for their tobacco.

Guthrie is the birthplace of Robert Penn Warren (1905—1989), America's first Poet Laureate and writer of the Pulitzer Prize winning novel *All the King's Men*, which was turned into an Oscar winning film in 1949. The plot focuses on the rise and fall of the ambitious and ruthless politician, Willie Stark, in the American South. Though a fictional character, Stark strongly resembles the flamboyant Louisiana governor and U.S. senator Huey Long who served in the 1920s and 1930s. To date, Warren is the only person to receive a Pulitzer Prize in both fiction and poetry. Warren was also noted for his insights into the myriad myths and issues of the Civil War and the Civil Rights Movement.

SIDE TRIP TO FORT CAMPBELL

Twenty miles to the west of Highway 41 is the massive **Fort Campbell Army Base**, which is located astride the Kentucky–Tennessee border between Hopkinsville and Clarksville, Tennessee. Approximately 70,000 acres, or two thirds of the total area of the installation, is in Tennessee; however, the official postal address for Fort Campbell is Kentucky.

Fort Campbell is home to the 101st Airborne Division—the "Screaming Eagles." The soldiers based here have usually been the first troops sent to overseas conflicts over the last two decades. Per Fort Campbell's website, the "...installation has the unique ability to deploy mission-ready contingency forces by air, rail, highway, and inland waterway."

Fort Campbell was originally established in 1942 as a mobilization camp and became a permanent installation in 1950. From 1948 to 1965, it was a top-secret nuclear weapons facility. The fort employs about 4,000 civilians, making it the area's largest employer and putting $2.6 billion into the local economy each year. Be aware that there is always heavy fort traffic.

The **Don F. Pratt Museum** was established at Fort Campbell in 1956 as a division museum for the 101st Airborne Division. The museum's central theme is the history of the 101st Airborne Division—the "Screaming Eagles"—and it covers the period from the early 1940s to present.

SIDE TRIP TO MAMMOTH CAVE AND BOWLING GREEN

Mammoth Cave National Park is approximately ninety-five miles east of Hopkinsville. The cave system comprises the world's longest network of cavern corridors. It is over three times longer than any other known cave system and a UNESCO World Heritage Site. The cave has been inhabited by humans for thousands of years; archeologists have found torches, gourd bowls, pottery, and woven cloth within the cave. A handful of dinosaur footprints exist as well.

Numerous hiking and biking trails wind through the park, and a variety of guided cave tours are provided as well. The website suggests you make reservations well in advance. According to the National Park Service website: "There are many different cave tours to choose from (and range) from a fully wheelchair accessible tour, short and long walking tours, lantern tours, and adventurous crawling tours. Some cave tours require a short bus ride to and from the cave entrance. Be sure to fully read the tour descriptions before purchasing your tour tickets."

Cave City lies outside the boundaries of Mammoth Cave National Park. The community has a number of attractions, including **Hidden River Cave** and the **American Cave Museum**, which features archeological exhibits. **Dinosaur World** has life-size models and a dino-themed playground for the kids.

And finally, if you are traveling back to Highway 41 from Mammoth Cave, you should make a stop in **Bowling Green** and check out the **National Corvette Museum**. As its name suggests, it is a museum that showcases the legacy of America's iconic sports car, the Chevrolet Corvette. If you love cars, this museum has over seventy classic Corvettes to admire. It is located

off I-65 just east of the city of Bowling Green:
https://www.corvettemuseum.org/

CONCLUDING THOUGHTS

Traveling on Highway 41 through western Kentucky is a trip back in time. If you are not tempted to blow through the state on I-69, you will see interesting small towns and farms along a lightly traveled road. The three cities of Henderson, Madisonville, and Hopkinsville are historic and interesting and worth a visit. Many of the natural attractions in the state are relatively easy to travel to from the road.

In the past, the people of western Kentucky were often characterized as "hillbillies," moonshiners, coal miners, and the like. But, like all stereotypes, these are unfortunate generalizations.

Many Kentuckians migrated to work in factories in the north in decades past due to the lack of economic prospects at home. There is much more industry now within the state, and it is a generally affordable place to live. The area through which Highway 41 travels is near larger locations and has thus not confronted some of the housing and congestion challenges Tennessee is managing.

Presently, Kentucky as a whole is prospering. Some of the state's largest employment sectors—automotive, metals, and the bourbon and spirits industry—have recently experienced record growth. The rapid rise of the electric vehicle and EV battery market has positioned the state for long term economic success, but the eastern portion of Kentucky is where most of the population growth is likely to be. The western portion remains agricultural with some manufacturing and less reliance on coal mining.

Kentucky has experienced some dreadful weather issues in recent years. A massive tornado in December 2021 flattened the far-western town of Mayfield, and the eastern part of the state has suffered serious flooding. There have been more frequent severe weather events in the area through which Highway 41 passes. According to meteorologists, "Tornado Alley" is shifting eastward from the Central Plains, and that will make Western Kentucky more prone to violent, dangerous storms in the future. This could have an impact on further development in the area.

Similar to other states, Kentucky has dealt with an opioid epidemic that continues to afflict those who live in the area. Substance abuse, including fentanyl, heroin, and methamphetamine use, is a critical public health and safety issue facing the state. The ease and availability of firearms within the state and from soldiers at Fort Campbell has also been a source of concern.

That said, some of the challenges the state now faces are the ones everyone wants. Kentucky's public and private sectors are working to improve workforce training and the education system to align more closely with high-demand skills. Homebuilders are trying to figure out when they will be able to meet demand. Whether or not Kentucky can retain its young people and avoid the brain drain that has afflicted some largely rural states will depend on good employment opportunities, affordable housing, and nearby interesting cultural activities that can attract and keep people in the state.

Kentucky is a conservative state where change occurs slowly. The small towns along Highway 41's Kentucky corridor will need outside investment to remain viable and necessary.

Postscript: In April 2025, generational flooding from torrential rains caused widespread damage to areas throughout Western Kentucky. The flooding severely impacted the city of Hopkinsville where much of the downtown area was submerged.

CHAPTER EIGHT
TENNESSEE

"*When I was governor, I was looking for a way to unify our state. I realized music is about the only thing that unifies Tennessee.*"

— *Lamar Alexander*

Highway 41 through Tennessee is 194 miles.

Key Towns/Cities: *Clarksville, Springfield, Goodletsville, Nashville, Murfreesboro, Manchester, Chattanooga*

Tennessee Counties along 41: *Montgomery, Robertson, Davidson, Rutherford, Coffee, Grundy, Marion, Hamilton*

Crossing from Kentucky, Highway 41 primarily traverses the "Middle Tennessee" section of the rectangular "Volunteer State." The highway goes through farming (and former farming) country that was once the province of the Cherokee Nation until the arrival of white settlers in the late 1700s. Highway 41 parallels Interstate 24 through much of its route and goes by a variety of places named for famous Tennesseans, including the James Robertson Parkway and Rosa Parks Boulevard in Nashville.

The state capital, Nashville, has grown markedly over the last decade; its metro area spreads north almost to the Kentucky border near the city of Clarksville, south to the satellite city of Murfreesboro, and beyond. Nashville has become one of the preferred locations for young professionals, and new construction abounds. Older, former farm-oriented towns along the road are being transformed into modern suburbs of Nashville as the metro area continues to grow in population.

Farther south of Metro Nashville, the highway goes through small towns, cities, and picturesque agricultural country. Farms along the road grow corn, soybeans, hay, cotton, and tobacco. Thick forest extends southeast from the town of Monteagle in the Cumberland Plateau region to the upscale historic town of Lookout Mountain just outside the city of Chattanooga, which sits on the bank of the Tennessee River near where Highway 41 exits into Georgia. Chattanooga has also grown into a major technology hub along with retaining its historic role as a transportation center.

The western edge of the Appalachian Mountains through central Tennessee is a mix of forest, woodland, and prairie on land formerly used for agriculture. The Interior Low Plateaus, as they are geologically known, are a series of gently rolling limestone landforms comprising the Pennyroyal Plateau and the **Nashville Basin**. Within the basin is the **Cumberland River**: present-day Nashville was founded on its banks. Surrounding the basin is the **Highland Rim**, an area of higher ground containing dense oak forests. The Nashville Basin was once an area of grassy meadows where bison, and later cattle and hogs, grazed. Tobacco and cotton were grown in this region, which also produced corn, soybeans, rapeseed, and a variety of other crops. The **Tennessee Valley**, which lies south of Nashville, is where cotton was grown and iron ore was mined.

A TENNESSEE ALBUM PLAYLIST

- Dolly Parton: *Jolene* 1974
- Tina Turner: *Private Dancer* 1984
- Kings of Leon: *Only by the Night* 2008
- Chet Atkins: *Chet Atkins in Three Dimensions* 1955
- Bessie Smith: *Bessie Smith Album* 1938
- Justin Timberlake: *Future Sex/Love Sounds* 2006
- Johnny Cash: *At Folsom Prison* 1968
- Rosanne Cash: *Black Cadillac* 2006
- Miley Cyrus: *Miley Cyrus & Her Dead Petz* 2015
- Paramore: *Riot!* 2007
- Kenny Chesney: *No Shoes, No Shirt, No Problems* 2002
- Jimi Hendrix: *Band of Gypsys* 1970
- Bob Dylan: *Nashville Skyline* 1969
- Taylor Swift: *Fearless* 2008
- Patsy Cline: *Showcase* 1961

IDENTITY

Tennessee is a southern state that has seen unprecedented growth over the last decade. Low taxes, mild weather, affordable living, and many employment opportunities have been big draws. Unfortunately, the transportation infrastructure has not kept up with the influx of people visiting and moving to the state. Prepare for some major congestion within the cities and on the main interstate highways.

At present, it is still possible to have good conversations (particularly about sports), listen to a variety of live music, and enjoy "southern hospitality" from friendly state residents. Tennessee is also the capital of country music in all of its different forms.

Tennessee has many parks, lakes, and forests for recreation, including the heavily visited **Great Smoky Mountains National Park** in the eastern part of the state. Tennesseans are quite religious with churches nearly everywhere. Politically, the state has moved from being moderately conservative to supporting a much harder right-wing contingent at the state level. This contingent is seeking to take control from local counties to place it within the state legislature. It will be interesting to see how this plays out in future years.

BY THE NUMBERS

Tennessee had a population of 7.1 million in 2023. It is among the fastest-growing states in the country, with many new residents coming from other parts of the United States. The population was 4.6 million in 1980, 5.07 million in 2000 and 6.09 million in 2020. The Nashville Metro population is approximately two million and growing. The Chattanooga metropolitan area (430,000) and Clarksville metropolitan area (177,000) are also fast-growing areas along Highway 41.

CLARKSVILLE

The journey south on Highway 41 through Tennessee can start with a quick detour a few miles east to Highway 41A, which skirts Fort Campbell and crosses the state line near the city of **Clarksville**. Clarksville lies along the Cumberland River and is the seat of Montgomery County. The city has grown in population over the last decade. It is the fifth-largest city in Tennessee, ranking just below Chattanooga in population. Ties to **Fort Campbell Army Base;** proximity to Nashville, to nearby recreational activities, and to facilities for several large corporations; and an affordable cost of living (there is no state income tax in Tennessee) have converged to increase the profile of the city. As the population has increased, so have traffic congestion issues in and around the area.

The Clarksville area has been inhabited for a millennia. **Dunbar Cave State Park**, located within the city, is a prehistoric site that has been used by humans for thousands of years. It is the site of significant Indigenous Mississippian cave art dating to the fourteenth century. Prior to European settlement, the Muscogee, Cherokee, Chickasaw, and Choctaw inhabited the area. The city was founded in 1784 as part of a reservation set aside by North Carolina to repay Revolutionary War soldiers and named for Revolutionary War hero George Rogers Clark.

A visit to Dunbar Cave also offers travelers an opportunity to understand the history of the African American experience in the region. From 1785 to 1865, Dunbar Cave was part of a plantation where more than 100 people were enslaved. The cave was a natural refrigerator of sorts for produce grown nearby. "Affricanna Town," near the entrance to the cave was a small village set up by refugees at the time of Emancipation. The place later became a segregated resort and tourist attraction in the era before air conditioning. The only African Americans allowed at the resort were those who worked for the facility. Country singer Roy Acuff later made it a concert venue. Abandoned in the early 1970s, it is a very interesting place to explore.

Dunbar Cave State Park, Clarksville, TN

Clarksville grew due to its access to the Cumberland River and nearby tobacco plantations. It was a strategically important city in the Civil War, occupied by Confederate troops until a flotilla of Union troops arrived by river. The Union occupied the city from 1862 until the end of the war. After the war, Clarksville remained prosperous due to the tobacco plantations, steamboat routes, and the railroad that made the city a transportation center.

In 1878, a great fire destroyed most of Clarksville's downtown area, which led to the rebuilding of the city center. It is now a historic area, including the **Roxy Theatre**, built in 1947 and used as a backdrop for numerous photo shoots, films, and commercials. A statue of Clarksville native Frank Sutton, who played the exasperated Sergeant Carter from the TV show *Gomer Pyle U.S.M.C.* stands right by the theater.

The **Customs House Museum & Cultural Center**, an ornate, Victorian building from 1898 in the city's historic district, was originally constructed as a U.S. post office during the tobacco boom. Today it houses local history and art exhibits as well as a fantastic children's museum in the basement that features a model train exhibit that is a sight to see.

The city has sustained large-scale damage from tornadoes and floods over the last twenty-five years and has rebuilt in each case. **Austin Peay State University** (enrollment 9,300), a regional state university, is located in Clarksville.

Customs House Museum and Cultural Center, Clarksville, TN

Roxy Theatre, Clarksville, TN

Frank Sutton, Sgt. Vince Carter statue, sculpted by Scott Wise, Clarksville, TN

There are two noteworthy historical plaques in the downtown area. One denotes the existence of Clarksville's pre-Civil War Slave Market. The marker denotes the corner where enslaved people were kept in a pen waiting to be sold at auction at the county courthouse. The sign notes that the enslaved population comprised half of the people living in Montgomery County in 1860. Very chilling to see.

The other plaque commemorates the city's ties and early 1960s connection with Jimi Hendrix, one of the most famous rock guitarists of all time. Hendrix was a soldier serving at Fort Campbell during his training as a parachutist. While living at the fort, he was also developing his guitar skills with a soldier friend. After being discharged from the Army, he stayed in Clarksville to play with a band at clubs there and in Nashville. Eventually, Hendrix moved to England where he became a star before returning to the United States with icon status at the Monterey International Pop Festival and Woodstock. He died in 1970 at age twenty-seven, leaving a musical legacy that has only grown over the decades.

One further musical note: the Monkees' hit song from 1966, "Last Train to Clarksville," is about a draftee trying to set up a meeting with his love before reporting to Fort Campbell for training prior to deployment to Vietnam.

VIGNETTE WILMA RUDOLPH

Wilma Rudolph (1940–1994) was a track and field star who overcame bouts of polio and scarlet fever and wore a leg brace during her childhood in Clarksville, Tennessee. She became a world-record-holding Olympic champion, winning a bronze medal in the 1956 Olympics in Melbourne and three gold medals at the 1960 Olympics in Rome. Her performances earned her the title of "the fastest woman in the world," and she became an international sports legend.

Upon returning home to Clarksville, she was celebrated with a parade and banquet in her honor. At her insistence (and refusal to attend otherwise), the parade and banquet were fully integrated—the first such integrated events ever held in the city. She won the Associated Press Female Athlete of the Year award in 1961.

Rudolph worked as a teacher while also serving as an ambassador for track and field events throughout the United States. Her Olympic success provided a boost to U.S. women's track. She was inducted into the U.S. Olympic Hall of Fame in 1983, and in 1990, she became the first woman to receive the National Collegiate Athletic Association's Silver Anniversary Award.

She died of a brain tumor in 1994. The life of Wilma Rudolph has been remembered in movies and publications, especially books for young readers. Clarksville has named a street after her as well as erected a bronze statue next to the local event center named in her honor. A section of Clarksville's history museum is devoted to her accomplishments. Wilma Rudolph is considered one of the greatest U.S. athletes of the twentieth century.

TOBACCO COUNTRY

Returning to Highway 41 past Clarksville, stay on the two-lane road through the **"Black Patch"** agricultural country once noted for tobacco production. While the barns in this area may look like they are on fire, they are actually curing tobacco leaves as part of the process of readying for market, which makes this an interesting place to see. Tobacco farming in Tennessee has been in decline for years, with fewer tobacco farms playing a smaller role in the state's economy.

In 2005, the $10 billion buyout of tobacco farmers and quota holders as part of the termination of the federal tobacco price support program sharply accelerated these trends. Smaller family tobacco farms are no longer the rule but the exception, as larger agribusinesses have taken their place. "Agritourism"—farms that link agricultural production and processing with tourism to attract visitors—is a growing industry in this area of the state, allowing some small farms to remain viable.

Tobacco curing in northern TN

ADAMS

The first locale on Highway 41 proper in Tennessee after crossing the border with Kentucky, is the picturesque little town of **Adams**. Adams's claims to fame for tourists are the **Bell Witch Cave** and **John Bell House**. Tradition says the Bell family purchased a tract of farmland from Mrs. Kate Batts, a neighbor with a reputation for meanness.

Mrs. Batts declared the Bell family cheated her, swearing on her deathbed she would come back and "hant" John Bell and all his kith and kin to their graves. The Bell family was allegedly tormented for years by the spirit of Old Kate Batts who sang, swore, and threw dishes and furniture at them. And Batt's anger extended beyond the Bell family. Old Kate reputedly terrified Andrew Jackson and some friends who came to the farm from Nashville to investigate. After a sleepless night, the harried Jackson left the farm saying to Bell that "I'd rather fight the British again than have any more dealings with that torment." The Bell Witch disappeared when John Bell died, but the Bell Witch Cave is still widely known for its paranormal activity and considered one of the most haunted places in the United States. The cave and Bell homestead are now privately operated venues that draw tourists.

Along the highway one will see signs for the **"Ring of Fire,"** a tourist trail that passes through the town of Adams and other scenic rural towns along the Cumberland Plateau. Sights along the trail include Dale Hollow Lake, the Cordell Hull Lock and Dam, and the Cumberland River.

To the west of Adams is **Port Royal State Historic Park**. Port Royal, established in 1797 and situated on the Red River, was a regional tobacco town and important trading post worked by enslaved African Americans. It was also a stop on the Trail of Tears in 1838. After the Civil War, the town was settled by new citizens—the formerly enslaved workers who became "shopkeepers, craftsperson's, ministers, and leaders" as indicated on a local historical marker. The town declined in the early part of the twentieth century as river traffic on the Red River and highways bypassed it. The state acquired a significant portion of the town in 1978 and developed it into the current preserved and protected historic site. Be sure to check out the old bridge across the Red River.

SPRINGFIELD

After passing through more farm country, you'll arrive in the town of

Port Royal State Historic Park Bridge, Port Royal, TN

Springfield, the Robertson County seat. Similar to many small cities along U.S. 41, Springfield has a civic square around the courthouse. Once an important venue for tobacco auctions, the Robertson County History Museum in the civic square extols the role of dark-fired tobacco of the city's past.

Dark-fired is a Burley type tobacco commonly used in cigarettes and sometimes in pipes and cigars. The cured tobacco leaves are known for their strong, distinct flavor. Due to Springfield's importance in the early part of the twentieth century, the "Bee Line," which eventually became Highway 41, was routed through the town. Stop along the highway at the **Dixie Maid Café**, established in 1953 and "the oldest café in town," or so says the sign.

The towns generally spruced up buildings and high-end stores speak to the fact that Springfield is within easy driving distance to Nashville. In a nod to the past, a monument to the fallen Confederate soldiers stands next to the courthouse, but the value of real estate in Springfield is propelling the old town into a new direction as a home for commuting professionals.

356

While the city boasts many restaurants, its closed movie theater, skating rink, and bowling alley are mourned by longtime residents.

Southeast of Springfield, Highway 41 passes through the small towns of Greenbrier and **Ridgetop**, "A beautiful small thriving community still welcoming with open arms and southern hospitality." Ridgetop, located at the edge of the Highland Rim at an elevation of over 800 feet above sea level, was settled in the early 1800s. Later, it became a vacation community for wealthy Nashville residents who could afford to take summer vacations. The resort was known as "The Enclosure."

Downtown Springfield, TN

Dixie Maid Café, Springfield, TN

GOODLETTSVILLE

Goodlettsville is the last city on southbound 41 before Nashville. It's also the location of the headquarters for **Dollar General**, the fastest-growing retail operation in the United States. The company was started in 1939 as J.L. Turner and Son. The name was changed to Dollar General in 1955, and the company went public in 1968. Dollar General is ranked among the top 100 companies in the United States by revenue. Locating many of its stores in rural areas of the nation, Dollar General's base customers are households earning $40,000 annually or less.

You'll see a lot of them along Highway 41, mainly outside small, underserved towns where most of the traditional main street retail establishments have disappeared. The chain is growing thanks to soaring inflation and the ongoing hollowing out of the middle class. Dollar stores provide a selection of goods of questionable quality and are often the only store within miles of the community. Unfortunately, such stores have also been places of violence due to minimal security.

The old-time general stores, produce stores, meat markets, and such, that populated many small downtowns are businesses of the past, except in higher income locations where a well-heeled customer base can pay the higher prices associated with more personal attention. Incidentally, in 2022 *Fortune* magazine ranked Dollar General among the most admired companies in the United States.

OPRYLAND

South of Goodlettsville, Highway 41 becomes congested with more stoplights. To the east is the **Gaylord Opryland Resort and Convention Center**, location of the **Grand Ole Opry** since 1974. It is quite an immense complex with a nine-acre indoor garden atrium, multiple restaurants and bars, a swimming aquatic center, a golf course, and, of course, the Opry. The Opry has been a going concern since 1925 which celebrates country music but has expanded to encompass bluegrass, folk, gospel, and comedy performances. Thirty years ago, this complex was quite far from Nashville's downtown in a more rural area on the outskirts of the city. Not anymore.

OPRYLAND USA

Situated next to the Cumberland River and just to the south of the current resort was the home of Opryland USA theme park, which operated between 1972 and 1997. The park offered roller coasters and carousels along with popular music shows featuring a variety of genres. Some of the most memorable Opryland rides included the Little Rock N' Roller Coaster for the kiddies, the Grizzly River Rampage, the Screamin' Delta Demon bobsled coaster, the Wabash Cannonball corkscrew coaster, and the Hangman suspended looping coaster. It was also home to an indoor "illusion" coaster called Chaos.

Though a major tourist attraction, the park was closed by Gaylord Properties, the park's parent company, to build a year-round attraction, **Opry Mills**—a super-regional shopping mall with over 178 stores. Older Nashville natives lament the closing of the old theme park, but amusement park fans may soon find some relief. In the summer of 2023, a development corporation unveiled planning for a theme park called **Storyville Gardens** to be situated in the city of Lebanon, thirty miles east of Nashville.

NASHVILLE

Highway 41 is known as Dickerson Pike as it proceeds into the city of **Nashville**. With a current population of over 700,000 within a metropolitan area of more than two million, Nashville is the largest city in Tennessee and is growing rapidly. It is gaining about 100 new residents daily. The city can be considered the capital of the "Mid-South," a term used to delineate the connection between northern parts of the South and southern parts of the Midwest. A born-and-raised long time resident of the city told me that, "Nashville is the dividing line between north and south; the city is 'in the south,' but not 'of the south.'"

Thirty years ago, Nashville's population was 445,000, and, for all intents and purposes, the city was a down-at-the-heels place known only for the state capital and the home of country music. The city and metro area have nearly doubled in population since 1990, transforming into a booming metropolis. The Greater Nashville Metro Area occupies approximately sixty-five miles along Highway 41, from Springfield in the north to just beyond Murfreesboro in the south. As of 2023, Metro Nashville is behind Austin and Houston as the fastest-growing area in the country.

Nashville has become a trendy destination for immigrants due to a healthy job market and a relatively low cost of living. The foreign-born population of the city has doubled over the past decade and comprises approximately twelve percent of the population. The city is home to large populations of Mexicans, Kurds, Vietnamese, Cambodians, Laotians, Arabs, and Bantus. Nashville is home to the largest Kurdish population in the country, and some 60,000 Bhutanese refugees have settled in the area. Nashville also has an active American Jewish community with a local history dating back more than 150 years.

In 2013, *The New York Times* anointed Nashville as the "It City"—the place to which everyone wants to move. Due to the city's very permissive zoning regulations, this has led to an amazing number of new buildings being constructed within the city. Neighborhoods have been completely transformed from small single-family worker cottages to townhouse developments and larger residential high-rises. Gentrification of former working-class areas has become a major challenge for housing affordability. Local wags have suggested that the new state bird is the "construction crane."

Nashville lies along the banks of the flood-prone Cumberland River. The Cumberland was (and still is) the source of the city's drinking water, but it was also where waste was disposed of, leading to periodic cholera outbreaks. Major efforts are underway to clean the river and overhaul the drainage system to better accommodate rainfall and prevent sewage backups in residences and offices throughout the city. This is a major and costly public works effort.

Because of the booming development, Nashville has a serious growing traffic problem. The freeway and arterial street networks are poorly designed for growth, becoming congested throughout the day. Many streets are also obsolete, with few sidewalks or areas for parking. The public transport system is not robust. In 2018, a transit plan initiative called "Let's Move Nashville" was put to voters. The proposal included the construction of an underground tunnel downtown, a twenty-six-mile-long light rail system, and the deployment of more rapid buses. To pay for the initiative, the plan proposed a half-cent sales tax hike and a surcharge on the business, hotel, and rental tax.

Additionally, bike lanes and paths have been proposed to expand infrastructure, but most have been shot down by the city council. However, scooters are abundant zooming around the downtown area. In November 2024, Nashville voters approved the "Choose How You Move" transit plan, appropriating $3.1 billion for a major overhaul of the city's bus systems, sidewalks, and traffic signals. It's worth spending a few days in Nashville to observe how hyper-growth defines its changing character.

NASHVILLE'S IDENTITY

Nashville is one of the more interesting cities along Highway 41. A small city that has grown into a big city, aspects of both are on display. As of late, Nashville has attracted many young people who like the laid-back lifestyle, but it will be interesting to see if they will stay to establish roots and raise families. In similar fashion to Hollywood and the movie business, many people come to Nashville aspiring to break into the music business. With fierce competition, these hopefuls may need to find other reasons to call the city home if they plan to stay. Nashville has become a hot spot for young techies as well which may become the future catalyst for growth.

NASHVILLE ISSUES

BASIC URBAN CHALLENGES

As Nashville has grown into a major city over the last two decades, it has faced a host of urban problems that are endemic to most American cities. Among these is a progressively growing chronic homeless population of women and children. An effort has been made to unify the city's response to homelessness, which has previously been spread among different offices. The city is also struggling with an opioid epidemic characterized by drug overdose deaths, mostly due to synthetic opioids like fentanyl.

GUNS

The state of Tennessee has some of the weakest gun laws in the country. In March 2023, a gunman killed three children and three staff members at Covenant Christian Primary School, leading to a heated confrontation in the state assembly over Tennessee's permissive gun regulations. Two African American legislators in Nashville were voted out of the assembly over the issue only to be voted back in by their constituents.

EDUCATION

In very controversial moves, the city has consolidated high schools and primary schools to save money. Charter schools have siphoned off many funds that once went to traditional public schools. Some longtime Nashville residents I spoke with were quite upset over these moves, as they impact communities in adverse ways. High school sports teams and other long-standing features of their neighborhoods are being taken away. Schools that communities were originally built around have disappeared without much resident input.

THE NAME

Nashville's name goes back to the late 1700s, when colonists established Fort Nashborough where the modern-day city is located now. The fort was named after **Francis Nash**, a North Carolinian who fought in the American Revolution. Nashborough was changed to Nashville in 1784.

NICKNAMES

Today Nashville is known by several nicknames. The most well-known is "Music City," but it is also known as "Cashville" in the African American community, and "Nashvegas" to those who see the downtown strip of bars on Broadway similar to the Las Vegas strip, minus the gambling.

Two names with a nod to Nashville's faith-based community are "Buckle of the Bible Belt," due to Nashville's large number of churches, and "The Protestant Vatican," given the city's number of denominational headquarters. Finally, the very popular Nashville Predators NHL hockey team have dubbed their city "Smashville."

NASHVILLE'S HISTORY

Nashville has been an important city since its official founding in 1806 when it also became the seat of Davidson County. It was designated the capital of the state of Tennessee in 1843. At that time, Nashville was one of the wealthiest southern cities due to iron production and its strong market in agricultural commodities. A historical marker in Nashville's present-day downtown denotes the location of the city's large slave market, once considered the heart of the city. As a major shipping port and rail center,

Nashville was the first Confederate state capital to be captured by Union troops in 1862, during the Civil War. In late 1864, the Confederate Army of Tennessee attempted to retake the city, but it suffered a significant defeat in the Battle of Nashville. A few months later, the Confederacy surrendered in Virginia, North Carolina, and, Texas.

In 1868, the Nashville chapter of the Ku Klux Klan was founded by disaffected Confederate veterans as a white supremacist organization. The Klan was one of the more violent organizations that originated in the city, which was referred to as the "cradle of the Lost Cause" after Reconstruction. In 1894, the United Daughters of the Confederacy was founded in Nashville. As a southern city, Nashville embraced Jim Crow policies, racially segregating public facilities until the early 1960s after a series of sit-ins were organized at lunch counters in downtown Nashville. A slow integration of most public facilities took place over the decade.

VIGNETTE DIANE NASH AND SNCC

Diane Nash (b. 1938) was born and raised in Chicago before attending Fisk University in Nashville as an English major. In Nashville, she was exposed for the first time to Jim Crow policies in 1959, when she was required to use the "Colored Women's" bathroom at the Tennessee State Fair. That experience led her to attend non-violence workshops, and in 1960 at age twenty-two, Nash became the leader of the Nashville student sit-ins targeting segregated lunch counters. The protests lasted from February to May, when the lunch counters began allowing African Americans to sit and eat with white customers. Later, Nash organized boycotts of grocery stores that refused to hire African Americans. She became one of the founders of the Student Nonviolent Coordinating Committee (SNCC).

SNCC would be involved in many campaigns during the Civil Rights era. Nash was one of the key leaders of the Freedom Riders in 1961. Volunteers, both white and African American, rode buses throughout the Jim Crow South to challenge segregation on interstate buses and in passenger facilities. During this period, she worked closely with Dr. Martin Luther King Jr. and the Southern Christian Leader Conference (SCLC). In 1963, President Kennedy appointed Nash to a national committee to promote Civil Rights legislation. She was involved in virtually every important Civil Rights action in the mid-1960s, including lobbying for the passage of the 1964 Civil Rights Act and the 1965 Voting Rights Act.

In December 2021, the Metropolitan Council of Nashville and Davidson County voted to name the landing in front of Nashville's courthouse the **Diane Nash Plaza**. *She received the Presidential Medal of Freedom in July 2022. Diane Nash is one of the last living links to the formative events of the Civil Rights era.*

In the 1970s, Nashville began to evolve from a sleepy, provincial state capital to national footprint due to the growth of the entertainment, healthcare, insurance, and automotive industries. Greater suburbanization in the metropolitan area occurred in the 1970s and 1980s, with the Grand Ole Opry moving from the Ryman Auditorium downtown to the self-contained resort hotel, convention center and amusement park called Opryland in 1974. By the late 1980s, downtown Nashville was quite dilapidated, with many closed-up buildings.

In 1975, just months before the celebration of the American bicentennial, Robert Altman's classic film *Nashville* was released. It is a docudrama about many things: opportunistic politics, family, marriage, music, greed, and loneliness. The film also offers a biting look at the "Nashville Scene," which revolved around the growing country music industry. While many things have changed in Nashville and the United States in the decades since its release, the film still resonates for its commentary on the city and the country.

A number of projects were initiated in the 1990s to provide much needed greenspace in the city. One of the most significant of these was **Bicentennial Capitol Mall State Park**, completed in 1996 and built to celebrate the 200th anniversary of Tennessee's statehood. The eleven-acre park tells the story of the state's history through plaques, plants, and fountains.

Bicentennial Capitol Mall State Park, Nashville, TN

Bicentennial Capitol Mall State Park, Nashville, TN

THE MUSIC BUSINESS

With its diverse music industry that includes all genres, Nashville has the highest concentration of musicians, talent managers and agents, and music-related companies in the nation. The city's music and entertainment companies are a combination of global corporations, small businesses, and independent artists, (including frontline musicians, backing vocalists, session musicians, composers, songwriters, lyricists, beat-makers, and studio producers). Music performance, composition, distribution, promotion, production, training and education, artists' rights groups, music organizations, live music venues, and builders and purveyors of equipment can all be found in Nashville. Within the greater Nashville Metro area, the industry is worth approximately $15.6 billion dollars.

Nashville is not only where country and gospel music began but also where it extended into pop and rock. Influential rock and pop artists associated with Nashville currently include Dolly Parton, The Allman Brothers Band, Kings of Leon, Garth Brooks, Kenny Chesney, Jack White, The Black Keys, Keith Urban, Paramore, Taylor Swift, and many more.

TOURISM & BACHELORETTE CAPITAL OF AMERICA

In the early 2000s, Nashville began backing a fresh tourism strategy that rebranded the "Music City" as both a music and a party destination. A formerly seedy stretch of the downtown "District," known for the adult entertainment industry, gave way to drinking establishments often tied to particular country music stars. The popular television show "Nashville," aired from 2012 to 2018, chronicled the lives of various fictitious country music singers in the city.

The **Music City Center** convention complex located downtown opened in 2013, bringing in additional visitors to the area. Nashville has become a melting pot of tourism extravaganzas, especially for music lovers. The city rebuilt Broadway, its entertainment district, with increased attention to historic preservation, and it moved a trash incinerator away from the river near the district. There are now over 180 live music venues throughout the city, a plethora of culinary offerings, many shopping centers, and more. Back in 1978, Nashville welcomed 7.7 million tourists. In 2023, the city hosted over 16.8 million visitors.

Nashville is now ranked among the top ten tourist destinations in the country, but with that growth has come growing alcohol overconsumption, drug use, and obnoxious tourist behavior that has brought negative attention and threatens to turn residents away from the area. The city is trying to balance its tourist success with the need to rein in bad behavior.

Among the tourist successes has been the growth of "Bachelorette" parties —one of the big reasons for visiting Nashville. Somewhere between 4,000 and 5,000 parties take place each month. This has been chronicled in articles, news programs, and even a documentary. Seeing a group of young women in boots and hats trooping through the downtown District or visiting one of the trendy hip neighborhoods throughout the city is not an unusual site.

Watching "Pedal Taverns" and "Party Barges" filled with revelers going down the street to various city locations for Instagram photos may be interesting for an observer like me, but many of those who call the city home regard such vehicles as a nuisance. A cottage industry of conspicuous leisure tours that feature shopping opportunities, dining options, hair and makeup application, and transportation to and from safe honky-tonk bars and distilleries for groups of bachelorettes has grown into a prosperous enterprise. Whatever the thoughts or jealousies of entitled, attractive young people, the money spent on bridal-related tourism in the city is undeniable.

Nashville Party Barge, Nashville, TN

HOUSING

Although Nashville is currently booming, affordable housing is an issue. Housing costs have skyrocketed in the metro area as more people move in. The familiar squeeze on lower-income families is in evidence with little being done to address it.

Close-in city neighborhoods are replete with "Tall Skinnies"—two tall, narrow homes in the place of an older, now demolished, one-story home. This satisfies the demands of young professionals for new housing where affordable land is scarce. Some neighborhoods are organizing to resist this change, but it is ongoing at present. Redevelopment of older working-class areas, many primarily African American, may be destroying what once made the city unique. And, as previously mentioned, Nashville, like most major cities, must deal with growing homeless issues. Encampments of unhoused individuals have been disbanded, but it's hard to ignore the homeless individuals who now live on the streets next to new construction in parts of the city.

CHURCHES

Nashville is said to be a city of churches, with a majority of born-and-raised Nashvillians attending one church or another. Local legend claims there is a church on every corner of the city. Life in Nashville has historically revolved around church activities and family connections. Gospel music has a legacy in the city in both the largely white and largely African American churches.

The **Downtown Presbyterian Church** and **St. Mary of the Seven Sorrows Church** (also downtown) date from the 1840s. **Spruce Street Baptist Church** is one of the oldest African American churches in Nashville that dates back from the mid-1800s.

Condominium construction nearby Bicentennial Capitol Mall State Park, Nashville, TN

SCHOOLS

Once called the "Athens of the South" due to the number of institutions of higher education in the city, Nashville is home to several noted colleges and universities. **Vanderbilt University** (enrollment 13,710) is a prestigious, highly rated institution with a large old campus. **Belmont University** (enrollment 8,910) is known for its lovely campus and music and arts programs. **Fisk University** (enrollment 1,050) is a prestigious HBCU (historically black colleges and universities) with a concentration in the liberal arts. Its campus is recognized as a National Historic Landmark. **Tennessee State University** (enrollment 8,077) is a state-funded HBCU. **Lipscomb University** (enrollment 4,650) is a private liberal arts school affiliated with the Church of Christ.

SPORTS

Major cities in the United States have professional sports teams, and Nashville is no exception. The city acquired a pro football team, the Tennessee Titans, in 1998 and a pro hockey team, the Nashville Predators, in 1997. The **Bridgestone Arena**, where the Predators play, is a multi-purpose venue that has hosted numerous concerts, sports, and other events since its completion in 1996. It is located near downtown Nashville. Because of its accessible location near Music Row, the arena is a popular place to attend country music performances.

The Tennessee Titans currently play in **Nissan Stadium**, a multi-purpose stadium along the Cumberland River that was built in 1999. The stadium is jointly owned by the city of Nashville and Davidson County. Despite being only slightly over twenty-five years old, the team and city recently agreed upon a replacement stadium that will cost $2.1 billion. This will make it one of the most expensive stadiums in the country. The new stadium will be fully enclosed and projected to open in 2027. The team and city hope to host major events such as the Super Bowl and college football championships at the stadium. Plans to renovate the area around the Cumberland River will add additional costs to the project.

Given the growth of Nashville, it is rumored that a Major League Baseball Team may consider moving to the city soon.

NEIGHBORHOODS

Highway 41 goes through and nearby several Nashville neighborhoods of note. To understand the city, it is worthwhile to go beyond the main tourist destinations to see where growth and change are occurring.

EAST NASHVILLE

Highway 41 skirts **East Nashville**, an area that looks to be quickly gentrifying. Between its size and proximity to downtown, East Nashville has begun to blur the line between urban and suburban. Neighborhood residents and business owners tend to be transplants from larger cities. The area boasts a number of businesses, bars, and restaurants, and the **Five Points** area of East Nashville has a number of art galleries and hosts several annual festivals including the Tomato Art Fest. The neighborhood's distinctive homes are generally larger and older, and the area is more settled than some of the Nashville neighborhoods closer to downtown. Lot sizes and proliferation of schools make it a much-desired place to put down roots.

Within East Nashville is an area called **Historic Edgefield**. On the National Register of Historic Places, residents are taking steps to limit commercial development to the corridor streets on its periphery to preserve its residential character.

As you drive by schools, churches, and car lots, Highway 41 becomes the James Robertson Parkway on its way past and into downtown Nashville.

East Nashville map, Nashville, TN

TENNESSEE STATE CAPITOL & BICENTENNIAL CAPITOL MALL STATE PARK

Highway 41 becomes Rosa L. Parks Boulevard as it rings around the bluff occupied by the **Tennessee State Capitol**. The building, which dates from 1859, is worth visiting to see a cool winding staircase up to bookshelves where all the legal statutes are housed. A statue of Andrew Jackson stands on the capitol grounds, as does the tomb of James K. Polk, the 11th President of the United States, and his wife Sarah Childress Polk. Another noteworthy statue is—the "Sergeant York" of World War I fame, a Medal of Honor recipient, and the subject of a classic movie made about his exploits.

The seat of government for the state has seen some raucous protests of late. Gun laws, abortion rights, school vouchers, corporate tax loopholes, and unfair taxation issues have been among the latest issues of protest.

Tennessee State Capitol Building, Nashville, TN

VIGNETTE   ANDREW JACKSON, DAVID CROCKETT, AND EDWARD CARMACK

On the capitol grounds is an imposing statue of Andrew Jackson (1767–1845). Inside the capitol building is a bust of David "Davy" Crockett (1786–1836), and, until it was torn down in 2020, a statue of Edward Carmack (1858–1908) stood outside of the capitol entrance. All three of these individuals were significant and are controversial to the present day.

Jackson, the seventh president of the United States and the face on the $20 currency note, had an outsized impact on the development of the country in his two terms as president. Known for his strong-willed and combative personality, Jackson was a populist hero who ushered in a key era of American exploration and westward expansion. He was also a wealthy slaveholder who supported and profited from slavery. He was a proponent of Indian removal and cruelty to Indigenous peoples of the southeast and Midwest. The Indian Removal Act he pushed through Congress, resulted in the forced displacement of 50,000 Indigenous nations off ancestral lands. Tens of thousands of Indigenous peoples died during forced removals like the Trail of Tears.

David Crockett was a statesman, backwoods orator, and man of the people. He is often referred to in popular culture as the "King of the Wild Frontier." He represented Tennessee in the U.S. House of Representatives and was fiercely opposed to Jackson's Indian Removal Act. After he was narrowly defeated for reelection in 1836, he left

Tennessee for Texas. He took part in the Texas Revolution and died at the Battle of the Alamo. Crockett's death secured his place as an antebellum American hero, but it was Walt Disney who brought his legend into the twentieth century. In 1954, Disney released the first of five episodes of the Davy Crockett television series starring actor Fess Parker. They were wildly successful and created a massive demand for frontier-themed children's toys including a mania for coonskin caps. Crockett's bust was unveiled in the capitol building in 2016.

Edward Carmack was a prominent late nineteenth and early twentieth century newspaper editor, a U.S. senator, an alcohol prohibitionist, and a segregationist. Carmack practiced law in Columbia, Tennessee before becoming editor of the Memphis Commercial (now the Commercial Appeal).

While in Memphis, Carmack was at odds with another newspaper writer, the pioneering civil rights activist Ida B. Wells. She was a full-time journalist and editor who had a one-third interest in an African American newspaper, the Memphis Free Speech and Headlight. She attacked segregation, lynching, and other racial injustices. When African American businessmen Calvin McDowell, Thomas Moss, and Henry Stewart—who owned a grocery store—were arrested, taken to the Shelby County jail, and lynched by being shot, Wells denounced the action. Carmack incited a mob against Wells, and her newspaper's office was destroyed. She was out of town at the time and did not return to Memphis. Wells became an internationally renowned anti-lynching activist, an early leader in the National Association of Colored Women, and a prominent suffragist.

Meanwhile, Carmack was elected to the U.S. House of Representatives and later the U.S. Senate. On November 9, 1908, Carmack attempted to shoot his publishing and political rival, Duncan Cooper. Carmack missed Cooper but wounded Cooper's son Robin, who returned fire and killed Carmack. The state legislature commissioned a large bronze statue of Carmack, which was erected in 1927 on the grounds of the Tennessee State Capitol building. The statue stood there until May 30, 2020, when it was damaged and torn down by individuals protesting the murder of George Floyd. There is a push to install a statue of David Crockett where the Carmack statue once stood. The fate of the Carmack statue is still being determined.

THE CAPITOL MALL AREA

Prior to continuing into downtown Nashville, it is worthwhile to walk through the **Tennessee Map Plaza**, the **Bicentennial Capitol Mall State Park**, the **Nashville Farmers' Market**, and the **Tennessee State Museum**.

The Map Plaza has a large granite state map detailing the topography of Tennessee's cities and counties.

As you walk through the Bicentennial Capitol Mall State Park, you can view a series of markers that explain the history of the state from prehistoric times to the present. A World War II memorial, a ninety-five-bell carillon, a plaque honoring the Civilian Conservation Corps, and planters with native plant species from different regions of the state are within the park.

Sitting next to the park is the Nashville Farmers' Market where you can buy fresh produce and artisanal food. The market also features an indoor section with shops and restaurants. I had a terrific lunch at the **Bowl & Roll**, a Korean-themed restaurant there. The indoor market is open daily from 8:00 am to 8:00 pm, and the outdoor farm sheds are open on weekends.

The **Tennessee State Museum**, which opened in 2018, sits at the end of the Capitol Mall and has an excellent set of exhibits that provide a more detailed background on the area's history.

GERMANTOWN AND NORTH NASHVILLE

Germantown is a redeveloped area across the street from the Bicentennial Capitol Mall State Park. One of the oldest areas of the city, Germantown, is on the National Register of Historic Places. The neighborhood is known for its dining opportunities. If you're in the mood for a Southern breakfast, stop at **Monell's**, one of Germantown's historic restaurants. **North Nashville**, where Fisk University is located, is next to Germantown and is an up-and-coming area.

JEFFERSON STREET

To the west of the Bicentennial Capitol Mall State Park and within North Nashville is **Jefferson Street**, the historic center of the African American community. It is currently undergoing much redevelopment.

When Interstate 40 was rammed through the neighborhood in 1968, the construction destroyed many of the local clubs that showcased African American performers. A committed group of individuals have kept the area alive. The **Jefferson Street Sound Museum** is a small but well curated museum on Jefferson Street dedicated to preserving Nashville's R&B (rhythm and blues) heritage. Each July, the **Jefferson Street Jazz & Blues**

Festival celebrates the vitality of North Nashville community with art, music, and food. Nearby **Fisk University** and **Tennessee State University** are also important to maintaining the viability of the neighborhood.

To the north of Jefferson Street is the **Buena Vista Historic District**, a neighborhood of older homes that is also threatened by redevelopment. Buena Vista's Hopewell Baptist Church, constructed in 1902, was badly damaged in a 2020 tornado. Rebuilt in 2022, the church is once again a center of worship in the African American community. The church is on the National Register of Historic Places.

DOWNTOWN

There is much to see in downtown Nashville. New construction is everywhere, and Highway 41 around downtown is highly congested. Your best bet is to explore this walkable area on foot. You can stop and see the **Musicians Hall of Fame and Museum**, the **Tennessee Performing Arts** Center, the National Historic Landmark **Hermitage Hotel**, and the **Ryman Auditorium**, the original home of the Grand Ole Opry. Ryman Auditorium, "the Mother Church of Country Music," fell into disrepair after the Grand Ole Opry moved in 1974, but by 1994, the acoustically perfect performance venue had been renovated and restored. Across the street from the Ryman is the recently established **National Museum of African American Music**, which opened in 2021, and the **Assembly Food Hall**, a huge food court and entertainment venue serving a variety of Nashville's favorite cuisines.

The Woolworth Theatre on John Lewis Way in downtown Nashville was a Woolworth "five and dime" store decades ago and, in February 1960, was the site of one of the first lunch counter sit-ins in the city. The Woolworth has a display showing the old lunch counter, but in its new function, the location provides a state-of-the-art venue for different live shows and events.

The **Nashville Public Library** downtown is a terrific resource for the city, with multiple rooms housing archives and exhibits documenting the Civil Rights movement in Nashville and the fight for women's rights. Tennessee was the thirty-sixth and final state needed to ratify the 19th Amendment to the Constitution in 1920, which granted women the right to vote.

Formerly owned by AT&T, the colloquially known as the **"Batman Building"** at 333 Commerce is a thirty-three-story office tower that is currently the tallest building in Tennessee. An unusual resemblance to the Caped Crusader makes it a favorite photo op for tourists, but the structure is privately owned and has no observation deck or tourist attractions inside.

Nashville Yards is a nineteen-acre project under construction in the heart of downtown Nashville. Completed in 2025, the mixed-use area encompasses a hotel, a newly renovated Union Station, restaurants, and several office towers.

Musicians Hall of Fame and Museum, Nashville, TN

"THE DISTRICT"

Just outside of the downtown area is **"The District,"** packed with live country music honky-tonk bars, themed restaurants, western wear and boot shops, and lots of country music kitsch, particularly on **Broadway Street**. Among the better-known venues are **Legends Corner, Tootsies Orchid Lounge, Layla's Honky Tonk, Nudie's Honky Tonk, Robert's Western World, Luke's 32 Bridge,** and **Ole Red**. Several venues are attributed to country stars such as Miranda Lambert, Jason Aldean, and Kid Rock. The **Ernest Tubb Record Shop**, a mainstay on Broadway Street for seventy years, closed its doors in the spring of 2022; however, a dedicated group of local musicians is working to reopen in 2025. All of the bars feature live music with most open to the outside. This is the "Nashvegas" strip that tourists come to see, and it's how Nashville is known to the world. You will also see intoxicated tourists in The District.

The "District," Nashville, TN

SoBRO

SoBro (South of Broadway) is a part of downtown. The neighborhood has bustling bars, cool restaurants, and a vibrant music scene. Interactive exhibits and musical artifacts are the draw at the **Country Music Hall of Fame and Museum** while local performance venues for big-name rock acts include the **Bridgestone Arena**—home of the NHL Nashville Predators—and the open-air **Ascend Amphitheater** on the banks of the Cumberland River. Next to the Country Music Hall of Fame is the 2.1-million-square-foot **Music City Center**, Nashville's chief convention center. The **Schermerhorn Symphony Center** is known for its modern neoclassical design and high-tech acoustics.

Two more museums to consider visiting in your travels to SoBro are the **Johnny Cash Museum** and the **Patsy Cline Museum**. Nearby, the **John Seigenthaler Pedestrian Bridge** crosses the Cumberland and affords a nice view of downtown Nashville.

GOO GOO CLUSTERS

The Goo Goo Chocolate Company is located across the street from the Johnny Cash Museum. Home of the Goo Goo Cluster, Nashville's official candy, this candy bar is a configuration of milk chocolate, caramel, marshmallow nougat, and fresh-roasted peanuts. It's called "America's First Candy Bar," and the company store is a unique place to visit.

THE GULCH

Located slightly southwest of the downtown, Highway 41 skirts by **The Gulch**, an upscale area of apartment buildings, hotels, high-end fashion boutiques, and an abundance of restaurants. The **Frist Art Museum** is housed in The Gulch in an Art Deco building that was once the post office. For excellent bluegrass music, check out the **Station Inn** (cash only), a tiny club that has been open since the 1970s, while **Cannery Hall** features indie, soul, and folk gigs. New construction is booming everywhere in The Gulch.

Frist Art Museum, Nashville, TN

MUSIC ROW

To the south and west of The Gulch is **Music Row**, the home of major entertainment company offices such as **Sony Music Publishing** and **Curb Word Entertainment**. Several recording studios are located in or near Music Row, including the iconic **RCA Studio B**, where legends like Elvis Presley and Dolly Parton recorded hits. Various country stars are honored with street names in the area, and in **Owen Bradley Park** there's a statue of the influential country music record producer seated at a grand piano. Trendy **Virgin Hotel Nashville** sits on Music Row.

VIGNETTE FAMOUS NASHVILLE ENTERTAINERS

Nashville has had an outsized influence on the American entertainment industry. Three individuals are noted here out of the multitude of famous Tennesseans with ties to the city.

Chester "Chet" Atkins (1924–2001) is known as "Mr. Guitar" and "The Country Gentleman." Atkins helped create the "Nashville sound," which extended the crossover appeal of country music with pop music to reach a larger audience. He is considered one of the greatest guitar players ever and received multiple Grammy awards. He is in the Rock & Roll Hall of Fame, the Country Music Hall of Fame, and the Musicians Hall of Fame. Atkins's legacy began as a producer and executive at the legendary RCA Studio B from 1957 until 1982. He was responsible for recordings by Elvis Presley, The Everly Brothers, Roy Orbison, Don Gibson, Charley Pride, Dolly Parton, Willie Nelson, Jerry Reed, and Waylon Jennings, among others.

Oprah Winfrey (b. 1954) is a talk show host, television producer, actor, author, and media purveyor. Winfrey was born in rural poverty in Mississippi and grew up in Milwaukee with her mother, who worked as a maid. She returned to live with her father in Nashville to finish high school. At age seventeen, Winfrey won the Miss Black Tennessee beauty pageant and was hired to report the news part-time on a local Black radio station. She won an oratory contest, which secured her a full scholarship to Tennessee State University. She went on to be the youngest news anchor and first Black female anchor at a TV station in Nashville.

From there she moved to a station in Baltimore before relocating to Chicago in 1984 to take over as the host of a local low-rated half-hour morning talk show. By 1986, that show evolved into The Oprah Winfrey Show, which remained on the air until 2011. She became a millionaire at age thirty-two, started her own production company at age forty-one, and is now a billionaire as well as one of the best known and most influential individuals in the United States.

Reese Witherspoon (b. 1976) is an actress, producer, and entrepreneur. She grew up in Nashville and began her acting career in 1991. A series of critically and commercially successful films—notably, Election in 1999 and Legally Blonde in 2001 —was followed by an Academy Award performance as June Carter Cash in the film Walk the Line (2005). Witherspoon has also appeared in a number of television shows in the last decade.

In 2012, she founded a production company, and in 2015, she launched a retail brand focusing on fashion and home decor. She founded her book club "Reese's Book Club" in 2017. The book club operates under a media company called Hello Sunshine. In 2023, Witherspoon was named by Forbes magazine as the world's highest earning actress and one of the richest women in the United States.

EDGEHILL

Nashville's older, lower-income communities have been hit hardest by redevelopment. One of these is **Edgehill**, a historically African American neighborhood to the east of Music Row and the Gulch that is in danger of being destroyed by tear-down fever and short-term rentals. Though many people seem to think that displacement and housing destruction is an unavoidable consequence of growth, this does not have to be the case. In 2024, a draft "Edgehill Neighborhood Plan" was proposed to provide a vision for long-range growth and development "to retain and preserve the historic neighborhood and mixed income and housing character."

WEST END-MIDTOWN

To the west of Edgehill is the upscale **West End**. The neighborhood is home to **Vanderbilt University** and **Centennial Park**, well-known for its full-sized 1897 reconstruction of the Parthenon in Athens, originally built for the Tennessee Centennial and International Exposition. Inside the **Parthenon** is a small art gallery and a huge forty-two-foot-tall sculpture of the goddess Athena. Completed by sculptor Alan LeQuire in 2002, the statue is gilded in gold leaf. A human-sized Nike stands in Athena's upturned palm, crowning her with a wreath of victory. If you look closely, you can spot other gods and mythical creatures: Zeus, Apollo, Poseidon, Pegasus, fighting Amazons, a sphinx, and the severed head of serpent-haired Medusa.

The Parthenon, Nashville, TN

Statue of Athena by sculptor Alan LeQuire, The Parthenon, Nashville, TN

West End is known for having a strong LGBTQ+ community with several clubs and bars located along Church Street including **Suzy Wong's Drag n' Brunch**. The neighborhood has some restaurants of note, such as **Pastaria** for Italian American and **Woodland's Indian Vegetarian Cuisine** for fresh vegetarian food. Not far from the Parthenon and Vanderbilt is **Elliston Place Soda Shop**, which has been serving classic "meat-and-three plates" and soda shop specials since 1939. All around it is new construction.

Elliston Place Soda Shop, Nashville, TN

BELMONT-HILLSBORO

To the south of Edgehill is another upscale neighborhood: **Belmont-Hillsboro**. **Belmont University** is located here as well as the ultra-hip area known as **12 South**. This retail district is full of hip designer stores such as **Draper James** (previously owned by Reese Witherspoon) and **Buck Mason**. It also boasts some fancy eateries. Be sure to take a look at **Gruhn Guitars, Inc.,** which has a beautiful mural on its facade and offers an amazing selection of new and vintage guitars. If you are a musician, this store is not to be missed. Theater buffs should watch a movie at the **Belcourt Theatre**, which shows a wide selection of new and old films.

NASHVILLE AIRPORT AND BEYOND

Highway 41 proceeds by **Nashville International Airport**, which has become quite a busy place in recent years. Auto dealers, vape shops, and chain stores line this stretch of the road. As you exit the city, you will pass by an Arabic supermarket, and the ubiquitous **Waffle House**, along with signs for many Hispanic businesses along the road. The **Antioch** neighborhood, located between Interstate 24 and Highway 41, is becoming more desirable due to its affordable housing, the neighborhood's decision to embrace diversity, and the recent addition of regional **Mill Ridge Park**, which features a five-story climbing tower and a fifty-two-foot slide.

As Highway 41 moves southeast out of Nashville, it exits Davidson County and enters Rutherford County. A large **Nissan** auto plant in **Smyrna**—the largest town in Tennessee—employs approximately 8,400 workers. Since you are still within the Nashville Metro area, expect to encounter a number of stoplights along this stretch of the highway.

Gruhn Guitars, Nashville, TN

OTHER THINGS TO SEE WHILE IN THE NASHVILLE AREA

Belle Meade Historic Site & Winery lies in far southeast Nashville. A former plantation that is now on the National Register of Historic Places, is a popular venue for multiple events. Approximately 5,400 acres were worked by 136 enslaved people prior to the American Civil War. The plantation was known for its ties to horse breeding and racing, including the Kentucky Derby. It contains Nashville's first and oldest winery, outbuildings, a museum, and an onsite restaurant.

The educational **Belle Meade Plantation Journey to Jubilee** walking tour focuses on the lives and stories of the African Americans who were enslaved on this plantation. Along the path, you can learn about the research performed by area institutions that dive into the history of enslavement and work under labor contracts after the passage of the 13th Amendment. Belle

Meade is a lovely place to visit where you can learn much about what life was like for both the privileged and the enslaved. You can easily spend a day visiting here.

To the south of Belle Meade is **Cheekwood**, a fifty-five acre botanical garden and art museum located on the historic Cheek estate. Originally built as the home of Leslie and Mabel Cheek in 1929, Cheekwood is one of the finest examples of a Country Place Era estate. The Country Place Era lasted from 1890 to 1930. During this stretch of time, wealthy Americans commissioned extensive gardens similar to those in Europe at their country estates. Since its conversion to an art museum and botanical garden in 1960, Cheekwood has presented world-class art exhibits, spectacular gardens, and a unique historic estate. Cheekwood welcomes over 400,000 visitors annually, making it one of the city's top cultural attractions.

Not far from Cheekwood is **The Bluebird Cafe**, a tiny but iconic music listening room. Unassuming in appearance (as it is tucked into a strip mall), some of the most significant songwriters and artists have performed on Bluebird's stage including Garth Brooks, Keith Urban, Vince Gill, Taylor Swift, Townes Van Zandt, Kathy Mattea, and many more. The Bluebird was featured on the TV show *Nashville* and was the subject of the 2019 documentary, *Bluebird*.

The Hermitage is 1,100-acre estate ten miles east of downtown Nashville. Built in 1821, it was the home of President Andrew Jackson and his wife Rachel. Jackson's estate grew cotton, thanks to the efforts of many enslaved people, who numbered over 110 at the time of his death. The estate is now a museum and a National Historic Landmark. A memorial to the enslaved was placed on the grounds in 2006. The Hermitage is one of the most visited presidential estates in the United States.

BRENTWOOD AND FRANKLIN

South of Nashville and East of 41 lie the cities of **Brentwood** and **Franklin**, which are home to several well-known celebrities. These communities have become desirable places to live due to their excellent school districts and large homes. Brentwood contains **Primm Historic Park**, which preserves some the largest prehistoric Mississippian mounds in the region. The park also features **Boiling Spring Academy**, an 1830 one-room schoolhouse built next to the mounds. In Franklin are remnants of the American Civil War

Battle of Franklin in 1864, which was one of the worst defeats for the Confederate Army. The city has several historic homes, and the national landmark designated downtown boasts restored Victorian buildings.

In-N-Out Burger, a West Coast fast-food restaurant chain has announced that it plans to open a corporate office in Franklin and restaurants in and around Nashville. This will be the company's first expansion east of Texas. Founded in 1948 by Harry and Esther Snyder as California's first "drive-thru" hamburger stand, In-N-Out is still owned and operated by the Snyder family.

STONES RIVER NATIONAL BATTLEFIELD

In Murfreesboro, right along Highway 41, is **Stones River National Battlefield**. Similar to other Civil War sites nationally, the site displays numerous statues and markers memorializing individuals and battle units from both the Union and Confederate armies that engaged in the battle. **Stones River National Cemetery** is a Union graveyard across the road from the visitor center. Visitors will see evidence of urban encroachment near the site, as new buildings are going up just outside of the battlefield.

Stones River National Battlefield Cemetery, Murfreesboro, TN

The Battle of Stones River is also known as the Second Battle of Murfreesboro (1862—1863). A Union victory when the North sorely needed one, both sides suffered high casualties. The outcome allowed the Union Army to retain control of Central Tennessee, which became crucial as the Civil War dragged on. The visitor center provides a short, informative film and offers an impressive display of battle artifacts. As always, the National Park Service workers are quite informative and can provide details even a Civil War buff may not know.

A short walk away, near the Highway 41 overpass, is the **Trail of Tears** pathway. There were several trails used during the forced migration, and this is the one that passed through Tennessee. Thousands died during the forced removal of the Cherokee Nation and other southeastern peoples from their homelands. As with all traces of the Trail of Tears, it is sobering to contemplate.

MURFREESBORO

The Greater Nashville Metro area continues through the city of **Murfreesboro**. The sixth-largest city in the state, Murfreesboro is one of the fastest-growing localities. Murfreesboro is home to **Middle Tennessee State University** (enrollment 20,000), "the number one source of graduates for the Greater Nashville economy", as their website proclaims. Murfreesboro is the seat of Rutherford County situated at the geographic center of the State of Tennessee. It has been a destination for many immigrant refugees from Somalia, the Kurdistan region of Iraq, and other areas affected by warfare. Murfreesboro's busy downtown possesses many restaurants and shops. Murfreesboro was the capital of Tennessee from 1819 to 1825 and a shipping point for cotton and dairy products. In 1862, during the Civil War, the First Battle of Murfreesboro resulted in a Confederate victory over the occupying Union troops.

The exurbs of Nashville, with their new housing developments, finally end several miles south of Murfreesboro, where the rural landscape begins again. A beautiful Hindu Temple, **Shri Krishna Pranami Mandir**, is located southeast of Murfreesboro in unincorporated **Christiana** just to the west of Interstate 24, which parallels Highway 41 in this section. The Pranami is a Hindu sect that worships Krishna as the Supreme God. The life and teachings of the saintly philosopher Mahamati Prannath form the basis of practitioners' religious lives. On my visit, I was warmly greeted to see inside the place of worship. The temple is the sect's North American headquarters. It is well worth a stop to see.

BEECHGROVE

Beechgrove, off Highway 41, is a tiny unincorporated village situated right next to Interstate 24. It is the location of **Beechgrove Confederate Cemetery and Park**. A Civil War skirmish called the Battle of Hoover's Gap was fought here in June 1863. The site includes several grave markers and a stone marker with General Nathan Bedford Forrest's farewell address to his troops at the end of the war. Forrest later became one of the founding members of the Ku Klux Klan. The site also features a marker commemorating the actions of the 18th Indiana Battery at Hoover's Gap, commanded by Captain Eli Lilly. If you have heard that name before, it is because Lilly went on to establish a pharmaceutical company in his name. This enterprise has become one of the largest pharma providers in the world.

Nearby the cemetery is an old Masonic lodge and **Gregory's Beechgrove Country Store**, a little general store that also serves food and drinks.

Hermon Masonic Lodge, Beechgrove, TN

MANCHESTER

A pretty drive from Beechgrove brings you to Manchester on the two-lane road that is U.S. 41. **Manchester** is the seat of Coffee County. You will cross the picturesque **Duck River** as you come into the city. The nearby Cumberland Mountains are in view. **Old Stone Fort State Archaeological Park** is right off the highway here, and it's well worth a visit. The Old Stone Fort was a ceremonial point for ancient Indigenous peoples who lived along the river. Hiking trails lead to some lovely waterfalls, and the visitor center provides information on Indigenous settlements in the area.

Outside Manchester, TN

Blue Hole Falls, Elizabethton, TN

Corporal Brian James Schoff Memorial, Manchester, TN

Manchester has a pretty city center with a craft beer brewery—**Common John Brewing Co**—which hosted a small musical festival the night I was there. You'll pass by the typical retail sprawl of new commercial buildings just outside of town. Manchester is the home of the **Bonnaroo Music and Arts Festival**, which is held annually over four days in June. Held on a 700-acre farm, the festival sold out in 2023, with an audience of approximately 70,000 attendees and more than 150 musical performances. This is one of the big outdoor concert venues in the United States with big-name bands and performers. I visited in mid-June as the venue was being set up. It was a major undertaking.

SIDE TRIP TO CUMBERLAND CAVERNS AND McMINNVILLE

The small city of **McMinnville** lies twenty-four miles to the east of Manchester. Known as the "Nursery Capital of the World" by virtue of the more than 300 nurseries in and around the city, it's a charming old town and a good place to stop for the night. Nearby **Cumberland Caverns**, the second-longest cave in Tennessee, is a "show cave" that offers tours, some of which include overnight underground stays. Cumberland Caverns hosts all kinds of events. I had a terrific rib dinner at **Collins River BBQ & Café** in McMinnville.

SIDE TRIP TO TENNESSEE WHISKEY TRAIL

For connoisseurs of Tennessee whiskey, there are several important stops nearby Highway 41. State Road 55 southwest of Manchester will take you about eleven miles into the town of **Tullahoma**. Located north of town on a beautiful twisting drive is the **Cascade Hollow Distilling Company**, which produces George Dickel Whisky. One of the oldest distilleries in Tennessee, the company has been making whiskey here for 130 years. I took a tour of the distillery and was able to sample some of the different varieties produced at the location.

Cascade Hollow Distilling Co. (George Dickel Distillery), Tullahoma, TN

East of Tullahoma is **Lynchburg**, the home of the **Jack Daniel's Distillery Visitor Center**. Jack Daniel's is a well-known whiskey ubiquitous in bars and stores across the country. The Jack Daniel's Distillery is the oldest registered distillery in the United States and receives over 250,000 visitors every year.

A relatively recent whiskey—Uncle Nearest Premium Whiskey—honors the world's first-known African American master distiller, Nearest Green. This is the first spirits brand in the world to be named after an African American. It is made at the **Nearest Green Distillery** in Shelbyville, approximately seventeen miles from Tullahoma on Highway 41A.

MANCHESTER TO MONTEAGLE

A pastoral drive on Highway 41 southeast of Manchester takes travelers through rolling farmland in the foothills of the Cumberland Mountains, which rise in the distance. The vast majority of through-traffic uses Interstate 24, so Highway 41 is a relaxed drive through very pretty scenery. Highway 41 continues over **Monteagle Mountain**, a section of the Cumberland Plateau. The small community of **Monteagle** features several historic sites and claims associations with an interesting collection of people, including Al Capone, Madame Chiang Kai-shek, and Dr. Martin Luther King Jr. Between 1932 and 1962, it was the site of the **Highlander Folk School**, where courses on nonviolent resistance to segregation were formative for Dr. King, Rosa Parks, John Lewis, and Eleanor Roosevelt. In 1838, a group of 700 Cherokee, led by John Bell, passed through Monteagle on the Trail of Tears as they followed the route to what is present-day Arkansas.

While in Monteagle, I had a fine dining experience at the **High Point Restaurant** in the **RyeMabee Home (also known as Castlewood),** which is on the National Register of Historic Places. The restaurant prepares food from scratch using locally sourced hand-picked ingredients. I had a dinner with pasta and sauteed Morell mushrooms that was fantastic.

North of Pelham, TN

Hillsboro, TN

Gallery 41, Pelham, TN

Highlander Folk School marker, Manchester, TN

SIDE TRIP TO SEWANEE

Sewanee: The University of the South (enrollment 1,735) is located five miles from Monteagle on Highway 41A. The 13,000-acre Sewanee campus overlooks the Tennessee Valley. The school was established by the Episcopal Church in 1858, blown up by Union troops in 1863, was rebuilt, and resumed operations in 1868. There are a number of stone buildings on campus, which makes it one of the most beautiful college campuses in the United States. The liberal arts school is quite prestigious, with a few traditions tied to southern culture. *The Sewanee Review*, founded in 1892, is the oldest continuously published literary magazine in the United States. While on campus, I witnessed a group of Southern women teachers at the chapel take a moment of silence for their departed colleagues who have passed away.

Many notable Southern authors have had ties to the school. Playwright Tennessee Williams left his literary rights to Sewanee, and his royalties have helped build the **Tennessee Williams Center**, a venue for theater performances with a dressing and design studio, a dance studio, costume and scenery studios, dressing and makeup rooms, and faculty offices.

University of South Sewanee, Sewanee, TN
(photo courtesy of Sewanee University)

University of South Sewanee, Sewanee, TN
(photo courtesy of Sewanee University)

A stop at **The Amish Hippie** as you take Highway 41A back from Sewanee to Monteagle, is well worth your time. It's a quirky little store that sells soaps, homemade jam, incense, and a lot of vintage stuff.

The Amish Hippie, Monteagle, TN

TRACY CITY

Tracy City is a cute little town on the twelve-mile **Fiery Gizzard Trail**, rated as one of the 25 best hiking trails in the United States. A marker in town commemorates the long-gone blast furnace where coke was processed from coal and used to make iron. I recommend a stop at the **Dutch Maid Bakery and Café** for coffee and lemon cake. The area is full of natural attractions, including **South Cumberland State Park**. Picturesque **Foster Falls** and **Denny Cove Falls** are just off the highway.

The scenic drive from Monteagle through Tracy City to the Tennessee River was one of the loveliest parts of my entire Highway 41 travels. Along the thickly wooded highway, you'll see some houses built right up against the road—a practice often used in the English colonies and the early United States. Note: there are steep grades down the road as it gets closer to the Tennessee River.

It was interesting to see how crowded Interstate 24 was compared to the very uncrowded Highway 41 as I crossed the river, which had lots of recreational boating.

SIDE TRIP TO RACCOON MOUNTAIN

I suggest taking a short side trip off the highway to check out the **Raccoon Mountain Pumped Storage Plant** that overlooks the Tennessee River. It is

394

the Tennessee Valley Authority's (TVA) largest hydroelectric facility. Water is pumped to a reservoir on top of the mountain and used to generate electricity within the TVA system. The TVA was created as part of President Franklin Roosevelt's New Deal in 1933. Today it is the nation's biggest government utility, serving about ten million customers in seven states.

Highway 41 over the Tennessee River looking at Interstate 24

LOOKOUT MOUNTAIN, RUBY FALLS & ROCK CITY

When you return to Highway 41, you will be in close proximity to **Lookout Mountain**. Expect traffic to get much heavier, particularly on weekends, as this is a major tourist destination. Multiple signs along the highway and on barns advertise **Ruby Falls** and **Rock City**. You'll climb up a winding road to a parking area with a sign that says, "Lookout Mountain—Welcome to Ruby Falls."

Ruby Falls is an underground waterfall in the commercial cavern that is part of the tourist complex on the mountain. If you want to visit this attraction, you'll need to buy tickets online ahead of time, and it's not cheap; when I visited the adult admission was $26. The natural landmark is home to the tallest and deepest underground waterfall open to the public in the United States. Visitors to the cave take an elevator as part of the guided tour to view the waterfall. The walk through the cave can be a bit of a slog shared with many other tourists, but the waterfall is truly spectacular.

Rock City Gardens, with an admission price of $34 for adults, is a one-mile stroll through some interesting rock formations and gardens. The views are very beautiful, particularly from the Lovers Leap and seven state viewing sites, but be warned: it can get very crowded.

Lookout Mountain Battlefield is a National Park Service site encompassing 3,000 acres of land on the summit and slopes of the mountain. The best views are found in **Point Park**, a ten-acre site on top of the mountain, which rises 2,000 feet above sea level and overlooks the city of Chattanooga. The views of the Tennessee River and the city are extraordinary. The view has always been an attraction as several markers suggest. A cool 1904 stone entrance leads into the park, which charges a nominal admission.

Across the river from Lookout Mountain is the **Moccasin Bend Archeological District**, also run by the National Park Service. The district contains remnants of 12,000 years of human habitation and is considered to be an area of cultural significance.

The land on and around the mountain figures heavily into American history. Lookout Mountain was the site of a September 1782 Revolutionary War engagement between the British-backed Chickamauga and Cherokee nations and a Continental Army contingent. The Continental victory occurred just before a peace treaty was signed in November 1782, officially ending the American Revolution. In the American Civil War, the Battle of Lookout Mountain, also known as the "Battle Above the Clouds," took place in 1863 and resulted in a Union victory. Commemorative markers are on display in the park.

The area around the national parklands contains some beautiful private homes. Aside from the tourist hordes, the neighborhood adjacent to Point Park seems to be a very attractive place to live. From Lookout Mountain, Highway 41 will take you into the city of Chattanooga.

CHATTANOOGA

Sitting on the border with Georgia, **Chattanooga** is the fourth-largest city in Tennessee. The city has been an important transportation site; first for riverboats and later for the railroads, since it was founded as a trading post called Ross's Landing in 1836. In 1838, the U.S. Army used Ross's Landing as one of the exile points for Native Americans before forcing them to begin their journey on the Trail of Tears. The city was a center of battle during the

American Civil War due to its strategic importance.

Chattanooga went through a difficult period of economic adjustment in the 1970s but managed to right itself and revitalize its downtown. Today Chattanooga is an attractive, interesting city, which *Lonely Planet* designated as one of the top U.S. travel destinations for its many attractions, and *Southern Living* magazine has called "one of the best places to retire to." In 2025, Chattanooga, once one of the most polluted cities in the United States, received the designation as the first "National Park City" in the United States by the United Kingdom based National Park City Foundation.

Lookout Mountain, TN

Highway 41 first proceeds through the **St. Elmo Historic District,** site of the **Lookout Mountain Incline Railway,** an 1895 funicular that runs from St. Elmo to the top of Lookout Mountain. If you can, take the Incline as a quick way to the top of Lookout Mountain. At the top, you'll face a three-block walk to Point Park. From the neighborhood's incline station, you can walk or drive over to the **Naughty Cat Café** on Tennessee Avenue, Chattanooga's first and (so far) only cat café. Signs in the window and outside mention that there are "30 Cats Inside" and that this is "NOT a strip club."

From there, you can make a stop at **International Towing & Recovery Museum**, replete with all kinds of old-time tow trucks. Chattanooga was where the tow truck was invented, and outside the museum is a sculpture garden dedicated to the "tow truck drivers" who have died in the line of service to the motoring public.

Point Park, Lookout Mountain, TN

Atop Lookout Mountain overlooking Moccasin Bend, TN

Sculpture at the International Towing & Recovery Museum
Chattanooga, TN

Highway 41 continues into the **Southside Historic District**, where **Terminal Station** is located. It is a lovely 1909 railway station that was the inspiration for the 1941 song **"Chattanooga Choo Choo,"** made famous by the Glen Miller Orchestra. Now the old station is a hotel and banquet complex with several bars and restaurants. I had a terrific Old-Fashioned cocktail at the Terminal bar. Some old rail cars have been fixed up for display with several older rail cars that will eventually be renovated as well.

Take Broad Street into downtown Chattanooga and park along the riverfront. **Hunter Museum of American Art** and **Tennessee Aquarium**— considered one of the best aquariums in the United States, are located along the restored riverfront. Nearby, the **Bluff View Art District** sits atop a stone cliff where it provides great views of the Tennessee River and downtown Chattanooga.

Walnut Street Pedestrian Bridge, erected in 1891, is one of the world's longest pedestrian bridges. It connects downtown Chattanooga with the north shore of the Tennessee River. The bridge is beautiful and provides a lovely walk but has a dark history. Two Black men were lynched on the bridge, one in 1893 and the second in 1906. A monument next to the bridge recounts this painful legacy.

Walnut Street Bridge, Chattanooga, TN

Chattanooga Rail Station, Chattanooga, TN

NICKNAMES

The official nickname of Chattanooga is the "Scenic City," in reference to the surrounding mountains and valleys. Other names for the town have been "River City," "Chatt," "Nooga," "Chattown," and "Gig City," reputedly due to having the fastest internet in the country.

COMMERCE

Chattanooga remains an important transportation center and the main city for a region encompassing Northwestern Georgia and Northeastern Alabama, as well as Southeastern Tennessee. The city was one of the first to offer internet access directly to the public. A big **Volkswagen** auto plant is located on the outskirts of Chattanooga, and **Amazon** has a large fulfillment center in the city. Numerous companies have manufacturing or distribution centers there too. Chattanooga is also becoming a technology hub with a number of startup firms. And Chattanooga is famous for the **"Moon Pie,"** a snack consisting of two round graham cookies with marshmallow filling, all of which is dipped in a flavored coating. This unique southern snack is made by **Chattanooga Bakery Inc**.

Highway 41 proceeds through the outskirts of Chattanooga replete with many chain stores before it crosses over into Georgia.

CONCLUDING THOUGHTS

Highway 41's journey through Tennessee is fascinating. You'll see both urban and rural locations along with a number of scenic attractions. I hope that you can find the time to see a good number of them.

The past, present, and future are all represented within the state. Tennessee's lower cost of living may be illusory for people thinking of moving to the state as congestion issues mount. The winter climate is milder than that of northern states, but it can get very hot and humid in the summer. In recent years, severe weather in the form of tornadoes and floods have afflicted many locations in the state. Additionally, I would hope that Tennessee lawmakers allow the state to remain a welcoming location.

CHAPTER NINE
GEORGIA

"My version of 'Georgia' became the state song of Georgia. That was a big thing for me, man. It really touched me. Here is a state that used to lynch people like me suddenly declaring my version of a song as its state song. That is touching."

— Ray Charles

"The only way that I could figure they could improve upon Coca-Cola, one of life's most delightful elixirs, which studies prove will heal the sick and occasionally raise the dead, is to put bourbon in it."

—Lewis Grizzard

"There ain't no revolution, only evolution, but every time I'm in Georgia I eat a peach for peace."

—Duane Allman

Highway 41 through Georgia is 387 miles.

Key Towns/Cities: Dalton, Calhoun, Cartersville, Kennesaw, Marietta, Atlanta, Jonesboro, Macon, Perry, Tifton, Valdosta

Georgia Counties along 41: Catoosa, Whitfield, Gordon, Bartow, Cobb, Fulton, Clayton, Henry, Spalding, Pike, Lamar, Monroe, Bibb, Houston, Peach, Dooly, Crisp, Turner, Tift, Cook, Lowndes, Echols

Crossing the Tennessee state line from the small city of East Ridge, Highway 41, known in this section as the **Dixie Highway**, begins its track through Georgia in the northwestern part of the state. The highway closely follows an ancient Indigenous trail that became part of the **Trail of Tears** forced exodus in the 1830s. Thirty years later, General Sherman and the Union Army followed the same route to Atlanta during the American Civil War. Highway 41 is paralleled by Interstate 75 for most of its route through the state. From its entrance into Georgia, the road first passes through small towns and cities where a number of carpet and flooring factories are located. Metropolitan Atlanta begins forty-three miles north of the city proper at Cartersville and runs to Barnesville, sixty miles to the south.

The road runs through the far southwestern portion of the **Appalachian Mountains** and into the **Piedmont**, which contains soil with a high iron oxide clay content—the famous Georgia red clay. The thickly forested Piedmont has numerous streams, waterfalls, and rapids. The highway goes through Atlanta, the Georgia state capital and its largest city. Beyond the Atlanta megaregion, the road runs into the flatter and sandier **Coastal Plain**. The "Fall Line" is a geological border between the Piedmont and the Coastal Plain that begins near the city of Macon and extends to New England. This is where 41 enters the eastern part of the United States as well as the Deep South. The Coastal Plain south of Macon is younger in geologic terms than the land west of the Fall Line, with wetlands, shallow stream valleys, forests, and cropland.

South of Macon, Highway 41 proceeds through a highly agricultural area where peanuts, peaches, blueberries, onions, cotton, watermelon, cucumbers, peppers, tomatoes, cantaloupes, and broilers (chickens) are raised. Several small towns line the highway as it proceeds south toward the city of Valdosta. From there, U.S. 41 reaches the Florida border.

GEORGIA

A GEORGIA ALBUM PLAYLIST

- The Allman Brothers Band: *At Fillmore East* 1971
- Ray Charles: *Modern Sounds in Country and Western Music* 1962
- Little Richard: *Here's Little Richard* 1957
- Otis Redding: *Otis Blue/Otis Redding Sings Soul* 1965
- James Brown: *James Brown Live at the Apollo* 1963
- R.E.M.: *Reckoning* 1984
- Gladys Knight & the Pips: *Everybody Needs Love* 1967
- Ludacris: *Word of Mouf* 2001
- Usher: *Confessions* 2004
- Indigo Girls: *Indigo Girls* 1989
- Alan Jackson: *A Lot About Livin' (And A Little 'Bout Love)* 1992

CULTURAL, INDUSTRIAL, AGRICULTURAL ROOTS

Prior to European contact, the land we now know as Georgia was inhabited by Indigenous mound building cultures for thousands of years. The Etowah people were a North American chiefdom society that emerged about 1000 BCE. Spanish explorer Hernando de Soto visited Etowah in what is now northwest Georgia in around 1540 and described a complex system of chiefdoms that fought wars for regional and political dominance. The British colony of Georgia was founded by James Oglethorpe in 1733 and named for King George II.

Oglethorpe's original plan for the colony envisioned an agrarian society of farmers that prohibited slavery—the only one of the thirteen colonies to have done so. That distinction did not last long. Pressure from planters resulted in slavery being legalized by royal decree in 1751. Georgia became the fourth state in the Union in 1788 after the American Revolution. Atlanta has been the state capital since 1868.

Land was forcibly taken from Indigenous peoples in Georgia during the presidency of Andrew Jackson, despite the Supreme Court's ruling in 1832 that U.S. states were not permitted to redraw tribal boundaries. The Trail of Tears—the route of the forced march to "Indian Country"—began in 1838 from **New Echota**, the capital of the Cherokee Nation, near present-day Calhoun. This location is now one of the most significant Indigenous sites in the nation.

The Antebellum period, extending from the formation of the federal government to the outbreak of the Civil War, was marked by the practice of slavery and the associated societal norms around it. By 1860, enslaved people constituted forty-four percent of the state's total population. Slavery was officially abolished in the United States by the 13th Amendment, which took effect in December 1865.

In 1861, Georgia joined the Confederacy, and the state became a major theater of the Civil War. Significant battles were fought throughout northwest Georgia. After the end of Reconstruction in 1877, Jim Crow policies mandating racial segregation were put into place to discriminate against and disenfranchise African Americans in the 1890s. Segregation lasted until the mid-1960s. Jim Crow spurred many African Americans to leave Georgia and other Southern states for the North during the Great Migration between 1910 and 1970.

Author's Note: the state of Georgia does an excellent job of utilizing historical markers to promote tourism and create better access to the state's history.

Atlanta-born minister Dr. Martin Luther King Jr., founded the Southern Christian Leadership Conference (SCLC) in 1957 as a guiding organization for the burgeoning Civil Rights movement. The city of Atlanta became a center of that movement in the 1960s. A new political era began in Georgia in the 1970s with the election of Jimmy Carter, a strong supporter of civil rights, as governor. Carter was elected president in 1976. Andrew Young became the first elected African American representative in Congress since Reconstruction in 1973, and Maynard Jackson was elected the first African American mayor of Atlanta that same year.

In 1980, Hartsfield-Jackson Atlanta International Airport was expanded and would eventually become the world's busiest passenger airport. The Atlanta metropolitan area became a national center of finance, insurance, manufacturing, real estate, logistics, and transportation. Atlanta was the site of the 1996 Summer Olympic Games. The greater Atlanta metropolitan area has continued to expand in the last two decades, with significant numbers of African Americans moving back to the South from northern cities. Overall, census data indicates Georgia has seen a dramatic boom in ethnic and racial diversity during that time, a trend that is already having a profound effect on the politics of both the state and the nation.

BY THE NUMBERS

The state of Georgia had a population of 10.71 million in 2020, and it is estimated to reach 14.7 million by 2030. The vast Atlanta metropolitan area comprises a population of 6.1 million, and this increase is being fueled by continued strong employment growth. Metro Atlanta's employment base has increased 5.4 percent since the pandemic began in early 2020. That's the fifth highest in the nation, trailing only Austin, Dallas, Las Vegas, and Orlando.

WEATHER

Georgia has a humid subtropical climate with short, comparatively mild winters and long, hot, humid summers. Cold snaps can occur, as they did in 2022 and 2023 when sub-freezing temperatures nearly wiped-out Georgia's entire peach crop. The state is prone to tornadoes and hurricanes and experiences major rainfall events. Studies show that Georgia is among a string of Deep Southern states that will experience more severe floods, droughts, and coastal flooding due to climate change.

IDENTITY

Georgia shows many faces to travelers who drive the length of the state on Highway 41. The road is only a few miles from I-75 in large part, yet you will see a different world along 41 than the retail and restaurant chains clustered along the interstate exits. In the Northwest corner of the state, the highway passes through a jumble of houses, trailer parks, churches, old truck trailer yards, and carpet and flooring factories. The vast Atlanta metropolitan area traversed by the road covers multiple suburban communities. Highway 41 also goes through several interesting neighborhoods within the city limits. Well south of Metro Atlanta and beyond the city of Macon begins the rural southern section of the state, which can seem like a trip back in time.

While Georgia is definitely a Southern state, it is important to note that there is a contradictory mix of the "Old South" and the "New South" within the state. Old school Southern hospitality abounds in the state, while Atlanta is considered the capital of "hip-hop," a popular genre of music with deep roots within the city. Confederate flags are flown not far from LGBTQ+ rainbow flags. Numerous churches coexist with numerous strip clubs. The state has also unfortunately become a major partisan political battleground that displays the contradictions inherent in America during the 2020s. Georgia is now considered a "swing state" or "battleground state" where Democratic and Republican candidates have an equal number of supporters.

NORTHWEST GEORGIA
CATOOSA COUNTY

As you cross the state line from Tennessee into Georgia on Highway 41, the first thing you'll encounter is a rock outcropping—a local landmark called **"The Cliff."** It's right next to a new housing development and just down the street from the Food City Gas 'N Go. It shows up as a historic landmark but no one I asked seemed to know why.

A little father down the highway you'll come to State Route 146. If you follow that road west for seven miles through the town of **Fort Oglethorpe**, you will reach the **Chickamauga and Chattanooga National Military Park**.

The Battle of Chickamauga was the first major battle of the Civil War in Georgia and the only one that resulted in a victory for the Confederate Army in September 1863. It was also among the bloodiest, with nearly 35,000 casualties. The Union forces retreated to the high ground and rail hub of nearby Chattanooga where they counterattacked the Confederates at the Battle of Chattanooga in November 1863, driving them away from the city. The following spring, General William T. Sherman launched his famous march from Chattanooga to Atlanta and on to the sea.

The U.S. Congress established the park in 1890 as the nation's first military park to memorialize the battlefield and it is now part of the National Park Service. Similar to other important Civil War sites, the park features historic statues, monuments, plaques, and markers. A video and a large diorama in the visitor center detail the battles and soldiers on both sides. It's a captivating historic site, with beautifully manicured grounds that is definitely worth a visit.

Battery H, 4th U.S. Artillery, Grose's Brigade, near Fort Oglethorpe, GA

26th Ohio Infantry, 1st Brigade, Buell, 1st Division, near Fort Oglethorpe, GA

RINGGOLD

Once you return to Highway 41, the first town you see will be **Ringgold**, the Catoosa County seat. The highway is two lanes through the town and beyond as you pass churches, trailer homes, and auto repair shops. In downtown Ringgold, you will pass by a mural of Dolly Parton (b.1946), the beloved country singer and songwriter. Dolly married her late husband, Carl Dean, in Ringgold in 1966.

If you are driving this route in early June, you'll encounter the **Dixie Highway Yard Sale**, an annual event held the first full weekend of the month. It spans ninety miles along Highway 41 from Ringgold to Marietta. All manner of stuff is along the road, and it's interesting to see families out buying and selling. You might even want to stop and pick up some treasures for yourself!

Just outside of Ringgold's downtown is a small park with plaques commemorating the Civil War **Battle of Ringgold Gap** and the start of **Sherman's Atlanta Campaign**. A statue of Confederate General Patrick Cleburne stands in the park with a very provocative marker that details Cleburne's Emancipation Proposal to the Confederate High Command. Cleburne suggested training a division of enslaved men to serve in the Confederate Army in exchange for their freedom. The idea never reached fruition.

Catoosa County Courthouse, Ringgold, GA

"Tie the Knot," mural painted by artist Kim Radford, Ringgold, GA

The Atlanta Campaign marker, outside of Ringgold, GA

The road continues past some abandoned homes before entering **Tunnel Hill**, a quiet town today that is named for the **Chetoogeta Mountain Tunnel**, and the site of another Civil War skirmish. The railroad tunnel was completed in 1850 for the Western and Atlantic Railroad. It was the first major railroad tunnel in the South and the first through the Appalachian Mountains. It was also where "The Great Locomotive Chase" came through in 1862. The Tunnel Hill Heritage Center and Museum offers tours of the tunnel along with offering unique artifacts on display.

VIGNETTE   THE GREAT LOCOMOTIVE CHASE

This memorable military raid took place in April 1862 during the Civil War. Led by civilian, James Andrews, a group of Union soldiers acting as "engine thieves" successfully hijacked a locomotive known as "The General" and drove it toward Chattanooga, doing as much damage as possible to the Western and Atlantic railroad along the way. The goal was to prevent Confederate forces from moving north on the railway. The Union soldiers were pursued by Confederate forces on several locomotives, including "The Texas," for eighty-seven miles. The Confederates eventually caught up with the train and captured Andrews and some of the Union raiders, whom they executed. Others were able to flee, and these surviving raiders were the first troops to be awarded the newly created Congressional Medal of Honor for their actions. The Great Locomotive Chase may be best known as a 1956 Walt

Disney adventure film. It starred actor Fess Parker as James Andrews.

Postscript: In the summer of 2024, two additional soldiers from the raid, Privates Philip G. Shadrach and George D. Wilson, were awarded the Medal of Honor posthumously.

WHITFIELD COUNTY
DALTON

As you continue south, Highway 41 becomes four lanes and passes many yards before arriving in the city of **Dalton**, the seat of Whitfield County and the self-proclaimed "Carpet Capital of the World." Dalton is home to many of the nation's floor-covering manufacturers, primarily those producing carpeting, rugs, and vinyl flooring. If you're standing on a carpet in a hotel, at an airport, or even in a friend's living room, there's a very good chance you're standing on a carpet manufactured in or around Dalton, Georgia. More than eighty-five percent of the carpets sold in the United States and around forty-five percent of the residential and commercial carpets found worldwide are made within a sixty-five-mile radius of this small city, nestled in the foothills of the Blue Ridge Mountains.

Dalton is the site of factories for such global carpeting behemoths as **Mohawk Industries, Beaulieu International Group, Ira Bernstein & Associates, J & J Industries, Shaw Industries Group, Tandus Floorcovering,** and many similar companies. These facilities create some 12.2 billion square feet of floor covering each year. The industry has its own lobbying trade association called the Carpet and Rug Institute, which is based in Dalton "to educate consumers, commercial stakeholders and the industry about carpet and rugs." In the last decade, carpets have been accused of causing asthma and of being unhygienic. Chemicals used in the manufacturing of carpets may release volatile organic compounds (VOCs). Carpet competes for the home market with laminate flooring.

VIGNETTE   CATHERINE EVANS WHITENER AND PEACOCK ALLEY

The multibillion-dollar carpet industry centered in Dalton owes much of existence to the woman who helped get it started: Catherine Evans Whitener (1880–1964), Dalton's "First Lady of Carpet." In 1892 at the age of twelve, Catherine saw a tufted bedspread at the home of a relative. The spread had been made using an old technique called "candlewick tufting.'" She experimented with tufting and created two quilts, with one crafted in 1895 for her brother's wedding. Family and friends who saw the quilts asked Catherine to make more for purchase. Demand for her bedspreads grew locally, and she taught female friends and neighbors the tufted technique to help her prepare quilts for sale. In 1917, she and her brother formed the Evans Manufacturing Company, which featured a line of bedspreads, bathmats, and bathrobes.

From this origin, a cottage industry of entrepreneurs grew along the stretch of Highway 41 from the Tennessee border to Marietta that became known as "Peacock Alley" for the popular peacock design utilized in many bedspreads. Throughout the 1920s and 1930s, tufted chenille bedspreads, pillowcases, bathmats, and rugs were hung on display on clotheslines and fences. Women would sell these handmade wares to travelers heading to and from Florida to supplement the income of family farms in the largely agricultural area. Increased demand nationally eventually moved manufacturing from homes into factories. Catherine Evans Whitener's legacy is long-lasting with over ninety percent of carpets produced in the United States using the tufted techniques she pioneered. There is mural of Whitener in downtown Dalton. Peacock murals and statues symbolizing the community's heritage adorn the downtown as well.

Peacock statue, Dalton, GA

A large Hispanic population (fifty-three percent) resides in Dalton. Many of them are employed in the carpet and flooring factories. As you drive through the city, you will see evidence of their presence in the number of Latinx groceries and restaurants that cater to these workers. On my drive, many were advertising employment opportunities, and significant expanded facilities were under construction. In downtown Dalton, murals celebrate the city's Hispanic culture.

Thanks in part to its Hispanic population, Dalton now advertises itself as "Soccer Town USA." Nationally ranked teams at both Dalton High School and Southeast Whitfield High School compete with each other and in national tournaments. A number of players from Dalton have received scholarships to play soccer at colleges around the country.

Dalton is also home to the **Georgia Athletic Coaches Association Hall of Fame**, an all-sports tribute to the best developers of young athletes and young people in the state's history. The coaching elite are enshrined in a special permanent exhibition at the **Dalton Convention Center**. Plaques honoring the inductees are displayed year-round.

SIDE TRIP EAST ON STATE ROAD 76

The vast Chattahoochee-Oconee National Forest is about forty-five miles east of Dalton on State Road 76, encompassing 867,000 tree-covered acres across twenty-six counties. People come to the forest to enjoy its streams and rivers, campgrounds, and recreational trails, including a section of the famed **Appalachian Trail**. This legendary hiking trail starts at **Springer Mountain** in Georgia's Fannin County and stretches 2,190 miles all the way to Maine.

The Appalachian Trail Conservancy estimates there are over 3,000 attempts to traverse the entire trail each year; about twenty-five percent succeed. South of Springer Mountain is **Amicalola Falls State Park**, where you can see the highest waterfall in Georgia. Twenty miles east of the falls is the town of **Dahlonega**, where gold was discovered in 1828. Check out the **Dahlonega Gold Museum** in the historic 1836 courthouse which chronicles America's first gold rush.

GORDON COUNTY

RESACA

Leaving Dalton, the road proceeds by the **Monastery of the Glorious Ascension**, a monastic institution of the Russian Orthodox Church, before continuing to **Resaca** and the **Resaca Civil War Battlefield Historic Site**, which is situated just north of the small town. Resaca was originally named Dublin by the Irish laborers who constructed the state railroad and built a large camp at the site of the present town. Resaca is also the location of a Confederate cemetery that contains the graves of 500 soldiers.

VIGNETTE SHERMAN'S ATLANTA CAMPAIGN AND MARCH TO THE SEA

William Tecumseh Sherman (1820–1891) served as a general in the Union Army during the Civil War. After Ulysses S. Grant was promoted to commander of all the Union armies, Sherman was made commander of all troops in the Western Theater and began to wage the type of warfare that brought him great notoriety in the annals of history. Sherman may not have been the first general to advocate "total warfare," but he was certainly the first to bring deliberate destruction upon civilian property in the path of his army. He considered such tactics to be necessary to destroy the Confederacy's material and psychological will to wage war. Fighting first against the Confederate Army under General Joseph Johnston and then John Bell Hood, Sherman consistently used his superior troop numbers to outflank the Confederates. After numerous battle engagements, he captured Atlanta on September 2, 1864. After turning the city into a military garrison, he ordered all civilians to evacuate and burned the city to the ground, an event immortalized in the novel and movie Gone with the Wind.

From Atlanta, Sherman began his famous "March to the Sea," carving out a forty-to-sixty-mile-wide path of destruction through Georgia's heartland. On December 21, 1864, Sherman wired Abraham Lincoln to offer him an early Christmas present: the city of Savannah. Rumors at the time claimed he spared the city from destruction as a favor to his local girlfriend, but evidence points more to the city's willingness to surrender without incident and its importance as a seaport. The March to the Sea split the Confederacy in two and hastened an end to the war. After capturing Savannah, Sherman marched north through South Carolina into North Carolina, where, on April 26, 1865, he accepted Confederate General Johnston's surrender of all "rebel" troops in Georgia, Florida, and the Carolinas. This was the largest surrender of Confederate troops during the war.

CALHOUN

As the highway enters the historic city of **Calhoun**, you will pass a rock memorial arch beside the road with a statue of a Confederate soldier on one side and another of a World War I "doughboy" on the other side. Facing the arch is the Statue of Sequoyah in bronze. Sequoyah, also known as George Gist or George Guess, was a Native American polymath and geographer of the Cherokee Nation. In 1821, he completed his independent creation of an eighty-six-character Cherokee syllabary, which made reading and writing possible in the Cherokee language.

Sequoyah statue, Calhoun, GA

Calhoun Memorial Arch, Calhoun, GA

Calhoun is the Gordon County seat named for John Calhoun, who served as Secretary of State under President Tyler. The city served as a headquarters for General Sherman in the Civil War and thus was spared destruction only to be leveled by a tornado in 1888 followed by a fire that destroyed what was remaining. The city was rebuilt in the aftermath and today has a touristy downtown that includes the **Harris Arts Center— Roland Hayes Museum**. Hayes was a Gordon County native who became a renowned concert singer and performed around the world.

Another attraction in Calhoun is **Sam's Tree House**, which boasts a submarine prop from a 1960's Elvis Presley movie, a helicopter, and an airplane section. The house has been noted on the *Roadside America* list of offbeat tourist attractions. The **Seventh Day Adventist Church Rock Garden** is located just outside with fifty hand-sculpted miniature buildings, including a structure modeled after Notre-Dame cathedral in Paris.

Just east of Calhoun is **New Echota Cherokee Capital State Historic Site**. New Echota was selected in 1819 as the capital of the Cherokee Nation. In 1820, the nation met, adopted a republican form of government, and elected Chief John Ross (Tsan-Usdi) as president. In 1825, the Cherokee national legislature resolved to build a permanent capital called New Echota at the headwaters of the Oostanaula River. During its short history serving as capital (1825–1838), New Echota was the site of the first Indigenous language newspaper, which was published using the new syllabary created in 1820 by Sequoyah. In 1838, the infamous Trail of Tears began on this site. John Ross, who had devoted his life to resisting the U.S. government's seizure of Cherokee lands in Georgia, was forced to assume the painful task of shepherding the Cherokee on their difficult journey to Oklahoma Territory.

The New Echota site is a National Historic Landmark. It has a museum, an excellent video about the site, several plaques, and a stone memorial, which stands next to the museum. The rangers operating the site are quite knowledgeable. You can easily walk around to see the reconstructed buildings within the 200-acre site. While I was there, a group of schoolchildren were touring the grounds, which most visitors realize is hallowed ground. Members of various Cherokee tribes in the United States continue to be involved with New Echota. The ranger mentioned two important gatherings each year: the high school graduation of the Oklahoma-based Cherokee and an annual bike ride covering the 950-mile journey from New Echota to Tahlequah, Oklahoma, following the northern route of the Trail of Tears.

SIDE TRIP TO SUMMERVILLE

I highly recommend a side trip to the small city of Summerville, thirty-four miles east of Calhoun, to see **Howard Finster's Paradise Garden**. Listed on the National Register of Historic Places, it was the home of Howard Finster (1916–2001), the "Grandfather of Southern Folk Art" who was a preacher for thirty years before deciding to become an artist.

In 1965, he claimed to have heard a voice from the Lord telling him to transform four acres of land in Summerville into a "Paradise Garden." Using junk, broken dolls, tools, and clocks, he embedded these materials in the concrete walls that surround both a thirty-foot tower built of bicycle parts and his own church called "The World's Folk Art Church." The World's Folk Art Church is fifty-six feet tall and opened to the public in June 2025. Finster created over 46,000 pieces of original artwork over his life, many of which are on display in museums throughout the United States or prized by art collectors.

Paradise Garden is truly beyond words. Wander throughout the garden to view the sculptures, the artwork, the mosaic sidewalks, the unusual buildings, and the inscriptions from Finster that often reference bible passages. It is weird and wonderful and truly a feast for the eyes.

The Paradise Garden Foundation maintains the site with assistance from the High Museum of Art in Atlanta. **Finster Fest**, an annual festival held in late September, brings together folk art, crafts, and fine artists from all over the world. Paradise Garden has been the site of numerous documentaries and music videos. The band R.E.M. made the music video for their single "Radio Free Europe" in the Garden and used Finster's cover art for their album *Reckoning*. The band Talking Heads used Finster's cover art for their album *Little Creatures*. Images of Finster's art were also used by the band U2 for the 1997/1998 PopMart Concert World Tour.

Paradise Garden, Summerville, GA

Paradise Garden, Summerville, GA

Paradise Garden, Summerville, GA

Paradise Garden, Summerville, GA

BARTOW COUNTY

ADAIRSVILLE

Continuing south on 41, you'll arrive in **Adairsville**, established in 1837 as a railroad point for the Western & Atlantic Railroad. This was another city General Sherman's army destroyed as the Confederate Army withdrew following The Battle of Adairsville in May 1864. The city was rebuilt after the war and has a historic town square. A devastating tornado struck the city in 2013 destroying hundreds of businesses and residences leaving one resident dead and dozens injured. Once again, the city has been rebuilt becoming an industrial hub for corporations in Northwest Georgia.

South of the city is the **Barnsley Resort**, once known as Barnsley Gardens. In the late 1840s, Sir Godfrey Barnsley, an English consul and wealthy merchant based in Savannah, purchased 10,000 acres and built a manor home for his wife Julia, who died before the house was completed. It is said that her ghost appeared to demand the house be completed and for years after workers at the estate viewed the property as haunted. Both the home and its elaborate gardens were inspired by the work of Andrew Jackson Downing, a pioneering landscape designer.

Over the years, the property has had a colorful and weird history. In 1906 a tornado damaged the roof of the manor home, so the Barnsley family moved into the kitchen building that held "a fireplace built to cook sufficient food for a hundred people." In the 1920s, Godfrey and Julia's great-grandson, Preston Saylor, became a prize fighter, adopting the name K.O. "Knockout" Dugan. He participated in 125 fights. In 1935, K.O. Dugan was sent to prison after shooting and killing his brother Harry Saylor after a dispute over the financial affairs of the estate.

The property was sold by the Barnsley family in 1942 and eventually became a cattle and poultry farm in the 1950s. The historic areas of the property were blocked off. The ruins of the great main house and the land, including all of the ruins, was bought in 1988 by Prince Hubertus Fugger of Bavaria, who restored the gardens and renovated the grounds into an upscale golf resort. Prince Fugger sold the estate in 2004 to a family that has since added conference facilities, a ballroom, and a shooting ground for quail hunting. The resort has become a major wedding venue in recent years.

CASSVILLE

The next place of note you'll encounter after proceeding south on U.S. 41 is **Cassville**, now an unincorporated town but once a center of trade and travel for the Cherokee Nation. Once the Bartow County seat, Cassville was burned to the ground by General Sherman's army in 1864 and never fully recovered. Points of interest in this small community include the **Cassville History Museum** and **Cassville Confederate Cemetery**, located on Cass-White Road.

SIDE TRIP TO ROME

The city of **Rome** is located at the confluence of the Etowah and Oostanaula rivers, which meet to form the Coosa River a little over twenty miles east of Cassville. The city is nestled in the foothills of the Appalachian Mountains and developed on seven hills with rivers running between them, similar to its namesake in Italy. Rome was founded in 1834 after Congress passed the Indian Removal Act and the federal government removed the Cherokee from their traditional homeland. In the Antebellum period, Rome was an important cotton trading center due to its river location.

Rome is home to the **Between the Rivers Historic District**, with many well-preserved Victorian era homes and buildings. Rome is the seat of Floyd County and a regional center for medical care and education. Rome also has two giant paper mills just outside of town: **International Paper**, the largest paper producer in the world, and **Georgia Pacific**, a division of Koch Industries. If you ever wondered where all the cardboard for boxes derives from, you are in the right place.

Situated outside of Rome is **Berry College** (enrollment 2,317), a private, liberal arts school founded by philanthropist Martha Berry in 1902. Its beautiful 27,000-acre campus is the largest in the world and features a vast ecosystem of woodlands, meadows, and streams. Berry College has been ranked among the country's most beautiful institutions of higher education.

CARTERSVILLE

Back on the road, U.S. 41 continues to **Cartersville**, the seat of Bartow County. This is where the Atlanta Metro region begins. Traffic on the highway picks up noticeably as you proceed into the attractive old downtown. Historic attractions include a brightly painted Coca-Cola sign on the Young Brothers Pharmacy building, which, according to a historic plaque, was the first sign to advertise Coca-Cola in 1894. It was restored in 1989.

Cartersville has many interesting things to see, and you could easily spend a day or two exploring "Museum City" for all the museums that are present within and nearby.

THE FRIENDSHIP MONUMENT

An old monument, the **Friendship Monument**, and its historical marker stand in the public square near the railroad tracks. Surrounded by an iron fence erected by Mark Cooper, the monument is a tribute to thirty-eight "friends and creditors." Cooper, who was the proprietor of the Etowah Manufacturing and Mining Company, needed to satisfy a $100,000 debt. His local friends covered that debt. Three years later, in 1860, he returned the paid notes and erected this monument, on which the names of his benefactors are inscribed.

ROSE LAWN MUSEUM

Listed on the National Register of Historic Places in 1973, **Rose Lawn Museum** is housed in a beautifully restored Victorian mansion owned by Bartow County that operates as a house museum with all types of period pieces on display. The house was formerly the home of the nationally known evangelist Sam Jones (1847–1906), for whom Nashville's Union Gospel Tabernacle (Ryman Auditorium) was built.

The museum has writings and memorabilia related to the life of Sam Jones and Rebecca Latimer Felton (1835–1930), who in 1922, became the first woman to serve in the U.S. Senate when she was honored with a one-day appointment. Felton was an ardent feminist and equally ardent white supremacist who was the last member of Congress to be a slaveholder (although long before she sat in the chamber).

Across the street from the mansion is an interesting marker celebrating the life of Lottie Moon (1840–1912), a Cartersville schoolteacher who in 1873 became a Southern Baptist missionary to China with the Foreign Mission Board. She served for nearly forty years. A feminist long before it was acceptable, she wrote from China in 1893, "What women have a right to demand is perfect equality."

Rose Lawn Museum, Cartersville, GA

THE BOOTH WESTERN ART MUSEUM

The world's largest permanent exhibition space for contemporary western art is in downtown Cartersville, at the **Booth Western Art Museum**. The Booth is an affiliate of the Smithsonian Institution in Washington D.C. and has an extensive collection of western art ranging from Frederick Remington to Andy Warhol. Several large sculptures stand on the grounds along with Indigenous artifacts, a presidential gallery, stagecoaches, photography, pottery, movie posters, and many paintings. Look to spend several hours at the museum to see the entire collection. If you have children, the museum has an interactive children's gallery.

ETOWAH INDIAN MOUNDS STATE HISTORIC SITE

Outside of Cartersville is **Etowah Indian Mounds State Historic Site**. This site near the Etowah River was home to Indigenous North Americans from 1000 CE to 1550 CE. The ceremonial earthen mounds on the site were constructed around 1000 CE. Etowah Mounds constitute the most intact Mississippian Culture site in the Southeast. Hernando de Soto came with his army to Etowah in 1540. Several artifacts have been unearthed that indicate his presence in the area. There are some artifacts and explanatory signs on display in the visitors' center, but most people come here to see and climb the mounds and walk the surrounding grounds next to the quiet, serene river.

THE SAVOY AUTO MUSEUM

The **Savoy Automobile Museum**, "Connects people to the cultural diversity of the automobile," according to its website. The museum is housed in a sleek and modern building that opened in 2021. A departure from a typical old car museum features a highly curated collection of cars and auto-related artwork. A rotating assortment of vintage vehicles, particularly classic sports cars from the 1930s through the 1970s, is well worth seeing.

TELLUS SCIENCE MUSEUM

Tellus Science Museum (north of downtown near I-75), is also a Smithsonian affiliate that occupies more than 125,000 square feet. The museum showcases more than 4,000 rocks, gems, and minerals in the Weinman Mineral Gallery. The Fossil Gallery has some impressive dinosaur fossils. The on-site planetarium hosts astronomy programs and stargazing events. Vintage motorcycles, model trains, and all kinds of other unique and special exhibits make this another multi-hour stop, particularly if you are traveling with kids.

OLD CAR CITY

To the north of Tellus Museum on State Road 411 in White, Georgia, is **Old Car City USA**, proudly advertised as the "World's Largest Knowd 'Old Car Junkyard" on its sign. Founded in 1931, it covers nearly forty acres and features seven miles of walking trails, which wind by the site's 4,000 classic cars on display in their rusted, falling-apart glory. If you like truly strange, amazing tourist attractions, Old Car City is a must. Plan on taking multiple pictures.

Inside, additional oddities include the owner's extensive Styrofoam cup folk art collection, Elvis Presley's last automobile, and thousands of Hot Wheels—the little die-cast cars made by Mattel. Presiding over all of this is the owner, Lewis Walter Dean, whom I had the immense pleasure of spending time with during my visit.

Old Car City USA, White City, GA

Cartersville is not just about museums. A massive solar energy factory is being built by **Hanwha Qcells Georgia, Inc.** to manufacture solar cells to convert sunlight into electricity near Cartersville. In 2019, Qcells, one of the world's largest and most recognized photovoltaic manufacturers, opened its first U.S. manufacturing facility in Dalton, Georgia. When completed, the Cartersville factory will become the largest facility of its kind in the Western Hemisphere.

Old Car City USA, White City, GA

Old Car City USA, White City, GA

EMERSON & ALLATOONA PASS

After Cartersville, the highway leads to the small city of **Emerson**, a gateway to **Red Top Mountain State Park** on Lake Allatoona. Emerson has served as the backdrop for many film and television productions, including several *Fast & Furious* movies. **Allatoona Pass Battlefield**, where an exceptionally bloody Civil War battle took place in 1864, is located near the city. Over thirty-percent of the 5,300 participants lost their lives in the five-hour battle. The earthworks and trenches are still visible today.

COBB COUNTY

KENNESAW

Cobb County lies squarely within the Atlanta metropolitan area. **Kennesaw**, now a suburb of Atlanta, was another point of attack on Sherman's march. Once known as "Big Shanty," it was incorporated in 1887 under the name of Kennesaw to preserve its association with the Civil War battle fought nearby. The **Southern Museum of Civil War and Locomotive History**, a Smithsonian Institution affiliate, is located in the city center and features train-related memorabilia and a collection of exhibits on the war. **Kennesaw State University** opened in 1966 and has grown substantially becoming Georgia's third-largest university at present. The university also has a campus in nearby Marietta.

Kennesaw has achieved some notoriety from a law passed in 1982 that states, "Every head of household residing in the city limits is required to maintain a firearm." This is outlined in section 34-21 of the city code, which goes on to say its purpose is to "provide for and protect the safety, security, and general welfare" of the city's residents. The law does provide an exemption for certain people, including those with physical or mental disabilities that prohibit them from using a firearm, those who are financially unable to purchase and maintain a gun, and those with religious beliefs opposing gun ownership. In accordance with federal law, anyone who has been convicted of a felony is also prohibited from gun ownership.

In a CNN interview, Lieutenant Craig Graydon, who served on the Kennesaw police force for over thirty years, explained that the law was passed as "More or less a political statement because the city of Morton Grove, Illinois, passed a city ordinance banning handguns from their city limits." He went on to say that the law is "meant to be a crime deterrent" and that it's not actively enforced by the local police. Kennesaw's mayor, Derek Easterling, told CNN the local law has garnered a lot of national and even international interest and that some people make incorrect assumptions about the town based on the law.

KENNESAW MOUNTAIN NATIONAL BATTLEFIELD PARK

Kennesaw Mountain National Battlefield Park is a 2,965-acre site that preserves a Civil War battleground. As part of General Sherman's Atlanta Campaign, opposing forces maneuvered and fought here from June 19, 1864, until July 2, 1864. The Battle of Kennesaw Mountain was one of the more significant clashes of the campaign. Confederate forces under General Johnston were dug in the mountain, and attacking Union forces under General Sherman were unable to break through the Confederate defensive line. Although the Battle of Kennesaw Mountain was a Confederate victory, it did not achieve Johnston's goal of slowing Sherman's advance to Atlanta. After the battle, Sherman performed another flanking maneuver to the left of Johnston's forces, forcing Johnston to retreat farther towards Atlanta to protect the city's outer defenses.

Like other National Park sites, the visitor center features exhibits and a film about the battle. I climbed the 664-foot trail from the visitor center to the mountain's summit. I can only imagine what it was like to do that as a soldier in battle. From the summit, you can see downtown Atlanta and other points in the metro area.

Note that Kennesaw Mountain Battlefield Park is one of the most visited national parks in the country with 2.5 million visitors per year. Part of the reason for all the visitor traffic is that the park remains the largest wilderness area in the metropolitan Atlanta area, and many locals enjoy walking and hiking there as well as satisfying historical interests. You can expect the parking lot to be packed most days. I made the mistake of visiting the park on a crowded Sunday as parking was very difficult. Consider visiting during the week in the spring or fall when there are fewer crowds.

MARIETTA

The city of **Marietta** is one of Atlanta's largest suburbs located along Highway 41. Marietta was created from Cherokee land and incorporated in 1834 as a railroad point for the Western & Atlantic Railroad. The city is over 1,100 feet above sea level and has mild summers by Georgia standards. After the Civil War, many northern visitors wintered in Marietta at the **Kennesaw House** now known as the **Marietta Museum of History**—then one of the main hotels in the city.

Several upscale restaurants, a ballet school, and a variety of shops are found downtown in historic Marietta Square. The square also boasts **Glover Park**, which is adorned with a large cast-iron fountain at its center. The **Strand Theatre**, a noted local landmark, was originally opened in 1935 as a movie theater. It is now a multiuse performing arts and film center. A microbrewery and large food hall are also located in downtown Marietta.

Of additional note is the self-guided **Marietta Black Heritage Walking Tour**. The tour includes notable churches, the Black business district from the age of segregation, schools, and homes, such as the **Henry Greene Cole House**, which was a stop on the Underground Railroad. Reputedly, the Cole House is haunted, with nearby residents seeing a woman in the house and lights turning on and off at night. The house sits across from the **Marietta National Cemetery** which contains the remains of more than 17,000 soldiers from the Civil War and beyond. Separately, the **Marietta City Cemetery** includes sections such as **Marietta Confederate Cemetery**, which holds the remains of over 3,000 soldiers, and the **Old Slave Lot**, the only burial ground for the enslaved in any major white Georgia cemetery.

Two must-see landmarks on the Marietta stretch of Highway 41 (known as the Cobb Parkway) are the **Marietta Diner**, a classic neon-lit diner open 24 hours a day featured on Food Network's *Diners, Drive-ins and Dives*, and **The Big Chicken**, "A Marietta landmark since 1963." Originally called "Johnny Reb's Chick, Chuck, and Shake," The Big Chicken has been a **Kentucky Fried Chicken** franchise restaurant since 1966. Stop inside to see the statue of Colonel Harland Sanders, the founder of the restaurant chain, holding a bucket of chicken.

On the outskirts of Marietta is **Lockheed Martin**, an aircraft manufacturer and one of the city's largest employers. Advanced military aircraft, including the F-35 fighter jet and the C-130 military transport aircraft, are built at this facility.

Kennesaw Mountain Summit, Marietta, GA

Old Marietta train station, "Wait for a Dream" mural, artist Helen Choi,
Marietta, GA

Marietta History Center, Kennesaw House, Marietta, GA

Marietta First Baptist Church, Marietta, GA

Ballet school, Marietta, GA

Marietta Diner, Marietta, GA

SMYRNA & VININGS

The city of **Smyrna** is approximately ten miles northwest of the Atlanta city limits on Highway 41. The town is known as the "Jonquil City" for the thousands of jonquils that flourish in gardens and along the streets in the early spring. From 2000 to 2012, Smyrna grew in population by twenty-eight percent, making it one of the fastest-growing cities in the state. Just off Highway 41 in Smyrna is the **Nam Dae Mun Farmers' Market**, a large venue that offers a wide selection of fresh fruits, vegetables, meats, and seafood, as well as a variety of Korean and other international products.

VIGNETTE   FANNY WILLIAMS AND AUNT FANNY'S CABIN

A piece of Smyrna history was demolished in August 2022. Aunt Fanny's Cabin was a well-known restaurant that featured overtly racist "Old South" themes. The restaurant operated from 1941 to 1992. The restaurant was also known for the "African American waiters [who wore] sign boards hung around their necks to announce the menu," which "re-assured the almost exclusively white clientele that all was still right with the world even as the shackles of segregation were beginning to weaken all across the South."

African Americans worked as cooks, hosts, servers, and busboys. Waitstaff were made to sing for white patrons. The uniforms for female employees included pinafore dresses and head wraps that evoked the era of slavery. It was, for a time, one of the best-known restaurants in the Atlanta area and inspired other local restaurants, including Mammy's Shanty on Peachtree Street and Johnny Reb's Dixieland on U.S. 41 at Akers Mill Road, both of which romanticized the region's plantation history.

The life of the restaurant's namesake, Fanny Williams (1868–1949), was generally obscured by the myth of "Aunt Fanny." She worked most of her life for the Campbells, the wealthy white family who owned the restaurant, but Williams had significant accomplishments of her own. Many of these were connected with her association with Wheat Street Baptist Church, one of the more activist of Atlanta's several African American churches. In Cobb County, she made her mark and endured the displeasure of the Ku Klux Klan through civil rights activities long before the Civil Rights movement began. She was one of the major fundraisers for Marietta's "Negro Hospital," the first hospital for African Americans in Cobb County. This institution broke ground in 1947. "Fanny Williams was an African American woman who impacted the community through her legacy of advocacy, economic stability, and social justice that gave agency to people who did not have a voice."

After Aunt Fanny's Cabin closed in the early 1990s, a long struggle began over the building. It sat empty for decades as the city grappled with whether to preserve it in some way or simply tear it down. Among those pushing hardest to save it were members of Smyrna's African American community, who argued that demolishing the cabin would erase a critical part of local Black history.

In the end, the city of Smyrna stated that the entity it had transferred the property to was "unable to obtain permission to move it to their property." Another party declined to take possession of the property, and the city voted in favor of a task force recommendation to demolish the structure. As of January 2024, the city of Smyrna finalized a sculpture design for a memorial to honor Fanny Williams as a civil rights icon. The memorial stands in front of Smyrna's history museum. https://www.whiteclouds.com/blog/fanny-williams-outdoor-statue/

TRUIST PARK AND THE BATTERY

Truist Park is a baseball stadium in the Atlanta metropolitan area, approximately ten miles northwest of downtown Atlanta in Cobb County's unincorporated community of Cumberland. Opened in 2017, it is a purpose-built stadium and the home field for the Atlanta Braves Major League Baseball Team. The team ownership built the stadium, complete with a multiuse entertainment district called **The Battery Atlanta**, which surrounds the ballpark. The Battery contains recreational facilities, housing, retailers, restaurants, bars, and corporate offices. The trend with big league sports teams is now to build stadiums that include many entertainment venues within walking distance. I visited Truist Park in the off season and was surprised at how well attended the area was just steps from the ballpark.

The last place of interest in Cobb County along Highway 41 is the **Chattahoochee River National Recreation Area**. The park's **East Palisades Trail** is one of the favorite hiking places in the Atlanta Metro area. The trail is 3.4 miles and moderately challenging. To increase the level of difficulty, visitors can undertake climbing several boulders and cliff outcroppings. Hikers pass by streams, rock formations, and a bamboo forest on the way.

GREATER ATLANTA

The **Atlanta Megaregion** is home to well over two-thirds of the population of Georgia and encompasses 8,376 square miles, roughly the area of the state of Massachusetts. Atlanta is part of the emerging megalopolis known as **Piedmont-Atlantic**, which includes the metro areas of Atlanta, Georgia; Birmingham, Alabama; Memphis and Nashville, Tennessee; and Charlotte, Raleigh-Durham, and Greensboro-Winston-Salem-High Point, North Carolina. This megaregion represents twelve percent of the total United States population and covers over 243,000 square miles.

In addition to Marietta and Smyrna, Greater Atlanta includes a number of significant satellite cities that surround the central city, such as the notable suburbs Sandy Springs, Roswell, Johns Creek, Alpharetta, Douglasville, Ellenwood, Tucker, Duluth, Newnan, Peachtree City, McDonough, Conyers, Dunwoody, and Covington. For those visitors familiar with the greater Los Angeles Metro area, Atlanta Metro will seem similar in its spread-out geography.

ITP AND OTP

ITP simply stands for "Inside the Perimeter," while **OTP** stands for "Outside the Perimeter." The Perimeter is the nickname for Interstate 285, a busy interstate beltway that encircles the city of Atlanta. It is one of the most heavily traveled roads in the United States because so many people choose to live on one side and work on the other.

OTP neighborhoods encompass the outlying Atlanta neighborhoods and suburbs, and some people use the term to refer to the entire Metro Atlanta area. Roswell, Marietta, Sandy Springs, Smyrna, Johns Creek, and Alpharetta are all popular OTP places to live due to lower taxes, more opportunities, less traffic, and an overall quieter lifestyle.

People who reside in ITP will almost always have an Atlanta address. New residents of Atlanta usually live in communities like Midtown, Morningside, Ansley Park, Buckhead, Virginia Highland, and Chastain Park. Short commute times, more cultural opportunities, walkability, and sophisticated dining and shopping opportunities are some of the reasons people choose to live in ITP neighborhoods.

VIGNETTE ATLANTA'S NOTORIOUS TRAFFIC

Atlanta consistently ranks in the list of America's most congested cities and is well-known for its terrible traffic. With Atlanta's wide area, commute times can be long and challenging. In fact, three-quarters of the population (or more) drive to and from work each day, packing major arteries as well as side streets and leading to serious traffic problems. As the Atlanta Metro area continues to grow, so will its traffic woes. I'm not sure there is much that can be done at this point to transform an ingrained car culture. Thus, you'll see traffic backups everywhere you go in the city. Some discussion has taken place about a BeltLine light rail system, and there are also many e-bikes and electric scooters on Atlanta's downtown streets.

There are two huge pain points on Atlanta highways:

- The Downtown Connector, aka the **"Grady Curve,"** is a 7.5-mile stretch of road in the heart of downtown Atlanta where I-75 and I-85 meet and merge. It was dubbed "Grady Curve" after Grady Hospital, the regional trauma center visible from the highway at that point. It is known as one of the worst bottlenecks in the United States. Counterintuitive exit directions, multiple lane changes, and tight weaves make the Grady Curve a major hotspot for traffic delays and accidents.

- The Tom Moreland Interchange, aka **"Spaghetti Junction,"** is another major chokepoint for Atlanta traffic. This is a flyover highway interchange at the intersection of I-85 and I-285, where research has established that major delays for semi-trucks are as bad as any in the nation.

FULTON COUNTY

Atlanta, with a current 2024 population of 514,000, is the state capital of Georgia, the seat of Fulton County, and the unofficial capital of the southeastern United States. Highway 41 cuts right through the middle of the city, where it is also known as Tara Boulevard, Metropolitan Parkway, and Northside Drive. While Atlanta is by temperament and history a southern city, it is also quite diverse and progressive with a host of ethnic groups, a large LGBTQ+ population, and a prominent African American population. Atlanta is an economic powerhouse where you'll find the headquarters of numerous Fortune 500 companies including **UPS, Coca-Cola, Cox Enterprises,** and **Delta Airlines**.

Georgia's largest city is an educational center, with forty colleges and universities, including some of the country's oldest Historically Black Colleges and Universities. Atlanta's prominence as a business and educational center has drawn numerous individuals from across the country and world who now call the city home. Due to all of the transplants, finding a born-and-bred Atlanta native can be challenging.

While Atlanta is lacking in some areas, such as public transit options and an increasing cost of living, the city continues to grow due to its diverse population and multiple businesses. Unfortunately, the city center is very car-dependent, but there are interesting areas to walk as well. These include Downtown, Midtown, and the college neighborhoods.

The Metropolitan Atlanta Rapid Transit Authority (**MARTA**) is limited at present but has ambitious plans to expand in the future. The **Atlanta BeltLine**, like New York City's High Line, is a significant repurposing of outdoor space, developed from the unused railroad tracks that circle several of the city's attractive in-town neighborhoods. The BeltLine provides access to green space and parks. Atlanta has the densest urban tree coverage of any major U.S. city.

Atlanta faces many of the same social issues that afflict other large cities in the United States: crime and violence, housing affordability, homelessness, substance abuse, and traffic congestion are problems that need attention. On the plus side, the city boasts diverse neighborhoods, a creative arts scene, and multiple museums, parks, and sports attractions. Spending several days in the Atlanta area is well worth your while and will give you a chance to run into at least one of the seventy-one streets in the city that are called "Peachtree."

BACKGROUND HISTORY: FOUNDING, CIVIL WAR, CIVIL RIGHTS, OLYMPICS

Atlanta is significant to the history of the United States. For thousands of years prior to the arrival of Europeans, the Creek and their ancestors inhabited the area. The city was founded in 1837 as the terminus of the Western & Atlantic Railroad. Atlanta was the main manufacturing center in the South prior to the Civil War and served that role for the Confederacy until it was captured by General Sherman and his Union troops in 1864 and almost entirely burned to the ground. Atlanta was rebuilt after the war and became a national industrial center due to its prominence as a rail transport hub.

After Reconstruction in the 1880s, Atlanta was promoted as a city of the "New South," which relied on modern economic thinking rather than being tied to the traditional "Old South" of agriculture and slavery. But for all its differences from much of the rest of the South, Atlanta was not spared from the burdens of racism.

In September 1906, competing newspapers published contrived and unsubstantiated stories of Black men assaulting white women and called for a vigilante patrol. The result is remembered as the **1906 Atlanta Race Riot**, where armed white mobs beat, shot, and stabbed African Americans to death over a four-day period. Black neighborhoods were destroyed in the process. In September 2023, on the anniversary of the riot, the African American community made efforts to draw attention to the massacre and uncover more details.

In 1913, Leo Frank, a Jewish-American factory superintendent, was convicted of murdering a thirteen-year-old girl in a trial that attracted national attention. Modern researchers generally agree that Frank was wrongly convicted. He was sentenced to death, but the governor commuted his sentence to life. A lynch mob took him from jail in 1915 and hanged him in Marietta. The Jewish community in Atlanta was horrified by this antisemitism. The Frank case led to a rebirth of the Ku Klux Klan in Atlanta in the 1920s.

In 1929, Dr. Martin Luther King Jr. was born and raised in the Sweet Auburn neighborhood of Atlanta. While there are many important people associated with the Civil Rights movement, Dr. King was a transcendent figure who has become mythologized in the years since his 1968 assassination. It is beneficial to visit the neighborhood where he was raised to understand the importance of his mission. January 15th, Dr. King's birthday, is a federal holiday in the United States.

On December 15, 1939, Atlanta hosted the premiere of *Gone with the Wind*, the film based on the best-selling novel by Atlanta native Margaret Mitchell. The film has been seen by millions and, when adjusted for inflation, remains the highest-grossing film in history. The gala event was attended by the producer David O. Selznick and the film stars Clark Gable, Vivien Leigh, and Olivia de Havilland, but Oscar winner Hattie McDaniel, the African American actor who won the Academy Award for Best Supporting Actress, was barred from the event due to Georgia's racial segregation laws at the time.

Atlanta continued to grow as a business center after World War II. William Hartsfield, a racial moderate, was the mayor from 1942–1962 during a time when the growing American Civil Rights movement was centered in Atlanta. The city was promoted in the 1950s as "The City Too Busy to Hate" to distinguish it from other southern cities. Hartsfield developed the city as a national aviation center and annexed several nearby communities, increasing the city's population. Ivan Allen, a successful businessman, succeeded Hartsfield as mayor in 1962 and desegregated Atlanta's public facilities. In 1973, Maynard Jackson became Atlanta's first elected African American mayor. He continued to modernize the city's Hartsfield-Jackson International Airport in the 1980s.

In 1990, Atlanta won its bid to host the 1996 Olympic Games, surprising many residing outside of the United States who had never heard of the southern city and assumed the centennial Olympics would be held in Athens, Greece. The '96 Olympics are remembered for the athletic feats of track star Michael Johnson, long jumper Carl Lewis, and gymnasts Dominique Dawes and Kerry Strug. During the opening of the games, boxing hero Muhammad Ali's lighting of the Olympic torch was one of the most inspirational moments in Olympic History.

However, the Atlanta Olympics were marred by a domestic terror incident at Centennial Olympic Park, which served as the town square for the games. Two people were killed in an explosion, and more than a hundred people were injured. Richard Jewell, a security guard, was initially suspected by the FBI, but later Eric Rudolph, an American domestic terrorist, was implicated. A skilled outdoorsman, Rudolph managed to elude law enforcement officials for years as he hid out in the mountains of western North Carolina. He was finally captured in 2003 and is now serving a life sentence at the Florence Supermax federal penitentiary in Colorado.

Since the turn of the twenty-first century, Atlanta has seen increasing gentrification. Old neighborhoods such as **Cabbagetown** have been transformed by numerous apartment buildings built to house young professionals. Many more apartment complexes are currently under construction. A tech corridor is developing along the State Route 400, which is commonly known as the **Georgia 400**. The city has also emerged as a top filming location for Hollywood movies and TV shows. The television series comedy/drama *Atlanta* about the Atlanta hip-hop scene ran from 2016 to 2022 and received much recognition.

In 2023 and 2024, large protests, acts of civil disobedience, and incidents of domestic terrorism occurred over the planned Atlanta Police Safety Training Center (APSTC), which became known as "Cop City." The eighty-five-acre facility, which featured a mock city to train firefighters as well as police, was built within **Weelaunee Forest**, the largest green space in Atlanta. Opponents claim the facility will harm the environment, while supporters say it is needed to replace outdated facilities. Many modifications have been made to the plan, and costs have climbed due to the need to defend against continued protests. The center was completed in December 2024.

VIGNETTE TRANSFORMATIVE FIGURES IN ATLANTA

Ivan Allen Jr., Robert Woodruff, Andrew Young, Billy Payne, and Ted Turner may be unknown to many readers, but each was instrumental in his own way in moving Atlanta forward.

Ivan Allen Jr. (1911–2003) was the mayor of Atlanta from 1962 to 1970, a watershed period for the city. He governed during a time of massive change due to the Civil Rights movement and was able, in the words of the New Georgia Encyclopedia, "To maintain calm and broker peaceful paths to integration unlike other southern cities." Significant physical and economic growth for Atlanta occurred during his time in office.

Robert Woodruff (1889–1985) was the president of the Atlanta-based Coca-Cola Company from 1923 until 1955 when he stepped down as president but remained on the board of directors and was the unofficial leader of the company until his death. He transformed the company's flagship product into one of the world's best-known and most-recognized brand names. He was also a major philanthropist who provided funds to many educational and cultural institutions in Atlanta. Many of these gifts were made anonymously. Woodruff exerted a powerful influence on Atlanta's business, cultural, and political development in the twentieth century. He left much of his personal wealth to a charitable foundation that still bears his name. A statue of Woodruff stands at Woodruff Arts Center.

Andrew Young (b. 1932) is an American politician, diplomat, and activist. A close confidant to Dr. Martin Luther King Jr., Young served as a U.S. Congressional representative from Georgia, the United States Ambassador to the United Nations during the Carter administration, and the mayor of Atlanta from 1981 to 1990. Due to his global experience, Young was instrumental in the building of modern-day Atlanta by attracting new businesses and billions in private investments. He is considered by historians to be one of the most effective large-city mayors to serve in the past century.

William Porter "Billy" Payne (b. 1947) is an American businessman based in Atlanta. Through the late 1980s and early 1990s, Payne was a leading advocate for bringing the Olympic Games to Atlanta. He gained the support of Atlanta leaders for this effort, which depended heavily on private funding to back the Games. In 1996, he was named president and chief executive officer of the Atlanta Committee for the Olympic Games. He later served as chairman of Augusta National Golf Club from 2006 to 2017, where he saw the introduction of the first women to the club's membership rolls. A statue of Billy Payne stands in Centennial Park.

Ted Turner (b. 1938) is an American entrepreneur, a media mogul, and a philanthropist best known for launching the Cable News Network, widely known as CNN, in 1980. CNN was the world's first 24-hour, all-news network that was first based in Atlanta. Turner turned the outdoor advertising company he inherited from his father into a global media company by first transforming cable television by creating the first TV superstation WTBS. A colorful Atlanta character, Turner raced yachts, once owned the Atlanta Braves baseball team, provided millions to the United Nations, and married actress Jane Fonda. He is one of the largest private landowners in the United States. Ted Turner Drive in downtown Atlanta is named in his honor.

THE NAME

As noted above, Atlanta was founded in 1837 at the end of the line of the Western & Atlantic railroad, but it's first name was Marthasville in honor of the then-governor's daughter. It was given the nickname "Terminus" for its rail location, and soon after its founding, the city's moniker was changed to Atlanta, the feminine of Atlantic, as a nod to the railroad.

NICKNAMES

Atlanta has a host of nicknames. It is called "The Big Peach," "The A'/'da' A," "The Big A," "A-Town," "ATL" (for its airport code), "Black Hollywood" (for its thriving African American entertainment industry), "Dogwood City," "Empire City of the South," "New York of the South," and "Hotlanta" (after a 1971 instrumental song by The Allman Brothers Band). Historically, Atlanta was often referred to as "Gate City of the South."

ATLANTA PORTRAYALS

Thanks to generous state subsidies and tax credits for the entertainment industry, Atlanta has been featured in a slew of movies and television shows. The city has been nicknamed the "Hollywood of the South," falling only behind California and New York in the number of productions filmed.

Television shows and movies are filmed on location in Atlanta due to the convenience of the region.

Atlanta is a global city with access to nearby coasts, mountain terrains, large cities, and rural areas—a production manager's dream. The airport is massive, and allows for easy travel for the equipment, props, and extra staff needed on set to complete the scenes. Georgia offers a twenty percent tax credit to companies filming productions with budgets of $500,000 or more in the state. If the company mentions Georgia in the logo, the tax credit jumps to thirty percent. This is a powerful incentive for the entertainment industry to produce within the state. Near the Atlanta airport is the 330-acre **Tyler Perry Studios**, located on the historic grounds of the former Fort McPherson army base.

BOOKS AND MOVIES

Atlanta has been featured in a range of books, movies, television series, and songs. *Gone With the Wind* by Margaret Mitchell and *A Man in Full* by Tom Wolfe are novels where the city is at the center of the characters portrayed. The movies *Gone With the Wind* (1939), *Deliverance* (1972), *Driving Miss Daisy* (1989), *Drumline* (2002), *ATL* (2006), and *Baby Driver* (2017) are all about the city, whether past or present. Atlanta is also the subject of songs in multiple genres, from gospel hymns to hip-hop.

CELEBRITIES

Many notable celebrities currently reside in Atlanta or have Atlanta roots. Singers include Justin Bieber, Cardi B, Ludacris, NeNe Leakes, Elton John, Kanye West, T.I., Future, Gladys Knight, Lil Baby, and Kelly Rowland.

Actors/Directors are represented by Dwayne "The Rock" Johnson, Halle Berry, Chris Tucker, Chloe Grace Moretz, Spike Lee, Kenan Thompson, Ed Helms, Steven Soderbergh, and Julia Roberts. Athletes include Dwight Howard, Shaquille O'Neal, and Cam Newton, to name a few.

MUESUMS

Atlanta has many notable museums, as befits a major city. The **High Museum of Art** in Midtown is the leading art museum in the southeast, with more than 14,000 paintings, sculptures, photographs, and drawings.

The museum is located in the **Woodruff Arts Center** complex, which also includes the **Atlanta Symphony Hall** and the **Alliance Theatre**.

The **Atlanta History Center** in Buckhead contains many interesting exhibits, including the "Atlanta Cyclorama," an immense circular painting of the Civil War Battle of Atlanta that is housed in the **Lloyd and Mary Whitaker Cyclorama Building**, purpose-built in 2015 for the painting. Behind the History Center is the **Swan House**, a 1928 mansion that you can tour as well as walk around the surrounding gardens. You can also walk on a trail through a small forest area near the Swan House. Another place to see on the grounds of the History Center is the **Smith Farm**, Atlanta's oldest surviving farmhouse. The farm represents what a farm that depended on enslaved labor looked like in the 1860s.

The **College Football Hall of Fame** is housed in downtown Atlanta and is definitely a destination for those with a particular interest in the college game. With many interactive activities and game experiences for the active visitor, the Hall of Fame store sells jerseys and other merchandise emblazoned with the name and logo of your favorite big college team.

Of particular note is the **National Center for Civil and Human Rights**, is located next to the Georgia Aquarium and the World of Coca-Cola Museum within the downtown area. The center has exhibits that detail the American Civil Rights movement with a focus on individuals who risked their lives to fight for equality for African Americans. The upper level has a global human rights perspective with pictures and descriptions of human rights defenders around the world. The center also contains many artifacts and papers related to Dr. Martin Luther King Jr.

MARTIN LUTHER KING JR. NATIONAL HISTORIC SITE

The **Martin Luther King Jr. National Historic Site** in Atlanta's Sweet Auburn District contains many exhibits and local landmarks, including the birthplace of Dr. Martin Luther King Jr.; **Ebenezer Baptist Church**, where he preached at an early age; the King Center, where Dr. King and his wife Coretta Scott King are buried; and the **Peace Plaza**, where the visitor center is located. You should make a special effort to visit this site in Atlanta.

THE JIMMY CARTER LIBRARY AND MUSEUM

The **Jimmy Carter Presidential Center**, located in the Poncey-Highland

Martin Luther King Jr. National Historic Site, Atlanta, GA

Martin Luther King Jr. National Historic Site, Atlanta, GA

neighborhood, houses former President Carter's papers and other material relating to the Carter administration. The library hosts special exhibits, such as Carter's Nobel Peace Prize and a full-scale replica of the Oval Office as it was during Carter's term. The **Carter Center** is located next to the museum. Honoring the work of President Jimmy Carter, the 39th President of the United States, and his wife Rosalynn, the Carter Center, in partnership with Emory University, was founded to prevent and resolve conflicts around the world, enhance freedom and democracy, and improve health. It is nonpartisan and seeks to work collaboratively with other organizations from the highest levels of government to local communities.

Ebenezer Baptist Church, Atlanta, GA

ATLANTA CUISINE

With quite a diverse food scene, you will not go hungry in Atlanta. Southern comfort food like chicken and biscuits and peach cobbler share space with all of the multicultural influences of the many ethnic groups that call the city home. If you are a serious foodie, I recommend driving to the city of Doraville in the northeast quadrant of the metro area to eat at one of the many restaurants located in strip malls along **Buford Highway**. A cool place to check out is the **Buford Highway Farmers' Market**. It is a massive place with just about every type of global ethnic food one could imagine, including fresh fruit and vegetables, seafood, meats, and more types of rice than I ever knew existed.

Several markets and restaurants of note in the Atlanta Metro area to check out are listed on the next page:

- **Mary Mac's Tea Room:** Southern comfort food, Midtown; I had a terrific fried chicken lunch at Mary Mac's Tea Room and highly recommend it!
- **The Flying Biscuit® Café:** Southern food, breakfasts and biscuits, multiple city locations
- **Ponce City Market:** the only farmers' market in Georgia primarily attended by pedestrians and cyclists; Midtown, located adjacent to the Beltline
- **The Colonnade Restaurant:** an Atlanta institution serving fare like fried chicken and coleslaw in an unpretentious space; Morningside, Lenox Park
- **The Sun Dial Restaurant, Bar & View:** a hotel restaurant and bar with 360-degree views of the city; downtown Atlanta
- **The Varsity:** a drive-in restaurant serving burgers, hot dogs, fries, shakes, and other American classics; an Atlanta institution, in Midtown near Georgia Tech
- **Ria's Bluebird:** breakfast and all-day brunch, including biscuits and rum-soaked French toast; across from Oakland Cemetery
- **Petit Chou Atlanta:** French-inspired breakfasts and lunches; Cabbagetown
- **Home Grown:** breakfast and Southern fare: Memorial Drive Corridor
- **Nick's Food To Go:** gyros and other traditional Mediterranean fare; Memorial Drive Corridor
- **Daddy D'z BBQ Joynt:** barbecue, wings, and pork ribs; Memorial Drive Corridor
- **Grindhouse Killer Burgers:** classic hamburgers; Memorial Drive Corridor
- **The Busy Bee Café:** soul food; Atlanta University Center
- **The Municipal Market in Sweet Auburn (The Curb Market):** indoor artisanal market with meat, produce, bakery, and prepared-food stalls, plus dine-in tables; Sweet Auburn
- **Southern Belle:** seasonal locally sourced cuisine; Poncey-Highland
- **Majestic Diner:** an old-school breakfast restaurant that's been serving since 1929; Poncey-Highland
- **Paschal's Atlanta Restaurant:** a soul food icon since 1947; Castleberry Hill

Mary Mac's Tea Room, Atlanta, GA

HIP-HOP AND ROLLER SKATING

From the neighborhoods of Atlanta have come hip-hop icons such as Outkast, T.I., TLC, 21 Savage, Ludacris, Gucci Mane, Lil Jon, and many more. While the popular focus is on the artists, great producers have also been the drivers of this explosion. The history of hip-hop in Atlanta started with many challenges. Hip-hop came to Atlanta in the late 1980s, but it did not immediately resonate. At first, it was considered a version of "Miami Bass" or "booty music," but gradually developed its own personality, giving rap a Southern twist that stood out from the hip-hop movements happening in Los Angeles and New York. Although many doubted Atlanta's potential, today this city is the nucleus of hip-hop. The **Trap Music Museum** is the first museum of hip-hop music.

To the west of U.S. 41, just outside the West End neighborhood, is the **Cascade Family Skating Rink**. This family roller skating rink was instrumental in the growth of hip-hop during the 1980s and 1990s. Roller skating is iconic to Atlanta, and this rink has seen some of hip-hop's biggest artists, such as TLC and Jermaine Dupri, take turns during their rise in the industry. In 2006, the rink caught even more attention after it was featured in the comedy-drama film *ATL*, starring Atlanta's own T.I. and Big Boi. Even Usher has been spotted here, on wheels.

THE STRIP CLUB CAPITAL OF THE SOUTH

Atlanta has a well-established reputation for being the strip club capital of America, although there are four U.S. cities that actually have more strip clubs per capita. Atlanta's strip clubs serve as business lunch points, testing grounds for up-and-coming hip-hop artists, and gathering spots for both men and women. The most iconic venue is the **Clermont Lounge**, Atlanta's oldest continuously operating strip club that has been in operation since 1965. **The Lounge** is female-owned and operated and features dancers of all ages. It is located in the basement of the **Clermont Motor Hotel** in the Poncey-Highland neighborhood and accepts cash only.

Clermont Lounge, Atlanta, GA

Other notable strip clubs in Atlanta are:
- **Magic City:** in business since 1985 and notable for ties to the hip-hop music industry and well-known athletes; South downtown
- **Blue Flame Lounge:** a family-owned business since 1983; Brookview Heights, (near Six Flags)
- **Onyx Gentlemen's Club:** female- and African American-owned; Northeast Atlanta (near The Colonnade Restaurant and Sprouts Farmers' Market)
- **Pink Pony:** Brookhaven (Northeast)
- **Cheetah Lounge:** in business since 1984; Midtown

HOUSING

Atlanta attracts many young singles who migrate to the city for work. The city tops many lists of good locales for singles and young professionals to start a career. According to data from the U.S. Census American Community Survey in January 2025, over fifty-one percent of Atlanta's population is single. Where single people reside, there are many entertainment venues and restaurants.

A report by the Metro Atlanta Chamber of Commerce predicts continued growth, with an influx of nearly three million people by 2050. New housing construction is hard to miss within the area close to downtown. Redevelopment of some of the formerly working-class neighborhoods continues to be a source of controversy as the city grows. And as Atlanta expands, housing costs will continue to climb.

BUSINESS

What brings people to call Atlanta home has been primarily work; there are numerous corporations that have located their headquarters in the area. Greater Atlanta has been recognized as the number one U.S. metro area for business formation, according to a recent LinkedIn Economic report. The economy has bounced back from the pandemic downturn, and the city is growing "at a breakneck pace," according to the *Fox 5 Atlanta* news outlet. The spillover from the many large corporations with headquarters in the area may have something to do with that.

NEARBY COLLEGES AND UNIVERSITIES

Atlanta is home to several colleges and universities of note, including the following:

- **The Georgia Institute of Technology,** aka **Georgia Tech** (enrollment 47,000) in Midtown, is one of the nation's top public research universities. Students attend in person at the main campus in Atlanta, at Georgia Tech—Europe in Metz, France, and through distance and online learning.
- **Georgia State University** (enrollment 52,400) has one of the most diverse student bodies in the nation. The university provides associate to graduate degree-level educational opportunities for tens of thou-

sands across its downtown Atlanta campus and five Permiter College campuses.

- **Emory University** (enrollment 14,830) is a highly-rated private, prestigious research university (#24 in the nation in 2025 per *U.S. News & World Report*). It is located just outside of the city in the Druid Hills neighborhood and is known for its graduate schools of Medicine, Law, and Business.

- **Atlanta University Center** in the heart of Atlanta is home to the city's four Historically Black Colleges and Universities (HBCUs). **Clark Atlanta University** (enrollment 4,252) founded in 1865, is a private Methodist institution. **Spelman College** (enrollment 2,588) was founded in 1881 as the Atlanta Baptist Female Seminary. It became Spelman College in 1924 to educate African American women. **Morehouse College** (enrollment, 2,200) founded in 1867, is a private men's liberal arts college that has graduated extraordinary leaders, visionaries, and pillars of the community. **Morehouse School of Medicine** (enrollment 891) is a private medical school. Originally a part of Morehouse College, the School of Medicine became independent in 1981.

SPORTS

Baseball: The Major League Baseball (MLB) Atlanta Braves have called the city home since 1965 and recently were World Series Champions (2021). They play in **Truist Park**.

Football/Soccer: The National Football League (NFL) Atlanta Falcons and Major League Soccer (MLS) Atlanta United FC play at **Mercedes Benz Stadium**, which opened in 2017.

Men's Basketball: The National Basketball Association (NBA) Atlanta Hawks play at the **State Farm Arena**, a venue that opened in 1999.

Women's Basketball: The Women's National Basketball Association (WNBA) Atlanta Dream play at the **Gateway Center @ College Park**, a multipurpose sports and entertainment venue opened in 2019.

NEIGHBORHOODS

Highway 41 goes by and through several Atlanta neighborhoods of note. For a visitor to the city, it is a very convenient road connecting many places of interest. Note that the road is often two lanes through much of the city.

BUCKHEAD

When you cross the Chattahoochee River into the city proper on Highway 41, you'll first travel through **Buckhead**, the wealthiest section of Atlanta. The road passes through an area with lots of high-end shopping and high-rise condominiums. The nearby residential streets are tree-lined and feature some beautiful and architecturally significant homes. The **Atlanta History Center** is located in Buckhead. Georgia's **Governor's Mansion**, built in 1967, is located in the **Tuxedo Park** area of Buckhead. Some residents of Buckhead would like to see the community secede from Atlanta. Buckhead has its own security police.

Buckhead has several neighborhoods with distinct identities: **Brookwood Hills** is a historic neighborhood comprised of single-family homes built in the 1920s. **Spring Lake**, right off Highway 41, is located across from the **Bobby Jones Golf Course**, with two unique nine-hole courses that feature multiple tees and pin combinations to allow for different course experiences. It's a beautiful setting with a clubhouse and restaurant overlooking the golf course. Atlanta native Robert Tyre (Bobby) Jones Jr. (1902–1971) was a lawyer and an American amateur golfer who was one of the most influential figures in the history of the sport. Jones founded and helped design the Augusta National Golf Club and co-founded the Masters Tournament.

Collier Hills is a residential area in Buckhead where the **Northside Beltline Bicycle Trail** runs from **Tanyard Creek Park** by the Bobby Jones Golf Course to **Atlanta Memorial Park**. South of Collier Hills is the **Loring Heights** subdivision developed by Edgar H. Sims Sr., an Atlanta builder and developer who also developed several other subdivisions in the Atlanta area during the 1930s and 1940s.

MIDTOWN

Proceeding south, Highway 41 goes through the western section of the **Midtown** neighborhood. There are many things to see to the east of the road. I suggest parking your car to take a walk, run, or bike around the area. It's a desirable place to live due to its proximity to downtown, so there are many high-rise apartments, but there also a number of historic early

Bobby Jones Golf Course, Atlanta, GA

Buckhead Theatre, Atlanta, GA

twentieth century single-family homes and mid-century apartment buildings. The neighborhood is listed on the National Register of Historic Places.

Berkeley Park is a neighborhood with a number of significant homes located in the **West Midtown** area of Atlanta. Much of Berkeley Park is listed as the **Berkeley Park Historic District** on the National Register for Historic Places.

Midtown is home to **Piedmont Park**, a heavily used historic 189-acre urban park with walkable trails and green space for various celebrations, concerts, and events in general. The park hosts an annual Pride Festival, a Jazz Festival, and numerous other activities making it the most visited green space in the city. A number of restaurants and shops border the park. Piedmont Park is adjacent to the **Atlanta Botanical Garden**, which stretches over thirty acres.

To the west of Piedmont Park within Midtown is a walkable stretch of street featuring the **Woodruff Arts Center**, located in a striking building that is also home to the **Atlanta Symphony Orchestra**, the **Alliance Theatre**, and the **High Museum of Art**. Nearby is the **Federal Reserve Bank of Atlanta**, the **Margaret Mitchell House** where she wrote the novel *Gone with the Wind*, and the restored **Fox Theatre**. The **Georgia Tech** campus is also located in Midtown.

East of Midtown and Piedmont Park are the neighborhoods of **Virginia-Highland** and **Poncey-Highland**. You'll see many trendy restaurants and bars are along the main roads through here. The landmark **Plaza Theatre**, built in 1939, screens indie films. The Carter Center and Freedom Park exist within its boundaries.

South of Midtown and Downtown, is the **Old Fourth Ward**, one of Atlanta's most desirable neighborhoods due to its proximity to the city center and parks. A former industrial area, the Old Fourth Ward is a trendy hub attracting foodies and shoppers. Hip eateries and indie fashion stores fill the popular **Ponce City Market** in the large 1920s Sears, Roebuck & Co. building. **Irwin Street Market** has local artisan foods. **Atlanta BeltLine's Eastside Trail** provides a path on a converted railway line for walking and cycling. Nearby, historic **Fourth Ward Park** has a skatepark.

Plaza Theatre, Atlanta, GA

DOWNTOWN ATLANTA

Highway 41 is known as Northside Drive as it skirts downtown Atlanta, the city's central business district. At downtown's heart is **Centennial Olympic Park**, with its centerpiece Fountain of Rings and regular lunchtime concerts. **Skyview Atlanta** is a popular feature of the park—it's a twenty-story Ferris wheel that provides a great view of the city. Nearby sights include the **College Football Hall of Fame**, the **Georgia Aquarium**, which is the largest aquarium in the world, and the **Center for Civil and Human Rights**, which has multimedia exhibits. **Georgia State University's** main campus is in the downtown area along with a number of student-friendly restaurants and shops nearby.

State Farm Arena, the multipurpose structure where the NBA Atlanta Hawks play as well as a place for concerts and special events, is within easy walking distance. An interesting (and free) place to visit is the **Georgia State Capitol**. Unfortunately, large parts of the building were receiving a major renovation when I was there. While in downtown, you should also take in the **World of Coca-Cola Museum** located next to Centennial Olympic Park.

Located across from the College Football Hall of Fame is the former CNN Center, once the headquarters of the CNN Broadcasting network. CNN's corporate headquarters are now in New York City. The new name of this landmark office building is **The Center**. When I visited, the interior atrium still sported a big globe, which I hope will remain. Several food chains were located in the structure along with some very bored security personnel. The big red and white CNN logo was removed from the sidewalk spot outside of the complex in the summer of 2024.

Underground Atlanta is a shopping and entertainment district in the **Five Points** neighborhood of downtown Atlanta. Underground has gone through many different iterations since the 1970s and is trending more along the entertainment line at present. Nearby Underground on Auburn Avenue is the **APEX (African American Panoramic Experience) Museum**, an African American history museum "presented from the Black perspective." Founded in 1978, it is listed as a site on the U.S. Civil Rights Trail.

Centennial Olympic Park, Atlanta, GA

The Spectacular, Centennial Olympic Park, Atlanta, GA

SWEET AUBURN

Just to the east of downtown Atlanta and south of the Old Fourth Ward is the **Sweet Auburn** neighborhood, famous for **Martin Luther King Jr. National Historical Park**. Sweet Auburn was the epicenter of Atlanta's African American community. It is quickly gentrifying due its attractive location. The neighborhood has seen dramatic rises in property values. Increasing rents are inspiring some difficult conversations within the city about how urban regeneration has forced longtime residents to leave. Atlanta is not the only city confronting this issue, but it is apparent as you walk around the neighborhood and see all of the new construction.

OAKLAND CEMETERY

Just to the south of Sweet Auburn is **Oakland Cemetery**, a historic burial ground since the 1850s for a number of Atlanta's notable citizens. An interesting place to explore and observe how times have changed, sections include an African American burial ground, a Confederate burial ground, and a Jewish burial ground. A bell tower dating from 1899 tops Bell Tower Ridge, where Atlanta's most prominent citizens are buried. A visitor could spend significant time investigating here.

Oakland Cemetery entrance, Atlanta, GA

CABBAGETOWN, INMAN PARK, & LITTLE FIVE POINTS

Next to Oakland Cemetery and adjoining Sweet Auburn is the **Cabbagetown** neighborhood, a cool, artsy area with old cottage homes, a lot of street art, and a number of restaurants. The **Krog Street Tunnel** is a funky pedestrian passageway under the local railroad tracks that features murals and other street art. The tunnel leads to the **Krog Street Market** in the hip **Inman Park** and **Little Five Points** neighborhoods, with a variety of independent stores, dive bars, burger joints, and a host of other unique places to eat. I suggest that you should see it now before a transformation leads to more clear-cut land to erect new multilevel condominiums for young professionals.

Back on Highway 41 heading south through downtown is a building that reminded me of a spaceship, the domed **Mercedes-Benz Stadium**, with its retractable roof and seating for 75,000 spectators. Home to the Atlanta Falcons and Atlanta United Football Club, the stadium has hosted numerous sporting events including the Super Bowl, the College Football National Championship, and the MLS (Major League Soccer) Cup. In 2026, the stadium will host several FIFA World Cup matches. Outside of the stadium is a plaque honoring the historic Friendship Baptist Church, which served the area for 142 years before being demolished in 2014. The church's congregation was relocated in 2017 in a new structure a couple blocks west of the stadium near the Historically Black Colleges and Universities in the **Vine City** neighborhood.

WEST END AND CASTLEBERRY HILL

Continuing past the stadium, U.S. 41 brings you to **Castleberry Hill** and its residential lofts and art galleries in old, repurposed warehouses. On the west side of Highway 41 is **Atlanta University Center**. **Hank Aaron Plaza**, with a statue of the famous Atlanta Braves ballplayer, is outside of the **Morehouse School of Medicine**.

The road continues through the primarily African American residential neighborhood of **West End** where you can tour the historic **Wren's Nest** heritage museum that was once the home of Joel Chandler Harris. Harris was the author who popularized the African folktales of Br'er Rabbit. Also in the West End is the **Hammonds House Museum**, a fine arts museum within a nineteenth century Victorian home that focuses on artists of African descent.

Nearby, the **Atlanta BeltLine West End Trail** is a paved multiuse path. The neighborhood has a number of vegetarian and soul food restaurants, including the **Busy Bee Café**, which has been in operation since 1947.

ADAIR PARK

Adair Park is a residential neighborhood traversed by Highway 41. It was one of the early single-family housing developments built outside the central city, with many American Craftsman bungalows. In the latter half of the twentieth century, Adair Park gradually slid into decline along with the Metropolitan Parkway corridor. By 2000, the neighborhood experienced revitalization as young people began to move back into the neighborhood, settling alongside many lifelong residents. They were attracted by the charming, affordable bungalows and community spirit.

PITTSBURGH

Adjacent to Adair Park is the **Pittsburgh** neighborhood, founded in 1883 as an African American working-class suburb. It was named Pittsburgh because it resembled that industrial city in Pennsylvania. Gentrification has dramatically increased prices for homes in this neighborhood.

FORT McPHERSON AND TYLER PERRY STUDIOS

Fort McPherson is slightly east of Highway 41 as you near the airport. Long ago, it was a U.S. Army base, but now is parkland with a portion serving as the location of **Tyler Perry Studios**. Tyler Perry is an American actor, director, filmmaker, and playwright who has written and produced many hit plays and movies. He opened the studio in 2019 and has made history as the first African American to own a major movie studio. The studio—one of the largest production facilities in the country—showcases forty buildings on the National Register of Historic Places, twelve purpose-built sound stages, 200 acres of green space, and a diverse backlot.

Highway 41 continues south under the name of Dogwood Drive through the **Hammond Park** neighborhood. Local landmarks include **Mount Zion Methodist Church**, one of the first churches in the area. Tombstones in the adjacent cemetery date from 1796.

The road continues to the outskirts of the vast **Hartsfield-Jackson Atlanta International Airport**. A SkyTrain whisks passengers to their appropriate terminal for flight. The **Delta Flight Museum** is an aviation and corporate museum located on the outskirts of the airport. It is housed in two 1940s aircraft maintenance hangers that are the oldest surviving buildings at Delta's corporate headquarters. The museum is an interesting place to visit if you want to see some of the passenger aircraft Delta has used in the past and other memorabilia, including a display of passenger flight attendants' uniforms over the years. Among the highlights is a retired Boeing 747 aircraft on the premises you can tour. The plane contains a second-floor stairway and mementos of a time when the general American public rarely traveled by plane, so flying was a much bigger deal.

The North American headquarters of the auto company **Porsche** is located along this stretch of U.S. 41. The twenty-seven-acre complex opened in 2015 and is the largest investment outside Germany for the sports car manufacturer. The **Porsche Experience Center** is complete with a driver development track, a classic car gallery, a restoration center, a human performance center, a driving simulator lab, and a fine dining restaurant. The Experience Center has been specifically designed as a destination for the public, including automotive enthusiasts and Porsche customers. A boutique hotel, the **Kimpton Overland**, sits next to the headquarters.

HAPEVILLE

The small historic city of **Hapeville** sits right next to Atlanta Airport and about eight miles from central Atlanta. The city was founded in 1891 as a suburban community that was used as a summer home by its first settlers. Later, Hapeville became more industrialized and run-down until the early 2000s when significant redevelopment began to take place. New construction has attracted more young professionals to the city.

Highway 41 proceeds through the **Hapeville Historic District**, a small, attractive old-time downtown that is listed on the National Register of Historic Places. Hapeville is also home to the **Dwarf House**, the original home of Chick-fil-A restaurant. The founder of the now-national chain was S. Truett Cathy, in 1946. A statue of Mr. Cathy sitting on a bench is outside of the restaurant. **Chick-fil-A** is headquartered in Atlanta. Inside the headquarters is a classic diner with a sit-down counter that was filled with patrons on my visit.

OTHER THINGS TO SEE IN THE ATLANTA AREA

Six Flags Over Georgia is a giant amusement park with high-speed roller coasters, thrill rides, water attractions, and more. The park opened in 1967 as the second park in the Six Flags chain, following the original in Texas, which opened in 1961. The park was built on the site of the oldest permanent Indigenous agricultural village in Georgia, dating from 200 BCE to 500 CE.

Stone Mountain Park lies about twenty-five miles east of Atlanta. One of the most popular and heavily visited parks in the Atlanta metropolitan area, the park covers 3,200 acres and features numerous recreational and family-friendly attractions. You can ride a cable car up to the mountain summit. The park's centerpiece is the Confederate Memorial Carving on the side of the mountain, conceived in 1912 and completed in 1972. The high relief carving features Jefferson Davis, Robert E. Lee, and Thomas "Stonewall" Jackson, and is larger in area than the carvings on Mount Rushmore. According to a recent article in *The New York Times*, the memorial is "slowly being obscured by lichen and being stained back to the color of surrounding rock." Organized groups desiring to repair the monument are now facing against groups calling for an end to its upkeep. I visited the park on a rainy, foggy day and saw the carving and surrounding area. Suffice to say that most people coming to the park are there for recreation rather than history.

ATLANTA METRO SOUTH

CLAYTON COUNTY

As it leaves Hapeville and proceeds south into Clayton County, Highway 41 once again resumes the name Dixie Highway and remains four lanes through the metropolitan area. This stretch of road is lined with Asian and African food distributors, car and tire repair facilities, pawn shops, trailer courts, bail bondsmen, chain eateries, and multiple stoplights.

To the east of the highway is the **Hindu Temple of Atlanta**, one of the five large Balaji temples in the United States. There are more than 40,000 Hindus residing in Georgia, and most of them are concentrated in and around Atlanta. To the west of Highway 41 is the **Ambaji USA Shree Shakti Mandir Temple** where another branch of the Hindu faith worships. In addition to the temple, this complex features a gated community.

JONESBORO

The highway proceeds next into **Jonesboro**, an Atlanta suburb and the seat of Clayton County. A wall mural celebrates Jesse "Lone Cat" Fuller (1896–1976) a blues singer who grew up in this segregated southern town and migrated to the West Coast. There, he became known as a one-man band for all of the instruments he could play and for his song "San Francisco Blues." Bob Dylan adopted his use of a harmonica brace from Fuller. The city's name was originally "Jonesborough," where yet another Civil War battle was fought. **The Battle of Jonesborough** resulted in the final fall of Atlanta to Union troops in 1864. You can visit an old Confederate cemetery there, and there are a number of markers to read that provide information about Jonesboro's historic homes.

Jonesboro was the inspiration for many of the settings in the novel and movie *Gone with the Wind*, and it continues to trade on this with the **Road to Tara Museum** located in the old railroad station. Posters of Hattie McDaniel and Butterfly McQueen adorn the museum along with a mural of Scarlett O'Hara uttering her famous line "Fiddle Dee Dee." The historic 1839 home known as **Stately Oaks** served as the model for Margaret Mitchell's imagined plantation, Tara. I received a tour of the **Stately Oaks Antebellum and Historic Community** from Mickie and Susan, two lovely docents dressed in period costume. Stop for an interesting tour of the home and grounds, but note that hours, unfortunately, are limited to Friday afternoons.

Mickie and Susan were interested in my travels and wanted to let me know that they refer to Highway 41 as "1941," as the road is both Highway 41 and Highway 19 for a stretch. The road is also known as "Tara Boulevard" in this area to fully confuse the occasional traveler!

SIDE TRIP TO PEACHTREE CITY

An eighteen-mile side trip southwest from Jonesboro will take you to **Peachtree City**, an Atlanta suburb noted for its extensive use of golf carts. There are over 13,000 households and 11,000 registered golf carts, and dedicated paths wind throughout most areas of the city. While most places with carts are considered retirement communities, Peachtree City has a significant number of younger families who utilize them as well. Once children turn twelve, they are allowed to drive a cart with a licensed parent,

Jesse "Lone Cat" Fuller mural, artist Shannon Lake, Jonesboro, GA

Scarlett O'Hara mural, artist Shannon Lake, Jonesboro, GA

grandparent, or guardian in the front passenger seat. At fifteen, once they have their driver's permit, they can go off on their own.

LOVEJOY

Back on Highway 41, the Atlanta suburban sprawl continues into the city of **Lovejoy**, which was once a cotton-processing city. The **Battle of Lovejoy's Station** was fought here during the Civil War, but most of the battle site has now disappeared. Lovejoy has been proposed as the southern endpoint of Metro Atlanta's first commuter rail line.

HENRY COUNTY

Atlanta Metro continues into Henry County and the city of **Hampton**, noteworthy as the location of the **Atlanta Motor Speedway**, located just off the highway. The speedway has been in operation since 1960 and hosts a variety of NASCAR and drag-racing events, car shows, concerts, and conventions. The track seats 70,000 to 128,000 spectators, depending upon the configuration. Former U.S. President Jimmy Carter once worked as a ticket taker at the track and later attended races as governor of Georgia and as U.S. president.

SPALDING COUNTY

Highway 41 continues into Spalding County and its county seat, **Griffin**. Griffin is a small town that was once an important railroad point. It has a small commercial historic district. The western part of the town was heavily damaged by a series of powerful tornadoes in January 2023, and the community is still rebuilding. Griffin is the hometown of Wyomia Tyus (b. 1945), a track and field star who won gold medals in the 1964 and 1968 games. The local **Wyomia Tyus Olympic Park** in Griffin is named in her honor.

MIDDLE AND SOUTH GEORGIA

PIKE COUNTY AND LAMAR COUNTY

After leaving Griffin, U.S. 41 passes through a small stretch of Pike County before entering Lamar County. At the city of **Barnesville**, we at long last bid the Atlanta Metro area farewell. Barnesville, an old railroad town, was once known as the "Buggy Capital of the South" during its heyday due to the production of buggies within the city. The city celebrates the annual Barnesville Buggy Days Festival in September with a number of events tied to the area's traditions. Its downtown has murals, antique stores, and an old Carnegie Library that has been restored as a fine arts studio.

MONROE COUNTY

From Barnesville, Highway 41 proceeds east to the city of **Forsyth**, where it once again becomes a two-lane road. Forsyth is the Monroe County seat and is almost in the exact center of the state, according to a sign along the road. The commercial district encompasses the Monroe County Courthouse and square, which is listed on the National Register of Historic Places. This historic town is worth stopping to see.

The venerable **Rose Theater**, once a movie house, now operates as a community theater. A plaque commemorates Joel Chandler Harris, the creator of the "Uncle Remus" stories. He once worked as a copy boy at the local Forsyth newspaper. Unfortunately, Forsyth is also home to a tragic racist event when, in 1912, white mobs drove out the town's African American population over an alleged crime. As with many small Southern towns, it has been a slow road from segregation to integration and more inclusive participation in the governance and development in the city.

When I passed by, a collection of old trucks on the outskirts of town was covered in kudzu. Kudzu is an invasive vine that has covered the landscape in many parts of the South.

As it proceeds through Monroe County, Highway 41 parallels the railroad track through the little town of **Smarr** with its tiny post office. From there, the road provides a pretty country drive south into the city of Macon.

Outside Forsyth, GA

BIBB COUNTY

Macon, "where soul lives," is the fourth-largest city in Georgia and the Bibb County seat. It is the retail, medical, financial, educational, and cultural center of rural middle Georgia and definitely a classic southern city. The **Ocmulgee River** flows through the heart of downtown Macon, with its spacious streets and parks. The area was first settled by Indigenous peoples in the Mississippian period more than 17,000 years ago. Earthen mounds that date from 1000 CE are located at **Ocmulgee Mounds National Historical Park**, just south and east of the city. A network of trails connects the various mounds within the park for hiking and birdwatching.

Monroe County Courthouse, Forsyth, GA

Macon celebrated its bicentennial in 2023, earning a place on the *Condé Nast Traveler's* list of "The 23 Places to Go in 2023." I visited in mid-summer, when it was quite hot, but if you visit during Macon's **International Cherry Blossom Festival,** held each March, you will be treated to over 350,000 Yoshino cherry trees in full bloom. This festival is a definite draw, so make travel plans early. Downtown Macon is walkable with a number of old buildings undergoing restoration on my visit, but, unfortunately, several of the local stores seem to be permanently closed.

The **Georgia Sports Hall of Fame & Museum**, the "largest state sports hall in America," is located downtown near the **Tubman African American Museum**, which is the "largest of its kind in the southeast dedicated to educating people about the art, history and culture of African Americans."

Also close by downtown is the **Hay House**, an 1859 mansion and National Historic Site. It features four levels and a two-story cupola. In fact, Macon is home to 5,500 National Register historic structures in eleven historic districts, which are spread across the city. Well-known restaurants in Macon include **H&H Soul Food Restaurant** and **The Rookery**. The **1842 Inn** is a boutique bed and breakfast hotel in a historic Greek Revival Mansion.

SCHOOLS

Wesleyan College (enrollment 700) was founded in 1836 in Macon, and it was the first college in the United States chartered to grant degrees to women. **Mercer University** (enrollment 9,164) a private research university with its main campus in Macon, was founded in 1833 and is the oldest private university in Georgia. **Middle Georgia State University** (enrollment 8,409) is a public university in Macon that traces its history to 1884.

MUSIC

The chief reason Macon attracts the majority of visitors is due to its musical heritage. Attractions throughout the city celebrate soul music, rock and roll, rhythm and blues, and the fusion of rock and R&B in what is known as Southern Rock. Famous performers and bands with links to Macon include The Allman Brothers Band, Little Richard, Otis Redding, James Brown, Bill Berry and Mike Mills from the band R.E.M., and Jason Aldean.

The Big House, where members of The Allman Brothers Band lived from 1970 to 1973, the **Otis Redding Museum** celebrating the King of Soul, and **The Little Richard House**, the childhood home and pioneer of rock and roll music are all open for tours. **Capricorn Sound Studios & Museum** celebrates Capricorn Records, the groundbreaking Southern Rock label where The Allman Brothers Band, The Marshall Tucker Band, The Charlie Daniels Band, and more recorded. Local live music venues include **Grant's Lounge, JBA, Society Garden, The Crazy Bull, The Hummingbird Stage and Taproom**, and **Serenity Entertainment Complex**.

VIGNETTE   ROSE HILL CEMETERY AND
THE ALLMAN BROTHERS BAND

*On my visit to Macon, I made a special pilgrimage to **Rose Hill Cemetery**, where* members of The Allman Brothers Band are interred. The cemetery is on the National Register of Historic Places and dates from 1844. It is a fascinating place to walk around and see a wide assortment of interesting gravesites and monuments. The cemetery is no longer open for burials, but many notable Macon citizens, some 600 Confederate troops, and an unknown number of enslaved persons rest here.

The cemetery has separate sections for Catholics and Jews. Rose Hill has at least one pet burial—in my rambles there, I found the grave of "Lieutenant Bobby, Just a Brown Dog, Loyal Pal and Pet of Capt. D.C. Harris." Another interesting monument is that of Little Martha, who died in 1836 at age twelve from disease. She is the namesake of the 1972, The Allman Brothers Band song, "Little Martha."

The Allman Brothers Band were an American rock band formed in Jacksonville, Florida, in 1969 by brothers Duane and Gregg Allman, as well as Dickey Betts (1943–2024), Berry Oakley, Butch Trucks, and Jai Johanny "Jaimoe" Johanson (b. 1944). The band was based in Macon and was known for its live shows and extended instrumental pieces that incorporated blues, jazz, and country music. The band would break up, reunite, tour, and compose with additional musicians until they performed their final show in 2014. Several band members struggled with drug addiction. Despite the ups and downs, The Allman Brothers Band is considered one of the most influential musical groups in history. **GABBA**, the Georgia Allman Brothers Band Association, was formed in the early 1990s to preserve The Allman Brothers' history. It produces a festival in Macon each year with live music to honor the band.

The Allman Brothers Band internment area is surrounded by an iron fence to avoid desecration and contains four graves. Duane Allman (1946–1971), slide guitarist and founding member of the band, died in a motorcycle accident at age twenty-four. He is considered to be one of the greatest guitarists of all time. His brother, Gregg Allman (1947–2017), the keyboardist and vocalist, struggled through life with drug addiction. He kept the band going after his brother's death. In the early 1970s, he embarked on a solo career. Around that time, he married (and immediately divorced) popular singer and actress Cher. Butch Trucks (1947–2017) was a drummer and founding member of the band. Berry Oakley (1948–1972) was a bassist and also a founding member of the band, and like Duane Allman, he died in a motorcycle accident. He is considered one of the greatest bass players of all time. On Oakley's tombstone is inscribed, "And the Road Goes On Forever."

As you leave Macon going south on Highway 41, you will pass lots of churches and suburban housing developments, and a great big **Armstrong World Industries** factory, which manufactures ceiling tiles and wall systems for commercial and residential properties. Other large factories line the highway as well.

Rose Hill Cemetery, Macon, GA

Lieutenant Bobby grave marker, Rose Hill Cemetery, Macon, GA

Rose Hill Cemetery, Macon, GA

Bearfoot Tavern, Macon, GA

Greenwood mural, Macon, GA

HOUSTON COUNTY

As Highway 41 crosses into Houston County, it skirts by the city of **Warner Robins**. This area was largely agricultural until World War II, when, in 1942, **Robins Air Force Base** was established as a major U.S. Air Force maintenance and logistics complex. The base is just outside of the city limits and has expanded over the years. It is one of the largest employers in the state of Georgia. The nearby **Museum of Aviation** is the U.S. Air Force's second largest aerospace museum. Historic and state-of-the-art aircraft are on display. The museum is a big draw; more than a half million visitors tour each year.

Warner Robins's other claim to fame is in kids' baseball and softball. The game of Tee-ball was invented here in 1958, and the city is the Southeast Region Headquarters of Little League Baseball and Softball. The city's teams have won both the Little League World Series and Little League Softball World Series, making Warner Robins the only Little League city to have won both a baseball and softball title.

A few miles south of Warner Robins is the city of **Perry**, the Houston County seat. Perry is known for the **Georgia National Fairgrounds and Agricenter**, where the Georgia State Fair is held annually in early October. Other events include the Dogwood Festival, the Perry Music Festival, and the city's New Year's Eve celebration, the highlight of which is the "Perry Buzzard Drop"—a plastic buzzard with real feathers that is dropped from the sky at midnight.

Perry has a picturesque, historic downtown with a courthouse square. To house travelers on their way to Florida, the **New Perry Hotel** was built in 1925. Enlarged over the years, the hotel is closed and awaiting renovation with a new life as an apartment complex. It is on the National Register of Historic Places. A landmark church dating from 1827, **Perry United Methodist Church** is an easy walk from downtown. While I was exploring Perry, I ran across a poster in the courthouse square asking remote workers to take a brief survey. Apparently, the city, which is a little over 100 miles from Atlanta, is becoming an attractive place for remote workers to live.

New Perry Hotel, National Historic Site, Perry, GA

DOOLY COUNTY

Leaving Perry and heading south, you'll enter Dooly County. From here, agricultural country stretches approximately 135 miles to the city of Valdosta. Farms line Highway 41 on this stretch of road, and many offer agritourism visits for a true farm experience. The highway is sparsely traveled for long stretches as it parallels I-75 a few miles away. The state of Georgia advertises the road in this juncture as **"Georgia Grown Trail 41"** with trail stops for attractions such as farm tours, unique stores, wineries, and farmers' markets.

I did not stop at all of the advertised places along the trail as I traveled this stretch of U.S. 41, but I still saw sights that seemed to come from another time. There were pickers in the fields working on a hot summer day. Converted school buses with all the windows cut out are utilized to carry watermelons. Produce warehouses, some abandoned homes and businesses taken over by vegetation, and interesting, but largely deserted, small towns lined the road.

In recent years, much of Georgia's agricultural country has been hit by crop damage from storms, floods, and early frosts, which have wiped out farm incomes. Farming as a way of life requires perseverance and patience. This is being tested as never before due to the effects of climate change. Numerous small towns in the vicinity of Highway 41 are in dire straits from the loss of income among residents.

Perry United Methodist Church, Perry, GA

UNADILLA

Highway 41 passes through small but not abandoned Unadilla; the slogan "Where People Make the Difference" is spelled out on its water tower. **Dooly State Prison**, a medium security facility, is located in Unadilla.

Along Highway 41, Dooly County, GA

Converted school bus transporting watermelons, Vienna, GA

VIENNA

Vienna, pronounced Vye-anna, is the Dooly County seat and a very old town incorporated in 1841. The entire downtown area is listed in the National Register of Historic Places, and it's definitely worth walking around. Stop at **We're Nuts—Ellis Bros. Pecans** to pick up pecans and peach ice cream. Also in Vienna is the **Georgia State Cotton Museum**, located in a 125-year-old schoolhouse. The museum outlines the history of cotton and contains some old farm tools. If you are fortunate, one of the curators will be available and happy to talk with you about the cotton industry and its integral part in Georgia's economy.

Since 1982, Vienna has been best known for the **Big Pig Jig**, put on by the Dooly County Chamber of Commerce. The event is held annually in early November and proclaims to be the Southeast's and Georgia's oldest official barbecue cooking contest. The contest draws approximately 100 teams cooking nearly 400 entries of hogs, shoulders, ribs, chicken, stew, and sauce. Cash prizes and trophies are awarded by more than 100 judges. This big spectator event has been recognized as one of America's top 500 festivals as listed by *Travel Agent* magazine.

SUGGESTED SIDE TRIPS

ANDERSONVILLE

About thirty miles east of Vienna is the small town of **Andersonville**, made infamous by the Confederate prison located there during the American Civil War. **Andersonville National Historic Site** preserves the former Andersonville prison and features a national cemetery and the National Prisoner of War Museum. The site was originally commanded by Captain Henry Wirz, who was tried and executed for war crimes after the war. Approximately 45,000 Union prisoners were held at Camp Sumter, as it was known during the war, and nearly 13,000 of them died of starvation and disease.

The conviction of Wirz was questioned by many in the South. In 1908, the United Daughters of the Confederacy erected a monument honoring Wirz in the center of Andersonville, "to rescue his name from the stigma attached to it by embittered prejudice." The monument blames the Union deaths on "the harsh circumstances of the times and the policy of the foe," and claims that Wirz was "the victim of misdirected popular clamor." The statue is evidence of the enduring power of the "Lost Cause" mindset that still survives in the rural south, and it remains the only U.S. monument to honor an adjudicated war criminal.

PLAINS

About thirty-eight miles from Vienna and slightly east of Andersonville is the little town of **Plains**, with a population of 538. It is home to **Jimmy Cart-**

er **National Historic Site**, which contains a museum and visitor center, a restored rail depot, and the boyhood home and farm of President Jimmy Carter (1924–2024) and First Lady Rosalynn Carter (1927–2023), who were both born and raised in Plains. They remained residents of the modest ranch home that Carter built in 1961. The Carters are buried beside a willow tree on the grounds of the house. At this writing, the National Park Service plans to turn the home into a museum.

CRISP COUNTY

Back on Highway 41, you'll travel from Vienna through farm country to the city of **Cordele**, the seat of Crisp County and the self-proclaimed "watermelon capital of the world." The town holds a **Watermelon Days** festival each July. The **Cordele State Farmers' Market** is north of town, where truckloads of melons were being offloaded and processed just off the highway when I stopped by. Peaches, peanuts, and pecans are also sold and processed at the farmers' market in season.

Downtown Cordele has seen better days, but you will enjoy a stop at the **Cordele Recreation Parlor Pool Hall**, which brags that it has been "Serving the best hot dog in the USA since 1939." A little west of town on Lake Blackshear is **Georgia Veterans State Park**, with a campground, veterans' monument, golf course, and picnic shelters.

Downtown Cordele, GA

Continuing on, the highway rolls into the little town of **Arabi** (pop. 465), where a sign proclaims it as the boyhood home of T. Graham Brown (b. 1954), a country singer. Check out **Sam's Country Store** as you enter town for a glimpse of how an old-time store should look.

TURNER COUNTY

The highway continues into **Ashburn**, the seat of Turner County and the self-proclaimed peanut capital of the world. I passed by the abandoned Ezy-Clean Car Wash on my way through town. It looked to be in an old service station with a boiled peanut stand on the premises. Every fourth weekend in March, Ashburn holds the **Fire Ant Festival**, to which, according to the festival website, welcomes visitors, "but not the ants themselves." The event has "wacky and off-the-wall activities for family fun" including the Fire Ant Pageant, where nine new Fire Ant Queens are crowned.

On my way out of Ashburn, I stopped by a granite monument erected by the Daughters of the Confederacy. Located next to the railroad track, the monument calls this part of Highway 41 the **"Jefferson Davis Highway."** A block from the monument is a cross street named Martin Luther King Drive.

TIFT COUNTY

From Ashburn, the highway continues through a rural landscape for some twenty-two miles before it enters **Tifton**, the seat of Tift County. Please make a point of stopping! Tifton is worth spending some time in. The city, once known primarily as Georgia's largest tobacco market, has a rich agricultural past that you can learn about at the **Georgia Museum of Agriculture.** Operated by **Abraham Baldwin Agricultural College** (enrollment 3,825) the museum has ninety-five acres of buildings, artifacts, gardens, and exhibits showcasing the past, present, and future of Georgia's number one industry.

Stop into **Espresso 41,** a café in an old, converted gas station to see lots of memorabilia and enjoy coffee and a hamburger. The café sports a colorful mural that welcomes visitors to Tifton. Also stop by the **Town Terrace Motel** (also known as the Pink Motel). Built in the 1940s, it was owned and operated by Violet Van Gundy, who played "Baby Violet" in some of the Little Rascals movies. The **Tift Theatre for Performing Arts** is located in the old Tift movie theatre, a downtown gem of a building that has survived since 1937.

The **Tifton Commercial Historic District** and **Residential Historic District** are both listed on the National Register of Historic Places. The local downtown offers some unique retail options. I bought some sale items at **The Big Store** and admired the signs for the **Little Hippie Chick** and the **Vintage 41** clothing store.

I stopped by the magnificent **Tifton City Hall** to pick up some information and saw the sign for the long-gone Myon Hotel, which was converted into the city hall in the mid-1980s. The Myon was constructed in 1906 and listed as the finest hotel south of Atlanta.

Tifton was a major railroad hub in the early 1900s and later became a stopping point for cars traveling on Highway 41. As the nearby interstate highway sucked up all the downtown businesses in the 1970s and 1980s, Tifton fell into disrepair. Thanks in large part to the vision of Harold Harper Sr. (1929–2019), a Tifton resident and real estate developer, several old tobacco warehouses and businesses were renovated in the 1980s and 1990s including the old Myon Hotel. When I visited, downtown Tifton was thriving with an eclectic mix of stores. A tip of the hat to Harold Harper, and others like him, who care about their communities and work to preserve them. A bronze sculpture of Harper seated on a park bench honors him in downtown Tifton.

Tifton mural at Espresso 41, artist Ridge Harper, Tifton, GA

Tift Theatre, Tifton, GA

COOK COUNTY

Leaving Tifton, Highway 41 proceeds another twenty-one miles before arriving at the quiet town of **Sparks**, which adjoins the city of **Adel**, the Cook County seat and self-proclaimed "City of Daylilies." Adel's name has an interesting history. The original name of the city was "Puddleville." The city's first postmaster, Joel "Uncle Jack" Parrish, wanted to change the name. Supposedly, he saw the name *Philadelphia* on a burlap sack and took out the four middle letters to create the name, *Adel*.

Downtown Sparks, GA

Traffic picks up on U.S. 41 as it nears the city of Valdosta, approximately twenty-five miles to the south. Toward the southern border of Cook County, the road passes through the tiny town of **Cecil** with a population of 281 by the **South Georgia Motorsports Park**, a drag strip and raceway that offers a full schedule of professional racing and events year-round. The grandstands can accommodate 6,000 fans, and offers VIP suites as well.

LOWNDES COUNTY AND ECHOLS COUNTY

Highway 41 continues into Lowndes County and the small agricultural

J&S BBQ, Sparks, GA

city of **Hahira**. The origin of Hahira's name remains a mystery. One suggestion claims it is derived from the Bible, and another holds that an American Indian named Hira stopped there to watch the trains pass, and one conductor would shout, "Hey Hira!" as his train rumbled by. The town had a cigarette manufacturer in the 1920s, and was the site of local fight promotions in the 1920s and 1930s. Later, beekeeping was introduced in the city. Today, Hahira maintains its agricultural roots. It is also an exurb of Valdosta, which lies about eleven miles to the south. The area is well known for the colorful azaleas that thrive there; a local azalea festival takes place in March.

VALDOSTA

Beyond Hahira, Highway 41 becomes "Old U.S. 41," a two-lane road through farm country, before it widens into a bypass around the city of **Valdosta**, the Lowndes County seat, known as the "Azalea City" and "A City Without Limits," as its motto proclaims. Valdosta is fortunate to be located next to Interstate 75, where most of the commerce is now clustered. Vacationers on their way to Florida have historically made Valdosta a pit-stop on their journey south to and from Orlando, Walt Disney World, and other attractions. If you take "Business 41," it routes you into Valdosta's historic downtown. Efforts are being made to revitalize the old downtown as a shopping and dining destination. There are some beautiful old buildings in Valdosta's downtown, but, unfortunately, there are also many empty storefronts.

Fountain in Downtown Valdosta, GA

Author's Note: In late September 2024, Hurricane Helene hit the Florida coast and continued north through Georgia, North Carolina, Tennessee, and Virginia. Many parts of these states were hard-hit by flooding from the hurricane. The Valdosta area was one of them. Numerous buildings in the historic business district suffered significant damage. Extensive flooding also occurred throughout Lowndes County.

Valdosta State University (enrollment 10,180) is located just north of downtown. The university, as an NCAA Division II member, has won multiple championships in many sports. The city has been dubbed "Winnersville" for the championship sports teams at local high schools and colleges. An interesting fact: the boys' high school football program at Valdosta High School has racked up more wins than any other American high school.

Valdosta is the "Naval Stores Capital of the World." Naval stores are products used in shipbuilding, such as turpentine, rosin, tar, and pitch.

These products are tapped from the longleaf pine trees that abound outside the city. Valdosta supplies eighty percent of the world's demand for these products.

Sadly, Valdosta has a very gruesome history of Ku Klux Klan involvement and lynching. Starting in 1915, KKK involvement in Valdosta became extensive. When a white planter was murdered by a mistreated African American farmworker in 1918, local lynch mobs killed thirteen local African Americans, including Mary Turner. Eight months pregnant, the mob cut her unborn baby and killed them both. There have been recent efforts made to commemorate the 1918 riots.

DASHER, LAKE PARK, AND THE FLORIDA BORDER

South of Valdosta, Highway 41 once again becomes a two-lane road with a pleasant drive through the small railroad towns of **Dasher** and **Lake Park**. You may well find yourself driving the only car on the road along this stretch. Lake Park has a series of interconnecting small lakes with several RV campgrounds nearby. The Georgia–Florida border lies fourteen miles south of Lake Park, although it passes through a tiny part of **Echols County** before it exits the state.

CONCLUDING THOUGHTS

A drive through Georgia on Highway 41 affords a glimpse of the past, present, and future along the road. While it is often only a few miles away from Interstate 75, Highway 41 provides much more to see along its route. You will need time and patience to do so; however, it will take much longer to travel on the highway than on the interstate due to the multiple communities it travels by and through. The road is heavily traveled through the Atlanta Metro area. Leisurely driving will not be possible there, and Atlanta's traffic issues are no joke. Still, to see and experience Atlanta using Highway 41 as a road to jump on and off is essential to understanding this incredibly important city.

The agricultural region that starts outside of Perry and extends to the Florida border is fascinating, beautiful, and well worth spending the time to drive through. The city of Macon is, in my opinion, a must-see, and I would like to spend more time there to discover even more of its highlights.

Georgia is complicated, as are all states. With multiple communities of first-generation Americans from nearly every country in the world, a traveler could spend a lot of time exploring these growing ethnic communities. The Atlanta area has always been a major hub of business that has only grown larger since the turn of the millennium. Understanding the multiple faces of this state means letting go of stereotypes of what the South is and is not. What is clear to me in my travels through Georgia is the sense of ownership shared by all its residents—even the "Yankee" newcomers. I admire places that embrace what America can be rather than looking to the past for a lost identity. Historical burdens must be scrutinized but not carried forward. Come to Georgia to see the United States.

CHAPTER TEN
FLORIDA PART ONE: FROM THE GEORGIA BORDER
TO TAMPA: OLD FLORIDA IN TRANSITION

"Florida is the world's greatest amusement park."

—Budd Schulberg

*"To Florida—it's dreamers, it's builders, it's mavericks, and it's scoundrels.
(Sometimes all four at once.)"*

—Beatrix Williams

*"Meanwhile, a Florida man got a DUI after crashing a lawnmower into a
police car. Yet another headline that did not need to specify what state it
happened in."*

—Stephen Colbert

*"Before you go to Florida, you have to decide if you want to see the Authentic
Florida, the Fake Florida, or the Authentically Fake Florida."*

—Joel Achenbach

486

Key Towns/Cities: *Lake City, Gainesville, Tampa, Bradenton, Sarasota, Port Charlotte, Fort Myers, Cape Coral, Naples, Miami, Miami Beach*

Florida Counties along 41: *Hamilton, Columbia, Alachua, Levy, Marion, Citrus, Hernando, Pasco, Hillsborough, Manatee, Sarasota, Charlotte, Lee, Collier, Dade*

Highway 41 through Florida is 479 miles, from the Georgia state line to downtown Miami. Of the eight states the highway passes through, this is the longest stretch. In Florida, Highway 41 is paralleled by I-75 for much of its route, and it passes through largely flat terrain that is barely above sea level. For the first quarter of the journey, the highway follows an ancient Indigenous trail later utilized by railroads through "Old Florida," a quiet, largely agricultural area with small towns and cities. The road crosses numerous rivers and passes many artesian springs. A short distance past the city of Dunnellon in the central part of the state, the highway starts to go through housing developments first built in the 1950s. South of Brooksville, you will enter the greater Tampa metropolitan area, which extends through the city and south to Ruskin. From Tampa to Miami, Highway 41 is known as the **Tamiami Trail**.

Beyond the Tampa Metro area, the highway traverses much of Florida's Gulf Coast and passes through the older cities of Sarasota, Punta Gorda, and Fort Myers. It also passes through many unincorporated, census-designated places (CDPs)—i.e., housing developments. The road continues by the city of Cape Coral, founded in 1957 and the largest city between Tampa and Miami in both population and area. At the city of Naples, U.S. 41 bears east through the scrub and swampland of **Big Cypress National Preserve** and the **Florida Everglades** to the city of Miami. In a portion of Miami, the highway is known as **Calle Ocho**, or Eighth Street. U.S. 41 officially ends in the Brickell neighborhood of downtown Miami, where it connects with U.S.1. Prior to 1999, the road ended in Miami Beach where it connected to U.S. A1A, which is also Collins Avenue in Miami Beach.

A FLORIDA ALBUM PLAYLIST

- Tom Petty and the Heartbreakers: *Damn the Torpedoes* 1979
- Gloria Estefan: *Cuts Both Ways* 1989
- Bo Diddley: *Bo Diddley* 1958
- Ariana Grande: *Thank U, Next* 2019
- Rick Ross: *Teflon Don* 2010
- Sam & Dave: *Hold On, I'm Comin'* 1966
- Lynyrd Skynyrd: *Lynyrd Skynyrd* 1973
- Enrique Iglesias: *Euphoria* 2010
- Flo Rida: *Wild Ones* 2012
- John Anderson: *Seminole Wind* 1991
- Dickey Betts: *Live at the Lone Star Roadhouse* 1988
- Chet Baker: *Chet Baker Sings* 1954
- Jimmy Buffett: *A1A* 1974

IDENTITY

Florida has many identities: Tourist haven, retiree outpost, seasonal "snowbird" paradise, capital of Latin America, haven for immigrants, haven for the wealthy, haven for ne'er-do-wells. Florida is, as a magazine article suggested, "America's Weirdest State." The sheer diversity of people who live in and visit the state can be head-spinning. A drive through the state on Highway 41 allows you to see the "Old Florida" as well as the continuing changes to "New Florida." The state's agricultural roots are still present in the cities and towns established prior to the existence of air conditioning and interstate highways. Residential developments abound, however, with many unincorporated communities throughout the state.

The old adage "see it now" is very true for travel on Highway 41 through Florida. What was put in place in the latter half of the twentieth century may well disappear by the end of this decade. Some areas, such as the Everglades and the Art Deco area of Miami's South Beach, are protected, for the time being, by federal legislation, but large swaths of the state will most likely become residential areas, and that will forever alter its character.

While it is not always easy to find a native Floridian, conversations with longtime residents can be very helpful in understanding some of the present issues. At the top of the list is the cost of living. Auto insurance, property insurance, and utility costs have soared in recent years. As the population continues to swell, increased housing and rental costs are impacting more working people with modest incomes.

Traffic congestion is another source of concern and afflicts much of the Gulf Coast that Highway 41 passes through. Many of Florida's highways, interstates, and bridge crossings can be parking lots during rush hour, and public transportation options are limited. Unless you have a great deal of time and patience, and you don't mind looking at endless retail strips while you stop and start through many traffic lights, there is a large swath of Highway 41 along the Gulf Coast that you may seek alternatives to traveling on.

Florida does not have a state income tax, nor does it tax transactions. This has made the state very appealing for retirees and high-income earners. Virtual workers have migrated to the state from elsewhere and have settled in metropolitan areas such as Tampa and Miami, further increasing home prices.

Florida's recent political history is one of single-party control. The Republican Party holds all of the state's key executive governmental positions and has a super-majority in the legislature. An aggressive set of restrictive laws impacting education, immigration, gun control, abortion rights, and building preservation have recently been enacted despite public objections that the laws are highly partisan in nature. This has caused much controversy within the state.

BY THE NUMBERS

When Florida became a state in 1845, it had a population of only 70,000. One hundred years later, the population had reached 2.4 million. Rapid growth began in the 1950s, with the population increasing to 9.74 million by 1980. Twenty years later, in 2000, the population was 16 million, and by 2020, 21.7 million. At this writing (2025), Florida has an estimated population of 23.2 million. It is the third most populous American state. Most of Florida's population is urban, concentrated near major cities. These include Jacksonville, Orlando, Tampa–St. Petersburg, and Miami–Fort Lauderdale, but there are also significant concentrations of people in real estate developments all along the Gulf and Atlantic coasts. Predictions by the state's Demographic Estimating Conference suggest continued population growth, which they predict will rise to 25 million by 2032 before leveling out.

RETIREES

For well over a century, Florida has been a retirement haven. With 20.9 percent of the population over age sixty-five, the state trails only Maine for the largest percentage of that demographic. During the months from October to April, millions of "snowbirds" migrate to Florida. Many snowbirds have achieved retirement age. Retirees from the Midwest of the United States have typically been most attracted to the Gulf Coast and central Florida. Numerous retirement villages are found in Florida, with **The Villages** (pop. 145,000), located just to the south of the city of Ocala, coming in as the largest age-restricted residential development in the world.

Other large, planned retirement complexes in the state are in Ocala (On

Top of the World), Sarasota (Lakewood Ranch), Tampa Bay (Sun City Center), and Fort Myers (Pelican Preserve). These developments have transformed the state and its priorities. Golf courses, dredged canals, and manmade lakes are often part of these developments.

CLIMATE

Florida is in one of the warmest regions in the United States, with an average temperature of 72 degrees (22.22° C). While most every other state has four seasons—winter, spring, summer, and fall—Florida has only two seasons: wet and dry. The wet season begins in late May, and the dry season normally begins mid-October. Summers can be intensely hot and extremely humid.

Florida's hurricane season arrives in mid-May and lasts to late November. Florida has a long history of hurricanes and severe weather with major storms occurring about once every five years, although some new evidence suggests the state will now experience such severe storms every other year. Recent climate change research suggests that Florida is vulnerable to rising water levels and extreme weather. The state's average temperature has risen more than 2 degrees Fahrenheit in the past decade. In recent years, hurricanes Milton & Helene (2024), Idalia (2023), Ian (2022), and Charley (2004) have caused widespread destruction. Due to climate change, intensifying storms may well become a permanent feature of life in Florida.

RED TIDE

A **red tide** is a naturally occurring phenomenon along Florida's Gulf Coast. It is caused by the toxic algae *Karenia brevis*. Scientists suggest that nutrients, which include nitrogen, originate in farm fields, agriculture, and waste, and often end up in waterways. These nutrients have the potential to intensify the growth of toxic algae blooms significantly when they flow into the Gulf of Mexico.

A red tide kills fish by producing a potent toxin called *brevetoxin*, which affects their central nervous systems. The toxin can also affect birds and other marine animals. Needless to say, tourism to coastal communities suffers when areas are closed due to dead fish washing up on beaches.

The Florida Fish and Wildlife Conservation Commission warns people to avoid swimming in or around a red tide due to the possibility of skin irritation, rashes, burning, and sore eyes. Red tides have been documented along Florida's Gulf Coast as far back as the 1840s, and scientists cannot predict precisely when one will occur.

HISTORICAL ROOTS

Indigenous peoples have lived in Florida for at least 14,000 years. The Calusa in southwest Florida descended from people who had lived in the area for at least 1,000 years prior to European contact. The Calusa were a nomadic people with a complex culture based on shellfish and estuarine fisheries rather than agriculture. European explorers brought diseases that killed scores of Indigenous peoples who had no natural immunities to them. Beginning in the early 1500s, smallpox and measles contributed to the Calusa's demise, and by the end of the 1700s, the Calusa had all died. There is a site complex northwest of Fort Myers with a research center dedicated to Calusa artifacts and ways of living.

Along with plundering Mexico and Peru, Spanish conquistadors sent expeditions to La Florida—land of the flowers—to search for gold and other wealth of any kind. Ponce de León landed on the Florida coast in 1513, searching for the elusive Fountain of Youth. His second expedition to Florida in 1521 landed on the southwest coast near what is now Charlotte Harbor to start a colony. It lasted five months before de León was wounded in a native attack and died in Cuba. The 1539–1543 expedition of Conquistador Hernando de Soto landed at what is now called Tampa Bay and traversed much of the present-day American southeast. De Soto died of a fever on the banks of the Mississippi in 1542.

Spain ruled Florida until the 1763 Treaty of Paris, which ended the Seven Years War. Spain traded Florida to Great Britain in exchange for control of Havana, Cuba. Spain regained Florida after Britain's defeat in the Revolutionary War. The region became a haven for fugitives from slavery and a base for Indigenous attacks against American territories, leading the United States to press Spain for reform. In 1821, the United States assumed control over Florida from Spain by treaty, even though the Seminole were sovereign rulers of much of the area and had never been consulted.

The Seminole, descendants of the Creek, were among the Indigenous nations slated for removal to western territories by the federal government, but they fought back effectively in three separate wars: the First Seminole War (1817–1818), Second Seminole War (1835–1842), and Third Seminole War (1855–1858).

The Seminole often took in African American fugitives from slavery, so the Seminole wars were as much "slave wars" as "Indian wars." Scholars estimate that the U.S. government spent $40 million dollars ($1.6 billion by 2024 calculations) in attempt to remove the Seminole from Florida, but the Seminole were never fully conquered.

Eventually, war-weary commanders tired of trying to find the Seminole in the vast swamps where they lived, the U.S. government could no longer afford the war. Even so, the government contested the status of the Seminole as legitimate residents of the United States until the middle of the twentieth century. While several thousand Seminole were force-marched west, others remained in the Everglades. Generations later, they remain on land along the Tamiami Trail, which is now part of Highway 41.

VIGNETTE OSCEOLA

Osceola (1804–1838), named Billy Powell at birth, was a Creek who was adopted as a Seminole as a child. A renowned leader of the Seminole tribe, he led during the Second Seminole War using guerilla tactics in the Everglades. The Seminole fought the much larger force of U.S. troops to a standstill. In 1837, Osceola went under a flag of truce to negotiate with U.S. General Thomas Jesup. By special order of the general, the treaty party was instead arrested and imprisoned. While in prison he had many visitors, including the artist George Catlin who painted his portrait. Osceola was removed to Ft. Moultrie in Charleston, South Carolina, where he died in jail, possibly from malaria. Jesup's treachery helped make the Seminole leader a hero, a martyr, and a legend.

Florida became the 27th state in 1845. In 1855, Florida's legislators passed the Internal Improvement Act, which allowed public land to be offered to people who wanted to build businesses in Florida. In 1861, Florida joined the Confederacy, but the state saw little military engagement during the Civil War. Union troops occupied many of the coastal towns and forts, while the central part of the state remained Confederate territory. Like other Southern states after Reconstruction, efforts to disenfranchise African Americans led to Jim Crow policies of segregation and voter suppression until the mid-1960s.

After the Civil War, Florida became a center for cattle-raising and growing citrus fruit such as oranges, grapefruit, and lemons. The discovery of large concentrations of phosphate led to the construction of many roads and railroad lines. An agreeable climate led to the growth of the state as a tourist mecca, first for the well-to-do prior to World War I and later for the growing middle class in the 1920s.

Powerful hurricanes hit the state in 1926 and 1928, badly hurting the economy. The Mediterranean fruit fly invaded the state in 1929, threatening the citrus groves as well. During World War II, Florida became a major training area for soldiers, sailors, and pilots. After World War II, Florida began to experience exponential population growth. New roads, airports, and the expansion of air conditioning to the average Florida home in the 1950s and 1960s contributed to this boom.

In the late 1950s, **Cape Canaveral** on Florida's east coast became the basis of space exploration operations for the newly created National Aeronautics and Space Administration (NASA) and brought much attention to the state overall. So, too, did the steady development of the tourist industry. **Walt Disney World** opened outside of Orlando in 1971, and other theme parks followed. People poured into the state from other parts of the United States and from many foreign countries. Miami became the unofficial capital of Latin America.

The Great Recession of 2008-2009 began in Florida and hit the state hard. Many people were unable to afford to stay in their homes. The state was able to slowly recover after 2010, but it has been hit with other tragedies in recent history, from major hurricanes to mass shootings. The question going forward for the state is whether it will be able to cope with large population increases while providing an affordable quality of life that has always been the allure of the Sunshine State.

REAL ESTATE

Florida's desirable climate and inexpensive land have attracted investors and developers throughout recent history with a real estate cycle of boom and bust. In 1881, during the post-Civil War era when the state had little money, Hamilton Disston (1844–1896), a Pennsylvania industrialist, purchased four million acres of Florida land—an area larger than the state of Connecticut—for 25 cents an acre. Disston's investment spurred growth around the state. Northern industrialists Henry Plant (1819–1899) and Henry Flagler (1830–1913) followed Disston's lead and built railroads, which helped establish Florida's tourist industry in the late 19th and early 20th centuries. Other individuals, such as Arthur "A.C." Frizzell (1890–1961), acquired land for ranching and logging in and around Charlotte County on the Gulf Coast.

Florida's first bona fide land boom happened after World War I. The state was marketed as "America's Riviera" to a new group of Americans, who were enjoying more disposable income and the ability to travel to Florida by train and automobile. Property was bought and sold to individuals by hucksters called "binder boys." Buyers had to only put down a ten percent deposit known as the "binder." Fortunes were made in some cases on property that was never seen. Pyramid and get-rich-quick schemes drove up prices on property that was often swampland or underwater to valuations far exceeding what the land was worth. Hurricanes in 1926 and 1928, followed by the stock market crash in 1929, led to a loss in confidence in Florida real estate, and the land boom turned into a land bust. Walter Fuller, a Gulf Coast real estate developer at the time said it best: "We just ran out of suckers."

Memphis businessman Barron Collier began purchasing Florida land after a visit in 1911, and his holdings eventually encompassed 1.2 million acres. At the time of his death in 1939, he was Florida's largest landowner. His road building project through the Florida Everglades became the **Tamiami Trail**, which connected Miami on Florida's east coast with Naples and Tampa on the west.

Starting in the 1950s and continuing over the next sixty years, land developers drained swamps, cleared trees, and built multiple housing projects, particularly in the areas of central and southern Florida traversed by Highway 41. Well-financed developers were aided by corrupt Florida politicians and the Florida Installment Land Sales Board, a regulatory body controlled by development interests that pushed "dredge and fill" development at any cost to lure many people into planned communities. Their primary targets were northern state retirees lured by low taxes and cheap housing. *The Swamp Peddlers: How Lot Sellers, Land Scammers, and Retirees Built Modern Florida and Transformed the American Dream* by Jason Vuic is a great book on the subject. It was published by Chapel Hill: University of North Carolina Press in 2021.

In the early 2000s, collateralized debt obligations (CDOs) exploded in popularity with investors nationwide when issuers began to use securities backed by subprime mortgages (held by borrowers with low credit rating) as collateral. Many of these mortgages were issued in Florida. The bottom fell out in 2008, when investors in CDOs were unable to find markets for their holdings. This led to the bankruptcy of major investment banks and brought on the Great Recession.

Southwest Florida was one of the hardest-hit areas in this economic meltdown, with Lee County on the Gulf Coast becoming the home foreclosure capital of the nation. The recession officially lasted only two years, but it took several more years for Florida's economy to bounce back. "The world had convinced itself that you could just borrow money in perpetude," said a real estate expert. "It was a mania... It was a lot of hot air and just collapsed on itself."

INSURANCE

In recent times (2024), an ongoing insurance crisis in the state has impacted Florida homeowners. Due to recent hurricanes such as Ian in 2022 and Helene and Milton in 2024, property insurance premiums have soared far above the national average. A number of private insurance carriers have failed or pulled out of the state entirely, leaving residents with limited alternatives. Citizens Property Insurance Corporation was established by the Florida Legislature in 2002 as an insurer of last resort for Florida property owners unable to find private market coverage. Natural disasters have become more common, more devastating, and more costly in Florida, resulting in massive payouts as well as litigation from homeowners suing their insurers over claim settlements. An exodus of longtime homeowners from the state may be underway.

FROM THE FLORIDA-GEORGIA BORDER TO LAKE CITY

HAMILTON COUNTY

The journey on Highway 41 south through Florida begins with a quiet drive across the Georgia state line. When I made the trip, mine was the only car on the road. At the border are some private homes on the Georgia side, and just a couple feet across the state line is an interesting historical marker dating from 1931 that honors Michael McKenzie Smith (1863–1929). Smith was a member of the Florida State Road Department from 1915 to 1919 and its chairman from 1919 to 1920. He laid plans for the pre-interstate Florida highway network. While his name is largely lost to history, he was obviously highly thought of by his peers, given this nice epitaph:

"He visioned and created a perfect network of highways for posterity—
This highway links birth with death, cementing friendships of cities and states—
His 'soul was like a star and dwelt apart'—"

Michael McKenzie Smith marker, Jennings, FL

JENNINGS

The highway proceeds through the woods before coming to **Jennings**, the first town on the road in Florida. A small "Welcome to Jennings" marker indicates that it is the birthplace of the actor Andrew Prine (1936–2022). Prine was a distinguished film, stage, and television actor, especially known for Westerns, who worked steadily from the late 1950s until well into the mid-2000s.

Long ago when cotton was grown in the vicinity, the tiny town of Jennings was a shipping point. Now it has a Dollar General, and a bar and restaurant called **Cooter Jacks**—"Where friends are family"—along Highway 41. Several miles south of Jennings, the highway crosses the Alapaha River, the first of many rivers U.S. 41 crosses as it runs through central Florida. The Alapaha and Suwannee rivers both have origins in southern Georgia, where they flow south into the Florida peninsula. **The Alapaha River Water Trail** covers about 128 miles of the 202-mile river, connecting the Sheboggy Boat Ramp in Berrien, Georgia, to the Alapaha's confluence with the Suwannee.

JASPER

The drive continues through a pine forest before arriving at the town of **Jasper**, the Hamilton County seat. Jasper was once in a region producing turpentine, cotton, and tobacco. A historical marker in town indicates it was on the Florida Branch railroad, established during the Civil War to try to evade the Union blockade of Florida ports. The line was completed one month before the end of the war in 1865. Its tracks later served as a conduit for the Atlantic Coast Line, a popular passenger railroad, before it was abandoned and finally removed in the 1980s.

Unfortunately, that is somewhat the current story of Jasper as well. The town has a myriad of empty old buildings, including one with a sign saying, "Let's Rebuild Jasper." The town is not a thruway for I-75, nor does it have much for a tourist to stop and see. On another empty storefront during my stop there were the words, "This is not the change we seek; it is the only chance for us to make that change." Before leaving Jasper, U.S. 41 continues past a sign that says, "The Triangle Motel—No Vacancy."

VIGNETTE NUTRIEN WHITE SPRINGS COMPLEX AND PHOSPHATE MINING

South of Jasper, Highway 41 passes by a large phosphate mine and processing plant owned by Nutrien, a Canadian fertilizer company based in Saskatoon, Saskatchewan. Nutrien is a large producer of potash and the third-largest producer of nitrogen fertilizer in the world. Phosphates are a natural source of phosphorous, used primarily to produce fertilizers for food production. Phosphates have been mined in Florida since the 1880s. Today, according to the Florida Department of Environmental Protection: "There are twenty-eight phosphate mines in Florida, covering more than 450,000 acres. Eleven phosphate mines are currently active. Ten mines are 100 percent reclaimed and released from reclamation obligations. The remaining mines are either not started or are shut down. Phosphate mines typically range in size from approximately 5,000 to 100,000 acres."

Phosphate mining disturbs between 3,000 to 6,000 acres annually in Florida. Approximately twenty-five to thirty percent of these lands are wetlands or other surface waters. Needless to say, there is concern about what is mined and what is left behind. By Florida law, companies are required to reclaim the land and analyze water quantity, quality impacts, and preservation of wildlife habitat and resources.

Nutrien is the second largest phosphate fertilizer production company in the U.S.A., after Mosaic (which dominates production in the massive "Bone Valley" phosphate mining district east of Tampa). Nutrien operates two mining areas in northern Florida, covering a 10-by-10 square mile region around White Springs, most of which has literally been turned over by years of strip-mining phosphates. What you see from the road are mountains of phosphate waste called "gypstacks," which contain tainted process water and other chemicals. Most people (and certainly, most tourists) don't even know they exist.

WHITE SPRINGS

White Springs lies at the southern end of Hamilton County. The town, located on the north bank of the Suwannee River, was long known as a health resort. The springs were considered sacred by local Indigenous peoples, who marked the springs with groves of trees. During the Civil War, the town was a Confederate refuge for wealthy plantation owners because it was out of the path of the Union invasion. Now the town is known for its antique stores and nearby recreational opportunities. There was not much stirring on the hot summer day I visited.

Just outside of the town is **Stephen Foster Culture Center State Park**. The park has numerous hiking trails, and a museum devoted to Foster, a prolific songwriter of the nineteenth century. Every Memorial Day weekend (the last weekend in May), the park hosts the **Florida Folk Festival**, "a three-day celebration of the music, dance, stories, crafts, and food that make Florida unique," according to the festival's website.

Jasper, FL

Stephen Foster State Park, White Springs, FL

Foster wrote the song "Old Folks at Home," which, incidentally, is the official state song of Florida. You probably know the song by its first line, "Way down upon the Swanee River." Foster named the river as "Swanee" because it better fit the music. Interestingly, Foster never visited Florida. Note that the song has a revised set of lyrics designated by the legislature in 2008 as the "official version."

Country Store, White Springs, FL

COLUMBIA COUNTY

LAKE CITY

Beyond White Springs, the highway remains tree-lined and sparsely traveled. Thirteen miles southeast of White Springs is **Lake City**, the seat of Columbia County. Highway 41 intersects at Lake City with Highway 90, the **Old Spanish Trail**, a transcontinental highway running from St. Augustine, Florida, west to San Diego, California. In the Jim Crow era, Lake City was considered a safe destination to stop at for African American travelers. The city has a downtown historic district on the National Register of Historic Places, with **The Blanche**, a restored 100-year-old hotel as its centerpiece. Built to service travelers coming to Florida by rail and road, the hotel was the first building in the state to have an elevator. Famous figures who have stayed at the Hotel Blanche include Johnny Cash and Al Capone. In the interstate era, Lake City is nearby the intersection of I-10 and I-75 and is known as "The Gateway to Florida." Servicing the travelers passing through is a big part of the community's economy.

In 2019, Lake City was the victim of a cyber ransomware attack that impacted all of the city services. The city's insurance company paid forty-two bitcoins ($460,000) to retrieve the city's files and data.

East of Lake City is the small town of Olustee, where you'll find **Olustee Battlefield Historic State Park**. Fought in February 1864, this Civil War battle was the largest military engagement in Florida. This park features a Confederate cemetery and battlefield markers.

If you continue south on Highway 41 from Lake City, you will intersect again with I-75 and one of the ubiquitous **Florida Welcome Centers**. Florida is still a tourism haven, and what better place is there to stock up on brochures? Stop in to use the restroom, see the knickknacks for sale, and talk with one of the travel experts. Once upon a time, the state's welcome centers provided a complimentary glass of orange juice, but I did not see that on my recent visits. Across the highway from the welcome center is **La Pinata Latin Market**, housed in an old gas station building that services the growing Latino population settling in the area.

The road continues through Columbia County's agricultural country where you'll pass by a few homes and signs for cattle or goat farms alongside. You'll also roll past the **All-Tech Raceway**, a dirt track for car racing aficionados.

HIGH SPRINGS TO TAMPA

ALACHUA COUNTY

As it crosses the Santa Fe River, the highway enters Alachua County. The **Santa Fe Canoe Outpost Park** on the south bank of the river is a pretty location and looks to be a good place for canoeing or kayaking.

HIGH SPRINGS

Nearby to the south of the park lies the small city of **High Springs**. The city is close to I-75 but far enough away from that busy conduit to retain its charm. Tourism is the biggest industry in town. Named for a hilltop spring, the city is known as the "Gateway to the Springs" due to its close proximity to **Poe Springs, Gilchrist Blue Springs,** and **Ginnie Springs**. High Springs is an old railroad town that once had a large number of residents, many of whom worked servicing locomotives on the Plant Railroad System and, later, the Atlantic Coast Line Railroad. Several phosphate mines operated nearby. High Springs was also an important locale for the surrounding agricultural area. Tobacco was the area's primary crop. Like many Florida locations, real estate booms and busts and changing transportation patterns adversely affected the growth of High Springs in the last decades of the twentieth century.

The railroad is long gone from High Springs, and the old rail depot is now the Chamber of Commerce. There, I found an enterprising lady who showed me around the city. Sharon, my guide, indicated that the city gets a number of European travelers passing through. Several antique stores are located on the main street, which retains an old-town feel. Check out **Chompers**, a drive-thru in High Springs with much more than your average hamburger place. Made-to-order chicken wraps, rice bowls, pasta bowls, seafood, fried green tomatoes, sandwiches and more are served up.

Chompers, High Springs, FL

The High Springs Emporium Rock Shop had some interesting information about the area's artesian springs and rivers. Over years past, the springs were advertised along with the state of Florida as "the land of eternal health and endless sunshine." In some respects, that is still the overriding message conveyed. But due to increased development and population, the springs now have lower water quality, suffer diminished flow, and are increasingly polluted. Much environmental concern centers on nitrate pollution from fertilizers and the pumping of too much water out of the underground aquifer.

High Springs is approximately twenty miles from Gainesville, and that is part of its allure. It has passed a referendum to limit real estate development within the city limits; however, existing housing developments and construction for more housing developments exist just a few miles to the south of High Springs.

NEWBERRY

Newberry is the next town you'll encounter as you drive south along Highway 41. This community was another railroad town that grew quickly in the late nineteenth century due to the mining of phosphates, with fourteen mines once operating nearby. The town had several hotels, boarding houses, and saloons for transient workers. The demand for phosphate ended abruptly in 1914 when the Allied Powers declared war against Germany—the principal customer for Newberry's phosphate—and World War I began. This caused the town's economy to collapse, a loss of jobs in the area, and heightened social tensions.

Newberry has a small historic district listed on the National Register of Historic Places with some storefronts that suggest the city's more vibrant past. But some of its past was quite awful. Racial violence against African Americans rose in Alachua County between 1891 and 1926, as twenty-one lynchings took place to enforce white supremacy. Times changed, fortunately, and in 1984 Freddie Warmack was elected Newberry's first Black mayor; he received sixty percent of the white vote. The current mayor as of 2025, is a National Development Officer for the John Birch Society.

After the collapse of the phosphate industry, the area became noted for agriculture, particularly the production of watermelons, which were brought to Newberry from nearby farms for shipment elsewhere. Since 1946, the town has held an annual watermelon festival in May to celebrate the fruit. The **Newberry Watermelon Festival Beauty Pageant** is a long-standing tradition of the event. The reigning queen and other members of the court have duties all year long, representing Newberry and competing for the title of Florida Watermelon Queen. There are pageant groups for all ages; from the festival website: "The Newberry Watermelon Queen must be reliable, responsible, dependable, neat and prompt at all times. She must also be knowledgeable in the watermelon industry. Dress code for the Newberry Watermelon Queen includes skirts."

Newberry Cold Storage, Newberry, FL

Newberry Barber Shop, Newberry, FL

SIDE TRIP TO GAINESVILLE

A half hour trip along FL-26, a very busy state road, will take you through multiple housing developments to the city of **Gainesville**. It is the Alachua County seat and home of the main campus of the **University of Florida** (enrollment 55,000), the fourth-largest public university campus by enrollment in the United States. The school's origin dates from the early

1900s when several colleges were consolidated into the state school. The school expanded rapidly after World War II, and it is considered one of the top-tier public universities in the country per the *U.S. News & World Report* standings. Many people associate the school with its Florida Gators sports teams, which have won multiple NCAA championships. The campus is quite large, with a number of historic buildings on the premises. The student union is huge. The campus is also a testimony to air conditioning, with giant units that cool the buildings in the stifling heat.

One of the main attractions on campus is the **Florida Museum of Natural History**, with millions of specimens and artifacts. If you plan on visiting the museum do not miss the **Butterfly Rainforest**, a screened, open-air exhibit containing hundreds of free-flying butterflies and birds. The campus's **Harn Museum of Art** is one of the largest university art museums in the south, with an interesting and varied multicultural collection. You should also check out the **University of Florida Bat Houses**, where you can watch the bats emerging at dusk to feed on insects.

A historical marker on campus signifies UF Medical College as the birthplace of Gatorade. The drink was developed by a team of researchers led by Dr. Robert Cade as a means to quickly replace nutrients in the human body lost from heat. It was tested in a Florida Gators' football game in 1965 and has gone on to become a popular drink for both athletes and non-athletes around the world.

RECENT CONTROVERSIES

While the University of Florida seems to be an enviable place to go to school on the surface, it is also, unfortunately, at the epicenter of a storm. The school has been caught up in the ultra-conservative politics of the state. As of early 2024, some prominent academics have left the university over new policies passed by the Florida legislature, which expand the power of the board of governors and trustees to dictate policies to campus administrations and faculties. In 2024, *The Wall Street Journal* ranked the school number one in the country among public universities. The University of Florida plummeted to number seven in the newspaper's 2025 rankings. Overall, the school ranks 30th among all national universities. Time will tell how the university will proceed in a changing state environment.

DOWNTOWN GAINESVILLE

As you would expect from a college town, downtown Gainesville has several restaurants. It also boasts the **Matheson History Museum**, which showcases the history of Gainesville and Alachua County and features a vintage postcard collection. The **Hippodrome State Theatre** is housed in a historic Federal building and hosts a regional theater company. The city is making efforts to contain suburban sprawl by introducing more apartments within the inner city. However, this also contributes to gentrification, which can price out many individuals looking for affordable living options.

ADDITIONAL ATTRACTIONS IN AND AROUND GAINESVILLE

Kanapaha Botanical Gardens is a sixty-eight acre facility comprised of twenty-four major collections, including a butterfly garden, a vinery, a bamboo garden, and a cool Azalea/Camelia Garden.

Devil's Millhopper Geological State Park features a limestone sinkhole that leads to a miniature rain forest. Geologic time can be measured in the rock layers exposed within the hole.

The **Retirement Home for Horses at Mill Creek Farm** is open to the public on Saturdays. The non-profit farm provides lifelong care for elderly horses that have been neglected, abused, or abandoned and seized by law enforcement agencies and other frontline rescue organizations. Retired police and military horses also find a home here. Bring carrots to feed the horses.

If you are a fan of vintage shopping or just someone who enjoys a good treasure hunt, **Waldo's Antique & Flea Market** in the town of Waldo, slightly north and east of Gainesville, sells all kinds of stuff.

Finally, much-loved rocker Tom Petty (1950–2017) was a Gainesville native, and among the eight 1960s and 1970s musicians and/or bands with musical roots in Gainesville that have been inducted into the Rock and Roll Hall of Fame. That is quite a legacy for this college town.

SIDE TRIP TO MICANOPY

South of Gainesville on Highway 441 is the tiny town of **Micanopy** (pop.

646), which calls itself "The Town that Time Forgot." Settled in 1821, it is believed to be Florida's oldest inland town. Featured in the magazine *Travel + Leisure*, Micanopy is the self-proclaimed antique capital of Florida. It has many shops, art galleries, cafés, boutiques, and a scenic landscape with plenty of nearby hiking options. The downtown has been designated the Micanopy Historic District and is listed on the National Register of Historic Places.

Nearby Micanopy is Cross Creek, the former home of Marjorie Kinnan Rawlings. Rawlings was a Pulitzer Prize winning author whose 1939 novel, *The Yearling*, was set in the area, which was far more isolated when she wrote the book. A movie starring Gregory Peck and Jane Wyman was made of the book in 1946. If you were in middle school or high school in the 1970s, you probably read *The Yearling* for English class. **Marjorie Kinnan Rawlings** homestead is now a Florida state park and historic site that features gardens and citrus groves.

ARCHER

Traveling south on Highway 41 from Newberry, you will soon pass through the little railroad-stop town of **Archer**. The town was the final home of Bo Diddley (1928–2008), an influential guitarist and singer who transitioned blues music to rock and roll and became famous for his "Bo Diddley beat" rhythm, which underpinned many of his hits.

According to his grandson at the time of his death, "There was a Gospel song that was sung, at his bedside, and when it was done, he opened his eyes, gave a thumbs up, and said, 'Wow! I'm goin' to Heaven!' The song was 'Walk Around Heaven,' and those were his last words."

LEVY COUNTY

WILLISTON

Between Archer and Williston, Highway 41 passes a number of horse farms as it crosses into Levy County. **Two Tails Ranch**, north of Williston, is worth a visit. The ranch is the only privately owned elephant facility of its kind in the country. The "Nature Coast" as this region is sometimes known, has a climate similar to that of lands where elephants are native species. The ranch provides a guided educational tour called "All About Elephants" to learn more about the animals in a protected setting.

Only twenty-one miles from Gainesville, the city of **Williston** is an attractive place for employees of the University of Florida to live. Williston is a crossroads town, with Highway 41, U.S. 27 leading to Ocala and Orlando, and State Road 121 meeting there. The city was once known as a headquarters for companies quarrying limestone and mining phosphates but now is pretty much a commuter town. The **Central Florida Peanut Festival** takes place in October and celebrates all things related to peanuts. The festival features the crowning of a Little Peanut King and Queen and of a Baby Peanut.

Williston is the location of limestone formations that are attractive to cave divers. The two most popular dive sites are **Blue Grotto Springs** and **Devil's Den Spring & Campground**. You'll need to make reservations ahead of time to dive and snorkel in these locations.

A final noteworthy place to visit in Williston is the **Kirby Family Farm**. This 110-acre non-profit farm hosts numerous children who are terminally ill, have special needs, are foster children, or are otherwise at-risk. It provides them with high quality educational, historical, recreational, agricultural, and community enrichment programs through a hands-on historical museum and agricultural experiences. The vision of the founders is to erect a facility where children of all ages can have a unique place to visit and learn as they prepare themselves for the future.

MARION COUNTY

ROMEO AND JULIETTE

Highway 41 continues from Williston into the far west portion of Marion County. The county was once in the center of a proposed waterway called the Cross Florida Barge Canal (sometimes referred to as the "Ditch of Dreams"). A large public works project that began in the 1930s, was touted as a shipping shortcut linking the Atlantic Ocean to the Gulf of Mexico through central Florida.

It was approximately one-third completed when construction halted. The project ran into opposition from environmentalists such as Marjorie Harris Carr (1915–1997) as well as concerns about the cost and benefits. President Nixon stopped construction of the project in 1971, and Congress de-authorized the project in 1990. Parts of the unfinished canal—one of the largest incomplete public works projects in the country—were eventually turned into **Marjorie Harris Carr Cross Florida Greenway**, a 110-mile linear park that has 300 miles of trails for hiking, mountain biking, paddling, equestrian, and a variety of other uses.

As you drive through farm and ranch country you will pass by some interesting old buildings, oak trees dripping with Spanish Moss, and the ghost town of **Romeo**, a former turpentine-producing settlement. You can stop at the **Silver Moon Tavern** with an outside memorial honoring the armed services of the United States "With respect, honor and gratitude."

Continue south on U.S. 41, and before too long you'll arrive in the ghost town of **Juliette**. It is now part of Rainbow Springs State Park. Juliette was once a small community of farms and homesteads surrounding what was then known as Blue Springs. The little community had a railroad depot, several general stores, a sawmill, a post office, and a hotel—the Rainbow Spring Lodge—that was built at the head of the springs. According to the 1939 *American Guide Series* to Florida, the towns of Romeo and Juliette were named, similar to the Shakespeare play, for a local legend that lovers lived in each of the settlements.

RAINBOW SPRINGS

Rainbow Springs is a definite must-see stop on your Florida journey. The springs consist of twelve named vents that discharge groundwater from the Floridian Aquifer System at an average of 485 million gallons per day making it one of the largest spring systems in the state. The 1,470-acre **Rainbow Springs State Park** is managed by the Florida Department of Environmental Protection and attracts over 300,000 visitors annually.

Similar to other areas in central Florida, the phosphate mining industry dug huge pits in the early 1900s to remove the phosphate located near the springs. Piles of discarded soil and rock from this effort were built into waterfalls when the area was turned into a privately owned theme park in the mid-twentieth century. The Rainbow Springs roadside attraction lasted from 1937 to the early 1970s and was advertised as a "jungle oasis." Beyond the waterfalls, there was a bird park, exotic animal park, gift shop, and dining terrace. Alas, the construction of I-75 and the opening of Walt Disney World in 1971 made Rainbow Springs an afterthought for tourists, and declining business forced it to close in 1973. The state of Florida acquired the property to be managed as a state park in 1990.

The park is a lovely place to spend some time. There are several pathways around the waterfalls, and the sapphire-blue translucent quality of the water in the springs and on the **Rainbow River** is unusual and eye-catching. The water's color is due to the minerals from the spring and riverbeds. This fragile ecosystem has experienced some degradation due to the use of nitrogen fertilizers and wastewater disposal in the area.

I was lucky enough to come on a weekday when there were few visitors. Unfortunately, park management must close the gates on weekends and holidays often once attendance reaches capacity. I left the park after being allowed to snap a picture of two ladies with their Jehovah's Witness pamphlets ready to distribute.

Rainbow Springs State Park, Dunnellon, FL

DUNNELLON

A few miles from Rainbow Springs, the historic city of **Dunnellon**, once a phosphate-mining boomtown, is now a pleasant place for a stop. It has antique shops and several good restaurants. Check out the "Blues Brothers" statue outside of the **Two Rivers Inn**. The town has no association with Jake and Elwood Blues; the statues are solely meant to catch the attention of tourists. Dunnellon's claim to fame was its role as a film location for the

2001 horror film, *Jeepers Creepers*.

South of Dunnellon, at the southern end of Marion County, is **Halpata Tastanaki Nature Preserve**, which sits along the Withlacoochee River and is named for a Seminole leader who was involved in the Second Seminole Indian War in 1836. The preserve is quite beautiful, with opportunities to see abundant wildlife. Adjacent to the preserve is **Ross Prairie Wildlife Management Area**, which features good trails for horseback riding, biking, and hiking.

Rainbow Springs State Park, Dunnellon, FL

Dunnellon, FL

CITRUS COUNTY

Across the Withlacoochee River from Dunnellon lies Citrus County. The county has a number of Census-Designated Places (CDPs), which are housing developments but not incorporated cities or towns. You will see many CDPs from this point on through Florida along Highway 41.

CITRUS SPRINGS

Unincorporated **Citrus Springs** has sprouted multiple houses and retail shopping areas but has no discernible city center. The Mackle Brothers developed Citrus Springs in the 1960s working under the auspices of the Deltona Corporation. They utilized intensive advertising to persuade perspective retirees from Chicago and Detroit to purchase low-cost retirement homes there. Citrus Springs is not exclusively comprised of retirees as it once was, but they still account for about a quarter of the population.

HERNANDO

The highway continues southward into the CDP called **Hernando**. Once an official city, Hernando was disincorporated in the 1970s. It sits on the banks of **Lake Hernando** and features a forty-six-mile former rail line, which has been repurposed as a bike trail known as **Withlacoochee State Trail**. A plaque in Hernando honors the former local **Church of the Nazarene,** which was built in 1934 and demolished in 1993. From 1994 to 2006, Hernando was the home of the **Ted Williams Museum,** a popular destination for baseball and fishing enthusiasts. The attraction in Hernando was closed in 2006 due to poor attendance and moved to Tropicana Field in St. Petersburg, the home of the Tampa Bay Rays baseball team, where it closed again in 2025. Ted Williams (1918–2002) was considered one of the greatest hitters in baseball history. He was also a resident of nearby Citrus Hills.

CITRUS HILLS

The CDP of Citrus Hills is a planned community, developed in the 1970s by Sam Tamposi (1924–1995) and Jerry Nash (1923–2014), real estate developers from New Hampshire. They parlayed a friendship with Ted Wil-

513

liams to assist in marketing the property to residents in the northeast, home of the Tamposi-Nash Company. Their "fly-down" program brought buyers from New England down to see the area during the 1980s and 1990s. Citrus Hills's website advertises that the community "combines the traditional country-club lifestyle with new amenities and member-driven activities, welcoming both retirees and working families in style!"

Hernando, FL

INVERNESS

Highway 41 continues south to the city of **Inverness**, the Citrus County seat. The city's motto is "Small Town Done Right." The architecturally significant **Old Courthouse Heritage Museum** was built in 1912 as the county courthouse and saved by the community from demolition in the early 1990s. It is on the National Register of Historic Places and is a beautiful vintage building right off the highway. In 1961, the old courthouse was used to film the courtroom scene in *Follow That Dream*, a film featuring Elvis Presley.

Inverness has a small but vibrant downtown. **Valerie Theatre and Cultural Arts Center** is housed in an old, renovated movie theater that hosts plays, concerts, and comedy shows. Several downtown buildings have historic plaques.

I found the **Dampier Building** plaque's inscription quite interesting:

"This building was built by Francis Marion Dampier Jr. as the Dampier

Department Store. The family operated the successful store from 1945 to 1967. It is remembered that "Frank" Dampier spent many hours on a wooden bench under an oak tree outside the store, visiting with acquaintances."

Inverness is located near **Flying Eagle Preserve**, an 11,000-acre mosaic of small lakes, marshes, and swamps, with numerous scattered islands of forested uplands. This broad mixture of hardwood and cypress swamps covers the floodplain of the Withlacoochee River. The preserve offers a large array of trails for hiking and biking, and lots of airboats are in use in the swamps.

Valerie Theatre, Inverness, FL

INVERNESS AND THE FLORIDA COOTER

Some restaurants in the area serve a famous food of the region: Florida Cooter. The cooter is a freshwater turtle that was once a meal for both Indigenous peoples and European settlers. The cooter is celebrated each October in the **Great American Cooter Festival**—or **"Cootertober,"** as the event's website proclaims—with concerts, a carnival, live entertainment, a Cooter King and Queen pageant, a pub crawl, and everything else that can be hosted by a small town.

Fort Cooper State Park, a quiet 700-acre park for bird and wildlife viewing, lies just south of Inverness. It was the scene of a battle in the Second Seminole War (1835–1842). Major battles of that war took place in this region in 1835 and 1836.

FLORAL CITY

Beyond Fort Cooper is a tree-lined drive that leads to **Floral City**, a definite stop to make along Highway 41. Floral City is often called "Old Florida," and a visitor can see why that makes sense here. The Avenue of the Oaks is a gorgeous stretch of road in a canopy of trees covered in Spanish Moss just off 41 on East Orange Avenue.

Stop by the **Ferris Grove** vegetable and fruit stand, which seems to have come from a past era. The city has some other retro places to see and hang out for a while. Check out the **Duval-Metz House**, built in 1863 and the oldest surviving residential building in Citrus County. The **Floral City Heritage Museum** is located across the street. The town holds **Floral City Heritage Days** the first weekend in December and the **Floral City Strawberry Festival** in early March.

Floral City, FL

HERNANDO COUNTY

South of Floral City, the road crosses into Hernando County and continues through a forested area before coming to **Chinsegut Wildlife and Environmental Area (WEA)**. *Chinsegut* is an Alaskan Inuit word that means "spirit of lost things." The property was deeded in 1932 to the U.S. Department of Agriculture as a sanctuary for wildlife study by Colonel Raymond Robins (1873–1954), an American economist, writer, prohibitionist, women's suffrage advocate, and supporter of diplomatic relations between the United States and post-revolutionary Russia after the First World War. He was friends with President Herbert Hoover, among others, and moved in politically well-connected circles. The land is now managed by the Florida Fish and Wildlife Conservation Commission. The forest trails are lovely for walking.

Near the wildlife area on one of the few hills in peninsular Florida is the historic house on a 114-acre site known as the **Chinsegut Hill Historic Site**. The site has been populated since prehistoric times and was part of plantation worked by slaves prior to Emancipation. In the 1920s and 1930s, Colonel Robins and his wife Margaret hosted many famous people of the day. The house is now operated by the **Tampa Bay History Center** and is open for weekend tours.

Just before you arrive at the city of Brooksville, you'll encounter the **Chinsegut Big Pine Tract**. It is the largest concentration of ancient old growth longleaf pine trees in America. Longleaf pine forests once stretched for miles in every direction through the region surrounding Chinsegut Hill. Timber companies cut down most of the trees decades ago, and I can only hope that the area continues to remain free of development.

BROOKSVILLE

Highway 41 continues through a forested area interspersed with some churches; ranches with sheep, goats, and horses; and nature preserves before arriving at the small city of Brooksville, the Hernando Country seat. Brooksville is a small, quiet town that has a welcoming bike trail called the **Good Neighbor Trail**. This bike path runs along a former rail line that links Brooksville's downtown with nearby **Withlacoochee State Trail**, and both are quite good for hiking and biking. Downtown, you'll encounter some old repurposed buildings in addition to the restored **Brooksville Train Depot**, which dates from 1885.

The **Hernando Heritage Museum** is located within the historic **May-Stringer House**. It is listed on the National Register of Historic Places and reputed to be haunted. When restoration work was taking place at the house in the early 1980s, volunteers heard footsteps and voices in empty rooms. Glowing lights, shadows, and the sound of a wailing child are among the supernatural experiences guides have reported.

Old neighborhoods canopied with oak trees, brick-paved streets, and large vintage homes make Brooksville a pleasant town to see. The city's website features a number of short videos extolling the down-home charm of the place. I spent the night in one of the grand old Brooksville homes that has been turned into a bed and breakfast. The B&B had a book titled *It's the Journey, Not the Destination* in which travelers could write notes and comments. This befits my journey through Florida on Highway 41. And if we could leave Brooksville with its placid present, that would be great, but unfortunately, the city has a controversial history.

First, the name: The town was named for Preston Brooks, the member of Congress from South Carolina who, in 1856, struck Senator Charles Sumner of Massachusetts with a cane on the floor of the U.S. Senate. The attack took place during a heated debate on slavery prior to the American Civil War. Sumner was a prominent Abolitionist whom Brooks believed had slandered the South in a speech. Sumner nearly died from injuries sustained in the attack and took years to recover, while Brooks became a hero in the South and received only a token punishment at his criminal trial. He was re-elected to the House but died of illness in 1857. The incident was one of several that set the nation on the path toward Civil War. The history of Preston Brooks that inspired the town's name does not fit its peaceful demeanor today. There have been periodic discussions about changing the town's name, but the idea has been opposed by residents in the past.

A Confederate soldier memorial statue, dedicated in 1916, is located on the grounds of the Hernando County Courthouse. There have been calls to remove the statue and equally vitriolic calls to keep the statue in place. A fence was installed around the statue in 2017.

Many of the town's early settlers were from southern states and some were slaveholders. The early economy of Brooksville was based on agriculture with several large plantations in the area. After the Civil War ended in 1865, many Confederate sympathizers moved into the area. Brooksville had a far more southern heritage than most other places in central west Florida. The area was the scene of many lynchings and other violent racial incidents after the Civil War and on into the 1930s. In the late 1930s, the "Lewis Plantation and Turpentine Still" was created to give tourists an idea of what an old-time plantation run after the Civil War by formerly enslaved people was like. African Americans were hired to play the roles of "impoverished ex-slaves, who sing, plunk banjos, and tell tall tales for the entertainment of visitors." This racially insensitive "entertainment" destination lasted until the late 1950s. In 1948, Brooksville instituted a zoning law segregating neighborhoods. Segregation remained in force until the late 1960s. The Ku Klux Klan staged marches in Brooksville as recently as the early 1990s.

SIDE TRIP TO WEEKI WACHEE

A twenty-five minute drive on State Road 50 from Brooksville will take you to **Weeki Wachee Springs State Park**, and a journey through Florida on Highway 41 must include this attraction. Weeki Wachi was placed on the National Park Service Register of Historical Places in 2020. It has been a roadside attraction since 1947 and became a state park in 2008. The park area has a natural spring that feeds the **Weeki Wachee River**, which flows through the park and into the Gulf of Mexico. The park features a boat ride on the river where you can see birds and other wildlife, kayak and paddle board rentals, Buccaneer Bay (a swimming area with a giant slide), some live animal attractions, and a store where visitors can purchase souvenirs and food.

The main reason most visitors come to the park is to see the mermaids. Newton Perry, a champion swimmer, movie stunt man, and trainer of World War II divers, founded the **Newton Perry Underwater Mermaid Theater** in 1947. Daily shows have entertained thousands of visitors over the decades. **The Mermaids of Weeki Wachee** perform underwater feats, including eating and drinking while submerged. If you cannot visit the park, several videos of the mermaid show can be found on YouTube, and there is an informative history of the attraction entitled *Weeki Wachee, City of Mermaids* by Lu Vickers and Sara Dionne (2007, University Press of Florida), which you can probably check out of a library.

I wanted to see more of the Weeki Wachee River as it looks closer to the seacoast, so I drove farther west to **Linda Pedersen Park** where there is a lookout tower and a wildlife area that has fishing, boating, and hiking opportunities. When I made my visit, an ongoing drought had reduced water levels on the river. In the summer of 2023, the river was dredged to reduce the level of sediment buildup. Invasive algae are also becoming a presence on the river.

Newton Perry Underwater Mermaid Theater, Weeki Wachee Springs State Park, FL

SPRING HILL

After I explored the Weeki Wachee River, I wanted to return back to Highway 41. This meant a drive through a sprawling, but unincorporated semi-city known as **Spring Hill**. Until the 1970s, Spring Hill was filled with long-leaf pine trees and sand pine scrub. The area was founded in 1968 as a planned community developed by the Deltona Corporation and the Mackle Brothers, who sold many of the properties in this region through intense advertising and the use of retired athletes as sales representatives to entice potential buyers to buy a piece of the Florida dream. One of these athletes was Bill "Moose" Skowron, a baseball player on the New York Yankees and a

Chicago native. Spring Hill now boasts the **Suncoast Parkway** (State Road 589), a toll road that connects directly to Tampa. The main entrance to the original development is marked by a waterfall. It has lots of houses and strips of retail establishments.

VIGNETTE THE MACKLE BROTHERS

Before Walt Disney began secretly buying the thousands of acres of central Florida forest in 1964, which ultimately became Walt Disney World, there were the Mackle Brothers, the "Sellers of Sunshine." The Mackle Company was founded in 1908 in Jacksonville by Frank Mackle Sr. (1881–1941) as a construction business. When he died, his sons Elliott (1908–1978), Frank (1916–1993), and Robert (1912–1983) took over the company. In the mid-1950s, they began buying hundreds of thousands of acres of land in rural parts of Florida and building retirement-oriented communities where land was cheap.

Gradually, they developed planned communities, including Citrus Springs, Marco Island, Port Charlotte, Port St. Lucie, Spring Hill, Deltona, Port St. John, and others. They pioneered the "installment land sales industry," which advertised $10 down and $10 a month to retiring northerners whose income depended on pensions and social security. Established in 1958, the General Development Corporation was the first installment company created by the brothers. After they sold that business, they created the Deltona Corporation in 1962. The Mackles kept home prices low by using techniques similar to those employed in the construction of Levittown in New York after World War II.

The Mackle Brothers were well connected politically and created a template of sorts used by developers ever since for the sprawling planned suburban and exurban developments that exist throughout the state, particularly around the Gulf Coast. Far more unscrupulous operators created housing developments by draining freshwater wetlands, digging canals, and chopping up thousands of acres into grid-like subdivisions and gated golf course communities that threaten the long-term sustainability of the state's water supply and infrastructure. Generations of northerners moved to Florida cheaply thanks to high pressure sales programs. But the long-term price continues to be paid in terms of overbuilt developments and environmental degradation. The legacy of the Mackle Brothers is a mixed one at best.

MASARYKTOWN

Highway 41 skirts Spring Hill as it passes through unincorporated **Masa-**

ryktown. Named for Tomáš Masaryk (1850–1937), the first president of Czechoslovakia, the town was established mainly by Czech and Slovak immigrants in the 1920s. It prospered for decades due to poultry raising. For many years, the community maintained cultural traditions celebrating the Old World at Independence Day festivities. Over time, the Slovaks left, and the poultry industry moved elsewhere. Today the legacy of the original settlement lives on in Slovak/Czech street names and the old Masaryk Hotel off Highway 41. In 1997, the hotel became **Café Masaryktown**, which serves "Fine Spanish Cuban Cuisine."

PASCO COUNTY
SHADY HILLS

Highway 41 continues into Pasco County and the census-designated place of **Shady Hills**. I stopped at the **U.S. 41 Bookstore** off the highway, but alas, it seems to be only open on weekends. Shady Hills's claim to fame is pigeon racing and is the headquarters of the **Gulf Coast Homing Club (GHC)**, the largest pigeon club in America. Pigeon races include an annual Gulf Coast Classic competition, where birds cover 600 miles back to their home lofts.

U.S. 41 Book Store, Spring Hill, FL

LAND O'LAKES

Highway 41 becomes a busy four-lane highway as it continues into the unincorporated town of **Land O' Lakes**. The town was once a railroad stop, and, before that, a stagecoach stop before becoming a series of gated estates. **Dupree Gardens** was a twenty-five-acre botanical garden called the "Blossom Center of Florida." The gardens are long gone, but the ruins of the former entrance are still located at the edge of a suburban housing development. When you leave this community heading south, you will soon find yourself within the metropolitan area of Tampa.

TAMPA METRO

The Tampa Bay Metropolitan Area starts along Florida's west coast in a population area that is among the fastest-growing in the United States. The Clearwater-Tampa-St. Petersburg 2024 population is estimated at 3,008,931. In 1950, the population was 299,530. The area surrounding **Tampa Bay** has continued to fill in with new arrivals which has put a strain on infrastructure, including roads and freshwater supplies.

HILLSBOROUGH COUNTY

From Land O' Lakes, Highway 41 proceeds south into Hillsborough County and the unincorporated town of **Lutz**. Lutz (pronounced "Loots") is another former railroad town. It features a replica of the original train depot, erected to replace the one that was torn down in 1966 to widen Highway 41. Along with other former small towns in Florida, Lutz is now mostly comprised of housing developments. A song called "Beautiful Downtown Lutz" was recorded in 1981 by country singer John Ritter and is still popular today. The **Old Lutz School**, established in 1927, is off Highway 41 and is on the National Register of Historic Places. Another claim to fame for Lutz is its role as one of the locations for the 1990 movie *Edward Scissorhands*, which was filmed in the Carpenter's Run neighborhood of the town.

To the east of Lutz is the CDP known as **University**. University, unfortunately, has a rough reputation. It is known as "The Box" by the Hillsborough County police and the pejorative nickname "Suitcase City" by local Tampa residents due to its large transient population. The area has been known for cheap, substandard housing, poverty, and crime. It sits next to the **University of South Florida**, which is located just southeast of the community and within Tampa's city limits. The community is also known as "University West," mainly due to its location relative to the university.

TAMPA

Tampa, with a population over 400,000 in 2024, is the Hillsborough County seat and one of the fastest-growing major cities in the United States. The city is drawing much attention as the Sunshine State's new "It" city per *Travel + Leisure* magazine. In 2023, *Money* magazine listed Tampa as one of the "Top Ten Best Places to Live in the U.S.," while *Time Magazine* proclaimed Tampa one of the "World's Greatest Places" alongside cities like Kyoto, Barcelona, and Vancouver. It is the third most populous city in Florida, after Miami and Jacksonville.

Tampa is a major financial and business center, and **Port Tampa Bay** is the largest seaport in the state by both tonnage and land. Unlike so many census-designated places and unincorporated cities located along Highway 41 in Florida, Tampa is a real city whose survival is not predicated on tourism or retirees. Year-round warm weather, nearby beaches, lots of recreational/cultural things to do, and many employment opportunities have made the city a magnet for young people.

The city is also becoming less affordable perhaps in part by growing interest and investment. Climbing housing costs and traffic congestion issues mirror other fast-growing cities in the southeast. The city's infrastructure is straining to meet growth demands. Trends show that the Tampa Bay area could swell to 5.3 million people by 2026 with traffic issues only getting worse. A historic streetcar line—the TECO Line Streetcar System—exists with expansion plans including additional public transit options.

Tampa's downtown, in particular, may become more walkable in time, but, unfortunately, the city is currently very car dependent. There are walkable neighborhoods in the Tampa Bay area, but most residents drive to what they need in the area.

Tampa is a southern city with a definite twist. It is, along with Miami, a historic hub of Latin-American culture. As a major commercial location, it is far more diverse and cosmopolitan than many other locations in the state. The **Tampa Riverwalk** and the area known as **Water Street Tampa** have substantially transformed the downtown Hillsborough River waterfront. The investors behind this development are Jeff Vinik, the owner of the Tampa Bay Lightning hockey team, and Bill Gates, the founder of Microsoft. You'll see tons of new construction in Tampa, similar to that in other major southern Highway 41 cities like Nashville and Atlanta.

The city's marquee festival, the **Gasparilla Pirate Fest**, takes place every January. It's named for the mythical Spanish Pirate Josè Gaspar, who terrorized the coastal waters of West Florida during the late eighteenth and early nineteenth centuries. The event features what is considered to be the largest parade in the United States, with more than a hundred floats following a 4.5-mile parade route along the shore of Hillsborough Bay and Bayshore Boulevard.

Highway 41 parallels Interstate 275 as it cuts right through the middle of Tampa, where it is also known as **Nebraska Avenue**. As it reaches the outskirts of the downtown area, U.S. 41 veers east through the East Tampa neighborhood before turning south again. I suggest you take **Business 41 (North Florida Avenue)** as you enter the city from the north, as it is a more interesting drive that will bring you into **Downtown Tampa** and the **Ybor City Historic District**. Tampa is a city of neighborhoods, many of which were former towns before being annexed. To really get to know the city is to see its neighborhoods up close.

Postscript: Until recently, the city of Tampa had not received a direct hit from a hurricane since 1921, but the twin hurricanes of Helene and Milton landed nearby the city within a two-week period in September/October 2024, resulted in much flooding in some of the city's neighborhoods. Numerous homes, roads, and infrastructure were destroyed or damaged. The costs to repair the damage that occurred within the Tampa Bay region will likely total several billion dollars.

BACKGROUND: BOOM AND BUST AND BOOM AGAIN

Tampa is very old. Indigenous peoples inhabited the area for thousands of years before the arrival of Europeans. The Timucua and Calusa were the largest Indigenous cultures in what is now the state of Florida. The Timucua lived in northern Florida and southern Georgia while the Calusa called southern Florida, including the Tampa Bay area, home. Other cultures that lived within the Tampa Bay area included the Manasota Civilization, the Tocobaga, the Mocoso, the Pohoy, and the Uzita. Numerous mounds were created in the region for ceremonial or spiritual purposes. Spaniards arrived in the early 1500s, searching for gold and bringing diseases such as measles, smallpox, and influenza, which decimated the Indigenous populations. The **Tampa Bay History Center** provides details of the clashes between conquistadors and the Indigenous peoples.

In the nineteenth century, the city was an isolated frontier outpost with **Fort Brooke** established in what is now downtown Tampa. During the American Civil War, Fort Brooke was occupied by the Confederates and bombarded by the Union Navy. The fort was subsequently occupied by Federal troops but was decommissioned after the war. In 1980, excavation for a downtown parking lot uncovered a burial site for the fort's soldiers, civilian employees, and local Indigenous peoples. The soldiers and civilians were reburied at a nearby cemetery, while forty-two Seminole were laid to rest with the essence of burning herbs at the Seminole Shrine at Orient Road in 1981.

Tampa's population was riven by Yellow Fever in the 1880s. The area was about to recede to nothing when the discovery of phosphate and the arrival of Henry Plant's 1884 railroad extension to the Hillsborough River led to a surge in population. The military also had a role in Tampa's development. In 1898, Teddy Roosevelt and the Rough Riders were staged in Tampa during the Spanish American War. By 1900, Tampa was one of the largest cities in Florida. The arrival of the railroad enabled the growth of cigar manufacturing, which began in Tampa in 1886.

Ybor City, located east of downtown Tampa, was named for Vincente Martinez Ybor, a Spanish entrepreneur and cigar manufacturer. The neighborhood soon became the center of cigar manufacturing in the United States. Tens of thousands of Latin immigrants came from Cuba and Spain to work in the cigar factories. They were soon followed by Italians and East European Jewish immigrants, who came to open businesses and shops that catered to cigar workers.

The Florida Land Boom of the 1920s got its start in South Florida and then spread to the Tampa Bay area. New communities of single-family homes, such as Davis Islands and Beach Park, were established, but the Great Depression impacted Florida, limiting development for many years. Tampa became a hotbed of organized crime, with illegal "bolita" lotteries, Prohibition bootlegging, general corruption, and lawlessness extending through the mid-1950s. **MacDill Air Force Base** was established during World War II with part of that land eventually becoming the site of **Tampa International Airport**. Today, the U.S. Central Command and U.S. Special

Operations Command are headquartered at MacDill.

On January 1, 1914, the world's first scheduled commercial airline service began with opening the St. Petersburg–Tampa Airboat Line. Piloting the airline's "flying boat" was Tony Jannus, the namesake of the Tony Jannus Award presented each year by the Tampa Chamber of Commerce for extraordinary accomplishments in the field of commercial aviation.

The population of Tampa surged in the 1960s and 1970s. New residential neighborhoods were created while businesses began moving out of the city's downtown into new office plazas. As with many southern cities in the 1960s, Tampa experienced racial unrest as Jim Crow segregation laws were dismantled. However, thanks to civic and business leaders, the violence seen in other parts of the country as stores and lunch counters were integrated was much less evident in Tampa.

A construction boom in the 1980s led to overbuilding, resulting in a real estate downturn in the early 1990s. In the early 2000s, a new real estate boom focused on downtown Tampa and the waterfront area known as Sparkman Wharf, only to suffer a severe downturn during the Great Recession of 2007–2009. The Tampa Bay economy took several years to recover. Time will tell how long the latest boom in Tampa will last.

NAME

The city's name is a point of speculation. Historians believe its linked to a Calusa town named "Tanpa," which was located well south of Tampa Bay. As maps were made in the 1700s, the British mapmaker Bernard Romans moved the location to the north and changed the name to "Tampa." Other historians believe "Tampa" may have been an anglicizing of a Calusa word for "sticks of fire." Still another explanation is that the name comes from a Spanish transliteration of *itimpi*, a Calusa word meaning "near it." People from Tampa can be known as Tampans, Tampanians or Tampeños, regardless of ethnic background.

NICKNAMES

"Cigar City" is a nod to the cigar-making past of Tampa. "The Big Guava" was coined in the 1970s by Steve Otto, a newspaper columnist.

LYKES GASLIGHT SQUARE PARK

Lykes Gaslight Square Park is located in downtown Tampa. It is the size of one full city block and is a pleasant place to have an outdoor lunch. The park is also known for musical events and the Tampa Police Department Memorial Run. The park is named for the Lykes family, a prominent Tampa-based family with interests in agribusiness for more than a hundred years. The family owns over 610,000 acres of land in Florida and Texas. Lykes Citrus grows fruit in Florida that is sold to orange juice brands such as Tropicana and Florida's Natural. The Lykes Cattle Ranch in Glades and Highlands counties spreads over 337,000 acres on one of the largest contiguous pieces of land in the state. At one time the family owned a shipping firm I once worked for called "Lykes Brothers Steamship Company," based in New Orleans.

GEORGE M. STEINBRENNER FIELD

George Steinbrenner III (1930–2010) was a prominent resident of Tampa. He was involved in the Great Lakes and Gulf Coast shipping and shipbuilding industry originally started by his grandparents in the early 1900s. In 1973, he bought a controlling interest in the New York Yankees Major League Baseball team, which he held until his death. During his time as owner, the Yankees won seven World Series championships and eleven American League pennants. Steinbrenner was highly controversial and outspoken, which earned him the nickname "The Boss." His micro-management of the Yankees was satirized in the *Seinfeld* television series. After his death, the ownership of the team went to his family, who own the Yankees to this day. **George M. Steinbrenner Field** in Tampa is named in his honor.

VIGNETTE TAMPA AND BASEBALL

Tampa has been a baseball hotbed since the nineteenth century. A Tampa baseball team was first organized in Ybor City in 1887. The city became a desired spring training location for Major League Baseball teams in 1913, with the Chicago Cubs, Cincinnati Reds, Boston Red Sox, Detroit Tigers, Washington Senators, Chicago White Sox, and New York Yankees all training in Tampa over the years. A minor league team, the Tampa Tarpons, continues to play in the city at Steinbrenner Field, while the Major League Tampa Bay Rays play at Tropicana Field in nearby St. Petersburg. Heavily damaged by Hurricane Milton, Tropicana Field is currently undergoing renovation.

Tampa has been the hometown of many Major League players. Al Lopez (1908–2005) was a Hall of Fame player and manager who is commemorated in Tampa with the name of a baseball stadium **(Al Lopez Field)**, a public park **(Al Lopez Park)**, and a trail **(Al Lopez Park Trail)**. His childhood home in Ybor City is the site of the **Tampa Baseball Museum**. Known as "El Senor" for his gentlemanly demeanor, he never had a losing record in eighteen years of managing ball teams. Other well-known players/managers associated with Tampa include Tony La Russa, Lou Piniella, Kevin Cash, Pete Alonso, Matt Joyce, Dwight Gooden, Fred McGriff, Dave Magadan, Tino Martinez, and Gary Sheffield.

CELEBRITIES

Tampa has had its share of well-known figures who have called the city home. Here are some:

- Cannonball Adderley (1928–1975): alto saxophone player with the Miles Davis jazz group
- Derek Jeter (b. 1974): retired Major League Baseball player and CEO
- Hulk Hogan (1953-2025): retired professional wrestler
- Tom Cruise (b. 1962): film actor and producer
- Robin Zander (b.1953): rock musician
- Sara Blakely (b. 1971): businesswoman

FOOD

Tampa is becoming known as an up-and-coming foodie destination due to its diverse restaurant scene. Tampa is the birthplace of the **Cuban sandwich**, according to local lore. The sandwich was first made in the Ybor City neighborhood to feed Cuban workers at local cigar factories. There are lots of sandwich places in town; **Tampa Magazine** lists these restaurants in 2024 as the best:

- **Columbia Restaurant:** The oldest restaurant in Florida established in 1905, located in Ybor City, has remained within the same family for five generations.
- **La Segunda Bakery and Café:** Ybor City
- **West Tampa Sandwich Shop:** West Tampa
- **Brocato's Sandwich Shop:** Oak Park

- **Stone Soup Company Café & Pub:** St. Petersburg

OTHER NOTABLE RESTAURANTS IN TAMPA

- **Skipper's Smokehouse:** (live music and southern eats) North Tampa
- **The Green Iguana:** (burgers and tacos) Bayside West
- **Rocca:** (Italian) Tampa Heights
- **Koya:** (Japanese) Hyde Park
- **Ebbe:** (Scandinavian) Downtown Tampa
- **Lilac:** (Mediterranean) Downtown Tampa
- **SuperNatural Food & Wine:** (Breakfast/Lunch) Downtown Tampa
- **The Pearl:** (Seafood) Water Street next to Amalie Arena
- **Predalina:** (Mediterranean) Water Street near Amalie Arena
- **Streetlight Taco:** (Mexican) South Tampa

HOUSING

As of 2024, Tampa is a hot real estate market. The median home price for a single-family home in early 2024 was $450k. The relatively high demand and low inventory are causing local real estate prices to skyrocket. Tampa is one of the fastest-appreciating markets in both Florida and the United States, and since September 2022, home values have increased by 9.22 percent. Faced with one of the most competitive housing markets in the country, Tampa housing officials have been exploring ways to incentivize the private sector to build housing for people across the income spectrum. Similar to other large cities, Tampa has a need for affordable housing.

According to a report presented to Tampa City Council, for a household to afford a median-priced home in the city right now requires an annual income of $150,000. The report also noted the average Tampa resident is currently paying fifty-three percent of their income on housing and transportation.

To make living in Tampa affordable, Jane Castor, the current mayor of Tampa, states the city needs to make sure there is a sufficient housing supply, including mid- and upper-income housing. "We have to provide housing at all levels. But" she adds, "the most critical need is affordable." One-third of Hillsborough County's residents pay over thirty percent of their monthly income on housing, making them among the most financially squeezed in the state, per the Florida Housing Coalition. Homelessness has increased as more low-income families lack the means to pay for housing.

BUSINESSES

Top Companies in Tampa:
- Cisco
- EPAM Systems
- Fisher Investments
- Gartner
- General Dynamics
- HDR
- IBM
- Novetta
- Procore Technologies

SCHOOLS

- University of Tampa (enrollment 11,000), a private university
- University of South Florida (enrollment 49,000), a public university
- Hillsborough Community College (enrollment 43,000), a public community college

SPORTS

- **Tampa Bay Rays:** Major League Baseball Team; plays at Tropicana Field in St. Petersburg.
- **Tampa Bay Buccaneers:** National Football League team; plays at Raymond James Stadium.
- **Tampa Bay Lightning:** National Hockey League team; plays at Amalie Arena.
- **Tampa Rowdies:** United Soccer League team; plays at Al Lang Stadium in St. Petersburg.
- **Tampa Tarpons:** Minor League affiliate of the New York Yankees; plays at George M. Steinbrenner Field.

TAMPA NEIGHBORHOODS AND ATTRACTIONS NEAR HIGHWAY 41

Highway 41 goes by and through several Tampa neighborhoods of note. When visiting the city, U.S. 41 is a very convenient road that connects you to many places to see.

UNIVERSITY OF SOUTH FLORIDA

Just to the east of the unincorporated University area and within the Tampa city limits is the 1,500-acre campus of the **University of South Florida**, the fourth-largest university in Florida. Established in 1956, USF is one of the fastest-growing research universities in the nation. The Tampa campus borders 735 acres of forest preserve and has a botanical garden that is home to more than 3,000 plants, animals, and natural habitats.

SULPHUR SPRINGS

Sulphur Springs is a neighborhood within Tampa annexed in 1953. From the late nineteenth century until the 1940s, its mineral springs made Sulphur Springs "Florida's Coney Island," a national tourist attraction hosting a unique shopping arcade/hotel, a forty-foot water slide, and an alligator farm. The **Sulphur Springs Water Tower** was built in 1927 and is a historic landmark. Today, the neighborhood is low-income and underserved, but it features an active **Sulphur Springs Museum and Heritage Center**.

BUSCH GARDENS TAMPA BAY

Directly east of Sulphur Springs is **Busch Gardens Tampa Bay**, a 335-acre animal attraction and theme park that opened in 1959. Originally operated by the Anheuser-Busch beer brewing firm, it has animal enclosures where you can see zebras, giraffes, rhinos, and many other animal species, including endangered ones. The theme park has thrill rides and roller coasters, which proclaims are among the "fastest, steepest, tallest coasters in the country." The park has an annual attendance of four million, ranking just behind Seaworld Orlando in popularity. Other nearby attractions include the **Adventure Island** water park and the **Museum of Science & Industry**.

SEMINOLE HEIGHTS

Seminole Heights is a historic neighborhood known for its many 1920s bungalow homes. It was once connected to Tampa's downtown by streetcar, which may happen again. It is known for its many interesting bars, eateries, and vintage shops. Lastly, the Zoo Tampa at Lowry Park is another attraction to visit. A sixty-three-acre nonprofit zoo exists as a center for Florida wildlife and biodiversity. The zoo is considered one of the best in the United States.

South Seminole Heights, Tampa, FL

TAMPA HEIGHTS

Tampa Heights is situated in the central part of the city and is one of the oldest neighborhoods within the city limits. Within proximity of Tampa's downtown, Tampa Heights has revived as an attractive place to stay when visiting. I stayed the night in Tampa Heights at **Gram's Place Bed & Hostel**, a music-themed hostel named for musician Gram Parsons. The Heights is a hip place that is home to the **Armature Works**, a mixed-use retail and food establishment in a former warehouse, and **Heights Public Market** food hall.

DOWNTOWN TAMPA

There are numerous interesting places to see in downtown Tampa, but the first stop for a visitor should be the **University of Tampa Plant Hall/Henry B. Plant Museum**. The building is a National Historic Landmark and quite extraordinary. It's an enormous structure covering six acres and situated on 150 acres that cost over $3 million to build between 1888 and 1891.

Originally named the Tampa Bay Hotel, it was designed to surpass all other grand winter resorts. The 511-room giant rose to a flamboyant height of five stories embellished by ornate Victorian gingerbread and topped by Moorish minarets, domes, and cupolas. It was built by Henry B. Plant (1819–1899), a businessman, entrepreneur, and investor in railroads and steamboats. The building was designed to be, and still remains, a symbol of the city of Tampa and its history. It is safe to say that Henry B. Plant transformed Tampa from a sleepy fishing village to the city that it is today. Opened in 1891 for the accommodation of winter visitors, in 1898 it became the military headquarters for the U.S. army during the Spanish-American War.

Now called **Plant Hall**, it has served as the main building for the University of Tampa since 1933. The Tampa Municipal Museum was also established in 1933 in the south wing of the first floor to preserve the legacy of the Tampa Bay Hotel. The museum became the **Henry B. Plant Museum** in 1974 and houses original hotel furnishings and art objects collected by Mr. and Mrs. Plant.

Henry B. Plant Museum, Tampa, FL

FRANKLIN STREET HISTORIC DISTRICT

The first street in Tampa to be paved, have sidewalks built, and install electric lights—**Franklin Street**—has served as Tampa's historic commercial epicenter since the late nineteenth century. An early twentieth century streetcar route and home to as many as five department stores, Franklin Street fell into decline during the 1960s as suburban development expanded across Tampa and Hillsborough County. Seeking to compete against suburban malls, including West Shore Plaza and Tampa Bay Center, city leaders converted a five-block section of Franklin Street into a pedestrian mall during the 1970s. However, Franklin Street continued to decline, partially due to a reduction in store visibility and parking. Reopened to vehicular traffic in 2001, the Franklin Street corridor is coming back to life along with the rest of downtown Tampa.

Other attractions in downtown Tampa worth seeing include the **Old Tampa City Hall**, constructed in 1915, and the renovated landmark 1926 **Tampa Theatre**. The **Tampa Museum of Art**, the **Glazer Children's Museum**, and the **Straz Center for Performing Arts** are situated next to the Hillsborough River. Restaurants and bars line the **Tampa Riverwalk**.

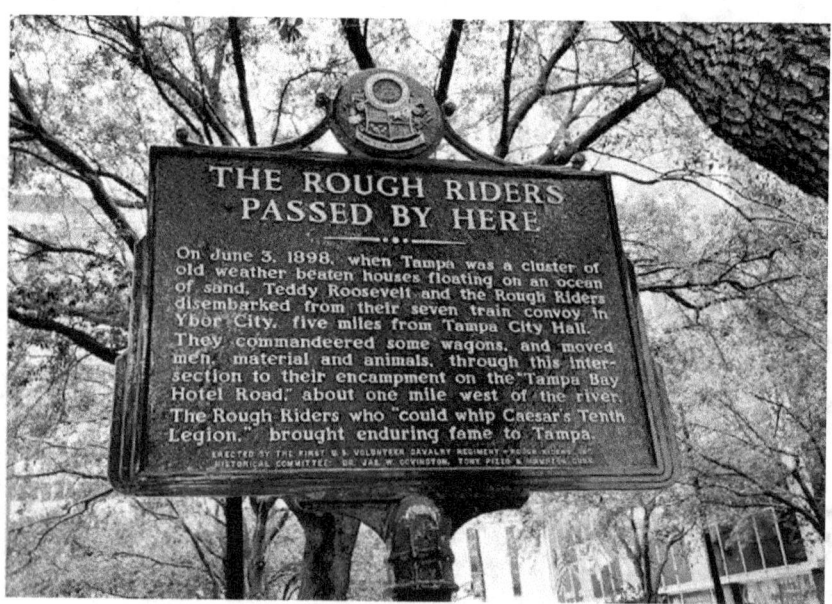

The Rough Riders Passed By Here plaque, Downtown Tampa, FL

Tampa Theatre, Tampa, FL

Riverwalk, Tampa, FL

536

Tampa Convention Center, Tampa, FL

HYDE PARK

Adjacent to the University of Tampa and downtown, the **Hyde Park** neighborhood is one of the most desirable places to live in Tampa. It is known for its historic homes, shady streets, high-end restaurants, and upscale stores. **Bayshore Boulevard** serves as Hyde Park's eastern boundary. This boulevard runs along Tampa Bay for 4.5 miles and has the longest continuous sidewalk in the United States.

YBOR CITY HISTORIC DISTRICT

The **Ybor City Historic District** is listed in the National Register of Historic Places for its Latin and cigar-manufacturing heritage, which is showcased at **Ybor City Museum State Park**. Ybor City is where Tampa residents go to have fun at its many restaurants and bars that line 7th Avenue. Many of these venues feature live music. You can get a hand-rolled cigar at one of several cigar lounges along 7th Avenue as well. The **Tampa Baseball Museum** is located here. If you visit **Centennial Park**, just off 7th Avenue, you will most likely see the Ybor City chickens walking around. These chickens are allowed to roam freely throughout Ybor City thanks to a City of Tampa ordinance that protects them. These birds are living memorials to the founding and early days of Ybor City.

Unfortunately, Interstate 275, built in the 1960s, cuts Ybor City off from the rest of downtown Tampa. Proposals to transform I-275 into a landscaped boulevard featuring bike and pedestrian paths have been shelved in favor of widening the road to add another lane and provide shoulders for bus travel.

Ybor City, Tampa, FL

VIGNETTE GUAVAWEEN

Guavaween was an extraordinarily popular annual Halloween festival in Ybor City for more than a decade. The first Guavaween was held in 1985. It was started by the Ybor City Chamber of Commerce as a fundraiser to help the Tampa Playmakers, a local drama company. By 1989, when Guavaween generated $100,000, it was becoming quite popular. Around dusk, the Mama Guava Stumble Parade, Guavaween's most popular attraction, made its way down 7th Ave, Ybor's main street. The parade, led by Mama Guava, featured floats and costumed individuals who threw candy and beads to the spectators. But as time passed, the event became increasingly difficult to control. In 1990, when 250,000 people were in attendance, the police had to step in to manage the crowds. In 1995, organizers decided to begin charging admission. In the 2000s, the event still drew large crowds, but the city enacted more restrictions, such as a dress code for costumes, due to the many risqué costumes that had been on display in the past. Ticket prices increased as well, rising *from $4 to $17. In 2009, only 15,000 people attended. In 2012, the Mama Guava Stumble Parade made its final run, and the final Guavaween festival was held in 2017. Although Guavaween declined in popularity over the years, many people still have fond memories of this once-beloved Halloween tradition.*

DAVIS ISLANDS

Historic **Davis Islands** is known for its views of downtown Tampa, as well as its lavish, pastel-colored Mediterranean-style buildings that date from the 1920s. It is one of the most desirable locations to live in Tampa.

PORT TAMPA BAY

South of downtown, Highway 41 passes by **Port Tampa Bay**. With an economic impact of more than $17 billion annually, Port Tampa Bay is the economic engine of West Central Florida and the state's largest port. Florida is responsible for more than a third of U.S. exports to the Caribbean and Latin America, and much of that trade passes through this port. Major industry clusters include food and beverage, citrus and juice products, furniture, general department store merchandise, steel, fertilizer, animal feed, and agricultural products. Port Tampa Bay is also a major cruise port, which welcomes ships from Carnival, Celebrity Cruises, Royal Caribbean, and NCL at its three cruise terminals.

AREAS TO SEE ACROSS TAMPA BAY

TARPON SPRINGS

Tarpon Springs is known for its Greek community and culture. Greek sponge divers settled there in the early 1900s and built the city's natural sponge industry. For 30 years, the sponge industry was the largest industry in Florida—larger than either citrus farming or tourism. Tarpon Springs was known as the "Sponge Capital of the World" until a blight in the 1940s and 1950s almost wiped out the industry. Sponges returned in the 1980s but climate change has reduced the number of sponges. The industry lives on, and the area remains a leader in the natural sponge market.

CLEARWATER

Clearwater is a city in Tampa Bay's Metro area known for sunny weather and Gulf coast beaches. Clearwater Beach is a three mile stretch of white sand backed by hotels and restaurants. Injured dolphins and sea turtles are rehabilitated at the **Clearwater Marine Aquarium**. The Philadelphia Phillies Major League Baseball team plays spring training games at the city's **Spectrum Field**.

ST. PETERSBURG

Twenty-two miles southwest of Tampa, across the bay, **St. Petersburg** is a community of retirees (twenty percent) and singles (thirty-six percent). Nicknamed "The Sunshine City" in years past, St. Petersburg was a magnet for retirees and often referred to as "God's waiting room." But now the city is becoming a hip place for younger people and features numerous waterfront cafés, restaurants, and bars to accompany its multiple beaches.

Things to see in St. Pete include **Central Avenue** in the heart of downtown, **Gulf Beaches Historical Museum**, and **Pass-a-Grille National Historic District**. **Jimmy B's Beach Bar**, is, as their advertising states, "St. Petersburg's hottest beachside hangout, with paved pathways from the wooden deck to the soft white sands of St. Pete Beach." Visitors will also enjoy **The Don CeSar Beach Resort and Spa, Fort De Soto Park, and The Dali Home** and **Salvador Dali Museum**.

Author's Note: St. Petersburg was hit hard by hurricanes Helene and Milton in the fall of 2024. Significant flooding and building damage occurred throughout the city; the fabric roof of Tropicana Field, where the Tampa Bay Rays baseball team play, was completely shredded. Immense piles of storm-related debris needed to be cleared. As sea levels rise, St. Petersburg will need to assess how to rebuild in areas of the city that are susceptible to the flooding and surges associated with large storms.

CONCLUDING THOUGHTS

Travel on Highway 41 from the Florida border to Tampa affords a view of an often overlooked portion of the state. Visitors to this region can still see what the state looked like before the large population increases that started in the 1980s. The towns along U.S. 41 are interesting from the standpoint of their historical locations and the natural environment around them. "Old Florida," as much of the area is known, still has small communities and open land with trees. Links with the "Deep South" of Louisiana, Alabama, and Mississippi can be found here. Change is taking place, however, as the many housing projects currently planned or under construction promise to alter the character of what once was a largely agricultural and mining country.

From State Road 60 (East Adamo Drive) at the southeast end of Tampa to Miami, Highway 41 is known as the **Tamiami Trail** and begins the final 284 miles of our drive to Miami. Part Two of our Florida journey takes place through what is known as "South Florida." It is the only region of the continental United States that has a tropical climate. Transplants migrating from northern states and nearby Caribbean countries provide a different vision and perspective, as we will see traveling through South Florida; the end of our trek down Highway 41.

CHAPTER ELEVEN
FLORIDA PART TWO: "SoFLO" SOUTH FLORIDA AND
THE TAMIAMI TRAIL

"That's sort of the price you may have to pay for living in paradise,"

—*Tampa Mayor Jane Castor*

In the space of two weeks, in late September/early October 2024, the state of Florida was hit by two massive back-to-back hurricanes from the Gulf of Mexico—hurricanes Helene and Milton. Both created storm surges, high winds, heavy rainfall, and tornadoes causing extreme flooding, property damage, and loss of life. The combined estimated damage in Florida from the two hurricanes is likely to exceed $100 billion. Along the Gulf coast of Florida where Highway 41 runs, the recovery from these weather-related events in some areas may take a long time. Gulf storms appear to be happening more frequently, which will impact the booming South Florida area in uncertain ways.

TAMPA TO NAPLES

From Tampa to Miami, Highway 41 is more famously known as the **Tamiami Trail.** Between Tampa and Naples, the road roughly parallels Florida's west coast for 169 miles, though it is a couple of miles inland and, for the most part, out of sight of the Gulf of Mexico. **Interstate 75**, which has been the main route for traffic since its completion in the 1980s, runs farther east. Through this area, Highway 41 is a commercial and service road with retail establishments and stoplights. The road passes through several cities and by multiple housing developments along the way. You will find much traffic congestion along a good part of this section of the route. Once, numerous truck gardens lined highway 41, but now the road passes through some of the fastest-growing population areas in the country.

South of the Tampa city limits, you'll drive through the CDP (census-designated place) of **Palm River–Clair Mel**. The ornate **Wat Mongkolratanaram Buddhist Temple** on the bank of the **Palm River** is an interesting place to stop and visit near this stretch of the road. Its Sunday market with Thai food is quite popular.

MOSAIC RIVERVIEW FACILITY & TAMPA BAY

Farther south along the road is the **East Bay Raceway Park**, an old clay racing car track first opened in 1977. It ran its final race in November 2024. Behind the track rises what appears to be a giant mountain that, at first glance, looks to be a large garbage mound. It is a phosphogypsum stack—a "mountain" of solid waste topped with an open retention pond holding millions of gallons of toxic wastewater from fertilizer production. The stack is 200 feet tall and covers approximately 380 acres. This "toxic mountain," called the **Riverview Phosphogypsum Stack**, is owned by the **Mosaic Company**, a Fortune 500 company headquartered in Tampa. This enterprise mines and processes phosphate and potash minerals for fertilizer. The old raceway was sold to Mosaic, which will likely expand the footprint of the Riverview stack location.

Several environmental advocacy groups have called this stack and others like it an ecological disaster waiting to happen. In 2004, heavy rain from Hurricane Frances caused a rupture in a reservoir at the Riverview facility, then owned by Cargill Fertilizer. In October 2024, rainfall from Hurricane Milton overwhelmed the stack and caused over 17,500 gallons of polluted water to spill into Tampa Bay. The stacks are highly susceptible to major rainfall events that can cause the containment wall of the stack to break down and leak materials like uranium, thorium, radium, and radon gas suspended in its wastewater. Two more stacks lie farther along the road. Nearby residents are concerned about health issues that might arise from proximity to Mosaic's waste stacks.

The waste stacks are located by Tampa Bay, Florida's largest open water estuary, which extends over 400 square miles. The bay is a habitat for wildlife, including fish, crustaceans, birds, and endangered manatees. At this writing, there are no state regulations in place mandating safeguards against future spills in Tampa Bay.

MacDILL AIR FORCE BASE

Across Tampa Bay from the Mosaic Riverview facility is **MacDill Air Force Base**, as noted in Florida Part One. Once slated for closure in the 1990s due to its proximity to the Tampa International Airport, it is currently home to the U.S. Central Command that runs U.S. Military operations in the Caribbean, Middle East, and elsewhere and Special Operations Command that is the only unified combatant command created by an Act of Congress. Approximately 7,000 military and civilian personnel work at the base. It is a major employer within the Tampa metropolitan region.

PROGRESS VILLAGE

To the east of the highway, in the shadow of the Riverview Stack, lies the unincorporated CDP community of **Progress Village**. This historically Black community was set up in the late 1950s to provide affordable housing for

African Americans who were forbidden by segregation real-estate covenants from living in most majority-white neighborhoods. In addition, flooding from Hurricane Milton in 2024 and a lack of adequate drainage systems have plagued the community. Longstanding residents have been forced from their homes without the means of making repairs.

RIVERVIEW

South of the gypsum stacks along the Alafia River is the CDP of **Riverview**, a fast-growing suburb of Tampa. Some 40,000 residents have been added since the 2010 census. Located in Riverview is the **Showmen's Museum**, which honors the outdoor traveling shows, carnivals, circuses, thrill shows, wild west shows, and other attractions that entertained people before television and video screens came about. The museum preserves the rides, games, costumes, and memorabilia of days gone by when the circus came to town.

In similar fashion to Progress Village, hurricanes Helene and Milton caused much flooding through some residential areas of Riverview near the Alafia River.

GIBSONTON

As you proceed south, the highway crosses the Alafia River into **Gibsonton**, sometimes nicknamed "Gibtown," another CDP. Gibsonton, once known as the "strangest town in America," was famous as a traveling sideshow wintering town for people who performed and worked in carnivals. Human oddities such as bearded ladies and fire-eaters resided there. A special counter for dwarfs was once part of Gibtown's post office. Special zoning laws allowed carnival trailers and circus elephants to be kept on front lawns. Today, sideshows are rarely found on carnival midways, which are now dominated by amusement rides, games, and food joints. At present, the town has the usual gas stations and convenience stores found in any other outlying community near a major city.

RUSKIN

Farther down the road lies **Ruskin**, yet another CDP that was once an incorporated town. The community was named for utopian John Ruskin—the English writer, philosopher, art historian, and critic—by the founders of the short-lived Ruskin College. This institution of higher learning existed from 1910 to 1918. For decades, Ruskin was a rural truck farming community. Its main crops were tomatoes, strawberries, flowers, and other assorted agricultural items. In the 1970s and 1980s, developers started buying up the farmland to use as lots for homes. Today, Ruskin is a Tampa suburb with a strip retail commercial area and a large Amazon fulfillment center.

If you can, please stop by and patronize the **Ruskin Family Drive-In Theatre** right off Highway 41. It's one of only seven such theaters left in Florida and the only one on the Gulf Coast. It has been projecting movies since 1952. It's owned by a husband-and-wife team. I hope that someone will want to keep it a theater when they retire, but one of the owners told me he receives frequent calls from real estate developers. You have to love their website:

"The Ruskin Family Drive-In Theatre, with over 50 years of continuous service to the Ruskin and South Hillsborough County, has been a community gathering place since its first movie, "Singing in the Rain" played in 1952.

We call it the "Last family drive-in" in the U.S.A. because families, dating couples, single parents with children and everyone else young and old can come and visit. We had family values when family values were the rule. We still have family values although by some we're not considered cool.

We offer great movies, good food, and peace and quiet on a continuous basis. We have a 2000 square foot screen, clean restrooms, a snack bar and a clean parking lot. We are open year-round—rain or shine, hot or cold, including holidays! We only accept cash, no checks or credit cards allowed!"

Ruskin Family Drive-In Theatre, Ruskin, FL

SUN CITY

Past Ruskin is the **River Valley RV Village**, built on the remnants of what was once called **Sun City**, which was developed during the Florida land boom of the 1920s. The 500-acre Sun City Motion Picture Studio was constructed here in 1925. It featured a visitor's gallery where residents and tourists could watch motion picture stars at work. Land was sold around the studio and plotted as streets named for famous screen actors of the day, such as Charlie Chaplin and Olga Petrova. Unfortunately, the local land boom went bust after a major hurricane in 1926. The studio went bankrupt, and the property was demolished in 1932. A second try at making Sun City an east coast Hollywood in the late 1930s ended up going nowhere, and today a mobile home park sits on the site.

MANATEE COUNTY

A few miles south of Sun City, Highway 41 enters Manatee County, named for the large, gentle, and vulnerable aquatic mammals native to Florida. The county population was 97,000 in 1970, 264,000 in 2000, and 460,000 in 2024. The highway goes through an agricultural area where strawberries are grown, but you'll see many more housing developments than cropland on your journey here. Still, several roadside stands sell strawberries off the highway.

VIGNETTE   THE PINEY POINT CRISIS

Off Highway 41 to the east and close to the Gulf of Mexico waterfront is the former **Piney Point Phosphate Plant**, *a phosphate-processing facility that once operated in Manatee County. Piney Point is the site of one of Florida's worst ecological disasters in recent years. In late March 2021, a leak in a wastewater reservoir liner caused a breach in the containment wall, triggering the Piney Point Crisis. To avoid collapse of the reservoir, some 215 million gallons of wastewater were pumped into Tampa Bay. In April, responding to the risk of catastrophic flooding should the leak become a larger breach, homes, businesses, and the Manatee County Jail were evacuated, and Florida Governor DeSantis declared a state of emergency.*

Despite objections from environmental organizations, in June 2021 the Manatee County Commissioners approved a plan to pump the contaminated wastewater deep underground. Critics argued that this could contaminate the aquifer and compromise the safety of Florida's groundwater. The wastewater removal was expected to be com-

pleted in December 2024. The plant is now closed, and it remains to be seen what further effects of the crisis might take place. Some individuals have suggested that the former plant should be turned into a bird sanctuary with no future commercial or residential development.

RUBONIA

Highway 41 skirts by the unincorporated community of **Rubonia**, an area first developed as housing for African Americans working in the area as migrant farmers. Rubonia's modern development suffered due to the construction of the modern four-lane Highway 41 in 1965, which bypassed the small town on the main route between Tampa and Bradenton. At present, Rubonia is an area with lots of manufactured home communities.

Rubonia hosts one of the only Mardi Gras parades in the area, known as the **Historical Rubonia & Terra Ceria Mardi Gras**. The event dates back to 1980, when Luanne Topp (aka Ruby Rubonia) wanted to go to Mardi Gras in New Orleans for her birthday. She couldn't manage to put the trip together, so to cheer her up, about a dozen friends jumped on a truck and threw their own parade through the town. The event was so popular among community members that it began to be held annually. At its peak, it was attended by over 20,000 spectators. It was cancelled in 2015 due to financial troubles, but was revived in 2017 and continues as an event each year.

MEMPHIS & PALMETTO

South of Rubonia lie Memphis and Palmetto. **Memphis** is a CDP that once was a predominately African American community. The **Old Memphis Cemetery** is the resting place of many African Americans who cultivated tomato, celery, cabbage, and citrus crops in the area's truck farming fields. Many of the graves are unmarked. The Old Memphis Cemetery has a historical marker that details the life and death of the now-abandoned graveyard, which closed in 1977.

The city of **Palmetto** is located on the banks of the Manatee River. Its **Palmetto Historic District** features several historic twentieth century buildings, including a Carnegie Library that dates from 1914 and is on the National Register of Historic Places.

ELLENTON

To the east of Palmetto is the unincorporated community of **Ellenton**, which is home to **Gamble Plantation Historic State Park**. Built by enslaved labor between 1842 and 1845 by order of Major Robert Gamble, the plantation grew sugar prior to the Civil War. Following the end of the Civil War, Judah Benjamin, the Confederate Secretary of State, supposedly sheltered at the Gamble Mansion as a fugitive from Union troops before escaping to England. A stone monument to honor Benjamin was erected by the United Daughters of the Confederacy on the mansion's grounds in 1942. The monument was removed in June 2020 and placed into storage.

BRADENTON

Crossing the Manatee River, you'll enter the city of **Bradenton**, which is the Manatee County seat. Bradenton's motto is "The Friendly City," and it's a little less glitzy than its neighbor Sarasota, thirteen miles to the south. Among the first things a visitor encounters after crossing the river are Bradenton's scenic **Riverwalk** and the **Mosaic Riverwalk Amphitheater**. The **Bishop Museum of Science and Nature** is worth a visit to see the **Parker Manatee Rehabilitation Habitat**, a temporary home for manatees that were rescued after they became sick or injured. Farther east is **Manatee Village Historical Park**, which was opened in 1976 to preserve the history of the county. Restored historical buildings are situated here.

Bradenton has a downtown historic district located just off the highway and surrounding the 1913 neoclassical **Manatee Courthouse**. Check out the gumball machine collection in the courthouse basement. **O'bricks Irish Pub & Martini Bar** in downtown Bradenton is a good restaurant where I had an excellent seafood dinner. The **Bradenton Public Market** is on Old Main Street and features local fresh produce for sale and seasonal events on Saturdays from October through May. Multiple art and music activities are held during the tourist season. Another cool place to see in Bradenton is the **Village of the Arts**, which consists of colorful, historic 1920s and 1930s homes that are now art galleries, studios, shops, and restaurants.

The city is also the spring training home of the Pittsburgh Pirates National League Baseball team. The Pirates play at **LECOM Park**, originally named McKechnie Field. Built in 1923, it is the oldest stadium still used for spring training. The park is just east of Highway 41, and while it has experienced renovations over the decades, it still retains the feeling of a classic neighborhood ballpark. The park's Spanish mission-style facade was constructed during a significant stadium facelift in the early 1990s.

If you are spending some time in the Bradenton area, you will probably want to visit the Gulf Coast beaches situated on **Anna Maria Island**, a barrier island that is a big tourist draw. The island suffered much damage from hurricanes Helene and Milton, particularly to waterfront homes, and it will take some time for the beaches to fully reopen. **Coquina Beach** is a personal favorite, but there are several lovely beaches along the island strip. Also worth checking out is the **De Soto National Memorial**. It marks the location where, in 1539, Hernando de Soto's army of soldiers, mercenaries, craftsmen, and clergy made landfall in Tampa Bay.

From Bradenton, Highway 41 travels through **South Bradenton**, a suburb with lots of mobile home parks, old motels, and advertisements for gun shows. A food pantry had a long line waiting for distribution when I passed by.

SARASOTA COUNTY

As you proceed south on Highway 41, you'll enter the county and city of **Sarasota**, which is also the county seat. The county population was 120,000 in 1970, 326,000 in 2000, and 489,000 in 2024. The county includes the barrier islands of **Longboat Key** and **Siesta Key** on the Gulf Coast, and the **Myakka River State Park inland**, which is one of the oldest and largest parks in the state.

THE RINGLING

Highway 41 skirts **Sarasota Bradenton International Airport**. As you enter the city, **The Ringling** is just off the highway, and this is definitely a stop you'll want to make on your Highway 41 journey. Once the estate of John and Mable Ringling, the property was bequeathed to the state of Florida in 1936. John Ringling (1866–1936) was an entrepreneur who is best known as the creator of the modern circus. With his brothers, he merged the Barnum & Bailey Circus with the Ringling Brothers Circus in 1907, monopolizing the circus business and achieving great personal wealth. In the mid-1920s, the winter quarters for the circus were moved from Bridgeport, Connecticut, to Sarasota. The Ringlings traveled the world collecting fine art for their Sarasota estate, and the site features several exhibits of their finds. I suggest spending several hours at The Ringling to cover all of the attractions on display.

The **Museum of Art** boasts collections ranging from ancient Indian sculpture to early photography to immersive contemporary installations to Baroque masterpieces. Ringling amassed the largest private collection of paintings by Flemish artist Peter Paul Rubens in the United States, and the museum has an entire room devoted to these large-scale paintings. A collection of some 600 old master paintings is also on display in the museum. The courtyard is filled with replicas of Classical, Renaissance, and Baroque sculpture, including a bronze cast of Michelangelo's *David*. Take your time here—there is a lot to see.

The **Circus Museum** contains all kinds of memorabilia from the history of the circus. Wagons, costumes, circus art, train cars, and some amazing dioramas that display the logistics of a circus coming to town are housed in two different buildings.

The winter home of John and Mable Ringling was called **Ca' d'Zan** (meaning "House of John" in the Venetian dialect). It was completed in 1926 and is a Venetian Gothic palace on Sarasota Bay. The mansion has forty-one rooms and fifteen bathrooms. The Ringling's were among the richest families in the United States, and it is not hard to imagine the lavish entertaining done at the estate.

The **Historic Asolo Theatre** was originally constructed in 1798 inside a Renaissance-era palace in Asolo, Italy. It remained there until 1931, when it was dismantled to make way for a cinema. The theater's historic paintings, decorative panels, ornate proscenium, and gilded stage boxes remained in storage until The Ringling Foundation purchased them in 1949 and reassembled them at the museum. The theater is equipped with modern technology and stages many productions each year. Finally, the museum grounds feature the **Bayfront Gardens** with plants, trees, sculptures, and trails.

Across the highway from The Ringling is the **Sarasota Classic Car Museum**. It was closed on my visit and may be moving to another location. The museum supposedly houses a large collection of 1960s and 1970s "muscle cars." Farther south on the highway is the **Marietta Museum of Art & Whimsy**, "dedicated to the creative human spirit and raising the importance of Whimsical Art." Stop by to see a collection of eclectic contemporary art and statues. A fun, cool place to stop and check out.

Marietta Museum of Art & Whimsy, Sarasota, FL

DOWNTOWN SARASOTA

Downtown Sarasota has many high-rise condominium developments, and the area appears overcrowded. My research suggests that many longtime residents and community leaders are saying the same thing. Overdevelopment could lead to many potential problems for an overburdened infrastructure. The city's increasingly gentrifying historic **Rosemary Art & Design District** has many cafés, bistros, and bars that feature live music. The Rosemary District was established in the 1890s as a neighborhood for African Americans. The district was first known as "Black Bottom," which was later changed to "Overtown" in the 1920s. It was renamed the "Rosemary District" in the 1990s, but little remains of the original community vibe aside from local murals. African Americans have largely moved away from the area.

The **Marie Selby Botanical Gardens** lie just to the south of downtown. The city also has a well-established arts and culture scene bolstered by the **Van Wezel Performing Arts Hall**, the **Sarasota Opera House**, and the **Florida Studio Theatre**. A couple of seafood restaurants of note in Sarasota are **Owen's Fish Camp** in the downtown area and **Walt's Fish Market** in South Sarasota.

Farther south on the Tamiami Trail through Sarasota is **Phillippi Estate Park**, a sixty-acre nature area on Phillippi Creek that is also a popular local hiking spot. Within the park is the historic 1916 **Edson Keith Mansion**, listed on the National Register of Historic Places. Edson and his wife Nettie were part of what was called the "Chicago Colony" of socialites who envisioned Sarasota as an American Riviera. Beginning in 1910, when Chicago socialite and businesswoman Bertha Palmer first visited the area, a number of wealthy Chicagoans descended upon the site and built lavish estates.

Sarasota has been a hub for baseball spring training since the 1920s. Six Major League teams have made Sarasota County their spring training home since 1924, including the Boston Red Sox, the Los Angeles Dodgers, the Chicago White Sox, the Cincinnati Reds, and, currently, the Baltimore Orioles who play at **Ed Smith Stadium**, a couple miles east of Highway 41.

The fifty miles along Highway 41/Tamiami Trail through Sarasota to Port Charlotte becomes very congested at this point. Many retail strip malls, car dealers, and housing developments line the highway here. You might be sorely tempted to take I-75 to escape the monotonous congestion.

To the south of Sarasota is the Gulf of Mexico barrier island known as **Siesta Key**. The island is known for wide sandy beaches and laid-back Gulf Coast lifestyle. It took a direct hit from Hurricane Milton on October 9, 2024, with much damage to hotels, homes, shops, and restaurants. Siesta Key is a big tourist draw that receives 350,000 annual visitors. More frequent hurricanes will require much resiliency on the part of its residents.

Author's Note: As this book went to press in September, 2025 the Florida Department of Transportation was considering naming a section of Highway 41 in Sarasota County after Dickey Betts, the Rock and Roll Hall of Fame performer who passed away in 2024 and was a founding member of The Allman Brothers Band. Betts lived for many years in the census-designated-place of Osprey, just to the south of the city of Sarasota.

VENICE

Twenty-three miles south of Sarasota, **Venice**, the "Shark's Tooth Capital of the World" due to the abundance of shark's teeth that wash up on its shore, is an attractive city along the Tamiami Trail. It's a good place to stop for a welcome respite from the monotonous traffic and retail strip developments you will encounter on this section of the highway. Venice was planned out during the 1920's Florida land boom, and has managed to retain the look of an Old Florida city. The downtown area has smaller stores and areas to walk around that are quite agreeable for a visitor. **The Soda Fountain of Venice** exudes a vintage vibe, and I enjoyed the ice cream cone I purchased there.

Centennial Park, near the downtown area, is a fun place to walk around. **Venice Theatre**, a performing arts venue, is located near the park. The **Heritage Park Trail** runs between the split lanes that make up West Venice Avenue and terminates at **Venice Beach**, a lively, vibrant, public beach that is right on the Gulf of Mexico.

Check out the hyperbolic paraboloid **Venice Beach Pavilion**. Designed in 1964 by architect Cyril Tucker, the pavilion has endured many tropical storms and remained intact. Venice was hit hard by the dual hurricanes of Helene and Milton in 2024 with the public waterfront requiring extensive rebuilding. The beaches will reopen, but it remains to be seen if (or how many) of the private residences are beyond repair.

Near the beach on Heritage Park Trail is a monument honoring the **Venice Army Air Base**, which was established as a training facility in 1942 during World War II. Within a year, the facility was operational and at its peak. It housed 6,000 airmen who were there to learn to fly P-39s, P-40s, P-47s, and P-51 Mustangs. In all, about 20,000 pilots, including some Chinese-American pilots, learned to fly in Venice for the war effort. At the end of the war, the army gave the airport to the City of Venice with the stipulation that if it were not used as an airport, it would revert to the United States government. **Venice Municipal Airport** now occupies the land. Many of the pilots who trained at the base later returned to Venice and became residents, business owners, and civic leaders.

Another plaque along the Heritage Park Trail close to the beach was dedicated at the American Bicentennial in 1976. I found it very moving:

JULY 4, 1976

DEDICATED TO ALL VETERANS OF ALL WARS. THE DISABLED AND THOSE WHO GAVE THEIR LIVES IN THE HOPE THEIR CHILDREN WOULD NEVER NEED TO FIGHT OR GIVE THEIR LIVES TO KEEP OUR

COUNTRY STRONG AND FREE, BUT ESPECIALLY DEDICATED WITH THE KNOWLEDGE THAT IF CALLED, THEY WILL EMULATE THEIR PARENTS IN UPHOLDING THE HONOR OF THESE UNITED STATES.

Venice Army Air Base, Venice, FL

Parabola, Venice, FL

Beach, Venice, FL

Downtown Venice, FL

CHARLOTTE COUNTY

From Venice, the highway turns inland and crosses into Charlotte County. Charlotte County's population was 27,000 in 1970, 141,000 in 2000, 186,000 in 2020, and 218,000 in 2024. In August 2004, the county was hit by Hurricane Charley, and in September 2022 it was struck by Hurricane Ian. Damage from Ian is still evident. Long ago, the Calusa populated this area of the Florida coast before the arrival of Europeans and their diseases decimated the Indigenous population. In the late 1700s and early 1800s, the area was a haven for pirates, but remained undeveloped aside from small fishing villages. The county was long a backwater with small fishing villages and farming until the land developers descended.

PORT CHARLOTTE/CHARLOTTE HARBOR

Port Charlotte and adjoining **Charlotte Harbor** are census-designated places. Their large real estate developments were built on former ranch land by the Mackle brothers (see the vignette about them in Chapter Ten) and others starting in the 1950s. There is no port at Port Charlotte. Canals were dug to drain the swampy land, and then the Mackles offered the resulting 80,000 acres of small lots for sale to northern retirees. Sales practices such as mass advertising and celebrity endorsements were used to entice buyers. One of these tactics involved displaying models of Port Charlotte in northern department stores. A large concentration of residents sixty-five years old and over were among the first residents, and that demographic still comprises one-third of the population.

When I visited, I went to **Port Charlotte Beach Park**, which required driving through many residential streets. Many canals cut through the area that are used for mooring boats. Otherwise, there is not much to see except homes and what little commerce lies beyond the retail strip of the Tamiami Trail. I stayed at a hotel in the area and had the weird experience of being checked in by a remote worker to whom I talked on a video screen. The hotel key came out of a machine. Very strange. I ate dinner at **Le Lambi** restaurant, which serves authentic Caribbean cuisine that was quite tasty.

PUNTA GORDA

Crossing the **Peace River** from Charlotte brings you into the city of **Punta**

Gorda, the Charlotte County seat and the only incorporated city in the county. This is an interesting locality to see, perhaps because the "Old Florida" vibe still exists here. It was established as a community in 1884 by Isaac Trabue, an attorney from Kentucky who purchased thirty acres of waterfront land. He originally called the town "Trabue" and named the residential streets after family members. He arranged streets and blocks to align with the Charlotte Harbor waterfront, where he built a long public promenade connecting a string of public parks. Over time, the parks were combined into present-day **Gilchrist Park**, named for Albert Waller Gilchrist (1858–1926), one of Punta Gorda's founders and governor of Florida in the early 1900s.

On the waterfront, check out the plaque honoring James Lockhart and his wife Josephine, who built the **First Punta Gorda Homesite** in 1876. The city became a shipping point for fish and citrus fruits as well as an attractive destination for northern visitors.

Tamiami Trail over the Peace River, Punta Gorda, FL

Unlike many other Gulf Coast locations with gated communities, Punta Gorda is an easy place to walk around. Unfortunately, the city was in the direct path of Hurricane Ian in 2022 and once again in 2024 with hurricanes Helene and Milton. When I visited in December 2023, local buildings still displayed significant damage from Ian and will most likely have much additional damage to overcome during the next couple years. To my dismay, when I visited the **Blanchard House Museum of African American History and Culture of Charlotte County**, which honors the significant role of the local African American community, it was closed due to damage from Hurricane Ian.

The city boasts a historic district featuring a number of buildings on the National Register of Historic Places that date from the late 1800s to the 1930s. The **Punta Gorda Historical Society** plays an active role in preserving the city's architecture. Across from Blanchard House is **Bailey Brothers Park**, dedicated to the seven African American brothers from Punta Gorda who served their country in World War II and the Korean War. Visitors to Punta Gorda can also visit the **Military Heritage Museum** near **Fisherman's Village**. As you might expect, you will find Fisherman's Village which features many shopping and dining options on the waterfront.

Significant hurricane damage occurred to **Ponce de Leon Park**, which is located on the Charlotte Harbor coast and features walking trails and natural scenery. The park is home to the **Peace River Wildlife Center**, a nonprofit organization dedicated to the treatment of injured Florida wildlife. The hospital and education center suffered extensive damage from the twin 2024 hurricanes and will be closed indefinitely.

Several subdivisions adjoining Ponce de Leon Park within Punta Gorda were developed for retirees in the late 1950s and platted with canals that connect to **Charlotte Harbor**. This area of modest homes was devastated by the 2024 hurricanes. Many of these homes were flooded with up to four feet of water.

CHARLOTTE HARBOR PRESERVE STATE PARK

As we leave Punta Gorda, the highway continues south through more land developments. Here, **Charlotte Harbor Preserve State Park**, comprised of 45,000 acres that protect more than 100 miles of shoreline, lies along Charlotte Harbor. It is the third-largest Florida State Park and preserves mangrove forests, marshes, scrub habitats, and pine flatwoods that can no longer be seen inland.

LEE COUNTY

"The story of Florida is the story of development happening at times and places where it probably shouldn't."

—*An Official of Florida Conservation Voters*

Highway 41 continues into Lee County, which has had an outsized impact on both the state of Florida and the United States. It is one of the fastest-growing population areas in the nation. The numbers are astonishing: from barely over 17,000 residents in 1940, the county population had risen to 105,000 in 1970, 440,000 in 2000, 620,000 in 2010, 790,000 in 2020, and 886,000 in 2024. Experts predict Lee County's population will well exceed one million residents by 2030. Driving this surge has been a huge number of baby boomers looking for affordable housing near the Gulf Coast to take advantage of the warm weather in their retirement.

Highway 41 runs the length of Lee County and is the county's main north–south arterial highway. It is a major commercial corridor with multiple traffic lights and congestion throughout its length. Numerous gated housing developments line the road. Lee County received a direct hit from Hurricane Ian in September of 2022, and parts of the region are still in a state of recovery. A report in 2023 ranked Ian as the third most costly hurricane to hit the United States since 1980, trailing only Katrina in 2005 and Harvey in 2017. In a dreadful postscript, the cost of hurricanes Helene and Milton in 2024 is expected to be in the tens of billions of dollars. Sadly, many homeowners' policies along the Gulf Coast are not covered by flood insurance.

CAPE CORAL

To the east of Highway 41 is the vast city of **Cape Coral**, the largest city in Lee County and also the largest city between Tampa and Miami. City planners expect Cape Coral to have 400,000 residents by 2050. The city has over 400 miles of navigable waterways, more than any other city on Earth. For the first-time visitor, it resembles nothing more than a huge suburban bedroom community of housing developments without any discernible city center. The city has become a major destination for people moving from the Chicago area.

VIGNETTE   THE ROSEN BROTHERS

Cape Coral was founded in 1957 by real estate developers Jack and Leonard Rosen, who reputedly flew over the land and purchased a 103-square-mile tract for a planned community. Brothers Leonard (1915–1987) and Jack (1919–1969) can be portrayed as both visionaries and scam artists in the same sentence. Without a doubt, they had a significant impact upon southwest Florida. The Rosens were from Baltimore and started as street vendors. Later, they marketed hair care products, furniture, and electrical appliances utilizing television marketing. They applied some of those same techniques to selling real estate. The brothers had no land development experience when they bought their Florida property. They received a loan from the Chicago financier Jay Pritzker to create a real estate development company that became Gulf American Land Corporation. For a time, it was the largest land sales company in the United States.

Upon purchasing the environmentally sensitive Cape Coral property, the brothers cleared the land of mangroves, saltmarshes, and sloughs utilizing dredge and fill techniques. They created canals with docks for boats. Planes and buses ferried potential customers to the massive land holding. Celebrities were brought in to pump up the interest of customers. The Rosens used deceptive high-pressure sales techniques to persuade individuals to commit to buying properties on installment plans. The brothers were eventually accused of fraudulent sales practices by the state of Florida, and they sold the company in 1969 after they had cleared a net profit of $100 million from property-related activities.

Cape Coral continues to grow, despite the potential impact of climate change to the area. Recent environmental analysis suggests the Cape Coral area faces an extreme risk of flooding, some risk of wildfire, and an extreme risk of high winds from hurricanes, tornadoes, and other severe weather.

Cape Coral gated community, Cape Coral, FL

New construction near Cape Coral, FL

FORT MYERS

The nearby city of **Fort Myers** is much better known than Cape Coral but smaller in population. This city along Highway 41 is the seat of Lee County and sits on the banks of the **Caloosahatchee River**. It began with a fort built by the U.S. Army in the mid-1800s during the Seminole Wars. The community grew around the fort. Fort Myers has long been a tourist and fishing destination. It is known as the "City of Palms" for the varieties of palm trees within its limits.

Edison & Ford Winter Estates lies just off the highway. This twenty-one-acre area features the former homes of Thomas Edison (1847–1931) and Henry Ford (1863–1947), a research lab, botanical gardens, and a museum. Edison, Ford, and Harvey Firestone tested various trees and plants for rubber that could be used if the product could no longer be obtained abroad. The property has several beautiful old Banyan trees that were planted by Edison in the 1920s to obtain latex rubber.

Nearby the Edison-Ford Estate site, you'll find the **Edison Park Historic District**, which has some of Fort Myers's most stately homes. From here, you can take a pleasant drive off 41 on **McGregor Boulevard** which runs south all the way to **Fort Myers Beach**. This community contained a number of older homes and small businesses, but it was all but wiped out by a direct hit from Hurricane Ian. Two years after the storm, some properties had been fully rebuilt while others were still in need of repair. Hurricanes Helene and Milton in 2024 did not cause the massive damage that occurred with Ian, but they flooded the homes and streets of many storm-weary residents. Some people may decide to leave the area rather than risk another catastrophic storm.

LEHIGH ACRES

Slightly to the east of Highway 41 as it traverses Fort Myers, **Lehigh Acres** is another census-designated place that has gone through booms and busts. This is not a tourist destination. Built on a former cattle ranch, Lehigh Acres is currently one of the fastest-growing communities in Lee County. By 2050, this ninety-six-square-mile residential community is predicted to have a population of 350,000. It is a sprawling community of retirees and working families, with a growing Hispanic population. It is currently comprised of mostly quarter- and half-acre single-family lots. There is no dedicated downtown, just retail commercial corridors and mixed-use centers. We have talked about places in Florida that still have some of the vestiges of "Old Florida." Lehigh Acres is what Florida is now, and it may well be a blueprint for the future.

ALICO ROAD CORRIDOR

South of Fort Myers, the highway makes its way through more housing projects and the CDP of **San Carlos Park**. Along the road you'll pass **41 Bistro**, an Italian restaurant that opened in 2023 proclaiming to be "your cozy retreat for delightful family meals and shared moments." Additionally, you will pass by **Matt's Red Hots**, a local favorite with hand-cut fries and a sign that boasts that the stand sells Sahlen's Hot Dogs (from Buffalo, New York) and Royal Scoop Ice Cream (from Bonita Springs).

The area around **Alico Road**, once a gravel thoroughfare, has been clear-cut for more development of shopping plazas, apartment complexes, and large warehouses. The auto company Tesla and the retail giant Amazon have built facilities along this corridor in anticipation of exponential local growth. **Florida Gulf Coast University** also lies along this route. It was established in 1991 to provide a state university for the swelling population of southwest Florida.

ESTERO

As the highway continues south, it enters **Estero**, an incorporated village in Lee County. The village has a few things of note for travelers. **Estero Bay Preserve State Park** is an undeveloped wetland along the Gulf Coast. It is accessible by land and boat from Fort Myers and Estero. The park contains hiking trails that allow you to see the scrubland near the Estero River, which is part of the Great Florida Birding Trail. If you go, wear good hiking shoes, bring insect repellent, and carry plenty of water. Kayaking the area is well worth doing to see the mangrove trees and aquatic wildlife.

Within the Estero Bay Preserve is the island of **Mound Key**. It is only accessible by boat, and there are no facilities. Mound Key was a ceremonial center for the ancient Calusa, and researchers believe it to have been the site of Calos, capital of the kingdom. You can hike the trails around the island to see the large shell mounds left by the Calusa.

Right off the highway is **Koreshan State Park**. The park has beautiful scenery, hiking trails, picnic areas, and campgrounds. The park also has a unique history. It was the settlement for the Koreshan Unity, a cult faith established in 1893 by Cyrus Teed. It was based on the ideals of celibacy, a belief in reincarnation, and the promise of immortality, at least for the cult's leader. Teed preached that women were slaves in their marriages and needed to be liberated through celibacy, so men and women occupied separate living quarters. New recruits were required to turn over all their worldly possessions to the community. Teed told his followers that ten million true believers would come to Estero. From the "1939 Florida guidebook" there is this nugget:

"Because Teed had convinced his followers that he was immortal, on his death his body was placed on a cypress plank and laid on the banks of the Estero River. For several weeks his disciples awaited a triumphal reincarnation. It finally became necessary to place the remains in a bathtub. Soon a hurricane swept the bathtub away, and no trace of it or the body was ever found. The plank, however, was found unmoved on the spot where it had served as a bier, and this was enough to restore the faith of the sect."

Teed died in 1908, after which sect numbers began to decline. The final member of the cult deeded the land to the state of Florida in 1961. The park is a nice bit of public green space among all of the local housing developments.

BONITA SPRINGS

At the southern end of Lee County, you'll find the city of **Bonita Springs**. It still conveys a bit of "Old Florida" (at least for now). Leave the Tamiami Trail and take the turn onto Old 41 Road, which routes you into the downtown historic area. When I visited, I had lunch at **Old 41 Restaurant**, a popular family-owned diner that serves "truly home cooked food," as they say on the menu.

Across the street from the restaurant was—you guessed it! —a residential development called **Bonita Isles**. A couple miles down the road, though, you'll run across **Everglades Wonder Gardens**, a "botanical jungle" opened in 1936, which makes it one of the oldest roadside attractions remaining in Florida. After three generations of private ownership, the gardens were purchased by a nonprofit entity in conjunction with the city of Bonita Springs to preserve this piece of old Florida tourism.

Riverside Park in downtown Bonita Springs is a small but pleasant park with a bandshell and some walking paths. Take a look at the old Atlantic Coastline railroad tracks behind the park. Bonita Springs has an active historical society "with its mission to record, preserve and promote its history."

Wonder Gardens, Bonita Springs, FL

Continue on Old 41 south, which will connect you back to the Tamiami Trail and take you into Collier County.

Bonita Springs, FL

Bonita Springs, FL

COLLIER COUNTY

Similar to Lee County, the population of Collier County has grown exponentially. The population was 38,000 in 1970, 254,000 in 2000, 315,000 in 2010, and 419,000 in 2024. The largest county in Florida by land area, a large chunk of that land lying within is **Big Cypress National Preserve**. Collier is the second-wealthiest county in Florida, after Monroe County, which includes the Florida Keys. It is also the 14th wealthiest county in the United States, with huge homes and growing development. As of 2024, the most expensive home in the United States was selling in the Port Royal section of Naples. The price tag? $295 million.

NORTH NAPLES

The Tamiami Trail enters the Naples Metro area through the unincorporated communities of **North Naples**, which includes Naples Park, Pelican Bay, and Pine Ridge. Beautiful shrubs and flowers line the road. Lots of high-rise condominium and upscale housing developments are located in the area. Unless you know someone who lives there, or who is staying at the **Ritz Carlton** or playing golf at one of the area courses, you are continuing on to Naples.

NAPLES

Continuing into the city of **Naples** on the Tamiami Trail will bring you into an area of massive homes near the Gulf Coast. The median home price in the city is $800k. The beach is beautiful and spacious, and it is likely you have plenty of money if you happen to live there. Naples is the self-proclaimed "Golf Capital of the World," with ninety-one eighteen-hole courses, thirty of which are open to the public.

Downtown Naples, also referred to as "Old Naples," boasts high-end art galleries, shopping opportunities, and fine-dining establishments. The community landmark, **Naples Fishing Pier**, was first built in 1888 as a point for transport for freight and baggage. The iconic pier was damaged by hurricanes in 1910, 1926, 1960, and 2022. At the time of my visit, it was closed for repairs due to Hurricane Ian. Money was appropriated to rebuild the pier in late 2024.

I stopped at the Naples Historical Society, located in **Palm Cottage** near the pier. Built in 1895 as the home of Walter Haldeman, the publisher of the *Louisville Courier-Journal* and one of the city's first settlers, the cottage lies within Naples' Historical District. Haldeman paid $50,000 in 1890 for the 8,000 acres that comprised the fishing pier, a large hotel, and the land surrounding these structures. Palm Cottage is the oldest house in Naples, and it has a colorful history.

Among the previous owners were Alexandra and Laurence Brown, who purchased the house in 1944. The Browns entertained lavishly, hosting Hollywood film stars and other notables along with neighbors. They would hoist a flag on the front porch to signify that cocktails would soon be served. Though childless, the couple would attend PTA meetings with their dogs and a portable bar in tow. Larry Brown raised cocks for fighting, and Alexandra provided free piano lessons to any child who wished to learn. Larry died in 1961, and Alexandra lived in the home until her death in 1978. The Collier County Historical Society purchased the Brown's home for $100k in 1979. We were told during the home tour that the property next to Palm Cottage, a small house on land valued at over $4 million, was acquired by the Historical Society to assure a massive home, which would have detracted from the Palm Cottage, would not be put up on the valuable property.

The Royal Harbor/Naples Bay area has a number of high-rise condominiums lining the waterfront. Near the bay and the Gordon River is the shopping district of **Tin City**, which includes lots of little touristy shops and seafood restaurants. I ate at **Kelly's Fish House Dining Room**, in business since 1952, and the oldest seafood restaurant in Naples. Lots of knotty pine and nautical memorabilia grace the restaurant.

After your meal (or before it), wander across the parking lot to check out **Kelly's Shell Shack** for interesting shell souvenirs. Florida used to boast many of these "souvenir shops," and I was glad to see this one continuing to operate although I was the only customer in the store at the time. I also want to provide a shout out to **Fernweh Ice Cream**, which offers homemade ice cream. I enjoyed a delicious root beer float there. **Turco Taco**, which serves gourmet tacos, also deserves kudos. **Bistro La Baguette** is a cute French-owned bistro on the Tamiami Trail.

Before leaving the discussion of this community, it is important to recognize the **Naples Swamp Buggy Races**, an ongoing tradition for seventy-five years. It operates at the **Florida Sports Park-Reception Pavilion** on the outskirts of Naples. It is a nod to Old Florida.

Naples, FL

Kelly's Shell Shack, Naples, FL

NAPLES AFFORDABILITY

In conversation with some residents and through a little research of my own, I was able to see one big problem that currently afflicts Naples and Collier County: due to the area's affluence, it is becoming unaffordable for middle- and lower-income people to live there. Home prices and rents are quite high and becoming higher as population growth triggers more demand. Widening wage gaps are forcing working people to commute to jobs in the county from communities increasingly farther away. Left unaddressed, this will create shortages of essential workers that will not be easily solved by technology.

NAPLES OUTSKIRTS & MARCO ISLAND

From Naples, the Tamiami Trail runs through **East Naples**, the Collier County seat, which contains yet more gated communities. But if you take Collier Boulevard south from Highway 41, you'll soon find yourself in **Marco Island**, an affluent beach community that sports a number of resort hotels. Marco Island is the largest of the **Ten Thousand Islands**, most of which are uninhabited, protected mangrove and marsh habitats on the Florida coast.

Marco Island was developed in the 1960s by the Mackle Brothers of the Deltona Corporation, who purchased the land with the vision of building many homes using the same techniques they had perfected in their other large Florida developments. Litigation brought by environmental groups, the U.S. Corps of Engineers, and the State of Florida against the firm limited what land could be utilized and classified a number of areas environmentally sensitive. This led to a 1982 settlement that restricted development on Marco Island but granted the right to build on vacant lands to the north. This may lead to the creation of many future developments, which could double the number of Collier County residents.

THE SWAMP–NAPLES TO MIAMI
COLLIER-SEMINOLE STATE PARK

Beyond Marco Island and some sixteen miles outside of Naples, **Big Cypress Swamp** begins. The 7,271-acre **Collier-Seminole State Park**, opened in 1947, is the first stop east on our journey through the Big Cypress/Everglades region. The park lies partly within one of the largest mangrove swamps in the world. The parkland was originally owned by Barron Collier who wanted the federal government to establish a national park there, but it was designated a state park instead. The park features a royal palm hammock, a tropical hardwood forest that is one of the few original stands of the trees in Florida. Other vegetation includes a variety of ferns, native plants, and salt marshes. Endangered wildlife inhabits the area, including alligators, birds of all types (I wish I had brought my binoculars), Florida panthers, tortoises, manatees, squirrels, and black bears. Did I mention mosquitos? Plan on using bug repellant, as the mosquitos can be quite intense. The park is also the site of a National Historic Mechanical Engineering Landmark, the last existing **Bay City Walking Dredge**. Built in 1924, it is a huge contraption that was used to build the Tamiami Trail Highway (U.S. 41) through Big Cypress Swamp and the Everglades.

At one end of the park is the **Barron Collier Memorial**. It is decorated with marble columns that frame a bronze bust of Barron Collier. It's a little weird to see this formal memorial in a wilderness park. Inscribed on the pedestal is the following:

TO THE MEMORY OF THE FOUNDER AND
FATHER OF COLLIER COUNTY FLORIDA AND
THE FAITHFUL FRIEND OF ALL MANKIND
ERECTED JAN. 1, 1941
BY
COLLIER COUNTY, FLA.

VIGNETTE BARRON COLLIER & THE TAMIAMI TRAIL

Barron Collier (1873–1939), the namesake of Collier County, was a Memphis, Tennessee-born entrepreneur who started his own advertising business and became a millionaire by age twenty-six. He was involved in numerous business ventures by the time he came to southwest Florida in 1911 and started buying land; he ultimately acquired 1.25 million acres stretching from the Gulf of Mexico to the Everglades, the largest private landholding in the state.

At first, Collier appeared to want nothing but to enjoy his lodge and fishing retreat. But a few years later, in 1915, the state started talking seriously about building a 264-mile-long road from Tampa to Miami. The idea came out of a meeting of the minds between the head of the Fort Myers Chamber of Commerce, Francis Perry, and the Dade County Tax Collector, Captain J.F. Jaudon, who completed surveys of the route. Jaudon, who ramped up enthusiasm for the phrase "Tamiami Trail," invested thousands of dollars of his own money to fund the building of sections of the road westward from Dade County. Construction began in 1917, but it proceeded slowly until 1923. The road took thirteen years to complete and cost $8 million (about $112 million in 2023 dollars).

The Tamiami Trail was an extremely laborious, expensive project. Over 2,000 workers carved, blasted, shoveled, and scraped their way along the designated route. Much of the work was done by African American convicts laboring on chain gangs. Convict leasing, as it was known, was a system where prisoner laborers were rented out to private entities and industries. Convicts worked long days clearing out tropical landscapes and laying roads in hellish temperatures without adequate food, water, or shelter.

The longest and toughest stretch of the Tamiami Trail—the seventy-six miles across the Everglades from Naples to the Miami-Dade County line—took three years to complete. The limestone bedrock was deep and the conditions sweltering. There was a big turnover in the non-convict workforce because the work was so hard, and the mosquitos were a constant menace. Chain gangs and Seminole workers used two-handed saws and machetes to clear the right-of-way for the Tamiami Trail. As many as 2.6 million sticks of dynamite were hauled in on oxcarts and then carried by men on foot through the swamp water to blast through the rock. The project ran out of money multiple times.

In 1923, Barron Collier provided crucial funding to the state of Florida to complete the project. In exchange for his funding the trail, a new county was carved out of Lee County and named after him. Thus, Collier County in Southwest Florida was establ-

ished. *Internal arguments between those who favored a coastal route and supporters of an inland route caused rifts among the planners. Eventually, the Tamiami Trail was declared to be "complete," and the grand opening took place on April 25, 1928. Building the trail literally paved the way for the South Florida of today, for better or worse. While the road was important to the economic development of the area, it also created an environmental disaster that has taken years to fix. The road cut off the natural flow of water through the Everglades, necessitating the need for extensive bridging to correct the problem. A series of culverts and tunnels have also been built that allow water to flow under the road.*

In 1950, Highway 41 was extended east to Miami via the Tamiami Trail. In 1968, "Alligator Alley," formally known as Everglades Parkway, was completed across the Everglades twenty-five miles north of the Tamiami Trail. It started as a two-lane toll road that was poorly planned. Eventually, in the 1980s, "Alligator Alley" was widened to four lanes and designated Interstate 75. Bridges were installed to allow water and wildlife to flow under the roadway. Today, I-75 is the main road across the state, and the Tamiami Trail functions as a secondary highway.

Barron Collier had many interests. He was involved with the national Boy Scouts and, while serving in New York state as the special deputy commissioner for public safety, he introduced the use of white and yellow traffic divider lines on highways. Collier was a close personal friend of both President Franklin Delano Roosevelt and financier J.P. Morgan. His descendants have holdings in numerous companies as well as in real estate development. The Collier family is among America's wealthiest, with a net worth of $2.3 billion as of 2021.

After Collier County was created and named, Collier was quoted as saying, "When I first came here on holiday with Juliet, I never expected that I would buy a whole region of it, nor did I expect to pay for the new Tamiami Trail, or half the things I've done. But I really didn't expect to have a whole county named after me."

TEN THOUSAND ISLAND NATIONAL WILDLIFE REFUGE

One of the great things about the Tamiami Trail is the ability to turn off the road easily to explore places of interest. I stopped at the **Ten Thousand Island National Wildlife Refuge** to walk some of the trail through the marsh and mangrove clusters where visitors can observe birds of all types. Within just a short distance from the highway you will feel like you are in a different world.

Collier-Seminole State Park, Naples, FL

Ten Thousand Islands National Wildlife Refuge, Collier County, FL

BIG CYPRESS BEND BOARDWALK

If possible, stop at the **Big Cypress Bend Boardwalk**, which is just off the highway. It is another free place to walk on a boardwalk that brings you into all of the wilderness that is the Everglades. The trail has facilities for the traveler, such as areas to sit and restrooms. You will find it within **Fakahatchee Strand Preserve State Park**, the largest state park in Florida. It has been called the "Amazon of North America."

EVERGLADES CITY

The Tamiami Trail continues east to **Carnestown**, an uninhabited junction where State Road 29 will take you south five miles to tiny **Everglades City**. It should definitely be a stop on your journey through the area. Everglades City inhabitants date back 1,000 years to the Calusa and later the Seminole. Starting in the 1890s, a trading post was operated there by pioneering landowner George Storter Jr. He also started to entertain early northern tourists coming to the region to hunt and fish.

Barron Collier bought the town in 1922 as headquarters for the building of the Tamiami Trail. He converted the trading post into the **Rod and Gun Club**, which he operated as a private club that grew famous for its surrounding fishing opportunities. The club's distinguished guests have included U.S. presidents. It still operates today with guest rooms and an interesting restaurant. When I visited, the restaurant was open but vacant, with only me to take in the large collection of memorabilia covering the walls and the eatery's old jukebox, which looked like it was last updated in the mid-1960s.

Down the street from the Rod and Gun Club is the **Bank of Everglades** building, which dates from 1927 and is on the National Register of Historic Places. It looked to be under renovation when I visited. A block away is the **Old Collier County Courthouse**, built in 1926. It is now Everglades City Hall. A plaque by the building is inscribed:

BARRON G. COLLIER
FOUNDER OF COLLIER COUNTY
ADMIRED FOR TALENTS
ESTEEMED FOR VISION
BELOVED FOR KINDNESS
TO WHOM THE NATION OWES THE TAMIAMI TRAIL
TO COMMEMORATE THE OPENING OF THE TRAIL
APRIL 25, 1928

Everglades City boasts residential homes on stilts, as befits an area right on the waterfront. The **Old Railroad Depot** is closed, but a banner on the station indicated there was a campaign to try to save it. After the railroad was torn out in 1959, the old depot was converted into a restaurant, which is now abandoned. In 1957, the station was featured in the movie *Wind Across the Everglades*, starring Burl Ives and Gypsy Rose Lee.

Down the street is the **Right Choice Supermarket Plaza**, a much-loved little local food market next to the **Everglades Community Church**. The church was founded in 1926, and Everglades City has declared the church building, which dates from 1940, a historic structure "because it provides links with the aspirations and attainments of the City's pioneers and their descendants."

Bank of Everglades, Everglades City, FL

OCHOPEE

Continuing east on the Trail through the Big Cypress Preserve, you will come to the **Nathaniel P. Reid Visitor Center**. It has public washrooms and another boardwalk to take in the swamp. A little farther down the road is **Ochopee** (pop. 129), an unincorporated village in an area once known for tomato farming. Right off the Trail is the **Ochopee Post Office**, the smallest post office in the United States. Once a storage shed to house mail, today it's a one-person building that is a must-stop for every tourist who wants a photo and for every stamp collector who wants an Ochopee postmark. While I was visiting with the postmaster, a film crew from Europe was setting up a shot to broadcast.

Old Rail Depot, Everglades City, FL

Smallest Post Office, Ochopee, FL

Smallest Post Office, Ochopee, FL

Joanie's Blue Crab Café is located just down the road from the post office, and it lives up to the motto on its sign: "Good Food, Cold Beer." The 1920s-era building was originally a cattle barn that converted to a restaurant in 1987. Check out the slogan over the bar: "If you want fast-food, keep traveling, forty-two miles west or sixty-six miles east. Happy Trails ya'll. Watch out for Gators!"

The waitstaff is super-friendly, and the restaurant has all kinds of memorabilia and postcards from all over the world on the walls. There is no doubt you will want to make a stop and eat at Joanie's! Next to the café is an old filling station that's said to be the first concrete block building in Collier County.

In a couple more miles, the Tamiami Trail brings you to a statue of a **Florida Panther**, the state animal. It stands in front of **Shealy's Skunk Ape Research Headquarters**, which claims it was established in 1961. It's a campground, a general store, and a souvenir stand. You know you're there when you see the big plastic skunk ape in front. The skunk ape is Florida's version of Bigfoot. It is a mythical, human-like creature that lives in the swamps and stinks badly!

Just a few more miles down the Trail will bring you to **HP Williams Roadside Park**, named for one of the engineers who worked with Barron Collier on the Tamiami Trail. It was designated a state park in 1965 and features parking, a restroom, and a picnic area. The main reason for the stop, though, is that you will most likely see some alligators along the **Turner River Canal**. If you have not seen some alligators already at other roadside stops, this is a place to see them safely, and at reasonably close range.

Joanie's Blue Crab Café, Ochopee, FL

Alligators first appeared during the late Eocene epoch about thirty-seven million years ago. The name *alligator* is likely an anglicized form of "El lagarto," the Spanish term for "the lizard," which is what early Spanish explorers and settlers in Florida called the alligator. These large reptiles can live forty to sixty years in the wild and are very cool to see in their natural habitat. Mostly, they sun themselves on the water bank. I am convinced that alligators will long outlive humans!

A few more miles on the Trail brings you to **Kirby Storter Roadside Park**, designated as a state park in 1971. Named for another engineer who worked on the last stretch of road across the swamp, the park has a nice long boardwalk that enables you to walk out into the cypress swamp. I did not see alligators here, but I observed quite a few birds in this altogether lovely location.

Back on the Tamiami Trail, in a few miles you'll arrive at **Clyde Butcher Big Cypress Gallery**, which features truly stunning black and white photos of Florida nature and other natural landscapes for sale. Take a walk around the gallery to admire the photos. They also sell postcards of the photos if the price point for the larger prints seems a bit too high for you. Out in back of the gallery is a little nature walk that quickly puts you into the tropical woods.

The Tamiami Trail is part of the **Florida National Scenic Trail**, which stretches 1,400 miles across Florida, from **Gulf Islands National Seashore** to **Big Cypress National Preserve**. Several roads off the Trail allow you to travel farther inland within the Big Cypress preserve. All along this part of the Trail are campgrounds where you'll see a large array of tents and RVs.

Alligators at HP Williams Roadside Park, Everglades, FL

DADE-COLLIER TRAINING AND TRANSITION AIRPORT

In the middle of your drive through this isolated, very beautiful part of Florida, is a road turnoff for the **Dade-Collier Training and Transition Airport**. Constructed in 1968, it is a single runway for what was supposed to be a giant airport for supersonic jets serving Miami—fifty miles to the east. The planned airport ran into significant environmental concerns, and the planned Boeing 2707 supersonic jets never went beyond prototypes due to cost overruns and the lack of a clearly defined market. Such an airport situated in this protected natural area could have potentially destroyed the Everglades. The plug was pulled on further construction in 1970. The runway today serves as a place for commercial flight training and occasional military flights. There are no aircraft based at the site.

Author's Note: In June, 2025 construction began on the site for a migrant detention center. Nicknamed "Alligator Alcatraz" the site will be used to hold migrants prior to deportation to outside of the United States. Outside observers, including the author, believe the facility has all the earmarks of being a concentration camp. Time will tell how it evolves.

MIAMI-DADE COUNTY

The Tamiami Trail crosses from Collier County eastward into Miami-Dade County, the largest county in Florida and the seventh-most populous county in the United States. Its population was 1,267,000 in 1970, 2,253,000 in 2000, 2,496,000 in 2010 and 2,700,000 in 2024. The Trail runs through the vast sprawling nature preserve called **Everglades and Francis S. Taylor Wildlife Management Area** on the north side of the road and **Everglades National Park** on the south. Beyond the Everglades (approximately twenty miles) is the vast Miami metropolitan area, which is home to 6.14 million people.

MICCOSUKEE INDIAN VILLAGE

Along this part of the Trail is the **Miccosukee Indian Village**. The village—a tribal-run cultural center—has a statue of a Miccosukee wrestling an alligator as you enter the parking area. Inside is a village history museum where you can learn more about the Miccosukee culture, a gift shop with Indigenous crafts, and a theater to watch dancing and listen to music. An outdoor replica village and an alligator demonstration area are on the grounds, as well as an alligator sanctuary. You can take an airboat tour with an Indigenous guide into the Everglades to the secluded "tree islands" deep within the swamps that housed the Miccosukee for generations.

Miccosukee Indian Village, Everglades, FL

VIGNETTE   THE MICCOSUKEE TRIBE

The Miccosukee tribe has approximately 600 members, but what they lack in population they make up for in influence over Everglades rehabilitation efforts and recent prosperity. The tribe has a historical relationship with the Choctaw and is one of three federally recognized Seminole tribes in the state of Florida. During the Seminole wars of the 1800s, some 100 Miccosukee hid out in the Everglades and eluded capture by the U.S. Army. The present tribal members are direct descendants of that small band. They lived within small camps spread throughout the Everglades that are now used as sites for ceremonies.

Until the Tamiami Trail was built, the Miccosukee were virtually unknown to the outside world. With the opening of the Trail in 1928, they built new villages along the roadway to sell crafts, offer boat tours, and develop tourist attractions. The advent of casino gambling in 1999 has changed that, and the tribe has become quite prosperous. At the edge of the Florida Everglades is the nine-story Miccosukee Casino & Resort— one of the pioneer gambling operations in South Florida.

An interesting story surrounds the United States federal recognition of the Miccosukee. Buffalo Tiger, a tribal elder, went with a group to Cuba in 1959 where the tribe asked for recognition from Fidel Castro as a sovereign country within the United States. To forestall potential issues during the Cold War, the United States government quickly recognized the Miccosukee in January 1962. This legally established the Miccosukee's existence within the nation and the state of Florida.

TIPPY'S OUTPOST

How can I adequately describe the iconic Tippy's Outpost, just a few miles southeast of the Collier County line? It is a cool, family-owned market that offers provisions for sale as well as educational airboat rides into the swamp.

According to Tippy's website:

"Tippy's is more than just a store, it's a local landmark and part of the community. It's a place where locals and travelers can feel welcome, shop, sightsee, and chat with one another. While we have always tailored our selection to meet local needs, we carry nearly any item needed at home, outdoors, or on the road. All structures were hand-built locally utilizing centuries-old construction methods of palm leaves and Cypress logs.

Local alligator wrestler 'Tippy' as he was known, envisioned a community market located between the two areas of residences on the reservation off US 41. Our founder lived right across the street, raising alligators as well as live bait and fresh produce, to be later sold at market. Our founder and his wife ran the store together for many years, gaining a following with the local community and travelers alike."

SHARK VALLEY

On the other side of the Trail from the tribal village is **Shark Valley Visitor Center**. You can take a tram, walk, or bike along a paved road to the **Shark Valley Observation Tower** viewing platform, the highest point in Everglades National Park. **Otter Cave Hammock Trail** is a rough limestone path that passes over small streams and through a tropical hardwood forest.

Author's Note: This is a VERY popular tourist stop, and parking is exceedingly limited. It's best to avoid weekends and try to go early in the day.

FLIGHT 592 MEMORIAL

A few miles east of the village on the Trail, you'll notice there are several pullovers advertising airboat tours of the area. At the pullover for **Everglades Nature Tours** and RV park is a grim memorial: the **ValuJet 592 Memorial**. On May 11, 1996, Flight 592 crashed in the Everglades, claiming the lives of 110 people, including all of the passengers and crew. The cause of the crash was due to expired oxygen generators that were improperly carried in the cargo hold. The memorial was built in 1999 for the third anniversary of the crash.

The airline had a poor safety record before the crash, and the accident brought widespread attention to its problems. ValuJet's fleet was grounded for several months after the crash. When operations resumed, the airline was unable to attract as many customers as it had before the accident. It acquired AirTran Airways in 1997, and the lingering damage to the ValuJet brand led its executives to assume the AirTran name. Air Tran was absorbed by Southwest Airlines in 2014. The demise of flight 592 remains the deadliest plane crash in Florida history.

Flight 592 Memorial, Everglades, FL

COOPERTOWN THE ORIGINAL AIRBOAT TOUR

Unless you have already done so with one of the many operators along the Trail, take in an airboat tour at **Coopertown the Original Airboat Tour**. In business for seventy-five years, the Coopertown Airboat Tour is rated "Florida's Best" by the *Miami Herald*. I took the tour into the **Everglades National Park** and can say that it is well worth doing. Airboats can be noisy, and it was great to be provided with ear protection. The guide knew where the alligators were along the route so passengers could take pictures. The guide also slowed down or stopped the craft so that we could see herons, frogs, and turtles as well. I thought the best part was simply the ride into the trackless "river of grass" that is the Everglades. It is a spiritual experience. The adjoining **Coopertown Restaurant** is an Old Florida eatery where you can sample frog legs, gator tail, and key lime pie.

Everglades, FL

VIGNETTE ERNEST F. COE AND MARJORY STONEMAN DOUGLAS

Before moving on from the Everglades, it is important to note the two people who may have been most responsible for preserving this irreplaceable natural treasure.

Ernest F. Coe (1866–1951) was a professional gardener from Connecticut who did not see the Everglades until he was sixty years old. Upon seeing these wetlands, he was both fascinated by their unique beauty and appalled at the destruction of plants, animals, and natural water flow in the name of progress and prosperity. From then on, he made it his life's goal to protect the Everglades by setting up a national park. He viewed his own efforts as a failure, as he was unable to gain full buy-in from government officials for the entire breadth of the Everglades, but he lived long enough to see the Everglades officially become a national park in 1947. Coe is considered the Father of Everglades National Park.

*Marjory Stoneman Douglas (1890–1998) was a journalist for the Miami Herald, an acclaimed author, a women's suffrage advocate, and a conservationist who spent much of her life in defense of the Everglades. Her book The Everglades: River of Grass, published in 1947, helped convince people that the Everglades was a special place and worth preserving. She lived to the age of 108, working until nearly the end of her life for Everglades restoration. In a sad postscript, **Marjory Stoneman Douglas High School**, named for her in the Miami suburb of Parkland just a couple miles from Everglades National Park, was the scene of a deadly mass shooting in February 2018, perpetrated by a nineteen-year-old former student in which seventeen people were murdered and seventeen others injured.*

COMPREHENSIVE EVERGLADES RESTORATION PLAN (CERP)

The CERP, authorized by Congress in 2000, is a massive water management project conducted by the U.S. Army Corps of Engineers to "restore, preserve, and protect the south Florida ecosystem while providing for other water-related needs of the region, including water supply and flood protection." At a cost of more than $10.5 billion and with a 35+ year timeline, the CERP is the largest hydrologic restoration project ever undertaken in the United States. A unique Federal/State partnership guides the interagency plan. The South Florida Natural Resources Center (SFNRC) has a critical role to play in this partnership by ensuring that the mission of the National Park Service—to protect park resources unimpaired for future generations—remains at the forefront of CERP decision making. The project will improve the Central and Southern Everglades by routing more fresh, clean water into the River of Grass.

MICCOSUKEE CASINO & RESORT

If you drive some five more miles east on the Tamiami Trail from the Coopertown Original Airboat Tours, the road will bring you to the **Miccosukee Casino & Resort**. The casino includes the usual video slot machines and gaming tables. A painting over the resort's front desk highlights the long Miccosukee association with the Everglades. Back on the Trail heading east, you'll soon find yourself traveling into the West End and the Miami Metro area.

WEST END/TAMIAMI

The **West End** is a collection of unincorporated communities in suburban western Miami-Dade County. **Tamiami**, adjacent to Highway 41, is one of them. Very quickly, the culture changes from that of the Everglades' Indigenous peoples to **Latine**—i.e., the culture of Spanish-speaking people originally from Latin America. Along the road is the restaurant **El Palacio de los Jugos**, a family run place since 1977 that "takes pride in preparing traditional home-cooked Cuban recipes and the freshest tropical juices that taste just like abuelita's [Grandma's] cooking, bringing you back to your nostalgic roots," according to its website. I had a tropical fruit juice that was quite tasty on my stop. Note that there are several other locations of this restaurant chain within the greater Miami area.

UNIVERSITY PARK/FLORIDA INTERNATIONAL UNIVERSITY

Continuing on the Trail takes you to the census-designated place of **University Park**, home to **Florida International University** (enrollment 48,624 in 2024), a public research university that has only been open since 1972. FIU is now the third-largest university in Florida and the eighth-largest public university in the United States by enrollment.

WESTCHESTER/PALMETTO EXPRESSWAY

Back on the Trail, you'll pass through the **Westchester** CDP, driving by some office buildings and **New Life Plastic Surgery** on the way. According to its website, this medical practice offers plastic surgery procedures including Brazilian butt lift, liposuction, and breast augmentation. Miami is a popular destination for affordable cosmetic surgery, with a number of clinics and renowned surgeons practicing in the city. Continue under the heavily used **Palmetto Expressway** (State Road 826), where you'll see a sign that says "Bienvenidos, A La 'Calle Ocho'" (Eighth Street).

Before you enter Coral Gables on the Tamiami Trail, you'll pass through the small city of **West Miami**. The view from the road includes modest office buildings, modest homes, a motel and trailer park, some ethnic restaurants, dry cleaners, supermarkets, and photo studios. None of this prepares you for what you are about to encounter.

CORAL GABLES

Turning south on State Road 959 will bring you into **Coral Gables**, a very affluent and glamorous city with many beautiful homes. It adjoins Miami. Called the "City Beautiful" and "Garden City," it was planned and designed by George Merrick (1886–1942) as one of the first planned communities in the United States. Merrick started selling lots for it in 1921. He designed the city to have four entry arches: the Country Club Prado Entrance (the first you will encounter off Highway 41), the Granada Entrance, the Alhambra Entrance, and the Douglas Entrance.

The **Prado Entrance** at S.W. 8th Street and S.W. 57th Avenue (Red Road) is the setting for many wedding and special occasion photos. Two walkways with trellises and fountains run down the street with beautiful homes on both sides. The **Granada Entrance**, also located at S.W. 8th Street and 57th Avenue, is an arch entrance that spans Granada Boulevard. The boulevard takes you into the heart of Coral Gables. The **Alhambra Entrance Arch**, located at S.W. 37th Avenue (Douglas Road) and Alhambra Circle, leads into the main shopping area for the city. The **Douglas Entrance**, located at S.W. 8th Street (Tamiami Trail) and S.W. 37th Avenue (Douglas Road), is the main entrance to the City of Coral Gables and listed on the National Register of Historic Places. A forty-foot curved arch spans the roadway. The entrance once included a commercial and residential complex that is presently offices.

Coral Gables, FL

BILTMORE HOTEL

To the south of Country Club Prado is the **Biltmore Hotel**. Built in 1926, it is a Registered Historic Landmark and a tourist must-see. It has a beautiful lobby. If you are thinking of staying there, it is definitely a splurge. The Biltmore is also home to the legendary **Biltmore Golf Course**—an eighteen-hole, par seventy-one championship course originally designed in 1925 by architect Donald Ross. Check out the swimming pools—they are huge. You can have lunch overlooking the pools and feel like a mover and shaker.

Biltmore Hotel, Coral Gables, FL

Beyond the Hotel Biltmore is the **University of Miami**, a private research university. The school is quite well known and attracts students from around the world. Many people know the school for its division 1 NCAA sports teams. The football team has won five national championships since 1983. The baseball team has won four national championships since 1982. In 2023, the men's basketball team advanced to the Final Four for the first time in program history.

Back on the Tamiami Trail, as you travel through Coral Gables, you will see the **Graceland Memorial Park North Cemetery** "serving families since 1936." It has an Art Deco style mausoleum built in the 1930s.

ORIGINAL UNCLE TOM'S BARBECUE

Just before the Tamiami Trail exits Coral Gables and enters the City of Miami, you'll encounter **Original Uncle Tom's Barbecue**. The restaurant has been in operation since 1948 with reputedly the best BBQ sauce in a vintage location. It has an iconic sign that is hard to miss. The restaurant was closed when I stopped by and the online reviews for their signature BBQ baby back ribs, coleslaw, and fries are all over the place. Some love it and some hate it. BBQ aficionados can be tough to please!

MIAMI

Florida's best-known city and one of the most international of all U.S. cities is **Miami** (pop. 456,229), the seat of Miami-Dade County. Miami is where Highway 41 officially ends. The city is a business center, an entertainment center, a cultural center, and a tourist center. It is the unofficial capital of Latin America and ever evolving. Separating fact from the rich trove of fiction about the city is something only a visitor can do. Depending on your age, you very likely have a mental picture of the city based on one or more of the numerous television shows or movies broadcast in the last forty years. These programs include stereotypes of bikinis, speed boats, salsa dancing, nightclubs, cocaine sniffing, expensive cars, and private jet travel. Suffice to say that if you are a first-time visitor, it is a place that can be hard to get a handle on because of the incredible diversity—and also because you are probably stuck in traffic. Miami is one of the most congested cities in the world according to recent studies.

A big draw for the many visitors to Miami, particularly in the winter months, is the tropical climate. The region is warm and sunny when much of the United States and Canada is cold and gray. If you come in the spring and summer months, however, it is very hot and humid to the point of discomfort. Hurricane season for Miami lasts from June 1st through November 30th. Historically, the city had been hit by a major hurricane every six to eight years according to the weather data. Long-time residents can provide horror stories of the hurricanes they have lived through. With changing patterns of climate and the unprecedented storms that have taken place in the Gulf over the past couple years, it is likely that major storms will occur more frequently in the future.

Numerous visitors fly into **Miami International Airport**, one of the busiest airports in the country, and quickly head to the tourist locations of Miami Beach or the Florida Keys. This would be a mistake, as there is much to see in the city itself provided you have some time to spend. Some wonderful Cuban food as well as Mexican, Venezuelan, and Colombian cuisine can be had at large and small restaurants throughout the city. Miami boasts a wide variety of neighborhoods for a visitor to explore. A couple of my personal favorites are **Wynwood**, a hip area north of downtown Miami with huge, colorful street murals, art installations, restaurants and bars, and Coconut Grove, known to locals as "The Grove," along Biscayne Bay southwest of U.S. 1 (Dixie Highway). **Coconut Grove** is Miami's oldest neighborhood, with large trees, quiet residential streets, and high-end shopping in and around the CocoWalk mall. Lots of sailboats are moored along the coast, particularly around **Dinner Key**. **Miami City Hall** is in Dinner Key in a National Historic Register building that was once a Pan American Airlines terminal building constructed in 1934.

Wynwood Miami Heat mural, artist, Kyle Holbrook, Miami, FL

To the north of Coconut Grove on Biscayne Bay and less than a mile from Highway 41 is **Vizcaya Museum & Gardens**, a National Historic Landmark and a definite must-see. The museum was originally Villa Vizcaya, the estate of James Deering (1859–1925), scion of the Deering Harvester Company started by his father. This business eventually became International Harvester Corporation, the largest producer of agricultural machinery in the United States. The estate was built between 1914 and 1922 at a cost of $15 million ($265 million in 2024 dollars). Deering traveled extensively, and the art he collected on his journeys is displayed at the estate.

The museum also features extensive Italian Renaissance gardens complete with statues, ponds, lavish landscaping, and village outbuildings (including a casino). When it was a residence, guests to the estate arrived by boat at a sculpted stone barge in the Bay, designed by Alexander Calder. A spiral staircase, an interior garden, and a whole host of other displays are wonderful to see. Needless to say, many wedding and quinceaneras photo shoots were under way during my visit.

BACKGROUND

As you would expect, Miami has an interesting history. It is the only major city in the United States founded by a woman. Julia Tuttle (1849–1898) is famous for being the "Mother of Miami." She owned much of the land upon which the city was built. Through her efforts, a city that was "an impenetrable thicket" with a population of about 300 when incorporated in 1896, was able to lure industrialist Henry Flagler to extend his Florida East Coast Railway from Palm Beach to Miami. The city grew swiftly as more northerners moved south during the Florida land boom of the 1920s. A 1926 hurricane leveled much of the city, and the Great Depression descended on Miami not long afterward. During World War II, the city became a major military training ground.

When Fidel Castro came to power in Cuba in 1959, an exodus of over one million Cubans sought refuge in Miami-Dade County, permanently changing the demographics of the population. Further immigration from Haiti, Jamaica, and other parts of Latin America followed in the 1980s and 1990s. In 1980, the Mariel Exodus created major issues for the city when Castro allowed the release of 125,000 Cubans who descended *en masse* upon the Miami area. A number of the people released (estimated to be 20,000) came from Cuban jails and mental institutions, which contributed to a spike in Miami's crime and violence in the early 1980s. Another huge influx of migrants, (officially reported at more than a million people), fled Cuba between 2022 and 2023. These immigrants have come on foot through Mexico as well as by sea. Many of them settled in Miami. Next to El Paso, Texas, Miami is the second largest American city with a Spanish-speaking majority. While it is not mandatory for a tourist, it is helpful for residents to have a working knowledge of Spanish due to the large concentration of residents for whom Spanish is the primary language.

NAME

Miami was named after the Miami River, derived from Mayaimi, the historic name of Lake Okeechobee and the Indigenous peoples who lived around it.

NICKNAMES

Nicknames for Miami include the 305, (the original Miami area code), "Magic City," "Gateway to the Americas," "Gateway to Latin America," "Capital of Latin America," and "Vice City."

Wynwood neighborhood mural, Miami, FL

LITERATURE/MOVIES/TELEVISION

Miami and Miami Beach have amassed a rich trove of books, movies, and TV shows about them. If you have not read or seen one of these treatments, you owe it to yourself to do so.

Recent books set in Miami per *Read Your Way Through Miami* by Jonathan Escoffery, *The New York Times* April 5, 2023:

- **Continental Drift**, by Russell Banks, 1985
- **Black Miami in the Twentieth Century**, by Marvin Dunn, 1997
- **In Cuba I Was a German Shepherd**, by Ana Menéndez, 2001
- **Miami Noir**, edited by Les Standiford, 2006
- **How to Leave Hialeah**, by Jennine Capó Crucet, 2009
- **Garvey's Ghost**, by Geoffrey Philp, 2015
- **The Book of Luke: My Fight for Truth, Justice, and Liberty City,** by Luther Campbell, 2015
- **Ordinary Girls**, by Jaquira Díaz, 2019
- **Everything Inside**, by Edwidge Danticat, 2019
- **Of Women and Salt**, by Gabriela Garcia, 2021
- A personal favorite: **Miami**, by Joan Didion, 1987

Authors (This is a short list of authors who have used Miami as a setting for their books.):

- Dave Barry
- Edna Buchanan
- Lauren Groff
- Carl Hiaasen
- Elmore Leonard
- John D. MacDonald

Television (This is a very short list. In addition, many Spanish language television shows are shot in Miami for the Latin American market.):

- *Que Pasa, USA?*, 1977–1980
- *Miami Vice*, 1984–1990
- *Golden Girls*, 1985–1992
- *CSI: Miami*, 2002–2012
- *Nip/Tuck*, 2003–2010
- *Dexter*, 2006–2013
- *Burn Notice*, 2007–2013
- *Jane the Virgin*, 2014–2019
- *Ballers*, 2015–2019

Films (This is also a short list of films with a Miami setting.):

- *The Godfather Part Two, 1974*
- *Absence of Malice, 1981*
- *Scarface, 1983*
- *Ace Ventura, 1989*
- *True Lies, 1994*
- *Bad Boys, 1995*
- *The Birdcage, 1996*
- *Out of Sight, 1998*
- *There's Something About Mary, 1998*
- *Any Given Sunday, 1999*
- *2 Fast 2 Furious, 2003*
- *Bad Boys 2, 2003*
- *Moonlight, 2016*

PEOPLE

Miami has had its fair share of prominent figures. Here are a few:

- Henry Flagler (1830–1913): His companies constructed the **Port of Miami** between Biscayne Boulevard and 6th and 9th Streets.
- Alexander Orr (1877–1958): He was Miami's mayor from 1940 to 1941 and the man who protected Miami's water supply. A water treatment plant is named in his honor.
- John Pennekamp (1897–1978): A *Miami Herald* editor, his efforts contributed to the establishment of Everglades National Park.
- Claude Pepper (1900–1989): He served as a U.S. Senator from Florida from 1936 to 1951 and a Member of Congress from the Miami area in the U.S. House from 1963 to 1989. He was an important spokesman for the elderly.
- Reverend Theodore Gibson (1915–1982): He was a prominent Miami Civil Rights leader.
- Don Shula (1930–2020): He was the Hall of Fame Coach of the Miami Dolphins from 1970 to 1995.
- Maurice Ferré (1935–2019): This six-term mayor of Miami from 1973 to 1985 is often referred to as the "Father of modern-day Miami."
- Bob Graham (1936–2024): This Coral Gables native served as Florida's governor from 1979 to 1987 and as a U.S. Senator 1987 to 2005.

- Jorge Mas Canosa (1939–1997): This Cuban American businessman founded the Cuban American National Foundation and spearheaded efforts to isolate Fidel Castro.
- Xavier Suarez (b. 1949): He served as the first Cuban-born Mayor of Miami from 1985 to 1993 and again from 1997 to 1998.
- Gloria Estefan (b. 1957): A Cuban-born American singer, actress, and businesswoman, Estefan is also an eight-time Grammy Award winner and a Presidential Medal of Freedom recipient. She has been named one of the Top 100 greatest artists of all time by *Billboard Magazine*.

CELEBRITIES LIVING IN MIAMI

- Cher: Singer and Actor
- Dwayne Wade: Athlete
- Jennifer Lopez: Singer and Actor
- Julio Iglesias: Singer
- LeBron James: Athlete
- Madonna: Singer and Actor
- Matt Damon: Actor
- Pitbull: American rapper and singer songwriter
- Shakira: Singer
- Sylvester Stallone: Actor
- Tommy Hilfiger: Fashion Designer

HOUSING

Miami's downtown skyline is dotted with construction cranes as endless new condos and apartments are built throughout the city center and beyond. But much research suggests that the greater Miami area has an affordability crisis. Per Annie Lord, executive director of Miami Homes For All, "Miami-Dade is facing the largest affordability crisis in the country." Per a recent 2024 report by Creditnews Research, an independent research bureau, Miami is one of the least affordable housing markets in the United States for families looking to buy homes. The median listing price in 2024 for a Miami home was nearly $650,000, according to Zillow.

Remote and onsite workers alike are being drawn to Florida—and particularly to Miami—by a booming employment market. The city is a hotspot for multinational companies offering attractive job opportunities.

Meanwhile, Miami's 2.2 percent unemployment rate (2024) is considerably lower than the national figure. But, as we have seen with other places along our journey down Highway 41 regarding housing, people of average or below-average income are being priced out of home ownership.

MIAMI & CLIMATE CHANGE

More than half of Miami-Dade County is six feet above sea level or lower. By 2040, scientists predict that Miami will have sea levels anywhere from ten to seventeen inches higher than they were in 2000. Miami is considered "ground zero" as one of the most climate-change-threatened cities in the United States per Sonia Brubaker, chief resilience officer for the City of Miami. Ocean warming will bring increasingly intense hurricanes and storms to the city and could quite possibly turn some streets near Biscayne Bay into rushing rivers as a regular occurrence. Despite the extreme vulnerability to coastal inundation, people are still moving to the city.

BUSINESS

Top Companies Headquartered in Miami (2024):
- Baptist Health South Florida
- Lennar
- Carnival Cruise Line
- World Fuel Services
- Ryder System, Inc.
- Royal Caribbean Cruises Ltd.
- Burger King
- Costa Farms
- Norwegian Cruise Line
- REEF Technology, Inc.

SCHOOLS

- **University of Miami** (enrollment 19,500), a private university
- **Florida International University** (enrollment 49,500), a public university
- **Miami Dade College** (enrollment 46,000), a public community college

SPORTS TEAMS

- **Miami Heat** National Basketball Association team plays at the **Kaseya Center** in downtown Miami.
- **Miami Dolphins** National Football League team plays at **Hard Rock Stadium** in Miami Gardens.
- **Miami Marlins** Major League Baseball team plays at **LoanDepot Park** on the site of the former Miami Orange Bowl in Little Havana.
- **Florida Panthers** National Hockey League team plays at **Amerant Bank Arena** in Sunrise.
- **Club Internacional de Fútbol Miami (Miami CF)** Major League Soccer plays at **Chase Stadium** in Fort Lauderdale.

MIAMI NEIGHBORHOODS ALONG HIGHWAY 41
LITTLE HAVANA

Highway 41/Tamiami Trail is the main road through **Little Havana**, where it goes by the name of **"Calle Ocho,"** or, in English, "Eighth Street." The best-known Cuban exile neighborhood in the world, Calle Ocho is a definite must-see stop on the Highway 41 journey, and you need to spend time exploring all of the business and cultural activities of the neighborhood. It is on the list of National Trust for Historic Preservation endangered places due to development pressure, demolition of historic buildings, displacement of existing residents, and zoning changes that could impact its affordability, cultural richness, and character. See it now.

HISTORY

Before Little Havana was known as such, the neighborhood was home to a large Jewish population, who ultimately moved farther northwest into Miami-Dade County. The Jewish population gave way to Cuban immigrants, who settled in the area in ever larger numbers with each new influx creating a cascading effect for additional Cubans to move in. These displaced Cubans sought areas that were pedestrian friendly. The Riverside neighborhood, as it was then known, offered affordable real estate and a concentrated infrastructure of churches, hospitals, and entertainment venues. Many incoming Cubans took residence near Flagler Street and SW 12th Avenue a few blocks to the north and established the first shops and restaurants catering to the early Cuban exiles.

In the 1970s, Flagler Street gave way to Calle Ocho as the main commerce street. Today, Little Havana has become a conglomerate of various Latin American communities. Immigrants from the Caribbean, Central America, and South America all make Little Havana their home, causing a "mixing bowl" effect in the historic neighborhood.

Little Havana, Calle Ocho, Miami, FL

CALLE OCHO

The first thing to do on a visit to Calle Ocho should be to have a meal or pasteles (pastry) with a cup of Cuban coffee at **Versailles—The World's Most Famous Cuban Restaurant®**. This venerable restaurant has been serving Cuban cuisine and culture to the local and international community for over five decades. Soon after it opened its doors in 1971, Versailles became the gathering place and unofficial town square for Miami's Cuban exiles. With its uniquely French-inspired aesthetic, the iconic establishment is a community landmark and remains the unrelenting gauge of the city's diversifying pulse. A walk-up window for coffee has an interesting quote on one of the outside walls: "Sometimes Life closes a Door and opens a Ventanita." Cuban coffee is an acquired taste. If you have never experienced it before, prepare for a heavily sweetened espresso drink.

Versailles Restaurant, Miami, FL

Versailles Restaurant, Miami, FL

Sights along Calle Ocho from Versailles heading east include the **Santana Cigar** shop with its beautiful mural; **Pollo Campero**, a Guatemalan fast-food restaurant chain; and a building with a mural painted in the style of a place-name postcard that says, "Welcomes You to Little Havana." You will pass by a branch campus of **Miami Dade College**, which serves a higher number of minority students than any other college in the nation.

Along the road are colorful fiberglass statues of roosters. They are part of the local **Rooster Walk**, first created in 2002. The street vibe includes lots of little shops and murals as well as a big mural of Ricky Martin (b.1971), a Puerto Rican singer, songwriter, and actor.

You'll see several memorials to Cuban patriots, including those lost in the aborted 1961 Bay of Pigs invasion. An interesting, or maybe perplexing, quote on a building enthuses "Congratulations to Drugs for Winning the War on Drugs." A mural of a dancer graces the exterior of the **Sala'o Cuban Restaurant & Bar, The House of Daiquiri.** The **Little Havana Visitor Center** is usually packed with loads of tourists. **D' Asis Guayaberas**, open "since 1972," specializes in classic Cuban attire, particularly the iconic Guayabera shirts that serve as formal dress attire in the Caribbean. If you are lucky, the owner will be there to have a chat.

Little Havana, Calle Ocho, Miami, FL

The **Tower Theatre** on Calle Ocho, first opened in 1926, used to be an art house cinema owned by Miami Dade College. Now owned by the City of Miami, it is one of Miami's oldest cultural landmarks. On my visit, the theater had an exhibit devoted to **Úrsula Hilaria Celia de la Caridad Cruz Alfonso** (1925–2003), whose stage name was **Celia Cruz**. She was a Cuban singer and one of the most popular Latin artists of the twentieth century. Cruz rose to fame in Cuba during the 1950s as a singer of *guaracha*, a lively genre of music and dance. Her performances earned her the nickname "La Guarachera de Cuba."

Walk across the street to check out **Maximo Gomez Park**, known by most as **Domino Park** because a group of regulars plays dominoes here all day, every day. Games are for members of the Maximo Gómez Domino Club only, so don't plan on playing! Still, the spirited games are lots of fun to watch. The small park features walkways of domino-decorated tilework, and a perimeter lined with benches for spectators. You can't miss the painted (and peeling) mural that serves as the backdrop for this popular hangout. Created by Dominican artist Oscar Thomas, the mural depicts the presidents of all the nations that attended the 1st Summit of the Americas, which was held in Miami in December 1994.

On the sidewalk near the park, you'll find the **Calle Ocho Walk of Fame**. Reminiscent of the Hollywood Walk of Fame in Los Angeles, California, the stars here are given to Latin American actors, writers, artists, and musicians.

Cross Calle Ocho to see the colorful ice cream mural at **Azucar Ice Cream Company**. This is a big tourist stop so prepare for a line of customers. I am a huge ice cream fan, and this is a great place to come for a treat. It offers lots of flavors to choose from, and the Café con Leche flavor is sublime.

Little Havana, Calle Ocho, Miami, FL

Next door to Azucar is another Little Havana and Miami landmark, the **Ball & Chain Bar and Lounge** with its iconic green and white awning. Opened in 1935, the Ball & Chain is a very cool place to visit. It boasts a pine ceiling, a green-colored interior, and walls covered with framed pictures and posters of some of the many artists who have played there. These luminaries include Count Basie, Billie Holiday, and Chet Baker, among many others. The Ball & Chain was integrated long before other performing venues in Miami. I went both during the day and at night to hear some great salsa music. Some well-practiced dancers were showing their stuff on the floor. I recommend to get yourself a perfectly made mojito at the bar.

Ball & Chain Bar & Lounge and Azucar Ice Cream Company,
Little Havana, Calle Ocho, Miami, FL

Another colorful mural adorns the **Little Havana Social Club**, which hosts events with handmade premium cigars. **El Santo Restaurant & Nightclub**, with its Day of the Dead-inspired décor, is another place to check out for its excellent tacos and nightlife.

THE BAY OF PIGS MONUMENT AND CUBAN MEMORIAL PARK

A short walk past Domino Park is the **Bay of Pigs Monument**, which honors the exiled Cuban fallen soldiers who failed in a military invasion to overthrow Fidel Castro at the height of the Cold War. The monument was dedicated in 1971. To the rear of the monument along SW 13ᵗʰ Ave. is **Cuban Memorial Park**, which has devoted a series of monuments to Cuban and Cuban American icons.

STREET SIGNS FOR FAMOUS CUBANS AND CUBAN AMERICANS

You will see many signs through sections of Calle Ocho and side streets dedicated to honor important members of the Little Havana Cuban community.

I'm not sure if I saw all of them but here is a sampling:

- **Armando Bucelo Jr. Way**-Armando Bucelo Jr. (1952) became the first Cuban American to ring the closing bell of the New York Stock Exchange.
- **Cesar Calas Jr. Way**-Cesar A. Calas Jr. (1949–2003) was a professional engineer with the Miami-Dade Public Works Department.
- **Lorenzo de Toro Way**-Lorenzo de Toro (1930–2018) was the publisher of *IDEAL* magazine. It was a publication he started in 1971 and was in almost every Cuban American home in Miami.
- **Martha Flores Way**-Martha Flores (1928–2020) was a Cuban radio announcer, journalist and singer. She continued her career in the United States, where she was known as the "Queen of the Night."
- **Felipe Valls Way**-Felipe A. Valls Sr. (1933–2022), a Cuban exile who invented Miami's hallmark walk-up coffee windows, started a Cuban-cuisine restaurant chain, and founded Versailles Restaurant.
- **Betty Pino Way**-Betty Pino (1948–2013), born Beatriz Pino and also known as La Reina de la Radio, was a famous radio host and announcer.
- **Manuel Capon Way**-Manuel Capon (1925–2009) fled Cuba in the 1960s and went on to build Florida's El Dorado Furniture, one of the largest U.S. furniture store chains.

- **Olga Guillot Way**-Olga Guillot (1922–2010) was a Cuban singer who was known as the "Queen of Bolero." She was a native of Santiago de Cuba.
- **Captains Padron, Perez and Sosa Way**-Bay of Pigs veterans who were killed in Vietnam.
- **Carlos Arboleya Blvd.**-Carlos Arboleya (1929–2020), a refugee from Cuba became vice chairman and chief operating officer of Bank of America before retiring in 1994. Arboleya was a pillar of the Miami Cuban community and heavily involved in youth scouting.

THE MIAMI ORANGE BOWL

North of Calle Ocho in the Little Havana neighborhood is **LoanDepot Park**, the home ballpark of the Miami Marlins Major League Baseball team. It was constructed in 2012, but when I visited, I wanted to see the place more for its past than its present. From 1937 until 2008, it was the site of the now-demolished Miami Orange Bowl athletic stadium. The Miami Orange Bowl hosted the Orange Bowl, one of the original annual New Year's football games. It also served as the home field for the Miami University Hurricanes football team and for the first twenty-one seasons of the Miami Dolphins NFL football team. A plaque sits at the site of the former stadium, accompanied by four forlorn spectator seats rescued prior to demolition.

Back on Calle Ocho, Little Havana becomes less touristy. Calle Ocho Plaza features some small shops, some cigar stores, and one small, terrific Spanish restaurant: **Las Tapas De Rosa**, where I had excellent tapas. The restaurant is also known for its paella and potato omelets. Just before I-95 is a sign indicating that Calle Ocho has ended. From there, Highway 41 proceeds into the Brickell neighborhood.

BRICKELL

The **Brickell** neighborhood is named for Mary Brickell (1836–1922), who with her husband opened a trading post at the mouth of the Miami River in 1871. The land they lived on was referred to as **Brickell Point**, a site that is now listed on the National Register of Historic Places. Mary was the head of the family business that purchased land in the area. That land became a resdential neighborhood that eventually transformed into part of Miami's downtown as the city grew. It is doubtful that Mary would be able to recognize the area today.

In 1998, as a portion of the Brickell area was being excavated for new construction, workers discovered a layout of holes over an oval of limestone, believed to be a prehistoric site. The discovery of the "Miami Circle" led to the creation of the **Miami Circle National Historic Landmark**. It is now preserved as an archeological site where remnants of the earliest Miami peoples were found. The site also features a park with trees, benches, a promenade by the Miami River, and a small kid's area where children on their way home from school can relax a bit.

Brickell is currently undergoing intense redevelopment. When I traveled to this area of the city in 2002, it was full of nondescript office buildings. That is not the case now. It is the city's financial center, where a veritable forest of glittering business towers and luxury condos tower over Biscayne Bay. Brickell has grown in importance since the $1.05 billion **Brickell City Centre** was completed in 2016. The Centre provides upscale shopping opportunities and has served as a catalyst for the development of other luxury buildings nearby. On my visit in January 2024, an existing structure was being prepared for demolition, while ground looked to have been recently broken for a sixty-eight-floor office tower called **One Brickell City Centre** at the corner of the Tamiami Trail and Brickell Avenue. Currently, the eighty-five-story **Panorama Tower** in Brickell on Biscayne Bay is the tallest building in Miami.

Brickell, Miami, FL

Brickell also has a number of mixed-use buildings in place or under development. One good example is **ORA**. According to its website, "ORA is poised to be one of the most striking buildings in Miami, set in the center of Brickell and surrounded by breathtaking water and city views. ORA rises above Miami, with short-term rental residences ranging from studio to four-bedrooms, and a sky garden at the center of the building. Abundant with amenities, including an expansive fitness & wellness center, rooftop pool & resort pool, social lounges, and co-working lounge—all alive with social, upbeat energy."

Brickell is filled with young professionals and chic restaurants all around. If you are looking to mix with the cool crowd, upscale restaurants **Komodo Miami** and **Truluck's Ocean's Finest Seafood and Crab** are the end of the Tamiami Trail as it connects to Brickell Avenue, the main road in the Brickell neighborhood.

Brickell is not completely filled with upscale developments quite yet. In the shadow of the Brickell City Centre is a two-story building called **Brickell Psychic**, where you can avail yourself of a psychic reading, have your Chakras aligned, undergo past-life regression, have a Tarot reading, and have your handwriting analyzed. There's even a little coffee shop on the first floor.

A couple of doors down from Brickell Psychic is **Kush Brickell Tobacco Road**, a re-creation of a famous local "dive bar" known as "Tobacco Road," which was closed in 2014. Some other small businesses in the neighborhood provide glimpses of what the area once was like and appear to be hanging on for the time being.

Brickell, Miami, FL

SEARCHING FOR THE HIGHWAY 41 END SHIELD

Since this book is all about the great and glorious Highway 41, I was hoping to find a **41 East End shield**. When I visited in 2002, I found such a sign and took a picture of it. In 2024, I could find no sign signifying the eastern end of Highway 41. The road simply ends its long southerly journey at **Brickell Avenue** and **U.S. Highway 1** surrounded by high-rises and nightlife.

If you go north for one block, you will encounter the easternmost sign for Highway 41—West. No plaque or marker honoring the highway's significance was to be found, but this was no great surprise given all of the construction around the area. This great, unlamented road starts in a forest of trees blanketing the shore of Lake Superior and officially ends in a forest of skyscrapers here near **Biscayne Bay**. Somehow this leaves our tale of Florida a little anticlimactic, so we are going to turn back the clock to 1999 when the road went all the way to Miami Beach.

DOWNTOWN MIAMI

Going north on Highway 1/Brickell Avenue (and once Highway 41), the road crosses the **Miami River** and becomes Biscayne Boulevard as it brings you into **Downtown Miami**. The city hums with energy here. Department stores, jewelry shops, hotels, and the **Kaseya Center**—home of the Miami Heat NBA team—are among Miami's many downtown attractions. As in other cities such as New York and Chicago, many individuals reside in high-rise residential buildings in the downtown area. Miami has become a magnet for young professionals. Certainly, having the waterfront with all its attractions and activities nearby makes this a hot area. And be aware that it can be choked with traffic.

The road goes by **Bayfront Park**, Miami's first public gathering space. The park has been in existence since the 1890s and serves as a welcome piece of green space right on Biscayne Bay. It spans thirty-two acres with walkways, a beach area, a fountain, and a rock garden. Adjacent to the park is **Bayside Marketplace**, with lots of shops and food options, and the **Skyviews Miami Observation Wheel**, a large Ferris wheel featuring enclosed gondolas that provide great views of the city from the top.

Across from Bayfront Park you'll find the 100-story, 1,049-foot-tall **Waldorf Astoria Miami** building, currently under construction. Slated for completion in 2027, the building will be Miami's tallest tower and its first super-tall skyscraper. The building is designed to resemble a pile of unevenly stacked glass cubes.

ADDITIONAL SIGHTS TO SEE IN DOWNTOWN MIAMI

THE HISTORYMIAMI MUSEUM

West of Biscayne Boulevard on Flagler Street in an area of government buildings are the **Miami-Dade Public Library** and the **HistoryMiami Museum**, which is chock full of pictures, kid-friendly exhibits, and rotating exhibits offering a glimpse of the city's past. Lots of pictures on display relate to the city's history as a transportation point, a refugee center, and a tourist destination.

DuPONT BUILDING

Miami's historic **Alfred I. DuPont Building** has been a Miami landmark since its completion in 1939. It is located at 169 East Flagler Street. This seventeen-story rectangular building, designed in the Moderne style with Art Deco embellishments, is a popular venue for weddings and elegant parties.

FREEDOM TOWER

Just off Biscayne Boulevard, and hard to miss, is the seventeen-story National Historic Landmark **Freedom Tower**. The building was constructed in 1925 to house the *Miami Herald* newspaper owned by James Cox, a former Ohio governor and presidential candidate who lost to Warren Harding in 1920. Cox also founded Cox Enterprises; a global conglomerate headquartered in Atlanta.

The Tower is modeled on the Giralda bell tower in Seville, Spain, and is one of the most famous early Miami buildings. The building became a major immigration facility in the early 1960s; it's where many Cuban Refugees to the United States were processed. The building is now operated by Miami Dade College and houses the **Museum of Art and Design (MOAD)** among other cultural attractions.

MAURICE FERRÉ PARK

Formerly called Museum Park, **Maurice A. Ferré Park** is a twenty-one-acre public urban green space in downtown Miami. The park features the longest waterfront bay walk in Miami, with a promenade from Biscayne Boulevard to Biscayne Bay that provides pedestrian access to the two museums within the park boundaries. The **Pérez Art Museum Miami (PAMM)** is a contemporary art museum showcasing South American, Cuban, and Mexican art. It is housed in a beautiful building with views of the bay. The **Phillip and Patricia Frost Museum of Science** includes a world-class planetarium and aquarium. "Frost Science" stands out as one of only a few institutions worldwide to have both an aquarium and a planetarium in one museum. The north and west wings provide six floors of interactive exhibitions dedicated to the ecosystem of the Everglades.

MacARTHUR CAUSEWAY BRIDGE

Next to Museum Park, the former Highway 41 leaves Biscayne Boulevard and crosses Biscayne Bay on the **General Douglas MacArthur Causeway**, a six-lane causeway connecting downtown Miami to Miami Beach. The highway connects **Watson Island** and the bay neighborhoods of **Palm Island, Hibiscus Island,** and **Star Island**. Watson Island is home to the **Miami Children's Museum** and **Jungle Island**, a zoological park that features some of the world's rarest and most exotic animals.

PORT OF MIAMI

Dodge Island is in sight as you cross the MacArthur Causeway. This is where you'll find the **PortMiami Cruise Terminal**—the largest passenger port in the world—and the **South Florida Container Terminal**—one of the largest cargo ports in the United States. Chances are good that you will see some of the immense cruise ships that call at PortMiami. As of 2023, this massive facility accounted for approximately 334,500 jobs, welcomed 7,299,294 cruise vacationers, and provided an annual economic revenue of $43 billion to the state of Florida. It is the second-largest economic generator in Miami-Dade after Miami International Airport. As many passengers as PortMiami now welcomes, it plans to exceed that number going forward, thanks in part to new state-of-the-art cruise terminals built with innovative funding by the cruise lines. This makes PortMiami the preferred departure site for cruises to destinations such as the Caribbean, Mexico, and beyond.

Much of my working life has been devoted to the maritime logistics industry, and the South Florida Container Terminal holds a special interest.

It is the closest U.S. port to the Panama Canal and a first port of call for Florida cargo from Latin America and Asia. The port has a close proximity to the airport via the **Port of Miami Tunnel**, which was opened in 2014 to provide a direct connection for trucks from the port via Watson Island to Interstate 395 and State Road 836. Adjacent to the airport is the **Greater Miami Free Trade Zone**. Trade through the Miami airport and seaport exceeds $100 billion annually. The MacArthur Causeway/FL A1A exits to Miami Beach on 5th Street.

MacArthur Causeway and PortMiami Cruise Port, Miami, FL

MIAMI BEACH

Miami Beach has been one of America's premier beach resort cities since the early twentieth century. It boasts an abundance of places to see and be seen. Several famous beaches, fantastic Art Deco architecture, shopping, art, restaurants, and nightlife make this a place of worldwide interest. Hotels, resorts, condominiums, apartments, bars, and restaurants abound along its entire nine-mile length, from South Point Park Pier to North Oceanside Park. Throngs of visitors from all over the world join locals to experience the "Hollywood of the East Coast." The city has also dealt in recent times with "Spring Break" violence and questions about the structural integrity of aging condominium towers. Miami Beach has a lot to unpack.

BACKGROUND

Modern-day Miami Beach begins with John Collins (1837–1928), a Quaker farmer who moved to South Florida from New Jersey at the turn of the century. At first, he tried to grow vegetables on the five-mile piece of barrier island swampland he purchased in 1891. He later turned to real estate development and, with business partners, started the Miami Beach Improvement Company. **Collins Avenue**, the main shopping and hotel thoroughfare in Miami Beach, is named in his honor.

The development of radio in the early 1900s is also connected to early Miami Beach, as the Marconi Wireless Telegraph Company erected radio towers on the beach to send and receive messages in Morse Code. As radio was perfected, Miami Beach gained its first radio station in 1925 to broadcast to audiences around the country.

The city of Miami Beach was incorporated in 1915 and, with lots of promotion, became an alluring destination for visitors and residents alike. Many affluent visitors who could not get enough of the island's weather and water decided to make the city their winter home. Among them were leaders of industry, finance, communications, and nouveau riche millionaires from the burgeoning auto industry, hailing primarily from the Midwest.

John Collins built a casino and a hotel on the island, but he needed funds to complete a bridge to the city of Miami on the mainland. He secured that loan from Carl Fisher, a millionaire auto pioneer who received 200 acres of Miami Beach swampland in return. Fisher planned to enlarge and develop the swampland into a winter playground for his millionaire friends. He is considered to be the "father" of early Miami Beach. John Collins, his family, and Fisher all became very wealthy from the development of Miami Beach, which experienced a 400 percent increase in residential population between 1920 and 1925.

From the 1910s to the 1930s, some forty mansions were built on a stretch of land along Collins Avenue that came to be called **"Millionaire's Row."** By the 1970s, most of these once-palatial homes had been demolished and replaced by apartment buildings and commercial hotels. The area is still referred to as Millionaire's Row, but if you decide to walk around looking for homes as I did, all you will see are upscale condos and hotels. While I'm sure the condos and hotels are luxurious, there is not much of interest on Millionaires' Row unless you live there.

VIGNETTE CARL GRAHAM FISHER

Carl Graham Fisher (1874–1939) was the P.T. Barnum of the Automobile Age. Among individuals instrumental in development of the road system we have today, Fisher stands out as a true visionary, but he was also a deeply flawed individual. Fisher was born in Greensburg, Indiana, and quit school at the age of twelve. Despite a humble background and an astigmatism disability, he became a true entrepreneur who opened a bicycle repair shop in Indianapolis at age seventeen. In 1898, he became one of the first people in the city to own an automobile, and he operated one of the first automobile dealerships in the country as well. He founded, along with James Allison, the Prest-O-Lite company in 1904, which manufactured the first effective headlight for automobiles. The technology was not based on electric lights—that came about in 1912—but rather acetylene gas ignited by a sparking switch. The patented headlight made him rich, and he sold the company to Union Carbide in 1913.

Fisher loved to race cars, and he set a land speed record in 1904 when he drove an automobile around a two-mile dirt track in 2.02 minutes. The idea of having a test track for cars led to his founding of the Indianapolis Motor Speedway in 1911. It still serves as the venue for the Indianapolis 500, which is held annually and attracts thousands of spectators.

In 1912, long before it was accepted that road building was the task of government, Fisher was one of the earliest proponents of privately funding a coast-to-coast road for automobiles. He put together the Lincoln Highway Association, which was composed of wealthy contacts who put up crucial funding to complete the Lincoln Highway in 1915. That highway later became U.S.30. By 1915, Fisher stepped away from any involvement with the road to begin work on a new idea—the Dixie Highway.

The multi-pronged Dixie Highway was Fisher's plan for a highway from the north that would funnel visitors to his Miami Beach hotels. The highway is discussed in detail in Chapter Two of this book: Wheels and Roads.

From the start, Fisher saw the potential of Florida real estate in Miami Beach, then a little-known barrier island. He bought thousands of acres and attempted with little success to develop this land for wealthy tourists prior to 1921. That year, a publicity gimmick involving Rosie, a baby elephant owned by Fisher, acting as a golf caddy for vacationing President-elect Warren Harding "fixed Miami Beach in the public's mind as a place you had to see to believe." ("Mr. Miami Beach," American Experience, 1998).

Other promotional stunts followed, and the population of Miami Beach began to grow exponentially. Fisher then decided to build a northern counterpart to Miami Beach at the tip of Long Island, New York. The community became Montauk Point, but it did not achieve the same wild success as Miami Beach. Fisher's wealth in 1925 exceeded $50 million ($900 million in 2024 dollars).

Fisher's life began to slide downhill in 1926 when he divorced Jane, his wife of seventeen years, and the land boom in Miami Beach was dealt a blow by a major hurricane. The city eventually rebounded, but not before Fisher had fallen into debt from overextended real estate deals. The Great Depression followed, and Fisher's fortune disappeared. His former business partners in the Miami Beach Improvement Company offered him a salaried position as a sales representative, which he took, although he continued trying to revive Miami Beach.

Fisher was an ardent antisemite who would only sell property to gentiles and a racist who encouraged "Whites Only" property deed restrictions and racial segregation. Thanks to Fisher, Miami Beach was a "Sundown Town"—it forbade people of color to live on or even be on the island after dark, with the exception of performers, hotel maids, and bus boys. Well into the 1960s, most of the African American population of Miami Beach were female live-in domestic workers.

Fisher started drinking heavily and bootlegged alcohol during Prohibition. By 1938, he had developed cirrhosis of the liver. A final project to develop the Key Largo Caribbean Club, "a fishing club for men of modest means," was still in process when he died of a gastric hemorrhage in 1939 at age sixty-five. Fisher was credited after his death with being the man who looked at Miami Beach swampland and envisioned a winter playground. Carl, however, hadn't looked at Miami Beach as romantically as that. "Wasn't any goddamned dream at all," he once said. "I could just as easily have started a cattle ranch." His demise inspired many wry eulogies, with humorist Will Rogers probably saying it best: "Fisher was the first man to discover that there was sand under the water... [sand] that could hold up a real estate sign. He made the dredge the national emblem of Florida."

*The **Carl Fisher Monument** was built in 1941 and consists of a bust of Fisher mounted on a large keystone. The monument is in **Fisher Memorial Park** at 50ᵗʰ Street on the Biscayne Bay side of the city and commemorates the man who helped to establish Miami Beach in the nation's consciousness.*

WORLD WAR II

During World War II, Miami Beach became an important training center for the Army Air Corps, which commandeered hundreds of resort hotels and apartments in what is now the Art Deco Historic District. Nearly half a million men, including movie star Clark Gable, were stationed there along with a group of young women in the Army Air Forces Communication Detachment who were credited with shortening the war by breaking enemy codes. The military saw the climate, flat terrain, and seaside location as an ideal training site. Soldiers trained in pools, on golf courses, and at rifle ranges. Numerous photos of that time can be viewed online and at the HistoryMiami Museum.

JEWISH ENCLAVE

Starting in the 1940s, Miami Beach became a haven for Jewish families and retirees. At one time, Miami Beach had the greatest concentration of Holocaust survivors in the United States. By the 1970s, about eighty percent of the population was Jewish. Many of them were involved in developing the tourist industry of Miami Beach and supporting museums and arts organizations. A number of important Jewish synagogues are located in the city.

The Jewish population started to decline in the mid-1980s as more Cubans from the Mariel Exodus of 1980 and Caribbean immigrants came to the city. A surge of violent crime during this period scared off both tourists and many longtime residents and inspired the groundbreaking television show *Miami Vice* (1984–1989). The production was filmed in the South Beach section of the city, which at the time was blighted by poverty and crime. The show integrated pop and rock music into its soundtrack, and the set design featured intense colors that focused attention on the Art Deco architecture and generated support for the renovation of these structures.

In the 1990s, South Beach became a trendy place frequented by celebrities and people in the fashion industry. Up until that point, the area just north of South Beach featured large resort hotels centering on Collins Avenue and one or two-story hotels constructed in the 1950s and 1960s that attracted many middle-class vacationers. Starting in the late 1990s, however, many of these quirky hotels started to disappear along with their concrete camels, mermaids, and pyramids. Condominium high-rises went up in their place.

ART DECO HISTORIC DISTRICT

The design style called American Art Deco gained popularity between the mid-1920s and approximately 1943. Many Miami Beach buildings, including hotels, apartments, and other structures, adopted this style, and today the world's highest concentration of existing Art Deco architecture can be found in Miami Beach. In 1979, Miami Beach's **Art Deco Historic District**, with over 800 buildings, was the first urban twentieth century neighborhood in the United States listed on the National Register of Historic Places. The movement to preserve the Art Deco Historic District's architectural heritage was led by former interior designer Barbara Baer Capitman, and a street in the district is now named in her honor. The **Art Deco Museum** and **Art Deco Welcome Center** on Ocean Drive offer a wealth of information about the district and are well worth a visit. The **Miami Design Preservation League (MDPL)** offers guided walking tours led by historians and architects who explain the Art Deco, Mediterranean Revival, and Miami Modern (MiMo) styles found in Miami Beach.

VIGNETTE BARBARA BAER CAPITMAN

*Barbara Baer Capitman (1920–1990) was born in Chicago and lived in New York City where she worked as a journalist. Capitman was an industrial designer, artist, and sculptor. In 1976, she rediscovered Art Deco buildings in Miami Beach, many of which had largely been ignored and were slated for demolition. She literally stood in front of bulldozers to protect these buildings. Capitman founded the Miami Design Preservation League (MDPL) and set to work orchestrating the repainting and renovating of the drab, rundown hotels on Ocean Drive. Her vision transformed South Beach into the current tourist destination it is today. Her life is personified in this quote: "My whole life has been Art Deco. I was born at the beginning of the period and grew up during the height of it. It's a thing of fate." Tenth Street in South Beach is also known as **Barbara Capitman Way**.*

Another historic area to explore here is Miami Beach's **Collins Waterfront Architectural District**. It includes 110 contributing buildings and structures dating from 1922 through 1962, with Collins Avenue at its center. The district's predominant styles include Art Moderne, Art Deco, and Mediterranean Revival architecture, as well as the local Miami Modern style. The chief contributing resources are large resort hotels. The district is bounded by the Atlantic Ocean, 24th Street, Indian Creek Drive, Pine Tree Drive, and the Collins Canal. The district is part of Mid-Beach and is listed on the National Register of Historic Places.

PRESERVATION CONTROVERSIES

In late 2023, Florida passed a law that made it easier for developers to demolish hotels and other architecturally noted structures. The new law pits hard-won, decades-long preservation efforts to keep and maintain iconic architecture along the Miami Beach coastline against developers who seek to remove aging properties they claim are subject to environmental and safety challenges having much to do with climate change. Recent news articles suggest that critics of the law believe the legislation is a pretext to facilitate the demolition of historical buildings—ones that give Miami Beach its distinctive look—to make way for more high-rise luxury condos.

In 2021, the partial collapse of a Florida condominium tower killed ninety-eight people in the town of **Surfside**, just north of Miami Beach, and sent shockwaves through the ocean residence community. It has been identified as a case in point necessitating the new law. The **Champlain Towers South** building was constructed in 1980, and investigators are still trying to determine why the structure collapsed and if other properties might be at risk.

THE UNOFFICIAL END OF HIGHWAY 41 (PART ONE)

Upon exiting the MacArthur Causeway, the road becomes **5th Street**, which proceeds several blocks to connect to **A1A** (Collins Avenue) near the southern border of Miami Beach. Until 2000, this marked the end of Highway 41. It was a non-descript intersection when I visited in January 2024, with a Walgreens on one corner and a couple of banks and a small two-story apartment building on the others. At present, there is no plaque or sign signifying that Highway 41 once terminated at this point. Ocean Drive is one block to the east, and the beach itself is only a few yards away.

SOUTH OF FIFTH

The enclave known as **South of Fifth**, or **SoFi**, is a small, affluent, exclusive neighborhood situated on the southern tip of Miami Beach. It begins at South Pointe Park and extends north to 5th Street, from east to west. Until the end of World War II, SoFi was the only area that could be settled by Jewish residents of Miami Beach.

Neighborhood attractions include the **Jewish Museum of Florida–FIU**, which is housed in a former synagogue. This is also the place to find **Joe's**

Stone Crab, one of Miami's most famous restaurants. It's often visited by politicians, actors, and athletes. In business since 1913, Joe's is the biggest buyer of Florida stone crab claws and plays a significant role in that industry. The restaurant has won numerous awards and is one of the highest grossing restaurants in the country. SoFi is a quiet and compact area to walk around in and features some stunningly rehabbed Art Deco apartment buildings.

Collins Av. Miami Beach, where Highway 41 ended prior to 2000

Miami Beach, FL

FISHER ISLAND

Across the inlet from SoFi and accessible only by sea or air is the census-designated place **Fisher Island** (pop. 1002). Named after Carl Fisher who once owned the island, it has the wealthiest per capita income in the United States. It draws celebrities, executives, and oligarchs seeking social distance from nearby Miami. A typical condo goes for $9 million, but in January 2023, one 10,200-square-foot, seven-bedroom manse hit the market at $36 million. It is a seven-minute ferry ride from Miami Beach, but you can't board the ferry without an invitation.

VIRGINIA KEY

Beyond Fisher Island and accessible from Miami via the Rickenbacker Causeway (State Road 913) is **Virginia Key**, where you'll find the **Historic Virginia Key Beach Park**. At the time of Miami's founding in 1896, segregation was in full force. African Americans, many of whom had a major role in the building and development of the city, were excluded from all of its beaches. It is hard to imagine now how sweeping this enforcement was. Virginia Key was an unofficial exception, and in 1945 it became an "official colored only" site. Virginia Key Beach became a popular gathering place for the African American community, which used the site for religious services as well as recreation. In the 1950s and early 1960s, Caribbean, South American, and Cuban immigrants also found the beach to be the only one that they could legally visit.

Due to high operation and maintenance costs, the City of Miami closed Virginia Key Beach Park to the public in 1982. In 1999, after plans were announced for a private development to be built on the site, a group of citizens established the Virginia Key Beach Park Civil Rights Task Force. In response, the Miami City Commission established Virginia Key Beach Park Trust to oversee the development of this historic property. In 2002, the park was added to the National Register of Historic Places.

Historic Virginia Key Beach Park reopened to the public in February 2008, featuring many of the amenities of the past as well as some new venues as suggested by the community. The park is open to the public today; ecosystem restoration projects, interpretive signage, and the construction of an interpretive/cultural center remain to be completed.

KEY BISCAYNE

South of Virginia Key is **Key Biscayne**, a Florida town on a barrier island across the Rickenbacker Causeway from Miami. It lies between two large parks—**Crandon Park** and **Bill Baggs Cape Florida State Park**—each with long, sheltered beaches, mangroves, and tropical forestland inhabited by birdlife, butterflies, and loggerhead turtles. The latter park is home to the nineteenth century Cape Florida Lighthouse.

SOUTH BEACH

South Beach or **SoBe**, offers the quintessential Miami Beach experience. It is bounded by Biscayne Bay and the Atlantic Ocean and encompasses everything south of **Dade Boulevard**. It has numerous nightspots and restaurants. It is famous for being THE place to engage in people-watching, and I suggest you try to stay at one of the SoBe hotels for a night or two if you can afford it. I think it's best to go in the off-season or during off-weeks when availability is more likely. Traffic can be brutal, so my other suggestion is to ditch the car in a parking garage and explore on foot.

FASHION

People involved in the fashion industry started to move into South Beach in the late 1980s. Irene Marie (b. 1950) and her company **Irene Marie Models** are often credited with being the first to see the virtues of South Beach for the modeling community in 1989. Other fashion professionals followed, with perhaps the most glamourous being Gianni Versace (1946–1997), the founder of Versace, an international luxury-fashion house. Unfortunately, Versace was murdered outside of his Ocean Drive mansion by Andrew Cunanan, who died by suicide eight days later. Today the **Versace Mansion and Villa Casa Casuarina** operates as a luxury boutique hotel, restaurant, and event venue.

LGBTQ+ COMMUNITY

South Beach is considered one of Miami's LGBTQ+ hubs. It is home to many hotels, clubs, and other nightlife venues that cater to the LGBTQ+ community. Every April, the **Miami Beach Pride** parade takes place in South Beach. It is one of the largest pride parades in the country. It was not always that way. Until 1976, when Anita Bryant (1940–2024) launched an all-out attack on the gay community, many people tried to keep their sexual orientation secret. Bryant was a national figure as a former beauty queen, a popular singer, and a spokesperson for the Florida Citrus Commission promoting Florida orange juice. Her strident opposition to a gay rights ordinance first passed by the Miami-Dade County Commission resulted in its repeal in 1977. But her actions led to the mobilization of and activism in the LGBTQ+ community against bigotry that had not been previously seen in the area.

Though Bryant may have enjoyed some additional years of fame, her anti-gay rhetoric ultimately caused her career prospects to plummet. Her booking agent dropped her, the Florida Citrus Commission stopped running her orange juice ads, and she filed for bankruptcy—twice. The anti-discrimination ordinance she helped repeal in 1977 was restored in 1998. Now, we are in a new era of state and federal legislators working to curtail LGBTQ+ rights, but same-sex marriage is still legal across the country, and federal law, so far, still prohibits anti-LGBTQ+ discrimination in the workplace.

JACKIE GLEASON

Long before South Beach was a "thing," there was **Jackie Gleason**, who brought his weekly variety series *The Jackie Gleason Show* (1952–1970) to South Beach from New York for taping in 1964. The show was shot in color on videotape at the Miami Beach Auditorium, now called **The Fillmore Miami Beach at The Jackie Gleason Theater**. Gleason, a popular performer known as the main star of the classic television series *The Honeymooners*, promoted the locality as the "sun and fun capital of the world" on camera and finished each show saying, "Miami Beach audiences are the greatest audiences in the world."

SPRING BREAK & URBAN BEACH WEEK

My visit to South Beach in mid-January did not coincide with two large-scale events involving massive crowds and much controversy that have taken place there each spring for several years. **Spring Break** occurs during the month of March, and in the three years leading up to 2024, violence led to states of emergency and midnight curfews for partying college students.

In response, a far more stringent set of public safety enhancements has now been approved, including security checkpoints, DUI inspections, and a greater presence of local law enforcement and Florida state troopers on site. As a result of the crackdown, city officials have had to balance revenue lost by entertainment venues that serve unruly Spring Break crowds with relative peace and quiet.

The second big event, known as **Urban Beach Week**, is held annually around Memorial Day and is one of the most entertaining hip-hop weekend events worldwide. It is considered to be one of the largest urban festivals catering to the hip-hop community. Approximately 350,000 participants trek to South Beach from all over the country for a period of entertainment and crazy partying. The events of Urban Beach Week are typically spread over five days. The city does not sponsor the event, and there is no one organizer. Instead, it is a weekend-plus of rolling performances in private venues.

WHAT TO SEE IN SOUTH BEACH

My first piece of advice is to take a walk along **Ocean Drive**, known for its well-preserved Art Deco hotels and outdoor cafés that offer a ringside view of the scene. Go during the day to see these places in the sunlight, and go at night to experience the party atmosphere. Even on a slow mid-weeknight during a non-holiday period the place is jumping. My late-night party days are over, but I could certainly appreciate the energy of all the happening nightspots.

Park Central Hotel, South Beach, FL

Chapter Eleven: Florida Part Two

South Beach, FL

On Washington Avenue, two blocks west of Ocean Drive, **The Wolfsonian —Florida International University** is a small but cool museum in the Art Deco District. When you visit, make sure to see the Geneva Window by Harry Clark—a masterpiece that was condemned by the conservative government of Ireland at the time. The Wolfsonian's holdings—including one of the largest university art collections in the United States—enhance understanding of the modern age, from 1850 to 1950. Ranging from fine, decorative, and propaganda arts to graphic design and artifacts, the museum serves as a window to all of the changes that have transformed our world.

Only a few doors up the street from the Wolfsonian to the north is **Bettant Bakery & Café**. It advertises as "French family bakers since 1935," and served the best croissants I have had outside of France. If you're looking for a filling meal, head a little farther north to the **11th Street Diner**. True to its name, it is housed in an old railroad car. It has been "serving hungry tourists and locals since 1992."

Mac's Club Deuce Bar, on 14th Street and Collins Avenue, is as close as you can get to the perfect "dive bar." Accepting cash only, this watering hole features loads of gorgeous neon lights throughout and a friendly group of regulars. Also, find an excuse to visit the Art Deco **Miami Beach Post Office** on Washington Avenue to see its murals and beautiful ceiling inside.

Although it's not a place for vacation revelry, I highly recommend you visit the **Holocaust Memorial Miami Beach**. This significant monument to the six million Jews who perished at the hands of the Third Reich from 1933 to 1945 is located near the northern end of South Beach and features an outdoor space highlighted by a huge sculpture of a human hand. A path connects the Holocaust Memorial to the **Miami Beach Botanical Garden**, which is a pleasant escape from the intensity of South Beach.

North of South Beach, **Bayshore** is a neighborhood in the center of the island, between South Beach and Mid-Beach. It was built around the **Miami Beach Golf Club**, which was originally designed in 1923 for Carl Fisher's wealthy friends. The area has single family homes and **Miami Beach Senior High School**.

United States Post Office Miami Beach, Miami Beach, FL

MID-BEACH

Mid-Beach is where you'll find the luxury condo buildings and swanky MiMo (Miami Modern) hotels. They line the shores of this trendy Miami Beach neighborhood. A super cool area to see is in the **Faena District** between 32nd and 36th Streets. It has lots of cutting-edge architecture and high-end bars and restaurants catering to those with lots of money.

Farther north is the **Fontainebleau Miami Beach**, which is in a league all by itself. This iconic hotel dates from 1954 and has been featured in a number of movies and television shows over the decades. Major entertainment stars have all performed there. A billion-dollar renovation of the hotel in 2008 has kept its history intact and also made it modern and cool. If you want to splurge for a night or two, this might be the place to go. Other well-known hotels in the area include the **Eden Roc** and **Ocean Spray Hotel**. The **Blue and Green Diamond** are twin condominium towers located in Mid-Beach. Each tower has forty-four floors.

NORTH BEACH

More low-key than South Beach, **North Beach** is a mellow residential area fringed by a wide stretch of sand. Mid-century hotels still line Collins Avenue, backed by MiMo-style apartment buildings. Locals attend concerts at the historic **Miami Beach Bandshell** and enjoy **North Beach Oceanside Park**, with its trails and native trees. The area has become a meeting point for Argentine expatriates in Miami. Check out the **Little Buenos Aires** neighborhood around 71ˢᵗ Street for Argentine-themed restaurants and **La Playa De Los Pájaros** beach.

BEYOND MIAMI BEACH TO THE NORTH

If you drive north past Miami Beach on A1A, you'll find the town of **Surfside**. This primarily residential beachside community is where the **Champlain Towers South** condominium collapse occurred in June 2021. Surfside is adjacent to **Surfside Beach**. The next town to the north is **Bal Harbour**, which features exclusive hotels such as the **Ritz Carlton,** the **Four Seasons**, and the **St. Regis**.

Across the water east of Surfside in Biscayne Bay is **Indian Creek Island**. Nicknamed "Billionaire Bunker," it features forty-one opulent waterfront properties that house some of the wealthiest people in one of America's most exclusive and highly secured residential neighborhoods. The island is connected by a bridge to Surfside, Florida, and is guarded by a police checkpoint that turns away non-residents and unauthorized persons who attempt to visit the island.

On the barrier island just to the north of Bal Harbour is **Haulover Beach**. This sunny strand is quite well known as Florida's oldest officially recognized public nude beach. It is ranked as one of the Top 10 nude beaches worldwide. If you continue north on A1A you will eventually make your way to the cities of **Hollywood** and **Fort Lauderdale**.

THE UNOFFICIAL END OF HIGHWAY 41 (PART TWO)

From 1952 to 1999, Highway 41 extended to Collins Avenue/A1A, now also known as the **Jimmy Buffett Memorial Highway**. For some reason in 2000, the Florida Department of Transportation decided to remove all references to Highway 41 east of its junction with U.S. 1 /Brickell Avenue. So, without a memorializing marker, I suggest we end at the ocean.

To find the most interesting unofficial end to Highway 41, head back south to **Lummus Park** in South Beach. Lummus Park extends for several blocks along Ocean Drive and features restrooms, showers, and walking paths that connect to the **Miami Beach Ocean Walk**. This walking path runs the length of the city and northward through Surfside and Bal Harbour. And finally, there is the beach—the most fitting conclusion to a major transcontinental U.S route that originates at the shore of Lake Superior and ends at the shore of the Atlantic Ocean. So, once you have made it all this way, park the car, take your shoes off, put on your swimsuit, wiggle your toes in the sand, walk along the beach, and get in the water. You won't regret it.

Where Highway 41 should end

CONCLUDING THOUGHTS

My first travel to Florida was in 1963 when I was eight years old. I will never forget driving along the coast and seeing the ocean all along our journey from the airport. We stayed at the **Hotel Waikiki** in **Sunny Isles Beach** just north of Miami Beach, and we had a terrific time. The hotel was torn down long ago, and in its place stand the **St. Regis Residences**—two recently constructed condo towers where prices will be $3.9 to $6 million per unit. That is out of the price range of most people. These monstrous skyscrapers will take their place in what is becoming a veritable wall of buildings along the beachfront. I have been back to Florida many times over the years for vacations and for business. Times do change and nostalgia for an older Florida is a luxury that is rarely present in the Florida of today.

Florida's sunny beaches are a powerful draw, but the state and local governments are also encouraging more people to move to the shores of the Sunshine State. With no state income tax, many local governments in Florida rely on property taxes, which creates an incentive to develop more property. As more people have moved to the state, they have put immense pressure on the infrastructure—roads, fresh water, power, etc.—which can end up making such a move less inviting. And climate change will impact the state in ways that are hard to predict. Many long-standing Floridians have left the state due to these issues.

Traveling on Highway 41 provides drivers with a window into Florida's past, present, and probable future. You will note that I did not say anything about orange groves and the citrus industry. You will see very little of either while traveling along U.S.41, not only due to their location farther inland, but also because of blight, disease, and pressure to turn the former groves into new housing developments. The state's size and significance put it at the epicenter of many of the challenges facing the country in coming years. Florida was always a place where people could visit to enjoy all of its natural beauty and tourist attractions. It can still be that, but its future sustainability is questionable. Is Florida today what the United States will look like in 2050? This is certainly something to ponder as you travel the length of Highway 41 in the Sunshine State.

PART FOUR
AMERICAN JOURNEY

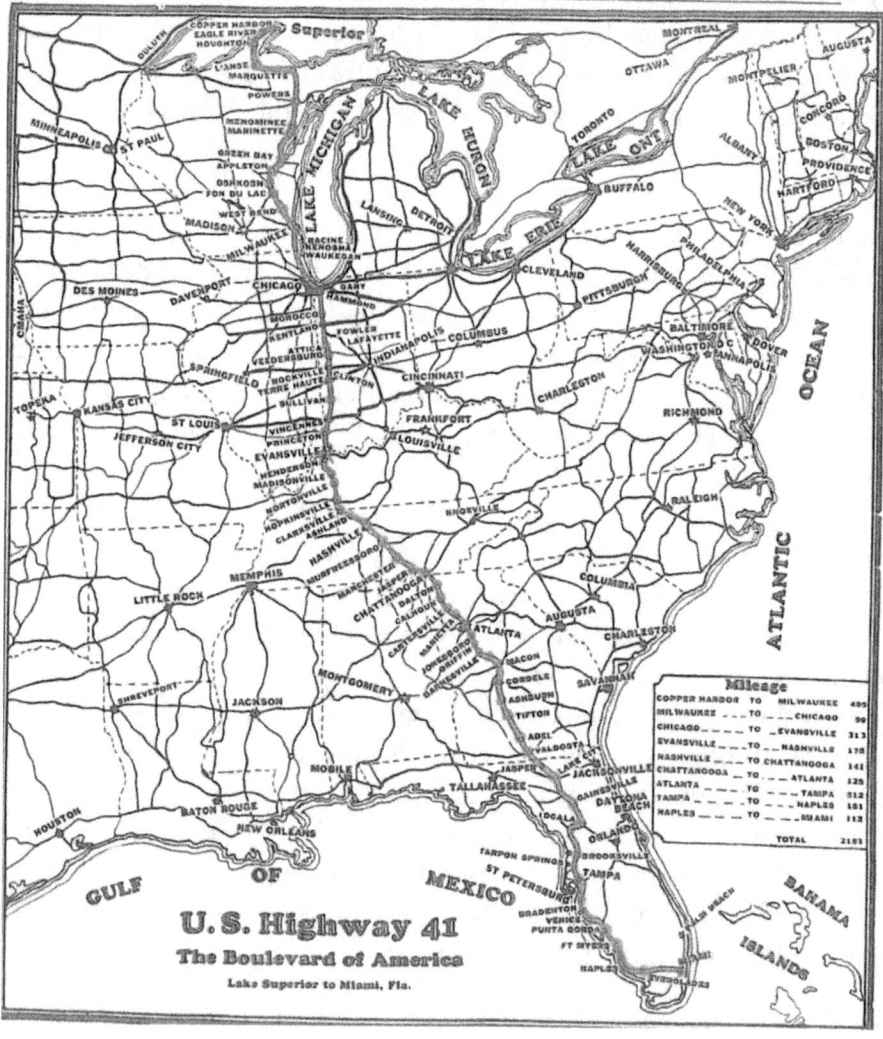

Map courtesy of the Henderson County Public Library Archives Collection

CHAPTER TWELVE:
THE BOULEVARD OF AMERICA

"It's not the destination, it's the journey."

—*Ralph Waldo Emerson*

Traveling through eight states and some 2,000 miles on Highway 41 over a three-year period of time has provided me with some interesting observations of the country I call home. For starters, it is immensely complex. Places on and near the road provide a smorgasbord of different sights—things you will never see if you are buzzing by on the interstate or flying overhead. I was continuously surprised, occasionally depressed, and altogether humbled by what I found on my journey. Here, in no particular order, are some of the things that bear mention.

OUR INDIGENOUS HERITAGE

I take no great pleasure in saying that prior to my 41 travels the amount of knowledge I had of our Indigenous peoples and their heritage of thousands of years within the land now designated as the United States could fill a thimble. During the time of my journey, I have learned and seen so many markers, museums, and land areas that speak to the long association Indigenous peoples have had with the land. The history of the United States did not begin with the European explorers. Suffice to say, there would not be a U.S. 41 to write about without an understanding of the Indigenous heritage along its route.

Despite all of the indignities heaped upon the Indigenous peoples over the centuries they have miraculously remained resilient with strong community networks and traditions that continue to influence the country in positive ways. A commitment to environmental stewardship and sustainability is part and parcel of what the tribes provide a country sorely in need of this knowledge. Travel along 41 opened my eyes to the Indigenous heritage and contributions and they will open yours too.

THE CIVIL WAR AND OUR AFRICAN AMERICAN HERITAGE

Thanks to a long-standing interest in the American Civil War, I was certainly aware that many battles were fought along the route of Highway 41. But to see the sites of these long-ago events in person provides a far greater understanding of the horrific nature of the conflict. What I learned far more about was the African American experience from enslavement to the Underground Railroad to emancipation and the onset of Jim Crow policies that lasted almost to the early 1970s.

Thanks to many markers and museums, travelers can gain a far more nuanced understanding of this aspect of American history. The truthful and sensitive coverage of these issues I found at sites related to the African American experience on the path of Highway 41 is a positive sign. Hopefully, the path of the country as a whole will move forward with the goal of establishing equity and equality for all in every aspect of society.

MEGAREGIONS

Urban megaregions are huge and expanding. The five big urban centers the highway passes through:

1) Greater Chicago- Milwaukee, WI–Chicago, IL–Northern Indiana.
2) Greater Nashville: Clarksville–Nashville–Murfreesboro, TN.
3) Greater Atlanta: Cartersville–Atlanta–Barnesville, GA.
4) Florida Gulf Coast: Greater Tampa–Cape Coral–Naples, FL.
5) Greater Miami, FL.

The above areas encompass thirty percent of the area covered by Highway 41. Chances are good that your journey on 41 started from one of these places. Planning for additional growth is going to require creativity, flexibility, cooperation, and vision. And the planning needs to incorporate more than real estate developers seeking to pocket profits at the expense of ensuring the infrastructure is adequate for continued growth. Big cities have big issues. Poverty, homelessness, housing affordability, safety, accessibility, etc. Nothing is easy about working and living in a big city, but few places can provide to support cultural venues and diversity that can be found in a large city.

The central city within each megaregion might begin and end in a somewhat logical order, but the sprawl around the central city from "edge cities" can seem like endless seas of housing developments, distribution centers, strip malls, auto dealers, pawnshops, the ubiquitous dollar stores, closed businesses, and abandoned buildings. Big shopping malls seen along the way seem to be entering the twilight of their usefulness as shopping patterns change. The challenge for planners will be what to do with these leviathans of another age.

Sometimes urban sprawl can reward the patient traveler by showing them things that speak to the variegated American experience—mosques and temples, food markets, ethnic restaurants, roadside stands, and unassuming historical sites that are not directly off the interstate or on the tourism bureau list of greatest hits. Highway 41 provides, within all the congestion, a slice of what America is today. Urban sprawl is not going away, but the opportunities for different cultures to meet and share and expand their understanding of others, as well as themselves, is a silver lining.

CONGESTION

Let's talk about congestion. Within the megaregions, the amount of auto and truck congestion on Highway 41 can be mind-numbing in some areas. The Gulf Coast of Florida; Lake County, Indiana; the exurbs south of Nashville and Atlanta—all come to mind when you contemplate stretches where the highway seems to be one giant service road. Portions of Highway 41 are being widened to accommodate more vehicles. This was not the answer in the 1970s when we first started to question why more road building was considered a good thing, and I'm not so sure that the answer in the present is more road building either. It will only beget more traffic.

There is very little in the way of public transportation along the highway. Urban planners, bike riders, and people unable to drive may desire alternatives to the automobile, but that competes with the fact the country still is wedded to the individual car. With nearly 300 million personal vehicles and an additional 13.5 million freight trucks on the road, we will not see an end to traffic congestion anytime soon.

On the optimistic side, steps are being taken by many of the cities along the highway to rebuild transit opportunities and promote biking and walking as transportation options. Opportunities to get people out of their cars need to be promoted and celebrated.

SMALLER CITIES

Green Bay, Wisconsin; Evansville, Indiana; Hopkinsville, Kentucky; Chattanooga, Tennessee; and Valdosta, Georgia are among the many smaller cities you'll travel through along the length of Highway 41. The road was once a vital lifeline to these locales, but it has largely been eclipsed by interstate highways as the main conduits of traffic.

Small cities face the same challenges as large megaregions but often with fewer resources and civic infrastructure to draw from. They are often reliant upon one or two large companies for employment and must be attractive and affordable to draw skilled young people who will want to stay. Adding and updating cultural amenities, including having interesting and thriving downtowns, are seen to be important. If these cities are fortunate, they have universities and community colleges that can provide support to the cultural factors that will keep people within the area. Nearby parks and recreation areas can also be a draw. And many of these smaller cities have a large enough medical infrastructure to serve the needs of both residents and those who live in outlying areas. In a sign of the times, medical complexes have become some of the largest employers within small cities. A heartening sign along Highway 41 was to see ongoing revitalization efforts in some older downtown areas. These efforts must continue.

AFFORDABLE HOUSING

A common refrain in my conversations with young people I met during my travels was the difficulty in procuring affordable housing. This was true throughout all the states. It is a quiet crisis of sorts. Housing, insurance, and rental costs, coupled with a lack of available supply to meet demand, are the critical issues, particularly in megaregions. We, as a country, need to start thinking creatively about housing and perhaps offer some incentives to aging baby boomers to move from larger homes to smaller ones.

While land redevelopment can have a net positive effect on many communities, the wholesale gentrification of long-time neighborhoods is counterproductive to residents of modest incomes. This is being addressed by neighborhood groups in Milwaukee, Nashville, Atlanta, and other points along the highway.

RURAL AMERICA AND SMALL TOWNS

A journey on Highway 41 still allows you to see glimpses of what the country was like a century ago. You'll travel through farmland that is still vital but under stress from climate change and consolidation. The United States has an aging agricultural base of farmers, and fewer young people want to make a go of all the uncertainties associated with farming. Rural America seems to be increasingly disconnected from urban America. The challenge will be to reestablish these connections and make a case for greater understanding. I saw some examples of farms that open their premises to visitors along the highway that may bridge some of the urban/rural divide.

Small-town America along the road is variegated. Thanks to greater tourism around state parks, some towns have turned their infrastructure into tourist-friendly vistas. Small towns that are home to colleges and universities also have some built-in advantages; a student and faculty population will support small shops and eateries if the traditional higher educational model remains viable. Highway 41 in its modern iteration is often routed just outside of the small towns it once went through, removing the traffic issues but also limiting who is visiting.

Some of the satellite towns of cities within a sixty-mile radius may provide housing opportunities for young families, but affordability and a welcoming, open location are question marks. Craft brew pubs, county fairs, sports teams, and musical events all are important to sustaining a sense of life in small towns. Some of the fast-growing rural exurbs on the edges of megaregions now face major congestion on country roads not built for heavy traffic.

Travelers on U.S. 41 may also see towns that have pretty much folded the tent. Small towns with empty storefronts, crumbling buildings, few to no people on the street, and closed manufacturing sites are a sad reality all along the highway. In a number of cases, the main business of the town has moved near the highway entrance or, if it is lucky, the interstate on-ramp. Along some stretches of the road, I felt as if I was seeing the underbelly of the country—places that have ceased to be relevant. There are no great answers here. Stores need people to shop, and a vicious cycle occurs when people move away for opportunities elsewhere, leaving mainly the elderly people who remain with fewer options. Investment only occurs when there is the potential of a return. People need to care more about the places that have little or no tourist interest but potentially can be reimagined for a new age.

RECREATIONAL AREAS

Rest, relaxation, and contemplation are important during a road trip, and I think the best way to get the most out of a journey is to plan some longer stops along the way. Highway 41 is blessed to have numerous parks and recreational areas along its traverse from north to south. Wildlife corridors are nearby, and they are essential to the birds and animals that share the country with humans. There are many places to hike, swim, fish, boat, and admire nature that lie close to the road. New bike paths have been created through many park areas. Travel through the Everglades in the south and the woods of the Upper Peninsula in the north have been celebrated aspects of the highway since its formation. The Tennessee foothills are especially beautiful. Take the time to enjoy the natural beauty of the country the road passes through.

GREAT UNDERTAKINGS OF THE PAST

It was striking to see how many structures along the highway date from the 1930s. Largely constructed during the Great Depression by the Works Progress Administration (WPA), they speak to achievements of the federal government that are enduring and remain essential. Many of these structures are in small cities and towns along the highway. Some have been landmarked and serve other purposes now than what they were originally intended for. Another set of primarily government buildings, including post offices, date from the early and mid-1960s. Nothing built since seems to have achieved the same permanence.

Similar to taking the time to visit areas of recreation I would suggest trying to see some of the many neighborhoods and buildings that are on the list National List of Historic Places and thus federally protected along the route of 41.

STATES AND COUNTIES STILL MATTER

State and county boundaries for most of the area traversed by Highway 41 were set and organized over 200 years ago. They were the result of surveys marking territories that were barely settled by Europeans at the time. Indigenous peoples were kicked off the land and forced far from their ancestral homes. The entire state of Florida, for example, had a population of 34,000 people in 1825. Today, these political boundaries make as much sense as the arbitrary lines drawn by the major European powers in the Middle East and Africa in the 1880s and after World War I. But here we are. Differences between crossing state lines from Wisconsin to Illinois to Indiana can be quite profound, not in terms of geography, but in culture and social makeup. Tennessee and Kentucky seem as if they could logically be one state, but it is quickly apparent they are not when you cross the border from one to another. Florida and Georgia might as well exist on different planets.

Counties, on the other hand, seem to change very little from one place to another. I noted them in my review of travel through the states on 41 and can say that a passing traveler will certainly not understand how an individual county delivers services to its residents. I'm not at all certain, however, that the arbitrary county lines drawn so many years ago are all that relevant at present. The one thing counties can do, however, is keep "county seats," comprising many small communities along the road from vanishing entirely. Counties that invest in older downtown districts and celebrate their historical legacy while performing the services of government can connect residents in a positive fashion.

IMMIGRANTS AND FACTORIES

"Give me your tired, your poor, your huddled masses yearning to breathe free..."

—from "The New Colossus" by Emma Lazarus

The welcoming tablet affixed to the base of the Statue of Liberty in New York Harbor was extended to a much-needed workforce in the last part of the nineteenth century. Factories needed able-bodied workers who would do jobs that many native-born Americans refused to do. They still do. You see this when you travel to the factory belt that extends from Indiana to Florida. If you care to listen, it might surprise you to hear many languages other than English spoken. It is interesting to hear the rhetoric directed at immigrants and observe the quiet, harsh reality that they are the bulk of blue-collar workforce now—whether or not anyone wants to acknowledge it. I would hope that travel on Highway 41 allows you to see the importance of recent immigrants to their communities. Without them, our nation will be worse off.

MONUMENTS/PLAQUES/MUSEUMS

If you seek to learn a fair bit about this country's founding, growth, and development, it will behoove you to stop and check out some of the many museums along Highway 41. I cannot vouch that every single one is worth a stop, but I can say that the curators and volunteer docents who staff each of these museums care a great deal about making sure you get a sense of the history of the location. And please give a listen to the professional national park rangers who staff many of the battlefield sites and monuments. Learning about the history of the country and the positives and negatives associated with that history is important to understand where we have been and where we are going. This is definitely true along the length of Highway 41. Insofar as plaques and the multiple stops for historic sites are concerned, take in as many as you can. The stories you will learn are often small ones, but they are so important to adding context to your knowledge of the country.

SCHOOLS

You will pass by a lot of them. And you will see yellow school buses picking up and taking kids back and forth to school and home. It is something you might take for granted, but please know that schools, particularly public schools, are the glue that binds this nation together and keeps it sane. When the schools close, that is often a death knell for the nearby community. Keeping public schools viable is a huge challenge for the country and well worth the effort—not whether or not libraries have the right books.

CHURCHES

You will also pass by many churches on your trip down Highway 41. A number of these churches were built in another time and now struggle to remain viable, particularly some of the older established Protestant and Catholic churches. Their congregations have moved on, and many find themselves unable to compete with the newer evangelical churches. Some of the churches you'll pass on the road are being repurposed for new congregations. The church was often the first public structure built by settlers when they established populated areas. Many of these old buildings are not in good shape. However, they are invaluable time capsules to the founding of the country and I think we need a way to document the churches remaining in a database, if only to know what we have.

CEMETERIES

Along with churches, you will see multiple cemeteries located near the highway. Most are quite anonymous—family plots for long ago townspeople with both large markers and small. Here and there, flowers or flags decorate the gravesites. Some plots are well kept while others are barely discernible. If you can take the time, it's worth it to wander around a small cemetery or two, if only to get a sense of all the people who have trod the ground before you and I came along. I hope these cemeteries can remain intact as final resting places, but I worry about what real estate developers, anxious to put in strip malls or dollar stores, have planned for these burial lands.

The military cemeteries near battlefields and national parks are an altogether different experience. Usually very well kept and more precisely laid out, these burial grounds speak to all of the wars of the country's past. Sobering, possessed of a stark beauty and quietude, these cemeteries spoke to me of the role of the military and the many Americans who have served throughout the country's history. Many young people have died due to war.

GUNS

I was struck by the number of billboard signs outside of the major cities along Highway 41 that advertise guns, gun shows, and gun dealers. If there was ever a debate about gun ownership in America, it seems to have largely ended. The availability and ease of procuring arms is an unfortunate reality within the United States. Mass murders garner headlines for a brief time and then simply recede into the recent history of each area affected. Too many of these murders target defenseless people. A collective will to change the terms of what constitutes responsible gun ownership, and a reinterpretation of the Second Amendment are not in cards at this time— and I'm not sure they ever will be.

CLIMATE CHANGE, FRESHWATER ACCESS, SEA LEVEL RISE, AND THE GROWING INTENSITY OF MAJOR STORMS

All of these environmental issues currently affect life along Highway 41, and their impacts will only increase in intensity as we peer down the road. During the time of my travels, some massive storms have seriously affected locales along U.S. 41, particularly in Florida and Georgia. It is often said that changes in thinking occur first along the coastal portions of the United States and slowly move inland. I would like to suggest a shift of that paradigm. The need to think carefully about the climate should not only be the province of scientists but also that of ordinary people within the interior of the country. How to communicate this clearly is a challenge, of course. The decline of local newspapers has greatly lessened understanding of local news and opportunities to promote community action. Ways of providing factual information clearly and without bias awaits innovation.

THE POLITICAL DIVIDE

I purposely sought to downplay the many partisan political issues that seem to so define living in the United States at this time. Partisanship has always been a feature of the American experience, so this is nothing new. Reading this book, a decade or two from now, you may see a very different picture from the one I have witnessed. Suffice to say, the journey along Highway 41 presents a complex picture of a nation that has little to coalesce around and much to disagree about. Sporting events and national holidays bring about some commonalities, but the larger picture of what it means to be an American is much more difficult when red and blue tribes are unable to understand one another with the lack of patience to try. I would like everyone, regardless of their political identity, to make the trip over the 2,000 miles of 41 and see the country for what it is—not what some algorithm tells you it is.

"THE FUTURE IS ALREADY HERE BUT THE PAST REFUSES TO DIE."

The above statement is from a book by R.C. Longworth called *Caught in the Middle* (Bloomsbury Press, 2008). It conveys much of what I witnessed on my Highway 41 journey. We are moving into an era that few people understand and even fewer know enough about to convey their knowledge in simple words. The dawn of Artificial Intelligence (AI) and Chat GPT promises to transform how we interact with information. On the plus side, these innovations might help to unlock solutions to difficult problems. On the negative side, they might further our descent into a miasma of deliberate misinformation and make us more suspicious of all facts and of each other. For people who now get most of what they know from looking at a cellphone or from talking heads screaming unfounded rumors and opinions at them, this is disconcerting to say the least. Content becomes key, and information gleaned strictly from podcasts and social media is highly suspect. I remain old-fashioned—I believe it's best to see things with one's own eyes, but I would be naive to think that we can go back to a simpler era.

Along Highway 41 are both prosperous communities and a number of poor ones. Technology serves everyone, but those who are technically sophisticated and economically advantaged benefit a great deal more than those who are in marginal circumstances. The past in the form of old cultural norms—racism, gender roles, isolationism, and distrust of government—is still present. On the positive side, you can still meet people along the road who might be wary of strangers but are generally friendly. Our society will have to learn how to integrate people who are in their nineties with those who are barely out of their teens. The America of a century ago no longer exists. In its place is a vibrant, interesting country that must embrace changing times or slowly become a fossilized relic.

At the end, I want to celebrate all of the places near Highway 41 that are part of Americana—diners, movie theaters, interesting little museums, parks, farmland, etc.—and hope that they still remain on my next journey down the road. It's a road that you should take as well. Travel on 41 to see the past, the present, and very possibly, the future.

ACKNOWLEDGEMENTS

I had thought about writing a book about Highway 41 some twenty-five years ago with brief trips through Indiana and Florida. As someone who always liked to do research, I started filling a laundry basket full of pictures, maps, and articles collected from a variety of sources starting in the late 1990s. (Mind you, this was before the Internet and search engines (and now AI) became the way most information is found these days). And there it sat for years, until we moved from downtown Chicago to a home in Western Springs, Illinois in 2021.

My wife asked me if I was ever going to do anything with the basket of material taking up space. That was a spur to get started writing in earnest. I joined a writer's group in Western Springs and reached out to some friends and acquaintances to figure out how to start what I first thought would be a relatively straightforward writing project. Having published work for academic journals in the past I was aware of being careful with facts. What I also had to learn was how to insert myself into a personal journey narrative. And I needed to travel the entirety of Highway 41.

Trying to determine a starting point for my narrative, I reached out to Dr. Anoush Pisani my friend and colleague during my PhD studies at the University of Illinois Chicago to help with an outline and format to make all of the gathered information complete. I owe her a big debt of gratitude in helping me get started. After completing a first draft I knew that I was going to need an editor. Cathy VanPatten, another long-time acquaintance who has been in the academic textbook publishing field for years agreed to edit the manuscript and I am indebted to her expertise that has made this book take shape. The book cover, maps and illustrations are all the work of Molly Miklosz, a visual art teacher and freelance artist who makes the book come alive with her pen and ink drawings. I am lucky to have met such a creative person.

Victoria Witkewitz, a former student of mine from long ago with an expertise in the publishing industry has taken this mass of work and transformed it into the book you see here. Without **Red Bicycle Books**, *Unearthing Highway 41 An American Journey* would not be seeing the light of day.

None of this would have been possible without encouragement and moral support from my wife, Emily Clott, a Chicago Architecture Docent, a former French Teacher, and Renaissance woman who I have been lucky enough to be married to over forty years. This book is dedicated to her.

The individuals noted here are all friends and acquaintances who have all been leaned on in one way or another for information and advice: Ellen Schubart, Paul Lurrie, Robin and Deb Snow, Greg Borzo, Eileen Donnersberger, Mauricio Araujo, Andrew Pudelek, Dennis Au, Bruce Hartman, Charlotte Brittan, Michael Broadway, Debbie Bissonnette, Molly Copeland, Kristy Vanderpool, Maggie Monteverde, Julie Chisholm, and the Western Springs Writers Group. I am thankful for all your assistance.

Finally, I would add that any author makes a personal journey. While I have received much information from many sources that I used to make this a hopefully useful and readable work, whatever mistakes made are mine to own.

BIBLIOGRAPHY

NOTE ON SOURCES

This book was compiled from visits by the author to multiple museums, libraries, tourist sites, chambers of commerce and state archives throughout the trail of Highway 41. In addition, voluminous materials from books, websites, newspapers, and magazines were consulted. Information on Highway 41 as a road is available but very scattered.

Note that Artificial Intelligence was not used for the creation of this book. We are soon to be in a world that is engulfed with AI and that is a rather depressing thought.

SONG

RAMBLIN' MAN

Words and Music by DICKEY BETTS
© 1973 (Renewed) UNICHAPPELL MUSIC INC. and FORREST RICHARD BETTS MUSIC
All Rights Administered by UNICHAPPELL MUSIC INC.
All Rights Reserved
Used by Permission of ALFRED MUSIC

BOOKS AND ARTICLES

Admire, Carlie. "Grand Opening." *Florida Weekly, Fort Myers Edition*, 13-19 December 2023.

Alderson, Doug. "The Great Florida Seminole Trail: Complete Guide to Seminole Indian Historic and Cultural Sites Sarasota." FL. Pineapple Press, 2013.

Aleaziz, Hamed. "Florida Builds 'Alligator Alcatraz' Detention Center for Migrants in Everglades." *The New York Times*, 23 June 2025. Retrieved from https://www.nytimes.com/2025/06/23/us/politics/florida-alligator-alcatraz-migrant-detention-center.html.

Algeo, Matthew. "The Sketchy Faith Healer Who Tried to Save New York From Vice." *Atlas Obscura*, 18 April 2017. Retrieved from https://www.atlasobscura.com/articles/john-alexander-dowie-zion.

American Experience. "Mr. Miami Beach. Carl and Jane Fisher." Aired 2 February 1998. Retrieved from https://www.pbs.org/wgbh/americanexperience/features/miami-carl-and-jane-fisher/.

American Guide Series, Works Project Administration. Florida: A Guide to the Southernmost State. New York, Oxford University Press, 1939.

American Guide Series, Works Project Administration. Georgia: A Guide to its Towns and Countryside. Athens, The University of Georgia Press, 1940.

American Guide Series, Works Project Administration. Illinois: A Descriptive and Historical Guide. Chicago, A.C. McClurg & Co. 1939.

American Guide Series, Works Project Administration. Indiana: A Guide to the Hoosier State. New York, Oxford University Press, 1941.

American Guide Series, Works Project Administration. Kentucky: A Guide to the Bluegrass State. New York, Harcourt, Brace and Company, 1939.

American Guide Series, Works Project Administration. Michigan: A Guide to the Wolverine State. New York, Oxford University Press, 1941.

American Guide Series, Works Project Administration. Tennessee: A Guide to the State. New York, Viking Press, 1939.

American Guide Series, Works Project Administration. Wisconsin: A Guide to the Badger State. New York, Duell Sloan and Pearce, 1941.

Anders, George. "For Anyone Starting a Business, these 10 Metros are Standouts." *LinkedIn*, 13 September 2023. Retrieved from https://www.linkedin.com/pulse/anyone-starting-business-10-metros-standouts-george-anders/.

Anderson, James. "Lakefront is No Place for an 'Expressway' Called DuSable Lake Shore Drive." *Chicago Sun-Times*, 29 December 2023.

Antaya, Nic; Storel, Marco. "America's Birthplace of Organized Skiing is in Michigan, Here's What it Looks Like." *The Picture Show NPR*, 5 February 2022. Retrieved from https://www.npr.org/sections/pictureshow/2022/02/05/1075890621/ishpeming-michigan-ski-jumping.

Applebaum, Noha. "On the Road Again." *The New York Times*, 15 July 1990. Retrieved from https://www.nytimes.com/1990/07/15/travel/on-the-road-again.html.

Baker, Ben. "Go Big or Go Bankrupt: Wisconsin Farmers Face Daunting Challenges as Factory Farms Flourish." *The Badger Herald*, 7 December 2021. Retrieved from https://badgerherald.com/features/2021/12/07/go-big-or-go-bankrupt-wisconsin-farmers-face-daunting-challenges-as-factory-farms-flourish/.

Barnett, Jonathan. *Designing the Megaregion: Meeting Urban Challenges at a New Scale.* Washington, Island Press, 2020.

Bateson, Ian. "Is there a place for Jefferson Davis?" *The New York Times*, 11 October 2020.

Belson, Ken. "Today, You Can Walk Around Like You Own the Place." *The New York Times*, 14 August 2022.

Beltran, Nicole. "DeSantis Challenges Federal College Accreditation Rules." *The Independent Florida Alligator*, 10 July 2023.

Benton, Emilia. "City Guide to Living in Atlanta and Its Neighborhoods." *NeighborWho.com*, 1 June 2022. Retrieved from https://www.neighborwho.com/real-estate/living-in-atlanta/?utm_campaign=Newsletter-NW-PROMO-P2-V1&utm_source=neighborwho&utm_medium=email.

Blackhawk, Ned. "The Rediscovery of America: Native Peoples and the Unmaking of U.S. History." New Haven. Yale University Press, 2023.

Blakemore, Erin. "Why Andrew Jackson's Legacy Is So Controversial." *History.com*, 29 August 2018. Retrieved from https://www.history.com/news/andrew-jackson-presidency-controversial-legacy.

Bloom, Nicolas. "Why the Humble City Bus is the Key to Improving US Public Transit." *The Conversation.com*, 2 March 2023. Retrieved from https://theconversation.com/why-the-humble-city-bus-is-the-key-to-improving-us-public-transit-199052?utm_source=pocket-newtab.

Boorstin, Daniel. *The Americans: The Democratic Experience.* New York, Vintage Books, 1974.

Bosman, Julie. "The City is So Resilient." *The New York Times*, 30 October 2022.

Bourdain, Anthony; Woolever, Laurie. *World Travel.* New York, Harper Collins, 2021.

Broadway, Michael; Broadway, John. "The UP at a Crossroads: Beyond the 2020 Census Results." *Rural Insights*, 15 December 2021. Retrieved from https://ruralinsights.org/content/the-up-at-a-crossroads-beyond-the-2020-census-results/.

Bruce, Cheryl Lynn. "My Chicago Journey." *New City Magazine*, February 2023.

Bruggers, James; Gearino, Dan. "Why Kentucky Is Dead Last for Wind and Solar Production." *Inside Climate News*, 31 March 2023. Retrieved from https://insideclimatenews.org/news/31032023/kentucky-coal-wind-solar/?utm_source=InsideClimate+News&utm_campaign=713e6e93ad-EMAIL_CAMPAIGN_2023_04_01_04_00.

Brunner, Nadja-Marie. "Cape Coral History." *NMB Realty, Cape Coral, FL*, 2009. Retrieved from https://www.nmbfloridavacationrentals.com/cape-coral-vacation/history-and-today.

Buchwald, Elizabeth. "Florida's Home Insurer of Last Resort is in Serious Trouble. Will Milton Put it Over the Edge?" CNN, 11 October 2024. Retrieved from https://www.cnn.com/2024/10/11/business/citizens-insurance-hurricane-milton/index.html.

Bunch, Riley; Eason, Brian. "How City's Share of Training Center Grew." *Atlanta Journal-Constitution*, 4 June 2023.

Burnim, Mellonee; Maultsby, Portia. *African American Music- An Introduction.* New York, Routledge, 2019.

Bush, Rudolph. "Chemical Weapon Site Haunts Indiana Town." *Chicago Tribune*, 30 December 2001.

Butko, Brian. Greetings from the *Lincoln Highway: A Road Trip Celebration of America's First Coast-to-Coast Highway. Centennial Edition*, Stackpole Books, Mechanicsburg, PA, April 2013.

Callahan, Ashley. *Peacock Alley: Highway 41 and the Growth of the Chenille Bedspread Industry.* Proceedings, Textile Society of America Symposium, 2002. Retrieved from https://digitalcommons.unl.edu/cgi/viewcontent.cgi?article=1375&context=tsaconf2002. DigitalCommons@University of Nebraska - LincolnDigitalCommons@University of Nebraska-Lincoln, 2002.

Cannariato, Nicholas. "Open City." *The New York Times Magazine*, 30 July 2023.

Cantor, George. *Old Roads of the Midwest.* Ann Arbor, MI. The University of Michigan Press, 1997.

Carruthers, Frances. "Nostalgic Images of American Road Trips from Every Decade." *Love Exploring.com*, 12 August 2024. Retrieved from https://www.loveexploring.com/gallerylist/135568/nostalgic-images-of-american-road-trips-from-every-decade.

Chase, Brett. "Groups Sue to Halt Expansion of Lakeside Dump on Southeast Side." *Chicago Sun-Times*, 13 March 2023.

Clampitt, Cynthia. *Destination Heartland.* Champaign, IL. 3 Fieldworks, Univ. of Illinois, 2022.

Clark, Thomas. *A History of Kentucky*. Ashland KY. The Jesse Stuart Foundation, 1992.

Committee for a Responsible Budget. "The Infrastructure Bill's Impact on the Highway Trust Fund." Committee for a Responsible Federal Budget, 3 February 2022. Retrieved from https://www.crfb.org/blogs/infrastructure-bills-impact-highway-trust-fund.

Cook, Kelsey. "Explore Indiana's Earliest History at Vincennes State Historic Sites." *Indiana State Museum of Historic Sites*, 19 March 2018. Retrieved from https://www.indianamuseum.org/blog-post/explore-indianas-earliest-history-at-vincennes-state-historic-sites/.

Cooke, Bill. "Remembering Miami Beach's Shameful History of Segregation and Racism." *Miami New Times*, 10 March 2016. Retrieved from https://www.miaminewtimes.com/news/remembering-miami-beachs-shameful-history-of-segregation-and-racism-8306647.

Coon, Anna. "The Biggest Airport that Never Was in the Florida Everglades." *UMTV Live*, 19 January 2024. Retrieved from https://www.youtube.com/watch?v=Rm-W3u8wvi8.

Cooper, Casey. "History of the US Highway System." GBCNET, 2004. Retrieved from https://www.gbcnet.com/ushighways/history.html.

Cottle, Michelle. "The Nihilism of the Golden Years." *The New York Times*, 6 March 2022.

Courter, Joe. "They Delivered Horrors." *The Gainesville Iguana*, July/August 2023.

Creamer, Colleen. "A Plan for Nashville's Meteoric Growth." Ledger, 26 May through 1 June, 2023.

Crumrin, Tim. *Hidden History of Terre Haute*. Mt. Pleasant SC, Arcadia Publishing, 2020.

Dairy Farmers of Wisconsin. "I'm a Wisconsin Dairy Farmer." Documentary Series, 2025. Retrieved from https://www.wisconsindairy.org/caring-for-wisconsin/wisconsin-dairy-farmers.

Danner, Jeff. "Bronze Age Part II: The Case of the Missing Copper." *Chapelboro.com*. Common Science, 18 June 2012. Retrieved from https://chapelboro.com/town-square/columns/common-science/bronze-age-part-ii-the-case-of-the-missing-copper.

Daryani, Connor. "A Revitalization Strategist Offers Nashville a Way Forward." *Nashville Scene*, 1-7 June 2023.

Davis, Mary; Berman, Joan, Graham, Mary; Mitten, Lisa. *Native America in the Twentieth Century-An Encyclopedia*. New York, Routledge, 2014.

Dellinger, Matt. *Interstate 69: The Unfinished History of the Last Great American Highway.* New York, Scribner 2013.

Didion, Joan. *Miami*. New York, Simon & Schuster, 1987.

DiMarco, Ed. "The Florida Affordability Crisis: An In-Depth Exploration with a Focus on Naples, FL." *Ed DiMarco Realty Blog*, 31 December 2024. Retrieved from https://www.naplesed.com/post/the-florida-affordability-crisis-an-in-depth-exploration-with-a-focus-on-naples-fl.

Dixon, Kristal; Fitzpatrick, Alex. "Half of Metro Atlanta Adults are Single." *Axios*, 14 February 2025. Retrieved from https://www.axios.com/local/atlanta/2025/02/14/half-of-metro-atlanta-adults-are-single.

Douglas, Deborah. *U.S. Civil Rights Trail: A Traveler's Guide to the People, Places, and Events that Made the Movement.* Berkeley, CA. Moon Books, 2021.

Drury, Robert; Clavin, Thomas. *Blood & Treasure: Daniel Boone and the Fight for America's First Frontier*. New York, St. Martin's Press, 2021.

Green Bay *Intensive Resource Survey Final Report*. City of Green Bay Redevelopment Authority, December 1988. Retrieved from https://www.greenbaywi.gov/DocumentCenter/View/1384/1988-Intensive-Resource-Survey-Final-Report-PDF-?bidId=.

Greenfield, John. "El of a Night: Twelve Hours on the Red and Blue Lines." *New City Magazine*, 3 May 2002.

Greenfield, John. "Hoosier Savior?" *New City Magazine*, 11 July 2023.

Grossman, James; Keating, Ann; Reiff, Janice, Editors. *The Encyclopedia of Chicago*. Chicago, The University of Chicago Press, 2004.

Grossman, Ron. "Op-Ed:'There Ain't No Road Just Like It.'" *Chicago Tribune*, 7 May 2021.

Gruszecki, Debra. "U.S. 41 Traffic Nearly Paralyzes Road." *The Times*, 6 August 1989.

Gurda, John. *The Making of Milwaukee*. Milwaukee, WI. Milwaukee County Historical Society, 2018.

Halpin, Jill. "Michigan National Forests Ultimate Travel Guide." *My Michigan Beach and Travel*, 11 March 2023. Retrieved from https://mymichiganbeach.com/michigan-national-forests/.

Hamalainen, Pekka. *Indigenous Continent*, New York, Liveright, 2022.

Hart, Richard. "Where the Buffalo Roamed – Or Did They?" *Great Plains Research: A Journal of Natural and Social Sciences. Americanprairie.org*. Spring 2001 DigitalCommons@University of Nebraska – Lincoln. Retrieved from https://www.americanprairie.org/sites/default/files/Where%20Buffalo%20Roamed%20-%20Or%20Did%20They.pdf.

Harvard Student Agencies. *Let's Go USA*, Cambridge, MA., St. Martin's Press 1999, 2008.

Heath, Glenn. "Nashville (1975)" *Little White Lies Magazine*, 25 June 2021. Retrieved from https://lwlies.com/reviews/nashville-1975/.

Heckman, Laura. "Littoral Combat Ship Still Fighting to Prove Its Worth." *National Defense Magazine*, NDIA, 26 March 2024. Retrieved from https://www.nationaldefensemagazine.org/articles/2024/3/26/littoral-combat-ship-still-fighting-to-prove-its-worth.

Helfen, Tim. *We Are EC: The Untold Story of East Chicago Basketball*. Documentary, Amazon Prime, 2017. Retrieved from https://www.cinemaclock.com/qc/montreal/movies/we-are-ec-the-untold-story-of-east-chicago-basketball-2017.

Henderson, Harold. *Chicago 101: History, Chicago Reader*, 22 September 2006.

Henri-Levy, Bernard. *American Vertigo: Traveling America in the Footsteps of Toqueville*, New York, Random House, 2006.

Ho Rodney. "Hundreds of CNN Alumni Bid Farewell to Network's Home." *The Atlanta Journal-Constitution*, 3 June 2023. Retrieved from https://www.ajc.com/life/photos-cnn-alumni-bid-farewell-to-downtown-atlantas-cnn-center/JSC2YQZUNBGHJLJY7SWXFVXU44/.

Hoekstra, Dave. "Corny Jokes, Clothes from Another Planet and Crimes of Passion: When the Supper Club Was King." *New City Communications*, 26 March 2024. Retrieved from https://music.newcity.com/2024/03/26/corny-jokes-clothes-from-another-planet-and-crimes-of-passion-when-the-supper-club-was-king/.

Hokansan, Drake. *The Lincoln Highway, Main Street Across America*, Univ. of Iowa Press, Iowa City, 1988.

Horn-Muller, Ayurella. "The Fight to Save Florida's Oranges." *Wired Magazine*, 3 August 2024. Retrieved from https://www.wired.com/story/the-fight-to-save-floridas-oranges-climate-change-farming-crop-shortages/?utm_source=pocket-newtab-en-us.

Horn-Muller, Ayurella. "Can Florida's Orange Growers Survive Another Hurricane Season?" *Grist Magazine*, 26 July 2024. Retrieved from https://grist.org/food-and-agriculture/can-floridas-orange-growers-survive-another-hurricane-season/?utm_source=pocket-newtab-en-us.

Hudson, John. *Across this Land*, Baltimore, MD. Johns Hopkins Univ Press, 2020.

Hull, Anne. *Through the Groves: A Memoir.* New York, Henry Holt & Co. 2023.

Hunter, Kala. "Three Hurricanes in Valdosta, Georgia Have Devastated His House. He Has No Home Insurance." *Columbus Ledger Enquirer*, October 17, 2024. Retrieved from https://www.ledger-enquirer.com/news/weather-news/article293610329.html.

Hurst, David. *The Native Americans: An Illustrated History.* Atlanta, Turner Publishing, 1993.

Hutter, Mark. *Experiencing Cities.* New York, Routledge, 2020.

Indiana Department of Natural Resources. "Historic Preservation & Archaeology: Underground Railroad." *DNR*, 10 January 2025. Retrieved from https://www.in.gov/dnr/historic-preservation/underground-railroad/.

Ingram, Tammy. *Dixie Highway, Road Building and the Making of the Modern South* 1900-1930. Chapel Hill, University of North Carolina Press, 2014.

Inskeep, Steve. *Jacksonland: President Andrew Jackson, Cherokee Chief John Ross, and a Great American Land Grab*, New York, Penguin Books, 2016.

Irfan, Umair. "The Ocean is Rising—and So is Miami's Skyline." Vox.com, 18 September 2023. Retrieved from https://www.vox.com/climate/23872640/coastal-climate-ocean-rising-miami-florida-building.

Isaacs, Deanna. "Sun, Sand—and Segregation." *Chicago Reader*, 20 July 2022. Retrieved from https://chicagoreader.com/columns-opinion/sun-sand-and-segregation/.

Jennings, Peter; Brewster, Todd. *In Search of America*, New York, Hyperion, 2002.

Jimenez, Jesus. "Four Decades Later, a Victim of the Highway Killer Is Finally Identified." *The New York Times*, 27 July 2023. Retrieved from https://www.nytimes.com/2023/07/27/us/larry-eyler-victim-keith-bibbs-identified.html.

Johnson, Michael; Hook, Richard. Encyclopedia of Native Tribes of North America, Ontario, Firefly Books, 2007.

Jones, Jay. "Hamburgers, a History." *Chicago Tribune*, 29 May 2022. Retrieved from https://digitaledition.chicagotribune.com/tribune/article_popover.aspx?guid=2a526e4d-8353-4f16-8212-f695c34563d5.

Jones, Tom. "Opinion | Florida Is Still Dealing with Hurricane Milton. So Where'd the National Coverage Go?" *Poynter.org*, 14 October 2024. Retrieved from https://www.poynter.org/commentary/2024/national-coverage-hurricane-milton-disappeared-florida/.

Jourard, Marty. "Gainesville: Where Tom Petty's Dreams Began. How One Sleepy Southern College Town Changed the History of Rock 'n' Roll." *Gainesville Magazine*, 4 October 2017. Retrieved from https://www.gainesville.com/story/news/local/2017/10/02/gainesville-where-tom-pettys-dreams-began/18644759007/#:~:text=Eight%20musicians%20with%20musical%20roots%20in%20Gainesville,remarkable%20showing%20for%20a%20small%20college%20town.

Kamin, Blair. "Invasion of the Lakefront." *Chicago Tribune*, September 2003.

Kamin, Blair. *Who Is the City For; Architecture, Equity, and the Public Realm in Chicago*, University of Chicago Press, 2022.

Kamp, Jon. "Rural Towns Are Aging, Cash-Strapped and in Desperate Need of Workers." *The Wall Street Journal*, 28 July 2024. Retrieved from https://www.wsj.com/us-news/rural-towns-are-aging-cash-strapped-and-in-desperate-need-of-workers-ae010a72.

Kaufman, Bydan. "How NAFTA Broke American Politics." Podcast. *The New York Times Magazine*, 8 October 2024. Retrieved from https://www.nytimes.com/2024/10/08/podcasts/the-daily/american-politics-trade.html.

Kelley, A.M. "Stone's Road Boss Rolls 'Till the End." *The Mining Journal*, 27 November 2002.

Kennedy, Frances. *American Indian Places: A Historical Guidebook*. Boston, Houghton Miflin, 2008.

Kho, Jennifer. "A 'Redefine' of DuSable Lake Shore Drive Must Make Street More Special, Not Less." Editorial, *Chicago Sun-Times*, 9 April 2023.

Knowlton, Christopher. *Bubble in the Sun: The Florida Boom of the 1920s and How It Brought On the Great Depression*. Simon & Schuster 14 January 2020.

Kotkin, Joel. "What Really Divides America." *New Geography.com*, 8 May 2023. Retrieved from https://www.newgeography.com/content/007817-what-really-divides-america.

Krishnavier, Kartik. "The Mackle Brothers – Makers of Modern Florida?" Florida History, *The Florida Squeeze*, 25 February 2017. Retrieved from https://thefloridasqueeze.com/2017/02/25/the-mackle-brothers-makers-of-modern-florida/.

Lang, Robert; Nelson, Arthur. "Megapolitan America." *Places Journal*, November 2011. Retrieved from https://doi.org/10.22269/111114.

Langston, Jacob. "Florida History: Did You Know Sunshine State Was Almost Split for a Shipping Shortcut?" *Click Orlando.com*, 18 November 2023. Retrieved from https://www.clickorlando.com/news/local/2023/11/15/bifurcate-our-state-how-florida-was-almost-split-in-two-to-create-a-shipping-shortcut/.

Lanham, J. Drew. "What Do We Do About John James Audubon?" *Audubon Magazine*, Spring, 2021. Retrieved from https://www.audubon.org/magazine/spring-2021/what-do-we-do-about-john-james-audubon.

Lavelle, Marianne. "Log and Burn, or Leave Alone? Indiana Residents Fight US Forest Service Over the Future of Hoosier National Forest." *Inside Climate News*, 4 June 2023. Retrieved from https://insideclimatenews.org/news/04062023/logging-indiana-hoosier-national-forest/?utm_source=InsideClimate+News&utm_campaign=d26d512e0b-EMAIL_CAMPAIGN_2023_06_10_01.

Leaming, Sarah. "Historical Sketch of Hernando County (WPA)." Early Hernando County History, Hernando County Public Library, 10 November 1936. Retrieved from https://www.fivay.org/hernando5.html.

Least Heat-Moon, William, *Blue Highways*, Boston, Little, Brown and Company, 1982.

Leonard, M.C. Bob. "Florida in the 1920's. The Great Florida Land Boom." Retrieved from https://floridahistory.org/landboom.htm.

Leonard, Kimberly; Markus, Nicole. "Republicans and Democrats Visited 'Alligator Alcatraz' for the First Time. Here's What They Saw." *Politico*, 12 July 2025. Retrieved from https://www.politico.com/news/2025/07/12/florida-alligator-alcatraz-visit-00449925?cid=apn.

Lewis, Helen. "The Magic Kingdom of Ron DeSantis." *The Atlantic*. 30 March 2023. Retrieved from https://helenlewiswrites.com/the-magic-kingdom-of-ron-desantis/.

Lin, Jan. *The Power of Urban Ethnic Places: Cultural Heritage and Community Life*, New York, Routledge, 2019.

Lippert, John. "113-year-old Dock a Drag on Economic Growth." *Chicago Tribune*, 27 August 2023.

Lippert, John; Freishtat, Sarah. "Belt Junction is a Notorious Bottleneck. Fixing it Could Increase Rail Capacity, but Benefits to South Side Residents Could be Mixed." *Chicago Tribune*, 4 February 2024.

Lodge, Thomas. *The Everglades Handbook- Understanding the Ecosystem, Fourth Edition*. Boca Raton, FL. CRC Press, 2019.

Longworth, Richard. *Caught in the Middle: America's Heartland in the Age of Globalism*. New York, Bloomsbury Press, 2007.

Lyons, Nick. "Hemingway's Many Hearted Fox River." *National Geographic*, Vol. 191, No. 6, June 1997.

MacManus, Elizabeth, MacManus, Susan. *The Lutz Depot: Tales of the "TN," the "Pea Vine," Rail Line Mergers & Spunky Pioneers*. Temple Terrace, FL: Pro-Copy, 2000.

Maguigad, Adriana. "How Devon Avenue Became the Hub for Chicago's Indian Community." WBEZ Chicago, 17 November 2022. Retrieved from https://www.wbez.org/stories/how-did-devon-avenue-become-chicagos-little-india/4fda96b4-7d02-4b9c-b6e9-147c3c72b992?utm_source=Newsletter_Weekly-Member&utm_medium+W.

Mahdawi, Arwa. "Hurricane Ian Was Less a Natural Disaster than a Human-made One. We Must Stop Building on Swamps." *The Guardian*, 5 October 2022. Retrieved from https://www.theguardian.com/commentisfree/2022/oct/05/hurricane-ian-was-less-a-natural-disaster-than-a-human-made-one-we-must-stop-building-on-swamps.

Mahoney, Olivia. *Chicago: Crossroads of America*. Chicago, Chicago History Museum, 2006.

Malmgren, Evan. "The Other American Frontier." *The Baffler*, 18 April 2022. Retrieved from https://thebaffler.com/latest/the-other-american-frontier-malmgren?utm_source=pocket-newtab.

Manning, Sturt. "Archaeologists Have a Lot of Dates Wrong for North American Indigenous History But They're Using New Techniques to Get it Right." *Getpocket.com. The Conversation*, 29 April 2020. Retrieved from https://getpocket.com/explore/item/archaeologists-have-a-lot-of-dates-wrong-for-north-american-indigenous-history-but-we-re-using-new?utm_source=pocket-newtab.

Mayer, Jane. "The Big Money Behind the Big Lie." *The New Yorker*, 2 August 2021.

Mazzei, Patrica. "The Mango is King of the Miami Summer." *The New York Times*, 8 July 2023.

McClendon, Dennis. "Interstate 494 Illinois. Encyclopedia of Chicago: Expressways, Chicago Historical Society," aaroads.com. Retrieved from https://www.aaroads.com/interstate-guide/i-494-il/.

McCrea, Megan. "A New Look at a Deadly Day." *The New York Times*, 18 October 2023.

McCue, Dan. "Does Ernie Pyle Still Matter?" The Well- News, 7 July 2023. Retrieved from https://www.thewellnews.com/fourth-estate/does-ernie-pyle-still-matter/.

McDonald, John. *Chicago-An Economic History*. New York, Routledge, 2015.

McKibben, Bill. "Wrong Turn: America's Car Culture and the Road Not Taken." Yale University, 8 June 2022. Published at the Yale School of the Environment. Retrieved from https://e360.yale.edu/features/wrong-turn-americas-car-culture-and-the-road-not-taken.

McMillen, Christian. "UVA and the History of Race: The George Rogers Clark Statue and Native Americans." *UVA Today*, 27 July 2020. Retrieved from https://news.virginia.edu/content/uva-and-history-race-george-rogers-clark-statue-and-native-americans.

McQuilkin, Steve. "Economy Bounces Back, but Many Still Recovering from Devastating Downturn." News-Press, 15 February 2018. Retrieved from https://www.news-press.com/story/news/local/2018/02/08/great-economy-bounces-back-but-many-still-recovering-devastating-downturn/861883001/.

Miami Design Preservation League. "Sunny Isles Motel Row." Archives, *Miami Design Preservation League*, 2020. Retrieved from https://mdpl.org/archives/2020/10/motel-row-sunny-isles/.

Miller, Abby. "Pritzker Moves Closer to Creating a 'Silicon Valley of Quantum Development' at Former South Works." *Chicago Sun-Times*, 26 July 2024. Retrieved from https://chicago.suntimes.com/technology/2024/07/26/pritzker-silicon-valley-quantum-development-south-works-crg-related-midwest.

Miller, Mike. "Old Florida Towns on US-41." *FloridaBackroadsTravel.com*, 16 November 2024. Retrieved from https://www.florida-backroads-travel.com/old-florida-towns-US41-Georgia-Tampa.html.

Miller, Mike. *Tampa*. Florida Backroads Travel.com July 2, 2022. Retrieved from https://www.florida-backroads-travel.com/tampa-florida.html.

Miller, Rich. "More Stadium Drama is on the Horizon." *Chicago Sun-Times*, 28 April 2024. Retrieved from https://chicago.suntimes.com/columnists/2024/04/26/bears-white-sox-red-stars-stadiums-chicago-nfl-mlb-taxpayers-rich-miller.

Monette, Clarence. *The History of Copper Harbor Michigan*. Calumet, MI. Greenlee Printing, 1976.

Moore, Natalie. *The South Side: A Portrait of Chicago and American Segregation*. Picador Paper, 2019.

Murphy, Patricia. "OPINION: Small Georgia Towns Struggle as Power Shifts North to Atlanta." *AJC Politics*, 30 July 2021. Retrieved from https://www.ajc.com/politics/opinion-small-georgia-towns-struggle-as-power-shifts-north-to-atlanta/NJ3MBNYDHFESXNO74JIWNMM2GY/.

Nelsen, James. *A History Lover's Guide to Milwaukee*. Charleston, S.C. The History Press, 2021.

Nussbaum, Emily. "Country Music's Culture Wars and the Remaking of Nashville." *The New Yorker*, 24 July 2023. Retrieved from https://www.newyorker.com/magazine/2023/07/24/country-musics-culture-wars-and-the-remaking-of-nashville.

Owens, Tracy. "How Barron Collier Got His County." *Gulf Shore Life Magazine*. June 25, 2018. Retrieved from https://www.gulfshorelife.com/2018/06/25/how-barron-collier-got-his-county/.

Pacyga, Dominic. *Chicago: A Biography*. Chicago, University of Chicago Press, 2009.

Paretsky, Sara. *Blood Shot*. New York. Delacorte Press, 1988.

Peace, Lauren; Prator, Jack. "More Cities Address 'Shade Deserts' as Extreme Heat Triggers Health Issues." *KFF Health News*, 28 August 2023.

Peace, Lauren; Prator, Jack. "Extreme Heat Causes Health Problems in 'Shade Deserts.'" *Tampa Bay Times*, 3 September 2023. Retrieved from https://kffhealthnews.org/news/article/cities-shade-deserts-extreme-heat-heatstroke-tampa/.

Pearson, Dan. "Hail Hitchcock." *Daily Southtown*, 6 January 2002.

Peeples, Scott. "Appleton Was Indeed a 'Sundown Town.'" *CelebrateDiversityFox Cities.com*, 16 April 2013. Retrieved from https://www.celebratediversityfoxcities.com/issues.

Peirce, Neal, Keefe, John. *The Great Lakes States of America: People, Politics, and Power in the Five Great Lakes States*, New York, Norton, 1980.

Peirce, Neal. *The Megastates of America: People, Politics, and Power in the Ten Great States*, New York, Norton, 1972.

Perry, Imani. *South to America: A Journey Below the Mason-Dixon to Understand the Soul of a Nation*, New York. Ecco, 2022.

Peterson, Tim. "'We Lost a Lot More Than That': The Toll of Losing 40K Wisconsin Dairy Farms in 4 Decades." *Wisconsin Public Radio*, 2 March 2022. Retrieved from https://www.wpr.org/we-lost-lot-more-toll-losing-40k-dairy-farms-4-decades.

Petroski, Henry. *The Road Taken: The History and Future of America's Infrastructure*, New York, Bloomsbury Publishing, 2016.

Petroski, Henry. *The Lines on the Road: Infrastructure in Perspective*, New York, Mechanical Engineering, 2016.

Piket, Casey. "Remembering Miami Pioneer Mary Brickell." *Miami History*, 13 January 2025. Retrieved from https://www.miami-history.com/p/remembering-miami-pioneer-mary-brickell.

Pomerantz, Gary. *Where Peachtree Meets Sweet Auburn: A Saga of Race and Family*, New York, Scribner, 1996.

Poole, Leslie. "To Preserve and Protect." Forum, *Florida Humanities*. Fall, 2023. Retrieved from https://floridahumanities.online/forum-archives/to-preserve-and-protect/.

Powers, R.E. "Seed & Sin: Lincoln Avenue's Motel Row," *A Chicago Sojourn*, 14 May 2012. Retrieved from https://achicagosojourn.wordpress.com/2012/05/14/seed-sin-lincoln-avenues-motel-row/.

Powers, Rebecca. "Michigan's Upper Peninsula, A World Apart." *The Washington Post*, 16 September 2021.

Prost, Gary. *North America's Natural Wonders: Appalachians, Colorado Rockies, Austin-Big Bend Country, Sierra Madre*. Boca Raton, FL. CRC Press, 2020.

Pults, Kathy. "The History of High Springs." High Springs Chamber of Commerce, 1992.

Rabin, Charles. "Fort Myers Beach Spared the Worst of Milton. But Some Still Ponder Moving On." *Miami Herald*, 13 October 2024. Retrieved from https://www.pressreader.com/usa/miami-herald/20241014/281573771148018?srsltid=AfmBOoqvyAuvdICul7LqxK3YEb5aADrKvMPys5aJqYsukG3hT4W-6dPT.

Rae, John. *The American Automobile Industry*. Boston, Twayne Publishers- GK Hall, 1984.

Rauf, Don. *Breaking History: Lost America: Vanished Civilizations, Abandoned Towns, and Roadside Attractions*. Guilford, CT, Lyons Press, 2019.

RedFin. "Cape Coral Housing Market." *Redfin.com*, December 2024. Retrieved from https://www.redfin.com/city/2654/FL/Cape-Coral/housing-market.

Reed, Atavia. "YouTubers And TikTokers Are Flocking To The South Side To Mock 'The Hood' — And Some Say The Trend Does Real Harm." BlockClubChicago.org, 13 October 2023. Retrieved from https://blockclubchicago.org/2023/05/16/youtubers-and-tiktokers-are-flocking-to-the-south-side-to-mock-the-hood.

Reed, Claire. "What to Know About the USS Beloit, Naval Combat Ship Being Commissioned Saturday in Milwaukee." *Milwaukee Journal Sentinel*, 21 November 2024. Retrieved from https://www.jsonline.com/story/news/2024/11/21/uss-beloit-naval-combat-ship-prepares-for-commissioning-in-milwaukee-photos-video/76458563007/.

Reed, Jennifer. "Stepping Into a Hidden World in the Everglades." *The New York Times*, 29 October 2024. Retrieved from https://www.nytimes.com/2024/10/29/travel/everglades-miccosukee-reservation.html.

Renkl, Margaret. *Graceland, at Last: Notes on Hope and Heartache From the American South*, Minneapolis, MN. Milkweed Editions, 2021.

Renn, Aaron. "The Semi-Elite City." *City Journal*, 9 August 2022. Retrieved from https://www.city-journal.org/article/the-semi-elite-city.

Reynolds, Jason; Kendi, Ibram. *Stamped: Racism, Antiracism, and You.* New York, Little Brown and Company 2020.

Riley, Betsy. "Highway Hub." *Atlanta Magazine*, August 2022.

Riley, Betsy. "What Home Means Now." *Atlanta Magazine*, April 2022. Retrieved from https://atlantamagazine.mydigitalpublication.com/articles/what-home-means-now.

Ring, Trudy; Salkin, Robert; La Boda, Sharon. *International Dictionary of Historic Places: Volume I Americas*, New York, Routledge, 1995, 2013.

Rockett, Darcel. "South Shore Facing its Future." *Chicago Tribune*, 15 November 2022. Retrieved from https://digitaledition.chicagotribune.com/tribune/article_popover.aspx?guid=5183ccbd-b591-4482-a299-e622bc6c7aa7.

Rodkin, Dennis. "What's That Building? Ford Calumet Environmental Center at Big Marsh Park." WBEZ Chicago, 26 May 2022.Retrieved from https://www.wbez.org/stories/whats-that-building-ford-calumet-environmental-center/4a8182d0-e22f-4801-90db-e7cee2d19dd9.

Rogal, Brian. "Microsoft to Build $1B Data Center." *Chicago Tribune*, 5 May 2023. Retrieved from https://digitaledition.chicagotribune.com/tribune/article_popover.aspx?guid=6958b633-d007-43f8-b47f-874ba3f4c8ca.

Rojas, Rick. "A City Where Teenagers Taste Independence at 10 m.p.h." *The New York Times*, 26 November 2023.

Rousso, Katie. "The Best 14 Things To Do in Atlanta, Georgia, Right Now." *Southern Living Magazine*, 9 July 2024. Retrieved from https://www.southernliving.com/travel/georgia/atlanta-ga.

Russell, Kent. *In the Land of Good Living: A Journey to the Heart of Florida*, New York, Knopf, 2020.

Salerno, Allison, "Hurricane Damage Puts Further Strain on Rural Areas in Georgia." *The Washington Post*, 4 October 2024. Retrieved from https://www.washingtonpost.com/weather/2024/10/04/georgia-agriculture-helene-damage/.

Sapien, Joaquin. "Eight Things You Need to Know About the Navy's Failed Multibillion-Dollar Littoral Combat Ship Program." *Propublica.org*, 7 September 2023. Retrieved from https://www.propublica.org/article/navy-littoral-combat-ship-takeaways.

Schlereth, Thomas. US 40: *A Roadscape of the American Experience*. Indianapolis IN, Indiana Historical Society, 1985.

Schoenberg, Nara. "The Ugly Illinoisan." *Chicago Tribune*, 21 August 2021.

Schwieterman, Joseph. *Route 41: The Chicago–Milwaukee Superhighway*. 2011. Retrieved from https://www.lakecountyil.gov/DocumentCenter/View/1011/Route-41-PDF.

Scottish Rite Blog. "A Funny Remembrance: The Life of Illustrious Brother Red Skelton, 33°." 2025. Retrieved from https://scottishritenmj.org/blog/red-skelton-freemason.

Sears, Stephen. *The Automobile in America*, Scribner Publishing, 1977.

Seidel, Jon. "Patrick Spilotro, Who Helped the Feds Nab Joey Lombardo After His Brothers' Murders, Dies at 85." *Chicago Sun-Times*, 5 May 2022.

Seiler, Cotten. *Republic of Drivers: A Cultural History of Automobility in America*. The University of Chicago Press, 2008.

Seminara, Dave. "Hidden Tampa: The Best of an Often-Overlooked Florida City." *The New York Times*, 21 March 2022. Retrieved from https://www.nytimes.com/2022/03/18/travel/tampa-travel-guide.html.

Sfondles, Tina. "IBM Will Join Illinois' Multibillion-dollar Sprawling Quantum Park on South Side." *Chicago Sun-Times*, 13 December 2024.

Shaer, Matthew. "Where Does All the Cardboard Come From? I Had to Know." *The New York Times Magazine*, 28 November 2022. Retrieved from https://www.nytimes.com/2022/11/28/magazine/cardboard-international-paper.html.

Sharp, David. "Navy Shipbuilding in 'Terrible State.'" *Chicago Tribune*, 16 August 2024. Retrieved from https://digitaledition.chicagotribune.com/tribune/article_popover.aspx?guid=9f3511f4-c535-499a-a376-b0a275fa6054.

Sharpton, Harley. "Dobyville: The Forgotten Black Tampa Community." *TampaHistorical.org*, 2019. Retrieved from https://tampahistorical.org/items/show/188.

Shepherd, Jean. *In God We Trust: All Others Pay Cash*. New York, Broadway Books, 1966.

Shilton, A.C. "A Look at What it Took to Construct 76-mile Tamiami Trail as We Celebrate 85th Anniversary of its Opening." *Naples Daily News*, 18 April 2013. Retrieved from https://archive.naplesnews.com/community/a-look-at-what-it-took-to-construct-76-mile-tamiami-trail-as-we-celebrate-85th-anniversary-of-its-op-331556511.html/.

Shul, Dave. "Historic Roads and Highways of Florida." 2002. Retrieved from https://losthistory.net/us-highways/flus.htm#US%2041.

Silverman, David. *Thundersticks: Firearms and the Violent Transformation of Native America*. Cambridge, MA. Harvard University Press, 2016.

Silverman, Mark. "City Guide to Living in Chicago and Its Neighborhoods." *NeighborWho.com*, 5 June 2022. Retrieved from https://www.neighborwho.com/real-estate/living-in-chicago/?utm_campaign=Newsletter-NW-PROMO-P17-V1&utm_source=neighborwho&utm_medium=email.

Skertic, Mark. *A Natives Guide to Northwest Indiana*, Chicago, Lake Clermont Press, 2003.

Smith, Talmon. "Can the F-150 Lightning Make Everyone Want a Truck that Plugs in?" *The New York Times*, 14 August 2022.

Society for Commercial Archeology. *Drivin' The Dixie: Automobile Tourism in the South*. Chattanooga, TN., Georgia Department of Transportation, Tennessee Historical Commission, 1998.

Solomon, Alan. "A Home Run Around Our Lake." *Chicago Tribune*, 21 September 2003.

Sommers, Lawrence; Darden, Joe; Harman, Jay; Sommers, Laurie. *Michigan: A Geography.* New York, Routledge, 1984, 2019.

Songwriters Hall of Fame. "Paul Dresser." *Songhall.org*, 2025. Retrieved from https://www.songhall.org/profile/Paul_Dresser.

Sorin, Gretchen. *Driving While Black: African American Travel and the Road to Civil Rights.* New York, Liveright Publishing, 2020.

Spencer, Terry. "Investigators Say Garage below Fla. Condo Tower Had Many Faulty Support Columns." *Chicago Sun-Times*, 7 March 2024.

Steinbeck, John. *Travels with Charley: In Search of America.* New York, Penguin Books, 1962, 1980.

Stewart, George. *US 40: Cross Section of the United States of America.* Boston. Houghton Mifflin, 1953.

Stinnett, Chuck. "Before There Was U.S. 41, There Was the Dixie Bee Line." Courier & Press, 5 January 2015. Retrieved from https://archive.courierpress.com/news/before-there-was-us-41-there-was-the-dixie-bee-line-ep-860516321-324821851.html.

Stroud, Hubert; Spikowski, William. "Planning in the Wake of Florida Land Scams." *Journal of Planning Education and Research*, 1998. Retrieved from https://web.archive.org/web/20101223021108/http://spikowski.com/landscam.htm#THE%20CASE%20OF%20LEHIGH%20ACRES,%20FLORIDA.

Sulski, Jim. "The Great Divide." *Chicago Tribune Sunday Magazine*, 6 July 2003.

Sweeten, Michelle; DeDecker, James. "Why Farm in Michigan's Upper Peninsula?" *Michigan State University Extension*, 2 May 2023. Retrieved from https://www.canr.msu.edu/news/why_farm_in_michigans_upper_peninsula.

Swihart, Tom. *Florida's Water- A Fragile Resource in a Vulnerable State.* New York, Routledge, 2012.

Tarkington, Booth. *The Magnificent Ambersons.* Garden City, NY. Doubleday, 1918.

Taylor, Candacy. *Overground Railroad: The Green Book and the Roots of Black Travel in America.* New York, Abrams Press, 2020.

Telander, Rick. "How's This For a Radical Idea?" *Chicago Sun-Times*, 14 May 2024.

Terkel, Studs. *Division Street: America.* New York, Pantheon Books, New Press, 1967, 2016.

The Upper Peninsula. "Timber, Iron Ore & Copper Mines." *Upper Peninsula Travel and Recreation Association*, 2025. Retrieved from https://www.uptravel.com/things-to-do/arts-history-and-culture/timber-iron-ore-copper-mines/.

Thomas, David; Miller, Jay; White, Richard; Nabokov, Peter; Deloria, Phillip. *The Native Americans: An Illustrated History.* New York, Turner Publishing, JG Press, 1993, 2001.

Thomas, James. "A 'Skate Migration' Is Changing How Atlanta Rolls." *The New York Times*, 2 May 2024.

Thompson, Erin. "The Most Controversial Statue in America Surrenders to the Furnace." *The New York Times*, 27 October 2023. Retrieved from https://www.nytimes.com/2023/10/27/opinion/robert-e-lee-confederate-statues.html.

Tompkins, Richard. "Beyond the Model T: How Henry Ford's Legacy Has Shaped Modern Life." *Financial Times*, 16 June 2003.

Townsend, Anthony. *Ghost Road: Beyond the Driverless Car.* New York, W.W. Norton, 2020.

Treur, David. "On Native Grounds." *The New Yorker*, 14 Nov. 2022.

Truer, Anton. "Atlas of Indian Nations." Washington D.C., *National Geographic*, 2014.

Tsui, Karina. "Florida to Detain Migrants in New Everglades Facility dubbed 'Alligator Alcatraz,'" 24 June 2025. Retrieved from https://www.cnn.com/2025/06/24/us/alligator-alcatraz-florida-everglades-migrant-detention-hnk.

U.S. Department of Agriculture. *Scenic and Historic Highway Connects North and South.* Washington D.C., 30 March 1930.

U.S. News and World Report. "250 Best Places to Live in the U.S. in 2024-2025." Retrieved from https://realestate.usnews.com/places/rankings/best-places-to-live.

V. Antoinette. "20 Things Atlanta Is Known and Famous For." *NomadsUnveiled.com*, 29 February 2024. Retrieved from https://nomadsunveiled.com/what-is-atlanta-known-for/.

Van Dam, Andrew. "What State Best Represents America?" *The Washington Post*, 10 May 2024. Retrieved from https://www.washingtonpost.com/business/2024/05/10/most-representative-most-unique-places-america/.

Veltman, Chloe. "So, You Began Your Event with an Indigenous Land Acknowledgment. Now What? *All Things Considered NPR*, 15 March 2023. Retrieved from https://www.npr.org/2023/03/15/1160204144/indigenous-land-acknowledgments?utm_source=pocket-newtab.

Vickers, Lu; Dionne, Sara. *Weeki Wachee, City of Mermaids: A History of One of Florida's Oldest Roadside Attractions.* Gainesville, FL. University Press of Florida, 2007.

Visit the USA. "Welcome to Atlanta – Vibrant, Cultural Hub of the Southeastern USA." *VisittheUSA.com*, 2025. Retrieved from https://www.visittheusa.com/destination/atlanta.

Vuic, Jason. *The Swamp Peddlers: How Lot Sellers, Land Scammers, and Retirees Built Modern Florida and Transformed the American Dream.* Chapel Hill, NC. University of North Carolina Press, 2021.

Warren, Leonard. *Maclure of New Harmony.* Bloomington, IN. Indiana University Press, 2009.

Weiland, Phil. "Didn't Anyone See This Coming?" *The Times*, 9 August 1989.

Weingroff, Richard. "From Names to Numbers: The Origins of the U.S. Numbered Highway System." *US Department of Transportation Federal Highway Administration, AASHTO Quarterly*, Spring 1997. Retrieved from https://www.fhwa.dot.gov/infrastructure/numbers.cfm.

Wendland, Michael. "The Calumet Tragedy." *American Heritage*, Vol. 37, Issue 3 April/May 1986. Retrieved from https://www.americanheritage.com/calumet-tragedy.

Wheeler, Ryan. "The Discovery and Preservation of the Miami Circle Site." *Trail of Florida Indian Heritage*, Florida Division of Historical Resources, 2025. Retrieved from https://www.trailoffloridasindianheritage.org/miami-circle/.

White, Jonathan; Sandage, Scott. "What Frederick Douglass Had to Say About Monuments. The Famed Abolitionist Wrote that 'No One Monument Could Be Made to Tell the Whole Truth.'" *Smithsonian Magazine*, 30 June 2020. Retrieved from https://getpocket.com/explore/item/what-frederick-douglass-had-to-say-about-monuments?utm_source=pocket-newtab.

Wilkerson, Isabel. "The Long-Lasting Legacy of the Great Migration." Washington D.C., *Smithsonian Magazine*, September 2016. https://www.smithsonianmag.com/history/long-lasting-legacy-great-migration-180960118/.

Wille, Lois. *Forever Open, Clear and Free: The Struggle for Chicago's Lakefront.* Chicago, Henry Regnery Co. 1972.

Wines, Michael. "In Nashville, a Gerrymander Goes Beyond Politics to the City's Core." *The New York Times*, 18 February 2022. Retrieved from https://www.nytimes.com/2022/02/18/us/nashville-gerrymandering-republican-democrat.html.

Wisniewski, Mary. "No Sanctuary: Are Historic Churches the Lost Souls of the City?" *New City Magazine*, 9 August 2023.

Wood, Junius. *Illinois, Crossroads of the Continent*. National Geographic, May 1931.

Wooten, Kristi. "'Call Me Ted' is a Riveting Look at the Life of CNN Cofounder Ted Turner." *Rough Draft Atlanta*, 17 November 2024. Retrieved from https://roughdraftatlanta.com/2024/11/17/ted-turner-documentary-call-me-ted/.

Wright, James. *The Dixie Highway in Illinois*. Charleston, S.C. The History Press, 2009.

Wright, John. *The Routledge Encyclopedia of Civil War Biographies*. New York, Routledge, 2012.

Yu, Yue Stella. "2020 Census Results: Middle Tennessee Drives Population Growth as State Becomes More Racially Diverse." *Nashville Tennessean*, 13 August 2021. Retrieved from https://www.tennessean.com/story/news/2021/08/12/census-2020-population-middle-tennessee-drives-state-growth-diversity/5559415001/.

Zoellner, Thomas. *The National Road: Dispatches from a Changing America*. Berkeley, CA. Counterpoint Publishers, 2020.

PHOTO CREDITS

Photos were taken by Christopher Clott on his journey of Highway 41 unless specifically noted, were used by permission in courtesy of the source. The author would like to thank the organizations that provided courtesy photos in the book as indicated for their assistance.

ABOUT THE AUTHOR

Christopher Clott is a former professor of international business and maritime logistics with a keen interest in how people live and work. After a long career in business and academia, this is his first book. When he is not on the road in search of fascinating places to see, he lives with his wife in the Chicago suburb of Western Springs.

To learn more about the story of Highway 41, visit Chris's website at www.highway41.org.